W9-BUR-255

The Parental Experience in Midlife

The John D. and Catherine T. MacArthur Foundation Series on
Mental Health and Development

STUDIES ON SUCCESSFUL MIDLIFE DEVELOPMENT

Also in the series

Sexuality across the Life Course
Edited by Alice S. Rossi

The Parental Experience in Midlife

Edited by

Carol D. Ryff and
Marsha Mailick Seltzer

The University of Chicago Press
Chicago and London

CAROL D. RYFF is professor of psychology and director of the Institute on Aging at the University of Wisconsin–Madison. MARSHA MAILICK SELTZER is professor of social work and coordinator of the Applied Research Unit of the Waisman Center at the University of Wisconsin–Madison.

THE UNIVERSITY OF CHICAGO PRESS, CHICAGO 60637
THE UNIVERSITY OF CHICAGO PRESS, LTD., LONDON

© 1996 by The University of Chicago
All rights reserved. Published 1996
Printed in the United States of America

05 04 03 02 01 00 99 98 97 96   1 2 3 4 5
ISBN: 0-226-73251-7 (cloth)

The University of Chicago Press gratefully acknowledges a subvention from the John D. and Catherine T. MacArthur Foundation in partial support of the costs of production of this volume.

Library of Congress Cataloging-in-Publication Data

The parental experience in midlife / edited by Carol D. Ryff, Marsha Mailick Seltzer.
   p.   cm. — (The John D. and Catherine T. MacArthur Foundation series on mental health and development. Studies on successful midlife development)
   Includes bibliographical references and index.
   ISBN 0-226-73251-7 (alk. paper)
   1. Empty nesters.   2. Parent and adult child.   3. Middle age.
4. Middle aged persons.   5. Parenthood.   I. Ryff, Carol D.
II. Seltzer, Marsha Mailick.   III. Series.
HQ1059.4.P37   1996
306.874—dc20   96-12012
                                                                CIP

⊗ The paper used in this publication meets the minimum requirements of the American National Standard for Information Sciences—Permanence of Paper for Printed Library Materials, ANSI Z39.48-1984.

CONTENTS

v

Contents

VII SUMMARY AND CONCLUSIONS

I Introduction

The Uncharted Years of Midlife Parenting

Carol D. Ryff and Marsha Mailick Seltzer

INTRODUCTION

The MacArthur Research Network on Successful Midlife Development (MIDMAC) provided the starting point for this volume. MIDMAC, part of the Health Program of the John D. and Catherine T. MacArthur Foundation, is made up of a multidisciplinary group of scholars studying midlife. Their broad objective has been to explore the main biomedical, social, and psychological factors that promote successful development during the middle years of adulthood. A variety of new research initiatives have grown out of MIDMAC, one of which is the present exploration of the parental experience in midlife. Most adults in American society are parents (see Marks, chapter 2). Thus, parenthood constitutes one of the most pervasive of all adult life experiences.

Social scientists have amassed knowledge about parenthood, but the extant research encompasses only certain segments of the whole experience. What has been extensively studied, largely by developmental and personality psychologists, is the transition to parenthood and the early years of caring for young children. At the other end of the life cycle, family sociologists and gerontologists have examined the period when aging parents begin to need care and attention from adult children. The middle territory, those years when children grow up and into adulthood but parents are not yet themselves elderly, has received surprisingly little scientific attention, although it is the longest period of the parental experience.

The existing literature also neglects how the having and raising of children affects parents themselves. Center stage is typically the reverse question, that is, how parents influence the growth and development of their children. We chose in this volume to emphasize the counterpoint, namely, how children, especially grown children, contribute to the lives and well-being of their parents. Scholars from diverse disciplines (anthropology, developmental psychology, demography, economics, sociology, social work) were thus invited to explore this uncharted period of parenthood and encouraged to address how the parental experience has influenced parents themselves.

Two broad themes guided the collective inquiry. First, we wanted to draw attention to the *diversity* of midlife parenting—that is, our aim was to illuminate variations in the parental experience with regard to broad sociodemographic factors (e.g., gender, social class, ethnicity) as well as specific parental or child characteristics (e.g., single parenthood, raising a disabled child). Second, we targeted *developmental features* of midlife parenting. Of interest was how the parental experience is influenced by the developmental changes and processes occurring in the lives of children (e.g., onset of puberty) and parents (e.g., death of parent).

To locate the volume in the context of prior research, our introductory chapter provides a brief synthesis of the kinds of questions that have guided earlier studies on parenthood. We highlight omissions in this literature to underscore the rationale for the present endeavor. Next, we introduce key questions to be investigated in the chapters that follow. These questions are woven together around the themes of diversity and development in the parental experience. We conclude the introduction with observations about the rich array of theories and methods evident in this multidisciplinary look at the midlife years of parenthood.

PRIOR RESEARCH ON PARENTING

Our review of prior parenting research distinguishes between studies in which parents have been included primarily to chart how they influence the growth and development of their offspring, and those investigations in which parents themselves are considered part of the outcome or are influenced by the process. By far, the largest number of studies are in the former category, as illustrated with several areas of inquiry. We further consider the temporal organization of the earlier literature, to address where in the unfolding of the parental experience most work has been conducted.

How Parents Influence Children

Most knowledge about parents deals with how they facilitate and enrich, or interfere with and diminish, the growth and development of their children. Certain topics in this literature represent longstanding areas of study, such as research on attachment (e.g., Ainsworth 1973; Bretherton and Waters 1985; Sroufe 1979). Parents (typically mothers) are intrinsic to understanding the nature of the bond between them and their children, but interest in this relationship serves primarily to clarify the subsequent socioemotional adjustment of the child, not that of the parent. Recent efforts to explicate the "parental side of attachment" (Bretherton, Biringen, and Ridgeway 1991) have examined how the mother experiences her baby and his/her development and how she deals with separation experiences and autonomy issues. But, again, these data are obtained to understand the parent-child relationship, not the mother as an individual or possible effects on her own development.

In the contemporary era, working mothers have been extensively studied by developmentalists interested in day care (e.g., Belsky 1990; Clarke-Stewart 1989). This literature examines how day care influences the relationship between mothers and children and, in turn, the child's general adjustment. Limited attention has been given to how day care influences the mother, apart from interest in how her attitudes and feelings about working might contribute to how she interacts with her child (e.g. Hock 1980).

Other work addresses how parents discipline and manage their children (e.g., Baumrind 1971, 1973; Dornbusch et al. 1987). Here again, parental approaches to the management of children are viewed as antecedents to the cognitive and social competence of children. Parenting styles may, however, also result in different experiences for the parent and subsequent variations in the gratifications and frustrations associated with parenthood. Such issues have not been studied.

Recently, a new genre of developmental scholarship has probed the nature of parental belief systems and ideas (Goodnow, 1995; Goodnow and Collins 1990; McGillicuddy-DeLisi and Sigel, 1995; Sigel, McGillicuddy-DeLisi and Goodnow 1992). This work goes beyond earlier studies of parents' discipline, control, or management strategies to questions of how parents *think* about children's development and how it occurs. For example, McGillicuddy-DeLisi (1992) examined whether parents construe developmental progress in children as due to the child's imitation of role models or to the child's social constructions or attributions. Additional questions pertain to parents' beliefs about children's competencies and personalities and whether these are seen as limited by background genetic factors, by the child's maturation, or by patterns of rewards and negative consequences. Related investigations examine parents' understanding of developmental timetables, their views of the causes of development, their cognitions about socialization as well as their beliefs about the causes of aggressive behaviors and how children acquire social skills (Rubin and Mills 1992). Parents' perceptions of their children's physical and cognitive abilities have also been studied as possible antecedents to how children perceive themselves (Martin and Johnson 1992).

Thus, an ever more differentiated understanding of how parents *construe* the development, natural tendencies, and abilities of their children is emerging, but across these endeavors the underlying rationale is to link parental beliefs to parental practices and, ultimately, to how children turn out down the road. Even the landmark studies of bidirectional effects in socialization processes (e.g., Bell 1968; Bell and Harper 1977; Peterson and Rollins 1987) do not focus on the parent as an individual. It is the parent-child system and episodes of interactive behavior between them that is of interest.

In combination, these literatures illustrate the many ways in which parents potentially influence the lives of their children. Paradoxically, this exclusive and pervasive emphasis on parent characteristics and parenting practices as independent variables strengthens the rationale for studying them as dependent variables as children grow up. That is, it is *because* parents are so widely construed to play central roles in their children's development that consequences for parents are particularly high. How children function in life becomes for many parents a major statement about their own resources and strengths or their limitations and weaknesses. As such, we thought it particularly important to understand not only the "products" of their efforts (i.e., their grown children) but also how these offspring and the experience of raising them impact their own lives, self-perceptions, and well-being.

How Children and the Parental Experience Influence Parents

Studies wherein parenthood is conceptualized as an experience that can influence the parent appear in the life-span developmental and adult personality literatures (Seltzer and Ryff 1993). Of interest has been how the transition to parenthood affects personality characteristics, such as levels of efficacy and control, or psychological functioning, such as anxiety or depression (Sirignano and Lachman 1985). These changes have been linked with various mediating factors, such as parents' perceptions of their infant's temperament. In other studies, parents' emotions and satisfactions have been related to parental expectations, attributions, and the actual work of parenting (see Goodnow and Collins 1990 for a review).

Others have examined changes in parents' gender-role orientations across the family life cycle (Abrahams, Feldman, and Nash 1978; Feldman, Biringen, and Nash 1981). Parenthood, contrasted with cohabitation or with marriage without children, is hypothesized to involve reallocation of roles along traditional lines with implications for profiles of parents' femininity and masculinity ratings. Still other studies, conducted largely in the sociological survey domain, have considered the impact of parenthood on the psychological well-being of parents. Here a central question has been how the well-being of parents differs from that of nonparents. This voluminous literature suggests that parenthood has negative consequences for psychological well-being (McLanahan and Adams 1987). Adults with children at home report they are less happy and less satisfied with their lives than do other groups, although overall differences appear small in magnitude. McLanahan and Adams (1987) suggest that the differences between parents and nonparents may stem from economic and time constraints related to women's increased labor force participation and increasing rates of marital disruption and single parenthood. Even within the group of parents that remain married, however, having young children is associated with diminished marital satisfaction.

Umberson and Gove (1989), in contrast, have argued that children have both positive and negative effects on parents—parents were shown to score better than nonparents, for example, on measures of life meaning. Other indicators, such as affective well-being and satisfaction, appeared more influenced by the context of parenting (e.g., when children are young, when parents are divorced). They also noted benefits of parenting for the affective well-being of parents whose children are adults and have left home and for parents who are widowed.

Several survey studies have suggested that mothers experience more parental role strain than do fathers (Scott and Alwin 1989; Umberson 1989). Efforts to explain the differences have implicated not variations in role experiences between mothers and fathers but the different expectations that mothers bring with them to parenting (such as the view that they are more responsible for relationships and hence more affected by emotional stress in family relationships). Mothers' well-being has also been linked with changes in employment roles (Wethington and Kessler 1989), more so, in fact, than with change in parenting roles. Another line of survey research has addressed the normative expectedness of parenthood (Menaghan 1989) and the idea that occupying normatively expected social roles is associated with psychological advantages (e.g., social integration, sense of meaning).

Thus, when parents have been studied from the perspective of outcome rather than antecedent variables, the focus has been on how their personality characteristics, such as self-concept, sex-role orientation, and well-being, are influenced by the parental experience. The children of these parents, their characteristics and needs, are generally absent from this literature. Parenthood is thus conceptualized primarily as a role that one does or does not occupy, with less emphasis given to the actual experiences of parenthood or to the characteristics of children that define one's role status and impact one's well-being.

Midlife Parenting: The Missing Segment

Temporally, most of the preceding investigations address the early years of the parental experience when children are newborn or young and when parents are likely to be young adults. At the other end of the life course is a literature about aged parents and their middle-aged children (see Seltzer and Ryff 1993). This intergenerational relations literature (Hagestad 1987) is conducted largely by family sociologists and gerontologists and tends to focus on patterns of contact, intergenerational transmission of values and attitudes, family norms and expectations, and patterns of assistance and support (Bengtson 1987; Bengtson and Schaeder 1982; Brody 1985; Cicirelli 1991; Hagestad 1987; Mancini and Blieszner 1989; Marshall, Matthews, and Rosenthal 1993; Rossi and Rossi 1990; Zarit and Eggebeen 1995).

The middle years of the parenting experience, when children grow into adolescence and young adulthood and parents themselves are not yet elderly, is the longest but least studied period of the parental experience (Lancaster et al. 1987; Rossi and Rossi 1990; Seltzer and Ryff 1993). Hence, Hagestad (1987) has argued that most of what we know is about the "alpha" phase, which includes studies of young children and new parents, or the "omega" phase, which includes old parents and their middle-aged children. The general paucity of knowledge about the middle years of the parental experience occurs, ironically, during a most interesting time in the parental experience: when parents watch their children grow from adolescence to adulthood and begin to see how their strengths and weaknesses are played out in life choices. It is also the time when parents begin to establish adult-to-adult relations with them.

An exception to this temporal characterization is represented by the research conducted by Rossi and Rossi (1990). They examined the reciprocity or imbalance in the flow of affection, comfort, and goods between the generations in the middle years of adulthood. Their work suggests that intimacy between parents and adult children increases over the adult years. Presumably such increments in intimacy have positive consequences for parents' well-being, although such claims have yet to be tested. Drawing on sex-role perspectives, Rossi and Rossi also hypothesized that the experience of parenthood "may encourage the flowering of tender, nurturant qualities in men" (305), whose prior socialization, unlike that of women, had not emphasized such qualities. As predicted, having children was found to have significant positive links with the expressivity levels of men but not those of women.

Other contributions to the emerging literature on the middle years of parenthood have been made by researchers included in this volume. Silverberg (Silverberg and Steinberg 1987, 1990), for example, has generated important findings on the ways in which children's progressions through adolescence are linked with the well-being of their midlife parents. Similarly, Aquilino (1990, 1991) has examined the return of adult children to the parental home and how this refilling of the nest influences parent-child relations and parental satisfaction. Their chapters in this volume include summaries of these previous findings as well as extensions of their work in new directions.

Summary

This selective summary of questions guiding the prior research on parenting is intended to set the stage for the work presented in this volume. Two conclusions emerge from this overview. First, parents have been conceptualized and studied primarily as critical input factors in understanding child development. Much less is known about how the parental experience influences the health, well-being, and development of parents themselves. Second, a particularly neglected period of the parental experience is middle adulthood, when children emerge as adults in their own right and parents are not yet elderly.

Posing Questions on the Diversity of Midlife Parenting

The chapters in this volume convey diverse definitions of midlife parenting, reflecting the variety present in methodological approaches, disciplinary orientations, and substantive concerns. For some, age of parent, age of child, or age of both parent and child have been used to define midlife parenting. Marks (chapter 2), for instance, defines midlife parenthood as the time of life when parents are between the ages of thirty-five and sixty-four. This straightforward approach focuses on the midlife period of the parent's life, regardless of the stage of parenthood the individual is experiencing. Thus, a thirty-five-year-old parent of an infant and a sixty-four-year-old parent of a forty-year-old son or daughter would both be considered to be midlife parents.

Bringing the age of the child and his or her living arrangement into the definition, Meyer (chapter 3) defines midlife parenthood as the stage of life when parents are between the ages of thirty-five and fifty-four and have a child under the age of eighteen still living at home. Ryff, Schmutte, and Lee (chapter 10) also take this approach, although their focus is on older children (aged twenty-one and older) whose parents are under the age of sixty-five. Studying an atypical example of the midlife parenting experience, Seltzer, Krauss, Choi, and Hong (chapter 12) examine parents aged fifty-five and older with coresident adult children who have a disability. Nydegger and Mitteness (chapter 14) investigate fathers, aged forty-five and older, with adult sons and daughters in their twenties and thirties. Wadsworth (chapter 5), in longitudinal perspective, tracks the midlife experiences, including parenthood, of a birth cohort born in and studied since 1946.

Another definitional strategy emphasizes the age of the child without regard to parental age. Silverberg (chapter 6), studying the early years of midlife parenting, selects families in which the oldest child is between the ages of ten and fifteen. Similarly, Graber and Brooks-Gunn (chapter 7) focus on the early to later adolescent years of daughters and their relationships with their mothers, independent of the mother's age. Allen, Aber, Seidman, Denner, and Mitchell (chapter 8) target urban minority mothers whose children are making the transition from elementary to junior high school. Following the same line, Spencer, Swanson, and Glymph (chapter 9) study African American families of children in middle school (grades six, seven, and eight).

Both Aquilino (chapter 11) and Pruchno, Peters, and Burant (chapter 15) include a wide age span of children (nineteen to thirty-four and thirteen to twenty-five, respectively), regardless of parent age. Umberson (chapter 13) defines the onset of midlife parenting as having a child aged sixteen or older and raises important questions regarding when this stage of parenthood ends. The complexity is made more difficult, as Blieszner, Mancini, and Marek (chapter 16) point out, because of the increasing diversity in the ages at which both men and women begin and end their parenting "careers" and the increasing frequency of blended families. Thus, defining the onset and end of midlife parenting for a *family* as a whole is even more problematic than indexing this stage of life to one parent or one child.

Together, these approaches indicate a continuum of family time that constitutes midlife parenting. This phase of life begins when the children reach puberty and enter junior high or middle school. The landmark event of the midlife parenting stage is the home leaving of the child. Subsequent to this turning point, midlife parents and their children struggle to develop adult-to-adult relationships. As Umberson (chapter 13) clarifies, however, there is no "magic moment" when this stage of life begins or ends but rather a series of gradual transitions in family life.

The definitional diversity of midlife parenting intersects with changes in contemporary American life and increased questioning of the notion of the normative family in midlife (Dannefer 1988). In past decades, the image of the idealized American family as white, middle-class, and consisting of mother and father who are both in their first marriage was broadly endorsed. Currently, however, what was once nonnormative is ever more common and accepted by society. For example, as Meyer (chapter 3) describes, single-father families are the fastest growing type of family in the United States today, constituting 18 percent of the midlife single parents. Just decades ago, this family form was unusual and highly stigmatized. Aquilino (chapter 11) examines the diversity surrounding the home leaving of adult children and reveals that for many families, home leaving is not a discrete event but a process, with some children moving away and subsequently returning, often repeating this sequence several times.

Alwin (chapter 4) elaborates diversity according to the broad sweep of historical time. Focusing on the values that parents bring to the socialization of children, he asks what socialization values have characterized American cohorts born in the 1920s onward. Change is implicated in such values as obedience and conformity contrasted with independence and autonomy. His analyses explore the extent to which support exists for two major interpretations of these changes: processes of cohort replacement or processes of social change within cohorts. We point to the significance of these value shifts for parental childrearing strategies and parent-child relationships and note their influence in introducing (or restricting) diversity in the midlife experience at any given point in time.

Wadsworth (chapter 5) also examines how social and historical changes affect intergenerational relationships, with a specific focus on the years after World War II in Britain. This period, characterized by a rising standard of living and expanded educational and occupational opportunities, contributed to increasing differences between the generations. He uses longitudinal data from midlife adults born during this era to explore the long-term effects of upward social mobility, particularly among children of working-class parents. Among a number of questions posed, Wadsworth asks whether a risk of isolation from parents and friends accompanies this upward mobility. Family-of-origin variables are thus used to predict not only children's educational attainment but also the emotional support and closeness they have as midlife adults with their aging parents. Looking to the past, Wadsworth also describes linkages between the early childhood experience (e.g., parents' enthusiasm for children's education) and the midlife experience (e.g., optimism about work). A recurring element of diversity evident in these analyses is differences between the generations.

Racial, ethnic, and social class diversity appear in multiple chapters. Allen et al. (chapter 8) and Spencer, Swanson, and Glymph (chapter 9) portray the midlife parenting experience for poor African American families in which the children are making the transition from elementary to junior high/middle schools, presenting a contrasting picture to Silverberg's (chapter 6) and Graber and Brooks-Gunn's (chapter 7) study of white, middle-class families at the same point in the family life course.

Of interest is how differing questions are brought to these same transitions as a function of the context in which they occur. Silverberg asks whether parents' mental health, their self-appraisal, and midlife concerns are affected by the development (physical, personal, social) of their adolescent children. Graber and Brooks-Gunn focus on the physiological change of adolescent daughters and how this reproductive transition influences conflict, cohesion, or discourse within mother-daughter dyads. In contrast, Allen et al. target the degree of risk faced by black and Latina youth in their transition from elementary to junior high school, whereas Spencer et al. elaborate the unique contexts of African American adolescents, emphasizing the dangerous and violent features of neighborhood contexts. Thus, children's adolescent transitions pose strikingly different challenges for midlife parents depending on racial/ethnic and socioeconomic statuses as well as environmental contexts.

12

These observations underscore Marks's point (chapter 2) that the "fault lines of diversity" in midlife parenting reflect broad factors such as socioeconomic status, race/ethnicity, parental marital status, family composition, and personal resources. To these variations, we bring accompanying questions regarding the well-being of families at this time of life (e.g., economic well-being, quality of parent-child relationships) and the well-being of the parent as an individual (e.g., purpose in life, depression). For example, Silverberg (chapter 6) asks how individual differences in parental well-being are linked with the work orientation of the parent as well as the parent's social class. Ryff, Schmutte, and Lee (chapter 10) investigate how children's attainment is linked to their parents' well-being as a function of the gender and educational level of parents. Nydegger and Mitteness (chapter 14) target the parental experiences of fathers of high socioeconomic status (SES) and emphasize differences in the quality of their relationships with adult daughters and sons. Similarly, Pruchno, Peters, and Burant (chapter 15) probe linkages between the frequency of parent-child disagreements and parental depression based on family SES.

Other manifestations of diversity of midlife parenting involve the different meanings that events and transitions take on in varying family contexts. For example, Aquilino (chapter 11) explores the process of launching adult children, as do Seltzer et al. (chapter 12). In the latter, however, the launching process occurs in families with an adult child with mental retardation (mean age equals thirty-five). These families have delayed launching beyond the time when children ordinarily move away owing to the continuing dependency needs of the adult child. When these children do move away from the family home, they ordinarily are placed in supervised settings. Seltzer et al. investigate how home leaving by these children is analogous to and different from launching in more typical families. The extent to which launching connotes gains or losses in the independence of the child illustrates the varieties of meaning brought to life transitions.

As noted earlier, an extensive body of research has contrasted parents and nonparents, with the conclusion that parenting has negative consequences for psychological well-being. Guided by our theme of diversity, the chapters in this volume shift the scientific discourse from whether parenting is stressful to questions about *the conditions under which* midlife parenting is stressful or is experienced positively. Thus, by highlighting the diversity *within* the midlife parenting experience, we move beyond the question of how parents compare with nonparents to a search for the sources of difficulties and gratification associated with the parent role and their consequences for the parent.

DEVELOPMENTAL ASPECTS OF MIDLIFE PARENTING

The study of midlife parenting could be organized around the development of children as they move into adolescence and adulthood and how such progressions influence their parents. Alternatively, developmental questions could also pertain to the life course progressions of parents themselves and how such change processes are linked to parental experience. We posit that developmental trajectories of both parent and child must be incorporated to understand the midlife parental experience. In the chapters that follow, some authors give greater emphasis to developmental processes and transitions in children (e.g., entrance into junior high or middle school, the focus of Silverberg; Allen et al.; and Spencer, Swanson, and Glymph) and their effects on parents. Others emphasize life transitions and developmental processes among parents (e.g., parents' experience of the death of a parent, as in Umberson) and how these are influenced by grown children. Still others emphasize the intersection and interdependence of these unfolding developmental trajectories (e.g., child's adolescent development vis-à-vis parents' midlife development, as in Graber and Brooks-Gunn and in Nydegger and Mitteness).

In addition to the question of *who* is developing, there is the related question of the temporal organization of development. In some formulations that follow, development refers to gradual processes, typically indexed by chronological age, such as children's physical development during adolescence or parents' possible progressions toward increased self-evaluation in midlife. In others, development is tracked in terms of visible life transitions or status changes. Those who focus on life transitions typically address more circumscribed time periods surrounding the event itself, whereas the emphasis on the unfolding of physical, psychological, or social developmental processes incorporates longer temporal comparisons.

Illustrating work on developmental processes and transitions of children, Silverberg addresses a variety of changes that occur in adolescents (e.g., pubertal processes, peer influences and relationships, and moves toward greater independence and autonomy) and links them to parental well-being. She hypothesizes that these changes take place at a time when parents themselves may be dealing with developmental

14

processes involving life reappraisal and personal reevaluation. Of interest is whether such parents may be particularly unsettled by confrontations with their youngster's sexual maturity, willingness to question parental authority, and the fact that such adolescents have all life's opportunities and choices ahead of them.

Graber and Brooks-Gunn ask how the reproductive transition—menarche—affects the mother-daughter relationship. Their analysis elaborates variations in this marker of biological development, for example, differences in reports of conflict for mothers with late-maturing versus early-maturing daughters. Variations are also examined with regard to the working status of the mother as well as her own reproductive status. Daughters' adjustment is further linked to how mothers and daughters perceive conflict as well as cohesion in their relationship. Examination of the role of puberty in separation-individuation processes constitutes another focus of this chapter, which is explored in terms of mother-daughter modes of discourse.

Allen et al. address a similar period in the development of children but target a social and educational transition commonly experienced during these years, namely, the move from elementary to junior high or middle school. This school transition signifies for many the first time a young person goes from a small personal environment to a larger, more impersonal one. For poor, minority urban youth who experience high levels of environmental stressors, this transition may be especially difficult, placing those who do not successfully negotiate it at risk for long-term negative developmental outcomes. Although parents in this transition have been studied, the predominant concern has been with understanding their influences on developing children. Allen et al. reverse this usual line of inquiry to examine how the potential difficulties of this transition in children are linked with parental efficacy.

The mutual influence of African American parents and their adolescent children on each other's development is further explicated by Spencer, Swanson, and Glymph. They consider the Eriksonian task of generativity, where the goal is to assist young individuals and to have interest in more global concerns, noting that this task may be particularly difficult and complex for minority parents dealing with low resources and ethnicity-linked experiences. Emphasis is given to the context of individual development, namely, the high-risk neighborhoods where many African American adolescents grow up. Among other issues, their analyses address the extent to which parents' depression and satisfaction are influenced by raising children who perceive the contexts of their lives as violent, conflictual, and dangerous. Although Wadsworth studies a largely white British sample, he also observes that social class is a powerful mediator of development during adolescence and exerts a lifelong influence on well-being.

As children grow into young adulthood, parents may be confronted with different issues and concerns. Ryff, Schmutte, and Lee address the question of how parents think their grown children have "turned out." They hypothesize that the achievements and adjustment of these adult children constitute an important lens through which midlife parents evaluate themselves and their accomplishments in life. Some parents may experience this as a time of fulfillment and pride as they watch children transform into well-adjusted and accomplished adults. For others, it may be a period of difficulty in which they see grown children struggle with life's challenges, perhaps prompting regrets about what they did or did not do as parents. The authors explore empirical linkages between grown children's adjustment and attainment and parent's psychological well-being, as moderated by particular social psychological processes (e.g., parents' views of how responsible they were as parents).

Aquilino further explicates this period of young adulthood with a focus on the propensity of adult children to return to the parental home. He provides surprising data on the prevalence of such returns and links their likelihood to other normative transitions of young adulthood (e.g., marriage, cohabitation, parenthood, work, schooling, military service). To understand the significance of these returns, he emphasizes the increasing independence and growing emotional autonomy that makes up the prime developmental task of these young adults. This work, in combination with that of Silverberg and Graber and Brooks-Gunn, points to possible developmental shifts in the consequences for parents of children's emerging autonomy. In early adolescence, children's progressions toward greater independence may be associated, for some parents, with negative well-being outcomes. As children move into young adulthood, however, the prediction is that parental well-being and parent-child relationships actually benefit from children's increasing autonomy.

Nydegger and Mitteness also emphasize the changing balance in the independence and dependence of the roles of both parent and child. Their perspective draws attention to the parallel role developments of fathers traveling through midlife into later life with those of their children traversing young adulthood through middle age. The focus is thus on role transformations and role maturity, such as children's moves toward more egalitarian relationships with fathers, and fathers' simultaneous shifts away from being authority figures to counselor and friend. The experience of distancing, both of children from fathers and vice versa, is examined as a feature of these parallel maturational processes. It is juxtaposed with observations about gains in the functional involvement of fathers in the lives of their adult children.

Continuing the theme of interdependent lives, Pruchno, Peters, and Burant posit that change in the life of one family member begets change in that of the others. They examine variations in parental well-being as a function of negative life events experienced by adolescent and young adult children (e.g., unwed pregnancy, involvement with drugs or alcohol, change of schools, personal injury or illness, beginning a serious relationship) as well as by the extent of disagreement between children and their parents. Emphasis is placed on the importance of considering such issues with data collected from multiple family members.

Umberson addresses the quality of the relationships between midlife parents and their grown children and how it affects parental well-being. Of primary concern is one's position in the social structure and what such position implies for the nature of the parent-child relationship and parental well-being. Reinvoking developmental questions, Umberson further examines how transitions in the lives of parents, namely, the death of one of their own parents, affects midlife individuals' relationships with their adult children. How this stressful life event, the most common form of bereavement in adulthood, is linked with such relational indicators as contact with or social support from children is the focus of analysis.

Seltzer et al. explore developmental questions related to parenting but in the context of the atypical family: parents who have a child with mental retardation. They suggest that parenting a child with mental retardation may transform usual conceptions of the family life course. Their exploration involves examining patterns of vulnerability and resilience in these mothers during the midlife and later years of parenting. Of particular developmental significance are the unique issues surrounding the launching stage of the family life course for these parents.

Blieszner, Mancini, and Marek come to the question of the midlife parental experience from the far end of the life course, namely, the literature on late-life parenting. They explore broad areas of inquiry, such as research on parent-child relations in later life, caregiving to aged parents, and intergenerational relations, with the aim of identifying possible midlife antecedents to these late-life topics. The emphasis is on understanding the long-term unfolding of the parental experience.

Finally, while not explicitly developmental in their focus, Marks and Meyer consider the age of midlife parents and its correlates with other sociodemographic variables (e.g., age of children, age of parents, socioeconomic status). These perspectives underscore the importance of considering position in the life course in the attempts to portray contours of the midlife parental experience. Alwin, in a portrayal of historical change in parents' values, probes the linkage between life-span developmental trajectories of individuals and the nature of social change.

THEORY AND METHOD IN THE STUDY OF THE MIDLIFE
PARENTAL EXPERIENCE

The chapters in this volume make up a rich array of diverse theoretical perspectives. Silverberg, for example, draws on psychoanalytic theory, stress theory, and role theory in framing questions about adolescent development and its possible links with parental well-being. Graber and Brooks-Gunn also utilize psychoanalytic theory to explore mother-daughter relationships during daughter's pubertal transitions, but this conceptual guide is combined with numerous other perspectives (e.g., family systems theory, biological models and their interaction with social and pscyhological processes, contextual models, cumulative events models).

Allen et al. review literatures on self-esteem in adolescence, parental efficacy, and childrearing practices to inform the study of school transitions among urban minority adolescents. Spencer, Swanson, and Glymph employ developmental theory to explore the challenges facing midlife minority parents, further enriching the query by utilizing contextual approaches to examine the challenges facing their adolescent children. Ryff, Schmutte, and Lee incorporate social psychological theories about social comparison and attribution processes to explicate possible mechanisms by which the lives of grown children are linked with the self-evaluations of their midlife-parents. Their work also employs developmental and clinical theories to define key dimensions of parental well-being.

These more psychological and individual perspectives are contrasted with societal and historical approaches. Wadsworth, for example, draws on ideas of relative deprivation and social change processes to understand the lifelong experiences of a cohort growing up in postwar Britain. Alwin takes an explicitly historical and social change perspective to examine parent socialization processes and their transformations over time.

Several contributors conceptualize their questions within life-course perspectives and family development theory. Aquilino, for example, speaks of the interconnectedness of intra-individual development of family members and changes in family relationships. His work also draws on models of parental expectations. Seltzer et al. examine family development theory and family stress theory to investigate the issues confronting parents of adult children with mental retardation. Nydegger and Mitteness draw extensively on family role theory, providing both a critique of earlier research and an elaboration of new concepts, such as role maturity. The literatures on parent-child relations and intergenerational relations are prominent in the formulations of Pruchno, Peters, and Burant and of Blieszner, Mancini, and Marek, although in the former such research illuminates the effects on a child of negative life events, whereas in the latter, the authors draw on it to elaborate midlife antecedents to late-life parental experiences. Finally, several contributors, including Marks, Meyer, and Umberson, utilize social structural theory with its emphasis on broad sociodemographic factors that set the larger stage on which midlife parenting is experienced.

Collectively, these perspectives convey the multidisciplinary vitality of research on midlife parenting. Guiding theories range from the micro- to the macroanalytic, with questions of development and family relationships evident in both. It is the dialectic and exchange between these multiple levels of theory (see Ryff 1987) through which rich, comprehensive understanding of the parental experience is to be achieved. This volume, with its diverse array of intellectual orientations, fosters such ends.

Among the methodological issues raised by the chapters that follow, we target four. A first observation is the call for studies that capture family life experiences from the perspective of *multiple family members*. Midlife parenting is the time when the greatest number of family members make independent contributions to the characterization of family life. Children are thus credible sources of data separate from their parents, mothers and fathers have both shared and distinct perspectives, and often grandparents are surviving and sufficiently healthy so as to provide their views on family life. Pruchno, Peters, and Burant emphasize, for example, that events in a family have a ripple effect, influencing not only the individual to whom the event occurred but also other family members. Describing and understanding these ripple effects requires input from multiple family members. Such data further clarifies the complexity of within-family relationships at the midlife stage. The relationship between a mother and one child might bear little resemblance, for example, to her relationship with another of her children. And, as these authors convey, relationships between adolescents or young adults and their mothers might be quite different from their relationships with their father. To sharpen these points, Graber and Brooks-Gunn focus on discrepancies that exist between how mothers and their adolescent daughters construe their relationships. Importantly, their data indicate the power of these discrepancies in predicting key outcome variables.

A second methodological consideration pertains to research design and the need for *longitudinal studies*. Although capturing the diversity of family perspectives at any one time enriches our understanding of family life, only longitudinal approaches can reveal the dynamic quality of family life and family interactions. Past formulations of bidirectional effects of parents and children (Bell 1968; Bell and Harper 1977) raise the "direction of effects" question. Longitudinal studies are best equipped to map the influence of parent on child, of child on parent, and of one stage of family life on another. Blieszner, Mancini, and Marek provide a useful framework for conceptualizing the bidirectional influences from a longitudinal perspective.

We note, however, that many influences of family life in the midlife parenting period may occur decades earlier, at times going back to the childhood of the parents or their early years of marriage. Viewed in the context of the total length of the parent-child relationship (roughly five decades), most longitudinal studies cover a small slice of time in which to sort out the causal ordering of variables. Wadsworth's analysis of a longitudinal sample that has been studied for nearly fifty years provides dramatic examples of the long-term reach of early life circumstances and experiences.

Third, we underscore the *multidimensional outcomes* of the parental experience represented in the volume. Many studies presented here differ from past work in that they measure both positive and negative aspects of the midlife parenting experience and content of family relationships. For example, Ryff, Schmutte, and Lee examine the influence of parental views of how their children have turned out on indicators of positive well-being (e.g., personal growth, purpose in life) as well as depression. Similarly, Umberson argues for the importance of measuring both positive and negative aspects of family relationships, showing that parental well-being is differentially related to positive and to negative content of relationships with children.

Related to these distinctions is the need for objective indicators of well-being in midlife parents and for subjective measures. Meyer characterizes midlife parents in terms of their income, access to resources, and employment status. In contrast, Ryff, Schmutte, and Lee clarify how the objective indicator of a phenomenon might be less useful in understanding a family process than are individual family members' interpretations of reality. The issue here is not whether objective or subjective indicators are superior but rather that they are differentially useful in explaining the well-being of parents during the midlife stage.

Finally, we draw attention to the issue of *meaning* in study of midlife parenting. Umberson cautions that differences in meanings may complicate empirical research on parenthood, such that sociocultural differences may exist in the interpretations made by parents of scientific concepts such as what is "adequate" social support or what expectations parents hold for patterns of contact with their children. Thus, differences obtained on dependent variables between racial, ethnic, or economic groups may reflect differences in meanings attached by parents to the questions asked of them, rather than "true" differences on these dimensions. Nydegger and Mitteness confront issues of meaning as a central objective of their inquiry and employ phenomenological methods to get to the essential meaning of the paternal role to midlife fathers. Their qualitative procedures add considerable richness and complexity to the understanding of parent-child relationships in midlife.

In sum, the parental experience in midlife, characterized by diversity as well as unfolding developmental processes, is a time ripe for theoretical and empirical study. It affords researchers the opportunity to explore both individual-level and family-level analyses and to examine how parenthood and the parent-child relationship affect parents and children. Midlife parenting also brings together theory from different disciplines and, as such, fosters scientific agendas that integrate social structural questions with concerns for individual well-being. It calls too for a richness and diversity of scientific methods. Finally, marked by the challenge of watching one's children grow up, the midlife parenting experience requires a long lens into the life course of individuals, as they leave young adulthood and the early parental period, on the one hand, and as they look toward old age, on the other. The studies in this volume bring together these many features of the midlife parental experience.

REFERENCES

Abrahams, B., S. S. Feldman, and S. C. Nash. 1978. Sex role self-concept and sex role attitudes: Enduring personality characteristics or adaptations to changing life situations. *Developmental Psychology* 14:393–400.

Ainsworth, M. 1973. The development of infant-mother attachment. In B. Caldwell and H. N. Ricciue, eds., *Review of child development research*, 31:1–94. Chicago: University of Chicago Press.

Aquilino, W. S. 1990. The likelihood of parent-adult child coresidence: Effects of family structure and parent characteristics. *Journal of Marriage and the Family* 52:405–419.

———. 1991. Predicting parents' experiences with coresident adult children. *Journal of Family Issues* 12:323–342.

Baumrind, D. 1971. Current patterns of parental authority. *Developmental Psychology Monograph* 4:1–103.

———. 1973. The development of instrumental competence through socialization. In A. D. Pick, ed., *Minnesota symposium on child psychology*, 7:3–46. Minneapolis: University of Minnesota Press.

Bell, R. Q. 1968. A reinterpretation of the direction of effects in studies of socialization. *Psychological Review* 75:81–95.

Bell, R. Q., and L. V. Harper. 1977. *Child effects on adults*. Hillsdale, N.J.: Lawrence Erlbaum.

Belsky, J. 1990. Parental and nonparental child care and children's socio-emotional development: A decade in review. *Journal of Marriage and the Family* 52:885–903.

Bengtson, V. L. 1987. Parenting, grandparenting, and intergenerational continuity. In J. B. Lancaster, J. Altmann, A. S. Rossi, and L. R. Sherrod, eds., *Parenting across the life span: Biosocial dimensions*, pp. 435–456. New York: Aldine de Gruyter.

Bengtson, V. L., and S. S. Schraeder. 1982. Parent-child relations. In D. J. Mangen and W. A. Peterson, eds., *Research instruments in social gerontology*. Vol. 2, *Social roles and social participation*, pp. 115–187. Minneapolis: University of Minnesota Press.

Bretherton, I., Z. Biringen, and D. Ridgeway. 1991. The parental side of attachment. In K. Pillemer and K. McCartney, eds., *Parent-child relations throughout life*, pp. 1–24. Hillsdale, N.J.: Lawrence Erlbaum.

Bretherton, I., and E. Waters, eds. 1985. Growing points of attachment theory and research. *Monographs for the Society of Research in Child Development* 50 (1–2, ser. no. 209).

Brody, E. M. 1985. Parent care as normative family stress. *Gerontologist* 25:19–29.

Cicirelli, V. G. 1991. Attachment theory in old age: Protection of the attached figure. In K. Pillemer and K. McCartney, eds., *Parent-child relations throughout life,* pp. 25–42. Hillsdale, N.J.: Lawrence Erlbaum.

Clarke-Stewart, K. A. 1989. Infant day care: Maligned or malignant? *American Psychology* 44:266–273.

Dannefer, D. 1988. What's in a name? An account of the neglect of variability in the study of aging. In J. E. Birren and V. L. Bengtson, eds., *Emergent theories of aging.* New York: Springer.

Dornbusch, S. M., P. L. Ritter, H. Leiderman, D. F. Roberts, and M. J. Fraleigh. 1987. The relation of parenting style to adolescent school performance. *Child Development* 58:1244–1257.

Feldman, S. S., Z. C. Biringen, and S. C. Nash. 1981. Fluctuations of sex-related self-attributions as a function of stage of family life cycle. *Developmental Psychology* 17:24–35.

Goodnow, J. J. 1995. Parents' knowledge and expectations. In M. H. Bornstein, ed., *Handbook of parenting.* Vol. 3, *Status and social conditions of parenting,* pp. 305–332. Mahwah, N.J.: Lawrence Erlbaum.

Goodnow, J. J., and W. A. Collins. 1990. *Development according to parents: The nature, sources, and consequences of parents' ideas.* Hillsdale, N.J.: Lawrence Erlbaum.

Hagestad, G. O. 1987. Parent-child relations in later life: Trends and gaps in past research. In J. B. Lancaster, J. Altman, A. S. Rossi, and L. R. Sherrod, eds., *Parenting across the life span: Biosocial dimensions,* pp. 405–434. New York: Aldine de Gruyter.

Hock, E. 1980. Working and nonworking mothers and their infants: A comparative study of maternal care-giving characteristics and infant social behavior. *Merrill-Palmer Quarterly* 26:49–101.

Lancaster, J. B., J. Altmann, A. S. Rossi, and L. R. Sherrod. 1987. *Parenting across the life span: Biosocial dimensions.* New York: Aldine de Gruyter.

Mancini, J. A., and R. Blieszner. 1989. Aging parents and adult children: Research themes in intergenerational relations. *Journal of Marriage and the Family* 51: 275–290.

Marshall, V. W., S. H. Matthews, and C. J. Rosenthal. 1993. Elusiveness of family life: Challenge for the sociology of aging. *Annual Review of Gerontology and Geriatrics.* 13:39–72. New York: Springer.

Martin, C. A., and J. E. Johnson. 1992. Children's self-perceptions and mothers' beliefs about development and competencies. In I. E. Sigel, A. V. McGillicuddy-DeLisi, and J. J. Goodnow, eds., *Parental belief systems: The psychological consequences for children,* 2d ed., pp. 95–114. Hillsdale, N.J.: Lawrence Erlbaum.

McGillicuddy-DeLisi, A. V. 1992. Parents' beliefs and children's personal-social development. In I. E. Sigel, A. V. McGillicuddy-DeLisi, and J. J. Goodnow, eds., *Parental belief systems: The psychological consequences for children,* 2d ed., pp. 115–142). Hillsdale, N.J.: Lawrence Erlbaum.

McGillicuddy-DeLisi, A. V., and I. E. Sigel. 1995. Parental beliefs. In M. H. Bornstein, ed., *Handbook of parenting.* Vol. 3, *Status and social conditions of parenting,* pp. 333–358. Mahwah, N.J.: Lawrence Erlbaum.

McLanahan, S., and J. Adams. 1987. Parenthood and psychological well-being. *Annual Review of Sociology* 13:237–257.

Menaghan, E. G. 1989. Psychological well-being among parents and nonparents: The importance of normative expectedness. *Journal of Family Issues* 10:547–565.

Peterson, G. W., and B. C. Rollins. 1987. Parent-child socialization. In M. B. Sussman and S. K. Steinmetz, eds., *Handbook of marriage and the family,* pp. 471–507. New York: Plenum.

Rossi, A. S., and P. H. Rossi. 1990. *Of human bonding: Parent-child relations across the life course.* New York: Aldine de Gruyter.

Rubin, K. H., and R. S. L. Mills. 1992. Parents' thoughts about children's socially adaptive and maladaptive behaviors: Stability, change, and individual differences. In I. E. Sigel, A. V. McGillicuddy-DeLisi, and J. J. Goodnow, eds., *Parental belief systems: The psychological consequences for children,* 2d ed., pp. 41–70. Hillsdale, N.J.: Lawrence Erlbaum.

Ryff, C. D. 1987. The place of personality and social structure research in social psychology. *Journal of Personality and Social Psychology* 53:1192–1202.

Scott, J., and D. F. Alwin. 1989. Gender differences in parental strain: Parental role or gender role? *Journal of Family Issues* 10:482–503.

Seltzer, M. M., and C. D. Ryff. 1993. Parenting across the life span: The normative and nonnormative cases. In D. L. Featherman, R. M. Lerner, and M. Perlmutter, eds., *Life-span development and behavior.* Vol. 12, pp. 1–40. Hillsdale, N.J.: Lawrence Erlbaum.

Sigel, I. E., A. V. McGillicuddy-DeLisi, and J. J. Goodnow. 1992. *Parental belief systems: The psychological consequences for children,* 2d ed. Hillsdale, N.J.: Lawrence Erlbaum.

Silverberg, S., and L. Steinberg. 1987. Adolescent autonomy, parent-adolescent conflict, and parental well-being. *Journal of Youth and Adolescence* 16:293–312.

———. 1990. Psychological well-being of parents with early adolescent children. *Developmental Psychology* 26:658–666.

Sirignano, S. W., and M. E. Lachman. 1985. Personality change during the transition to parenthood: The role of perceived infant temperament. *Developmental Psychology* 21:558–567.

Sroufe, L. A. 1979. The coherence of individual development. *American Psychologist* 34:834–841.

Umberson, D. 1989. Relationships with children: Explaining parents' psychological well-being. *Journal of Marriage and the Family* 51:999–1012.

Umberson, D., and W. R. Gove. 1989. Parenthood and psychological well-being: Theory, measurement, and stage in the family life course. *Journal of Family Issues* 10:440–462.

Wethington, E., and R. C. Kessler. 1989. Employment, parental responsibility, and psychological distress: A longitudinal study of married women. *Journal of Family Issues* 10:527–546.

Zarit, S. H., and D. J. Eggebeen. 1995. Parent-child relationships in adulthood and old age. In M. H. Bornstein, ed., *Handbook of parenting.* Vol. 1, *Children and parenting,* pp. 119–140. Mahwah, N.J.: Lawrence Erlbaum.

II Demographic and Economic Aspects of Midlife Parenting

Social Demographic Diversity among American Midlife Parents

Nadine F. Marks

INTRODUCTION

Midlife parents are not all equal. There is great diversity in the experience of midlife parenting. Disparities in the range of personal resources (or lack of resources) midlife parents bring to the role of parent contribute significantly to this diversity. Additional diversity stems from differences in the characteristics of children being parented—for example, number, types (step, biological, and/or adopted), ages, and relative independence. Midlife parents also differ on whether they have living parents of their own who are physically and economically thriving and who might be available for potential or actual support or, conversely, whether midlife parents have living parents who are becoming increasingly frail and dependent. Developmental processes occurring with the aging of midlife parents themselves—such as changes in health and in work careers, as well as the concurrent aging of spouses, children, and others in their social networks—add to variation. Diversity sometimes has a cultural component to it, based in shared values and practices tied to affiliation with an ethnic group identity or a racial group identity. Social organizational patterns create diversity—for instance, through covert or overt categorical discrimination in the labor market that often puts women and/or nonmajority ethnic and racial groups at a disadvantage (Blau 1984; Marini 1989; Ross and Reskin 1984).

This research was supported by the John D. and Catherine T. MacArthur Foundation Research Network on Successful Midlife Development. The National Survey of Families and Households (NSFH) was funded by CPR-NICHD grant HD21009. NSFH was designed and carried out at the Center for Demography and Ecology at the University of Wisconsin–Madison under the direction of Larry Bumpass and James Sweet. Fieldwork was conducted by the Institute for Survey Research, Temple University. I thank the other Workshop on Midlife Parenting participants, University of Wisconsin–Madison Sociology Department Life Course and Aging Training Seminar participants, and University of Chicago Press reviewers for helpful comments on previous versions of this chapter.

Idiosyncratic personal choices and unexpected events, such as accidents that create lifelong handicaps, also contribute to differences between midlife parents.

A number of techniques and methods can bring the fault lines of diversity among midlife parents to light. One approach, the one I take, is to examine differences and similarities among midlife parents along a number of social demographic dimensions. Specifically, I chart differences in the midlife parenting population in terms of personal resources, characteristics of children, characteristics of this population's own parents, and selected multiple role configurations by gender, age, marital status, and race/ethnicity. Although this exercise is predominantly descriptive, I intend it as an empirical foundation that may suggest hypotheses to test in further work and as a basis from which to evaluate better the likely generalizability of ideas about the experience of midlife parenting that are developed in work on more restricted samples. Such an analysis also provides grounds from which to consider inequities in the resources and demands among midlife parents that should lead to considering what public policy and other social intervention efforts are needed to create a social environment in which more midlife parents have the opportunity to optimize their development and the development of their children.

Historically, social science has tended to focus on the "average" or "central tendency" in a population—usually the dominant cultural group population—and define this as the "normative" experience. Life-span developmental psychologists, however, have noted that adulthood is a life period of great plasticity and variability—and that studying variance must be seen to be as important as studying central tendency (Baltes 1987). In family sociology, too, because family life has been undergoing such dramatic changes in recent decades—with high divorce rates, greater likelihood of experiencing multiple marriages, and more life years spent in an unmarried state, even after having children—it has become particularly questionable to think about midlife parenting only in terms of one "ideal type" or "normative" pattern with all other patterns considered "deviant" (Bumpass 1990; Schoen, Urton, Woodrow, and Baj 1985; Sweet and Bumpass 1987; Watkins, Mencken, and Bongaarts 1987). There are just too many people who do not fit into any one pattern.

Simply describing a single variance around a total population mean is often not enough to make apparent how variance is *patterned* among subgroups within a population. Social demography provides a useful tool for a middle-ground approach to descriptive social science. Dividing a total population along a number of significant demographic dimensions helps delineate subgroups of persons exposed to similar social structural opportunities and constraints. Evaluating these demographic patterns helps flesh out the "variance" in a population more effectively than can a single population mean with a single population standard deviation.

For those interested in what is in fact "typical" and the relationship between what is statistically typical and what is socially condoned and held to be ideal, evaluating actual social demographic differences can be instructive. For example, what is statistically typical for the dominant social group in a society often defines what is institutionally supported and attended to by social policies more than does what is statistically typical for subordinate social groups in a society.

Investigating patterns across age groups can also be suggestive of developmental differences, but using cross-sectional data requires cautious evaluation because historical cohort differences may be confounded in what appear to be developmental trends. In cases where little developmental change can be expected over the adult years under study—for years of education and family size, for example—it is more plausible to infer historical cohort change.

Data

The data used for this analysis came from the first wave of the National Survey of Families and Households (NSFH), which includes information from personal interviews conducted in 1987–88 with a nationally representative sample of 13,017 noninstitutionalized American adults, nineteen years old and older. Interviewees included a main sample of 9,643 people, together with an additional oversample of 3,374 blacks, Mexican-Americans, Puerto Ricans, single parents, stepparents, cohabitors, and recently married persons. The interview response rate was 75 percent. Within this total adult population sample, 5,643 primary respondents were ages thirty-five to sixty-four; 4,992 of these midlifers were parents of biological, adopted, and/or stepchildren, and these respondents became the analytic subsample used here. Sampling weights correcting for selection probabilities and nonresponse allow this sample to match the composition of the U.S. population on age,

TABLE 2.1. Weighted Percentage Distribution of Family Status
by Age: Total U.S. Population Ages 35–64 (%)

| | Age | | | | | |
| | 35–44 | | 45–54 | | 55–64 | |
Family Status	Men	Women	Men	Women	Men	Women
% parents[a]						
First marriage	56.0	52.5	57.9	53.6	59.7	52.6
Remarried	17.1	16.7	18.9	16.3	17.7	12.4
Separated	2.0	3.6	3.5	3.9	3.0	2.6
Divorced	7.5	12.8	7.8	13.6	6.2	7.2
Widowed	.4	1.6	1.0	5.6	3.1	16.0
Never married	1.0	2.8	.9	1.0	.6	.5
% nonparents						
First marriage	4.2	3.3	2.4	1.8	4.2	3.0
Remarried	1.1	.6	1.0	.2	.5	.1
Separated	.0	.2	.2	.3	.7	.2
Divorced	2.8	2.5	1.0	.7	.7	.7
Widowed	.0	.3	.7	.3	.4	1.7
Never married	7.8	3.2	4.7	2.7	3.2	3.0
Population subtotals						
% parents	84.1	90.0	90.0	94.0	90.3	91.4
% nonparents	15.9	10.0	10.0	6.0	9.7	8.6
TOTAL[b]	100.0	100.0	100.0	100.0	100.0	100.0
Unweighted N	1,120	1,618	613	920	553	819

Source: National Survey of Families and Households, 1987–88; primary respondents. Total
unweighted N = 5,643.
[a]Includes biological, adoptive, and stepparents.
[b]Column totals do not always sum to 100 percent because of rounding error.

sex, and race (see Sweet, Bumpass, and Call 1988 for additional design
details).

DIVERSITY IN PERSONAL CHARACTERISTICS OF MIDLIFE PARENTS
Prevalence of Parenthood

To begin with, it is useful to consider midlife parents in the context
of the entire United States population. Table 2.1 addresses this issue.
Overall, about 90 percent of all adults ages thirty-five to sixty-four in
1987–88 (birth cohorts from 1923 to 1953) reported being parents of
biological, adopted, and/or stepchildren. The rates were lowest for the
youngest midlife men (84.1 percent) and women (90.0 percent). Part

of the difference between the youngest men and women may reflect the fact that men typically become parents at somewhat older ages than women (Schoen et al. 1985). A small portion of the nonparents at these ages may still become parents. However, some demographers are also projecting a significant increase in levels of childlessness for cohorts born during the 1950s (see Rindfuss, Morgan, and Swicegood 1988), so something of a genuine historical cohort effect in the direction of increased childlessness may be reflected here. Still, even with some possible diminishment of parenthood rates over cohorts, parenting remains a very typical experience of the midlife years.

The proportion of the total midlife adult population parenting in a *first* marriage, however, is not much more than half of women (52.5–53.6 percent) and just under three-fifths (56.0–59.7 percent) of men. Remarried parents and single parents have become increasingly common among the younger cohorts. In the birth cohorts aged thirty-five to forty-four, even never-married parenting has gained ground among the women (and is likely to be underreported among the men [Cherlin, Griffith, and McCarthy 1983]).

Having described how the midlife parenting population fits in the context of the *total* U.S. midlife population, for subsequent analyses I included only midlife *parents* as the base population of interest and made all contrasts *within* the subpopulation of midlife parents.

Marital Status of Midlife Parents

The distribution of marital statuses among all midlife parents is displayed in table 2.2. This table also details separately marital status breakdowns for three major race/ethnic groups: non-Hispanic whites (81.3 percent of midlife parents), blacks (10.8 percent of midlife parents), and Hispanics (6.8 percent of midlife parents—including Mexican-Americans [4.1 percent], Puerto Ricans [1.2 percent], Cubans [.5 percent], and other Hispanics [1.0 percent]). It would have been preferable to analyze Mexican-Americans, Puerto Ricans, and Cubans separately, because patterns in certain outcomes might be expected to vary somewhat between these different cultural groups. However, sample sizes of these subgroups at these ages were not large enough to make analyses at such a level of disaggregation viable with these data.

Many demographic analyses do not distinguish first-married and remarried persons. These analyses make this distinction wherever possible among midlife parents because of increased evidence from family research that differences in well-being and family dynamics exist be-

TABLE 2.2. Weighted Percentage Distribution of Marital Status by Age and Race/Ethnicity: U.S. Parents Ages 35–64 (%)

| | Age | | | | | |
| | 35–44 | | 45–54 | | 55–64 | |
Marital Status	Fathers	Mothers	Fathers	Mothers	Fathers	Mothers
Total[a]						
First married	66.6	58.7	64.6	56.7	66.8	57.8
	(506)	(587)	(267)	(359)	(273)	(319)
Remarried	20.1	18.0	20.6	17.4	18.6	13.2
	(211)	(271)	(129)	(142)	(99)	(99)
Separated/ divorced/ never married	12.7	21.5	13.7	19.9	11.1	11.5
	(198)	(562)	(127)	(273)	(86)	(131)
Widowed	.5	1.8	1.2	6.0	3.6	17.6
	(12)	(46)	(15)	(73)	(26)	(181)
TOTAL	100.0	100.0	100.0	100.0	100.0	100.0
(Unweighted N = 4,992)	(927)	(1,466)	(538)	(847)	(484)	(730)
Non-Hispanic white						
First married	69.2	62.9	67.2	58.8	68.2	62.5
	(377)	(437)	(204)	(271)	(214)	(272)
Remarried	20.3	19.7	20.9	19.6	19.6	13.6
	(168)	(229)	(103)	(121)	(81)	(77)
Separated/ divorced/ never married	10.0	16.1	10.9	16.8	9.0	7.7
	(128)	(325)	(76)	(166)	(52)	(66)
Widowed	.5	1.3	1.0	4.8	3.3	16.2
	(8)	(29)	(10)	(45)	(20)	(120)
TOTAL	100.0	100.0	100.0	100.0	100.0	100.0
(Unweighted N = 3,599)	(681)	(1,020)	(393)	(603)	(367)	(535)

TABLE 2.2. (*Continued*)

Marital Status	Age					
	35–44		45–54		55–64	
	Fathers	Mothers	Fathers	Mothers	Fathers	Mothers
Black						
First married	52.7	34.9	41.2	38.1	56.7	26.7
	(82)	(80)	(35)	(48)	(35)	(28)
Remarried	19.3	10.3	22.0	8.9	14.2	15.5
	(29)	(22)	(21)	(15)	(11)	(18)
Separated/ divorced/ never married	27.4	51.4	33.5	41.5	26.5	28.4
	(51)	(173)	(44)	(83)	(28)	(43)
Widowed	.5	3.4	3.3	11.6	2.5	29.4
	(2)	(13)	(5)	(19)	(3)	(45)
TOTAL	100.0	100.0	100.0	100.0	100.0	100.0
(Unweighted N = 933)	(164)	(288)	(105)	(165)	(77)	(134)
Hispanic						
First married	59.0	54.2	70.2	63.6	70.9	44.5
	(40)	(60)	(25)	(35)	(23)	(17)
Remarried	19.0	13.9	18.2	6.6	10.4	6.3
	(11)	(16)	(5)	(5)	(6)	(4)
Separated/ divorced/ never married	20.8	31.3	11.6	20.7	8.7	36.0
	(16)	(62)	(5)	(20)	(4)	(21)
Widowed	1.2	.6	.0	9.2	10.0	13.2
	(2)	(1)	(0)	(6)	(3)	(13)
TOTAL	100.0	100.0	100.0	100.0	100.0	100.0
(Unweighted N = 400)	(69)	(139)	(35)	(66)	(36)	(55)

Source: National Survey of Families and Households, 1987–88; primary respondents who are biological, adoptive, and/or stepparents.

[a] Includes other race/ethnic (unweighted N = 60) as well as non-Hispanic white, black, and Hispanic parents.

tween first-marriage families and remarriage families—especially when there are stepchildren involved (e.g., White and Booth 1985). Remarried parents now constitute about one in five midlife parents.

Likewise, separated, divorced, and never married parents were collapsed into one category, but a distinction between these single parents and widowed parents was made when the total population of midlife parents was examined. Although widows and widowers are "single" parents too, previous research has shown that making this differentiation reveals economic, emotional, and social differences between these groups (Kitson et al. 1989). Data in table 2.2 for "all parents" indicate little widowhood among midlife parents until the third decade of midlife (ages fifty-five to sixty-four) among women, where 17.6 percent are in this category. Because of gender differences in mortality and higher rates of remarriage for men (Glick and Lin 1986), even at the older bounds of midlife less than 5 percent of men are widowers.

Unmarried parents, overall, constitute approximately another one in five midlife parents. Single parenting as well as remarried parenting is more common in the younger midlife cohorts, with the proportions of midlife parents who are in nontraditional families expected to grow in the future (Bumpass 1990). (It is also worth remembering that those in the "remarried" category now were also at one time in their lives either divorced or widowed.)

In parallel statistics for non-Hispanic white parents only, we find patterns similar to those found in the total population for marital status, except for somewhat higher proportions in first marriages and lower proportions in nonwidowed single status. Blacks evidence a significantly lower likelihood of being in first marriages and a higher likelihood of being single. For the youngest cohorts of black mothers, more than half (54.7 percent) are in the single-parent categories. On the other hand, Hispanic parents fall between non-Hispanic whites and blacks in rates of single parenting.

Even with the aggregation of Mexican-Americans, Puerto Ricans, Cubans, and other Hispanics, sample sizes for the separate marital statuses used to generate statistics for Hispanics become rather small, especially for single Hispanic parents, and are subject to high standard errors. Therefore, when a race/ethnic breakdown was made in subsequent tables, first-married and remarried cells were collapsed into a "married" category, and separated/divorced/never married and widowed were collapsed into a "single" category. Particular caution is urged in overinterpreting estimates of Hispanic marital status differences.

TABLE 2.3. Mean Years of Education by Sex, Age, Marital Status, and Race/Ethnicity: U.S. Parents Ages 35–64

	Age					
	35–44		45–54		55–64	
Marital Status	Men	Women	Men	Women	Men	Women
Total[a]						
First married	14.1	13.3	13.2	12.5	12.3	11.9
Remarried	13.3	13.2	12.7	12.2	12.2	11.6
Separated/ divorced/ never married	12.9	12.3	12.3	11.9	11.7	10.5
Widowed	13.2	12.6	11.6	12.0	10.4	11.2
TOTAL	13.8	13.0	13.0	12.3	12.2	11.6
(Standard deviation)	(3.1)	(2.9)	(3.6)	(2.8)	(3.7)	(3.0)
Non-Hispanic white						
Married	14.2	13.6	13.6	12.7	12.7	12.1
Single	13.5	12.8	13.1	12.3	12.2	11.7
TOTAL	14.1	13.4	13.6	12.6	12.6	12.0
(Standard deviation)	(2.8)	(2.5)	(3.2)	(2.5)	(3.3)	(2.6)
Black						
Married	12.9	12.7	10.5	12.0	10.2	11.6
Single	11.7	12.3	11.2	11.1	9.3	10.5
TOTAL	12.6	12.5	10.7	11.6	10.0	10.9
(Standard deviation)	(3.0)	(2.2)	(3.5)	(3.1)	(4.3)	(2.9)
Hispanic						
Married	11.3	9.8	8.9	9.0	8.5	7.8
Single	11.7	9.3	6.3	11.1	9.4	7.2
TOTAL	11.4	9.6	8.6	9.6	8.6	7.5
(Standard deviation)	(4.3)	(3.9)	(4.4)	(4.2)	(4.4)	(4.2)

Source: National Survey of Families and Households, 1987–88; primary respondents who are biological, adoptive, and/or stepparents. Total unweighted N = 4,992. Estimates are based on weighted data.

[a]Includes other race/ethnic as well as non-Hispanic white, black, and Hispanic parents.

Education

Table 2.3 first provides estimated means for years of formal education among all midlife parents. For the vast majority of people, lifetime educational attainment is completed before the age of thirty-five, thus the differences across the ages in this case can probably be best interpreted as historical cohort differences, with higher educational attainment apparent among younger cohorts in comparison with older co-horts. The total gender group means for all parents suggest that over twenty years of birth cohorts, educational attainment has increased for both men and women by about a year and a half—from 12.2 years for the oldest men to 13.8 years for the youngest men, and from 11.6 years for the oldest women to 13.0 years for the youngest women. Men, therefore, continue to have an educational advantage. Parents in first marriages tend to have more years of education than do those in other marital statuses. Separated/divorced/never married parents have the lowest levels of education in each age group.

Race and ethnic comparisons indicate that non-Hispanic whites have higher overall levels of education in every case than blacks; His-panics have the lowest levels of education—more than one population standard deviation lower in every case of comparison with non-Hispanic white parents. This may be due, in part, to language obstacles and/or immigration from third world conditions. Single parents gener-ally are at an educational disadvantage in comparison with married parents.

Employment

In a similar way, table 2.4, displays employment levels (including both part-time and full-time) among midlife parents. Fathers work more than mothers, but rates of mothers' employment are still quite high for parents aged thirty-five to fifty-four. The lower levels of em-ployment among mothers aged fifty-five to sixty-four likely reflect a cohort effect—somewhat lower levels of employment for older cohorts of women—as well as developmental age trend toward somewhat re-duced employment beginning around age fifty-five and accelerating after age sixty. In future decades it is still an open question whether men and women will increasingly opt to retire as early as possible, or whether gradually pushing back the eligibility for full social security to age sixty-seven will encourage lengthening years of labor force par-ticipation for both men and women. Currently, some extension of la-bor force participation into later middle age has been observed for women, with shortened years of labor force participation occurring among men (Bianchi and Spain 1986).

Single non-Hispanic white mothers are more likely to work than married non-Hispanic white mothers. Married black mothers, how-ever, are employed at higher rates than single black mothers and mar-ried non-Hispanic white mothers. Married Hispanic mothers are least

TABLE 2.4. Weighted Percentage Employed by Sex, Age, Marital Status, and Race/Ethnicity: U.S. Parents Ages 35–64 (%)

	Age					
	35–44		45–54		55–64	
Marital Status	Fathers	Mothers	Fathers	Mothers	Fathers	Mothers
Total[a]						
First married	95.5	68.8	90.1	68.0	66.2	35.0
Remarried	90.4	70.8	86.0	68.8	63.2	42.8
Separated/ divorced/ never married	88.3	74.9	78.8	72.7	65.6	52.5
Widowed	91.0	62.2	76.0	71.4	43.2	49.8
TOTAL	93.5	70.4	87.6	69.3	64.8	40.6
Non-Hispanic white						
Married	95.4	68.9	89.9	69.8	66.9	36.2
Single	90.0	79.1	86.1	78.3	66.3	54.7
TOTAL	94.9	70.7	89.5	71.6	66.8	40.6
Black						
Married	88.9	80.2	85.6	70.5	61.0	49.2
Single	90.6	70.8	64.3	60.7	54.2	45.9
TOTAL	89.4	75.0	77.8	65.3	59.1	47.3
Hispanic						
Married	89.4	61.6	81.9	44.7	58.7	26.8
Single	81.0	56.9	100.0	58.5	40.2	31.1
TOTAL	87.5	60.1	84.0	48.8	55.3	28.9

Source: National Survey of Families and Households, 1987–88; primary respondents who are biological, adoptive, and/or stepparents. Total unweighted N = 4,992.

[a]Includes other race/ethnic as well as non-Hispanic white, black, and Hispanic parents.

likely to be working, especially in the older cohorts, which may represent a greater gender role traditionalism as well as low levels of educational preparation for employment in this group. Yet among younger cohorts (those thirty-five to forty-four) of Hispanics, more married mothers are in the labor force, and similar to young midlife black mothers, married parents have higher rates of employment than do single parents.

Higher unemployment among minority fathers than non-Hispanic white fathers in the peak midlife earning years is noteworthy. Unemployment for black and Hispanic fathers at ages thirty-five to forty-four is *double* that for non-Hispanic white fathers (10.6 percent versus

5.1 percent). During the highest earning age period for households, between the ages of forty-five and fifty-five (see also table 2.5 and figure 3.1 in Meyer, this volume), nine out of ten (89.5 percent) non-Hispanic white fathers are working, whereas only a little more than three of four (77.8 percent) black fathers are employed. The rate for Hispanic fathers falls in between (84.0 percent). This pattern of disparity is also evident for the older cohorts, although the proportionate gap narrows somewhat. These figures are not a good sign about minority fathers' ability to maintain successfully the "breadwinning" roles so critical to family life. Nor are they encouraging about minority fathers' prospects for an economically secure transition to older age.

Household Income

Table 2.5 displays median total household incomes. In survey work, data on income are some of the most difficult on which to receive accurate reports. Much more data is missing here (for about 23 percent of respondents) than on any other measure. Those for whom income data were lacking were less well educated, more likely to be black, less likely to be married, and more likely to be older. These demographic statuses are associated with lower incomes, so the medians presented here are likely to be higher than an even better subsample representation would provide. Total household income is a measure that includes all types of income (earned and unearned) by all members in the household.

Income figures for the total sample of parents indicate that the marital status ranking of household income is first-married, remarried, widowed, and separated/divorced/never married. Developmentally across the age periods there is a trend toward peak household income during ages forty-five to fifty-four. In the age fifty-five to sixty-four decade, household income already begins to taper off, probably due to the lower levels of employment apparent in table 2.4. Single mothers are found having less than half the household incomes of married mothers. Single fathers also show the single-earner reduction, although it is not as steep as it is for single mothers. In the younger two decades, married mothers appear to have household incomes even a bit higher than those of married fathers, probably because of the tendency for women to be married to slightly older (and higher-earning) men.

Blacks consistently trail non-Hispanic whites in household income, and except among the oldest cohorts (age fifty-five to sixty-four), Hispanics do even more poorly overall. Single mothers of all race and

TABLE 2.5. Median Total Household Income by Sex, Age, Marital Status, and Race/Ethnicity: U.S. Parents Ages 35–64 ($)

	Age					
	35–44		45–54		55–64	
Marital Status	Fathers	Mothers	Fathers	Mothers	Fathers	Mothers
Total[a]						
First married	41,350	42,688	45,950	45,357	38,735	35,500
Remarried	40,003	41,159	37,900	43,057	34,018	26,419
Separated/ divorced/ never married	26,963	16,978	31,290	17,576	25,162	12,100
Widowed	29,124	18,151	21,434	20,905	12,744	11,817
TOTAL	40,039	37,501	42,281	35,456	33,250	26,132
Non-Hispanic white						
Married	42,100	45,725	48,442	45,750	39,491	35,589
Single	29,705	19,163	33,720	20,073	25,142	13,990
TOTAL	41,337	40,350	45,950	39,362	36,234	30,332
Black						
Married	33,743	37,588	34,344	38,178	22,063	24,500
Single	23,763	12,441	30,100	10,104	12,585	6,754
TOTAL	31,131	25,311	32,073	20,775	20,200	9,505
Hispanic						
Married	23,445	21,141	17,228	26,930	23,641	26,100
Single	20,015	9,946	22,405	21,167	16,851	6,166
TOTAL	21,910	16,013	17,604	24,665	23,151	19,467

Source: National Survey of Families and Households, 1987–88; primary respondents who are biological, adoptive, and/or stepparents. Total unweighted N = 4,992. Estimates are based on weighted data.

[a]Includes other race/ethnic as well as non-Hispanic white, black, and Hispanic parents.

ethnic groups are clearly disadvantaged, with significant deterioration in household income evident in later middle age. It will remain to be seen whether younger cohorts of working women will be able to decrease this developmental disadvantage in late midlife by more continuous and more equitably paid labor force participation (Marini 1989).

Use of Public Assistance

Another way of evaluating economic disadvantage is found in table 2.6, which displays the proportion of persons who indicated that they

TABLE 2.6. Weighted Percentage of Persons Who Received Public Assistance at Any Time since 1982 by Sex, Age, Marital Status, and Race/Ethnicity: U.S. Parents Ages 35–64 (%)

	Age					
	35–44		45–54		55–64	
Marital Status	Fathers	Mothers	Fathers	Mothers	Fathers	Mothers
Total[a]						
First married	3.0	4.0	2.3	2.2	2.5	0.6
Remarried	8.0	9.0	10.4	5.9	7.0	1.0
Separated/						
divorced/						
never married	9.0	27.2	10.2	20.4	10.3	16.8
Widowed	9.0	14.0	15.4	15.3	3.4	9.6
TOTAL	4.8	10.1	5.2	7.3	4.3	4.1
Non-Hispanic white						
Married	3.2	4.1	2.6	2.3	3.0	0.4
Single	8.3	20.0	11.0	13.2	4.1	9.6
TOTAL	3.7	6.9	3.6	4.7	3.1	2.6
Black						
Married	6.8	4.6	4.8	3.3	7.2	1.6
Single	7.2	31.6	8.0	34.3	8.7	22.4
TOTAL	7.0	19.3	6.0	19.6	7.6	13.6
Hispanic						
Married	12.2	18.3	15.4	13.1	6.6	5.8
Single	9.4	46.8	0.0	31.5	10.4	12.9
TOTAL	11.6	27.4	13.5	18.6	7.3	9.3

Source: National Survey of Families and Households, 1987–88; primary respondents who are biological, adoptive, and/or stepparents. Total unweighted N = 4,992.

[a]Includes other race/ethnic as well as non-Hispanic white, black, and Hispanic parents.

had received public assistance since 1982 (representing a period of about five years when interviewed in 1987–88). For "all parents," re-marrieds were more likely than first-married adults to have encountered such a period of economic difficulty. Having a "spell" of poverty is not a rare event in the American population (Bane and Ellwood 1986). It often occurs after a divorce, but within a few years people often leave poverty either through remarriage or better employment. The highest five-year incidence of utilizing public assistance occurs for those still single, especially among the younger two midlife groups. Black single mothers are the most likely to have received public assistance. This fits with the profile of relatively low education, employment, and total household incomes seen previously for them. And, again, this proportion of black parents is not small—for those thirty-five to forty-four, about 55 percent of black mothers are single mothers (table 2.2)–and almost a third of them reported depending on public assistance at some time in the last five years.

Single Hispanic mothers in the youngest middle-aged decade also have relatively high levels of public assistance receipt, but they are a much smaller proportion of the parent population (about 27 percent, see table 2.2). Public assistance is relatively common for both married and single Hispanic parents, perhaps because Hispanic parents' education, employment, and income levels are often so poor.

Home Ownership

Still another way to consider family resources is to examine home ownership. Table 2.7 provides estimates of the proportion of parents owning a home. Again, first-married parents lead in this indicator of wealth, followed by remarrieds. Widows are next most likely to own homes. Other single parents are least likely to own a home. Not every home is better than every apartment for family life, to be sure, but home ownership has certainly been a part of the "American dream" and must generally be seen as an advantage for providing a home life for children, their friends, and, in later middle age, grandchildren. Also, home ownership in middle age is likely to be translated into equity, wealth, and reduced home expense as homes are paid off in late middle age and older age.

Race and ethnic differences in home ownership are glaring. While about four out of five non-Hispanic white, early midlife parents (thirty-five to forty-four) own their own homes, only a little more than one in two minority parents do. Less than one in three single minority parents (fathers or mothers) own their own homes. And this is during the period of midlife when parents are most likely to have younger children at home.

Net Worth

Net worth is another important indicator relevant to intergenerational relationships and the relative ease with which midlife parents might be able to give to children or might be in need of help from children. It is not easy to get complete data from respondents for a calculation of total wealth, but the NSFH tried to get enough indicators

TABLE 2.7. Weighted Percentage Homeowners by Sex, Age, Marital Status, and Race/Ethnicity: U.S. Parents Ages 35–64 (%)

	Age					
	35–44		45–54		55–64	
Marital Status	Fathers	Mothers	Fathers	Mothers	Fathers	Mothers
Total[a]						
First married	85.6	85.7	89.8	88.7	92.7	88.4
Remarried	75.0	73.5	74.1	80.2	85.7	83.0
Separated/ divorced/ never married	36.8	38.6	49.0	52.2	42.6	50.6
Widowed	91.0	67.4	72.0	66.0	70.0	64.9
TOTAL	77.4	73.1	80.7	78.6	85.0	79.2
Non-Hispanic white						
Married	86.9	85.3	89.2	87.5	93.0	89.5
Single	46.5	45.9	58.6	59.6	54.8	66.4
TOTAL	82.7	78.4	85.6	81.4	88.3	84.0
Black						
Married	69.3	76.2	76.3	89.0	87.0	80.1
Single	22.2	32.1	34.9	44.5	36.3	41.6
TOTAL	56.3	52.2	60.8	65.4	72.3	57.9
Hispanic						
Married	54.6	63.0	64.1	72.2	68.0	62.0
Single	29.7	30.6	34.2	50.6	56.4	52.7
TOTAL	49.2	52.6	60.6	65.8	65.8	57.4

Source: National Survey of Families and Households, 1987–88; primary respondents who are biological, adoptive, and/or stepparents. Total unweighted N = 4,992.

[a]Includes other race/ethnic as well as non-Hispanic white, black, and Hispanic parents.

to create at least a rough assessment. The measure used here first took the difference between respondent estimates of the selling price and the amount owed on personal property assets—home, other real estate, business or farm, and motor vehicles (including cars, trucks, campers, boats, and other recreational vehicles)—and added these amounts together. Then the approximate total value of respondent (and her or his spouse's) savings (including savings accounts, savings bonds, IRAs, money market shares, and certificates of deposit) as well as the approximate total value of respondent (and spouse's) investments (including stocks, bonds, shares in mutual funds, or other investments) were added in. Finally, amounts that the respondent reported he or she owed

on credit cards or charge accounts, installment loans for major pur-
chases (other than auto), educational loans, personal loans from banks
and other businesses other than mortgage or auto loans, personal loans
from friends or relatives, other bills owed for more than two months,
and home improvement loans were subtracted. Most people answered
these questions without refusal, but where data were missing for any
of these questions (or in the case of the property assets, if information
was missing on *either* value or debt), a zero was imputed. Thus, a net
worth amount was calculated for every person in the sample, even if
there was some incomplete information. It is important to be cautious
about overinterpreting these actual amounts though; this measure is
offered here more as a heuristic for a rough ranking of population
subgroups than as a measure reflecting exact numerical accuracy.

Estimates for the group of all parents in table 2.8 reveal a developmental trend of continuous accumulation continuing into late middle
age, even though it has already been noted that employment and yearly
household income begin to decrease during this period. It is the net
worth accumulated by late middle age, in fact, that is supposed to provide the "cushion" for good management of the lower earning years
of older age. But is this optimal developmental trend evident for all
groups of parents?

For men who remain in their first marriages, continuous accumulation over time is clear. Remarried fathers show evidence that disrupted
lives (often including a point when assets were split to some degree)
have taken a toll on their ability to accumulate wealth. Early widowed
men also show signs of disadvantage in relation to married men but are
clearly better off than other single fathers. Separated/divorced/never
married fathers fare the worst among fathers, but still not so poorly
as do separated/divorced/never married mothers, who are doing most
poorly among mothers. Remarried mothers also show an obvious
wealth disadvantage in comparison with first-marriage mothers as well
as remarried fathers.

The race and ethnic contrasts are instructive here. Perhaps it is net
worth trajectories that illustrate most clearly the effects of categorical
discrimination and disadvantage over the life course. Non-Hispanic
white fathers are consistently revealed to be substantially better off than
black fathers and Hispanic fathers. Married non-Hispanic white mothers report less wealth than married non-Hispanic white fathers but
are still very sizably advantaged in comparison with minority married
mothers. Single non-Hispanic white fathers are not doing as well as

TABLE 2.8. Median Net Worth by Sex, Age, Marital Status, and Race/Ethnicity: U.S. Parents Ages 35–64 ($)

	Age					
	35–44		45–54		55–64	
Marital Status	Fathers	Mothers	Fathers	Mothers	Fathers	Mothers
Total[a]						
First married	58,150	45,699	85,694	77,638	111,588	85,461
Remarried	39,620	31,873	51,936	50,000	71,500	44,621
Separated/ divorced/ never married	5,009	2,000	22,884	8,269	11,338	3,465
Widowed	24,151	19,747	65,550	28,644	69,233	37,071
TOTAL	47,001	28,074	66,286	58,384	90,499	60,654
Non-Hispanic white						
Married	66,499	50,000	88,553	80,860	130,299	88,235
Single	15,167	6,092	37,220	24,732	48,998	37,893
TOTAL	57,999	39,588	84,192	73,001	115,000	75,001
Black						
Married	13,222	13,092	15,602	17,329	23,039	40,304
Single	961	6	4,075	2	3,973	751
TOTAL	7,102	1,216	8,571	2,821	12,685	3,916
Hispanic						
Married	15,103	2,682	6,202	31,204	45,007	12,250
Single	252	2	902	4,540	43,405	1,405
TOTAL	12,001	1,166	6,051	25,007	45,108	4,249

Source: National Survey of Families and Households, 1987–88; primary respondents who are biological, adoptive, and/or stepparents. Total unweighted N = 4,992. Estimates are based on weighted data.

[a]Includes other race/ethnic as well as non-Hispanic white, black, and Hispanic parents.

their married counterparts but do considerably better in accumulating wealth than either single non-Hispanic white mothers or most minority group parents. The disadvantaged status of black single mothers is quite glaring here; median estimates of less than eight hundred dollars across all the ages suggest that half these mothers are living in debt not covered by other assets and at a considerable disadvantage in meeting unexpected needs and looking forward to retirement and old age. The pattern for single Hispanic mothers is one of similar economic vulnerability.

Physical Health

Another often neglected but nonetheless important personal resource of parents is health. It is during the midlife years that physical health problems often begin to become a concern. And variations in health are likely to be a factor in how easy or difficult it is for parents to fulfill their role obligations with their children, parents, and others. Health is associated with subjective evaluations of parenting; for example, poorer parental health has been linked with less satisfaction with adult child coresidence (see Aquilino, this volume).

NSFH respondents were asked whether they had a physical or mental condition that limited their ability to care for personal needs, such as dressing, eating, or going to the bathroom; move about inside the house; work for pay; do day-to-day tasks; climb a flight of stairs; or walk six blocks. Respondents who indicated a limitation in one or more of these activities were classified as having a functional health limitation. All other respondents were classified as not having such a limitation.

Table 2.9 displays midlife parent differences in functional health limitation. The developmental trend is in the direction of poorer health for older aged parents as might be expected; among all parents, less than one in twelve (5.2 percent–7.2 percent) midlife parents begin midlife limited, whereas about one in five (18.5 percent–20.7 percent) midlife parents has functional limitations in later midlife. Mothers report more health limitations than fathers. Single parents in the vast majority of cases report substantially higher rates of functional limitation than married parents. Minority parents also evidence much higher rates in every instance than do majority group white parents.

Mental Health

Psychological well-being is another resource necessary for successful functioning in the responsibility-laden middle years of adulthood. Table 2.10 describes differences among parents in one measure of mental health—psychological distress. Distress is measured in the NSFH using a modified form of the Center for Epidemiological Studies Depression Index (CES-D; see Radloff 1977). Each respondent was asked how many days during the last week he or she had experienced the following symptoms: (1) felt bothered by things that usually weren't bothersome,

TABLE 2.9. Weighted Percentage with Functional Health Limitation by Sex, Age, Marital Status, and Race/Ethnicity: U.S. Parents Ages 35–64 (%)

	Age					
	35–44		45–54		55–64	
Marital Status	Fathers	Mothers	Fathers	Mothers	Fathers	Mothers
Total[a]						
First married	3.0	4.9	7.3	8.8	15.1	18.6
Remarried	7.4	8.4	11.3	17.1	25.3	22.9
Separated/ divorced/ never married	13.2	11.6	10.4	21.1	20.0	28.8
Widowed	12.4	20.1	21.2	22.5	40.7	20.5
TOTAL	5.2	7.2	8.7	13.5	18.5	20.7
Non-Hispanic white						
Married	3.5	5.3	8.4	10.3	17.1	19.0
Single	9.5	10.3	5.4	16.9	19.1	20.1
TOTAL	4.1	6.2	8.0	11.7	17.3	19.2
Black						
Married	5.5	4.7	5.3	17.8	26.7	23.3
Single	15.3	15.7	28.4	24.5	16.0	35.0
TOTAL	8.2	10.7	13.7	21.3	23.6	29.9
Hispanic						
Married	7.9	7.8	4.2	9.1	12.2	21.9
Single	23.9	11.9	0.0	47.9	59.8	27.5
TOTAL	11.4	9.1	3.7	20.7	21.1	24.7

Source: National Survey of Families and Households, 1987–88; primary respondents who are biological, adoptive, and/or stepparents. Total unweighted N = 4,992.

[a]Includes other race/ethnic as well as non-Hispanic white, black, and Hispanic parents.

(2) did not feel like eating, (3) could not shake off the blues even with help from family or friends, (4) had trouble concentrating, (5) felt depressed, (6) felt that everything one did was an effort, (7) felt fearful, (8) slept restlessly, (9) talked less than usual, (10) felt lonely, (11) felt sad, and (12) could not get going. Answers to these questions were totaled, resulting in an index of symptom days during the past week ranging from zero to eighty-four. Mean score for midlife parents was 12.8, with a standard deviation of 16.3, indicating a significant skew toward the low end of the distribution. Internal consistency (Cronbach's alpha) for this scale is .94.

TABLE 2.10. Mean Number of Psychological Distress Symptom Days during the Last Week by Sex, Age, Marital Status, and Race/Ethnicity: U.S. Parents Ages 35–64

	Age					
	35–44		45–54		55–64	
Marital Status	Fathers	Mothers	Fathers	Mothers	Fathers	Mothers
Total[a]						
First married	9.9	12.1	10.5	11.5	8.0	13.1
Remarried	10.7	15.5	11.4	16.6	13.1	16.8
Separated/ divorced/ never married	20.0	19.3	12.9	18.7	15.4	15.3
Widowed	5.3	22.4	19.7	20.3	14.7	17.5
TOTAL	11.3	14.5	11.1	14.3	9.9	14.6
(Standard deviation)	(15.3)	(16.6)	(15.6)	(16.8)	(15.3)	(17.5)
Non-Hispanic white						
Married	10.0	12.6	10.5	12.3	8.4	13.8
Single	17.0	19.3	13.3	16.6	12.7	16.4
TOTAL	10.7	13.7	10.8	13.2	8.9	14.4
(Standard deviation)	(14.1)	(16.1)	(15.2)	(15.3)	(14.2)	(17.7)
Black						
Married	10.9	14.6	14.0	10.6	15.3	14.3
Single	22.7	21.3	14.6	24.9	12.2	15.5
TOTAL	14.1	18.2	14.2	18.4	14.4	15.0
(Standard deviation)	(19.1)	(17.9)	(19.1)	(20.2)	(17.7)	(17.0)
Hispanic						
Married	10.6	13.3	9.0	20.1	10.4	13.6
Single	25.0	17.8	10.3	20.4	27.3	19.8
TOTAL	13.7	14.7	9.2	20.2	13.4	16.2
(Standard deviation)	(19.7)	(17.5)	(13.9)	(24.3)	(19.7)	(17.1)

Source: National Survey of Families and Households, 1987–88; primary respondents who are biological and adoptive parents. Total unweighted N = 4,992. Estimates are based on weighted data.

[a]Includes other race/ethnic as well as non-Hispanic white, black, and Hispanic parents.

Mothers, overall, report more psychological distress than fathers. Remarried parents report more symptoms than first-marriage parents. Single parents—both mothers and fathers—report the highest levels of psychological distress. Black single mothers aged thirty-five to forty-four and forty-five to fifty-four, for example, report a mean of 21.3 symptom days and 24.9 symptom days, respectively. By contrast, black married mothers aged thirty-five to forty-four report a mean of 14.6 symptom days, and those forty-four to fifty-four, a mean of 10.6 symptom days—much closer to the mean for the entire sample of midlife parents. Overall, similar gender and marital status patterns can be observed for each of the three race/ethnic groups, except minority group parents consistently report higher levels of distress symptoms than majority group (non-Hispanic) white parents.

DIVERSITY IN CHARACTERISTICS OF MIDLIFE PARENTS' CHILDREN

Having examined several indicators of diversity in parental resources over the middle years, I turn to an exploration of differences in the characteristics of midlife parents' children. Many studies of parents either ignore child differences or make only minimal attempts to control for them. With the interdependence of lives characteristic of the parent-child relationship, however, it would seem all the more important to consider which and how child characteristic differences influence the experience of midlife parenting (see also in this volume Aquilino; Allen et al.; Pruchno, Dempsey, and Burant; Ryff, Schmutte, and Lee; Seltzer et al.; Silverberg; Umberson).

Number of Biological and/or Adopted Children

Table 2.11 displays the mean number of biological and/or adopted children of midlife parents. The base population for this table includes only parents who reported biological and/or adopted children. About 3 percent of parents who reported only stepchildren were excluded. Considering estimates across the age decades provides for the most part a picture of historical cohort variability here, because the majority of childbearing is completed before age thirty-five; Bianchi and Spain (1986) report that for those who had completed their childbearing by 1980, 82 percent had done so by age thirty-five and 95 percent had done so by age thirty-nine. A trend toward smaller families over these birth cohorts is clearly observable—for parents overall, about one less child.

Looking at race/ethnic differences reveals that that tendency for mi-

TABLE 2.11. Mean Number of Biological and/or Adopted Children by Sex, Age, Marital Status, and Race/Ethnicity: U.S. Parents Ages 35–64

	Age					
	35–44		45–54		55–64	
Marital Status	Fathers	Mothers	Fathers	Mothers	Fathers	Mothers
Total[a]						
First married	2.5	2.5	3.1	3.2	3.3	3.5
Remarried	2.4	2.5	3.3	3.0	3.2	3.2
Separated/ divorced/ never married	2.2	2.6	2.7	3.2	3.0	3.6
Widowed	2.5	2.7	2.9	3.1	3.9	3.6
TOTAL	2.4	2.6	3.1	3.2	3.3	3.5
(Standard deviation)	(1.2)	(1.3)	(1.6)	(1.6)	(1.7)	(2.0)
Non-Hispanic white						
Married	2.4	2.5	3.0	3.1	3.1	3.3
Single	2.1	2.4	2.5	2.9	2.9	3.4
TOTAL	2.3	2.4	3.0	3.0	3.1	3.3
(Standard deviation)	(1.1)	(1.2)	(1.4)	(1.5)	(1.5)	(1.8)
Black						
Married	2.8	2.5	3.5	3.5	4.7	3.9
Single	2.6	2.9	3.2	4.0	4.4	4.0
TOTAL	2.8	2.7	3.4	3.7	4.6	4.0
(Standard deviation)	(1.4)	(1.5)	(1.9)	(2.2)	(2.4)	(2.5)
Hispanic						
Married	3.0	3.4	4.5	4.0	4.0	4.9
Single	2.5	3.2	4.3	3.2	4.6	3.8
TOTAL	2.9	3.4	4.5	3.7	4.1	4.4
(Standard deviation)	(1.9)	(1.7)	(2.8)	(2.2)	(2.3)	(2.7)

Source: National Survey of Families and Households, 1987–88; primary respondents who are biological and adoptive parents. Total unweighted N = 4,992. Estimates are based on weighted data.

[a]Includes other race/ethnic as well as non-Hispanic white, black, and Hispanic parents.

nority parents to have more children remains, but it has decreased among younger cohorts. Hispanics are the most likely to have larger families, although younger cohorts show an even higher rate of birth reduction over these birth cohorts than is apparent for non-Hispanic whites.

Parents with Stepchildren

Next, table 2.12 returns to the full population of midlife parents, including parents of stepchildren only, and details the proportion of parents in each population subgroup who have stepchildren. Not surprisingly, remarried persons are most likely to have stepchildren, but even some first-married persons have stepchildren from marrying someone who has been married before. Single males evidence somewhat higher rates of being a stepparent than do single females, in part because "singles" in this analysis include cohabitors, and the measure of stepchildren used here includes children in the respondent's household who are the children of a cohabiting partner (usually a mother).

This table illustrates that being a stepparent is hardly a rare event of midlife—especially for men and for younger cohorts. About one in six or seven midlife parents is a stepparent today because of high divorce rates and remarriage rates during early adulthood. Blacks have the highest rates of stepparenthood; about one in five black midlife fathers reports being a stepparent. The lifetime rate of stepparenting would be even somewhat higher, because a respondent is less likely to name a former stepchild when surveyed if a remarriage has failed, (Cherlin, Griffith, and McCarthy 1983). As mentioned earlier, however, only about 3 percent of midlife parents are parents *only* to stepchildren. Therefore, most of the stepparenting that takes place occurs *together with* parenting of biological and/or adopted children (either in the same household or separate households). The complexity that this may provide in terms of obligations and responsibilities to one's own and one's stepchildren—and in relationship to a spouse who has children from another marriage—are factors that certainly must be included now in thinking about the challenges of midlife parenting and the diversity of midlife parenting experiences.

Child Age Differences

Table 2.13 displays how the ages of children being parented are changing during the three decades of midlife under evaluation here. Current marital status would not be expected to have a significant im-

TABLE 2.12. Weighted Percentage with Stepchild(ren) by Sex, Age, Marital Status, and Race/Ethnicity: U.S. Parents Ages 35–64 (%)

| | Age | | | | | |
| | 35–44 | | 45–54 | | 55–64 | |
Marital Status	Fathers	Mothers	Fathers	Mothers	Fathers	Mothers
All Parents[a]						
Unweighted						
N = 4,992						
First married	6.3	7.4	5.8	6.1	3.7	3.7
Remarried	34.5	41.2	44.4	52.9	63.5	43.9
Separated/						
divorced/						
never married	16.4	10.2	17.4	4.6	15.1	2.8
Widowed	6.9	19.0	4.5	15.6	20.7	7.3
TOTAL	13.3	14.5	15.4	14.4	17.2	9.7
White parents						
Unweighted						
N = 3,599						
Married	11.6	15.4	15.6	17.4	18.1	10.5
Single	13.5	9.9	9.6	9.1	16.4	5.3
TOTAL	11.8	14.4	14.9	15.6	17.9	9.2
Black parents						
Unweighted						
N = 933						
Married	22.6	25.9	19.9	18.4	18.4	31.7
Single	19.9	11.8	24.3	3.0	14.9	4.5
TOTAL	21.8	18.2	21.5	10.3	17.4	16.3
Hispanic parents						
Unweighted						
N = 400						
Married	14.7	7.8	7.1	6.2	6.9	5.0
Single	26.1	7.2	46.7	0.0	29.1	8.9
TOTAL	17.3	7.6	11.7	4.3	11.1	6.9

Source: National Survey of Families and Households, 1987–88; primary respondents who are biological, adoptive, and/or stepparents.

[a]Includes other race/ethnic as well as non-Hispanic white, black, and Hispanic parents.

TABLE 2.13. Weighted Percent Distribution of Child Age Types by Sex, Age, Marital Status, and Race/Ethnicity: U.S. Parents Ages 35–64 (%)

Child(ren)'s Age(s)	Age					
	35–44		45–54		55–64	
	Fathers	Mothers	Fathers	Mothers	Fathers	Mothers
Total[a]						
Only 18 and under	73.8	60.8	15.0	4.9	1.0	0.4
Both 18 and under and 19 and older	20.8	29.9	44.1	32.5	13.3	5.8
Only 19 and older	5.4	9.4	40.9	62.7	85.7	93.7
TOTAL	100.0	100.0	100.0	100.0	100.0	100.0
Non-Hispanic white						
Only 18 and under	74.6	62.5	14.9	4.4	0.3	0.2
Both 18 and under and 19 and older	19.9	28.2	42.4	31.4	11.6	4.4
Only 19 and older	5.5	9.3	42.7	64.1	88.0	95.4
TOTAL	100.0	100.0	100.0	100.0	100.0	100.0

pact on ages of children at midlife, so for this table three child age contrasts are described for all marital statuses combined across the three midlife decades: having nonadult children *only* (age eighteen and under only); having *both* nonadult children *and also* adult children (age eighteen and under and also age nineteen and over); and having adult children only (children nineteen and older only).

For the youngest decade of midlife, childrearing for the majority is confined to rearing nonadult children. A sizable proportion of parents also juggle children who are both young adults and nonadults. A relatively small proportion of parents has only adult children by the time they are age forty-five. Women have children at younger ages and watch children age at correspondingly somewhat younger ages themselves than men do. Blacks have children at younger ages and also

TABLE 2.13. (Continued)

Child(ren)'s Age(s)	Age					
	35–44		45–54		55–64	
	Fathers	Mothers	Fathers	Mothers	Fathers	Mothers
Black						
Only 18 and under	62.1	48.4	12.3	4.6	1.2	0.6
Both 18 and under and 19 and older	31.7	38.7	46.5	33.6	22.0	10.6
Only 19 and older	6.2	12.9	41.2	61.8	76.8	88.8
TOTAL	100.0	100.0	100.0	100.0	100.0	100.0
Hispanic						
Only 18 and under	78.8	59.9	19.4	8.4	5.4	3.4
Both 18 and under and 19 and older	19.9	33.7	61.5	42.5	25.9	14.1
Only 19 and older	1.4	6.4	19.1	49.1	68.7	82.5
TOTAL	100.0	100.0	100.0	100.0	100.0	100.0

Source: National Survey of Families and Households, 1987–88; primary respondents who are biological, adoptive, and/or stepparents. Total unweighted N = 4,992.
[a]Includes other race/ethnic as well as non-Hispanic white, black, and Hispanic parents.

begin to see them move into adulthood when they themselves are at somewhat younger ages.

By ages forty-five to fifty-four, substantially fewer parents have only nonadult children. The vast majority now either have only adult children or have *both* adult children and nonadult children. By the last decade of midlife, very few parents have children under nineteen anymore. Slightly larger families for blacks and Hispanics mean that this process of "aging out" children spans a somewhat longer period for them than for non-Hispanic whites.

Coresidence with Children

Table 2.14 describes demographic differences in the likelihood that midlife parents have a child (any age) living in their household. This

TABLE 2.14. Weighted Percentage with Child(ren) Living
in Household by Sex, Age, Marital Status, and Race/Ethnicity:
U.S. Parents Ages 35–64 (%)

| | Age | | | | | |
| | 35–44 | | 45–54 | | 55–64 | |
Marital Status	Fathers	Mothers	Fathers	Mothers	Fathers	Mothers
Total[a]						
First married	96.8	96.2	76.0	69.7	36.9	31.7
Remarried	81.8	83.7	73.3	48.4	34.6	17.8
Separated/ divorced/ never married	34.2	86.9	28.6	71.4	22.0	43.8
Widowed	87.1	84.6	64.0	58.2	43.9	45.1
TOTAL	85.9	91.7	68.9	65.7	35.1	33.5
Non-Hispanic white						
Married	93.0	93.4	73.8	63.1	32.5	25.5
Single	37.0	85.8	30.8	62.8	24.7	35.9
TOTAL	87.2	92.1	68.8	63.1	31.5	28.0
Black						
Married	91.1	89.4	77.9	71.2	56.8	49.5
Single	32.2	87.2	28.0	74.7	28.1	59.8
TOTAL	74.8	88.2	59.9	73.1	48.7	55.3
Hispanic						
Married	93.3	93.2	75.3	64.7	36.4	29.1
Single	36.3	86.7	31.3	68.3	27.4	44.6
TOTAL	85.9	91.7	68.9	65.7	35.1	33.5

Source: National Survey of Families and Households, 1987–88; primary respondents who are biological, adoptive, and/or stepparents. Total unweighted N = 4,992.
[a]Includes other race/ethnic as well as non-Hispanic white, black, and Hispanic parents.

table makes apparent the important difference between single (particularly separated, divorced, or never-married) fathers and single mothers in parenting. About two-thirds of single fathers are not living with children—and a number of the ones who *are* being counted here as living with a child are actually living with a cohabiting partner's child(ren). The fact that single fathers often do not live with their children might lead us to hypothesize that their experiences of midlife parenting will differ greatly from that of either single mothers with resident children or married parents with children. They do not have some of the day-to-day responsibilities, but they may also be missing the development of close ties with children that coresidence facilitates—ties that may become more significant to them as they age and have the potential for increased dependency (Cooney and Uhlenberg 1990).

Remarried mothers also evidence reduced rates of having children in residence, likely due to in part to the greater propensity of children in remarried households to leave home at an earlier age (Aquilino 1990; Goldscheider and Goldscheider 1989; White and Booth 1985).

Coresidence with Adult Children

Table 2.15 provides another vantage point on the process of children becoming adults: the percentage of parents in each subgroup (keeping the total population of parents as a base) who have an adult child (age nineteen or older) living at home. These children may never have left home, or they may have "left the nest" and returned. This table reveals that watching children reach the magic age of eighteen or nineteen is hardly always the end of in-house parenting of children (see also Aquilino, this volume). In the earliest decade of midlife, the fact that the majority of parents don't yet have children over nineteen keeps the figures down (see also table 2.11). The highest rates of having adult children at home occur during ages forty-five to fifty-four. The level is highest for first-married parents: among mothers it is 49.8 percent, and among first-married fathers the rate is 45.9 percent. Remarried parents have clearly lower rates: 26.4 percent of remarried mothers and 17.7 percent of remarried fathers ages forty-five to fifty-four have adult children at home. This additional evidence is congruent with the research about earlier home leaving in stepfamilies (Aquilino 1990; Goldscheider and Goldscheider 1989; White and Booth 1985).

Single mothers are again more likely than single fathers to have adult children living with them. Younger widows and widowers are also quite likely to have adult children living with them. In most cases delineated here, black and Hispanic parents have higher rates of adult child coresidence than non-Hispanic whites.

Grandparenting

One of the significant social transitions of midlife is the event of becoming a grandparent to one or more grandchildren. Table 2.16 displays how in a relatively short span of midlife years the grandparenting role is acquired by most midlife parents. A sharp increase is noted in the decade around age fifty, and by ages fifty-five to sixty-four a large majority of midlifers have become grandparents.

Nadine F. Marks

Table 2.15. Weighted Percentage with Adult Child(ren) (Age 19+) Living in Household by Sex, Age, Marital Status, and Race/ Ethnicity: U.S. Parents Ages 35–64 (%)

| | Age | | | | | |
| | 35–44 | | 45–54 | | 55–64 | |
Marital Status	Fathers	Mothers	Fathers	Mothers	Fathers	Mothers
Total[a]						
First married	13.8	17.0	45.9	49.8	31.4	28.3
Remarried	9.2	15.2	17.7	26.4	14.2	11.2
Separated/ divorced/ never married	3.9	19.7	16.8	49.4	16.8	35.4
Widowed	20.5	30.8	22.9	42.3	42.4	41.2
TOTAL	11.7	17.5	35.8	45.2	26.8	29.0
Non-Hispanic white						
Married	12.7	16.3	38.1	43.7	25.2	22.3
Single	3.1	16.3	16.3	43.4	21.8	33.2
TOTAL	11.7	16.3	35.6	43.6	24.8	24.9
Black						
Married	14.3	22.8	37.6	48.8	42.8	43.7
Single	11.2	25.1	16.0	54.9	15.4	45.8
TOTAL	13.4	24.1	29.8	52.0	35.1	44.9
Hispanic						
Married	14.5	15.6	50.9	53.9	38.9	47.8
Single	0.0	25.3	46.7	59.1	64.0	53.8
TOTAL	11.3	18.7	50.4	55.4	43.6	50.8

Source: National Survey of Families and Households, 1987–88; primary respondents who are biological, adoptive, and/or stepparents. Total unweighted N = 4,992.

[a]Includes other race/ethnic as well as non-Hispanic white, black, and Hispanic parents.

Women tend to become grandparents at earlier ages than men because they are usually somewhat younger when they begin having children. Becoming a grandparent is often hastened for the remarried through older stepchildren having children. Earlier ages of childbearing for blacks and Hispanics translate into somewhat earlier transitions to grandparenthood. Black grandparents have been found to be more likely to take on a "pseudoparental" role with their grandchildren, often coresiding with grandchildren and actively helping to raise grandchildren (Cherlin and Furstenberg 1986). How becoming a grandparent changes parent-child relationships and the midlife experience of

58

TABLE 2.16. Weighted Percentage with Grandchild(ren) by Sex, Age, Marital Status, and Race/Ethnicity: U.S. Parents Ages 35–64 (%)

| | Age | | | | | |
| | 35–44 | | 45–54 | | 55–64 | |
Marital Status	Fathers	Mothers	Fathers	Mothers	Fathers	Mothers
Total[a]						
First married	5.1	9.4	39.3	49.0	75.6	75.8
Remarried	9.8	24.9	47.1	67.7	79.8	86.3
Separated/						
divorced/						
never married	10.2	17.4	44.7	59.8	58.0	73.1
Widowed	5.4	28.0	44.4	55.0	77.5	83.4
TOTAL	6.7	14.3	41.7	54.7	74.6	78.2
Non-Hispanic white						
Married	5.9	12.1	41.4	51.4	77.1	77.8
Single	5.3	12.7	41.3	54.4	61.5	79.2
TOTAL	5.8	12.2	41.4	52.0	75.2	78.1
Black						
Married	10.4	21.4	52.5	70.4	78.7	89.7
Single	22.7	28.7	56.5	71.3	73.5	80.8
TOTAL	13.8	25.3	54.0	70.9	77.2	84.7
Hispanic						
Married	5.6	19.5	28.3	54.8	70.0	51.5
Single	13.5	16.0	46.7	52.9	52.3	72.3
TOTAL	7.3	18.4	30.5	54.2	66.4	61.7

Source: National Survey of Families and Households, 1987–88; primary respondents who are biological, adoptive, and/or stepparents. Total unweighted N = 4,992.
[a]Includes other race/ethnic as well as non-Hispanic white, black, and Hispanic parents.

parenthood for all race and ethnic groups is only beginning to be understood (Bengtson and Robertson 1985; Cherlin and Furstenberg 1986).

Disrupted Marriages of Adult Children

Another event in the lives of children that can have consequences for the parenting relationship with adult children and for midlife parents' experience of parenting and sense of well-being is the disruption of an adult child's marriage. Usually, on marriage, an adult child would be presumed to be "launched" into independence and a nuclear family of his or her own—with a certain amount of dependency on parents

TABLE 2.17. Weighted Percentage with a Separated, Divorced, or Widowed Adult (Age 19+) Child by Sex, Age, Marital Status, and Race/Ethnicity: U.S. Parents Ages 35–64 (%)

	Age					
	35–44		45–54		55–64	
Marital Status	Fathers	Mothers	Fathers	Mothers	Fathers	Mothers
Total[a]						
First married	0.6	1.2	9.8	13.9	19.2	22.3
Remarried	3.4	7.6	21.0	28.4	42.7	38.7
Separated/ divorced/ never married	2.5	5.7	13.6	26.6	25.8	37.4
Widowed	0.0	2.9	6.1	26.8	37.2	41.4
TOTAL	1.4	3.4	12.6	19.6	25.1	29.6
Non-Hispanic white						
Married	1.3	2.9	13.8	16.3	23.7	24.1
Single	1.8	5.5	8.3	25.0	23.9	35.7
TOTAL	1.4	3.4	13.2	18.1	23.8	26.8
Black						
Married	2.1	3.7	7.1	26.9	35.7	43.8
Single	3.1	6.6	19.5	28.4	37.8	42.7
TOTAL	2.4	5.2	11.2	27.7	36.3	43.2
Hispanic						
Married	0.0	0.0	3.5	15.4	24.5	30.3
Single	4.4	3.4	46.7	36.6	54.9	51.6
TOTAL	1.0	1.1	9.3	21.2	30.4	41.4

Source: National Survey of Families and Households, 1987–88; primary respondents who are biological, adoptive, and/or stepparents. Total unweighted N = 4,992.

[a]Includes other race/ethnic as well as non-Hispanic white, black, and Hispanic parents.

becoming funneled into interdependency with a spouse. When a separation, divorce, or widowhood occurs, adult children often turn to parents for help—especially if they have children to raise (as is the case for many single mothers). Such a sequence of events requires yet another reorientation of the parent/adult-child relationship.

Table 2.17 provides evidence that such disruptions in young adult children's lives are common events for midlife parents. Earlier childbearing again makes such an event for an adult child somewhat more likely to occur at younger midlife ages for women; about one in five mothers at the age of forty-five to fifty-four has a separated, divorced, or widowed adult child. By late middle age (ages fifty-five to sixty-four) more than one-quarter of mothers and fathers report having a child who is single because of marital disruption. In considering this table, one should keep in mind that after disrupted marriages, many young adults remarry (although at different rates by gender and race). This table provides only one-time, cross-sectional prevalence estimates. Lifetime incidence estimates would be higher at older ages.

Children's marital stability appears highest among stably married parents—who, as noted previously, also possess the highest levels of resources to provide for lengthened child dependence and educational support. Marital disruption rates are higher among minority group parents—the same parents with the least material resources for providing a "safety net."

Diversity in Characteristics of Midlife Parents' Parents

Looking "up" a generation to explore differences among midlife parents in terms of characteristics of their own aging parents is as important as looking "down" a generation to differences in characteristics of children. Midlife parents remain adult children themselves whose lives remain interdependent with their now aging parents. Some theorization about midlife suggests that this time is when midlifers are increasingly likely to "switch roles" with their parents, that is, they begin to give more to parents than they receive from them, possibly becoming responsible for economically and/or physically dependent aging parents. Older parents, on the other hand, if they are healthy and prosperous, may well provide an important backup and support for midlife parents, for example, through helping with the finances of college educations, through providing mentoring and friendship to teenage and young adult grandchildren (midlife parents' children), and/or through providing direct day-to-day emotional and instrumental support to midlife parents (Rossi and Rossi 1990).

Living Parents

First, how likely are various demographic groups of midlife parents to have living parents? Table 2.18 addresses this question, revealing that experiencing the death of a parent (or both parents) is a typical social transition of midlife (Winsborough, Bumpass, and Aquilino 1991). Because of gender differences in mortality rates (favoring women) and the fact that fathers are usually somewhat older than mothers, the parental death most likely to come first is that of father.

TABLE 2.18. Weighted Percentage with a Living Father/Living Mother by Sex, Age, and Race/Ethnicity: U.S. Parents Ages 35–64

| | Age | | | | | |
| | 35–44 | | 45–54 | | 55–64 | |
	% with Living Father	% with Living Mother	% with Living Father	% with Living Mother	% with Living Father	% with Living Mother
Total[a]	60.3	79.7	29.5	60.6	7.2	29.3
Non-Hispanic white	61.7	80.6	29.8	60.8	7.1	29.9
Black	49.6	70.9	27.6	56.5	10.7	23.2
Hispanic	58.6	84.1	28.8	63.9	3.9	27.3

Source: National Survey of Families and Households, 1987–88; primary respondents who are biological, adoptive, and/or stepparents. Total unweighted N = 4,992.
[a]Includes other race/ethnic as well as non-Hispanic white, black, and Hispanic parents.

At ages thirty-five to forty-four, about 40 percent of midlife parents' fathers have already died. For cohorts twenty years older, more than 90 percent of fathers are dead. There have been some increases in life expectancy and an overall lowering of the average age of parents— as viewed from children's perspective—among younger birth cohorts (mainly because of smaller families; see Eggebeen and Uhlenberg 1989). These factors would mean that this table is likely to be an inexact representation of the expected developmental trend for all cohorts. However, historical changes over thirty years have not been so great as to change the basic age-trend story altogether.

The vast majority of midlife parents leave middle adulthood without having a living father. Younger midlife (thirty-five to forty-four) black and Hispanic parents are more likely to be without a living father than are non-Hispanic white fathers of the same age.

Mothers of midlife parents, comparatively younger when becoming parents and with a longer life expectancy than fathers, are more likely to be living. About 80 percent of young midlife parents have living mothers; at ages fifty-five to sixty-four, about 29 percent still have living mothers.

Parental Vulnerability

Table 2.19 takes into consideration two factors that can create a feeling of greater responsibility for their older parents among midlife adults: having only one parent living (in most cases for the cohorts of parents represented here, this means that the parent is widowed) and

TABLE 2.19. Weighted Percentage with Only One Living Parent/ Limited Health Parent by Sex, Age, and Race/Ethnicity: U.S. Parents Ages 35–64

| | Age | | | | | |
| | 35–44 | | 45–54 | | 55–64 | |
	% with One Parent	% with Limited Health Parent	% with One Parent	% with Limited Health Parent	% with One Parent	% with Limited Health Parent
Total[a]	38.7	49.7	46.1	39.7	28.9	22.0
Non-Hispanic white	37.8	48.6	46.1	38.1	29.1	21.9
Black	46.5	46.9	46.6	45.1	27.4	24.7
Hispanic	38.2	63.4	46.7	50.1	27.0	19.4

Source: National Survey of Families and Households, 1987–88; primary respondents who are biological, adoptive, and/or stepparents. Total unweighted N = 4,992.
[a]Includes other race/ethnic as well as non-Hispanic white, black, and Hispanic parents.

viewing one or both parents to be in either very poor, poor, or fair health, rather than in good or excellent health.

Across every midlife age decade, between about a quarter (27 percent) and a half (47 percent) of all midlife parents have only one parent living—and potentially face having additional responsibility for that solitary parent. And it should be remembered again that this is a cross-sectional view of the population. Lifetime rates for *ever* having had a period with only one living parent would, of course, show significant increases at each age increment. The point to be observed here, though, is that during some part of midlife, a midlife parent will very likely experience at least some concern about a parent who is aging and alone (usually a mother). If parents-in-law were included here, again, rates would also increase.

Similarly, the proportion of midlifers reporting one or both parents in poor or fair health is quite substantial; half of all midlife parents report such in early midlife. Proportions are lower in the oldest decade largely as a function of there being fewer parents alive during this age period. For the about one in four midlife parents in these later midlife years with a limited health parent, this parent is likely to be increasingly dependent. Although an aging parent in only fair health may not require hands-on care, such a parent is probably becoming at the very least a cause for some concern and possibly worry and less likely to

TABLE 2.20. Weighted Percentage Who Live with a Disabled Parent or Give Out of Household Care to a Disabled Parent by Sex, Age, Marital Status, and Race/Ethnicity: U.S. Parents Ages 35–64 (%)

| | Age | | | | | |
| | 35–44 | | 45–54 | | 55–64 | |
Marital Status	Fathers	Mothers	Fathers	Mothers	Fathers	Mothers
Total[a]						
First married	6.5	10.8	12.9	15.4	8.1	10.9
Remarried	7.1	9.9	9.9	17.0	14.5	10.0
Separated/						
divorced/						
never married	10.1	7.2	6.7	7.9	7.9	5.5
Widowed	4.3	12.0	5.5	10.4	6.7	11.1
TOTAL	7.1	9.9	11.3	13.9	9.3	10.2
Non-Hispanic white						
Married	7.3	11.5	13.6	16.3	9.8	11.5
Single	6.0	7.3	6.8	7.6	9.4	11.6
TOTAL	7.2	10.8	12.8	14.4	9.8	11.5
Black						
Married	3.4	7.3	7.4	15.4	4.5	8.2
Single	19.1	9.8	3.3	14.5	5.7	5.4
TOTAL	7.8	8.7	5.9	14.9	4.8	6.6
Hispanic						
Married	2.3	4.5	0.0	5.1	8.7	0.0
Single	15.1	3.7	0.0	1.5	0.0	0.0
TOTAL	5.1	4.2	0.0	4.1	7.0	0.0

Source: National Survey of Families and Households, 1987–88; primary respondents who are biological, adoptive, and/or stepparents. Total unweighted N = 4,992.

[a]Includes other race/ethnic as well as non-Hispanic white, black, and Hispanic parents.

be regarded by the midlife parent as a potential source of aid and instrumental support.

Helping a Disabled Parent

Midlife is the age period in the life span when providing in-household or out-of-household caregiving to parents peaks (Marks, forthcoming). Table 2.20 is a more direct assessment of how many midlife parents are coming to the aid of a truly disabled parent. The percentage estimates here are for those midlife parents who reported living with a parent, parent-in-law, or stepparent who required care or assistance because of a disability or chronic illness and/or who indicated that during the past twelve months they had given care to a parent, parent-in-law, or stepparent who was seriously ill or disabled but lived in another household.

More of such caregiving is evident among mothers than fathers and appears to peak during the decade around age fifty when about one in eight parents overall is involved in such care. Married and widowed mothers are more likely to provide this care than are nonwidowed single mothers. Married fathers, overall, probably with the help of their wives, are much more likely to be giving care to dependent parents than unmarried fathers. Again, this is a cross-sectional view; lifetime incidence figures would be higher at each increasing age.

Parental Coresidence

Table 2.21 provides lifetime incidence rates for another indicator of filial responsibility for aging parents over midlife: the proportion of parents who reported ever having had a parent come to live with them since they had been on their own. This should exclude, then, reports of respondents who have returned to their *parent's* households in need— although it does not exclude the possibility that older parents who moved into their adult child's household actually still provided more help to the child than vice versa.

At any rate, although cross-sectional estimates of extended family living are rather low (Tienda and Angel [1982] reported a rate of 7 percent based on the 1980 census), the lifetime incidence reports in the NSFH indicate that a substantial number of midlife adults have experienced parental coresidence with them, for however long or short a period—by the end of midlife, almost a third have experienced some period of this.

Single parents, overall, are less likely to have experienced a parent moving in with them, possibly because they have had fewer resources to provide such refuge for a parent. Some research indicates a higher incidence of black extended family living than white extended family living (e.g., Beck and Beck 1989). Possibly because the direction of movement was specified here—parent moving *into* the adult child's residence—there appears to be no major race/ethnic rate difference.

Diversity in the Midlife Squeeze

Finally, it is worthwhile to consider the prevalence of "midlife squeeze," that is, midlife parents "in the middle" of multiple role re-

TABLE 2.21. Weighted Percentage Who Have Ever Had a Parent or Parent-in-Law Live with Them by Sex, Age, Marital Status, and Race/Ethnicity: U.S. Parents Ages 35–64 (%)

| | Age | | | | | |
| | 35–44 | | 45–54 | | 55–64 | |
Marital Status	Fathers	Mothers	Fathers	Mothers	Fathers	Mothers
Total[a]						
First married	6.9	8.1	14.2	15.6	24.3	33.5
Remarried	9.0	9.7	18.8	17.2	22.1	18.1
Separated/						
divorced/						
never married	7.8	8.8	12.6	10.3	16.0	21.9
Widowed	20.5	8.1	18.2	15.0	33.2	29.1
TOTAL	7.5	8.6	15.0	14.8	23.3	29.4
Non-Hispanic white						
Married	6.8	7.6	15.8	16.9	22.1	30.4
Single	6.7	9.5	11.4	9.6	20.9	27.7
TOTAL	6.8	8.0	15.2	15.3	22.0	29.7
Black						
Married	6.2	11.4	16.5	14.4	32.9	27.8
Single	6.6	8.9	12.1	11.3	20.9	24.2
TOTAL	6.3	10.0	14.9	12.8	29.5	25.7
Hispanic						
Married	10.1	10.3	35.3	42.8	22.5	26.1
Single	46.7	28.5	19.5	9.7	29.1	14.6
TOTAL	14.7	15.8	32.3	25.2	23.8	19.8

Source: National Survey of Families and Households, 1987–88; primary respondents who are biological, adoptive, and/or stepparents. Total unweighted N = 4,992.

[a]Includes other race/ethnic as well as non-Hispanic white, black, and Hispanic parents.

sponsibilities (Oppenheimer 1981; Brody 1981, 1985, 1990; Spitze and Logan 1990). It has been postulated that midlife adults are uniquely situated to be experiencing economic, emotional, and time pressure from commitments to the older and younger generation and to both work and family. Some argue that caregiving for older parents is becoming a "normative" event of midlife (especially for women) (Brody 1985). Other researchers suggest that significant hands-on help to parents while parenting young children is not really very prevalent (Spitze and Logan 1990). What do the data from the NSFH suggest?

TABLE 2.22. Weighted Percentage Who Have Child(ren) in the Household and Have a Limited Health Parent by Sex, Age, Marital Status, and Race/Ethnicity: U.S. Parents Ages 35–64 (%)

| | Age | | | | | |
| | 35–44 | | 45–54 | | 55–64 | |
Marital Status	Fathers	Mothers	Fathers	Mothers	Fathers	Mothers
Total[a]						
First married	47.7	45.8	31.7	25.1	6.7	8.1
Remarried	38.1	47.5	33.0	18.2	10.1	5.9
Separated/ divorced/ never married	15.6	46.2	12.3	35.9	12.5	4.0
Widowed	75.1	48.7	35.4	27.5	2.8	6.7
TOTAL	42.0	46.3	29.3	26.0	7.9	7.1
Non-Hispanic white						
Married	44.0	45.6	30.5	21.7	5.7	7.2
Single	19.3	45.2	13.2	33.7	13.0	5.9
TOTAL	41.5	45.5	28.4	24.2	6.5	6.9
Black						
Married	40.3	42.8	33.5	26.4	11.7	14.8
Single	12.1	41.5	11.6	39.1	6.8	8.8
TOTAL	32.4	42.1	25.4	32.9	10.4	11.5
Hispanic						
Married	69.1	58.6	46.7	43.9	27.5	6.4
Single	28.0	57.3	46.7	22.1	0.0	0.0
TOTAL	60.0	58.1	46.7	37.1	21.5	3.0

Source: National Survey of Families and Households, 1987–88; primary respondents who are biological, adoptive, and/or stepparents. Total unweighted N = 4,992.
[a]Includes other race/ethnic as well as non-Hispanic white, black, and Hispanic parents.

Children at Home and Limited Health Parent

Table 2.22 describes how many midlife parents were in the position of having a child living at home (any age) and also had at least one parent in fair to poor health. Due in part to the age structure of children and also the death rates of parents, the data in table 2.22 suggest that it is during the young and middle period of midlife that the "generational squeeze" may be greatest. For some midlife parents this, no doubt, means a much heavier burden than for others. But across the years from thirty-five to fifty-five, at least, at any given time about one in three midlife parents is likely to be providing day-to-day support for a child or for children and have some measure of concern about a parent (or parents) at the same time.

Nonwidowed single fathers are the least likely group to deal with this double burden, mainly because they are so much less likely to have children living with them. Hispanic parents are particularly likely to be experiencing the concerns this combination of family factors may bring (with, as noted earlier, fewer resources).

Children at Home and Employed

Table 2.23 provides a similar analysis of the double role challenge of working and having children at home. Here, again, the greatest pressure seems to be evident among those in their late thirties and early forties. In the second decade of midlife, younger children are being phased out, and in the last decade, employment levels are reduced. Hispanic mothers, having lower levels of employment, have somewhat lower rates than non-Hispanic white mothers and black mothers.

Single fathers—again, less apt to have children at home—are less likely to be facing this dual role challenge. Nonwidowed single mothers, generally having higher rates of employment and children at home, have the highest levels overall of this double role challenge, with fewer economic resources and without a partner to share the load. Among fathers, it is first-marriage fathers—with resources and a partner—who are most likely to have this double role commitment.

Limited Health Parent and Employed

Another potential double role challenge is that of being employed and having a limited health parent. As the "woman in the middle" hypothesis has been empirically explored, it has been noted that often the challenge of an older parent may come after children are relatively grown up, that it is *employment* and caring for an older parent that is really the midlife challenge many will face (Cantor 1991). Table 2.24 displays the proportion of parents who are both employed and who have a fair to poor health parent. Substantial proportions of such parents exist in all age groups.

Parent health is probably deteriorating even more severely among the parents of parents in the later midlife years, such that caregiving may be more intensely needed during these years. The potential for employment and elder care conflicts appears to be very real, especially over so many years of relative "risk" of such conflict.

68

TABLE 2.23. Weighted Percentage Who Have Child(ren) in the Household and Are Employed by Sex, Age, Marital Status, and Race/Ethnicity: U.S. Parents Ages 35–64 (%)

| | Age | | | | | |
| | 35–44 | | 45–54 | | 55–64 | |
Marital Status	Fathers	Mothers	Fathers	Mothers	Fathers	Mothers
Total[a]						
First married	92.5	65.9	69.0	46.0	25.3	9.8
Remarried	73.6	59.9	61.9	35.4	24.1	8.0
Separated/						
divorced/						
never married	34.2	63.8	25.4	51.3	13.5	22.0
Widowed	78.1	49.7	52.9	42.3	16.0	24.7
TOTAL	81.2	64.1	61.5	45.0	23.4	13.5
Non-Hispanic white						
Married	88.6	64.4	66.8	43.8	23.4	8.0
Single	36.6	65.6	31.0	49.4	15.4	21.5
TOTAL	83.2	64.6	62.8	45.0	22.5	11.2
Black						
Married	82.8	71.7	66.7	47.8	40.6	21.6
Single	33.0	61.9	18.5	47.1	9.7	25.9
TOTAL	69.1	66.4	49.4	47.4	31.9	24.0
Hispanic						
Married	89.4	55.1	69.7	35.2	30.9	24.0
Single	44.3	49.5	46.7	54.8	19.5	22.9
TOTAL	79.3	53.3	67.0	41.0	28.8	23.5

Source: National Survey of Families and Households, 1987–88; primary respondents who are biological, adoptive, and/or stepparents. Total unweighted N = 4,992.

[a]Includes other race/ethnic as well as non-Hispanic white, black, and Hispanic parents.

Children at Home, Employed, and Limited Health Parent

Finally, who is likely to be dealing with all three challenges: young children, employment, and a limited health parent? Table 2.25 addresses this question. Again, early midlife appears to be the period when these multiple challenges are most likely: 37.4 percent of fathers and 30.5 percent of mothers report this constellation of responsibility. During the decade around age fifty, 24.9 percent of fathers and 16.0 percent of mothers make similar reports.

Nonwidowed single fathers once again have the lowest rates because

TABLE 2.24. Weighted Percentage Those Who Have a Parent with Limited Health and Are Employed by Sex, Age, Marital Status, and Race/Ethnicity: U.S. Parents Ages 35–64 (%)

Marital Status	Age					
	35–44		45–54		55–64	
	Fathers	Mothers	Fathers	Mothers	Fathers	Mothers
Total[a]						
First married	47.0	32.4	35.6	20.5	11.0	10.4
Remarried	41.8	44.1	36.4	24.0	20.9	9.9
Separated/						
divorced/						
never married	39.9	36.3	38.3	35.2	23.7	12.0
Widowed	66.1	35.4	33.7	34.7	7.5	6.8
TOTAL	45.2	35.4	36.1	24.7	14.2	9.9
Non-Hispanic white						
Married	44.6	34.5	34.9	21.0	12.1	9.7
Single	40.5	38.1	39.6	38.1	23.1	9.4
TOTAL	44.2	35.1	35.4	24.6	13.4	9.6
Black						
Married	40.3	41.5	38.6	28.5	23.5	21.2
Single	43.1	32.4	32.1	33.7	9.1	8.9
TOTAL	41.1	36.7	36.2	31.1	19.4	14.5
Hispanic						
Married	66.4	37.6	40.5	19.1	19.4	6.4
Single	48.4	32.4	65.8	13.6	17.8	6.9
TOTAL	62.3	35.9	43.5	17.4	19.1	6.7

Source: National Survey of Families and Households, 1987–88; primary respondents who are biological, adoptive, and/or stepparents. Total unweighted N = 4,992.

[a]Includes other race/ethnic as well as non-Hispanic white, black, and Hispanic parents.

children are less likely to be living with them. Overall, in the middle midlife period, nonwidowed single mothers have about twice the likelihood of shouldering this triple role challenge than do their first-married mother peers (25.5 percent versus 13.9 percent), whereas nonwidowed single fathers have less than half the likelihood of this triple role challenge than first-married fathers *or* nonwidowed single mothers (11.7 percent versus 26.7 percent and 25.5 percent).

The rates reported here show similar age patterns but are considerably higher than those reported by Logan and Spitze (1991), who defined their triple role challenge somewhat differently, including em-

TABLE 2.25. Weighted Percentage Those Who Have a Parent
with Limited Health, Are Employed, and Have Child(ren)
at Home by Sex, Age, Marital Status, and Race/Ethnicity:
U.S. Parents Ages 35–64 (%)

| | Age | | | | | |
| | 35–44 | | 45–54 | | 55–64 | |
Marital Status	Fathers	Mothers	Fathers	Mothers	Fathers	Mothers
Total[a]						
First married	42.9	29.8	26.7	13.9	4.3	2.7
Remarried	33.0	34.3	27.7	11.3	6.8	3.2
Separated/						
divorced/						
never married	14.4	29.4	11.7	25.5	8.1	2.7
Widowed	66.1	27.6	28.2	18.4	0.0	2.3
TOTAL	37.4	30.5	24.9	16.0	5.1	2.7
Non-Hispanic white						
Married	39.9	30.5	26.1	13.1	4.0	2.4
Single	17.7	30.8	12.4	25.6	8.8	2.5
TOTAL	37.6	30.5	24.5	15.7	4.6	2.4
Black						
Married	33.8	34.7	27.2	18.1	11.4	10.4
Single	11.6	24.9	9.8	24.0	0.0	4.0
TOTAL	27.7	29.4	20.9	21.2	8.2	6.8
Hispanic						
Married	57.2	31.4	34.3	11.7	9.9	2.5
Single	21.9	28.8	46.7	9.8	0.0	0.0
TOTAL	49.4	30.6	35.7	11.1	8.1	1.3

Source: National Survey of Families and Households, 1987–88; primary respondents who are biological, adoptive, and/or stepparents. Total unweighted N = 4,992.
[a]Includes other race/ethnic as well as non-Hispanic white, black, and Hispanic parents.

ployment of thirty-five or more hours a week, having children living at home or helping an adult child three or more hours a week, and living with a parent or parent-in-law or helping a parent or parent-in-law three or more hours a week. They found that no more than 13 percent of midlife adults were involved in three active roles, thus defined. By including part-time employment and using a measure of parental health limitation rather than the more stringent criterion of hands-on help to a parent, this analysis has broadened the net somewhat and thereby found more evidence for the likelihood that midlife adults will experience something of a "squeeze."

Summary and Conclusion

Midlife parents evidence important differences from one another on many dimensions. Gender differences are usually noteworthy. A sizable proportion of midlife parents (about two in five) are either remarried or single parents, and many substantial disparities between parents cluster around marital status differentiations. Contrasts between non-Hispanic white majority parents, black parents, and Hispanic parents also help identify important differences between parents in middle adulthood.

Dramatic differences exist, particularly, in the personal resources of midlife parents. First-married, non-Hispanic white parents fare best on all measures of personal resources. Unmarried parents, especially mothers, are significantly disadvantaged in relation to married parents. Minority parents overall do much more poorly than do non-Hispanic whites. Inasmuch as fulfilling the parental role well is contingent on having the economic wherewithal to provide adequately for children's needs, especially during the more expensive teenage and transition to adulthood years, clearly nonmajority race/ethnic group members, as well as single female parents, are at a handicap.

Family sizes are decreasing among younger midlife parents. Children are becoming adults in terms of chronological age during the period of midlife parenthood, but a significant proportion of midlife parents between the ages of thirty-five and fifty-four especially, and even after age fifty-five, continue to have children (including substantial numbers of adult children) living in their households.

About one in six midlife parents has a stepchild. Stepparenting is apt to create a very different experience of midlife parenting, as is single parenting, both in being the sole primary caretaker for children (the case for many single mothers) or in being relatively removed from the day-to-day lives of children (as are many single fathers). The experiences of the nontypical but growing groups of custodial single fathers as well as noncustodial single mothers should also not be ignored (see also Meyer, this volume). Grandparenthood is an expectable event of midlife parenting. Experiencing the marital disruption of one or more children is also relatively common.

Midlife parents will probably experience the death of one or both parents. A substantial proportion of midlife parents will also experience some period of parental coresidence with them, possibly also providing aid to a parent because of chronic illness or disability. Overall, married parents (especially mothers) appear to be somewhat more likely to provide coresidence and care for aging parents when it is needed.

The multiple role challenges of employment, having at least one child at home, and having a parent in limited health are highest among younger midlife parents. In the years to come, if employment rates continue to increase and stay steady throughout the midlife years for women and men and if the parents of midlifers live longer (if not always healthier lives), one might expect these multiple role challenges to persist over more years of midlife and to be present for even larger proportions of midlife parents at any given age.

For midlife parents with the fewest resources to meet these challenges—single mothers and minorities—there is and will continue to be experience of the midlife period, and midlife parenting especially, very different from that found for subgroups of the population with the most resources—non-Hispanic white, first-married men and women. Social policies that assume midlife parents all fit the profile of the non-Hispanic white, first-married population and are, for example, involved in their peak earning years, accumulating considerable assets and wealth (including paying off a home), maintaining good physical and mental health, and well situated to support the educational aspirations of their children and provide any necessary support in the "launching" of children and to meet crisis needs of their own aging parents, are missing the needs of the approximately two in five midlife parents who do not fit this profile.

Recognizing these differences should make even more apparent the need for an increased variety of formal as well as informal support for differing midlife parents and their children. For example, financial aid programs for higher education tailored to the needs (and payback capabilities) of many types of families, formal caregiving supports to complement the informal caregiving efforts of midlife parents helping aging parents and other relatives, and employment supports (including retraining and placement) for midlife parents who have become displaced workers in a very competitive employment market should be important priorities to help more midlife parents successfully meet their family and work responsibilities and experience optimal mental and physical health.

A plurality of midlife parenting experience is organized significantly along social demographic divisions of gender, age, marital status, and race/ethnicity. We need more research to understand this diversity of parental experience and development. Better social policy and practices responsive to the diverse challenges and needs of all types of parents are also necessary to reduce the *disadvantage* currently associated with many aspects of *difference* among America's midlife parents.

REFERENCES

Aquilino, W. S. 1990. The likelihood of parent-adult child coresidence: Effects of family structure and parental characteristics. *Journal of Marriage and the Family* 52:405–419.

Baltes, P. B. 1987. Theoretical propositions of life-span developmental psychology: On the dynamics between growth and decline. *Developmental Psychology* 23: 611–626.

Bane, M. J., and D. T. Ellwood. Winter 1986. Slipping into and out of poverty: The dynamics of spells. *Journal of Human Resources* 21:1–23.

Beck, R. W., and S. H. Beck. June 1989. The incidence of extended households among middle-aged black and white women. *Journal of Family Issues* 10:147–168.

Bengtson, V. L., and J. Robertson, eds. 1985. *Grandparenthood*. Beverly Hills, Calif.: Sage.

Bianchi, S. M., and D. Spain. 1986. *American Women in Transition*. New York: Russell Sage.

Blau, F. D. 1984. Occupational segregation and labor market discrimination. In B. F. Reskin, ed., *Sex segregation in the workplace: Trends, explanations, remedies*, 117–143. Washington, D.C.: National Academy Press.

Brody, E. M. 1981. "Women in the middle" and family help to older people. *Gerontologist* 21:471–479.

———. 1985. Parent care as a normative family stress. *Gerontologist* 25:19–29.

———. 1990. *Women in the Middle: Their Parent-Care Years*. New York: Springer.

Bumpass, L. L. 1990. What's happening to the family? Interactions between demographic and institutional change. *Demography* 27:483–498.

Cantor, M. H. 1991. Family and community: Changing roles in an aging society. *Gerontologist* 31:337–346.

Cherlin, A. J., and F. F. Furstenberg Jr. 1986. *The New American Grandparent: A Place in the Family, a Life Apart*. New York: Basic.

Cherlin, A., J. Griffith, and J. McCarthy. 1983. A note on maritally-disrupted men's reports of child support in the June 1980 Current Population Survey. *Demography* 20:385–389.

Cooney, T. M., and P. Uhlenberg. 1990. The role of divorce in men's relationships with their adult children after midlife. *Journal of Marriage and the Family* 52: 677–688.

Eggebeen, D. J., and P. Uhlenberg. 1989. Changes in the age distribution of parents, 1940–1980. *Journal of Family Issues* 10:169–188.

Glick, P. C., and S. L. Lin. 1986. Recent changes in divorce and remarriage. *Journal of Marriage and the Family* 48:737–747.

Goldscheider, F. K., and C. Goldscheider. 1989. Family structure and conflict: Nest-leaving expectations of young adults and their parents. *Journal of Marriage and the Family* 52:87–97.

Kitson, G. C., K. B. Babri, M. J. Roach, and K. S. Placidi. 1989. Adjustment to widowhood and divorce: A review. *Journal of Family Issues* 10:5–32.

Marks, N. F. Forthcoming. Caregiving across the lifespan: National prevalence and predictors. *Family Relations.*

Marini, M. M. 1989. Sex differences in earnings in the United States. *Annual Review of Sociology* 15:343–380.

Oppenheimer, V. K. 1981. The changing nature of life-cycle squeezes: Implications for the socioeconomic position of the elderly. In R. W. Fogel, ed., *Aging: Stability and change in the family,* 47–82. New York: Academic Press.

Radloff, L. S. 1977. The CES-D scale: A self-report depression scale for research in the general population. *Applied Psychological Measurement* 1:385–401.

Rindfuss, R. R., S. P. Morgan, and G. Swicegood. 1988. *First Births in America: Changing Patterns of Parenthood.* Berkeley and Los Angeles: University of California Press.

Roos, P. A., and B. F. Reskin. 1984. Institutional factors contributing to sex segregation in the workplace. In B. F. Reskin, ed., *Sex segregation in the workplace: trends, explanations, remedies,* 235–260. Washington, D.C.: National Academy Press.

Rossi, A. S., and P. H. Rossi. 1990. *Of Human Bonding: Parent-Child Relations across the Life Course.* New York: Aldine de Gruyter.

Schoen, R., W. Urton, K. Woodrow, and J. Baj. 1985. Marriage and divorce in twentieth-century American cohorts. *Demography* 22:101–114.

Spitze, G., and J. R. Logan. 1990. More evidence on women (and men) in the middle. *Research on Aging* 12:182–198.

Sweet, J. A., and L. L. Bumpass. 1987. *American Families and Households.* New York: Russell Sage.

Sweet, J. A., L. L. Bumpass, and V. A. Call. 1988. The design and content of the National Survey of Families and Households. NSFH Working Paper no. 1. Madison: Center for Demography and Ecology, University of Wisconsin.

Tienda, M., and R. Angel. 1982. Headship and household composition among blacks, hispanics, and other whites. *Social Forces* 61:508–531.

Watkins, S. C., J. A. Mencken, and J. Bongaarts. 1987. Demographic foundations of family change. *American Sociological Review* 52:346–358.

White, L. K., and A. Booth. 1985. The quality and stability of remarriages: The role of stepchildren. *American Sociological Review* 50:689–698.

Winsborough, H. H., L. L. Bumpass, and W. S. Aquilino. 1991. The death of parents and the transition to old age. NSFH Working Paper no. 39. Madison: Center for Demography and Ecology, University of Wisconsin.

THREE

The Economic Vulnerability of Midlife Single Parents

Daniel R. Meyer

The economic vulnerability of single parents is well known and is increasingly being recognized as a public policy concern. Two trends have contributed to the interest in the special issues and problems faced by single parents. First, the number of single parents has increased dramatically. Whereas almost 88 percent of American children were living in a married-couple family in 1960, by 1990 that percentage had decreased to 72.5 percent (House 1992). Recent estimates are that over half of all children born today will spend some time in a single-parent family (Bumpass 1984).

Second, the economic vulnerability of these famlies is drawing increased attention. In 1959 only 18 percent of the poor families were single-mother families with children, but by 1991 almost half of the poverty population consisted of single-mother families with children (Bureau of the Census 1991b). Single-parent families with children, especially mother-only families, have *very* high poverty rates: 44.5 percent of mother-only families with children were poor in 1990, as were 18.8 percent of father-only families, compared with 7.8 percent of married-couple families with children (Bureau of the Census 1991b, table 4). And not only are mother-only families the poorest of all major demographic groups, their spells of poverty are the longest (Garfinkel and McLanahan 1986).

These trends have spurred several public policy changes. The Family Support Act of 1988 made significant changes in the Aid to Families with Dependent Children (AFDC) program, the primary cash assistance program for single-parent families, including a requirement that more recipients work or prepare for work. The children support system

This research was supported in part by a grant from the U.S. Department of Health and Human Services to the Institute for Research on Poverty. Some of the data were gathered under a contract with the Wisconsin Department of Health and Social Services. Any opinions and conclusions expressed here are solely those of the author and should not be construed as representing the opinions or policy of the sponsoring institutions.

has also been substantially changed in the last fifteen years: state child support offices have been instituted, and a variety of reforms have attempted to increase the amount of child support received by single-parent families.

Accompanying these trends and policy changes has been increased research attention to issues related to single parenting (for reviews, see Garfinkel and McLanahan 1986 and McLanahan and Booth 1989). Almost all this research has focused on single mothers, primarily because there are many fewer single fathers (McLanahan and Booth 1989). Yet recent research (Meyer and Garasky 1993) has documented that single-father families are growing at a faster rate (in percentage terms) than single-mother families, suggesting that this group merits more research attention. In addition, much of the research on single mothers has not looked specifically at age differences; when it has, the focus has been almost exclusively on teenage or very young mothers.

In this chapter I seek to expand our knowledge about economic vulnerability and single parenthood in four ways. First, I do not follow the traditional pattern in examining teen parents but look at *midlife* single parents, defined here as those between the ages of thirty-five and fifty-four who still have a child less than age eighteen at home. Second, this chapter includes information on midlife single fathers as well as midlife single mothers, filling a gap in the prior research. Third, I evaluate the relative well-being of midlife single parents on several measures of economic vulnerability beyond the traditional poverty measure. Finally, I provide information on the extent to which economic policies directed at improving the economic status of disadvantaged families are being used by single parents.

Reasons for a Focus on Economic Well-Being

Well-being is clearly a multidimensional concept (see Umberson; Ryff, Schmutte, and Lee; and Silverberg, this volume). One dimension of a broad concept of well-being is how one is faring economically. Indeed, some research has shown that economic issues play a vital role in determining well-being: for example, when Americans (and those in twelve other countries) were asked their personal hopes, the most frequent categories mentioned were their own health and having a "decent standard of living" (Cantril 1965). Partly because economic issues are such a major part of hopes and dreams, family income has been found to be positively correlated with overall life satisfaction in many studies (Easterlin 1974). Finally, when life satisfaction has been broken into two realms, economic and noneconomic, family income has been found to be related to satisfaction with the noneconomic sphere as well as the economic sphere (e.g., Douthitt, MacDonald, and Mullis 1992).

Economic problems have been associated with a number of other problems for children and adults. In a review of the effects of economic hardship on African Americans, McLoyd (1990) presents an exhaustive list of the problems that seem to be a result of poverty: increased mental health problems, emotional distress, marital dissolution, social isolation, decreased resiliency, decreased capacity for adequate parenting, and even child abuse. Another more recent summary of the literature found that poverty is associated with numerous other problems, including poor health, poor housing and homelessness, increased mortality, violence, and behavior problems for children; the effects even span the generations, with poor children likely to experience failure as adults (e.g., National Commission on Children 1991). In this volume, Pruchno and her colleagues find that mothers with low socioeconomic status (SES) are more depressed and their children have experienced more negative life events than occur in high SES families.

Economic problems may have different effects for men and women. In particular, men's earnings may have direct effects on their levels of depression because men put more emphasis on the income-producing role: by contrast, wives' earnings may have only an indirect effect on depression, mediated by their perception of economic hardship, because they place more emphasis on the homemaking role (Ross and Huber 1985). Yet this research that focuses on husbands and wives is probably less relevant for single-parent families, who must fulfill both income-producing and homemaking roles.

THEORY AND PRIOR LITERATURE ON THE RELATIONSHIP BETWEEN AGE, MARITAL STATUS, AND GENDER AND ECONOMIC WELL-BEING

Age

Human capital theory suggests that midlife should be the time of least economic vulnerability (Mincer 1974). Earnings are thought to depend, at least in part, on the value of a worker's contribution to the employer (e.g., Mincer 1974; Marini 1989). If workers become more productive as they gain more experience, their wages should increase as they age. Earnings may decrease after a certain age, however, as workers begin to think more about retirement and invest less of themselves into their work. National statistics provide some support for this

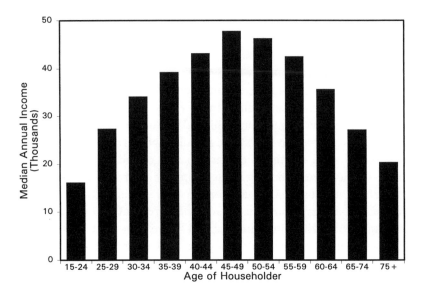

FIGURE 3.1. Median family income, 1990 (all families). *Source:* Bureau of the Census 1991a, table 17.

hypothesized age-earnings profile. Figure 3-1 shows median family incomes in 1990 by the age of the householder. The poorest families are those whose householder is either very young or very old. The highest median incomes are those in which the householder is between forty-five and forty-nine, followed by those with householders aged fifty to fifty-four, then aged forty to forty-four. Poverty rates show a similar pattern, with only 7.8 percent of those aged forty-five to fifty-four poor in 1990, compared with 16.1 percent of those aged fifteen to twenty-four and 12.2 percent of those aged sixty-five and over (Bureau of the Census 1991b).

Marital Status

But these generally positive aggregate numbers may mask a great deal of diversity. The parents in a married-couple family may be able to divide their tasks so that one parent specializes more in work-related and income-producing activities and the other parent specializes more in home-related, non-income-producing activities (Becker 1981). Families who have organized their lives in this way may find that the partner specializing in work-related activities is realizing the results of the years of investments in work by receiving a large salary (Mincer and Polachek 1974). At the same time, the partner who specialized in home-related tasks may find fewer demands at home and may be free to take a higher-paying, more demanding job. Thus this two-parent family may be at the peak of their income during midlife.

Single parents, however, do not typically have the luxury of dividing tasks between two adults in the home (Ellwood 1988). They must be both the income producer and the nurturer and thus they may select careers that allow more flexibility, that allow them to be more available to their children. In addition, they may have to pay for child care from a single income rather than from two incomes, as would be the case for a two-earner couple needing child care. This double burden may depress their income in these and other ways, and thus they may not experience the lessening of financial burdens in midlife. Further, the role strain of attempting to meet the roles of income producer, home-maker, and nurturer may make them especially vulnerable to psychological as well as economic distress (McLanahan and Adams 1987).

Gender

The economic vulnerability of single-parent families may also be compounded by gender issues. The wages of women tend to be less than 70 percent of men's wages (Marini 1989). Several factors have been used to explain this difference: discrimination, differential education and training, more sporadic work histories for women, and segregation into certain jobs (Marini 1989).

Because of these gender differences, a single mother may face greater job discrimination and may not be able to earn as much as a single father with comparable education and training. Indeed, the literature concerned with poverty in single-parent families has typically focused only on single-mother families (McLanahan and Booth 1989). Single-mother families are poorer than single-father families, with a poverty rate more than twice as high. Yet recent research has shown that single-father families, although not as economically disadvantaged as single-mother families, are also economically vulnerable: when compared with men in married-couple families, they are less likely to work, have lower hourly wages, have lower incomes, and are more likely to live in poverty (Meyer and Garasky 1993).

In summary, theory and prior research would suggest that midlife is typically a time of relative financial security. Single parents, however, are more likely to be economically insecure, particularly single mothers. Whether *midlife* single parents are less disadvantaged than young single parents and whether midlife single fathers are less disadvantaged than midlife single mothers are two of the questions this research addresses.

DATA, MEASURES, AND METHODS

Data

A description of single fathers and single mothers requires a large dataset because single-father families make up only about four percent of the families with minor children (Meyer and Garasky 1993), and the number within a specific age range is, of course, smaller. For this research, then, I have selected two different data sources: the Current Population Survey (CPS) and the Wisconsin Court Record Database (WCRD). The CPS has a large sample of single fathers and is thus the best source of economic information on them. No national dataset provides information about the child support awards of single fathers, so the WCRD, although not nationally representative, provides child support data.

Current Population Survey (CPS). The CPS provides a variety of demographic and income data on a large, nationally representative sample. I have analyzed data from the 1990 CPS (which includes demographic information from March 1990 and income information from 1989). For single-father families, I selected the families and subfamilies coded "other male head" (i.e., not "husband-wife families" or "other female head") that included an own (biological and/or adopted), never married child under age eighteen.[1] Of these families, 478 had a head between the ages of thirty-five and fifty-four, and 354 were thirty-four or younger. Single-mother families were selected in a similar fashion; 2,170 of these families had a head between the ages of thirty-five and fifty-four, and 3,042 were thirty-four or younger.[2] For comparison, I also examined married men and women in "husband-wife families" who have an own, never married child under age eighteen. Note that the CPS does not differentiate between families in which a child lives with two parents from those in which a child lives with a parent and a stepparent, calling both "two-parent families." There are 9,737 married fathers between the ages of thirty-five and fifty-four and 8,416 married mothers in this age range in the 1990 CPS.

Wisconsin Court Record Database (WCRD). The WCRD provides information on the child support awards and payments for custodial fathers and mothers. It is a sample of divorce and paternity cases from the family court records of twenty-one Wisconsin counties in which at least one child is potentially eligible for child support. (For a more complete description of the sampling design, see Garfinkel et al. 1988.) For this analysis I have used families that came to court between January 1984 and June 1987. In each year 30 to 150 cases were selected in each county, and if these cases came back to court, new information was collected. Because all child support payments are required to go through the courts in Wisconsin, this court record database also includes monthly amounts of child support paid and owed. I have analyzed payment and award information from the period 1 July 1987 through 31 December 1987 (multiplying by two to get annualized figures). Selecting only cases that did not change physical custody during July to December 1987 provides a total sample of 392 midlife (aged thirty-five to fifty-four) custodial fathers and 4,680 midlife custodial mothers, with 213 midlife fathers and 1,179 midlife mothers for whom we have full information.[3] In addition, we have full information on 165 young (less than age thirty-five) custodial fathers and 3,127 young custodial mothers. Note that these custodial mothers and fathers are not representative of all custodial families because they are drawn only from families who have been through a court process; for example, some families who are informally separated and nonmarital unions in which paternity has not been established are not included. Note too that some remarried fathers and mothers may be included in this sample because the court record does not always update the marital status of the parents.

This is a cross-sectional study using cross-sectional data. Some men and women who headed single-parent families before 1989 will have married or remarried and appear as married-couple families in this 1990 data. This research, then, does not describe those who were *ever* single-parent families, which obviously is a much larger group than those who are currently single-parent families. Further, those who are currently single parents may differ from those who were ever single parents. For example, if better-off single parents remarry more quickly, then the group of men and women who were ever single parents will be better off than the group of single parents at a particular point in time. Similarly, this research does not include those who no longer have children under age eighteen. Although many of the authors in this volume explicitly include those who have ever been a parent, limitations of the data require that I focus on those with minor children in the home.[4]

Measures

Before presenting information on specific measures of economic vulnerability, I provide background information on labor market outcomes (earnings, wages, hours of work, the percent unemployed, and so on). I present four different measures of economic vulnerability in this paper. First is the percent poor, using the government's official measure of poverty.[5] The poverty line, in use since the mid-1960s, is a measure of the level of income at which a family can no longer meet its basic needs. The line was originally set by identifying the cost of a basic food budget for families of different sizes and then multiplying that food cost by three, because it was thought that families should spend no more than one-third of their income on food (Orshansky 1965). While the line has been adjusted to reflect changes in the general price index, it has not been adjusted to reflect current expenditure patterns in which about one-sixth of income is now typically spent on food (Ruggles 1990). A family's annual gross cash income is compared with the line to determine who is poor.[6] The poverty line in 1989 was $9,885 for a family of three. Those below the poverty line are the "income poor."

Problems with health insurance coverage provide a second indicator of economic vulnerability. Although these data do not provide information on health status other than disability, they do provide information on health insurance coverage. Clearly those without health insurance coverage would sustain large expenses if they had a serious illness, and they are therefore quite vulnerable to economic catastrophe. Others, even though they have insurance coverage, may have to purchase their own coverage rather than having it provided by their employer. Those who have to pay the full cost of their coverage (often over two hundred dollars per month) who have incomes below 200 percent of the poverty line may be considered vulnerable in that providing themselves with coverage puts them near or below the poverty line. These two groups make up the "health insurance poor."

A concern with future economic security provides the third indicator of economic vulnerability. The Social Security program was originally designed to be a "floor of protection" during retirement, rather than the sole source of income (Derthick 1979). Thus many employers offer pensions and many people have accumulated assets to fund their retirement. Others may not have accumulated assets yet but if they have sufficiently high incomes may be able to accumulate assets before retirement. Those whose employers provide no pension, who have asset income of less than five thousand dollars per year, and who have incomes below twice the poverty line can be considered "pension poor."

A final indicator of economic vulnerability is not having a telephone in the household, suggested by Jencks and Torrey (1986). In this country, telephones have become almost a necessity. Those without one are without fast access to a variety of help in times of need and thus can be considered "access poor."

In addition to providing information on measures of vulnerability, I then present information on whether programs intended to lessen vulnerability are providing help to these families. I first focus on the welfare system, examining whether poor and near-poor families were recipients of several major means-tested programs in 1989. I then examine the child support system to see whether single-parent families have child support awards, the level of these awards, and the percentage paid.

Methods

Because so little is known about midlife parents, particularly about midlife single parents, my statistics are descriptive. For most characteristics, I make five comparisons: midlife single fathers are compared with midlife single mothers to see whether gender differences exist between single parents. Midlife single fathers are compared with midlife married fathers and midlife single mothers are compared with midlife married mothers to document the extent of economic disadvantage associated with single parenthood when gender is held constant. Finally, midlife single fathers are compared with young single fathers and midlife single mothers are compared with young single mothers to determine if the disadvantage associated with single parenthood diminishes in midlife. On each indicator I present information on the distribution of individuals, thus allowing us to examine the level of diversity within each of the six categories. To keep the results more accessible, I have limited the presentation to these six categories. Comparisons among racial and ethnic groups within each of these six categories are also informative, and for selected indicators these results will be presented in the text rather than on the tables.[7]

RESULTS

An estimated 727,500 unmarried men aged thirty-five to fifty-four had at least one child under the age of eighteen living with them in 1989. There were 3.350 million unmarried mothers in this same age range, so almost 18 percent of the midlife single parents are fathers, a much higher percentage than for single parents younger than age thirty-five, of whom 10.3 percent are fathers. Of all the men and women aged thirty-five to fifty-four who have at least one child living with them, 46.8 percent are married men, 40.1 percent are married women, 2.3 percent are single men, and 10.7 percent are single women.

There are racial differences in the composition of these groups. Single-parent families are more likely to be African Americans than are two-parent families: 16 percent of the midlife single fathers are African Americans, as are 27 percent of the midlife single mothers, compared with 7 percent of the midlife married fathers and mothers. Hispanics are not extraordinarily overrepresented among single-parent families: 8 percent of the midlife single fathers and 11 percent of the midlife single mothers are Hispanic, compared with 8 percent of the midlife married fathers and mothers.

Table 3.1 provides information on personal economic characteristics of six groups—midlife single fathers, midlife married fathers, young single fathers, midlife single mothers, midlife married mothers, and young single mothers—including earnings, employment status, insurance coverage, and disability status. The first two columns allow us to compare midlife single fathers with midlife married fathers. They show that midlife single fathers have lower annual earnings than midlife married fathers (panel 1), in part because they work less (panel 2) and in part because they have lower hourly wages (panel 3). Midlife single fathers have a somewhat higher unemployment rate, but it is still fairly low at 5.5 percent, and the difference is not statistically significant. Almost twice as many of the midlife single fathers are without health insurance coverage.

The midlife single fathers, however, are generally better off than the young single fathers. They earn more, partly because they work more and partly because they have higher hourly wages. Their unemployment rate is only half as high, and they are more likely to have health coverage. In fact, young single fathers have the worst insurance coverage of any of the parental groups, with almost one-third uninsured.

Midlife single mothers fare worse in the labor market than midlife single fathers. The midlife single mothers earn substantially less, both

Table 3.1. Personal Employment, Earnings, Health Coverage, and Disability Status of Parents by Gender, Marital Status, and Age Groups (%)

	Fathers			Mothers		
	Midlife Single (35–54)	Midlife Married (35–54)	Young Single (<35)	Midlife Single (35–54)	Midlife Married (35–54)	Young Single (35–54)
Annual personal earnings ($)						
0	15.4	13.0	14.0	25.7[a]	30.8[b]	35.3[b]
1–4,999	5.8	3.4[a]	10.5[a]	10.5[a]	15.2[b]	20.2[b]
5,000–9,999	6.4	3.5[a]	13.9[a]	12.1[a]	12.8	15.1[b]
10,000–19,999	18.0	14.3[a]	33.7[a]	28.0[a]	21.5[b]	19.6[b]
20,000–29,999	21.3	19.7	15.2[a]	14.4[a]	12.5[b]	7.6[b]
30,000–49,999	25.4	30.8[a]	11.2[a]	8.5[a]	6.2[b]	2.1[b]
50,000+	7.7	15.4[a]	1.3[a]	0.8[a]	1.0	0.1[b]
Annual hours expressed as a percentage of full-time full year (2080 hours)						
0	6.2	3.4	9.2	22.7[a]	25.0	34.0[b]
.01–24.99	1.6	1.1	4.6	4.8[a]	9.3[b]	10.7[b]
25.00–49.99	2.9	1.7	5.7	5.0	9.1[b]	7.6[b]
50.00–74.99	5.8	3.3	7.8	7.7	10.6[b]	8.7
75.00–99.99	13.0	9.4	16.5	14.5	13.4	13.5
100–109.99	40.4	42.9	37.5	33.3[a]	25.4[b]	21.2[b]
110+	30.1	38.3[a]	18.8[a]	12.0[a]	7.1[b]	4.3[b]
Average hourly wage (those with hours and earnings, $)						
0.01–3.34	4.3	3.2	7.3	7.9[a]	8.3	16.9[b]
3.35–4.99	6.6	3.3[a]	13.1[a]	13.0[a]	12.5	20.7[b]
5.00–6.99	9.7	6.5	22.9[a]	21.8[a]	18.5[b]	23.2
7.00–9.99	18.2	13.7	22.3	24.7[a]	23.2	20.9[b]
10.00–14.99	25.8	26.5	21.5	20.0	22.7[b]	12.8[b]
15.00+	35.4	46.8[a]	12.9[a]	12.5[a]	14.9[b]	5.4[b]
Unemployment rate	5.5	3.0	11.6[a]	7.2	3.0[b]	14.6[b]
Percent uninsured	22.7	11.0[a]	33.7[a]	18.9	16.4	20.1
Percent disabled	9.9	6.8	7.9	11.6	5.1[b]	8.5[b]

Source: Author's calculations from the 1990 CPS.
Notes: Wages do not include anyone with self-employment or farm income. Annual hours are defined as number of weeks worked times hours usually worked per week when working. Sample sizes are 478 midlife single fathers, 9,737 midlife married fathers, 354 young single fathers, 2,170 midlife single mothers, 8,416 midlife married mothers, 3,042 young single mothers. Because the sample for wages includes only those with hours and earnings, these samples are smaller.
[a]The difference between the percentage of midlife single fathers and the percentage of midlife married fathers (or young single fathers or midlife single mothers) is significantly different from zero at the .05 level (two-tailed).
[b]The difference between the percentage of midlife single mothers and the percentage of midlife married mothers (or young single mothers) is significantly different from zero at the .05 level (two-tailed).

annually and hourly. Many more of them are not working at all or working only part-time. The gap is particularly large at the highest wage level, with more than one-third of the midlife single fathers but only one-eighth of the midlife single mothers earning more than fifteen dollars per hour. The unemployment rate, uninsurance rate, and percent disabled do not differ significantly for these mothers from those data for midlife single fathers.

In contrast with the finding that midlife single fathers earn less than midlife married fathers, midlife single mothers generally earn *more* than midlife married mothers. However, these higher earnings are due to their working more hours, since they have lower hourly wages. Their unemployment rate is more than double that of midlife married mothers, and the percentage that are disabled is more than twice as high as midlife married mothers. No significant difference exists in the percent uninsured.

As expected, in comparison with young single mothers, midlife single mothers earn more annually, work more, and earn more per hour. Their unemployment rate is half as large. Neither of the age groups of single mothers has as high a rate of uninsurance as the two age groups of single fathers.

In summary, midlife parents fare better in the labor market than young parents, as expected. The effect of single parenthood is different for men and women: whereas single fathers earn less and work less than married fathers, single mothers earn more annually (though they earn less per hour) and work more than married mothers. Finally, women fare much worse than men, regardless of whether they are married or single. A different picture emerges for health insurance coverage, with little difference by age or marital status for women but large differences for men, with young single fathers three times as likely to be uninsured as midlife married fathers, and midlife single fathers twice as likely to be uninsured as midlife married fathers.

Family income and poverty status of the six groups are shown in table 3.2. (Whereas table 3.1 focused on individuals, table 3.2 looks at families. Family incomes are simply the sum of the incomes of each individual in the family.) Comparing the first two columns shows that family income in midlife married-father families is much higher than in midlife single-father families, probably because married couples have the potential of two adult earners in the family. In fact, more than three times as many married fathers as single fathers have family incomes over fifty thousand dollars. The second group of data shows

TABLE 3.2. Family Income and Poverty Status by Gender, Marital Status, and Age Groups (%)

	Fathers			Mothers		
	Midlife Single (35–54)	Midlife Married (35–54)	Young Single (<35)	Midlife Single (35–54)	Midlife Married (35–54)	Young Single (35–54)
Annual family income ($)						
0	1.0	0.2	2.5	2.3^a	0.2^b	5.9^b
1–4,999	5.8	0.8^a	13.5^a	11.2^a	0.7^b	29.0^b
5,000–9,999	7.6	2.1^a	13.5^a	16.2^a	2.1^b	25.6^b
10,000–19,999	19.5	7.8^a	30.3^a	28.9^a	7.2^b	24.3^b
20,000–29,999	21.9	12.4^a	19.9	19.5	12.0^b	10.0^b
30,000–49,999	30.0	33.0	14.8^a	16.4^a	32.1^b	4.6^b
50,000+	14.1	43.8^a	5.6^a	5.6^a	45.7^b	0.6^b
Annual family income compared with poverty						
<50% of poverty	6.3	1.5^a	10.7	13.5^a	1.4^b	25.4^b
51%–100% poverty	6.1	4.0	12.9^a	16.5^a	3.8^b	24.8^b
101%–200% poverty	18.7	12.8^a	23.3	27.4^a	12.3^b	25.6
201%–300% poverty	21.8	19.3	24.7	19.5	18.5	12.0^b
Over 300% poverty	47.1	62.3^a	28.4^a	23.2^a	64.0^b	12.3^b

Source: Author's calculations from the 1990 CPS.
Note: Sample sizes are 478 midlife single fathers, 9,737 midlife married fathers, 354 young single fathers, 2,170 midlife single mothers, 8,416 midlife married mothers, 3,042 young single mothers.
[a]The difference between the percentage of midlife single fathers and the percentage of midlife married fathers (or young single fathers or midlife single mothers) is significantly different from zero at the .05 level (two-tailed).
[b]The difference between the percentage of midlife single mothers and the percentage of midlife married mothers (or young single mothers) is significantly different from zero at the .05 level (two-tailed).

annual family income compared with the poverty line. Because the poverty line varies with the number of people in the family, this comparison recognizes that income has to stretch further when there are more people in the family. Poverty rates for midlife single-father families are more than twice as high as for midlife married-father families, 12.4 percent versus 5.5 percent. Yet almost half the midlife single fathers have incomes more than three times the poverty line, so the group as a whole is not extremely poor. This point is underlined by comparing the midlife single-father families with the young single-father families, who are much worse off. Only half as many young single-father families earn over thirty thousand dollars, and almost twice as many, 23.6 percent, are below poverty.

Midlife single-mother families have substantially lower family incomes than do midlife single-fathers. Only 22 percent of the single-mother families have incomes above thirty thousand dollars, compared with 44 percent of the single-father families. The poverty rates of midlife single-mother families are *much* higher, with 30 percent below poverty, and only half as many of the single mothers are in the highest income/poverty category. These midlife single mothers are also substantially disadvantaged compared with midlife married mothers, whose family incomes and income/poverty rates are quite high. Similar to young single fathers, young single mothers do even worse than midlife single mothers, with half living in poverty. Indeed, young single mothers are by far the poorest group, with about 75 percent of them below twice the poverty line. In summary, family income and poverty status show a clear ranking among the six types, with midlife married men and women by far the best off, midlife single fathers next, young single fathers and midlife single mothers about the same, and young single mothers clearly the worst off.

Table 3.3 shows the indicators of economic vulnerability for the six family types. The poverty indicator in row 1 shows that single-parent families, especially single-mother families and young single-parent families, are at greatest disadvantage (as we saw in table 3.2). The second row, those who are "health insurance poor," shows a different picture. Here, single-parent families are again more vulnerable than married-couple families, but there is no gender difference at midlife: single fathers are as vulnerable as single mothers. And young single fathers are the most vulnerable, whereas age makes no difference among the single mothers. Most of the "medically poor" are uninsured, rather than those who are insured but have to pay large amounts for insurance, as can be seen by comparing this row to the row for the uninsured in table 3.2.

The third row focuses on future vulnerability by indicating those who are without pensions, poor or near-poor, and have few assets (the "pension poor"). Again, marital status matters, with single parents faring worse than married parents. Gender and age also matter, as single mothers are not doing as well as single fathers, and young single parents are doing considerably worse than single parents at midlife. The final indicator is the access poor, those without telephones, shown in the fourth row. Single parents are once more worse off, but there is no gender difference. Young single parents are much more likely not to have a telephone in the household than single parents at midlife.

The bottom panel shows the combinations of the four indicators

TABLE 3.3. Indicators of Economic Vulnerability by Gender, Marital Status, and Age Groups (%)

	Fathers			Mothers		
	Midlife Single (35–54)	Midlife Married (35–54)	Young Single (<35)	Midlife Single (35–54)	Midlife Married (35–54)	Young Single (35–54)
1. Income poor	12.4	5.5[a]	23.6[a]	30.0[a]	5.2[b]	50.2[b]
2. Health insurance poor	23.8	11.5[a]	35.6[a]	20.4	16.6[b]	21.4
3. Pension poor	25.8	13.0[a]	36.8[a]	43.0[a]	14.2[b]	59.4[b]
4. Access poor (no phone)	8.6	3.0[a]	24.0[a]	10.7	2.5[b]	20.7[b]
At least one of the above	39.6	20.8[a]	58.3[a]	53.1[a]	26.1[b]	71.5[b]
At least two of the above	20.6	8.8[a]	38.2[a]	35.8[a]	9.1[b]	54.7[b]
At least three of the above	8.8	3.0[a]	19.0[a]	13.4	3.0[b]	23.1[b]
All four of the above	1.7	0.5	4.6	1.8	0.4[b]	2.4

Source: Author's calculations from the 1990 CPS.

Note: Sample sizes are 478 midlife single fathers, 9,737 midlife married fathers, 354 young single fathers, 2,170 midlife single mothers, 8,416 midlife married mothers, 3,042 young single mothers.

[a]The difference between the percentage of the families of midlife single fathers and the percentage of the families of midlife married fathers (or young single fathers or midlife single mothers) is significantly different from zero at the .05 level (two-tailed).

[b]The difference between the percentage of the families of midlife single mothers and the percentage of the families of midlife married mothers (or young single mothers) is significantly different from zero at the .05 level (two-tailed).

of vulnerability. While very few parents have all four indicators of vulnerability, more than 39 percent of each of the categories of single parents have at least one indicator of vulnerability, compared with between 20 and 30 percent for the married couples. There is a clear pattern to those measures, with young single mothers being the most vulnerable, followed by young single fathers and midlife single mothers, midlife single fathers and, last, midlife married parents. Although midlife single parents fare better than young single parents, their rates of vulnerability are quite high, with more than one-fifth of the midlife single fathers and more than one-third of the midlife single mothers experiencing two or more areas of disadvantage. Gender differences persist at midlife, with single fathers substantially better off than single mothers, even if they are worse off than married fathers.

Not shown on the table are differences among racial and ethnic groups within each of the six gender/marital status/age groupings. As might be expected, African Americans and Hispanics are more likely to be poor within each category (not shown on table): for example, among midlife single mothers, 39 percent of the African Americans and 52 percent of the Hispanics are poor, compared with 21 percent of the whites. Similarly, for all six groups, African Americans and Hispanics are more likely to be pension poor than whites and at least as likely to be access poor as whites. A different pattern exists for health insurance: among the four midlife groups, African Americans and Hispanics are more likely to be health insurance poor than whites. But among the young single fathers and mothers, whites are slightly more likely to be health insurance poor than African Americans, 35.8 percent to 27.6 percent for young single fathers and 21.3 percent to 18.1 percent for young single mothers. This occurs because more African Americans than whites are covered by Medicaid among young single parents, so they are less likely to be uninsured.

Putting all four indicators of vulnerability together underlines the cumulative disadvantage faced by African Americans and Hispanics within each of the six groups. For example, among midlife single fathers, 69 percent of the whites have no indicators of vulnerability, compared with 33 percent of the African Americans and 41 percent of the Hispanics. Among midlife single mothers, the comparable figures for no vulnerability are 55 percent for whites, 41 percent for blacks, and 24 percent for Hispanics. Correspondingly, the percentage with multiple areas of vulnerability is quite high for some groups of African Americans and Hispanics: among midlife single mothers, for example, 17 percent of the African Americans and 27 percent of the Hispanics had three or four areas of vulnerability, compared with 9 percent among whites.

Table 3.4 provides information on whether the programs that have been instituted to help disadvantaged families are reaching these groups. This table is limited to the near-poor (incomes less than twice the poverty line), since the programs shown are limited to the poor and near-poor. The bottom row shows that a majority of the near-poor families of each type receive at least one welfare program. The program that has the most participation is the reduced price hot lunch program for children in school, with between 57 percent and 82 per-

TABLE 3.4. Welfare Recipiency of Families with Incomes below Two Times Poverty by Gender, Marital Status, and Age Groups (%)

	Fathers			Mothers		
	Midlife Single (35–54)	Midlife Married (35–54)	Young Single (<35)	Midlife Single (35–54)	Midlife Married (35–54)	Young Single (35–54)
AFDC recipient	17.0	10.2	13.5	30.2[a]	9.7[b]	46.7[b]
Food stamps recipient	21.4	18.8	34.4	40.2[a]	18.4[b]	53.7[b]
Of those with children under 15: Children receive either Medicaid or Medicare	30.5	15.3[a]	30.5	37.7	15.1[b]	52.6[b]
Public housing recipient	6.3	5.1	11.4	18.4[a]	4.4[b]	26.2[b]
Energy assistance recipient	11.4	8.4	11.0	15.9	8.2[b]	16.9
Of those with children aged 5 to 18: Children receive reduced price hot lunches	68.1	57.4	73.3	72.7	58.4[b]	81.8[b]
Recipient of any of the above	63.4	50.6	58.2	70.7	50.0[b]	77.2[b]

Source: Author's calculations from the 1990 CPS.

Note: Sample sizes (those with incomes less than twice the poverty line) are 150 midlife single fathers, 1,909 midlife married fathers, 173 young single fathers, 1,274 midlife single mothers, 1,573 midlife married mothers, 2,301 young single mothers. Sample sizes for Medicaid are 129, 1,747, 173, 1,060, 1,371, and 2,276, respectively. Sample sizes for hot lunches are 109, 1,424, 77, 986, 1,164, and 1,379, respectively.

[a]The difference between the percentage of the families of midlife single fathers and the percentage of the families of midlife married fathers (or young single fathers or midlife single mothers) is significantly different from zero at the .05 level (two-tailed).

[b]The difference between the percentage of the families of midlife single mothers and the percentage of the families of midlife married mothers (or young single mothers) is significantly different from zero at the .05 level (two-tailed).

cent of the families in each group participating. Few families receive public housing or energy assistance, with the other programs in between these extremes in usage. In general, few significant differences exist in welfare use between midlife single fathers and midlife married fathers, and age does not make a difference for single fathers. However, single-mother families use AFDC, food stamps, and public housing more than single fathers, and single-mother families receive every type of welfare more frequently than married mothers. Young single mothers are even more frequent users of welfare than midlife single mothers, perhaps reflecting their lack of human capital.

TABLE 3.5. Child Support Agreements and Payments
by Gender and Age Groups (%)

	Fathers		Mothers	
	Midlife Custodial (35–54)	Young Custodial (<35)	Midlife Custodial (35–54)	Young Custodial (<35)
Percentage with current child support award	24.9	30.8	83.3[a]	80.1[b]
Amount of child support due annually (of those supposed to receive)				
$1–1,199	36.5	32.7	11.4[a]	27.3[b]
$1,200–2,399	36.5	46.9	19.9[a]	32.3[b]
$2,400–4,799	17.3	16.3	30.8[a]	27.6
$4,800–7,199	5.8	4.1	21.1[a]	9.1[b]
$7,200 and over	3.8	0.0	16.8[a]	3.6[b]
Percentage of child support award that is paid				
0	53.8	40.8	24.4[a]	25.9
1–50%	3.8	8.2	8.7	11.8[b]
51–99%	15.4	20.4	18.2	19.9
100% or more	26.9	30.6	48.7[a]	42.4[b]

Source: Author's calculations from the WCRD.
Notes: Includes awards and payments for July–December 1987 (times two for the annual amounts). Some custodial parents have remarried. Sample sizes for the percentage with award are 209 midlife custodial fathers, 159 young custodial fathers, 1,135 midlife custodial mothers, and 2,969 young custodial mothers; for amount of award, 55 midlife custodial fathers, 49 young custodial fathers, 945 midlife custodial mothers, and 2,378 young custodial mothers; and for percentage paid, 52 midlife custodial fathers, 49 young custodial fathers, 929 midlife custodial mothers, and 2,355 young custodial mothers.
[a]The difference between the percentage of midlife custodial fathers and midlife custodial mothers (or young custodial fathers) is significantly different from zero at the .05 level (two-tailed).
[b]The difference between the percentage of midlife custodial mothers and young custodial mothers is significantly different from zero at the .05 level (two-tailed).

The child support system is the other major area of policy addressed specifically at the needs of single parents. Table 3.5 shows child support awards and payments for fathers and mothers who have been through the Wisconsin courts. This entire table should be viewed cautiously because of the small samples of custodial fathers in the different age ranges. Mothers in both age groups are much more likely to have a child support award than are fathers, around 80 percent, compared with 25–30 percent. When there is an award, awards for mothers are much higher; among mothers, substantial variation exists across the two age ranges: awards among midlife mothers are higher than among young mothers. About one-third of the fathers in each age range who have awards are supposed to receive less than one hundred dollars per month, compared with about one-tenth of the midlife mothers and one-fourth of the young mothers. Correspondingly, almost 40 percent of the midlife single mothers have awards of four hundred dollars per month or greater, compared with fewer than 15 percent of the other groups. The percentage of the award that is received by custodial fathers is substantially lower than the percentage received by custodial mothers: 40–54 percent of the custodial fathers with awards receive nothing versus about one-fourth of the custodial mothers. About 30 percent of the fathers receive the full amount due, compared with 40–50 percent of the mothers. There are no significant differences between midlife custodial fathers and young custodial fathers in any category, perhaps in part because sample sizes are small. On the other hand, age makes some difference for mothers: midlife mothers are slightly more likely to have awards, and their awards are quite a bit higher than those received by young mothers. The percentage of the award that is paid is also somewhat higher for midlife mothers.

Discussion and Some Thoughts on Future Research

The indicators used here are somewhat crude and certainly incomplete. If the dataset had more information, other indicators of vulnerability could include those without social supports, those living in inadequate housing, those who went to bed hungry at least once in the last month, and so forth. The four measures used here, though imperfect, do provide some indication of the severity of economic vulnerability on a variety of dimensions.

These results have generally shown that age tends to increase economic well-being, that single parenthood tends to decrease economic well-being, and that single mothers fare considerably worse than single fathers. These broad generalizations, however, mask a great deal of diversity within each population group. So although *most* single fathers at midlife are better off than young single fathers and single mothers of any age and are worse off than married men and women, many individuals do not fit this pattern. For example, while 44 percent of the midlife single-father families have family incomes over thirty thousand dollars, 14 percent have incomes below ten thousand dollars. Similarly, although 30 percent of midlife single-mother families have family incomes below ten thousand dollars, 22 percent have incomes over thirty thousand dollars.

Marital status, gender, and age have complicated interactions, and each measure of well-being is influenced somewhat differently by the interplay of these factors. For example, age seems to be quite important in influencing who is "pension poor," with young single fathers and mothers most disadvantaged. In the case of pensions, however, age interacts with gender so that while midlife single parents are doing better than young single parents, midlife single fathers are doing considerably better than midlife single mothers. Gender is important to the number of hours worked, with men working more than women, but the interaction of gender and single parenthood produces single fathers who are less likely to work long hours than married fathers and single mothers who work more than married mothers. Certainly the finding that men work more than women is not a surprise, being consistent with prevalent norms (Ross and Huber 1985). But because single fathers are trying to fulfill several roles—provider, nurturer, and household manager—this may cause them to work less than married men. Single mothers, on the other hand, are at such economic disadvantage that perhaps they cannot afford to work less to fulfill their multiple roles.

Single mothers as a group have very low family incomes and very high poverty rates. The disadvantage associated with being female and with being a single parent is clear, and the general story holds across many measures of well-being. On one measure, however, the likelihood of being uninsured, young single fathers are worse off than young single mothers, and the percentage of midlife single fathers uninsured is higher than midlife single mothers (although at midlife, the difference is not statistically significant).

Further, single fathers are less likely to receive economic help from either the welfare or the child support system. Some of the difference in welfare receipt is due to the fact that even within the categories of poor and near-poor, single mothers are worse off than single fathers. But despite fairly narrow income/poverty groups, single mothers still have higher participation rates than single fathers. Perhaps there is more stigma for men in receiving welfare, perhaps they have more resources (savings, friends with money) than single mothers, or perhaps they prefer to use other resources rather than receive welfare. Another difference may be information: many fathers may believe that welfare programs are available only to single mothers. It is also possible that the welfare system treats men differently from women, discouraging their application or examining their assets and income more carefully.

The child support system is providing much less assistance to custodial fathers than to custodial mothers, and this holds true at each step of the system: fewer custodial fathers have awards, the ones that do have smaller awards, and a smaller percentage is paid. The lower percentage with awards may reflect fathers who agree not to ask for money if they can have the child, or it may be that when fathers have custody, the noncustodial mothers have very poor economic circumstances and thus are not asked to pay. It could also reflect a reluctance on the part of the court to order women to pay, or it could be due to some other factors. Similarly, the fact that fathers with awards have lower awards than mothers may reflect the desires of fathers, the relative earning capacity of the noncustodial parent (noncustodial fathers probably have higher earnings than noncustodial mothers), the fact that fathers with custody generally have custody of fewer children, or systematically different treatment on the part of the courts. While the first two portions of table 3.5 (whether there is an award and its amount) refer to outcomes that are set by a judge (or negotiated by the parents and approved by a judge), the bottom part does not and thus is a purer reflection of the actions of the noncustodial parent. As noted above, many more fathers than mothers receive nothing, and a much smaller percentage receive the full amount. The factors associated with the payment of child support by mothers are not well understood, and these data cannot shed much light on this issue or the other questions about the potential differential treatment of men and women by the courts. Yet these questions are quite important: clearly the policy implications of the finding that men receive less child support depends a great deal on whether this is due to private agreements or to a difference in the way courts treat men and women. Further research using different data, particularly interviews of divorcing mothers, fathers, and judges, may prove fruitful.

Despite recent increases in the numbers, single fatherhood is still a relatively rare and nonnormative experience, with reasons for the increase not well understood. The increase in single fatherhood could occur because men are seeking custody more frequently when partnerships fail, because women are seeking custody less frequently, or because the court is responding to custody conflicts differently from how it has in the past. Men could be seeking custody more often because they are more involved in parenting or because they believe they now have a chance to be awarded custody. Some women may no longer see parenthood as one of the core parts of their identity, thus being willing to give up custody. Yet another line of thinking is that men may have discovered that if they do not have custody, they will have to bear significant economic costs in child support, and they therefore fight for custody more frequently.

Because the number of single fathers is increasing rapidly, the composition of this group may be changing. Ten years ago, two types of single fathers likely existed: trendsetters (higher-income men) and those whose partners were unable to cope with the children (perhaps more likely to be of low income). If increases continue, this family type may become less nonnormative, perhaps spreading throughout the income distribution.

This brief discussion highlights several unanswered policy questions. First, why do single fathers make less use of welfare programs? Is this related to knowledge, stigma, or some other factors? If fathers do not believe they are eligible for these programs, then an information campaign that informs single fathers about the availability of various benefits could be conducted. If their lack of participation in these programs is mainly because poor single fathers rely on other resources, then policymakers interested in minimizing welfare costs might be interested in examining whether single mothers could also take advantage of these other resources.

Second, what accounts for the rise in single-father families? Is this increase related to changes in laws that require a gender-neutral determination of custody, to the preferences of the parties involved, or to other factors? If this increase is due to legal change, then perhaps research is needed that compares the outcomes of children growing up in single-father families with those growing up in mother-only families. If the outcomes for children differ, even when other factors are held constant, perhaps this should be considered in laws governing the determination of custody. And what accounts for custodial mothers and custodial fathers having different outcomes from the child support system? Are the courts treating noncustodial fathers and mothers who have the same income similarly? Should they?

This research has also opened several other questions. For example, what is the interaction between age, gender, and marital status on broader measures of economic well-being? Other indicators could include the number who live in overcrowded housing, those who live in substandard housing or in dangerous neighborhoods, those who pay a high percentage of their income for food and housing, those who go to bed hungry, those who do not get consistent medical care, and the like. Clearly, economic well-being is a multifaceted concept and is strongly related to well-being in noneconomic spheres. What is the relationship between economic well-being and psychological well-being, and does it differ within age, gender, and marital status groups? Measures of depression or of global life satisfaction could be examined in this type of framework, looking closely at the interactions between age, gender, and marital status. And would a longitudinal examination of economic well-being for these groups reveal a different picture? More recent data show that 21 percent of those who were poor in 1990 were not poor in 1991, and 3 percent of those not poor in 1990 became poor in 1991 (Bureau of the Census 1995). What are the interactions of age, gender, and marital status if we examine those who are persistently poor? Examining data over a long period would help us understand whether young single parents who are poor are likely to be poor single parents when they reach midlife.

Finally, this research has provided simple descriptive information on single-parent families. Further work using a multivariate framework is needed. For example, single fathers are more likely to be white and to have higher education levels than single mothers (Meyer and Garasky 1993). Thus single fathers could be expected to have fewer economic problems than single mothers. Multivariate analyses would clearly further our understanding of disadvantage and vulnerability.

SUMMARY

Single parents are disadvantaged on nearly every economic indicator. They have lower incomes, higher levels of unemployment, less medical coverage, and less security for the future than do married parents. Although some of these indicators of disadvantage improve substantially in the midlife group (such as the percentage with pensions and with telephones and the employment rate), others do not (for example, the rate of uninsurance is nearly as high for midlife single mothers as for young single mothers). Gender differences persist at midlife among single-parent families on most indicators: single-mother families are more likely to be poor, are less likely to have pensions, and have higher welfare participation rates. One exception is in health insurance coverage, which seems to be just as problematic among men, if not worse.

Some of the economic policies intended to help the disadvantaged may not be reaching these groups. Less than one-fourth of the near-poor midlife single-father families and less than one-half of the near-poor midlife single-mother families receive AFDC, food stamps, public housing, and energy assistance. Perhaps programs not targeted on the poor (and thus not carrying so much stigma) would be more effective in addressing the needs of the disadvantaged. Finally, although the child support system has been substantially improved in the last decade, not much is being provided to single-father families, with fewer than 30 percent having an award and with less than half of those with awards receiving some payment.

NOTES

1. Some cohabiting couples are coded as single-parent families in this dataset. Although the number of cohabiting couples who have children living with them has grown rapidly (Spanier 1983), only about 15 percent of the father-only families in the CPS (n = 125) were men who were living with a female partner, and thus almost all of the children cannot be living with both their parents.

2. An additional forty single father and ninety-seven single mothers were fifty-five or older. Because these do not fit my definition of "midlife," they were not included in the following analyses.

3. I also excluded cases with split custody (one or more child to each parent) and those with joint physical custody (each parent has the child(ren) half the time).

4. This definition therefore differs from that used by Marks in this volume in two ways: first, she includes those with children of any age, whereas I have only those with minor children. Second, she includes all those who have parented children, in contrast with my counting those who have children currently living with them. Thus her "single parents" group includes both custodial parents (those on whom I focus) and noncustodial parents (who I do not include).

5. A recent summary of the reasoning behind the poverty line, a discussion of the issues involved in establishing a line, and a summary of critiques of the official poverty measure has been provided by Ruggles (1990).

6. Statistics using the line have been criticized because income does not incorporate the value of in-kind benefits (e.g., food stamps or medical care) and taxes have not been subtracted. The Census Bureau now provides information on what the poverty rate would be if these adjustments and others were made (Bureau of the Census 1992).

7. I have made comparisons among four groups: non-Hispanic whites (called "whites" in this chapter), non-Hispanic African Americans (called "African Americans" in this chapter), Hispanic, and others.

8. Jencks and Torrey (1986) provided information on a number of indicators of well-being for children and the elderly, including the percentage without automobiles, without enough money to buy food at some point during the past year,

without full bathroom or kitchen facilities, in overcrowded housing, and so forth. These measures, while quite interesting, are not available in this dataset. Cook and Kramek (1986) also report on a variety of similar measures for the elderly, including, for example, those who were evicted in the last year, those who had their "utilities cut off because of no money," and those who "would have no support system if they needed help with food, sickness, place to stay, and money."

References

Becker, G. S. 1981. *A treatise on the family.* Cambridge, Mass.: Harvard University Press.

Bumpass, L. 1984. Children and marital distribution: A replication and an update. *Demography* 21:71–82.

Cantril, H. 1965. *The pattern of human concerns.* New Brunswick, N.J.: Rutgers University Press.

Cook, F. L., and L. M. Kramek. 1986. Measuring economic hardship among older Americans. *Gerontologist* 26:38–47.

Derthick, M. 1979. *Policymaking for Social Security.* Washington, D.C.: Brookings Institution.

Douthitt, R. A., M. MacDonald, and R. Mullis. 1992. The relationship between measures of subjective and economic well-being: A new look. *Social Indicators Research* 26:407–422.

Easterlin, R. A. 1974. Does economic growth improve the human lot? Some empirical evidence. In P. David and M. Reider, eds., *Nations and households in economic growth,* pp. 89–125. New York: Academic Press.

Ellwood, D. T. 1988. *Poor support: Poverty in the American family.* New York: Basic Books.

Garfinkel, I., T. J. Corbett, M. MacDonald, S. McLanahan, P. K. Robins, N. C. Schaeffer, and J. A. Seltzer. 1988. Evaluation design for the Wisconsin child support assurance demonstration. Report prepared for the Wisconsin Department of Health and Social Services. Madison University of Wisconsin.

Garfinkel, I., and S. S. McLanahan. 1986. *Single mothers and their children: A new American dilemma.* Washington, D.C.: Urban Institute Press.

Jencks, C., and B. B. Torrey. 1986. Beyond income and poverty: Trends in social welfare among children and the elderly since 1960. In J. L. Palmer, T. Smeeding, and B. B. Torrey, eds., *The vulnerable: America's young and old,* pp. 229–273. Washington, D.C.: Urban Institute Press.

Marini, M. M. 1989. Sex differences in earnings in the Uniterd States. *Annual Review of Sociology* 15:343–380.

McLanahan, S., and J. Adams. 1987. Parenthood and psychological well-being. *Annual Review of Immunology* 5:237–257.

McLanahan, S., and K. Booth. 1989. Mother-only families: Problems, prospects, and politics. *Journal of Marriage and the Family* 51:557–580.

McLoyd, V. C. 1990. The impact of economic hardship on black families and children: Psychological distress, parenting, and socioemotional development. *Child Development* 61:311–346

Meyer, D. R., and S. Garasky. 1993. Custodial fathers: Myths, realities, and child support policy. *Journal of Marriage and the Family* 55:73–89.

Mincer, J. 1974. *Schooling, experience, and earnings.* New York: National Bureau of Economic Research.

Minder, J., and S. Polachek. 1974. Family investments in human capital: Earnings of women. *Journal of Political Economy* 82:S76–S110.

National Commission on Children. 1991. *Beyond rhetoric: A new American agenda for children and families.* Washington, D.C.: National Commission on Children.

Orshansky, M. 1965. Counting the poor: Another look at the poverty people. *Social Security Bulletin* 28:3–29.

Ross, C. E., and J. Huber. 1985. Hardship and depression. *Journal of Health and Social Behavior* 26:312–327.

Ruggles, P. 1990. *Drawing the line: Alternative poverty measures and their implications for public policy.* Washington, D.C.: Urban Institute Press.

Spanier, G. B. 1983. Married and unmarried cohabitation in the United States: 1980. *Journal of Marriage and the Family* 45:277–288.

U.S. Bureau of the Census. 1991a. *Money Income of Households, Families, and Persons in the United States: 1990.* Current Population Reports, ser. P-60, no. 174. Washington, D.C.: U.S. Government Printing Office.

———. 1991b. *Poverty in the United States: 1990* Current Population Reports, ser. P-60. no. 175. Washington, D.C.: U.S. Government Printing Office.

———. 1992. *Measuring the effect of benefits and taxes on income and poverty: 1979 to 1991.* Current Population Reports, ser. P-60, no. 182-RD. Washington, D.C.: U.S. Government Printing Office.

———. 1995. *Dynamics of economic well-being: Poverty, 1990 to 1992.* Current Population Reports, ser. P-70, no. 42. Washington, D.C.: U.S. Government Printing Office.

U.S. House. 1992. Committee on Ways and Means. *1992 Green book: Overview of entitlement programs.* Washington, D.C.: U.S. Government Printing Office.

III Historical and Social Changes and the Parental Experience

FOUR

Parental Socialization in Historical Perspective

Duane F. Alwin

> True, men and women will always go on loving one another,
> will always go on having children. That is not the question at
> issue. The point is that the ideas entertained about these relations
> may be dissimilar at moments separated by lengthy periods of
> time.
>
> Philippe Aries, *Centuries of Childhood*

INTRODUCTION

Though fertility rates have been declining, and fewer people are opting for parenthood, childrearing continues to be a major preoccupation of the majority of adults. Changes in society and in the family, however, have altered some aspects of childrearing and the relations between parents and children (see Levine and White 1986; Vinovskis 1987). Parents can see some of these changes within their own lifetime, because they can, with some degree of distortion perhaps, compare themselves with their parents and compare the nature of their relationships with their children with the way they were raised (see Alwin 1988a). But we need to take a longer perspective, as well as a more objective one, to trace the patterns of childrearing over time. This chapter focuses on historical changes in the qualities parents want to see embodied in the behavior of their children. The perspective offered here suggests that there have been remarkable changes in the parental experience over past centuries—and especially over recent decades—manifest in changing parental value orientations. Parental conceptions of what children should be like have, by a number of empirical indications, undergone systematic changes in the direction of granting children greater independence and expecting less obedience and con-

Preparation of this chapter and the collection of data on which it is based were supported by grants from the National Institute of Mental Health (MH37289 and MH39761), the National Science Foundation (SES-8712119), and the National Institute on Aging (AG04743). I acknowledge the research assistance of Tom Carson, Xiaohe Xu, Merilynn Dielman, and Rachel Murray. Generous comments by Carol Ryff and Marsha Seltzer greatly improved the paper.

formity. The changes in parental experience are reflected in transformations of both the contexts of childrearing and the nature of parent-child relations. Whatever their source—and there may be many— these changes have implications, not only for children but also *for parents themselves:* shifts in what society wants from children and expects of them have altered the task of childrearing (see Hogan 1987). Thus, the historical changes to which this chapter attests reflect patterns of change in the nature of parenting, as much as they do changes in the nature of children.

The chapter begins with a discussion of the ways in which conceptions of childhood and the parent-child relationship have evolved in modern psychological and social science. Of course, how childhood is conceived has implications for assumptions made about the nature of parental socialization. Thus, to the extent that the nature of childhood is seen as something that varies across time and across place, so too should the nature of parenthood be viewed. Of particular interest in this regard is the emergence of a broad perspective incorporating developmental, social, and historical conceptions of the context of parent-child relationships (see, e.g., Elder, Modell, and Parke 1993). The discussion of this emergent perspective leads to an articulation of a concern with "parental socialization values"—standards of desirability that parents use to evaluate their children's behavior and their successes in childrearing—which are known to vary historically, socially, and developmentally. Although limited in some respects, the study of parental values can provide a key empirical reading on changes in both childhood and parenthood—one that can help disentangle the sources of historical change in the nature of the family.

In taking all three aforementioned sources of variation—developmental, social, and historical factors—into account, I first review the existing empirical record on *historical* changes in parental values. This provides documentation, to the extent possible, of changes in parental orientations toward children from roughly the Industrial Revolution until the present. For obvious reasons, most of the evidence regarding what parents themselves say about their childrearing values comes from the relatively recent historical record, although some studies reach back to the beginning of this century. In this context I also review what is known about ahistorical patterns in childrearing values, that is, variation linked to the structure and organization of modern society, as well as to the developmental factors.

After this brief reconnaissance of the available evidence on factors

linked to variation in parental values, I then focus exclusively on historical changes, examining the extent to which support exists for two major interpretations for this change—changes in parental values due to
processes of *cohort replacement* or processes of social *change within
cohorts.* For this purpose I examine data from the Child-Rearing in
Detroit Project, developed to chart patterns of social changes in parental orientations and their sources. The Detroit data span the thirty-
year period between 1958 and 1988. Relatively clear patterns exist in
these data, reported through 1983 in an earlier paper (Alwin 1990b),
supporting to some extent the cohort replacement model of social
change. I also examine *new* data from the General Social Survey, although it exists for a much shorter period of time, to confirm our
Detroit findings on a broader-gauged national database. There has
been some indication of convergence between the Detroit results and
national data in previous research, but those results were based on a
weaker set of measures than we now have available (see Alwin 1989b).
Finally, in the process of analyzing these materials, I confront one of
the major assumptions of the cohort replacement model of social
change, specifically, the assumption of the life-cycle stability of values
(see Alwin 1990b) and the implications for such theories of developmental evidence with respect to the life-cycle variations in parental
values. This leads to a more detailed inspection of the 1982–83 data
from the Child-Rearing in Detroit Project (Alwin 1994b) to examine
the question of whether there are detectable changes in parental values
over the life cycles of parents and the developmental stages of their
children.

Conceptions of Childhood and Parenthood

There are several prevailing conceptions among behavioral scientists
and laypersons about the relation between child development, parent-
child relations, and social change. One view, which is very common,
especially among developmental psychologists, is that certain elements
about the nature of childhood are experienced universally, regardless
of culture and historical time. This view is rooted in the assumption
that there are psychobiological universals to which cultures respond
more or less sympathetically, regardless of time or place, and given the
genetically driven nature of physiological and psychological development of children, there are certain regularities of experience, which
strongly affect "normal" childhood development whatever the sociohistorical context in which it occurs. "Psychologies" of childhood, for

example, the Freudian interpretation of processes of individuation, or the Piagetian processes of assimilation and accommodation with respect to the individual's relation to the environment, are interpretations of innate, universal psychogenetic processes.

An alternate view, more commonly but not exclusively held by anthropologists, sociologists, and historians of the family, is that the phenomenon of childhood and its associated characteristics are a function not only of developmental stages but of cultural and historical factors as well (see Elder, Modell, and Parke 1993; Richards and Light 1986). This view contrasts with the above "timeless" and "placeless" view of childhood. Indeed, it is the recognition of these facts that leads Aries (1962) to suggest that the nature of children and of adult orientations to aspects of childrearing and/or socialization may change as a function of demographic changes and/or changes in social institutions and the resultant changes in the conditions of life experienced by parents. Theoretically, then, as the institutional bases for the definition of "childhood" and the desired characteristics of children change, so also will the treatment of children and expectations for their behavior.

Both of these views, naturally, are credible. There is no denying the genetic basis for human possibilities and its consequences for shaping and constraining the potentials for and limitations on human development. But, with its physical and psychological development, the social nature of the child changes as well. The norms and customs defining the role of children in the family and their desirable characteristics for functioning in the larger society have a sociocultural basis, as well as a developmental one. The requirements of social life and the nature of the culture also dictate what the child is like, and with institutional and cultural changes, then, so also come changes in the conditions of family life and childrearing. Such social changes have direct implications for parental experiences, parental shaping of children, and the "nature" of childhood and parenthood.

It is also the case that developmental trajectories and stages of the life cycle for children interact in significant ways with historical period. For example, Elder (1980) develops an interesting argument regarding the linkage between social changes and the life-cycle definition of adolescence, which has a more general applicability to the issues being addressed here. He suggests that in a society characterized by a lengthy youthful stage in which the individual experiences a great deal of independence and a period of flexibility and openness to change, it may be reasonable to theorize about the lifelong impact of youthful socialization experiences (see Alwin, Cohen, and Newcomb 1991). On the other hand, in a society characterized by a rather abrupt transition from childhood to adulthood, with fewer choices open to the individual, there may not be such a youthful stage during which the individual is preoccupied with the pursuit of identity and autonomy. Elder's (1980) argument illustrates the great value of recent theorizing with respect to the consideration of the interaction of social change and life-span development, and his recent collaborative project on the implications of a changing society for children's growth and development is a landmark accomplishment (Elder, Modell, and Parke 1993; see also Cahan et al. 1993 and Elder, Caspi, and Burton 1988).

This broader view fits well with Alex Inkeles's (1955) observation that the family is an important mechanism for the mediation of social change and that parental approaches to childrearing are as much an effort to prepare children for a life in society's future as they are reflections of current life circumstances. One can only speculate about the motivational basis for parental behavior, as it is no doubt strongly affected by "current" conditions of life (Elder 1974), but it is also clearly the case that in theory parents would prefer their children to survive in the future society, as well as the present one. Thus, what parents perceive the future to be potentially has a direct bearing on their approaches to the socialization of children and their perceptions of desirable qualities of children.

Elder (1974, 13) suggests such a perspective assumes too great a degree of "future awareness, rationality, and choice in parental behavior" and may not be relevant in all situations. He argues specifically that during times when family survival is at stake, the parental generation focuses on the immediate needs of children, not on "future adult roles." His research into the impact of the economic deprivation experiences connected to the Great Depression suggests that "the socialization environment and the response of parents to children in deprived situations during the 30s had much less to do with their anticipation of life in the future than with the immediacy of survival requirements" (Elder 1974, 13). If only from the point of view of self-preservation of the family grouping, however, one can assume that parents have some considerable motivation to prepare their children for the future, as well as the present, so in a very real sense parents contribute to social change through the socialization of their children. Presumably, in addition to the conditions of life they face during their parental years, parents are also affected by their own experiences as children, as adolescents, or as young adults, and their past experiences contribute greatly to their present orientations to children. Parental experiences thus reflect changes carried forward by previous generations, and given that with "biographic" time, the most basic of human orientations (e.g., beliefs and values) tend to stabilize over individual life-course trajectories (see Alwin 1994a), we would expect that parental orientations to children will reflect something "stable" about the individual. That is to say, while we normally assume that parents are relatively adaptive and orient themselves toward preparing their children for a future life in the society, at some point parents may be unable to adapt to change, given the crystallization of beliefs and values in their own cognitive organization and world view.

Therefore to comprehend the nature of social change, we must also conceptualize the influence of time along the biographic dimension of the parental life cycle. It is often assumed that parental orientations are relatively persistent over the biographies of individuals (see Alwin 1990b), but this dimension is relatively unexplored. Even though children are changing through time, due to developmental and historical factors, do parental orientations to children remain stable? This raises a complex set of questions regarding the sources of parental childrearing orientations. Do they originate exclusively in the parents' own socialization experiences and current social experiences, or are they responsive to the nature and direction of their childrens' development? To what extent is there flexibility in the preferences of parents for what they want to see embodied in their children? This raises the possibility that, although parents may maintain considerable continuity in their underlying values, the external manifestation of those values may differ across the child's development. For example, how one socializes a four-year-old for *autonomy* is presumably different from how one socializes an adolescent toward the embodiment of the same value. There has been extensive work on the link between life-span development and parent-child relationships, but these issues have largely been ignored (but see Altmann 1987; Draper and Harpending 1987).

Parental Values and Socialization of Children

As indicated earlier, in this chapter I use the concept "parental values" as the main indicator for charting historical changes in parent-child relations. Parental values are the "standards of desirability" that parents use to evaluate the behavior and attitudes of their children. Conceived of as "standards," parental values are assumed to be the criteria used as the basis for asserting what are the desirable qualities of children (Kohn 1969). Of course, a wide range of desirable child qualities exists, and parental values are the standards that serve as a basis for choosing among them. A principle contrast of interest here, which is in line with several scholarly treatments of parental socialization values, is the contrast between *autonomy* and *obedience* or, put simply, between "thinking for oneself" and "obeying" adult authority. This contrast has been written about widely. Lynd and Lynd (1929, 131–152) contrasted parental values for "independence" and "obedience." Duvall (1946) distinguished "traditional" from "nontraditional" values, aligned along this dimension. Miller and Swanson (1958, 55–58) came even closer to a dimension of sociological relevance in contrasting parental orientations that were "entrepreneurial," which emphasize child self-control and a manipulative stance toward the environment, with those that were "bureaucratic," which stress reliance on external forms of behavioral control and an accommodation to the environment. Lenski (1961) used the terms *intellectual autonomy* and *intellectual heteronomy* to contrast parental preferences that stressed "thinking for oneself" versus "obedience." Similarly, Kohn and his colleagues (Kohn 1959, 1969, 1981; Pearlin and Kohn 1966; Kohn et al. 1983; Kohn and Slmoczynski 1990) popularized the contrast between "self-direction" and "conformity to external authority" to refer to this same dimension. More recently, Schaefer and his colleagues (e.g., Schaefer 1987; Schaefer and Edgerton 1985) have used the term *parental modernity* to refer to an orientation among parents that stresses self-reliance, self-control, and independence. And, finally, Baumrind (1989, 1991) contrasts parental behavior that is "authoritarian" (behavior that is demanding and directive but not responsive, stressing obedience and respect for authority) with that which is "authoritative" (behavior that is both demanding and responsive, assertive, but not intrusive or restrictive).[1]

Regardless of the particular language used, it is remarkable that these various scholars have all pinpointed the same dimensions of relevance in describing the nature of values underlying parent-child relations. Such contrasts in values are central to the dimensions along which substantial social change has occurred, although the two concepts of "autonomy" and "obedience" should probably *not* be viewed just in terms of their contrast but separately, especially to the extent they are changing independently. In any event, this contrast is definitely linked to the central dimension of historical social development in western industrialized societies, which have increasingly required the exercise of independent thought and action (Stone 1977; LeVine and White 1986). In addition, this set of distinctions is also developmentally relevant, since it is normally believed that children progress from a relatively "obedient" to a relatively "autonomous" state as they mature cognitively, emotionally, and socially (see Piaget 1932).

This is especially interesting, as mentioned earlier, to the extent that "developmental" trajectories and "historical" trajectories interact to produce different requirements of children at different historical periods. Indeed, the very conception of childhood, as an extended period of dependence on adults, is a relatively modern invention, tied to particular historical circumstances. Aries' (1962) provocative essays on the history of childhood should remind the contemporary observer of the necessity of viewing childhood, and all stages of human development, in historical perspective. Social historians have pointed to differences over time in conceptions and treatment of children in Europe and America through the past few centuries—resulting from cultural changes, as well as from the evolution of technology, demography, and social organization (Greven 1970; Stone 1977; Elias 1978; Schlumbohm 1980).

Finally, a third reason for the importance of this dimension should be noted. The contrast between the emphasis on "autonomy" and on "obedience" is also relevant to social stratification. Research on class differences in childrearing orientations in U.S. society, in part due to the early work of the Lynds (1929), has appropriately focused on modes of promoting child development. In the 1940s and 1950s, for example, researchers debated whether the working class was more permissive in childrearing than was the middle class (see Davis and Havighurst 1948; Havighurst and Davis 1955) or vice versa (see Maccoby and Gibbs 1954; Sears, Maccoby, and Levin 1957). Later interpretations (e.g., Bronfenbrenner 1958; Kohn 1959) focused explicitly on the goals of childrearing rather than the means. Kohn (1963, 1969, 1981), for example, emphasized the concept of parental values as embodying the standards of desirability parents use in evaluating the behavior of their children, regardless of the particular childrearing practices, that is, regardless of the means they use to achieve their childrearing goals. In this tradition, the principle contrast in parental values used almost universally is again the contrast between "autonomy" and "obedience." The results of a vast amount of research on class differences in childrearing orientations have done much to confirm the observations of the Lynds (1929), namely, that the middle and upper classes tend to express a greater preference for autonomy or self-direction in children, whereas the working classes give a relatively greater emphasis to obedience and conformity to authority and tradition (see reviews by Alwin 1989a; Gecas 1979; Kerckhoff 1972; Kohn 1977).

THE FAMILY: CONTINUITY OR CHANGE?

Historically, although it is apparent from a number of sources that American culture is distinct in its emphasis on *individualism,* parental orientations over this century have gradually shifted away from an emphasis placed on *obedience* or *conformity* to greater valuation of *independence* or *autonomy* (see Alwin 1984, 1988a, 1990a). This is an example of what Inkeles (1984) refers to as "continuity and change in American national character." He describes a striking degree of continuity in the core values held by Americans since the early days of this nation, despite massive changes in the nature of the family and the levels of education and relative affluence, patterns of residence, and forms of work. It is thus possible for there to be considerable continuity at the level of the "deep structure" of cultural values and beliefs and at the same time substantial shifts in the expression of those values and beliefs at another level.

As Inkeles (1984) noted, Tocqueville's (1835–40) observations about the distinctiveness of American "individualistic" values in the period before the Industrial Revolution thus tend to stand in the way of a purely social structural interpretation of family change. This view calls into question some very popular assumptions that the twentieth-century transformation of the American family was exclusively the result of industrialization, in which the population shifted from rural to urban residence, from agricultural to industrial production, from primary to secondary education levels, and from large to smaller family sizes (Goode 1963). What may seem to be basic value shifts, from one point of view, may be seen as changes in the embodiments of values that have high levels of stability, from another. This poses an interesting set of questions, then, regarding whether value change is best viewed as a fundamental shift in orientations or as a changing expression of basic values, which themselves have considerable continuity.

Whether it reflects continuity or change, mounting evidence indicates that relationships between parents and their children have changed in important ways in industrialized societies over major periods of the past two centuries. But what seems to be most apparent from these changes, changes that I document in the next section, is that they may be relatively unresponsive to many demographic and economic factors normally thought to shape relationships in the family (see Alwin 1984). Although it may be difficult in most studies to ascertain the extent to which values are changing in response to these more fundamental demographic and economic changes, there have been dramatic historical changes in the culture of childrearing, ones associated with the expansion of secondary and tertiary education and with the assimilation of religio-ethnic groups (Alba 1981). Whether cultural changes are in part dependent on sociodemographic changes in the family or mainly responsive to the broader structural changes in the mode of production is not clear.

It could be argued that what has changed is linked to basic changes in social organization. Coleman (1990), for example, contends that one fundamental organizational/institutional change throughout human history is the nature of the society's mechanisms for the exercise of authority (658–660). He maintains that the principal structural change in society with respect to authority relations has been away from the total institutional control of the individual toward authority directed by individual corporate actors. This shift clearly parallels the changes in parent-child relations noted above, and Coleman (1990, 660) cites the evidence on changes in parental values as indicative of evidence in support of his argument.

The movements away from communal forms of social control to more internalized, individual control seems evident in many other aspects of modern life as well, and some would bemoan the losses to "community" that would come about because of the movement toward greater opportunities for emphasis on individualism and self-reliance (Bellah et al. 1985; Popenoe 1988). Regardless of changes in the nature of the modern family, however, it remains apparent that responsiveness to children and a concern for their development is as important in modern life as it was in earlier society. It does seem reasonable to inquire regarding the trade-offs to the emergence of the primacy of the individual in modern life, and I later address this to some extent in the nature of changing parental socialization values in probability samples of the Detroit area. Specifically, we can examine the extent of evidence that increases in expressions of the value of "individualism" in children are emerging at the expense of "community" values.

HISTORICAL CHANGES IN PARENTAL SOCIALIZATION VALUES[2]

Regardless of rather dramatic changes in the nature of the modern family (see Popenoe 1988), many of the basic functions regarding *socialization* of children have remained intact. The family continues to be the primary organizational entity responsible for the care and nurture of children. In virtually all known societies, the family recognizes the child as an object of affection and attention from the time of its birth. In one way or another, the child is given a place in the family grouping, and this helps shape her/his behavior. Of course, what constitutes the family grouping and the nature of the family structure in any given culture at any particular time is variable, but the existence of the parental role, lodged in the nature of the domestic environment of the family, is relatively constant historically. What is done with and to the child, however, depends on a number of factors: it depends in part on the level of physical, psychological, and emotional maturity of the child but, as suggested earlier, also on social, cultural, and historical factors. What the family defines as the "ideal" child and the associated behavioral qualities or traits expected of the child are given meaning through norms and values reflected in adult orientations to children, which culturally and structurally help define and constrain the conditions of life experienced by the family unit.

Since the Industrial Revolution

To some, the history of childhood since the Industrial Revolution is a nightmare from which "we have only begun to awaken," referring to past periods in which children were subjected to exploitation, abuse, abandonment, and murder (DeMause 1974).[3] To others, such as Aries (1962), the development of the idea of the individuality of children, the acceptance of their inherent worth, and the emergence of the awareness of the innocence and purity of childhood all reflect the "privileged age" of the nineteenth-century childhood (see Sommerville 1982). For still others, the Industrial Revolution was a period of both the greatest glorification of childhood and its greatest exploitation (Sommerville 1982, 160). According to this latter view, life in an industrialized society was very difficult for children of the working classes, given their involvement in the labor force. By contrast, the lives of children of the elite classes were comfortable and relatively isolated from the "ravages" of working-class life.

Stone's (1977) vivid historical account of class differences in child-rearing during the seventeenth and eighteenth centuries in England and America presents an argument that social change may not occur universally across social classes. Among the upper classes during this period, he argues, a number of dramatic changes came about in child-rearing practices, indicating a more child-centered, developmental orientation. As the mother became more of a dominant figure in the children's lives, "swaddling gave way to loose clothing, mercenary wet-nursing to maternal breast-feeding, breaking the will by force to permissiveness, formal distance to empathy" (284). But this change toward a "maternal, child-oriented, affectionate and permissive" mode of childrearing did not occur in all social classes. Stone refers to the principle of "stratified diffusion" in his interpretation of the dynamics of the change among classes, wherein new attitudes and values "take hold among those classes which are most literate and most open to new ideas" (285) and only later are adopted, if at all, by lower socioeconomic groups. Stone's argument alerts the student of historical trends in parental socialization values to take account of class differences, where possible. But it should also alert the student of class differences to take account of historical trends, if possible. (This argument made by Stone [1977] has considerable similarity to the argument made by Bronfenbrenner [1958] about class differences in childrearing.)

The increased emotional commitment to children and an interest in their development among the elite classes was clearly present in many Western European cultures by the end of the eighteenth century. Schlumbohm (1980) refers to the differing orientations of social classes in eighteenth-century Germany, for example, wherein the upper classes developed explicit models for rearing children, devoting time, care, and thought to their upbringing. The children of these classes often enjoyed a cloistered existence, removed from the influences of "the street" and of other children. The dominant emphasis was on the development of the internal capacities of the child, especially his/her intellect and character. Although strict adherence to rules and conformity to adult authority was often stressed, the rationale for these practices was given in terms of their achievement of specified developmental outcomes.

Consistent with Stone's analysis of England and America, the emphasis on the individuality of the child recorded by Schlumbohm among the more educated, bourgeoisie classes of Germany was not replicated among the working classes. The conditions of a subsistence orientation among the guild craftsmen of this period, he argues, meant that they often had "little time for their children [and] did not concern themselves much with their education and the aims of child-rearing," and where there was a concern for childrearing, it often revealed itself in a strict orientation to the obedience of children (Schlumbohm 1980, 77, 79). Children of the working classes, according to Schlumbohm, were often ignored to the extent they were not economically useful. Schlumbohm's claim that working-class children were ignored makes it seem possible that working-class parents, while manifestly demanding obedience, may have been fostering the latent phenomenon of autonomy, for in practice children were left to be pretty much responsible for themselves.

Some of these class differences in orientations to children can also be followed into the nineteenth and twentieth centuries. Zelizer (1985), for example, has argued that the "economically useful" child of nineteenth-century industrialized society was eventually replaced by the economically worthless, but emotionally priceless child of the twentieth century. She contrasts two views of childhood, expressed in a variety of historical public documents she examined (child labor legislation, life insurance for children, compensation for the death of children, and patterns of adoption and foster care). One historically relevant view is of the child engaged in labor, for which an economic value existed and in terms of which the value of the child was assessed. The second, now contemporary, view is of a nonlaboring, "priceless child" whose moral value far outweighs any associated economic value. Zelizer traces the conflict of these values in public and private institutions from 1870 to 1930, observing the gradual prevalence of the second view over the first and the tendency toward defining the value of children in terms of sentimental or moral considerations. This is, of course, indicative of the orientations both Stone and Schlumbohm attribute to the upper classes in Europe and America during the eighteenth century.

The nineteenth-century value conflicts to which Zelizer refers also reflect important class differences. Working-class children were those exploited by the industrial economy and to some extent by the circumstances of their own families. But middle-class reforms against child labor eventually denied them access to income from jobs in factories and stores. The children of the elite and business classes were rarely involved in paid labor and were removed from the public environments of day-to-day life. The promulgation of the "sentimentalized" conception by middle-class reformers thus conflicted with working-class strategies to obtain optimal economic well-being for the family unit through the labor-force involvement of their children.

The Twentieth Century

Considerable empirical evidence indicates that relationships between parents and their children have changed in important ways in industrialized countries over major periods of this century. One of the best early quantitative descriptions of the family and parent-child relations in the early twentieth century is Robert and Helen Lynds's ethnographic account, embodied in *Middletown* (1929). Whereas the Middletown of nineteenth-century America had emphasized the importance of childbearing, because of its link to the agrarian economy of middle America, the more urban Middletown of the 1920s, having shifted its technological base, showed evidence of a greater emphasis on *childrearing*. Parental orientations to children had changed from a concentration on fitting children into society to one of providing for children in a way that would enhance their development (131). They observed that the traditional conception of childrearing in the late nineteenth century had consisted primarily of "making children conform to the approved ways of the group," securing the maximum of obedience from them. The Middletown of the 1920s, by contrast, was seen as more differentiated in responsibilities toward children and the family as a less potent force in securing adherence to established group sanctions.

The decline of the influence of the traditional institutions of church and family and the increasing role during this period of the school in the socialization of young people in American society is confirmed by the observations of Ogburn (1922), Sorokin (1927), and Thomas and Thomas (1929). The concerns of parents were often with the fact that their children had too much independence and that their socialization through the formalized social system of the school made many demands on children for independence of action for which parents did not believe they were prepared (Lynd and Lynd 1929, 131–152). Thus, adults often wanted young people to pay greater attention to their parents and to behave in ways consistent with institutional definitions for appropriate behavior. From the perspective of social scientists, young persons were often viewed as having to adapt to rapid social change and were particularly vulnerable given that the new social forms of regulation and preparation for life had not yet stabilized. This situation led W. I. Thomas and D. S. Thomas (1929) to comment that it was "widely felt that the demoralization of young persons, the prevalence of delinquency and crime, and profound mental disturbances are very serious problems, and that the situation is growing worse instead of better" (xiii). Thus parental emphases in childrearing often stressed obedience to parents and loyalty to institutional authority, although perhaps somewhat less so than was true in the earlier era. According to the Lynds (1929, 149), however, this type of concern was motivated by a *developmental* orientation toward children. They remarked, for example, that "one cannot talk with Middletown mothers without being continually impressed by the eagerness of many to lay hold of every available resource for help in training their children" (149).

The Great Depression. The Lynds conducted their initial ethnographic research in the few years before the Great Depression, but they returned to Middletown in the postdepression era (Lynd and Lynd 1937), witnessing several indications of continued changes in social life relevant to childrearing. Rather than the continued impact of growing size and the mechanization of the industrial process, the major impetus for social change was exogenous. The institutional arrangements and social structure of the community were viewed as the major sources of stability in the behavior of Middletown residents, whereas the external economic, social, and political events of the late 1920s and early 1930s were seen as the ultimate sources of change. The Lynds observed a disintegration of traditional family roles, especially changes in the options available to women, and the continued widening of a gap in mutual understanding between parents and their children. They saw many indications of the emergence of a "more self-conscious subculture of the young in Middletown" in the mid-1930s (167). The increased acceptance of contraception, the postponement of marriage, increasing levels of premarital sexual activity, the importance of the peer group, the emphasis on social activities tied to the high school, and the desire for employment of young women were all indications of their general observation that "adult-imposed restraints of obedience to parents, school, and public opinion have weakened further as the adult world has crumbled under the depression" (168).

But there were obvious strengths to be found in the parent-child relationship of the depression era. Elder's (1974) famous study of the adaptation of families to the experience of economic loss stressed the vulnerability of the parent-child relationship to economic loss. How-

119

ever, he found that families reacted differently to economic hardship, depending on the way economic loss was interpreted. I noted earlier that Elder (1974, 13) has questioned the idea that the "future orientation" of parents is all that pervasive. He specifically argues that during times when family survival is at stake, parents focus more directly on the present needs of their children, not future adult roles. Even if a "future" orientation is not exclusively assumed, however, to the extent that the parental generation experiences social change, there may be consequences to their own childrearing values.

If we take the main premise of the above discussion seriously, then we will conclude that the "generation" of parents experiencing the Great Depression may have had a distinctive set of sociohistorical conditions, and in part as a consequence of this, they possess a different view of what is possible and desirable for their children (see Elder and Hareven 1993). The plausibility of such effects rests on the potency of historical influences on the affected persons, namely, those charged with the care and nurture of children—and the impact of such events on parental values and childrearing practices. In any event, the factors, both historical and ahistorical, shaping social life at a given time—a time at which a new "generation" undergoes the parental experience— are presumed to have an important influence on values, including those relevant to childrearing. As a result of such shifts in cohort experiences, social changes in the family in general and parental values in particular, are potentially due to the phenomenon of "cohort replacement." At the same time, one would assume that some factors producing social change would affect all persons regardless of cohort, in which case one would speak of intracohort change, involving either "life cycle" change or "period" effects.

There is little evidence, however, that because of such experiences, the "children" of the Great Depression developed a distinctive set of values with regard to their own future childrearing. We do know (see below) that cohorts growing up during the depression have more traditional views with respect to childrearing, which could be due in part to the experience of the depression but also to a dozen other possible factors. I argued earlier that changes in the contexts of childrearing can potentially change the nature of parental values not just for those who are enacting the parental role but for the children themselves as well. That is, what children learn about the parent-child relationship during their formative years has potential effects that show up much later, for example, in effects on the values they later bring to the childrearing experience. The critical change in childrearing contexts due to the depression was the situation of economic loss and its consequences for parental roles; however, we have very little evidence that this actually affected values. Elder's (1974) study provided a laboratory for the discussion of historical influences on aspects of family functioning, aspirations, and expectations for the future, but because of the inherent limitations of small, single-cohort studies (see Riley 1973), social change cannot be fully studied by reliance on such types of designs. Rather, one needs data on several cohorts measured over time, although not necessarily on the same people over time, as long as the samples are representative of a well-defined population.

World War II. In the case of the Second World War, the alteration of childrearing contexts was much more episodic in nature and considerably less confounded with other cultural and economic changes. With respect to childrearing the major change linked to the war was one of father absence, which can be argued to have an effect on children's development (see Tuttle 1993). This, of course, raises the more general question of the role of father absence, or single parenthood, as a condition experienced during childhood, on the development of childrearing orientations. This is beyond the scope of the present study, but we can at least examine the question by looking for distinctive patterns among those cohorts growing up during the war. We should, however, perhaps be guided by the null hypothesis in that there is, as with the depression, precious little evidence that such effects are known to exist. Tuttle (1993, 32–33) implicates several features of the American experience between 1940 and 1945 "that deeply affected the home front children's lives," even suggesting that the war had an effect on "professional child-rearing advice and, presumably, on child-rearing practices." He is not specific, although he does register some caution in alleging that children suffered neglect because their mothers worked to help the war effort (39). There is no evidence from his study of changes in parental socialization values that resulted from the Second World War per se.

The Postwar period. Within the past few decades more research has been conducted on these matters. Findings from several countries, including the United States, West Germany, and Japan over a variety of different time periods and using a variety of different measures, all show that greater value has been placed on independence or autonomy in children and declining importance has been attached to the obedi-

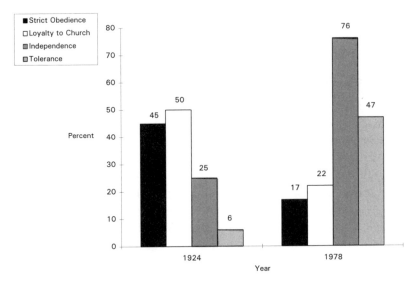

FIGURE 4.1. Percentage selecting quality as one of the three most important emphases in childrearing (Middletown data).

ence of children to traditional institutional authority. Alwin (1988), for example, used data from the replication of the famous Middletown studies described earlier (Lynd and Lynd 1929; Caplow et al. 1982; Caplow and Chadwick 1979) to show that between 1924 and 1978, parental valuation of independence in children increased dramatically and emphasis on obedience declined. The key features of these findings are reproduced in figure 4.1, which presents a fairly clear pattern of increasing preferences for autonomy in children and a decline in the valuation of obedience. Dramatic increases in preferences for "independence" and "tolerance" in children are accompanied by contrasting levels of decline in "strict obedience" and "loyalty to church," which suggests a substantial shift in the nature of parental socialization values over this more than fifty-year period.

The same conclusion was reached using data from the Detroit metropolitan area, although gathered over a much shorter period of time. Several studies of the Detroit area have revealed similar patterns of an increase in the valuation of autonomy, specifically the value of children "thinking for themselves," and a decrease in preferences for "to obey" as a factor parents would choose as the most important quality to emphasize to prepare children for life (Alwin 1984, 1986; Duncan, Schuman, and Duncan 1973; Duncan 1985). Figure 4.2 shows that from 1958 to 1983, within religio-ethnic categories, there have been relatively clear patterns of change. For explainable sociohistorical reasons, the pattern is most evident among Catholics (see Alwin 1984, 1986). I return to a detailed examination of these and more recently collected data from the Detroit Area Studies, below. Suffice it to say at this point that as a proxy for "culture," religio-ethnic category seems to interact in an interesting way with social change. In the late 1950s, respondents identifying themselves as white Protestants exceeded Catholics in the extent to which they preferred autonomy over obedience; but by the 1970s, these earlier differences had vanished, and by the early 1980s, they had been reversed.

These patterns are also evident in national-level data for the United States (Alwin 1989b; Wright and Wright 1976). It is of considerable significance that Kohn (1969, 193–194) actually predicted these changes, speculating that "a major historical trend probably has been—and will continue to be—toward an increasingly self-directed populace." He cited rising educational levels and increasing levels of occupational self-direction experienced by the labor force. Wright and Wright (1976) used two studies by the National Opinion Research Center (NORC)—Kohn's 1964 survey and the 1973 General Social Survey (GSS)—to try to substantiate Kohn's prediction, and reported a rather dramatic shift in parental values over the decade of the 1960s. The percentage of fathers valuing the quality "obeys parents well" as the most important quality declined from 24 percent to 13 percent in the short space of a single decade. And the quality "good sense and sound judgment" increased in importance from 10 to 15 percent. Other indicators showed the same pattern, and Wright and Wright (1976, 531) concluded that these data were indicative of a trend toward less "authoritarian or conformist values, or alternatively, an overall population increase in the value of self-direction." Looking at the same data, however, Kohn (1976, 541) saw "no justification for inferring change in parental valuation of self-direction." Rather, the change observed by the Wrights "reflects nothing more than a methodological artifact."[4]

Uncertain about the generality of the findings from the Middletown and Detroit studies and to verify the nature of the change in the data examined by Wright and Wright, I reexamined the data used for comparison and tabulated data from later GSS surveys as well (see Alwin 1989b, 1990a). These results showed strong support for the change

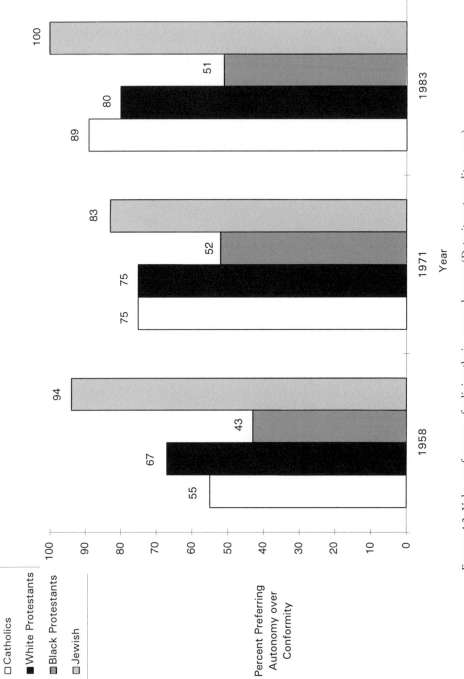

FIGURE 4.2. Value preferences of religio-ethnic groups by year (Detroit metropolitan area).

interpretation of the data examined by the Wrights and that the change lasted into the 1970s. Data are given in figure 4.3, which depicts a systematic historical shift in the expected direction from the mid-1960s through the late 1970s, with valuation of qualities reflecting obedience declining and those reflecting autonomy increasing. The trend may have abated into the early 1980s, as the GSS data reflect little apparent further change and may even suggest a slight reversal of the trend. The source of such a reversal may lie in differences in the experiences of the youngest cohorts: the very youngest cohorts in the GSS data showed considerably more valuation of obedience and less emphasis on independence (see Alwin 1989b). I return to this issue later in the chapter.

These patterns have also been demonstrated outside the United States, particularly in Germany (Mohler 1989; Reuband 1988) and Japan (Trommsdorff 1983), testifying to the pervasiveness and far-reaching nature of these trends. The German case is shown in figure 4.4, which gives the level of endorsement in national samples to the qualities "independence and free will" (*Selbstandigkeit und freier Wille*) and "obedience and deference" (*Gehorsam und Unterordnung*). These data result from the question, addressed to national samples at varying intervals since 1951, "In rearing children which set of qualities should be stressed most: obedience and deference, love of order and industriousness, or independence and free will?" Although independence and obedience were similarly endorsed in the early 1950s in these data, there has been a significant and systematic trend in the direction of favoring independence in children and an accompanying deline in preferences for obedience (see EMNID 1983, 1986).

Therefore, on the basis of the vast majority of research into this question, considerable evidence indicates a major historical trend in the childrearing values of parents—from values stressing obedience to those giving more emphasis to autonomy. The evidence spans many continents, many different time periods, and many different types of measures. And while one may question the methodological adequacy of any given study, a reasonable reading of the available research would suggest that important changes have occurred in parental values for autonomy and obedience, among other things (see below).

MODELS OF SOCIAL CHANGE

What accounts for these changes? Previous explanations can be grouped, for present purposes, into three categories: (1) explanations referring to important structural or compositional changes in society,

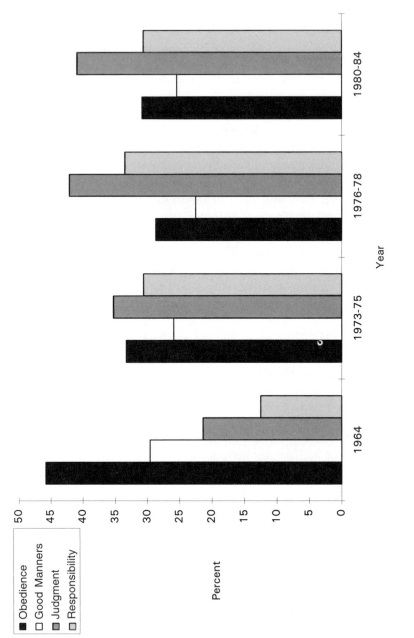

FIGURE 4.3. Percentage of parents choosing quality as one of three most important by year of survey.

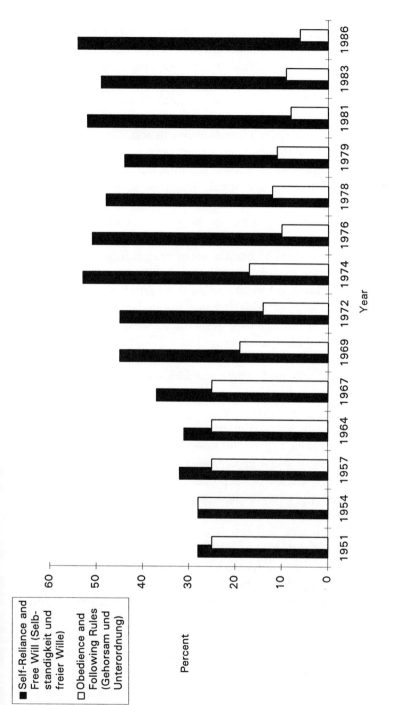

FIGURE 4.4. Trends in desirable child qualities: Germany, 1951–1983. Source: EMNID, Erziehungsziele: Stagniert der Trend zur emanzipatorische Erziehung? *EMNID Informationen* 8/9 (1983).

particularly changes in the nature and distribution of education and work (see Alwin 1984, 1989b; Kohn 1969); (2) explanations that emphasize other exogenous cultural changes affecting some or all of the population, especially changes in religion and cultural values (see Alwin 1986; Zelizer 1985); and (3) explanations that point to "generational" phenomena, or "cohort effects," implicating factors associated with the distinctiveness of socialization experiences during youth (see Alwin 1992, 1993; Lesthaeghe and Surkyn 1988).

All these explanations have some potential for placing the changes in parental values in an appropriate historical perspective, but we need to elaborate further on their potential by consideration of several specific questions regarding the general processes by which social changes in parental values occur. Specifically, how do these social factors introduced to explain social change in parental values operate to produce the observed changes? What are the potential consequences of historical factors on different generations of parents? What are the effects of social change on individuals, and which categories of individuals? Posed somewhat more broadly, what is the linkage between life-span developmental trajectories of individuals and the nature of social change? These questions can be addressed both generally (Alwin 1991, 1994) and with specific aspects of social change in mind, such as changes in the family and parent-child relations.

Social changes in parental orientations to children, as with other more general attitudes, beliefs, and values, can happen through one or both of *two* types of social processes—via *cohort replacement* or via *intracohort change.* These types of processes are not mutually exclusive, as both may be happening simultaneously. However, theories of social change tend to emphasize one or the other process in explaining why social values, attitudes, and beliefs change over time. For example, Ryder (1965) argued that the potential for social change resides in the youngest cohorts, who are relatively uncommitted to social roles and relationships. It may also be the case that these processes may interact with other factors, such as cultural or structural variables, wherein one or another process may be apparent within some subgroups of society but not in others. For example, the findings from the Detroit data discussed above (Alwin 1984, 1986), and verified to a remarkable extent in national data (Alwin 1989b), strongly suggest that the values of American Catholics have changed in ways different from those of American Protestants. And more recent analyses (see Alwin 1990b) suggest that the youngest cohorts—those born after 1930—were those most affected by the historical factors bringing about the differential change.

Processes of Cohort Succession

Whether or not there are such interactions with "culture" or "social structure," theories emphasizing cohort replacement give attention to the potency of historically linked socialization experiences that produce different parental orientations as a result of cohort membership. This can be visualized with respect to figure 4.5, adapted from Riley, Johnson, and Foner (1972, 10), which depicts the intersection of biographical and historical times in the lives of four hypothetical cohorts. Stated compactly, the assumptions of the theory of cohort replacement in this context are twofold: (1) since members of each cohort experience a unique slice of history during their youth, presumed to be the "critical" period for the acquisition of values, attitudes, and beliefs, distinctive cohort differences exist in the value orientations relevant to parental approaches to socialization; and (2) cohort differences endure over time, due principally to the stability inhering in the life-span trajectories of individuals, which typically "crystallize" into stable value orientations during midlife. These two assumptions combine, then, to form a picture of social change driven primarily by the natural processes of "social metabolism" wherein the passage of historic time results in the replacement of old cohorts—and their ideas—with new ones (Mannheim 1952; Ryder 1965).

According to White (1992), cohorts become "actors" only when they cohere enough around historical events, in both their own and others' eyes, to be called "generations." In this sense, we would distinguish between "cohorts" and "generations" in that the former refers simply to *year of birth*, whereas a generation is a "joint interpretive construction which insists upon and builds among tangible cohorts in defining a style recognized from outside and from within" (White 1992, 31). Through such mechanisms "cohort effects" are given life through these interpretive and behavioral aspects. The term *generation*, despite its popularity in theorizing about the influences of cohort turnover on social change, is somewhat less precise than might otherwise be desirable. "Generation" has several meanings, referring variously to kinship status (e.g., parental generation), a unit of time separating members of kinship groups (a generation is often thought to be about thirty years), as well as to groups of persons affected uniquely by partic-

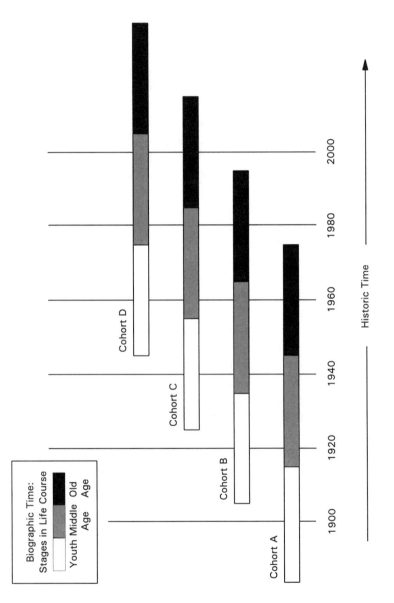

FIGURE 4.5. Intersection of biographic and historic time.

ular historical periods (e.g., the Vietnam generation). Obviously, since human species do not replace themselves according to any regular cycle, there can be no exact equivalence between "generations" in the sense of kinship relationships and "cohorts" (see Blau and Duncan 1967). And, given the difficulties of establishing the definitional and interpretive aspects of designating "generations" in the sense referred to by White (1992), it is perhaps best simply to use the term *birth cohort* or *cohort* to refer to the placement of differential socialization experiences in historical time.

The idea that social change occurs, at least in part, by a process of cohort succession, with each new cohort being exposed to a unique climate of ideas and eventually replacing older ones in the overall composition of society, is an extremely important one. In a paper regarding social change in Western democracies, Lesthaeghe and Surkyn (1988) argued that the long-term trends toward individualism and away from institutional control to which I referred at the beginning of the chapter are due to cohort differences and processes of cohort replacement. Their research shows that for a number of important indicators from the 1981 European Values Survey, including measures of values regarding parental emphasis on the autonomy and obedience of children, there are tangible cohort differences. Compared with older cohorts (born in 1936 or before), the younger cohorts (born after 1936) showed greater preference for an emphasis on the imagination and independence of children and lesser preference for social conformity and obedience to traditional institutional authority. Lesthaeghe and Surkyn (1988) maintain that these intercohort differences result from a historical process tied to different "generational" experiences of the type mentioned in theories of cohort replacement (see Mannheim 1952; Ryder 1965). These changes result, they contend, from a permanent ideational or cultural imprinting that arises from unique cohort experiences, which generates a momentum of its own. Thus, each new set of cohorts potentially possesses it own particular value orientations, its own particular set of orientations to children.

Intracohort Change

The alternative to this "cohort succession" model of social change is that societal-level changes are reflections not of cohort differences but of individual-level changes occurring within cohorts. Two classes of intracohort factors influence individuals, causing them (and their cohorts) to change: factors tied to life cycle or aging, and factors tied to historical or "period" influences. Due to either or both period factors or to life-cycle/aging factors, there will be substantial intracohort change, rather than change due just to cohort turnover or replacement. But, regardless of the source of the within-cohort change, this model for how social change occurs is very different from one that relies solely on cohort replacement ideas.

If the cohort replacement hypothesis is applicable in the present context, then differences will be observed among birth cohorts in parental orientations to children. As noted earlier, the plausibility of this type of interpretation rests on two things: (1) the potency of unique historical influences on each cohort or set of cohorts, such that cohort differences can be said to exist, and (2) a set of assumptions about the nature of individual stability over the life course. The latter poses a particularly interesting set of issues, as the assumption about the stability of individuals over most of their life span is critical. Thus, distinct historical experiences may exist and distinguish cohorts for a time, but if individuals are not stable after some early point in their life cycle, such intercohort differences may not persist through time. Humans are often thought to be susceptible to change in their early lives but to become increasingly stable in important respects with age, remaining relatively resistant to change throughout most of adult life. But this may not be the case, and an emergent view sees the adult life course as essentially "open-ended," in which human life is characterized to reflect a lifelong openness to change rather than growing stability and resistance to change.

METHODS

In the remainder of the chapter, I consider the extent of social change that we can document into the recent past and the extent to which these contrasting images of social change can be supported in the available empirical data. I examine two sets of data—data generated on parental values in the Detroit Area Study series mentioned earlier, and data generated from a recent series of surveys undertaken as part of the General Social Survey, from 1985 to 1991. Each of these surveys uses the same measures of parental values—a measure developed in Gerhard Lenski's (1961) work, which contrasts values for "obedience" and "autonomy"—and each permits us to look at whether social change is produced primarily through cohort replacement versus intracohort change.

Measurements

In surveys, parental values are typically measured by asking people either how important it is to instill certain qualities in children or what qualities of children are deemed to be most desirable to prepare children for life. Because many child qualities are highly desirable, most value researchers insist on using rankings of importance rather than ratings (see Alwin and Krosnick 1985). If such ranked preferences can be administered for a well-defined population at more than one point in time, some evidence can be gained about the extent of social change in parental values. For this purpose I have relied on a question that Gerhard Lenski (1961) included in the 1958 Detroit Area Study and replicated in 1971 (see Duncan, Schuman, and Duncan 1973), in 1983 (see Alwin 1984, 1986), and again in 1988 (see Alwin 1988c). The question has also been included in the General Social Surveys since 1985. From a set of five choices, respondents are asked to select the quality or trait most important to prepare a child for life:

> If you had to choose, which thing on this list would you pick as the most important for a child to learn to prepare him (or her) for life?
> a. To obey
> b. To be well-liked or popular
> c. To think for himself or herself
> d. To work hard
> e. To help others when they need help
> Which comes next in importance? Which comes third? Which comes fourth?

Data from such questions are very useful for charting trends in parental values. They are, however, not without limitations and potential lack of clarity, and it is important to understand the variety of possible interpretations to such survey questions. First, valued qualities of children may be seen as *absolute,* in the sense that certain qualities may reflect "markers" along a dimension of social and/or moral development. Some developmental outcomes, as exemplified by certain child qualities, may be seen as important *as objectives or goals of childrearing.* There may, however, be no consensus on what is developmentally desirable, and there may be criteria other than developmental ones that govern parental choices of desirable child qualities. For example, a parent may desire obedience to family customs or to religious teachings as being most important in an absolute sense, but this may bear no explicit relationship to any objectively defined level of moral or social development. A second way we might interpret parental valuation of child qualities is in their reflection of "unmet" desires or objectives, in contrast to values as absolutes. Thus, as statements of preferences, values may reflect the disparity between what one has in reality achieved and that which one aspires to or hopes for. For example, a parent whose child is well-behaved, orderly, and generally obedient may not choose such a response in a survey. The parent enjoys such a childhood state but because the child's obedience is plentiful, the parent may take it for granted and desire other qualities, for example, independence, which while not necessarily more desirable in an absolute sense may represent a desired outcome yet to be attained. On the other hand, a parent who may desire independence equally in an absolute sense, but whose child is not very obedient, may rank obedience higher than independence on the scale of importance, mainly because it is relatively harder to come by. Finally, parental responses to questions concerning desirable child qualities may in some instances reflect a fait accompli. Children may acquire certain qualities through exposure to the larger culture, and parents may simply accept these as realities they must accept. Thus, a parent may desire independence in children not just because it is desirable in some absolute or relative sense but because she has observed it in her child's behavior and has learned to accept it. It comes a goal of childrearing through a process of absorption of values already embodied in children's behavior.

Yet another problem exists with the interpretation of social changes in rankings of parental preferences for child qualities. Because most research on parental values uses rankings of the importance of child qualities, it is possible to know only the relative preferences and not absolute ones (see Alwin and Krosnick 1985). Rankings are ipsative, and thus, the sum of the scores for an individual (or the sample as a whole) is always the same. This means that if the interpretation of social changes in the rankings of a particular quality or qualities is desired, it must be made within the framework of what other changes are taking place. If more than one dimension of change is embedded within a single set of ranked qualities, that is, more than one central phenomenon of change, it may not be possible to isolate specific dimensions of change. I return to this issue later in the context of interpreting the available change data, but mention it here simply to indicate that rankings may be the most preferable way to measure values, but their ipsative nature makes it more difficult to measure social change.

Aside from the more technical measurement problems (e.g., ratings versus rankings for measuring values), because of these conflicting interpretations of parents' responses on their preferences, the results of research on parental values are often ambiguous. In short, if we admit that responses to survey questions have more than a single interpretation and we do not know in what proportion particular interpretations exist at any one time or at different times, then there may be little basis for arriving at intertemporal assessments of changes in parental values. Or, if different cohorts respond to such survey questions in different ways, then the situation for assessing social change via the replication of surveys may be even more hopeless. If we cannot unambiguously assess change over time in measures of parental values because of ambiguities in the meaning of responses to such questions, then conclusions may be risky. At the same time, however, despite these limitations, we still have some basis for drawing inferences about social change, even if our current level of understanding is limited due to lack of complete precision. I proceed, therefore, with both anticipation over the revelations we are to find in patterns of variation in these measures over time and warranted caution in what meanings we should place on the discovered patterns.

In the present study I focus primarily on just two of the five qualities on the list given above, one reflecting preferences for autonomy—"to think for self"—and the other reflecting preferences for obedience—"to obey." These qualities permit the assessment of the relative value placed on autonomy and obedience (or conformity). In the analysis presented below, I assigned a high score (5) to the quality if it was selected as the most important, a four (4) if it was chosen as second in importance, and so on, so that a low score (1) was assigned to the quality if it was chosen as the least important. In an earlier analysis of the 1971 data, we performed an "ipsative factor analysis" of these measures (see Alwin and Jackson 1982), establishing that the contrast between "thinks for self" and "obey" conforms to the main factor underlying these responses. Thus, in some of the analyses presented here, I use a measure computed by taking the rank given to "thinks for self" minus the rank given to "obey," which assesses this contrast directly (see Lenski 1961, 200–201).

This measure is similar in many respects to Kohn's (1969) measure of parental values for self-direction versus conformity in children, in that it represents the contrast between preferences for autonomy and obedience in children. Kohn's measure is much more complicated than the Lenski measure described above and has a number of deficiencies for our present purposes (see Krosnick and Alwin 1987, 1988), but it also has certain advantages in that it takes into account the age and sex of a specific child. The Kohn question presents respondents with a list of thirteen qualities, essentially asking them to sort these qualities into five categories: (1) the quality most desired, (2) the two qualities highly desired but not the most desired, (3) the quality least desired, (4) the two undesirable qualities but not the least desired, and (5) all others.[5] This measure was obtained in the 1982–83 Child-Rearing in Detroit study, and I use these data later with Kohn's measure to detect life-cycle patterns in parental values for *autonomy* and *obedience*.

Samples and Data

I rely on (a) three comparable cross-sectional studies of the Detroit metropolitan area conducted over a thirty-year period, undertaken in 1958, 1971, and 1987–88, (b) two Detroit samples of parents undertaken in 1982 and 1983, and (c) six surveys obtained by the General Social Survey (GSS) annually since 1985. The two Detroit samples of parents were based on probability samples of the Detroit, Michigan, metropolitan area (the three-county metropolitan area made up of Wayne, Oakland, and Macomb counties). The 1983 Detroit sample consisted of parents with children between the ages of two and eighteen (N = 520) in which black households were oversampled.[7] For our later analysis of developmental trajectories in parental values, I combine the 1982 and 1983 data. The 1982 data unfortunately altered the wording of Lenski's (1961) question and therefore is not useful for analyzing trends.[8] Also, given the noncomparability of sampling, we exclude the 1983 data from the trend analysis presented here. The 1958, 1971, and 1988 Detroit surveys were standard cross-sections of the adult population, with the following sample sizes: 1958, N = 609; 1971, N = 1,833; 1987–88, N = 1,035).[6]

The GSS is an annual cross-section of the noninstitutionalized residential population of the continental United States aged 18 years and over (Davis and Smith 1991). It has been conducted nearly every year since 1972 on approximately fifteen hundred respondents per year to monitor social trends in attitudes and behavior. Since 1985, the above Lenski (1961) question on parental values has been included in the survey, and although we cannot do much with this series in terms of studying social change, given the short time span involved, it is possible to examine differences among birth cohorts and processes of cohort replacement and intracohort change so as to verify what we report for Detroit in a more broadly representative database.

Methods of Analysis

To capture inter- and intracohort variation, I analyze these data using multivariate methods in which historical time is indexed by the year of the survey and biographical time is indicated by the year of birth. For purposes of tabular presentation, however, I reduce birth year to the following birth cohort categories (where applicable): (1) born before 1920, (2) born 1920–29, (3) born 1930–39, (4) born 1940–49, (5) born 1950–59, (6) born 1960 and after. I also control for variation in the amount of schooling and religio-ethnic identification in a subsequent analysis, since variation in these factors bears heavily on preferences for qualities in children. I assessed the amount of schooling using a measure of the number of years of schooling completed. The measure of religious preference was based on a survey measure, common to all survey data sets used here, that asked if the respondent had a religious preference and, if so, what it was. For present analytic purposes we focus on two major groups: those identifying themselves as Roman Catholics and those who were white Protestants. Other groups—black Protestants, Jews, other religions, or those with no religious preference—are ignored for some purposes in the following analyses because of the relatively small subsample sizes.

In addition to the tabular presentation of the data, I also employ multivariate techniques. Specifically, my model for describing social change involves a simple linear decomposition of change into a component representing cohort replacement and a component that represents intracohort change. The approach, due to Firebaugh (1989, 253), is to first regress the variable of interest on survey year and cohort (birth year), as follows:

$$y = b_0 + b_1 \, \text{Year} + b_2 \, \text{Cohort} + e$$

The slopes from the estimation of this equation are then used to estimate the cohort replacement and intracohort change components, defined as:

intracohort change (IC) $= b_1 \, (t_T - t_1)$, and
cohort replacement (CR) $= b_2 \, (C_T - C_1)$,

where $t_T - t_1$ represents the amount of historical time elapsed between time 1 and time T, C_T is the mean birth year at time T, and C_1 is the mean birth year at time 1. As Firebaugh (1989, 253) notes, because the model is often misspecified in positing linearity and additivity of year and cohort, the two components rarely sum to $Y_T - Y_1$, the amount of social change in y. But, "the discrepancy should not be large; a large discrepancy suggests that the effects of year (intracohort, the period-age effect) and cohort (intercohort, the cohort-age effect) are not linear-additive." After comparing this method with other techniques that decompose differences of means across time, Firebaugh concluded that the linear decomposition method expressed above provides reasonably good estimates of cohort turnover and intracohort influences on means. In the present analysis, I supplement this approach by adding control variables to the equation, which may account for the cohort replacement effects (for example, schooling), *and* I develop a rationale to conduct the decomposition within categories of other variables (religio-ethnic groups, for instance) to examine hypotheses regarding the interaction of cohort replacement processes with other processes of social change.

HISTORICAL CHANGES IN PARENTAL VALUES

In this section I examine *new* data from the Child-Rearing in Detroit Project and the General Social Survey in order to focus on the extent to which we can find support for the principal models of social change discussed earlier—cohort replacement versus intracohort change— and begin to sort out the implications of these models with respect to changes in parental values across biographical and historical time. First, I examine the secular shifts in parental values in the Detroit area over the past thirty years as well as patterns of cohort differences and intracohort shifts as revealed in that setting. I then examine these issues in recent data from the General Social Survey, in this case not to chart the secular trends in parental values but to confirm our Detroit findings regarding cohort processes in a broader-gauged national database.

Parental Values in Detroit, 1958 to 1988

As noted earlier, we can examine changes in parental values in three cross-sectional Detroit surveys between 1958 and 1988. These results are given in table 4.1 for all five child qualities presented by the Lenski (1961) measure. Consistent with previous reports using the Detroit data, there is a secular trend in these data from 1958 through 1988,

TABLE 4.1. Mean Rankings of Child Qualities: Detroit Metropolitan Area, 1958, 1971, and 1988

Child Quality	Year of Study			F	p
	1958	1971	1988		
Obey	3.17	3.10	2.92	9.13	0.000
Popular	2.18	1.60	1.45	174.25	0.000
Think for self	3.91	4.10	4.01	4.31	0.014
Work hard	2.64	2.93	3.40	150.39	0.000
Help others	3.08	3.27	3.19	5.74	0.003
Sample Size	609	1833	1035		

Note: Question Wording: If you had to choose, which thing on this list would you pick as the most important for a child to learn to prepare him or her for life?
A. Obey
B. Be popular
C. Think for self
D. Work hard
E. Help others

which suggests a shift in parental values in the direction of greater preferences over time for the quality associated with autonomy—"think for self"—and a declining preference for the quality "obey" (Alwin 1984, 1986, 1990a, 1990b). The 1988 survey results reveal somewhat of an inconsistent pattern with respect to the trends just mentioned, in that trends in preferences for autonomy seem not to have continued in the same manner since 1971. The overall results do provide support, however, for the conclusion that over the thirty-year period since 1958, choices favoring autonomy have increased, and preferences for obedience have declined. As indicated by the F statistics provided in the table, the secular trends in all qualities are statistically significant, although in some cases this results from the large sample sizes, given that the differences are essentially of trivial magnitude.

One difficulty with the interpretation of these results, as noted previously, is that these measures reflect the "relative" rather than "absolute" preferences of these five qualities, and it is not necessarily possible to interpret the changes in absolute terms. If preferences for "think for self" and "obey" were the only values changing and preferences for the other qualities were more or less constant over time, then our task would be easier. But this is not what has been happening. In table 4.1 we can also see that preferences for "work hard" have also dramtically and systematically increased over this time period. Interpreting this increase as a change in the direction of greater autonomy provides even more support for our overall conclusion. Such may be possible, for "hard work" may reflect several other qualities associated with autonomy, such as self-reliance, responsibility, good judgment and the like, but we should note that it may be as much a reflection of conformity or obedience to cultural norms than it is of independence.

Regardless of how we interpret this change in the valuation of the quality "work hard," we must take this into account when assessing the shifts in "think for self" and "obey." Clearly, if the value of "work hard" increased, then given the ipsative nature of rankings, something else must have decreased in importance, which makes it harder for us to see true changes in the relative preferences for "think" and "obey." Thus, perhaps the safest way to interpret these results is in purely relative terms. If we take this course, we can see that, despite the shifts in mean ranks, the major changes over this period of time are in the relative positions of "obey" and "work hard." The other qualities remain fairly constant in terms of relative rankings. "Think for self" is consistently the most popular quality over the entire period, and "popular" is the least. In 1958, the quality "obey" was relatively highly valued, as it was judged in the aggregate to be second only to "think for self" in importance, but it had slipped to fourth in overall average rank by the time of the 1988 survey. By contrast, in 1958 the quality "work hard" was ranked in fourth place, but by 1988 it had become second in importance among the five qualities on this list. In effect, between 1958 and 1988, the qualities "obey" and "work hard" have exchanged places with respect to their relative positions. This provides support for the suggestion mentioned above that the shift in valuation of "work hard" is actually indicative of the shift away from obedience and in the direction of autonomy, insofar as that contrast is concerned.

With respect to the argument of Bellah et al. (1985) that Americans are becoming more individualistic at the expense of communal values, there is little support for it here. Indeed, if one takes the "help others when they need help" quality as an indication of this factor, there is virtually no change over this period, and to the extent there is, it is in the positive, not negative, direction. Of course, one needs to recognize all the same caveats noted above regarding the interpretation of ranked preference data over time, but only this trait shows little change over time.

The theoretical questions raised above suggested that secular shifts in values might be due to a "succession of cohorts" or, alternatively, to changes occurring within cohorts. Table 4.2 presents the average

TABLE 4.2. Mean Rankings of Child Qualities of Autonomy and Obedience by Year of Study and Birth Cohort Category

Cohort	Year of Study 1958	1971	1988	Total	F	p
		Think for Self				
Pre–1920	3.67	3.76	3.49	3.65	2.93	NS
1920–29	4.09	4.17	4.08	4.11	0.32	NS
1930–39	4.28	4.39	4.02	4.19	5.93	<.003
1940–49	—	4.26	4.08	4.15	3.14	NS
1950–59	—	4.33	4.11	4.12	0.12	NS
1960+	—	—	4.07	4.08	—	—
TOTAL	3.91	4.10	4.01	4.05		
F	11.64	20.52	4.69	24.20		
p	<.000	<.000	<.000	<.000		
		Obey				
Pre–1920	3.30	3.46	3.48	3.40	1.67	NS
1920–29	3.09	3.08	2.98	3.04	0.43	NS
1930–39	2.96	2.87	2.83	2.88	0.33	NS
1940–49	—	2.84	2.80	2.81	0.14	NS
1950–59	—	2.67	2.90	2.89	0.11	NS
1960+	—	—	2.68	2.68	—	—
TOTAL	3.17	3.10	2.93	3.06		
F	2.29	16.33	4.99	20.11		
p	NS	<.000	<.000	<.000		
		Think minus Obey				
Pre–1920	0.37	0.30	0.00	0.25	1.86	NS
1920–29	1.00	1.09	1.10	1.07	0.12	NS
1930–39	1.32	1.52	1.18	1.31	1.22	NS
1940–49	—	1.42	1.29	1.33	0.53	NS
1950–59	—	1.67	1.22	1.22	0.15	NS
1960+	—	—	1.39	1.40	—	—
TOTAL	0.74	1.00	1.09	0.98		
F	7.50	23.98	6.21	28.42		
p	<.001	<.000	<.000	<.000		
	Sample Sizes					
Pre–1920	312	584	120			
1920–29	174	432	150			
1930–39	123	356	140			
1940–49	—	446	207			
1950–59	—	15	284			
1960+	—	—	125			
TOTAL	609	1,833	1,026			

ranking for the two qualities of central interest here ("think for self" and "obey"), as well as their contrast ("think" minus "obey") by birth cohort categories and year of survey. The table also contains the results of an Analysis of Variance (ANOVA) of these averages across available cohort categories within each survey (down the columns of the table) and between surveys within each of the cohort categories (across the rows of the table). The relevant F statistics and p values for the former are given at the bottom of each column in the table, and those for the latter are given on the right-hand side of each row. These comparisons provide an initial basis for evaluating the extent of intracohort (within cohort) versus intercohort (between cohort) changes in these indicators of parental values (see Glenn 1977, 1980).

The numbers in table 4.2 provide some support for the cohort succession model, as cohorts born later give systematically greater emphasis on autonomy and less on obedience. This is most clear in the 1958 survey but is generally true of the later surveys as well. The "think for self" ranks have come close to the "ceiling" in the 1988 survey, and it is more difficult to see the cohort differences, which are mainly between cohorts born before 1920 and all others born later. This is not true of the scores for "obey," which have declined systematically across cohorts in all surveys. To give clear testimony to this pattern of findings, I have also presented the means for the "Think minus Obey" score, contrasting values for autonomy and obedience. In addition to these intercohort patterns, the means for the cohort categories appear to be relatively stable over time. This can be seen from the fact that the intracohort F statistics are generally nonsignificant, whereas the F statistics for the intercohort comparisons are, by and large, significant. These results parallel those presented in my earlier research (Alwin 1990a), which focused solely on parents, and those presented by Lesthaeghe and Surkyn (1988).

I now implement Firebaugh's (1989) linear decomposition technique, as described earlier, to partition the net social change into two components: that due to intracohort change, and that due to cohort differences. While these decompositions give very useful information, we must caution that we have *not* solved the classic "age-period-cohort" confounding (see Mason and Fienberg 1985). For example, it should be clear from our foregoing discussion that the *intracohort change* component contains both period influences and changes due to aging or life-cycle factors. And, the component due to *intercohort differences* could be due to age differences among cohorts, as well as to differing cohort experiences, or both. This confounding of these factors makes interpretation virtually impossible without the benefit of strong theoretical "side information." But despite the confounding of these factors, these decompositions help with the analysis and interpretation of the data. Results are given in table 4.3.

This table shows several pieces of information relevant to interpreting the social changes in parental values between 1958 and 1988. It presents an overall indicator of the amount of *social change* in autonomy and independence for the 1958–88 period as well as a decomposition of that change into two components: *cohort replacement* and *intracohort change*. The later estimates convey the extent and magnitude of either type of process in producing the observed social change. In addition, the table presents the results of a similar decomposition while controlling for cohort differences in the amount of schooling, permitting an assessment of the extent to which the intercohort turnover component of change is dependent of cohort effects on educational experiences. Finally, the same type of decomposition is provided for Catholics and white Protestants in order to gauge religio-ethnic differences in the rate of change in either component.

These results confirm, using new data and new means of assessing the role of cohort replacement versus intracohort change factors, that in the Detroit area at least, change has indeed been in the direction of greater valuation of autonomy and diminished interest in obedience in children. The table summarizes these results in its most revealing sense in the comparison of the two traits—using the "think-obey" score (hereafter referred to as the Lenski score). The results here indicate that the largest component of this change is the decline in valuing obedience, in that for reasons given above, positive changes in the valuation of autonomy are weaker. As indicated in previous research (see Alwin 1984, 1986, 1989a), the change has been greatest relative to other groups, among those members of the population identifying themselves as Catholic. Moreover, these data reveal that for both groups, the largest component of the change is that linked to cohort succession, that is, more recent cohorts prefer significantly greater independence and less obedience in children than do earlier ones. Again, this result is strongest among the Catholics, although the results are also significant for white Protestants.

Essentially *no* intracohort change exists in valuing the quality "obey" over this time period, but what is perhaps most novel in these results is, despite an overall positive shift in preferences of autonomy,

TABLE 4.3. Decomposition of Social Change in Preferences for Child Qualities of Autonomy and Obedience into Intracohort and Cohort Replacement Components: Detroit Metropolitan Area, 1958, 1971, and 1988

Dependent Variable	Time Period	Social Change[1]	Unadjusted		Adjusted for Schooling		St. Dev.
			Intracohort[2]	Cohort Replacement[3]	Intracohort	Cohort Replacement[3]	
Total sample (N = 3577)							
Think for self	1958–88	0.096	−0.270***	0.339***	−0.330***	0.182***	1.406
Obey	1958–88	−0.249**	0.060	−0.313***	0.150*	−0.130**	0.667
Think − obey	1958–88	0.346*	−0.330**	0.651***	−0.480***	0.313***	2.667
White Protestants (N = 1169)							
Think for self	1958–88	−0.011	−0.270**	0.277***	−0.360***	0.185***	1.271
Obey	1958–88	−0.229	0.060***	−0.323***	0.210	−0.208**	0.659
Think − obey	1958–88	0.218	−0.330*	0.600***	−0.600***	0.392***	2.542
Catholics (N = 1289)							
Think for self	1958–88	0.295*	−0.240*	0.443***	−0.270**	0.234***	1.528
Obey	1958–88	−0.669***	−0.180	−0.443***	−0.180	−0.261***	1.614
Think − obey	1958–88	0.964***	−0.030	0.886***	−0.090	0.495***	2.707

[1] p value calculated as difference of two means (Y_t and Y_1). Critical values for the two-sided z statistic are: 1.96 = .05, 2.576 = .01, 3.09 = .001.
[2] p value taken from b_1 coefficient: $*p < .05$, $**p < .01$, $***p < .001$.
[3] p value taken from b_2 coefficient: $*p < .05$, $**p < .01$, $***p < .001$.

a negative intracohort shift in the valuation of "think for self" over this time. This result appears to some extent for both religio-ethnic groups, but it is essentially nonsignificant for Catholics. It suggests that among white Protestants there has been a slight decline within cohorts in preferences for autonomy. In this case the negative shift seems to offset the otherwise consistent set of patterns observed, and while relatively minor in its overall contribution to these results, it deserves further examination.

The table also presents figures that help assess the role of intercohort differences in the amount of schooling in producing these results. Schooling is among the most important determinants of parental values (see Kohn 1969; Alwin 1989a), and there have been broad-based differences in cohort exposure to schooling. Vast differences exist in the extent of schooling to which different cohorts have been exposed over this century. In the early part of this century, few adolescents attended secondary school. Now, few do not go on to some form of postsecondary schooling. Thus, it is not surprising that cohort differences in the number of years of schooling completed account for a substantial portion of the cohort replacement effect. Among white Protestants, schooling accounts for about one-third of the part attributable to cohort succession, whereas among Catholics it is between 40 to 50 percent of the intercohort component of change. This clearly reflects cohort experiences, since schooling levels are not confounded with life-cycle variation in the present survey data: virtually all respondents had completed their education when interviewed.

Parental Values in National Surveys

In six annual surveys since 1986, the GSS has collected data on the Lenski child qualities. This obviously does not help us in the quest for historical patterns to socialization values, but it does permit a comparison with a national sample of the intercohort findings reported for Detroit. The average rankings of the five qualities on the list for these surveys are given in table 4.4. These data show a pattern of rankings that is completely consistent with the 1988 Detroit survey: specifically, "think for self" is viewed as the most important quality, "work hard" is the second in importance, followed in third place by "help others," in fourth place by "obey," and, last, "to be popular." Thus, the relative importance of autonomy compared with obedience in the American population is confirmed, as well as the emergence of "work hard" as a relatively valuable quality for children to have to prepare them for life.

TABLE 4.4. Mean Rankings of Child Qualities by Year and Gender: General Social Survey of the U.S. Population, 1986 to 1991

Item	1986	(N)	1987	(N)	1988	(N)	1989	(N)	1990	(N)	1991	(N)
					Total Sample							
Obey	3.058	732	2.840	1800	2.953	977	2.845	1000	2.823	871	2.852	982
Popular	1.398	732	1.492	1800	1.465	977	1.418	1000	1.414	871	1.391	982
Think for self	3.993	732	4.001	1800	3.908	977	4.004	1000	3.963	871	3.935	982
Work hard	3.283	732	3.369	1800	3.379	977	3.427	1000	3.484	871	3.473	982
Help others	3.269	732	3.298	1800	3.290	994	3.306	1000	3.317	871	3.349	982
					Male							
Obey	2.869	315	2.836	772	2.976	430	2.908	432	2.956	390	2.950	408
Popular	1.508	315	1.583	772	1.508	430	1.472	432	1.478	390	1.463	408
Think for self	3.944	315	3.893	772	3.813	430	3.884	432	3.722	390	3.811	408
Work hard	3.387	315	3.389	772	3.418	430	3.423	432	3.546	390	3.479	408
Help others	3.291	315	3.299	772	3.285	430	3.313	432	3.299	390	3.297	408
					Female							
Obey	3.215	417	2.843	1028	2.934	547	2.794	568	2.710	481	2.775	574
Popular	1.307	417	1.417	1028	1.429	547	1.373	568	1.360	481	1.335	574
Think for self	4.033	417	4.090	1028	3.990	547	4.103	568	4.166	481	4.032	574
Work hard	3.196	417	3.353	1028	3.346	547	3.430	568	3.431	481	3.469	574
Help others	3.250	417	3.298	1028	3.294	558	3.300	568	3.333	481	3.390	574

We can also examine the GSS data from 1986 to 1991 by year of survey and birth cohort category, as presented in table 4.5. These data reveal, with one possible exception, the same pattern of results as found for Detroit. In general, earlier birth cohorts give greater approval to obedience in children and prefer less emphasis on autonomy. Consistent with the above findings, significant differences exist between the cohort categories within surveys. The main exception to the above findings is that in the GSS data, post-1950 birth cohorts have a very clear tendency to report greater preference for obedience and less preference for autonomy than we would expect given the trend over earlier cohorts. This reversal in pattern has been discussed with respect to other measures of parental values (see Alwin 1989b) and in other types of attitude measures (Yankelovich 1984).

There is a high degree of stability within cohort categories over surveys in the GSS, as evidenced by the overwhelming number of nonsignificant F statistics on the rows, compared with the columns, of table 4.5. This is not surprising, given the small amount of time between the first and last surveys. In this regard, the results presented for the Detroit samples with respect to intracohort change are all the more remarkable, given very little change within cohorts over a period of thirty years. The intercohort patterns in the GSS data also reinforce the Detroit findings, which is even more apparent if we again implement the linear decomposition technique, as we did with the Detroit data, in which we partition the net social change into that due to intracohort change and that due to cohort differences. These results are given in table 4.6.

I indicated earlier that our reason for looking at the GSS data was to confirm the conclusions reached from the Detroit data in a broader-based sample. The time period covered by the GSS is a mere six years, so it is hardly possible to say something about social change. On the other hand, if we compare the findings presented in table 4.6 with those presented for Detroit in table 4.3, in virtually every instance the pattern of findings is the same. Specifically, the national results confirm the pattern of intercohort differences and the component of change attributable to cohort turnover. More recent birth cohorts (if not the *most* recent) generally prefer more autonomy and less obedience in children, this pattern is much stronger among Catholics than among white Protestants, and a substantial portion of this effect for either group is due to cohort differences in the amount of schooling.

The convergence of the GSS results with the Detroit findings also

TABLE 4.5. Mean Rankings of Child Qualities of Autonomy and Obedience by Year of Study and Birth Cohort Category

Cohort	1986	1987	1988	1989	1990	1991	TOTAL	F	p
					Think for Self				
Pre–1920	3.67	3.68	3.53	3.60	3.65	3.61	3.63	.26	NS
1920–29	3.79	3.91	3.87	4.03	3.85	3.87	3.89	.36	NS
1930–39	4.07	4.00	3.93	4.16	3.93	3.91	4.00	.52	NS
1940–49	4.34	4.18	4.22	4.11	4.05	4.04	4.16	1.13	NS
1950–59	4.02	4.20	3.98	4.09	4.10	4.06	4.10	1.01	NS
1960–74	3.88	3.84	3.81	3.92	3.96	3.88	3.88	0.29	NS
TOTAL	3.99	4.00	3.91	4.00	3.96	3.94	3.97		
F	3.75	5.19	3.83	3.08	1.51	1.65	16.09		
p	0.00	0.00	0.00	0.01	0.18	0.14	0.00		
					Obey				
Pre–1920	3.39	3.46	3.51	3.42	3.17	3.24	3.39	.78	NS
1920–29	3.35	3.15	3.05	3.31	3.39	3.15	3.22	.89	NS
1930–39	3.11	2.88	3.08	2.80	2.63	3.05	2.92	1.50	NS
1940–49	2.91	2.63	2.78	2.64	2.78	2.82	2.73	1.10	NS
1950–59	2.80	2.63	2.71	2.64	2.65	2.70	2.68	.45	NS
1960–74	3.09	2.71	2.92	2.76	2.70	2.69	2.78	1.85	NS
TOTAL	3.06	2.84	2.96	2.84	2.82	2.85	2.88		
F	2.91	11.08	5.29	7.19	5.58	3.54	32.03		
p	0.01	0.00	0.00	0.00	0.00	0.00	0.00		

Think minus Obey

Pre–1920	.28	.23	.02	.18	.48	.37	.24	.41	NS
1920–29	.44	.76	.82	.72	.46	.72	.67	.46	NS
1930–39	.96	1.12	.85	1.36	1.30	.86	1.08	.80	NS
1940–49	1.43	1.55	1.44	1.48	1.26	1.22	1.43	.55	NS
1950–59	1.22	1.57	1.27	1.45	1.45	1.37	1.42	.81	NS
1960–74	0.79	1.13	0.88	1.16	1.27	1.19	1.10	0.91	NS
TOTAL	0.93	1.16	0.95	1.16	1.14	1.08	1.09		
F	3.84	9.34	5.56	5.40	3.77	2.80	28.50		
p	0.00	0.00	0.00	0.00	0.00	0.02	0.00		

Sample Sizes

Pre–1920	108	254	143	118	107	105	835
1920–29	101	217	133	122	110	108	791
1930–39	82	219	101	128	89	114	733
1940–49	151	335	174	169	149	151	1,129
1950–59	178	444	207	232	217	266	1,544
1960–74	109	320	215	229	199	237	1,309
TOTAL	729	1,789	973	998	871	981	6,341

TABLE 4.6. Decomposition of Social Change in Preferences for Child Qualities of Autonomy and Obedience into Intracohort and Cohort Replacement Components: General Social Survey of U.S. Population, 1986 to 1991

Dependent Variable	Time Period	Social Change[1]	Intracohort[2]	Cohort Replacement[3]	Intracohort[2]	Cohort Replacement[3]	St. Dev.
Total Sample (N = 6362)			*Unadjusted*		*Adjusted for Schooling*		
Think for self	1986–91	−0.058	−0.035**	0.024***	−0.050***	−0.005	1.292
Obey	1986–91	−0.206**	0.025	−0.058***	0.035*	−0.029***	1.397
Think − obey	1986–91	0.148	−0.065*	0.083***	−0.085***	0.024**	2.343
White Protestants (N = 3085)			*Unadjusted*		*Adjusted for Schooling*		
Think for self	1986–91	0.027	−0.025	0.019**	−0.030	0.010	1.279
Obey	1986–91	−0.172	0.045*	−0.062***	0.055*	−0.053***	1.405
Think − obey	1986–91	0.198	−0.070	0.082***	−0.085*	0.058***	2.381
Catholics (N = 1518)			*Unadjusted*		*Adjusted for Schooling*		
Think for self	1986–91	0.022	−0.045	0.050***	−0.050	0.035***	1.295
Obey	1986–91	−0.336**	0.015	−0.075***	0.020	−0.060***	1.389
Think − obey	1986–91	0.359	−0.065	0.125***	−0.710	0.095***	2.298

[1] p value calculated as difference of two means (Y_t and Y_1). Critical values for the two-sided z statistic are: 1.96 = .05, 2.576 = .01, 3.09 = .001.
[2] p value taken from b_1 coefficient: *p < .05, **p < .01, ***p < .001.
[3] p value taken from b_2 coefficient: *p < .05, **p < .01, ***p < .001.

extends to the intracohort portion of the change, even though, as we stated earlier, there is little temporal room for such change. As with Detroit, we find a small, but significant intertemporal trend among white Protestants that espouses obedience at the expense of independence. This runs counter to the intercohort pattern, which means that the two sources of influence cancel each other, making it appear as if little social change is occurring. The effects of controlling for schooling are much the same as we observed for the Detroit data, although the reduction of the intercohort effects is slightly less visible in the present data. We should also note that although we were able to explain some of the intercohort patterns by recourse to cohort differences in schooling, this is not possible with the intracohort portion of the change. Indeed, net of schooling, the intracohort change among Protestants is even stronger (see table 4.6).

Developmental Differences in Childrearing Orientations

At several points in the earlier discussion we suggested that parental orientations to children potentially depend on the life cycle of the parental role. This suggests some intracohort change, and yet in the above results we have found little support for this idea. This in no way means that such developmental or life-cycle factors do not impinge on parent-child relationships and parental values. They evidently do, as we shall explore in greater detail in this part of the chapter; however, their influence may be more subtle than can be detected with the types of measures used in the foregoing. Moreover, parental age is confounded with birth cohort, so it is virtually impossible in cross-sectional studies to tease out the aspect of parental values that is due to life-cycle factors. One solution to this problem is to conceptualize it in terms of developmental differences in children and to ask whether parental values vary according to the developmental stage of the child.

Based on a Piagetian view of moral development, I would entertain a model in which the child is expected to develop from (1) a premoral stage governed by situational reinforcement contingencies to (2) a stage of conventional morality, in which established group sanctions push for conformity and obedience to the norms and/or authority of the social group or social institutions and, finally, to (3) the postconventional "principled" morality, in which the child/adult develops an internalized set of abstract principles that allow him/her to evaluate situations and behaviors with regard to a set of standards or values. In our framework, the second stage of moral development stresses the importance of obedience or conformity to norms, whereas the third stage involves the principle of independence or thinking for oneself. It should be no surprise that Piaget referred to the contrast between these two stages in terms of the state of "moral heteronomy" versus one of "moral autonomy" (see Piaget 1932). Thus, from a developmental point of view it could be argued that parental values are strongly conditioned by the developmental stage of the child.

Here I examine this hypothesis in greater depth, through a more detailed inspection of the 1982–83 data from the Child-Rearing in Detroit Project (Alwin 1994b) in order to examine the question of whether there are detectable changes in parental values over the life cycles of parents. This is accomplished through an investigation of differences in parental orientations linked to the developmental stages of their children. For this purpose I examine responses to Kohn's (1969) measure of parental values, which elicits choices to a list of thirteen qualities (see note 5). This is necessary because, as noted earlier, global assessments of child qualities reveal few differences with respect to the ages of children (Alwin 1989b), whereas assessments of desirable child qualities with particular children in mind are more prone to reveal such developmental differences (Alwin 1991).

To understand these data, it is necessary to provide some brief background in the ways this measure performs in the study of parental values for autonomy and obedience. These measures are very difficult for most respondents, say, compared with the Lenski measures used above.[9] Also, it is not completely clear that the qualities on the Kohn (1969) list adequately reflect the concepts of interest here (see Alwin 1989b, 202). Kohn (1969, 58) argues that there is a strong factor underlying responses to this measure reflecting *self-direction versus conformity,* a bipolar factor with a mixture of qualities associated with each component. In Kohn's (1969, 58) analysis, the qualities associated with *self-direction* were "considerate," "interested in how and why things happen," "responsible," "self-control," and "good sense and sound judgment." Some of these clearly reflect the notion of independence or autonomy, as we have used it here, but with some ambiguities. The quality "considerate" may actually imply a certain degree of obedience to social norms about the treatment of other people more than it reflects the idea that one should think for onself. "Self-control," rather than reflect self-direction, may actually refer to the internalization of social norms to conform to society's dictates. The traits associated with *conformity* in Kohn's analysis were "obey parents," "good manners," "being neat and clean," and "good student." There is less ambiguity here with respect to measuring the concept of obedience as we have defined it (in terms of obedience to institutional authority). Despite considerable utility in the Kohn measure and in his results, several problems exist with his analysis. He does not, for example, take the age of the child into account in his factor analysis of these data, therefore ignoring a feature of the data (in terms of how the issues are addressed to the respondent, namely, "Which qualities would you say are desirable for a [boy/girl] of [child's] age to have?"). This clouds the issue somewhat, as our own preliminary analyses of these data suggest that the notions of *self-direction versus conformity* values in parents' minds are very different depending on the age of the child (see below). For these reasons we present the detailed rankings of each child quality rather than combining them into an overall composite score that would reflect what Kohn identifies as the concept of relevance (see Kohn 1969, 58).

Table 4.7 presents the average ranking of each of the qualities on Kohn's (1969) list for the 1982–83 Detroit samples. A trait picked as the most important was assigned a score of five, one picked as one of the three most, but not the most, important trait was given a four, and so forth such that our scale ranges from one to five, with five indicating the trait most highly valued. These data are presented separately for mothers and fathers because of potential parental gender differences.[10] These results show that the younger the child, the more likely the parent will be to desire the qualities "interested in how and why things happen," "obeys parents," "getting along with other children," "sex-role conformity," and "good manners." With increasing age of the child, parents increase their preferences for qualities such as "responsible," "being a good student," and "having good sense and sound judgment." The meanings of the concepts of *autonomy* and *obedience* seem to depend on the age of children. Thus, in younger children the notion of *autonomy* or "independence of thought" involves curiosity, whereas later on parents formulate it in terms of being responsible and having good judgment. In the case of *obedience,* the traits favored in young children are "to obey parents," "sex-role conformity," and "good manners," whereas in older children "consideration of others" and being a "good student" are obedience-type qualities that are more highly valued.

In addition to these findings, some other patterns in the Detroit data are worth mentioning with respect to Kohn's measures. The quality revealed to be most important using this measure is "honest" and

TABLE 4.7. Parental Preferences of Child Qualities by Gender of Parent and Age of Child: Detroit, 1982–83

	Mothers					Fathers				
Age of Child	2–6 N = 210	7–12 N = 245	13–17 N = 206	F	p	2–6 N = 101	7–12 N = 87	13–17 N = 110	F	p
1. Manners	3.25	3.07	3.04	4.29	.01	3.09	2.97	2.93	1.15	.32
2. Succeed	2.90	2.97	3.15	3.92	.02	2.70	2.91	3.02	3.12	.04
3. Honest	3.61	3.81	3.73	2.54	.08	3.66	3.93	3.87	2.54	.08
4. Neat and clean	2.57	2.49	2.66	2.18	.11	2.80	2.56	2.70	2.08	.12
5. Judgment	3.00	3.50	3.75	28.96	.00	3.14	3.42	3.64	6.72	.00
6. Self-control	3.03	3.08	3.04	.37	.70	2.92	2.94	2.90	.07	.93
7. Role	1.97	1.80	1.89	1.66	.19	2.09	2.00	1.80	2.10	.12
8. Amicable	3.36	2.89	2.64	37.59	.00	3.15	2.83	2.71	8.29	.00
9. Obeys	3.85	3.48	3.35	15.40	.00	3.82	3.43	3.33	8.9	.00
10. Responsible	2.86	3.29	3.44	28.70	.00	2.93	3.31	3.53	12.20	.00
11. Considerate	3.10	3.25	3.11	2.83	.06	3.16	3.11	3.16	.22	.81
12. Curious	3.03	2.46	2.21	37.27	.00	3.09	2.49	2.30	15.69	.00
13. Good student	2.47	2.92	2.98	25.12	.00	2.43	3.10	3.11	24.10	.00

to be least important is "acts like a boy/girl should." Thus, conformity to sex roles seems relatively unimportant to parents, but the virtue of being an honest person stands out as extremely important in most parents' minds. At the same time, "to obey parents" is second in importance only to "honesty," so it is clear that obedience has not necessarily declined in overall importance, at least with respect to specific children. Of course, for children in general, people are increasingly coming to believe that it is much better if children think for themselves than to have someone else do it for them.

DISCUSSION AND CONCLUSIONS

More than fifty years ago Schumpeter (1988/1942) predicted that parenthood would be regarded as too heavy a personal sacrifice under modern conditions. Have we reached that point? Declining birthrates certainly indicate that more and more people are opting out of parenthood, or have at least limited the number of their children. Parents appear to be spending less time in child care (see Gershuny and Robinson 1988), in part because of reductions in family size but also because of increased rates of maternal employment (Hoffman 1989). Some have interpreted this as a decreased commitment on the part of parents to the childrearing task, blaming inadequacy in the parental role for apparent declines in adolescent well-being (e.g., Uhlenberg and Eggebeen 1986). But the parental role and childrearing tasks have changed, and the future of parenthood should be addressed within this changing sociodemographic context and within this changing framework of parental demands, priorities, and choices (see Hogan 1987).

In this chapter I have documented *one* aspect of the changing family in Western industrialized societies—the transformation of the nature of parental values—that reflects an increasing desire for children to be able to act and think independently. What parents want from their children has thus shifted in significant ways, from what might best be described as a dual emphasis on obedience to authority and independence of thought to an orientation that gives even greater emphasis to autonomy and puts much less stress on obedience. These trends reveal something about the changing nature of society, the development of the modern family, and the shifting task of childrearing. The transformations in parental experience, reflected by these value shifts, have implications both for understanding the changing contexts of childrearing and for the nature of parent-child relations in modern society. Both "childhood" and "parenthood" have undergone change.

A detailed discussion of the implications of these findings for the future of parent-child relationships and parental childrearing strategies is beyond the scope of the present chapter. My main task was to look backward rather than forward. Thus, I have taken for granted that, as well as documenting their direction and magnitude, it was worthwhile to consider the sources of these changes. In one sense, I have simply documented the predictions made by others. Kohn (1969, 193–194) suggested, for example, that due to educational expansion and increases in the complexity of work, "a major historical trend (would move) toward an increasingly self-directed populace." We have definitely witnessed an important trend in self-direction, at least in the values expressed for the desirable qualities of children, and a substantial part of that trend is directly attributable to increases in the amount of schooling. And Lenski (1971, 50), in response to historically naive criticisms by Schuman (1971), predicted that changes within the American Catholic Church during the 1950s and early 1960s (brought on in part by the Second Vatican Council) would result in a continued erosion of observed differences between Catholics and other groups, because of changes occurring to the Catholic subpopulation (see also Alba 1981; Alwin 1986; Greeley 1977). We have documented the shifts foreseen by Lenski, although the finding of a recent countervailing trend in the youngest cohorts of white Protestants was unexpected and warrants further investigation.

What has been lacking in our understanding of changes in parental socialization values up to this point, which this chapter has attempted to clarify, is the extent to which the social changes are attributable to the effects of cohort succession versus intracohort change. This issue was addressed in earlier research, but the inclusion of more recent data has made it possible to give a stronger empirical basis for addressing this question. These results have essentially bolstered the earlier cohort-replacement interpretation of these changes (see Alwin 1990b). We have shown that majority of these changes have been rooted mainly in differing historically related experiences of birth cohorts, wherein the youngest, most influential cohorts are most affected by social change. There is only minor support for the notion that these changes have been felt across the age structure of the population in the form of period effects or that other types of intracohort change exist. We did find support for life-cycle variations in parental values, but these seemed to have more to do with subtle variations in developmentally linked child qualities, rather than value orientations themselves.

If the main changes are due to the different experiences of cohorts entering (and eventually) leaving the social scene, what are their origins? From what experiences do they emerge? Do they reflect a kind of exogenous shift in cultural values, as Zelizer (1985) argues, reflecting more deeply felt changes in individuation and secularization (see also Lesthaeghe and Surkyn 1988)? Or, are they linked to basic changes in the technological and structural features of society, reflected in the expansion of education (Kohn 1969) and changes in organizational authority structures (Coleman 1990)? There is clear evidence for the role of schooling, in that substantial portions of the cohort replacement effects on parental values are contributed by differences among cohorts in amounts of schooling, but this is only one component of such an explanation. Finally, are these changes linked to factors that are uniquely affecting the family, for example, to the changing composition and structure of the family and, specifically, the substantial declines in fertility in the United States since 1960 and increases in the labor-force participation of women with children (Becker 1981; Rossi 1987)?

The seeming regularity of the trends from obedience to autonomy and their consistency with other changing aspects of family life pushes for an interpretation of these changes as simply one part of a larger picture of change, perhaps one suggesting they are the result of more fundamental economic and demographic change (Thornton and Fricke 1987; Thornton 1990). There is little question that changes in the American family over the past several decades have been in the direction of granting greater autonomy to its members, even to the point that some have wondered if the family is in jeopardy (see Popenoe 1988). For example, the changing direction of parental values over this century—particularly the past four to five decades—seems to be consistent with declines in fertility (Ryder 1980; Westoff 1986); changing styles of independent living (Kobrin 1976); changing norms of sexual intimacy (Giddens 1992); changing patterns of marriage, cohabitation, and divorce (Westoff 1986; Thornton 1990); changing aspects of sex roles and household division of labor (Giele 1988; Gershuny and Robinson 1988; Mason and Lu 1988; Thornton, Alwin, and Camburn 1983); declines in church attendance (Alwin 1988c); and changing patterns of domestic living more generally (Bumpass 1990; Goldscheider and Waite 1991). From this point of view, changes in parental socialization values are simply one aspect of a myriad of changing aspects of the family, similarly responsive to whatever exogenous factors are shaping changes in the family (see Thornton 1990). In this sense, one would expect other indicators of family change to be linked to some extent to the sociohistorical processes identified here as important for the development of changes in parental socialization values.

On the other hand, rather than reflections of some basic value change in the nature of society or in the nature of the family, we should bear in mind the possibility that the types of value shifts observed in this analysis may simply be manifestations of continuity rather than change. I earlier referred to Inkeles's (1984) argument that the increased expression of preferences for the independence of the child may reflect continuity in the core values of individualism in our culture. From this point of view, it is not the basic values of our culture that have changed but the circumstances that permit their expression. Thus, preferences for increased autonomy in children reflect as much continuity in American values as they do changes in the nature of the family, rising affluence of the population, and the circumstances of increased educational opportunity. Perhaps it is the case that we can now afford to express attitudes and beliefs about childrearing that have been at the heart of our cultural heritage, the core values of which have not changed.

Whether they reflect continuity or change and whether they reflect shifts in the institution of the family or broader-based cultural and structural changes, if parental values are indeed valid reflections of what qualities of children the society desires as "products" of socialization, then these patterns of change reflect an important consideration in the understanding of the parent-child relationship in modern life. The parental socialization role may have changed, and family members may be achieving independence in exchange for adherence to traditional norms. At the same time, however, in certain of its institutional functions, the family has not changed but continues to be the primary agent for the care and nurture of children; the sociodemographic contexts in which families are formed, maintained, and changed are now different. The historical factors that help shape these family contexts are also expressed in the values parents use to determine what qualities children should have to prepare them for a future life. Whatever the future course of preferences for desirable child qualities, I expect that they will be established through the medium of the social, cultural, developmental, and historical contexts in which parents find themselves.

NOTES

1. Baumrind's classification describes how parents reconcile the joint needs of children for nurturance and limit setting and is based on the fourfold classification of the dimensions of parental demandingness and parental responsiveness, dimensions she claims result from factor anlyses of parents' behavior, citing Maccoby and Martin (1983). The resulting four types are authoritarian, authoritative, permissive, and rejecting-neglecting.

2. This portion of the chapter is based on a reworking of similar material presented in earlier papers (Alwin 1988b and 1990a).

3. This refers to the massive changes in social and economic organization resulting from the replacement of hand tools by machine and power tools and the development of large-scale industrial production, which occurred at approximately 1760 in England and somewhat later in other industrialized countries in Europe and North America.

4. Kohn (1976, 541) was in agreement that a change could be observed in comparing the two samples but attributed it to an artifact of measurement rather than real social change. This, despite his earlier (Kohn 1969, 193–194) prediction of a continuation of "a major historical trend . . . toward an increasingly self-directed populace." The issue raised by Kohn involves the fact that the questions from his 1964 sample asked about parental values of child qualities with respect to a specific child, whereas the GSS adaptation of his question (the data used by the Wrights for the 1973 time point), refers to children in general terms. To the extent possible, I explored the potential bias in asking these questions and found none (Alwin 1989b).

5. This measure is discussed extensively elsewhere (see Alwin and Krosnick 1985; Krosnick and Alwin 1987, 1988), so I do not discuss it here in detail. The qualities given are: good manners, tries hard to succeed, honest, neat and clean, good sense and sound judgment, self-control, acts like a boy should (acts like a girl should), gets along well with other children, obeys his parents well, responsible, considerate of others, interested in why and how things happen, good student. Given this list of qualities, the following questions are posed: (a) The qualities listed on this card may all be important, but which three would you say are the most desirable for a (boy/girl) of (child's name) age to have? (b) Which one of these three is the most desirable of all? (c) All of the qualities listed on this card may be desirable, but could you tell me which three you consider least important? (d) And which one of these three do you consider least important?

6. The 1988 data actually combine two studies, one conducted as a part of the Detroit Area Study series in 1987 and a supplemental sample of equal size undertaken in 1988. Both studies were initiated by the author to study changes in religious attitudes and behavior and are combined here and for present purposes simply referred to as the 1988 study. The response rates in the 1987 and 1988 surveys were 70 and 68 percent, respectively (see Alwin 1988c).

7. The sample sizes given here refer to the number of respondents for whom complete data existed on all variables used in the analysis presented.

8. The 1982 and 1983 surveys were initated by the author to study factors re-

lated to childrearing and adaptation to the parental role. The 1982 sample was a standard cross-sectional probability sample, stratified by race and geographical location. The design of the 1983 study was different, involving a disproportionate oversampling of households in high-density black areas. The interviews in both studies were conducted by professional interviewers trained and employed by the Survey Research Center of the University of Michigan, with the exception of one-half of the 1982 interviews, for which trained graduate student interviewers were employed. The response rates in the surveys were approximately 80 percent. In the present analysis of the 1983 data, the data are weighted to take into account the disproportionate sampling fractions.

9. Our research shows (see Alwin and Krosnick 1985; Krosnick and Alwin 1987, 1988) that about 10 percent of the sample typically does not complete the ranking task, presumably because of its extreme level of difficulty. Moreover, the respondents who do are sometimes affected by the order in which the response choices are offered, which suggests that responses are a somewhat crude indication of the phenomena of interest.

10. I ignore the sex of the child for present purposes, although it is often argued that developmental differences vary by sex of child (Block 1978, 36–38). Past analyses of these data indicate no statistical interaction of sex of child with age of child (see Alwin 1991, 213).

References

Alba, Richard. 1981. The twilight of ethnicity among American Catholics of European ancestry. *Annals of the American Academy of Political and Social Science* 454:86–97.

Altmann, Jeanne. 1987. Life span aspects of reproduction and parental care in anthropoid primates." In J. B. Lancaster, J. Altmann, A. S. Rossi, and L. R. Sherrod, eds. *Parenting across the life-span: Biosocial dimensions,* pp. 15–29. New York: Aldine de Gruyter.

Alwin, Duane. 1984. Trends in parental socialization values: Detroit, 1958 to 1983. *American Journal of Sociology* 90:359–382.

———. 1986. Religion and parental child-rearing orientations: Evidence of a Catholic-Protestant convergence." *American Journal of Sociology* 92:412–440.

———. 1988a. From obedience to autonomy: Changes in traits desired in children." *Public Opinion Quarterly* 52:33–52.

———. 1988b. "The times they are a-changin": Reflections on the changing culture of child-rearing in American society. Paper presented at the annual meeting of the American Sociological Association, Atlanta, September.

———. 1988c. Religion in Detroit. Unpublished paper, Institute for Social Research, University of Michigan, Ann Arbor.

———. 1989a. Social stratification, conditions of work, and parental socialization values. In N. Eisenberg, J. Reykowski, and E. Staub, eds., *Social and moral values: Individual and societal perspectives,* pp. 327–346. New York: Erlbaum.

———. 1989b. Changes in qualities valued in children in the United States, 1964 to 1984. *Social Science Research* 18:195–236.

————. 1990a. "Historical changes in parental orientations to children. In N. Mandell and S. Cahill, eds., *Sociological studies of child development* 3:65–86. Greenwich, Conn.: JAI.

————. 1990b. Cohort replacement and changes in qualities valued in children. *Journal of Marriage and the Family* 52:347–360.

————. 1991. Changes in family roles and gender differences in parental socialization values. In N. Cahill, ed., *Sociological Studies of Childhood* 4:201–224. Greenwich, Conn.: JAI.

————. 1992. Aging, cohorts, and social change: An examination of the generational replacement model of social change. In H. A. Becker, ed., *Dynamics of cohort and generations research*, pp. 53–95. Amsterdam: Thesis.

————. 1993. Socio-political attitude development in adulthood: The role of generational and life-cycle factors. In D. Krebs and P. Schmidt, eds., *New directions in attitude measurement*, pp. 61–93. New York: Walter de Gruyter.

————. 1994a. Aging, personality, and social change: The stability of individual differences over the adult life span. In D. L. Featherman, R. M. Lerner, and M. Perlmutter, eds., *Life-span development and behavior*, pp. 135–185. Hillsdale, N.J.: Lawrence Erlbaum.

————. 1994b. Child-rearing in Detroit project. 1982–83 Detroit Survey Data Sets. Ann Arbor, Mich.: Inter-University Consortium for Political and Social Research.

————. 1994c. From child-bearing to child-rearing: What do we want from our children? Workshop on Expanding Frameworks for Fertility Research, National Research Council/National Academy of Sciences, Woods Hole, Mass., September.

Alwin, Duane, Ronald Cohen, and Theodore Newcomb. 1991. *Political attitudes over the life-span*. Madison: University of Wisconsin Press.

Alwin, Duane, and D. J. Jackson. 1982. Adult Values for Children: An Application of Factor Analysis to Ranked Preference Data. In R. M. Hauser, D. Mechanic, A. O. Haller, and T. S. Hauser, eds., *Social structure and behavior: Papers in honor of William H. Sewell*, pp. 311–329. New York: Academic Press.

Alwin, Duane, and Jon A. Krosnick. 1985. The measurement of values: A comparison of ratings and rankings. *Public Opinion Quarterly* 49:535–552.

————. 1991. "Aging, cohorts, and the stability of socio-political orientations over the life-span. *American Journal of Sociology* 97:169–195.

Aries, Philippe. 1962. *Centuries of childhood: A social history of family life.* New York: Knopf.

Baumrind, Diana. 1989. Rearing competent children. In W. Damon, ed., *Child development today and tomorrow*, pp. 349–378. San Francisco: Jossey-Bass.

————. 1991. Parenting styles and adolescent development. In R. M. Lerner, A. C. Petersen, and J. Brooks-Gunn, eds., *Encyclopedia of adolescence*, pp. 758–772. New York: Garland.

Becker, Gary S. 1981. *A treatise on the family.* Cambridge: Harvard University Press.

Bellah, Robert, Richard Madsen, William M. Sullivan, Ann Swidler, and Steven M. Tipton. 1985. *Habits of the heart: Individualism and commitment in American life.* Berkeley: University of California Press.

Blau, Peter M., and Otis Dudley Duncan. 1967. *The American occupational structure.* New York: John Wiley.

Block, Jean H. 1978. Another look at sex differentiation in the socialization behaviors of mothers and fathers. In J. A. Sherman and F. L. Denmark, eds., *The psychology of women: Future directions in research,* pp. 29–87. New York: Psychological Dimensions.

Bronfenbrenner, Urie. 1958. Socialization and social class through time and space. In E. E. Maccoby, T. M. Newcomb, and E. L. Hartley, eds., *Readings in social psychology,* pp. 400–425. New York: Holt, Rinehart and Winston.

Bumpass, Larry L. 1990. What's happening to the family? Interactions between demographic and institutional change. *Demography* 27:483–498.

Cahan, Emily, Jay Mechling, Brian Sutton-Smith, and Sheldon H. White. 1993. The elusive historical child: Ways of knowing the child of history and psychology." In G. H. Elder Jr., J. Modell, and R. D. Parke, eds., *Children in time and place,* pp. 192–223. Cambridge: Cambridge University Press.

Caplow, Theodore, Howard M. Bahr, Bruce A. Chadwick, Reuben Hill, and Margaret Holmes Williamson. 1982. *Middletown families: Fifty years of change and continuity.* Minneapolis: University of Minnesota Press.

Caplow, Theodore, and Brucke A. Chadwick. 1979. Inequality and life style in Middletown, 1920–78. *Social Science Quarterly* 60:367–386.

Coleman, James S. 1990. *Foundations of social theory.* Cambridge: Harvard University Press, Belknap Press.

Davis, Allison, and Robert J. Havighurst. 1948. "Social class and color differences in child-rearing." *American Sociological Review* 11:698–710.

Davis, James A., and Tom W. Smith. 1991. *The general social surveys, 1972–1991: Cumulative codebook.* Chicago: National Opinion Research Center.

DeMause, L. 1974. The evolution of childhood. In L. DeMause, ed., *The history of childhood,* pp. 1–73. New York: Psychohistory Press.

de Tocqueville, Alexis. [1835–40] 1956. *Democracy in America.* New York.: Mentor.

Draper, Patricia, and Henry Harpending. 1987. Parent investment and the child's environment. In J. B. Lancaster, J. Altmann, A. S. Rossi, and L. R. Sherrod, eds., *Parenting across the life-span: Biosocial dimensions,* pp. 207–235. New York: Aldine de Gruyter.

Duncan, Otis Dudley. 1985. Generations, cohorts, and conformity. In W. M. Mason and S. E. Fienberg, eds., *Cohort analysis in social research,* pp. 289–321. New York: Springer.

Duncan, Otis Dudley, Howard Schuman, and Beverly Duncan. 1973. *Social change in a Metropolitan community.* New York: Russell Sage Foundation.

Duvall, Evelyn M. 1946. Conceptions of parenthood. *American Journal of Sociology* 52:193–203.

Elder, Glen H., Jr. 1974. *Children of the Great Depression.* Chicago: University of Chicago Press.

———. 1980. Adolescence in historical perspective. In Joseph Adelson, ed., *Handbook of adolescent psychology,* pp. 3–46. New York: John Wiley.

Elder, Glen H., Jr., Avshalom Caspi, and Linda M. Burton. 1988. Adolescent transitions in developmental perspective: Sociological and historical insights. *Minnesota Symposium on Child Psychology* 21:151–179.

Elder, Glen H., Jr., and Tamara K. Hareven. 1993. Rising above life's disadvantages: From the Great Depression to war. In G. H. Elder Jr., J. Modell, and R. D. Parke, eds., *Children in time and place,* pp. 47–72. Cambridge: Cambridge University Press.

Elder, Glen H., Jr., John Modell, and Ross D. Parke. 1993. Studying children in a changing world. In G. H. Elder Jr., J. Modell, and R. D. Parke, eds., *Children in time and place,* pp. 3–21. Cambridge: Cambridge University Press.

Elias, Norbert. [1st German ed., 1936] 1978. *The history of manners: The civilizing process.* Vol. 1. New York: Random House.

EMNID. 1983/1986. Goals of child-rearing: Stagnation in the trend toward non-authoritarian child-rearing? *EMNID Informationen* 8/9 (1983); 3/4 (1986).

Firebaugh, Glenn. 1989. Methods for estimating cohort replacement effects. In C. C. Clogg, ed., *Sociological methodology 1989,* pp. 243–262. Oxford: Basil Blackwell.

Gecas, Viktor. 1979. "The influence of social class on socialization. In W. R. Burr, R. Hill, F. I. Nye, and I. L. Reiss, eds., *Contemporary theories about the family,* pp. 365–404. New York: Free Press.

Gershuny, Jonathan, and John P. Robinson. 1988. Historical change in the household division of labor. *Demography* 25:537–552.

Giddens, Anthony. 1992. *The transformation of intimacy: Sexuality, love, and eroticism in modern societies.* Stanford, Calif.: Stanford University Press.

Giele, Janet Z. 1988. Gender and sex-roles. In N. J. Smelser, ed., *Handbook of sociology,* pp. 291–323. Beverly Hills, Calif.: Sage.

Glenn, Norval D. 1977. *Cohort analysis.* Beverly Hills, Calif.: Sage.

———. 1980. Values, attitudes, and beliefs. In Orville G. Brim Jr. and Jerome Kagan, eds., *Constancy and change in human development,* pp. 596–640. Cambridge: Harvard University Press.

Goldscheider, Frances K., and Linda J. Waite. 1991. *New families, no families?* Berkeley: University of California Press.

Goode, William J. 1963. *World revolution and family patterns.* New York: Macmillan.

Greeley, A. M. 1977. *The American Catholic.* New York: Basic.

Greven, Philip J., Jr. 1970. *Four generations: Population, land, and family in colonial Andover, Massachusetts.* Ithaca, N.Y.: Cornell University Press.

Havighurst, Robert J., and Allison Davis. 1955. A comparison of the Chicago and Harvard studies of social class differences in child-rearing. *American Sociological Review* 20:438–442.

Hoffman, Lois W. 1989. The effects of maternal employment in the two-parent family. *American Psychologist* 44:283–292.

Hogan, Dennis P. 1987. Demographic trends in human fertility and parenting across the life-span. In J. B. Lancaster, J. Altmann, A. S. Rossi, and L. R. Sherrod, eds., *Parenting across the life-span: Biosocial dimensions*, pp. 315–349. New York: Aldine de Gruyter.

Inkeles, Alex. [1955] 1983. Social change and social character: The role of parental mediation. *Journal of Social Issues* 11:12–23; rpt., *Journal of Social Issues* 39:179–191.

————. 1984. The responsiveness of family patterns to economic changes in the United States. *Tocqueville Review* 6:5–50.

Kerckhoff, Alan C. 1972. *Socialization and social class.* Englewood Cliffs, N.J.: Prentice-Hall.

Kobrin, Frances. 1976. The primary individual and the family: Changes in living arrangements since 1940. *Journal of Marriage and the Family* 38:233–239.

Kohn, Melvin L. 1959. Social class and parental values. *American Journal of Sociology* 64:337–366.

————. 1963. Social class and parent-child relationships: An interpretation. *American Journal of Sociology* 68:471–480.

————. 1969. *Class and conformity: A study in values.* Homewood, Il.: Dorsey. Reprint, Chicago: University of Chicago Press, 1977.

————. 1976. Social class and parental values: Another confirmation of the relationship. *American Sociological Review* 41:538–545.

————. 1977. Reassessment 1977. In *Class and Conformity*, pp. xxv–lx. 2d ed. Chicago: University of Chicago Press.

Kohn, Melvin L., and Carmi Schooler, Joanne Miller, Karen A. Miller, Carrie Schoenbach, and Ronald Schoenberg. 1983. *Work and personality: An inquiry into the impact of social stratification.* Norwood, N.J.: Ablex.

————. 1981. Personality, occupation, and social stratification: A frame of reference. In D. J. Treiman and R. V. Robinson, eds., *Research in social stratification and mobility*, pp. 267–297. Greenwich Conn.: JAI.

Kohn, Melvin L., and Kazimierz M. Slomczynski. 1990. *Social structure and self-direction: A comparative analysis of the United States and Poland.* Cambridge, Mass.: Basil Blackwell.

Krosnick, Jon A., and Duane F. Alwin. 1987. An evaluation of a cognitive theory of response-order effects in survey measurement. *Public Opinion Quarterly* 51: 201–219.

————. 1988. A test of the form-resistant correlation hypothesis: Ratings, rankings, and the measurement of values. *Public Opinion Quarterly* 52:526–538.

Lancaster, Jane B., J. Altmann, A. S. Rossi, and L. R. Sherrod, eds. 1987. *Parenting across the life-span: Biosocial dimensions.* New York: Aldine de Gruyter.

Lenski, Gerhard. 1961. *The religious factor: A sociological study of religion's impact on politics, economics, and family life.* Garden City, N.Y.: Doubleday.

————. 1971. The religious factor in Detroit: Revisited. *American Sociological Review* 36:48–50.

Lesthaeghe, Ron, and Johan Surkyn. 1988. Cultural dynamics and economic theories of fertility change. *Population and Development Review* 11:1–45.

LeVine, Robert A., and Merry White. 1986. *Human conditions: The cultural basis for educational development.* London: Routledge and Kegan Paul.

————. 1987. Parenthood in social transformation. In J. B. Lancaster, J. Altmann, A. S. Rossi, and L. R. Sherrod, eds., *Parenting across the life-span: Biosocial dimensions,* pp. 271–293. New York: Aldine de Gruyter.

Lynd, Robert S., and Helen M. Lynd. 1929. *Middletown: A study in contemporary american culture.* New York: Harcourt, Brace.

————. 1937. *Middletown in transition: A study of cultural conflicts.* New York: Harcourt, Brace.

Maccoby, Eleanor E., and P. K. Gibbs. 1954. Methods of child-rearing in two social classes. In W. E. Martin and C. B. Standler, eds., *Readings in Child Development,* pp. 380–396. New York: Harcourt, Brace.

Maccoby, E. E., and Martin, J. A. 1983. Socialization and the context of the family: Parent-child interaction. In E. M. Hetherington, ed., *Socialization, personality, and social development,* pp. 1–101. New York: John Wiley.

Mannheim, Karl. 1952. The problem of generations. In Paul Kecskemeti, ed., *Essays in the sociology of knowledge,* pp. 276–320. London: Routledge and Kegan Paul.

Mason, Karen O., and Yu-Hsai Lu. 1988. Attitudes towards women's familial roles: Changes in the United States, 1977–1985. *Gender and Society* 2:39–57.

Mason, William M., and Stephen E. Fienberg, eds. 1985. *Cohort analysis in social research.* New York: Springer.

Miller, Daniel R., and Guy E. Swanson. 1958. *The changing American parent.* New York: Wiley.

Mohler, Peter Ph. 1989. Wertkonflict oder Wertdiffusion? Ein Vergleich von Ergebnissen aus Bevölkerungsumfragen und einer Inhaltsanalyse von Leitartikeln der FAZ (Value conflict or diffusion of elite values? A comparison of results from the polls and a content analysis of editorials from the Frankfurter Algemeine Zeitung). *Kölner Zeitschrift für Soziologie und Sozialpsychologie* 1:95–122.

Ogburn, William F. 1922. *Social change.* New York: Viking.

Pearlin, Leonard I., and Melvin L. Kohn. 1966. Social class, occupation, and parental values: A cross-national study. *American Sociological Review* 31:466–479.

Piaget, Jean. 1932. *The moral judgement of the child.* New York: Free Press.

Popenoe, David. 1988. *Disturbing the nest: Family change and decline in modern societies.* New York: Aldine de Gruyter.

Reuband, Karl-Heinz. 1988. Von äußerer Verhaltenskonformität zu selbständig Handelin. In Heinz Otto Luthe and Heiner Meulemann, eds., *Wertwandel— Facktum oder Fiktion? Bestandsaufnahmen und Diagnosen aus kultursoziologischer Sicht,* pp. 73–97. Frankfurt: Campus Verlag.

Richards, Martin, and Paul Light, eds. 1986. *Children of social worlds.* Cambridge: Harvard University Press.

Riley, Matilda White. 1973. Aging and cohort succession: Interpretations and misinterpretations. *Public Opinion Quarterly* 37:35–49.

Riley, Matilda White, Marilyn Johnson, and Anne Foner. 1972. *Aging and society: A sociology of age stratification.* New York: Russell Sage Foundation.

Rossi, Alice S. 1987. Parenthood in transition: From lineage to child to self-orientation. In J. B. Lancaster, J. Altmann, A. S. Rossi, and L. R. Sherrod, eds., *Parenting across the life-span: Biosocial dimensions,* pp. 31–81. New York: Aldine de Gruyter.

Ryder, Norman B. 1965. The cohort as a concept in the study of social change. *American Sociological Review* 30:843–861.

———. 1980. Components of temporal variations in American fertility. In R. W. Hiorns, ed., *Demographic patterns in developed societies.* London: Taylor and Francis.

Schaefer, Earl. 1987. Parental modernity and child academic competence: Toward a theory of individual and societal development. *Early Child Development and Care* 27:373–389.

Schaefer, Earl, and Marianna Edgerton. 1985. Parent and child correlates of parental modernity. In Irving E. Sigel, ed., *Parental belief systems: The psychological consequences for children,* pp. 287–318. Hillsdale, N.J.: Lawrence Erlbaum.

Schlumbohm, Jurgen. 1980. "Traditional" collectivity and "modern" individuality—some questions and suggestions for the historical study of socialization: The examples of the German lower and upper bourgeoisie around 1800. *Social History* 5:71–103.

Schuman, Howard. 1971. The religious factor in Detroit: Review, replication, and reanalysis. *American Sociological Review* 36:30–48.

Schumpeter, Joseph. 1988. Decomposition. *Population and Development Review* 14: 499–506. Originally published in *Capitalism, socialism, and democracy* (New York: Harper and Row, 1942).

Sears, Robert R., Eleanor E. Maccoby, and Harry Levin. 1957. *Patterns of child-rearing.* Evanston, Ill.: Row, Peterson.

Sommerville, John. 1982. *The rise and fall of childhood.* Beverly Hills, Calif.: Sage.

Sorokin, Pitirim A. 1927. *Social mobility.* New York: Harper and Row.

Stone, Lawrence. 1977. *The family, sex, and marriage in England, 1500–1800.* New York: Harper and Row.

Thomas, William I., and Dorothy Swain Thomas. 1929. *The child in America.* New York: Alfred Knopf.

Thornton, Arland. 1990. Changing attitudes toward family issues in the United States. *Journal of Marriage and the Family* 51:873–893.

Thornton, Arland, Duane Alwin, and Donald Camburn. 1983. Causes and consequences of sex-role attitudes and attitude change. *American Sociological Review* 49:784–802.

Thornton, Arland, and Deborah Freedman. 1983. The changing American family. *Population Bulletin* 38 (4):2–44.

Thornton, Arland, and Thomas E. Fricke. 1987. Social change and the family: Comparative perspectives for the West, China, and South Asia. *Sociological Forum* 2:746–779.

Trommsdorff, Gisela. 1983. Value change in Japan. *International Journal of Intercultural Relations* 7:337–360.

Tuttle, William M., Jr. 1993. America's home front children in World War II. In G. H. Elder Jr., J. Modell, and R. D. Parke, eds., *Children in time and place,* pp. 27–46. Cambridge: Cambridge University Press.

Uhlenberg, Peter, and David Eggebeen. 1986. The declining well-being of American adolescents. *Public Interest* 82:25–38.

Vinovskis, Maris A. 1987. Historical perspectives on the development of the family and parent-child interactions. In J. B. Lancaster, J. Altmann, A. S. Rossi, and L. R. Sherrod, eds., *Parenting across the life-span: Biosocial dimensions,* pp. 295–312. New York: Aldine de Gruyter.

Westoff, Charles. 1986. Perspective on Nuptiality and Fertility. In K. Davis, M. Bernstam, and R. Ricardo-Campbell, eds., *Below-replacement fertility in industrialized societies,* pp. 155–170. Cambridge: Cambridge University Press.

White, Harrison. 1992. Succession and generations: Looking back on chains of opportunity. In H. A. Becker, ed., *Dynamics of cohort and generations research,* pp. 31–51. Amsterdam: Thesis.

Wright, James D., and Sonia R. Wright. 1976. Social class and parental values for children: A partial replication and extension of the Kohn thesis. *American Sociological Review* 41:527–537.

Yankelovich, Daniel. 1984. American values: Change and stability. *Public Opinion,* December/January, pp. 2–8.

Zelizer, Viviana A. 1985. *Pricing the priceless child: The changing social value of children.* New York: Basic.

Social and Historical Influences on Parent-Child Relations in Midlife

Michael E. J. Wadsworth

INTRODUCTION

For the majority, midlife is the time of greatest family size, with one generation and sometimes more on either side, each of which is likely to contain, at some stage, dependents or semidependents. The expectations and demands of such family relationships will be reduced by the passage of time, as children grow up and move out of the home and as parents die. The nature of these expectations and demands is conditioned by the current circumstances of families and of their society, as are perceptions of relationships of those in midlife with family members in the following and in the previous generations. In this chapter I examine aspects of intergenerational relationships with the previous and the following generation which are likely to be affected by longer-term social and historical circumstances, and I describe how midlife perspectives on work and family life are affected by earlier life circumstances, both social and individual.

It has been well demonstrated that generations who live through times of great and historically imposed stress, such as the American Great Depression, are likely to carry the imprint of that time in their occupation and economic life chances, as well as in their styles of behavior, and that doing so has an impact in the following generation (Elder, Liker, and Cross 1984). It seems likely now that these sociopsychological effects have their parallel in biology, in that, for example, generations who live through epidemics of tuberculosis, parental smoking, or poor educational opportunities will carry the associated health risks into their later life, with the possibility of some degree of risk being transferred into the following generation (Wadsworth 1991; Barker 1992). It is, however, unlikely that only such dramatic events as epidemics or social upheavals on the scale of the depression affect health and styles of behavior. Poverty, for instance, and shifts in the distribution of income and in the opportunities to gain it, will also have a powerful effect. In a high-technology society with a market economy, social instability and change is in many respects inherent, bringing the associated risk of relative deprivation for a sizable proportion of the population.

Increasing awareness of relative deprivation—and the consequent discontent—has been an evident problem in most urbanized countries during the last fifty years. In Britain, Masterman (1909) observed that social discontent "propagates and triumphs in times of plenty, withers up and vanishes in times of depression. This is exactly the reverse of the accepted belief, which thought that the poor are stung into Socialism by suffering, as poets are stung into poetry by wrong" (quoted in Runciman 1966, 22). Politicians, historians, and sociologists have therefore been greatly concerned with the social development of risk of discontent and its effects on individuals and on families (Runciman 1966; Goldthorpe and Llewellyn 1980; Young and Willmott 1973). Often these concerns have been with the immediate effects of relative deprivation, as is appropriate, for example, in the study of young people. But in studies of parents and those in midlife, a longer-term perspective is necessary, because they may well be prepared to tolerate perceived relative deprivation in the light of potential future opportunities for escape from that situation for their children and even themselves. Present social context and past personal experience will condition parents' and children's perceptions of the availability of benefits, as well as costs in endeavoring to help children escape present relative deprivation.

The years since the end of the Second World War have, in Britain, been a time of great social change in terms of rising standards of living and, more recently, of widening gaps between the rich and the poor, as well as changes in educational and occupational opportunities. These changes have brought new demands on family life and increasing differences between generations. This period presents, therefore, a valuable opportunity to study the interactions of individuals with changing social circumstances.

The Social Circumstances

In the immediate postwar years in Britain, there was a popular desire for change, particularly among the manual working-class mass of the population, which was proportionately much greater than today. As at the end of the First World War, people in 1944 wanted to remove the prewar barriers which class had placed to opportunity and communication. In future they wanted greater freedom of choice and equality of access not only to medical care and education but also to home ownership, better standards of living, and divorce (Addison 1985; Summerfield 1986). The election of a Labour government as the first administration after the wartime coalition revealed the strength of feeling on these subjects. This new administration was concerned not only with welfare development and housing improvement but also with restructuring the country's economy, which had to be moved from its foundation on heavy industry and undermechanized agriculture toward a new wealth-generating base. The newly elected postwar government was therefore particularly concerned with industrial policy, as well as with education, welfare, and health. Although in the short term the change in the national economic base had to be achieved by capital expenditure, it would evidently be sustained in the long run only with a better-educated and fitter work force. Thus new policies were introduced to improve health, welfare, and education to satisfy popular demand but also as a vital aspect of the future requirements of the economy (Bartlett 1977; Barnett 1986; Wadsworth 1991).

At the same time, there was also a desire for stability and a return to aspects of prewar life, especially to what was, following the disruption of war, easily perceived in retrospect as order. Many aspects of postwar pro-natalist and pro-family policies in health and welfare sought to preserve national stability (Marquand 1988; Clark 1991) and to return to prewar custom, for example, in the pressure for women not to take up paid employment after childbearing (Finch and Summerfield 1991) and usually not to undertake higher education (Halsey 1988). Contemporary changes in the arts and expansion of higher education were interpreted by some as indicators of risk to established institutions (Marwick 1982; Sissons and French 1986), just as an awesome source of change was seen in the expansion of higher education, which would enable a much greater proportion of the future generation to emerge "into social and political consciousness" (Carr 1964, 149).

In education, proposals for change were divided into those concerned to prepare children for life by means of a wide-ranging and traditional education and those motivated by the need for a better-trained work force, for whom education was to be, far more than before, a preparation for the labor market. The decisive factor in the design of the new system was the psychological premise that children's abilities and aptitudes for either academic or, alternatively, more concrete, applied work could be measured by the time they reached ten to eleven years of age. Measures at this age could, it seemed, be used to distinguish children who could best be "groomed for positions of influence . . . owing nothing to family influence or money, sifted out by intelligence tests, separated from the rest" (Sampson 1962, 185). The resulting national system of selection by tests and examinations to decide whether a child was suited either for academic or for applied education after age eleven years experienced, in practice, two kinds of difficulties. Studies of the operation of the selection system, which were published in the mid-1960s, showed an evident bias, in favor of the middle classes, in the selection of "bright" children for the academic preparation intended to lead to further or higher education (Douglas 1964). They revealed a "waste of talent," in that a surprisingly small proportion of the children of high measured intelligence were, in practice, selected for academic education from among those in manual–social class families. It looked as if the new education system embodied all the old problems of differential opportunity that it had been popularly hoped to avoid, and no amount of talk about "meritocracy" could cover the evidence or the pressure for further change, which followed in due course, for a nonselective and comprehensive system of education.

Perceptions of risk associated with change, as well as the necessity for change, which had been discussed at a national level, were equally a problem for parents whose children were to be the products of the welfare state, subjected to educational testing and possible selection for higher education. There were reasons why the prospect of higher education for their children was not of unmitigated attraction to all parents. The working-class majority of parents, who had at that time much lower purchasing power than today, were sometimes reluctant to lose the increase in household income associated with a child staying on at school and into further and higher education (Douglas 1964), particularly since few mothers were then in paid occupation and the great majority of families relied on the earnings of the father, the family member likely to live for the shortest time. Parents also foresaw a risk of future alienation from children who had been to academically inclined schools or to university and had learned other ways and other interests. For working-class children, selection for academic school was to risk ridicule from class peers and social and family divisions created by the demands of homework (Young and Willmott 1962); it was also a source of anxiety for working-class parents that "their grammar-school-educated children will be ashamed of them" (Stacey 1960, 140).

For manual–social class parents, therefore, the prospect of easier access to better education for children presented a dilemma. On one hand, education was popularly seen as the route to advancement in occupation and income and thus to the greater freedom of choice in many aspects of life that was then collectively greatly desired. On the other hand, at a personal level, a child who pursued the more academic route to extended education might in many respects, it was feared, be lost to the family and to the community of origin, whereas children who did not take that route would continue to belong to the same community (Young and Willmott 1962).

To assess the results of such far-reaching change, especially that of the expansion of higher education, the long-term effects of upward social mobility have been widely studied. Researchers have explored the extent to which newly increased opportunities for upward mobility have been evenly distributed (Glass 1954; Lipset and Bendix 1959; Goldthorpe and Llewellyn 1980), whether the experience of social mobility carried with it a raised risk of isolation from contemporaries and family of origin (Blau 1956; Musgrove 1963; Stacey 1967; Goldthorpe and Llewellyn 1980); and whether the traditional family structure of extended kin relations—living close by and stable in terms of occupation and location over a number of generations—could possibly be maintained in such circumstances (Anshen 1949). Answers to these kinds of questions about social structure remain of great importance for social policy and for understanding how social change occurs.

Several aspects of these questions have been examined in a longitudinal study of British children born soon after the Second World War. These children come from a nationally representative sample of families (Wadsworth et al. 1992). They were among the first to experience the new educational system designed to provide a more highly educated work force, and the working lives of their parents were touched by the beginnings of this change, as seen in the unusually high rates of social mobility among their fathers (Douglas 1964; Wadsworth 1991). As already described, the social context at that time also exerted pressures to conform to prewar stereotypes of higher education as a predominantly masculine province, recruiting largely from the upper, nonmanual social classes; of occupation as largely for men and a matter for women only in the years before family life; and of caring for elderly parents as a matter for women. This cohort has been studied regularly since birth and most recently in middle life, thus presenting the chance to ask whether the postwar opportunities for upward social mobility,

173

newly introduced through education, had in the long term the expected effect of decreasing contacts with families of origin. This continues to be an important question, particularly now that the cohort's parents are in later life and likely to be in increasing need of care.

The Longitudinal Study and Chapter Objectives

The birth cohort study was begun in 1946 as an investigation of the medical and social circumstances of birth in Britain. A cohort of all births in one week (N = 13,687) was studied, with a follow-up undertaken of a national sample stratified by social class (N = 5,362). In this chapter, the findings have been weighted to compensate for this social class stratification. Using a wide range of methods, researchers have collected information from that sample nineteen times since birth: ten times in childhood and adolescence (at two to fifteen years of age), and nine times in adult life, most recently at ages forty-three to forty-four. At that age contact was achieved with 85 percent (N = 3,854) of the targeted sample, which excluded those in the follow-up sample who had died (7 percent of those selected for follow-up), were currently resident abroad (eleven percent), or who had previously refused further cooperation (10 percent) (Wadsworth et al. 1992). First offspring born to members of this birth cohort when they were aged nineteen to thirty-six were followed up at ages four and eight (N = 1,805) in a home interview study of childrearing, based on interviews with mothers. Findings on mental and physical health, education, and social circumstances of the birth cohort and their offspring have been summarized elsewhere (Wadsworth 1991).

In this chapter I will examine six aspects of midlife that may well have been affected by childhood experience of social and family pressures for and against educational attainment: occupational attainment and satisfaction, satisfaction with family life, care of elderly parents, recall of own childhood, and two aspects of the upbringing of the firstborn child. Data used include information collected during childhood, at interviews with cohort members in adult life, particularly that at ages forty-three to forty-four, and from the study of cohort mothers' upbringing of their firstborn offspring.

FINDINGS
The Perspective in Midlife

In midlife (at ages forty-three to forty-four) 35 percent of cohort members still had both parents alive, 46 percent had one living parent, and 19 percent had experienced the death of both parents. The great majority had at least one child (89 percent of women and 82 percent of men), and 8 percent of men and 14 percent of women had one or more than one grandchild. Most had married (92 percent of men and 97 percent of women), and 13 percent of men and 17 percent of women had been married more than once. Figure 5.1 summarizes the circumstances at this age.

There were clear distinctions in family circumstances in midlife according to the circumstances of family of origin. Those from manual–social class families of origin experienced significantly higher rates of parental death and divorce and of own death, marriage, and divorce (Wadsworth 1991), and they were significantly more likely to have children and grandchildren and at younger ages compared with those from nonmanual families of origin.

Father's change of social class during the time when the cohort member was aged four to fifteen (1950–61) also influenced midlife circumstances (summarized in table 5.1). Rising paternal social class during this time was associated with a significantly greater chance of parents' survival, at least until their cohort offspring's midlife. Rising paternal social class was also associated with reduced risks of divorce in both generations, but the experience while aged four to fifteen years of falling paternal social class was associated with parents' and, later, own divorce. Falling social class, which was less common (3 percent of fathers experienced downward social mobility), was associated with an increased chance among cohort members of having children and of having the first birth at an age significantly younger than did other cohort members. On the other hand, rising class was also associated with increased chances of having children, but at a later age.

Education played an important part in these associations in both generations.[1] Manual-social class fathers were significantly more likely to have risen in social class and nonmanual fathers less likely to have fallen if one or the other parent had a higher school-leaving qualification. In turn, cohort members whose fathers had risen in social class had a greatly increased chance of gaining higher-level qualifications (28 percent gained higher qualifications), and those who experienced a fall in paternal social class had significantly reduced chances of gaining higher qualifications (15 percent). Although this was true for all cohort members, the gender difference (table 5.2) is striking. As with men, women's chances of education and training attainment benefited from high or rising paternal social class and were eroded by falling social

FIGURE 5.1. Study Members at Ages 43–44 in Relation to Older and Younger Generations, Divided by Social Class of Family of Origin.

Neither Parent Alive (19% of the population, of whom 20% are NM and 80% are M)	One Parent Alive (46% of the population, of whom 25% are NM and 75% are M)	Both Parents Alive (35% of the population, of whom 30% are NM and 70% are M)
18% of NM origin & 14% of M origin have no children	13% of NM origin & 15% of M origin have no children	18% of NM origin & 12% of M origin have no children
82% of NM origin & 86% of M origin are parents	87% of NM origin & 85% of M origin are parents	82% of NM origin & 88% of M origin are parents
6% of NM origin & 16% of M origin are grandparents	3% of NM & 13% of M origin are grandparents	5% of NM & 11% of M origin are grandparents

Note: NM = father in nonmanual class occupation when cohort member aged 4 years. M = father in manual class occupation when cohort member aged 4 years.

TABLE 5.1. Changing Paternal Social Class and Its Relation to Other Family Circumstances of Study Member (SM)

Change in Paternal Class, SM Aged 4–15 Years (1950–61)	% Both Parents Dead When SM Aged 43 Years (1989)	% Parents Divorced When SM Aged 0–15 Years (1946–61)	% SM Divorced by Age 43 (1989)	% with First Child Born after SM Aged 31 Years	% SM with Grandchildren by Age 43	Mean (SD) Score (range 0–50) of Parents' Interest in SM's Education while Aged 5–11 Years	
						Boys	Girls
Static (nonmanual occupation, 22%)	12	5	13	13	4	37 (11.5)	37 (11.9)
Falling (nonmanual to manual, 3%)	19	7	21	1	9	30 (13.4)	35 (11.1)
Static (manual occupation, 69%)	19	6	15	8	13	26 (13.7)	28 (13.4)
Rising (manual to nonmanual, 7%)	14	4	16	15	7	31 (12.2)	33 (13.6)
TOTAL (N = 8,468)	Both parents dead = 977 $p < .001$	Parents divorced = 471 $p < .03$	SM divorced = 835 $p < .01$	Children born after SM 31 years = 549 $p < .001$	Grandchildren = 516 $p < .001$	Total parents = 4,097	Total parents = 3,885

TABLE 5.2. Changing Paternal Social Class of Origin and Its Association with Subsequent Highest Educational Training Attainment for Men and Women

| Paternal Social Class and Its Change, Cohort Member Aged 4–15 Years | Gender of Cohort Member | Highest Level of Education/training (%) | | | | |
		No Qualification	Minimum School-Leaving Qualifications	Maximum School-Leaving Qualifications[a]	University-Level Qualifications[a]	TOTAL (=100%)
Nonmanual throughout	Men	23.4	17.5	34.1	25.0	901
	Women	26.8	28.6	35.6	9.0	863
Falling from nonmanual to manual	Men	63.5	19.1	13.0	4.3	115
	Women	61.8	26.0	11.5	0.8	131
Manual throughout	Men	61.0	13.2	21.7	4.1	2,807
	Women	67.2	22.3	9.5	1.0	2,736
Rising from manual to nonmanual	Men	47.4	22.8	20.2	9.6	302
	Women	47.4	26.3	19.4	6.9	232

[a]Described throughout this chapter as high levels of educational attainment.

class. But rising social class did not lift the chances of attainment of those who began life in manual-social class families to the level of those who were always in a high (nonmanual) social class. Women's rates of high attainment in education were considerably less than those of men, whatever the social class circumstances, because of generally held lower expectations of attainment by women and consequently fewer opportunities in Britain at that time (Halsey 1987; Wadsworth 1991). At five to ten years of age, however, parental interest in education was significantly higher for girls than for boys (table 5.1) in families in which the father was in a nonmanual occupation or rose to or fell from a nonmanual occupation during that time; in families in manual social circumstances throughout this period, parental enthusiasm did not vary with the gender of the child. There was greater enthusiasm for the education of girls, at this age, than for boys, regardless of birth order, but by children's adolescence, parental ambitions for girls' and boys' careers had changed to the opposite position, and ambitions for boys in manual-class families began to lag behind those in nonmanual-class circumstances (Douglas 1964; Douglas, Ross, and Simpson 1968).

Perceptions of occupation in midlife. Educational attainment was strongly associated not only with earlier family and social circumstances but also with subsequent income and occupation (Kuh and Wadsworth 1991), and by midlife, which must have seemed for many the peak time in their career, it was associated with perception of satisfaction in occupation. By this time (age forty-three to forty-four years), 91 percent of men and 80 percent of women were in paid employment, and three questions were asked about current perceptions of occupation (see table 5.3). In answer to the question, "How satisfied are you with what you have accomplished in your working life?" many (49 percent) felt "very satisfied" with their current employment, but women reported significantly more dissatisfaction than did men. Practically a third (32 percent) of the study population, in answer to the question, "Do you feel that you have achieved all you are likely to in your working life or do you have further ambitions for the future?" said that they had nothing more to achieve; women were strikingly less inclined than men to feel they had, in this sense, "much more to achieve." Similarly, in answer to the question, "Looking back, would you say that you have had the opportunity to do what you wanted to do in your working life or have your opportunities been limited?"

TABLE 5.3. Occupational Satisfaction and Expectations in Midlife
(43–44 years)

Perceptions of	Low Qualifications		High Qualifications	
Occupation	Men (%)	Women (%)	Men (%)	Women (%)
Working life opportunities described as				
Hardly limited at all	55	44	61	46
Limited a little	31	36	33	38
Very limited	14	20	6	16
N	2,255	2,757	1,259	689
Satisfaction with accomplishments in working life				
Very satisfied	52	48	46	48
Fairly satisfied	31	31	41	34
Dissatisfied	17	21	13	18
N	2,272	2,755	1,259	685
Amount to achieve at work in future				
Much more to achieve	26	14	32	21
Something more to achieve	46	40	56	54
Nothing more to achieve	28	46	12	25
N	2,257	2,745	1,255	686

women much more often than men perceived opportunities at work as very limited.

Men and women whose parents had been enthusiastic over their education were, in midlife, significantly more optimistic than others about future work achievements and opportunities. This long-term positive effect of parental enthusiasm, assessed before eleven years of age, was evident in men's optimism about current work and future achievements and opportunities at forty-three to forty-four years of age at all levels (i.e., all five social classes) of occupation but, in women, among only those in nonmanual occupations. Perceptions of having much more to achieve in working life and of few limitations to occupational opportunities were greatest in men and women who had attained higher educational qualifications.

Work satisfaction scores from each of the three indicators shown in table 5.3 were summed and the relationship of satisfaction scores with earlier and contemporary life factors examined; the findings are shown in table 5.4. Data from earlier life showed that for both men and women, social class of family of origin, father's social mobility, parents' enthusiasm for education, and own attainment in education were associated with work satisfaction, but experience of parental divorce was not related. In men, higher education raised the likelihood of work satisfaction, whatever the class of the family of origin, but most among those from nonmanual families. In women this pattern was the same in those from manual origins, but higher education scarcely differentiated work satisfaction among those from nonmanual families. High parental enthusiasm for education was associated with high work satisfaction in both sexes, as was rising paternal social class.

In adult life a rise in social class compared with that of the father's class and current nonmanual occupation were associated in both sexes with high work satisfaction. Differences between partner's and study member's education was of note only in men, where low attainment in education for both study member and partner was associated with least likelihood of high work satisfaction. Family life circumstances seemed more important to women's assessment of work satisfaction than to that of men. Women who had never married and women who had no children expressed highest levels of work satisfaction, whereas in men, the opposite was found.

The combined score of occupational satisfaction was used in a regression analysis to examine the relative power and independence of all associated factors. Although the total explanation of variance (R^2) was low (7.1 percent in men and 6.4 percent in women), in women the childhood variables explained a smaller proportion of variance (2.1 percent) than did the adult factors (4.3 percent), but in men childhood information explained more of the variance (4.0 percent) than the adult factors (3.1 percent). Of all the childhood variables, level of qualification made the greatest contribution in both sexes, but in men, parental enthusiasm for education was of much greater importance than in women. When the effect of parental enthusiasm for education was removed from the analysis, the adult variables accounted for the greater part of the variance explained, as in women. Of the adult variables, social class of occupation was the most powerful among men, with small contributions from the other variables; in women, marital history, having children, and partner's level of education also made significant contributions.

Work satisfaction in midlife was evidently associated with a number of important factors from the previous generation, which may be sum-

TABLE 5.4. Percentage of Men and Women with High Work Satisfaction (top two-fifths of scores)

Childhood and Adult Life Factors	Men		Women	
	%	N	%	N
Social and educational origins				
Nonmanual family of origin				
Low educational attainment	37	347	24	477
High educational attainment	48	468	22	348
Manual family of origin				
Low educational attainment	31	1,910	15	2,268
High educational attainment	37	787	26	338
	(***)		(***)	
Father's social mobility while study member aged 0–15 years				
Nonmanual static	44	642	23	636
Falling nonmanual to manual	43	92	26	106
Manual static	32	1,915	17	1,912
Rising manual to nonmanual	37	211	22	151
	(***)		(**)	
Parents' enthusiasm for education while study member aged 5–10 years				
Lowest fourth	26	1,081	16	897
Second fourth	33	855	19	751
Third fourth	42	629	19	757
Highest fourth	45	651	21	748
	(***)		(*)	
Parents' divorce				
Not divorced	35	3,431	19	3,303
Divorced while study member aged 0–15 years	40	277	15	279
	(NS)		(NS)	
Intergenerational social mobility				
Nonmanual in both generations	49	676	23	647
Rising manual to nonmanual	24	172	15	149
Manual in both generations	24	1,440	12	916
Falling nonmanual to manual	44	1,325	21	1,618
	(***)		(***)	

TABLE 5.4. (*Continued*)

Childhood and Adult Life Factors	Men		Women	
	%	N	%	N
Own social class at age 43				
Nonmanual	46	2,001	22	2,265
Manual	24	1,612	12	1,065
	(***)		(***)	
Study member's and spouse/partner's education				
Study member has high educational attainment				
Partner has high educational attainment	42	504	23	432
Partner has low educational attainment	41	605	19	128
	(NS)		(NS)	
Study member has low educational attainment				
Partner has high educational attainment	38	358	18	777
Partner has low educational attainment	31	1,525	17	1,443
	(**)		(NS)	
Marital history by age 43				
Married once and still married	36	2,907	19	2,818
Married more than once	36	500	15	581
Never married	30	254	25	110
	(NS)		(**)	
Parenting by age 43				
Children	36	3,062	17	3,178
No children	32	620	32	396
	(*)		(***)	

$*p < .05.$ $**p < .01.$ $***p < .001.$

marized as those indicating optimism and energy in the parental generation—namely, parental enthusiasm for education—and the social class and social mobility of the family of origin.

Perceptions of family life. Satisfaction with family life at forty-three to forty-four years of age was assessed with the question, "Looking back, how satisfied are you with what you have accomplished in your home and family life?" Women (93 percent), a little more often than men (91 percent), were satisfied or very satisfied. Past and present characteristics of those currently dissatisfied with family life are provided in table 5.5.

Men, but not women, with experience of parental divorce were significantly less satisfied with family life at age forty-three to forty-four years, but only if they themselves had not been divorced. Men and women who had experienced falling paternal social class during their own childhood were significantly less satisfied than others with home and family life, and greatest satisfaction was reported by those who had experienced rising paternal social class during childhood. Women who had experienced the death of both parents felt significantly less satisfaction than did other women with their family life, but parental death did not affect men in this respect.

Men and women with low qualifications who had been raised in nonmanual-social class families of origin had significantly lower levels of satisfaction with family life, as did women with high qualifications who originated from manual-social class families. Those with low qualifications were now, in midlife, particularly dissatisfied with family life if their parents had expressed high interest in their education during childhood. In other words, those who may have fallen short of their parents' expectations in education were overrepresented among the dissatisfied.

Men and women who had never married reported the most dissatisfaction with family life in midlife; there was no variation with the numbers of own marriages experienced. Those who had never been parents were significantly less satisfied compared with those who were parents, and the later the age at first parenting, the greater the likelihood of reported satisfaction at forty-three to forty-four years of age. Men currently in manual-social class occupations expressed significantly more dissatisfaction with current family life than men in nonmanual occupations, as did women who had not changed their social class between generations.

Logistic regression analysis showed that of all the significantly associated variables, current manual social class, manual social class of family of origin, parental divorce, and having no children were the factors significantly associated with dissatisfaction with family life among men, once the effects of all associated variables have been taken into account. Among women, only experience of marriage and age at birth of first child remained significant.

Care of Elderly Parents by Cohort Members in Middle Life

When cohort members were forty-three to forty-four years old, the mean age of their surviving mothers was 70.6 years (SD = 5.2), and fathers, 72.1 years (SD = 5.1). The majority (70 percent) of cohort subjects who lived within an hour's drive of their parents saw them once a week or more often, and the only variation in rate of contact among this population who lived nearby was the significantly fewer contacts made by men and women from nonmanual families of origin who had received further or higher education. As anticipated, significantly greater proportions of those with high educational qualifications lived at a distance (one hour's drive or more) from their parents (28 percent of men and 38 percent of women), compared with those with low qualifications (15 percent of men and 15 percent of women). Those who came from manual families of origin and had high qualifications were less inclined to live at a distance (26 percent of men and 35 percent of women) than were those with similar qualifications but from nonmanual families of origin (33 percent of men and 41 percent of women), just as those with low qualifications lived closer to home if they had begun life in a manual- rather than a nonmanual-class family. High parental interest in education added to the effect of high qualifications in increasing the likelihood of residence at a greater distance, in both sexes and regardless of social class of the family of origin.

Emotional support for parents. Cohort members at age forty-three to forty-four described their current (midlife) provision of emotional support for parents and the degree of help they provided with household tasks and with finance. Regular provision of emotional support for parents was reported more often by women (45 percent) than by men (29 percent), and men more often never gave emotional support (36 percent of men) compared with women (23 percent). Support was significantly less often provided by those who lived more than an hour's drive from parents (54 percent of men and 72 percent of women) than by those who lived within an hour's drive (67 percent of men and 79 percent of women). The association of earlier life and contemporary life characteristics with propensity never to provide emotional support to elderly parents is given in table 5.6.

A number of aspects of childhood were strongly associated with midlife emotional support of elderly parents. Parental divorce or separation, experienced while the subjects now in midlife were aged zero

TABLE 5.5. Percentage of Men and Women Who Were Dissatisfied with Family Life at Age Forty-three to Forty-four

	Men		Women	
Childhood and Adult Life Factors	%	N	%	N
Social and educational origins				
Nonmanual family of origin				
Low educational attainment	13	358	9	500
High educational attainment	8	470	5	353
Manual family of origin				
Low educational attainment	9	1,918	6	2,335
High educational attainment	8	787	8	346
	(***)		(***)	
Father's social mobility while study member aged 0–15 years				
Nonmanual static	10	656	7	662
Falling nonmanual to manual	14	92	12	106
Manual static	8	1,915	7	1,955
Rising manual to nonmanual	8	211	5	163
	(**)		(**)	
Parents' enthusiasm for education while study member aged 5–10 years				
Lowest fourth	8	1,088	8	935
Second fourth	9	859	4	767
Third fourth	10	636	7	785
Highest fourth	10	649	10	766
	(***)		(***)	
Parents' divorce				
Not divorced	9	3,443	7	3,401
Divorced while study member aged 0–15 years	15	285	9	289
	(***)		(NS)	
Intergenerational social mobility				
Nonmanual in both generations	9	675	8	653
Rising manual to nonmanual	11	176	6	154
Manual in both generations	11	1,444	7	926
Falling nonmanual to manual	7	1,327	6	1,618
	(***)		(**)	

TABLE 5.5. (*Continued*)

Childhood and Adult Life Factors	Men		Women	
	%	N	%	N
Study member's and spouse/partner's education				
Study member has high educational attainment				
Partner has high educational attainment	5	506	4	440
Partner has low educational attainment	4	606	5	131
	(*)		(NS)	
Study member has low educational attainment				
Partner has high educational attainment	5	358	3	1,491
Partner has low educational attainment	7	1,529	6	796
	(**)		(***)	
Marital history by age 43				
Married once and still married	8	2,917	5	2,901
Married more than once	9	500	12	597
Never married	20	264	15	115
	(***)		(***)	
Parenting by age 43				
Children	8	3,071	6	3,280
No children	15	631	11	402
	(***)		(***)	
Parents' survival when study member aged 43 years				
Neither alive	10	685	9	681
Only mother alive	10	1,245	5	1,356
Only father alive	8	406	8	366
Both alive	8	1,317	7	1,219
	(NS)		(**)	

*$p < .05$. **$p < .01$. ***$p < .001$.

TABLE 5.6. Percentage of Men and Women Who Never Provided
Emotional Support for Elderly Parents

	Men		Women	
Childhood and Adult Life Factors	%	N	%	N
Social and educational origins				
Nonmanual family of origin				
Low educational attainment	45	300	25	413
High educational attainment	38	399	24	317
Manual family of origin				
Low educational attainment	34	1,476	22	1,786
High educational attainment	36	608	20	277
	(**)		(NS)	
Father's social mobility while study member aged 0–15 years				
Nonmanual static	40	572	25	585
Falling nonmanual to manual	43	75	26	81
Manual static	36	1,514	21	1,555
Rising manual to nonmanual	41	177	31	140
	(NS)		(**)	
Parents' enthusiasm for education while study member aged 5–10 years				
Lowest fourth	35	829	30	685
Second fourth	35	656	21	625
Third fourth	43	524	21	609
Highest fourth	33	519	20	638
	(**)		(***)	
Parents' divorce				
Not divorced	35	2,749	22	2,709
Divorced while study member aged 0–15 years	49	199	35	200
	(***)		(***)	

to fifteen years, was powerfully associated for both sexes with greatly
reduced frequency of emotional support for parents. Among women,
the relation was to age at experience of parental divorce, with lowest
levels of current support coming from those who experienced parental
divorce when less than five years old; in men there was no comparable
relationship with age. The second aspect was the relationship of parent's enthusiasm and concern for the study subject's education during
childhood with current emotional support for parents. Study members
were significantly inclined to give less emotional support to parents

TABLE 5.6. (*Continued*)

Childhood and Adult Life Factors	Men		Women	
	%	N	%	N
Marital history by age 43				
Married once and still married	35	2,303	23	2,307
Married more than once	45	409	22	470
Never married	41	204	18	82
	(***)		(NS)	
Parenting by age 43				
Children	35	2,446	23	2,557
No children	40	481	21	324
	(***)		(NS)	
Study member's own social class according to occupation at age 43–44				
Nonmanual	35	1,582	20	1,834
Manual	37	1,270	27	814
	(NS)		(***)	
Parents' survival when study member is aged 43–44				
Widowed mother	25	1,241	15	1,335
Widowed father	50	398	35	366
Both parents alive	43	1,309	28	1,208
	(***)		(***)	

$*p < .05.$ $**p < .01.$ $***p < .001.$

who had not been enthusiastic for their education. Women who had received high parental enthusiasm for education but then not gained higher qualifications gave more support to parents than did other women. Men whose parents had been enthusiastic for their education but who had gained only low qualifications were significantly less inclined than other men to give regular emotional support. Men from manual-social class families of origin gave more support than others, and men who had not conformed to the generally expected pattern of educational attainment (with low attainment and from nonmanual families or with high attainment and from manual class families) were least inclined to offer emotional support. Women whose fathers had risen in social class during their childhood were the least likely in midlife to give emotional support to their parents.

In middle life, women in nonmanual social classes were most inclined not to give regular emotional support to elderly parents. Women and men gave significantly more support to widowed parents, especially mothers, than to others, but not to those widows who had been divorced during the study member's childhood. Own marital history was associated with men's likelihood of giving emotional support: those who had always been single up to age forty-three and men who had been married more than once by that age gave least emotional support to parents. However, among cohort subjects who were offspring of divorced parents, greatest emotional support was given by those who by midlife had themselves experienced more than one marriage. Men with no children reported giving less emotional support, but there was no comparable association in women.

Logistic regression analyses showed the variables that independently and significantly increased the risk of never giving emotional support to parents (see table 5.7). For women, these are, in childhood, low parental enthusiasm for education and, in adult life, manual social class, living at a distance of more than one hour's drive, and having both parents alive. The analysis for men showed that of the childhood factors, parental divorce was independently significant in its association with high likelihood of never giving emotional support to parents; in adulthood the significant variables were being married more than once or never having married, being in manual social class, living at more than one hour's drive from parents, and having both parents alive.

Practical support for parents. Those who lived within one hour's drive of their elderly parents were more inclined to give help regularly with such things as decorating, gardening, and spring cleaning and with getting out and about. An additive score was made for help giving, and in the results presented below and in table 5.8, help giving is compared between those who scored in the top third of this scale, indicating a high level of helping, and those who scored in the bottom two-thirds. In this section, only data from those living within one hour's drive are analyzed. Women, more than men, gave more practical help of this kind to their parents (35 percent of women did so regularly, compared with 33 percent of men; $p < .01$).

As table 5.8 shows, widowed parents received significantly more help of this kind than others. But divorced parents received significantly less, which may be accounted for to some extent by remarriage and new forms of independence after the divorce; information on parental remarriage following divorce is not available in this study for a

TABLE 5.7a. Logistic Regression Analysis of Variables Associated
with Never Giving Emotional Support to Parents: Women Only

Childhood and Adult Life Factors	Odds Ratio	Standard Error	Significance
Childhood			
Parental divorce	1.00		
No parental divorce	0.89	.236	NS
Parental enthusiasm for education is high (top three-fourths)	1.00		
Parental enthusiasm for education is low (bottom fourth)	0.63	.128	$p < .001$
Nonmanual family of origin and low educational attainment or manual family of origin and high attainment	1.00		
Nonmanual family of origin and high attainment or manual family of origin and low attainment	0.97	.041	NS
Father's social class rising	1.00		
Father's social class static or falling	0.93	.293	NS
Adult life			
Has children	1.00		
Has no children	0.95	.184	NS
Never married or married more than once	1.00		
Married once and still married	1.26	.146	NS
Manual social class	1.00		
Nonmanual social class	0.78	.123	$p < .04$
Lives within one hour's drive of parents	1.00		
Lives farther than one hour's drive	1.36	.140	$p < .02$
Widowed parent alive	1.00		
Both parents alive	2.48	.121	$p < .001$

TABLE 5.7b. Logistic Regression Analysis of Variables Associated with Never Giving Emotional Support to Parents: Men Only

Childhood and Adult Life Factors	Odds Ratio	Standard Error	Significance
Childhood			
Parental divorce	1.00		
No parental divorce	0.51	.210	$p < .001$
Parental enthusiasm for education (continuous variable)	0.99	.004	NS
Nonmanual family of origin and low educational attainment or manual family of origin and high attainment	1.00		
Nonmanual family of origin and high attainment or manual family of origin and low attainment	0.97	.031	NS
Father's social class rising	1.00		
Father's social class static or falling	1.18	.176	NS
Adult life			
Has children	1.00		
Has no children	0.80	.136	NS
Never married or married more than once	1.00		
Married once and still married	0.67	.125	$p < .001$
Manual social class	1.00		
Nonmanual social class	0.73	.103	$p < .01$
Lives within one hour's drive of parents	1.00		
Lives farther than one hour's drive	2.14	.123	$p < .001$
Widowed parent alive	1.00		
Both parents alive	2.50	.103	$p < .01$

sufficiently long period, however, to enable this to be further explored. Most help was given by those who were only or second or subsequently born offspring, and least, by those who were firstborn of several; significantly more help was reported as given by those who had never had children and those who had most recently had their first child. These findings may be because of the increased likelihood of those with no children living by age forty-three to forty-four with their elderly parents. Among men, those currently in manual social classes gave most help, and least was given by men who had experienced downward social mobility. Among women most support was also given by those in manual social classes. There was no variation in relation to educational attainment, and only in men was practical help associated with parental enthusiasm for education.

Multiple regression analyses were used to explore the independent significance of the associations with the provision of practical help to parents. In men, data from childhood information accounted for only 0.6 percent of the variance, compared with 4.3 percent accounted for by adult information. Greatest contribution was made by information on current social class and widowhood of parents. Similarly, among women, only a small amount (2.4 percent) of all variance accounted for was due to the childhood data, with 8.0 percent due to adult data; the most salient contributions were made by information on parental divorce, achieved level of education and its association with current own social class, and widowhood of parents.

Financial help was given regularly a little more often by men (12 percent) than by women (11 percent), and the associations of regular giving with other factors are shown in table 5.9. Naturally, those who were likely to have higher incomes—those in nonmanual occupations or who had risen to nonmanual occupations and those with higher educational attainment—were the most likely to be able to offer financial help to elderly parents. Those with more education gave significantly more often if they had come from manual–social class families of origin, as did those who had risen, intergenerationally, in social class: in other words, those who had attained more in their adult generation than their parents had in the previous generation had been more inclined to give financial help. Conversely, those with the least education, especially those with partners who also had low education attainment, were less likely to help regularly with finance. Those who had never married or had never had children were more often helpers than others because of their high likelihood of living with their parents. And, as in other aspects of relationships, divorced parents were helped least, and widows, most.

In multiple regression analyses of men's data, a total of 12.2 percent of the variance was accounted for, almost entirely by the variables from adulthood (12 percent) describing current social class, level of partner's qualifications, proximity of residence in relation to that of parents,

TABLE 5.8. Percentage of Men and Women Who Had Regularly
Given Most Practical Help (top third of scores) to Parents

	Men		Women	
Childhood and Adult Life Factors	%	N	%	N
Parents' enthusiasm for education				
Lowest fourth	35	733	35	548
Second fourth	40	514	37	526
Third fourth	30	391	35	483
Highest fourth	31	363	35	467
	(*)		(NS)	
Parents' divorce				
Not divorced	34	2,176	37	2,127
Divorced while study member aged 0– 15 years	25	133	16	151
	(***)		(***)	
Birth order				
Only child	34	78	35	263
First of several	30	665	26	691
Second- or later-born	37	1,198	40	1,145
	(***)		(***)	
Marital history by age 43				
Married once and still married	33	1,825	34	1,794
Married more than once	25	309	37	371
Never married	63	148	67	66
	(***)		(***)	
Parenting by age 43				
Children	32	1,936	35	2,026
No children	42	356	39	248
	(***)		(NS)	
Own social mobility				
Nonmanual static	32	384	30	382
Falling nonmanual to manual	19	124	70	96
Manual static	43	996	30	985
Rising manual to nonmanual	25	730	31	622
	(***)		(***)	

whether the respondent was single or married or had any children,
and whether the parent was widowed. Among women, only 6.4 percent
of variance was accounted for by similar analyses, again with by far
the greater part of the explanation (5.6 percent) coming from variables
describing adult circumstances. The most contributory variables were

TABLE 5.8. (*Continued*)

Childhood and Adult Life Factors	Men %	Men N	Women %	Women N
Own adult social class of occupation at age 43–44				
Nonmanual	27	1,114	31	1,367
Manual	40	1,120	44	718
	(***)		(***)	
Parents' survival				
Widowed mother	40	1,000	46	1,055
Widowed father	36	275	20	299
Both parents alive	27	1,034	28	924
	(***)		(***)	
Age at birth of first child				
<19	18	76	29	294
20–25	32	843	34	1,149
26–29	35	635	39	395
>30	32	382	41	188
	(**)		(**)	

$*p < .05.$ $**p < .01.$ $***p < .001.$

widowhood of parent, own experience of more than one marriage, childlessness or otherwise, and proximity of residence.

Childhood in Retrospect

Recollection of childhood was investigated using information given by women cohort members (N = 1,805) at ages twenty-three to thirty-seven years in the course of a home interview about the upbringing of their firstborn when that child was four (Wadsworth 1986). Women were asked to rate the general level of happiness, or otherwise, of their childhood, and 11 percent recalled their childhood as unhappy. These 11 percent were significantly more inclined to recall relationships with their mother and with their father as reserved, rather than affectionate, and to recall their parents' relationship with each other as poor (63 percent of those who had been unhappy in childhood compared with 13 percent of those who recalled childhood as a happy time). Parents of those who looked back on childhood as an unhappy time were also more often divorced (23 percent) compared with parents of those who recalled a happy childhood (7 percent). A high level of parental interest in education, on the other hand, provided significant protection

TABLE 5.9. Percentage of Men and Women Who Had Regularly
Given Financial Help to Parents

Childhood and Adult Life Factors	Men %	Men N	Women %	Women N
Social and educational origins				
Nonmanual family of origin				
Low educational attainment	7	295	9	422
High educational attainment	15	401	6	320
Manual family of origin				
Low educational attainment	12	1,517	11	1,815
High educational attainment	13	613	14	277
	(**)		(**)	
Parents' enthusiasm for education while study member aged 5–10 years				
Lowest fourth	10	832	11	686
Second fourth	15	650	12	613
Third fourth	12	525	11	601
Highest fourth	14	504	7	637
	(**)		(**)	
Parents' divorce				
Not divorced	13	2,754	11	2,719
Divorced while study member aged 0– 15 years	10	236	3	236
	(NS)		(***)	
Intergenerational social mobility				
Nonmanual in both generations	15	562	8	582
Rising manual to nonmanual	15	1,036	12	1,280
Manual in both generations	10	1,144	11	723
Falling nonmanual to manual	3	151	14	116
	(***)		(***)	
Study member (SM) and partner education				
SM high educational attainment				
Partner high educational attainment	13	420	10	371
Partner low educational attainment	11	466	12	133
	(NS)		(NS)	
SM low educational attainment				
Partner high educational attainment	17	286	14	617
Partner low educational attainment	9	1,208	9	1,163
	(***)		(*)	

TABLE 5.9. (*Continued*)

Childhood and Adult Life Factors	Men		Women	
	%	N	%	N
Marital history by age 43				
Married once and still married	11	2,337	9	2,336
Married more than once	14	417	16	476
Never married	26	204	16	88
	(***)		(***)	
Parenting by age 43				
Children	11	2,472	10	2,618
No children	19	497	13	329
	(***)		(***)	
Survival of parents				
Widowed mother	19	1,225	16	1,333
Widowed father	6	395	11	365
Both parents alive	8	1,304	6	1,192
	(***)		(***)	
Proximity of own home to that of parent(s)				
Living within one hour's drive	14	2,312	12	2,284
Living farther than one hour's drive	6	579	7	579
	(***)		(***)	

$*p < .05.$ $**p < .01.$ $***p < .001.$

against recollection of an unhappy childhood (8 percent were unhappy when parental interest was high), compared with low parental interest (14 percent recalled an unhappy childhood), but it did not offset the effect of a poor parental relationship. Remembered childhood unhappiness was associated with another indicator of parental problems, namely, father's falling social class: 27 percent of women with this experience recalled an unhappy childhood, compared with 8 percent of women from all other circumstances. This effect was not offset by high parental interest in education or by own high educational attainment.

Consideration of all significant childhood factors together, in a logistic regression analysis, showed the statistically independent variables related to recall of childhood as unhappy to be parental divorce, falling paternal social class, recollections of reserved relationships with mother, and a poor relationship between parents (table 5.10). Looking forward from the ages at which this information was collected to age forty-three to forty-four, it was clear that recollection of an unhappy childhood while a young parent was a precursor of later, midlife, per-

TABLE 5.10. Logistic Regression Analysis of Variables Associated with the Dependent Variable, Recollection of Childhood as Generally Happy or Unhappy

Childhood Factor	Odds Ratio	Standard Error	Significance
Recollection of parents' relationship			
(3-point scale)	1.00		
	3.40	.299	<.001
Social class of father			
Static (N = 1,377)	1.00		
Falling (N = 55)	5.99	.355	<.001
Relationship with mother			
Affectionate (N = 663)	1.00		
Reserved (N = 769)	3.46	.251	<.001
Parents' marital status			
Not divorced (N = 1,325)	1.00		
Divorced (N = 107)	3.39	.299	<.001
Relationship with father			
Affectionate (N = 647)	1.00		
Reserved (N = 785)	1.97	.251	<.01
Parental interest in education			
(score 0–50)	0.99	.008	NS

ception of significantly greater dissatisfaction with work and family life compared with others in this subsample of cohort mothers, as well as a greater number of marriages. But it was not associated with care of elderly parents or with midlife emotional relations with parents.

Cohort Members' Upbringing of Firstborn Children

Two aspects of child upbringing by cohort women have been studied, using information collected at home interviews with mothers when their firstborn child was four years old and eight years old. The first aspect is parental enthusiasm for the education of this child. Like the comparable data about cohort subjects used above, this information on their offspring was derived from mothers' and teachers' reports about the child up to age eight and about parents' relationships with the school. The second aspect of upbringing is provided by information on the nature of expressions of affection between mother and child, reported by the mother when the child was aged four years.

Parental enthusiasm for firstborn offspring's education. There was proportionately greater enthusiasm for education among parents of eight-
year-olds in the cohort generation of mothers (born 1946) than among
their mothers (born between 1898 and 1931). In the older mothers'
generation, 33 percent had been in the top quartile of scores of enthusiasm for their offspring's education (42 percent of those who were
mothers of firstborn children), compared with 50 percent in the cohort
generation of mothers of firstborn children. In both generations, significantly higher parental enthusiasm existed for the education of girls
than for boys.

Table 5.11 shows how high levels of enthusiasm for their eight-
year-old child's education were most often expressed by mothers with
higher education, whose own mothers had, in their generation, also
been enthusiastic for their child's education. High enthusiasm was also
associated with rising social class in both generations. Mothers who
had been only offspring in their families of origin had the greatest
chance of high enthusiasm for education, and high enthusiasm was
associated as well with current adulthood recall of the parents' relationship during own childhood as good and with recall of own relationship
with father as demonstrative. But relationship with mother was more
inclined to be recalled as reserved by those who now had high enthusiasm for their eight-year-old's education.

The extent of variance accounted for by these factors in cohort
member parents' enthusiasm for their child's education is shown in
table 5.12. Childhood variables made the greatest contribution, followed by those describing mothers' recollections of their childhood
and by level of education they had attained.

Affection between cohort mother and firstborn. Mothers' answers to a
question about how they and their firstborn four-year-old showed affection toward each other were grouped into those describing the relationship as affectionate and mutually initiated (71 percent), affectionate but usually initiated either by the mother or by the child (23
percent), or generally fairly reserved (6 percent). Information on circumstances of family of origin and mothers' recollections of their
childhood was used to seek explanation for this differentiation of styles
of affection.

Mothers from manual-social class families of origin were significantly less likely to describe their relationships as mutually warm (69
percent), compared with mothers from nonmanual origins (78 per-

TABLE 5.11. Percentage of Cohort Mothers Expressing
High Levels of Enthusiasm (top fourth of scores)
for Their 8-Year-Old Child's Education

Childhood and Adult Life Factors	%	N
Social and educational origins		
Nonmanual family of origin		
Low educational attainment	15	91
High educational attainment	46	78
Manual family of origin		
Low educational attainment	16	469
High educational attainment	52	71
	(***)	
Father's social mobility while study member aged 0–15 years		
Nonmanual static	34	115
Falling nonmanual to manual	11	37
Manual static	15	409
Rising manual to nonmanual	51	47
	(***)	
Own parent's enthusiasm for daughter's education		
Lowest fourth	9	173
2nd fourth	10	136
3rd fourth	24	169
Highest fourth	44	162
	(***)	
Parents' divorce		
Not divorced	23	669
Divorced while study member aged 0–15 years	18	55
	(*)	
Intergenerational social mobility		
Nonmanual in both generations	34	122
Rising manual to nonmanual	24	316
Manual in both generations	20	103
Falling nonmanual to manual	9	23
	(***)	

cent), and more likely to say that they were not mutually initiated (17 percent, compared with 25 percent of those from nonmanual families); reserved relationships were not significantly differentiated by class of origin. Similarly, in the current generation, when social class of the partner was manual, there was a significantly raised likelihood that the

TABLE 5.11. (*Continued*)

Childhood and Adult Life Factors	%	N
Highest level of educational attainment		
Below school-leaving exams	16	560
All higher levels	49	149
	(***)	
Mother's birth order		
Only child	30	81
First of several	26	199
Second or later born	18	381
	(***)	
Recollection of parents' relationship		
Very good	32	234
Good	19	246
Not good	11	104
	(***)	
Recollection of own relationship with mother		
Reserved or fairly reserved	26	335
Demonstrative	20	248
	(**)	
Recollection of own relationship with father		
Reserved or fairly reserved	21	335
Demonstrative	23	240
	(*)	

*$p < .05$. **$p < .01$. ***$p < .001$.

mother would describe her relationship with the firstborn child as not mutual (26 percent, compared with 18 percent in nonmanual families) or as reserved (7 percent, as compared with 3 percent) rather than mutually affectionate. This association with current social class was significant only when the mother had been in a manual–social class family in both generations. The extent of mutually warm relationships was significantly increased among mothers from manual-class origins by the experience of their parents' enthusiasm for education and, independently, by their own high educational attainment. Relationships with children among mothers from nonmanual origins were not associated with these effects of parental enthusiasm and own high educational attainment.

These associations with social class of origin seem to reflect both the class-differentiated affectional style of relationships between moth-

TABLE 5.12. Multiple Regression Analysis of Variables Significantly Associated with the Cohort Parents' Interest in the Education of Their Firstborn

Variables Entered in This Order	Beta	For Each Block of Variables Entered	
		Significance of F	R^2, % of Variance Accounted For
Step 1			
Social mobility of father	0.06		
Birth order	−0.22		
Parental divorce	0.16		
Cohort member parents' enthusiasm for education	0.27	$p < .001$	14.5
Step 2			
Level of education attained	0.22	$p < .001$	3.1
Step 3			
Intergenerational social mobility	−0.06		
Own social class	−0.11		
Partner's level of education attained	0.03	$p < .001$	1.3
Step 4			
Recollection of parents' relationship	0.08		
Recollection of relationship with father	0.17		
Recollection of relationship with mother	0.15	$p < .001$	4.9
TOTAL VARIANCE ACCOUNTED FOR			23.8

Note: Each level takes account of variables at the preceding levels.

ers and children, noted in another British study undertaken at this time (Newson and Newson 1968), and also the importance of parental concern for the child, shown here in parental enthusiasm for education. The social class effect may be a reflection of the irritations and hopelessness of life in poor social circumstances. It was seen here particularly in the mothers of manual origin whose first child was born when they were under twenty-one. They reported much lower rates of mutually warm relationships (42 percent, as compared with 73 percent in other manual-origin mothers whose first child was born later and

84 percent in mothers from nonmanual origins). Mothers who had been in manual-social class families of origin throughout their childhood were the least likely to report relationships with their firstborn as mutually affectionate (68 percent), compared with those who lived always in nonmanual-social class families (76 percent). Moving to a nonmanual status as a result of the father changing occupations was associated with reduced frequency of reports of mutually affectionate relationships (57 percent). There may be an element in the nonmanual class, as well as among educated mothers, of being more eager to give the "right answer" to these kinds of questions.

The importance of parental concern and interest was reflected, too, in women's recollections of childhood. Mothers who recalled that their parents' relationship with each other had been poor more often reported relationships with their firstborn as reserved (13 percent) than did mothers who remembered their parents as getting on well (4 percent). Reserved relationships with offspring were also more often reported by women who recalled reserved relationships with their parents. Recollection of childhood as generally unhappy significantly increased the likelihood of reserved relationships with the firstborn (13 percent, as compared with 5 percent among those who described their childhood as happy) and decreased the chance of describing relationships as mutually warm (61 percent of those with an unhappy childhood and 72 percent of those who remembered childhood as a happy time). Experience of parental divorce, however, had the reverse effect, being associated with a significantly increased likelihood that relationships with the firstborn child were described as mutually affectionate, perhaps as a form of intergenerational redress.

A polytomous logistic regression analysis showed that the variables that significantly and independently differentiated those with reserved and not mutual relationships from those with relationships described as mutually affectionate were reports of the nature of relationships with mother and father during childhood, parental enthusiasm for education, and partner's social class. Other variables in the analysis, but not contributing significantly, were parental divorce, social class of family of origin, parents' relationship, and the mother's recollection of happiness during her childhood.

CONCLUSIONS

Just as childhood social circumstances were associated with adult life chances in terms of survival, education, and family structure, so, as anticipated, aspects of childhood were also significantly associated in midlife with relationships with members of the previous and the following generations and with work satisfaction and attainment. Stability of parental relationships in the family of origin, rising paternal social class during the study member's childhood and school years, parental enthusiasm for education, and attainment of higher education formed a basis for midlife optimism about work and family life, recollection of a happy childhood, and enthusiasm for the education of offspring. However, women who had experienced higher education were least satisfied with family life. Instability in the family of origin—parental divorce or separation, falling paternal social class, low parental interest in education, and relatively low educational attainment—was associated with increased risk of negative midlife perceptions.

Midlife relationships with elderly parents and some aspects of satisfaction with work were, however, not so straightforwardly associated with childhood. The pathway from parental enthusiasm for education to high educational attainment led to greater geographical distance between study members and parents. Men whose parents had been enthusiastic for their education but who had then not gained higher qualifications had weak supportive relationships with parents, but the effect was the opposite for women. Study members of either sex tended to be more supportive of widowed parents and less supportive of those who had been divorced, which was mitigated by a study member's own experience of divorce.

Gender differences in satisfaction with work were associated with family of origin. Women in nonmanual occupations were least satisfied if they came from nonmanual families of origin, but men in similar occupations were least satisfied if they had originated in manual–social class families. Women who were parents reported less midlife work satisfaction than did men who were parents. Whereas findings of associations between childhood factors and adult family ties and work satisfaction were anticipated from earlier work in this study (Douglas 1964; Wadsworth 1991) and from that of others (Rossi and Rossi 1990), the gender differences in these associations were not expected. Gender differences in work satisfaction may be the result of differences in work and educational experience. Men had a greater likelihood than women of unbroken links over time from childhood and education into occupation and of continuing occupation in adulthood. In this cohort, however, women had much less opportunity for higher education and in most cases had experienced the disruption of occupation through childbearing. For them, family factors in both their families of origin and their own adult families had been sources of disruption of education and career, whereas for men, there was a much greater chance that families had, in both generations, been perceived as supportive. Gender differences in job satisfaction in relation to family of origin were probably of a different origin. The greater pessimism in well-qualified men who were from manual families of origin, compared with well-qualified men from nonmanual families, probably reflects the midlife awareness of how far work opportunities were differentiated by family of origin, another aspect of "the problem of gaining acceptance, as a conspicuous outsider, into established social circles" (Goldthorpe and Llewellyn 1980, 200). By contrast the greater optimism about work among well-qualified women from manual–social class families of origin, in comparison with well-qualified women from nonmanual families, may reflect their pleasure at having "made it to the top" despite great odds. These same women also had the highest levels of enthusiasm for the educational progress of their firstborn children. In addition, it may be that these high levels of optimism reflect a defensive position and an awareness of vulnerability. There is a suggestion that these women were coping with perceived vulnerability, as seen in this study in an alcohol intake significantly higher than in other women (Braddon et al. 1988).

Gender differences in relations with elderly parents may be associated with differences in views generally held at the time of the study population's childhood of what upbringing was to achieve. The aims then were to make men independent and to make women homemakers, responsible for the perpetuation of family life. Another study in a working-class London suburb, carried out at the time members of this birth cohort study were thirteen years old, found the following:

> In the middle classes children are usually dependent on parents until they are adult; their delay in reaching economic independence may make the break all the more complete when at last it does come. On the other hand, in Bethnal Green, as in other working class districts, nearly all the people left school at fourteen or fifteen and were earning their living not long after puberty, at an age when their fellows in other classes were still sitting at school-desks. Some of them did (and certainly do) use that independence to assert their own personalities by making at

least a partial break from their families whilst still adolescent. Having previously experienced some freedom from
parental influence, the women at least seem ready, by the
time of marriage, to re-form their ties with their families
of origin. . . . A closer tie [existed] between mother and
daughter than between the son and either of his parents.
(Young and Willmott 1962, 187–88)

These authors explain that the gender difference in contact with families of origin arose because men usually moved away from their father's
type of occupation, whereas women were drawn closer to their families
of origin for support, particularly with their mothers, when child upbringing began. And at that time, far fewer married women with children worked, and those who did were rarely in career or professional
occupations (Wadsworth 1991).

Confirmation of such strong gender differentiation also comes from
two sources of evidence about educational experience in the present
study. First, table 5.2 presents evidence of gender differences in education attainment: 9 percent of men versus 3 percent of women gradua-
ted with university-level qualifications, despite the absence of significant gender differences in attainment scores (Wadsworth 1991). The
second source of evidence comes from this same study population's
self-reports on gender differences in educational aptitude. Undergraduate university students observed that, for example, "women do not
have the same reasoning power as men," that "girls, in their own subjects, are as good, if not better, than the boys," and that "women make
bad teachers" (Wadsworth 1991, 109).

In occupation, by midlife many women had evidently broken away
from earlier stereotypical expectations of their being homemakers. But
although a high proportion were by then in paid employment (80 percent), the choice of employment was constrained by the education they
had attained, which had been subject to the mores of the population's
time of childhood.

The childhood factors associated with those aspects of midlife studied here exerted their influence largely through educational career,
which was itself greatly influenced by family circumstances. Parental
divorce and separation significantly reduced the chances of higher educational achievement (Wadsworth and Maclean 1986), probably because of school changes and reduced income; high parental enthusiasm
for the child's education tended to overcome this effect. Rising paternal

social class significantly improved educational attainment (Douglas 1964), perhaps because it was likely to raise parental hopes, aspirations, and income; it also significantly raised parental enthusiasm for the study child's education. These apparent long-term family influences may also include the effects of emotional perceptions, which may act to change the life course through their effects on family circumstances and as prisms through which earlier life is seen from midlife. Family instability caused by parental divorce or separation or by falling paternal social class is generally likely to have had concomitant adverse emotional effects for study members as children, and for some these effects may have continued into adult life (Wadsworth et al. 1990). Low parental concern for the child's education may also represent a generally low level of concern. Recovery from such adverse childhood experience can, of course, be achieved in adult life through partner choice, temperament, work, and other opportunities. But the childhood experience cannot be unmade, and as the needs of elderly parents increase with age, demands on children in midlife will be seen both in the current context and in the light of past remembered resentments and affection (Isaacs, Livingstone, and Neville 1972). It is also possible that fresh awareness of the nature of parents' earlier concerns (during childhood) may come with age. For example, it may become clear that an elderly mother has carried with her "a bit of her 'unmastered past,' " which she has, perhaps unconsciously, handed on, giving a new awareness to the daughter in midlife of having been seen by the mother as someone "through which she may live, and achieve all her lost hopes" (Steedman 1989, 105).

Although the emphasis in this chapter has been on the interactions of individuals with changing social circumstances, particularly those brought by increased educational opportunities, the power of educational effects should not overshadow the importance of those of family circumstances. Although the available information includes little about the nature of emotional relationships, their evident importance is clear in the salient impact of parental divorce, widowhood of parents, and the recollection of childhood. In this study, women's recollection of childhood as unhappy was associated at a mean adult age of twenty-six years with greater contemporary likelihood of reserved relationships with their firstborn child and at age forty-three with greater expression of dissatisfaction with family life and employment and a more than averagely disturbed marital history. Although reports of recollected emotions are not the ideal means through which to study intergenerational associations, the information available in this investigation suggests intergenerational continuities of affect.

This review of findings has touched on only some of the important questions raised by the opportunity to study intergenerational relationships. Ryff et al. (1994) showed that relationships between generations were not to be seen as a one-way process. Parents' perceptions of success or failure of offspring in education, work, marriage, and other areas of life may have potent effects on parental health, decision making, and way of life not only during the childhood and adolescence of their offspring but throughout life as well.

Intergenerational relations should also be considered from the social and historical perspective, as well as in terms of the life of the individual. This may be illustrated again using the example of expansion of education availability in Britain. In terms of social outcomes, evidence from this study and elsewhere indicates that positive effects result from making higher education available to greater numbers. Experience of higher education has been associated in this study population with greater community participation in voluntary social and political activities and in the arts, as well as providing a more skilled and adaptable work force (Wadsworth 1991). Expanding higher education has also brought an increase in parental enthusiasm for the education of offspring in the following generation, with consequent increased demand for better educational facilities. Yet there may also have been negative effects on a social scale, and many aspects of this question still remain to be investigated. There may have been changes in popular conceptions of the likely benefits of education, and there have certainly been changes in the perception of its value as an experience. Historians and others have wondered whether the cause of a perceived "slump in authority was paradoxically better education. Young people were trained to observe and judge and came sometimes to the conclusion that those in authority over them were fallible, intellectually or indeed morally. . . . The effects in schools were peculiarly disruptive" (Calvocoressi 1978, 167). At the individual level, positive outcomes of the experience of higher education have been shown in the subsequently improved access to better work opportunities and incomes (Kuh and Wadsworth 1991) and in the wider range of leisure interests described (Wadsworth 1991). It has yet to be discovered whether the broader view that higher education provides has increased the sense of social responsibility in relation, for instance, to life in the community and whether during this same period there have been changes in

moral views, especially those associated with public and private perceptions of responsibility for the care of family members. A further negative aspect of expanding higher education for individuals has been the
increased risk of later dissatisfaction with aspects of work and family
life in those who went against what was then the direction of the social
grain: those who undertook higher education having come from a
manual-social class family of origin or were women. It will be of particular interest to see whether the offspring of this group differ from others in terms of attainment of education and relationships with their
families of origin.

These kinds of interrelationships and adjustments of balance between politically activated social change and changes in individual
views and behavior may be how some aspects of social change take
place. But over time, social change and changes in perceptions of individuals are not likely to keep pace together because of the effect of age
in the individual. This study has shown that some perceptions have
changed with age. For example, at age twenty-six, study members who
had left home to take higher education courses were the most likely
to have moved away from the religious and political affiliations of their
families of origin, reflecting perhaps not only how much easier it is
for those who leave home to change their pattern of life but also the
tendency for higher education to encourage independent thought and
to be a source of pressure to conform to new surroundings. Confident
expectation of future change of social class was also seen much more
strongly in this group than in others (Wadsworth and Freeman 1983).
Ten years later there was evidence of a return to religious affiliations
and interests in those who had experienced higher education, contrary
to the trend of the time and in contrast with the opposite movement
among those study members who had not gone on to further or higher
education (Wadsworth 1991).

Many of the associations described in this chapter are bound to the
history of their time and their culture and are therefore not likely to
provide reliable indicators of what may happen in the future or in
other cultures. In Britain, as in America, new patterns of social factors
seem likely now to exert long-term effects on children because of the
rise in poverty and associated problems and the increase in unemployment (Fuchs and Reklis 1992; Wadsworth and Kuh 1993). These
changes will bring different prospects and different concepts of goals—
and of social and personal responsibility to children now—and in due
course in midlife.

Within the broader sweep of social change, however, will attitudes to personal and family relations also change? Will what seems here to be reduced contact with divorced parents change as divorce becomes much more usual? Will widows and widowers come to receive less care than the high levels received in this study population? It seems unlikely, but guessing future possible change of this kind is unreliable. It would, however, be surprising to find substantial change in the future in the finding that children from families of origin characterized by stability, concern for the children's education, and expressions of affection tend to become energetic and optimistic adults who have positive relationships with their children.

NOTE

For this chapter, education and training qualifications have been combined into one score. Higher-level qualifications include university entrance–level examinations, which were generally taken by those who stayed on at school for two years after the compulsory leaving age (then fifteen years), and all education and training equivalent qualifications at that level and above, including university degrees, and professional qualifications. Those with qualifications at lower levels or with no qualifications are described as having lower qualifications.

REFERENCES

Addison, P. 1985. *Now the war is over: A social history of Britain, 1945–51.* London: British Broadcasting Corporation.

Anshen, R., ed. 1949. *The family: Its function and destiny.* New York: Harper.

Barker, D. J. P. 1992. *Fetal and infant origins of adult disease.* London: British Medical Journal.

Barnett, C. 1986. *The audit of war: The illusion and reality of Britain as a great nation.* London: Macmillan.

Bartlett, C. J. 1977. *A history of postwar Britain, 1945–74.* London: Longmans.

Blau, P. M. 1956. Social mobility and interpersonal relations. *American Sociological Review* 21:290–295.

Braddon, F. E. M., M. E. J. Wadsworth, J. M. C. Davies, and H. A. Cripps. 1988. Social and regional differences in food and alcohol consumption and their measurement in a national birth cohort. *Journal of Epidemiology and Community Health* 42:341–349.

Calvocoressi, P. 1978. *The British experience, 1945–75.* London: Bodley Head.

Carr, E. H. 1964. *What is history?* London: Penguin.

Clark, D., ed. 1991. *Marriage, domestic life, and social change.* London: Routledge.

Douglas, J. W. B. 1964. *The home and the school.* London: MacGibbon and Kee.

Douglas, J. W. B., J. M. Ross, and J. R. Simpson. 1968. *All our future.* London: Peter Davies.

Elder, G. H., J. K. Liker, and C. E. Cross. 1984. Parent-child behaviour in the Great Depression: Life course and intergenerational influences. In P. B. Baltes and O. G. Brim, eds., *Life-span development and behaviour,* pp. 109–158. New York: Academic Press.

Finch, J., and P. Summerfield. 1991. Social reconstruction and the emergence of companionate marriage. In D. Clark, ed., *Marriage, domestic life, and social change,* pp. 7–32. London: Routledge.

Fuchs, V. R., and D. M. Reklis. 1992. America's children: Economic perspectives and policy options. *Science* 255:41–46.

Glass, D. V., ed. 1954. *Social mobility in Britain.* London: Routledge.

Goldthorpe, J. H. and C. Llewellyn. 1980. Class mobility in Britain: Three theses examined. In J. H. Goldthorpe, C. Llewellyn, and C. Payne, eds., *Social mobility and class structure in modern Britain,* pp. 175–216. Oxford: Clarendon.

Halsey, A. H. 1987. *Change in British society.* Oxford: Oxford University Press.

———. 1988. *British social trends since 1900.* London: Macmillan.

Isaacs, B., M. Livingstone, and Y. Neville. 1972. *Survival of the unfittest: A study of geriatric patients in Glasgow.* London: Routledge.

Kuh, D., and M. Wadsworth. 1991. Childhood influences on adult male earnings in a longitudinal study. *British Journal of Sociology* 42:537–555.

Lipset, S. M., and R. Bendix. 1959. *Social mobility in industrial society.* London: Heinemann.

Marquand, D. 1988. *The unprincipled society: New demands and old politics.* London: Cape.

Marwick, A. 1982. *British society since 1945.* London: Penguin.

Masterman, C. F. G. 1909. *The Condition of England.* London: Methuen.

Musgrove, F. 1963. *The migratory elite.* London: Heinemann.

Newson, J., and E. Newson. 1968. *Four years old in an urban community.* London: Allen and Unwin.

Rossi, A., and P. Rossi. 1990. *Of human bonding: Parent-child relations across the life course.* New York: Aldine de Gruyter.

Runciman, W. G. 1966. *Relative deprivation and social justice.* London: Routledge and Kegan Paul.

Ryff, C. D., Y. H. Lee, M. J. Essex, and P. S. Schmutte. 1994. My children and me: Midlife evaluations of grown children and of self. *Psychology and Aging* 9:195–205.

Sampson, A. 1962. *Anatomy of Britain.* London: Hodder and Stoughton.

Sissons, M., and P. French, eds. 1986. *Age of austerity.* Oxford: Oxford University Press.

Stacey, B. 1967. Some psychological consequences of inter-generation mobility. *Human Relations* 20:3–12.

Stacey, M. 1960. *Tradition and change.* Oxford: Oxford University Press.

Steedman, C. 1989. *Landscape for a good woman.* London: Virago.

Summerfield, P. 1986. The "levelling of class." In H. L. Smith, ed., *War and social change,* pp. 179–207. Manchester: Manchester University Press.

Wadsworth, M. E. J. 1986. Effects of parenting style and preschool experience on children's verbal attainment: A British longitudinal study. *Early Childhood Research Quarterly* 1:237–248.

————. 1991. *The imprint of time: Childhood, history, and adult life.* Oxford: Clarendon.

Wadsworth, M. E. J., and S. R. Freeman. 1983. Generation differences in beliefs: A cohort study of stability and change in religious beliefs. *British Journal of Sociology* 34:416–437.

Wadsworth, M. E. J., and D. Kuh. 1993. Are gains in child health being undermined? *Developmental Medicine and Child Neurology* 35:742–745.

Wadsworth, M. E. J., and M. Maclean. 1986. Parents' divorce and children's life chances. *Children and Youth Services Review* 8:145–159.

Wadsworth, M. E. J., M. Maclean, D. Kuh, and B. Rodgers. 1990. Children of divorced parents: A summary and review of findings from a national long-term follow-up study. *Family Practice* 7:104–109.

Wadsworth, M. E. J., S. L. Mann, B. Rodgers, D. J. L. Kuh, W. S. Hilder, and E. J. Yusuf. 1992. Loss and representativeness in a 43 year follow-up of a national birth cohort. *Journal of Epidemiology and Community Health* 46:300–304.

Young, M., and P. Willmott. 1962. *Family and kinship in East London.* London: Penguin.

————. 1973. *The symmetrical family.* London: Routledge.

IV Adolescents in Transition and Their Parents

SIX

Parents' Well-Being at Their Children's Transition to Adolescence

Susan B. Silverberg

The adolescent years in the family are likely to be a time of personal change and new developmental tasks for both young people and their middle-aged parents (Hill 1980; La Sorsa and Fodor 1990; Smith 1976). It is curious, however, that for the most part, researchers have investigated adult development and well-being at midlife independently from the study of adolescent development and parent-adolescent relationships (Bassoff 1987). An intriguing question that warrants greater research attention is whether the life/self questioning and reappraisal and personal stresses experienced by many adults at midlife (Anderson, Russell, and Schumm 1983; Eisler and Ragsdale 1992; Farrell and Rosenberg 1981a; Neugarten 1977; Rubin 1979; Vaillant 1977) are prompted or intensified, in part, by the presence of adolescents in the family and by the changing nature of parent-child relationship that typically occurs during the transition and through adolescence. This intuitively appealing proposition—that parents' mental health, personal reevaluation, and concerns at midlife may be affected by the development of their adolescent children—has been raised repeatedly not only in popular literature (Sheehy 1976) but also in clinically based work and other scholarly writings (e.g., Cohen and Balikov 1974; Farrell and Rosenberg 1981b; Kidwell, Fischer, Dunham, and Baranowski, 1983; Lidz 1969). Changes that have been assumed to be especially provocative to parents as middle-aged adults range from youngsters' sexual maturation to their willingness to question parental authority, to the fact that they—in contrast with their parents—have all their life's choices and opportunities ahead. Parents, according to many popular and clinical writings, are likely to respond to these changes with a sense of envy, feelings of being challenged, or possible regret

This chapter is based on a paper presented at the John D. and Catherine T. MacArthur Foundation Conference on Midlife Parenting, Chicago, Ill., 16–17 October 1992. The research was supported in part by funds from the W. T. Grant Foundation and the graduate school of the University of Wisconsin (awarded to Laurence Steinberg).

about their present life circumstances and previous life choices (Bassoff 1987; Farrell and Rosenberg 1981b; Lidz 1969; Rollins 1989; Sheehy 1976; Smith 1976).

The present research project was an attempt to respond to the need for more systematic, empirical study in this area on nonclinical samples. Its focus is on adults who are parents of early-adolescent children. These adults were studied because at the start of the research project, which extended over a twelve-month period, their oldest child was between the ages of ten and fifteen, not because of their own chronological age; most of the parents were, however, in their thirties or forties. By way of introduction, the following section will describe in somewhat greater detail specific theoretical and empirical sources of motivation for conducting the research.

MOTIVATIONS FOR THE RESEARCH
Theoretical Propositions

Interestingly, theories from a variety of perspectives suggest, implicitly or explicitly, that signs of youngsters' development and transformations in the parent-child relationship at adolescence may lead to increases in life/self questioning and reappraisal and/or to diminished well-being among midlife parents. Although each theory emphasizes a somewhat different mechanism or process at work, they all lead one to conclude that the psychological world of parents may be "at risk" at this point in the family life cycle.

Psychoanalytic theorists have long argued that the child's transition to adolescence is of critical importance to the quality of relationships within the family (Freud 1958). Expanding on the psychoanalytic-based ideas of Benedek (1959), Farrell and Rosenberg (1981b) argue that middle-aged parents identify with and see their inner selves reflected in their adolescent children, who are beginning to develop a separate sense of self and are struggling for increased independence by testing the boundaries and rules of the family. According to these authors and others (e.g., Colarusso and Nemiroff 1982), parents may in response become defensive or ambivalent about themselves and are likely to engage in a period of questioning and reassessment of their values and present life situation. Mothers and fathers from this perspective may also envy their adolescent youngsters, especially their *same-sex* youngsters' increasing sexual attractiveness (Bassoff 1987; Boxer et al. 1984; Lidz 1969). In short, the psychoanalytic-based view suggests that parental mental health and engagement in life/self reappraisal are intimately dependent on the transformations in the child and in the parent-child relationship at adolescence. Although there is a tendency from this perspective to emphasize the potential negative outcomes of identification with one's maturing teen (e.g., defensiveness, envy), it is certainly possible that positive outcomes such as a genuine or vicarious sense of pride or satisfaction could emerge as a result instead.

Role theory provides an alternative framework within which to consider the possible link between adolescent development, on the one hand, and the likelihood of self-reevaluation and life dissatisfactions of midlife parents, on the other. From this perspective, the self is regarded as "the sense of identity that comes from playing one's roles" (Breytspraak 1984, 38; see Biddle and Thomas 1979); and a positive sense of self and life satisfaction are based on continued performance of roles to which the individual is committed and which the individual considers valuable (Birnbaum 1975; McCall and Simmons 1978). As youngsters move into their adolescent years, several dimensions of the parenting role begin to diminish, be altered, or be challenged to some extent. The child's transition to adolescence, therefore, may be associated with temporary disruptions in parental sense of self or life satisfaction and with an increased likelihood of midlife identity concerns. Parental control over youngster's behavior—through the setting of limits and rules or through coercion—is one dimension of parenting that is likely to diminish or be challenged during the adolescent years. Farrell and Rosenberg consider what this may mean for a parent's sense of well-being: "[A father's] authority diminishes [when he has adolescent children] and he must deal with the loss of control associated with earlier phases of the fathering role. These strains create pressures to redefine his basic assumptions about himself, find new outlets, and alter his approach to the problem of giving meaning and purpose to his life" (1981a, 28). That certain parents may be more sensitive or vulnerable to such role diminishment for their sense of self and life satisfaction (Silverberg and Steinberg 1990) will be discussed further below.

The potential significance of youngsters' transition to adolescence for parental well-being can also be explored from a *stress paradigm* on adult mental health (Chiriboga 1989; Julian, McKenry, and McKelvey 1991; Lazarus and Folkman 1984). Psychological stress, according to Lazarus and Folkman (1984), "is a particular relationship between the person and the environment that is appraised by the person as taxing or exceeding his or her resources and endangering his or her well-being" (19). We know from several studies regarding the difficulty of parenting children of different ages that many parents do feel least adequate and least comfortable in parenting adolescents (Ballenski and Cook 1982; Pasley and Gecas 1984; Veroff and Feld 1970) and that parenting adolescent youngsters—in particular, early adolescents—is more worrisome, anxiety-provoking, and stressful than parenting children of other ages (Hoffman and Manis 1978; Small, Eastman, and Cornelius 1988). Parents may perceive their youngsters' disagreements, for example, not only as a challenge or threat to parental control, as was suggested above, but also as a general stressor within the context of family life (Pearlin and Lieberman 1979) and as a cause to feel less positive about their life situation, less than competent in the parental role, and/or less sure about themselves in general. Mothers may be at greater risk than fathers for mental health problems when they experience persistent strains or stresses in their ongoing relationships with their children (McGrath et al. 1990; Scott and Alwin 1989), because as women they are more likely to base their identity and self-conception in relationship terms (Gilligan 1982). Thus, mothers may be especially vulnerable to the challenging transitions and stresses at adolescence.

In sum, three rather diverse theoretical models appear to support the notion that adolescent development and realignments in the parent-child relationship during adolescence are likely to provoke or intensify midlife concerns, reappraisals, and dissatisfactions among parents. Given this strong theoretical convergence, it seems quite possible that a causal link may indeed exist not only for clinical samples but also for parents of adolescents in the general population. An important question to consider first, however, is, What do existing empirical studies suggest might be features of the transition to adolescence that would be especially provocative to parents?

Empirical Work on Parent-Child Relations at Early Adolescence

We know from three decades of rather systematic research on nonclinical samples of families at adolescence that the vast majority of adolescents feel fairly close to their parents rather than emotionally detached and that typically no dramatic changes occur in parent-child relationships at the transition to adolescence (see, for reviews, Collins 1990; Silverberg, Tennenbaum, and Jacob 1992; and Steinberg 1990). Nonetheless, this transition does seem to mark a time of important realignments in parent-child relations as well as a time of normative biological and social changes in children, all of which may be sufficiently challenging or provocative to parents to cause unfavorable consequences for their sense of self and well-being or, at least, a temporary period of heightened reappraisal of life/self.

Research on the consequences of youngsters' *pubertal maturation* for the quality of parent-child relationships raises this normative developmental change as a prime candidate for provoking midlife concerns and dissatisfactions among parents. A number of studies indicate, for example, that youngsters' pubertal maturation is associated with a temporary period of strained parent-child interactions marked by slight elevations in conflict, somewhat diminished parent-child closeness, and, especially among males, youngsters' attempts to play a more forceful, assertive role in the family and family decisions (e.g., Flannery 1991; Hill and Holmbeck 1987; Steinberg 1981, 1987a). The increase in assertiveness, along with the heightened levels of conflict, is especially likely to be directed toward mothers. And of special interest to the present research is Steinberg's (1981) finding that as sons move toward full pubertal maturation, it is *mothers* who display a complementary pattern of "backing off," that is, of yielding to their son's interruptions more often and of commanding less influence in family-based decisions relative to their sons (at least in a structured task situation). One wonders, then, what pubertal maturation per se, its symbolic meaning, and its accompanying relationship changes mean for parents' personal adjustment. How do mothers, in particular, perceive themselves and their life situations as their youngsters move through the pubertal cycle?

Although a high degree of conflict and dramatic increases in the level of *parent-child conflict* at adolescence are not universal, most parents and adolescents report quarreling or bickering on a regular basis (Montemayor 1986; Hill and Holmbeck 1986). Most important, perhaps, to the issue of midlife parents' psychological well-being is that "conflict and arguments are the primary complaints of parents about relations with their adolescents" (Montemayor 1986, 16). The present research project is the first effort, however, to examine whether parent-adolescent conflict leads to parents' reports of heightened midlife concerns and diminished psychological well-being. Its short-term longitudinal approach will permit some account of whether there is more than merely a concurrent association between difficulties in the parent-adolescent relationship and personal distress among parents.

Finally, while emotional ties to parents are maintained throughout adolescence for most individuals (Kenny 1987), a degree of psychological separation or *emotional autonomy* vis-à-vis parents develops as youngsters attempt to differentiate some aspects of the self from significant others (Blos 1967; Hill and Holmbeck 1986; Josselson 1980). For example, starting at early adolescence, youngsters begin to de-idealize their image of their parents (Steinberg and Silverberg 1986); and by middle adolescence, most youngsters have disengaged somewhat from an inner representation of their parents as "all-knowing" and "all-powerful" (Smollar and Youniss 1989). Gradually adolescents begin to sever childish dependencies on parents while taking responsibility for their own behavior, and begin to form a more individuated sense of self—a sense of oneself as a self-governing, separate individual. Although empirical research demonstrates that youngsters become more emotionally autonomous over the early adolescent years (Steinberg and Silverberg 1986), the present project is the first, to this author's knowledge, that has examined the way in which the adolescent's individuation may affect parents.

Individual Differences in Parent Vulnerability

It is tempting to assume that all parents will experience a period of heightened identity concerns and psychological strain as their children move into and through adolescence. To do so, however, would blur the diversity among parents that is undoubtedly present. Any links that do exist between parental well-being and the normative developmental and relational changes of early adolescence are likely to be moderated by characteristics of parents themselves that act as filters, buffers, or intensifiers—leaving some parents more sensitive or vulnerable than others. Potential moderating variables examined in the present research include *gender of parent and gender of child, socioeconomic status,* and *parenting- and work-role orientation* (i.e., psychological investment in one's parenting and paid-work roles, respectively). The rationale for examining the moderating role of these particular factors is described in the next section. Of course, other factors such as the parent's own experiences in adolescence, the parent's belief system regarding what is normative behavior during the period of adolescence, and the parent's personal characteristics (e.g., sense of control and level of neuroticism), most likely serve as moderators as well and deserve careful future research attention.

Gender

Studies documenting differences in family relations as a function of adolescent and parent gender (Hill 1988; Richardson et al. 1984; Steinberg 1987b; Youniss and Smollar 1985); scholarship focusing on the experiences of men and women during their midlife years (Barnett and Baruch 1978; Farrell and Rosenberg 1981a); and psychoanalytic and stress theories all highlight the importance of examining gender differences in the context of the present research. Two questions arise: first, will the normative developmental and relational changes of adolescence affect mothers and fathers in different ways, and second, will parents be affected differently by sons and daughters? If the process of *identification* discussed above underlies the relation between parental well-being and transformations in the child and in the parent-child relationship, then one would expect stronger relations for same-sex dyads. If, on the other hand, the *stress* induced by the transformations in the parent-adolescent relationship is crucial, one might expect mothers to experience more negative effects than fathers regardless of the gender of the child, because mothers traditionally play a more central role in childrearing and may have more opportunities to engage in conflictual-like interactions with their youngsters (McGrath et al. 1990; Montemayor 1986). Furthermore, mothers may be more likely than fathers to base their sense of self and psychological well-being on the quality of their relationships with their children (Baruch, Barnett, and Rivers 1983; Gilligan 1982) and therefore may be more sensitive or vulnerable to changes that challenge or transform these relationships.

Role Orientation

Role theory also would suggest that certain parents are more likely to respond unfavorably to their youngsters' development than are others. From this perspective, parents who have a strong psychological investment in or orientation toward their role as parent may be among those most susceptible to any negative consequences of their child's development. Indeed, it is clear from research on the transition out of active parenting (so-called empty-nest studies) that parents who are greatly invested in the parental role respond more negatively to disruptions in that role than do others (e.g., Bart 1971; Oliver 1977; Powell 1977). On the other hand, this same body of research suggests that parents who have a commitment to work roles outside the family adjust well to the disruption of their parenting role that occurs when their children leave home (Powell 1977). Moreover, studies on adult physical and mental health indicate that work outside the home (and, conceivably, an orientation toward that role) is related to higher self-esteem, a lack of depression, and better physical health (Adelmann et al. 1990; Baruch, Barnett, and Rivers, 1983; Birnbaum 1975; Coleman and Antonucci 1983) and may serve to buffer experiences in the family that might otherwise weaken one's sense of identity, cause one to reassess life commitments, or lead to symptoms of dysphoria and life dissatisfaction. Thus, it seems reasonable to propose that parents with a strong psychological investment in, or orientation toward, roles outside the family sphere (e.g., as a paid worker) will be less sensitive and more resistant than will other parents to any potential detrimental consequences of the normative developmental and relational changes that occur at adolescence.

Socioeconomic Status

Previous investigations also suggest that parents' socioeconomic status may moderate the ways in which transformations in the parent-adolescent relationship affect parental sense of self and well-being (Jacob 1974). Because working-class parents tend to value their youngsters' conformity and obedience to a greater extent than do parents from middle-class families, who appear to place greater value on youngsters' development of autonomy and independence (Kohn 1977), working-class parents may be more likely to perceive their youngsters' disagreements, arguments, and emotional autonomy, for example, as challenges or threats to their role as parent. As a result, parents in working-class families may be more adversely affected by conflict and distancing in the parent-adolescent relationship than parents from middle-class families.

THE RESEARCH PROJECT
Overall Goals

The research project presented in this chapter had three main goals but was part of a larger study of the family at the transition to adolescence (see, for example, Steinberg 1988; Steinberg and Silverberg 1986, 1987). Its first goal was to examine whether parents' reports of midlife identity concerns (life/self questioning and reappraisal) and psychological well-being (e.g., self-esteem, life satisfaction) are related *concurrently* to signs of their youngster's transition to adolescence (e.g., pubertal maturation, involvement in mixed-sex social relations); to indicators of the quality of the parent-adolescent relationship (e.g., conflict, emotional autonomy); and to perceived increases in challenge/distance in the parent-child relationship. The second goal was to determine whether factors such as family socioeconomic status (SES) and parental work- and parenting-role orientation moderate these concurrent relationships, that is, to determine whether parents' sensitivity or vulnerability to the changes at adolescence vary as a function of their SES or their investment in parenting and paid work. Results of analyses addressing some of these initial questions have been presented in earlier reports (Silverberg 1986; Silverberg and Steinberg 1987, 1990) but will be summarized and discussed further here.

The final goal of the present research and the major piece of this chapter that has not been discussed elsewhere was to examine whether signs of the transition to adolescence, quality of the parent-child relationship, and perceived increases in challenge/distance in the parent-child relationship all measured at the start of the study predict *changes* in level of parent psychological well-being and midlife concerns over a twelve-month period. This goal is noteworthy because only with longitudinal data can we begin to shed light on the question of whether youngsters' developmental status and the perceived quality of parent-adolescent relations lead to changes in parents' sense of self and well-being. As in the concurrent analyses, we were also interested in whether the strength of any longitudinal connections is moderated by family SES and parent work-role orientation.

In light of theoretical predictions regarding the role of gender and previous studies suggesting that parent-child relations vary as a function of child and parent gender (see Steinberg 1987b; Youniss and Smollar 1985), separate analyses were conducted throughout for mother-son, mother-daughter, father-son, and father-daughter dyads.

Study Participants

The sample for the present study is composed of 129 two-parent intact families with a firstborn (target) child between the ages of ten and fifteen at the time of the first wave of data collection. Participating families lived in a medium-sized midwestern city and were surveyed in their homes in 1985 and again twelve months later in 1986 (see Steinberg, Elmen, and Mounts 1989 for a detailed description of sample recruitment and participation rates). The sample is predominantly white (92 percent), evenly divided with respect to the sex of the target adolescent, socioeconomically heterogeneous (33 percent blue-collar, 36 percent white-collar, and 31 percent professional/technical, as determined by head of household occupation), and varied in terms of maternal work patterns (51 percent employed full-time, more than twenty-five hours per week; 40 percent part-time; and 9 percent not employed). At the time of the first data collection, the average age of mothers was 37.77 (SD = 4.10), of fathers, 39.59 (SD = 4.49), and of youngsters, 12.64 (SD = 1.65).

Measures

Of interest to the present report are four measures of parental sense of self and well-being: midlife identity concerns, self-esteem, life satisfaction, and psychological symptoms (Waves 1 and 2); two measures of adolescent intra-individual development: pubertal maturation and heterosocial involvement (Wave 1); two measures of parent-child relations: parent-adolescent conflict and emotional autonomy vis-à-vis parents (Wave 1); a measure of parents' perceptions of change in the parent-child relationship in the domains of control, guidance, and emotional support (Wave 1); and two measures of adult role orientation; parenting-role orientation and paid work-role orientation (Wave 1). Information on family socioeconomic status was also used in several analyses.

Measures of parental sense of self and well-being. Because men and women—and individuals from different social class backgrounds—may manifest stress and concerns differentially (e.g., Farrell and Rosenberg 1981a; Turner and Turner 1982), it was important to assess multiple dimensions of parental well-being: self-esteem, midlife identity concerns, general life satisfaction, and psychological symptoms. All four scales were scored so that *higher scores* indicate *positive adaptation.* The correlations among the parental well-being variables are presented in table 6.1.

Parents' *self-esteem* was assessed via a series of ten Likert-scale items taken from Rosenberg (1965) and Gould (1972). The internal consistency of the measure, as determined by Cronbach's alpha, is .83 among mothers and .84 among fathers. Scores could range from ten to forty, with higher scores indicating higher self-esteem. Mothers' and fathers' *midlife identity concerns* were assessed via a scale that incorporates items from Farrell and Rosenberg's (1981a) "midlife crisis scale" and from the work on adult identity issues and well-being by Gould (1972)

224

TABLE 6.1. Correlations Among Parent Well-Being Variables

Variables	1	2	3	4
1. Absence of midlife identity concerns	—	.53	.59	.55
2. Self-esteem	.44	—	.54	.30
3. Life satisfaction	.50	.42	—	.46
4. Lack of psychological symptoms	.39	.32	.37	—

Notes: Correlations for mothers are above the diagonal; correlations for fathers are below the diagonal. Ns range from 121 to 127. For all entries, $p < .01$.

and Keniston (1963). The measure, composed of ten Likert-scale items, inquires about the degree to which respondents are presently experiencing a period of reevaluation of their life situation, their life choices, and themselves. The internal consistency of the measure is .79 and .80 among mothers and fathers, respectively. Scores could range from zero to thirty, with higher scores indicating an absence of midlife concerns. Parents' *general life satisfaction* was assessed via an eight-item semantic differential instrument developed by Campbell, Converse, and Rodgers (1976) for use in their national study of the quality of adult life. The instrument asks respondents to describe their present life according to a series of adjective pairs (e.g., miserable-enjoyable, useless-worthwhile) along a seven-point scale. Life satisfaction scores are expressed in terms of the average rating given across the eight items (i.e., a range from 1.0 to 7.0), with the higher scores indicating greater satisfaction. In the present sample, the internal consistency of the measure is .92 for mothers and .90 for fathers. The parents' questionnaire battery also contained a measure of *psychological symptoms* adapted from the Center for Epidemiological Studies Depression Scale (CES-D) (Radloff 1977). This measure, developed for use with nonclinical samples, asks respondents to indicate the frequency, during the past year, of feelings of tension, depressed mood, and similar problems. The internal consistency of the scale is .77 for mothers and .71 for fathers. Scores could range from zero to twenty, with higher scores indicating less frequent symptoms and, thus, greater psychological health.

Measures of adolescent intra-individual development. Pubertal maturation was assessed by the research team members via a scale (differing appropriately for males and females) focused on three aspects of visible somatic and secondary sex characteristics associated with pubertal development: facial appearance (e.g., facial shape, acne); body proportions (e.g., chest development, limb length-to-torso production); and body coordination (e.g., gait). Scores range from three (no sign of pubertal development) to fifteen (pubertal maturation complete). The measure has an interrater reliability of .81 (see Garbarino et al. 1978; Steinberg 1987a). Adolescent *heterosocial involvement* was measured via a six-item (seven-item for boys) true-false scale based on a behavioral checklist completed by the adolescent. The measure, developed for the present research project, taps the youngster's involvement in mixed-sex peer and dating activities, including attending mixed-sex parties, having a boyfriend or girlfriend, and going out on dates. The scale has an internal consistency, as determined by Cronbach's alpha, of .77 for boys and .80 for girls. To compare girls' and boys' scores, scale scores were adjusted for the number of items in the measure; scores could range from 1.0 to 2.0. The correlation between pubertal status and heterosocial involvement is the same for girls and boys in the sample: $r = .24$, $p < .05$.

Measures of parent-adolescent relations. Parental report of *adolescent-parent conflict* was measured via a series of questions about the intensity of discussions that may have occurred with the adolescent across seventeen areas of day-to-day decision making (e.g., chores, clothing, curfew, friends) during the previous two weeks. The measure is modeled after one developed by Robin and his colleagues (see Robin and Weiss 1980). Discussion intensity was rated on a five-point scale from "very calm" to "very angry." The internal consistency of the measure for mothers is .75 and for fathers is .80. The adolescent's *emotional autonomy* vis-à-vis parents was assessed with a twenty-item, Likert-scale measure completed by the adolescent. The measure is grounded in psychoanalytic conceptions of adolescent autonomy (e.g., Blos 1979) and contains items that measure the adolescent's realistic perception of his or her parents; individuation from parental objects; de-idealization of parents; and nondependency on parents. The measure has an internal consistency of .75 (for details, see Steinberg and Silverberg 1986). Emotional autonomy and parental reports of conflict are not highly correlated in this sample (sons and mothers, $r = .28$; sons and fathers, $r = .00$; daughters and mothers, $r = .04$; daughters and fathers, $r = -.25$; cf. Ryan and Lynch 1989).

Measure of parents' perceptions of change in the parent-child relationship. A measure was designed to assess parents' perceptions of increases in

TABLE 6.2. Perceived Change in Parent-Child Relationship:
Scale Items in Three Domains

Domain	Items
Control	At times, my child disagrees with what I ask him/her to do.
	My child and I argue about rules.
	My child tells me where he/she will be before leaving the house.[a]
	My child sometimes thinks that my opinions don't count.
Emotional support	My child spends free time away from home with his/her friends.
	The talks I have with my child are frustrating.
	My child seeks out privacy when at home.
	My child comes to me for support when he/she is upset or troubled.[a]
Guidance	My child seeks my advice in solving day-to-day problems.[a]
	My child acts impatient when I talk with him/her about his/her nonschool activities.
	My child's values seem to differ from mine.
	My child sometimes thinks that my opinions don't count.

[a]Item was scored in reverse.

challenge to—or diminishment of—three dimensions of parenting: control, guidance, and emotional support. Parents were asked to consider a list of twelve statements, which included items such as "At times, my child disagrees with what I ask him/her to do" (control) and "My child's values seem to differ from mine" (guidance), and to indicate whether each item is more true of their child than it was two years ago, less true now than two years ago, or just about the same as two years ago. Table 6.2 presents the items that made up the three domains; some of the items were adapted from Robin and Weiss (1980). Summary scores were calculated for each area so that *higher scores* indicated perceptions of *increased* challenge to or distance in the parent-child relationship compared with two years earlier.

Measures of adult role orientation. Mothers' and fathers' *parenting-role orientation* was assessed via a five-item (six-item for fathers) Likert scale designed to determine the degree to which respondents invest themselves in their role as parent. The items reflect themes including, among others, thinking or talking about parenting when not actively engaged in that role (e.g., "When spending time with friends or neighbors I talk mostly about my child[ren]") and the subjective sense of importance of the parenting role. The scale has an internal consistency, as determined by Cronbach's alpha, of .72 for mothers and .70 for fathers. To compare mother's and fathers' scores, scale scores were adjusted for the number of items in the measure; scores could range from 1.0 to 4.0, with higher scores indicating a stronger parenting-role orientation. Parents' *paid-work role orientation* was assessed via a scale similar in format to that measuring parenting-role orientation. It includes Likert-type items such as "I often find myself thinking about my job when I am not working" as well as questions concerning the frequency with which parents take work home with them or remain at work after usual hours. This seven-item (eight-item for mothers) scale has an internal consistency of .66 for mothers and .71 for fathers. Scale scores were adjusted for the number of items in the measure; scores could range from 1.0 to 4.0, with higher scores indicating a stronger work-role orientation.

Findings and Discussion

Wave 1 data: Pubertal maturation, heterosocial involvement, and the moderating effects of parents' work-role orientation. In our first look at the data, we examined whether parents' reports of midlife identity concerns and psychological well-being are *concurrently* related to their youngster's pubertal status and heterosocial involvement at the transition to adolescence (Silverberg and Steinberg 1990). Simple correlational analyses revealed only a few significant and rather modest relations between parents' sense of self and well-being and these indicators of their youngster's development (table 6.3). They are noteworthy nonetheless. We found, for example, that daughters' pubertal maturity was related to mothers' reports of more intense midlife identity concerns and to mothers' reports of lower self-esteem. This pattern is consistent with the psychoanalytic perspective on parental development (Benedek 1959; Farrell and Rosenberg 1981b; Lidz 1969) that suggests that mothers may identify with their more adult-appearing adolescent daughters and be provoked to reflect on their own life situations and personal commitments. Clinicians might even propose that mothers are envious of their daughter's mature, yet youthful appearance and

TABLE 6.3. Correlations between Wave 1 Parent Well-Being Variables and Indicators of Youngsters' Transition to Adolescence

Adolescence Indicator	Absence of Midlife Concerns	Self-Esteem	Life Satisfaction	Lack of Psychological Symptoms
	Mothers of daughters			
Pubertal status	−.43***	−.18†	−.06	−.02
Heterosocial involvement	−.19	.09	−.18†	−.17†
	Mothers of sons			
Pubertal status	−.06	−.23*	−.03	−.11
Heterosocial involvement	−.21†	−.03	−.07	−.14
	Fathers of daughters			
Pubertal status	.07	.02	−.06	.00
Heterosocial involvement	−.15	−.07	−.19†	−.09
	Fathers of sons			
Pubertal status	.10	−.06	.06	−.05
Heterosocial involvement	−.07	.22†	.07	−.20†

Note: Ns range from 55 to 65.

†$p < .10$. *$p < .05$. **$p < .01$. ***$p < .001$.

respond by feeling more negatively about themselves, as reflected in reports of lower self-esteem; we could not examine this dynamic with our dataset, however. Interestingly, a trend also suggested that sons' involvement in heterosocial activities is associated with somewhat *higher* self-esteem among their fathers. Why might this be? It is possible that some fathers identify with their sons' social "achievements" and share in feelings of pride and higher self-esteem as a result.

If we were to have concluded our analyses at this point, we might have interpreted these sparse significant correlations as evidence that few meaningful or strong connections exist between the psychological well-being and concerns of parents, on the one hand, and their youngster's developmental status at the transition to adolescence, on the other. We proceeded, however, to explore potential *individual differences* in parental sensitivity or vulnerability to their youngster's pubertal and social development that may have been masked in the simple correlational analyses. Via a series of hierarchical regression analyses, we examined whether level of work-role orientation and whether level of parenting-role orientation had a moderating impact on the relation between these indicators of child maturation and parental well-being.[1]

Separate analyses were performed for each of the parent well-being variables in relation to each domain of adolescent development. To control for the effects of socioeconomic status, a dummy-coded SES variable was entered on the first step of each analysis, followed by the main effects of a domain of adolescent development (e.g., pubertal status) and parents' work-role orientation. In the final step, a term representing the interaction between the adolescent development variable and parent work-role orientation (e.g., the product of pubertal status and work-role orientation) was entered into the equation. Using this method and focusing on the increment in R^2 associated with this final step, we examined whether the interaction term significantly contributed to the prediction of parent well-being and beyond the separate effects of adolescent development or parental work-role orientation (see table 6.4).

A significant interaction indicates that the relation between parental well-being and the indicator of adolescent development differs as a function of parents' work-role orientation; however, it does not reveal the exact nature of this difference. A more illustrative picture of the significant interactions was revealed via post hoc analyses of regression slopes at two different levels of work-role orientation (determined by a median split). The results of these post hoc analyses (computed after controlling for SES) clarify whether, as predicted, unfavorable relations between signs of youngsters' adolescent status and parental well-being are more apparent for low as compared with high work-role orientation parents.

Results strongly suggested that the extent and manner in which parental well-being is related to pubertal and social indicators of youngsters' development varies as a function of the parent's level of orientation toward their role as paid worker—notably to a role outside the boundaries of the family per se (see table 6.4). With some variation—the chief exception being mothers of daughters—higher levels of youngsters' dating behavior and involvement in mixed-sex peer group activities were associated with more intense midlife concerns, lower self-esteem, lower life satisfaction, or more frequent psychological symptoms on the part of their parents, but these effects were found only among parents who are not strongly invested in their paid-work role. For example, mothers who are not strongly oriented toward their role as paid worker reported more intense midlife concerns ($b = -7.81$), and lower self-esteem ($b = -4.17$), and lower life satisfaction ($b = -1.29$) if their son was heterosocially active. Similarly, fathers

TABLE 6.4. Significance of Interactions between Adult's Work-Role Orientation and Indicators of Youngster's Development in Predicting Parent Well-Being (wave 1)

Well-Being Domain/ Interaction Term	B	R^2 Change[a]	B	R^2 Change[a]
		Mothers of sons	*Mothers of daughters*	
Absence of midlife identity concerns				
Puberty × work orientation	3.17	.34**	0.53	.01
Heterosocial × work orientation	3.86	.23**	−2.72	.08*
Self-esteem				
Puberty × work orientation	2.98	.30***	1.36	.05
Heterosocial × work orientation	2.20	.08*	−1.52	.03
Life satisfaction				
Puberty × work orientation	2.86	.28***	1.45	.06
Heterosocial × work orientation	3.19	.16**	−0.86	.01
Lack of psychological symptoms				
Puberty × work orientation	0.51	.01	−2.78	.21*
Heterosocial × work orientation	1.51	.04	−0.06	.00
		Fathers of sons	*Fathers of daughters*	
Absence of midlife identity concerns				
Puberty × work orientation	−0.82	.02	−0.80	.01
Heterosocial × work orientation	5.70	.54**	0.20	.00
Self-esteem				
Puberty × work orientation	−1.65	.10*	0.82	.01
Heterosocial × work orientation	4.21	.29**	1.43	.05
Life satisfaction				
Puberty × work orientation	−1.62	.10*	−0.17	.00
Heterosocial × work orientation	2.27	.09*	2.94	.22**
Lack of psychological symptoms				
Puberty × work orientation	−0.93	.03	−0.22	.00
Heterosocial × work orientation	−2.24	.08*	2.35	.14**

[a] R^2 change for the interaction term was determined after socioeconomic status and the separate contributions of the adolescence indicator and work-role orientation were entered into the regression equation. Ns range from 51 to 63 across analyses.
*$p < .05$. **$p < .01$. ***$p < .001$.

who are not strongly oriented toward their role as paid worker reported more intense midlife concerns ($b = -6.08$) and more frequent psychological symptoms ($b = -3.14$) if their son was heterosocially active.[2] We tentatively interpreted these results by proposing—from a role theory perspective (McCall and Simmons 1978)—that because parents with a low work-role orientation lack a strong basis outside of the family for their sense of self and satisfactions, they may experience concern at the prospect of losing their adolescent child and/or have difficulty facing the signs and occasional challenges of their youngster's maturity and expanding social world. A psychological investment and satisfaction in work—and perhaps in other outside interests—may buffer parents by supporting their sense of competence and self-worth and thus adding a layer of "psychological protection" against the challenges that are sometimes a part of adolescence (Steinberg and Steinberg 1994).

An interesting question arises: Is it because parents with a low work-role orientation are so greatly invested in their role as parent that they are more susceptible to changes in their youngster? We did not find support for this idea. First, correlational analyses indicated that a weak orientation toward work did not necessarily imply a strong orientation to parenting in this sample: $r = -.153$, $p < .05$ for mothers and $r = .063$, NS for fathers (comparable correlations are reported by Greenberger and Goldberg [1989] in their study of parents of preschoolers). Second, regression analyses indicated that *parenting*-role orientation as measured here did not moderate the relation between children's maturation and parental well-being (see note 1). Taken together, these results suggested to us that parents' level of orientation toward work outside the family, rather than their orientation toward parenting per se, is a crucial moderator of the effects of early adolescents' development on parents' mental health.

There is an alternative explanation for the association between signs of youngsters' maturation and diminished well-being among parents who report a low investment in their jobs, however. This explanation inheres in the possibility that early adolescent maturation may be influenced by parental well-being—rather than the reverse—and that this effect may depend on level of parental work-role orientation. It is conceivable, for example, that when mothers or fathers are less psychologically involved in work and are low in well-being (a combination that is perhaps a sign of general discontent), early adolescents begin to look elsewhere for close, intimate relationships and become more involved in heterosocial activities. In fact, a reciprocal process may be set in motion in families of parents without a strong work investment, if adolescents' distancing themselves, in turn, further diminishes their parents' mental health.

Our analyses also indicated that among parents who are strongly invested in their paid-work role, social and physical indicators of their youngsters' transition into adolescence appeared to be either unrelated or *favorably* related to well-being. For example, we found that mothers who are more strongly oriented toward their role as paid workers have somewhat *higher* life satisfaction ($b = 0.80$) and self-esteem ($b = 0.11$) if their son is heterosocially active. Moreover, it was among these mothers that sons' more advanced pubertal maturation was associated with less intense maternal midlife concerns ($b = 0.44$) and with higher levels of maternal life satisfaction ($b = 0.12$). We also found that, in contrast with fathers who are not strongly oriented toward their role as paid worker, fathers who are more strongly oriented toward their role as paid worker have less intense midlife concerns ($b = 6.66$) if their son is heterosocially active.

In short, we were seeing a pattern in our Wave 1 data—in mother-son, father-son, and to some extent father-daughters dyads—that suggested that psychological investment in a nonfamilial role at this point in the family life cycle may permit easier accommodation to potentially stressful or provocative changes in the family (cf. Thoits 1983). Our findings even suggested that parents with a strong extrafamilial investment may welcome signs of their child's maturation and the actual independence that their child displays. These signs may indicate an imminent reduction in parenting demands. Thus the maturation of the child may be interpreted by these parents as permitting them to spend more time with and to devote more energy toward their work or other extrafamilial interests.

Wave 1 data: Parent-adolescent relations and the moderating effects of socioeconomic status. In our next look at the data, we examined whether parents' reports of midlife identity concerns and well-being are related to the quality of parent-child relationships at the transition to adolescence, specifically, to intensity of parent-child conflict and to youngsters' level of emotional autonomy vis-à-vis their parents (Silverberg and Steinberg 1987). Here again we began by conducting analyses on mother-son, mother-daughter, father-son, and father-daughter dyads but with no further differentiations made among the parents. Several

TABLE 6.5. Correlations between Wave 1 Parent Well-Being
Variables and Quality of Parent-Adolescent Relationship

Parent-Adolescent Relationship Measure	Absence of Midlife Concerns	Self-Esteem	Life Satisfaction	Lack of Psychological Symptoms
	Mothers of daughters			
Mother-child conflict	.01	−.26*	−.32**	−.23*
Emotional autonomy	−.29*	−.17†	−.15	−.14
	Mothers of sons			
Mother-child conflict	−.16	−.03	−.38**	−.10
Emotional autonomy	−.13	−.10	−.18†	−.16
	Fathers of daughters			
Father-child conflict	.01	.04	−.09	−.01
Emotional autonomy	−.02	−.09	−.11	−.11
	Fathers of sons			
Father-child conflict	−.11	−.02	−.08	−.08
Emotional autonomy	−.39**	−.17	−.38**	−.04

Note: Ns range from 55 to 65.
†*p* < .10. *p* < .05. **p* < .01.

interesting findings emerged even from these initial analyses (see table
6.5). First, we found that fathers in the sample were more likely to
report midlife identity concerns when they had sons who were more
emotionally autonomous, that is, sons who have adopted less idealized
images of their parents, have relinquished some of their childish dependencies on them, and have formed a more individual sense of self;
mothers in the sample were more likely to report these heightened
feelings of reevaluation and introspection when they had daughters
who were more emotionally autonomous. This pattern of results offered some additional support for the psychoanalytic perspective on
parental development (Benedek 1959; Farrell and Rosenberg 1981b;
Lidz 1969). Mothers of daughters and fathers of sons may reconsider
their own life choices, personal commitments, and life situation when
they see their youngsters developing into independent adults. That fathers report lower life satisfaction in addition to more intense midlife
identity concerns in the face of emotional autonomy of their sons suggests that sons' emotional distancing may be particularly difficult for
fathers. Although perhaps surprising, this finding coincides with literature that suggests that fathers, more than mothers, have difficulty ad-

justing to an adolescent son's leaving home for college (Sullivan and Sullivan 1980; see also Glenn 1975 and Farrell and Rosenberg 1981a). Sons' increasing emotional autonomy in early adolescence may serve as a first signal to fathers that their son's departure is imminent.

A second important pattern of results to emerge from this portion of our data analyses indicated that mothers, but not fathers, seem to be adversely affected by the intensity of conflict they experience with their youngsters regarding such day-to-day issues as curfew, chores, free time, and style of clothes. One reason may be that mothers tend to play a more central role than fathers in childrearing and in the daily running of the household, whether or not they are employed outside the home (Maret and Findlay 1984). As a consequence, they may simply have more opportunities for engaging in conflictual discussions with their youngsters (Montemayor 1986); and they may be more likely to base their perceptions of self and of life in general on the quality of their familial relationships, including their relationships with their children (see Baruch et al. 1983; Gilligan 1982). That mothers seem to be adversely affected by conflict with sons *or* daughters lends some additional support to the stress hypothesis (Small, Eastman, and Cornelius 1988), suggesting that conflict (unlike children's emotional autonomy) may affect mothers directly, rather than through a mediating process of identification.

At this point in our analyses we began to explore the potential moderating impact of family socioeconomic status on the relation between parental well-being and the quality of parent-adolescent relationships. Most notable in our findings was that the relation between sons' emotional autonomy and fathers' midlife identity concerns mentioned above appeared to be stronger for *blue-collar* fathers ($r = .49$, $p < .05$) than for white-collar and professional fathers ($r = .21$, NS). This difference can be interpreted in at least two ways. First, children's emotional autonomy vis-à-vis parents during the early-adolescent years may be perceived as a challenge to parental control, particularly by working-class fathers, who generally place greater value on their youngsters' conformity and obedience and lesser value on their youngsters' autonomy and independence (Kohn 1977). As Rubin (1976) has noted, whereas white-collar and professional fathers have outlets for exercising authority and control in their work outside the family, "for the working-class man, there are few such rewards in the world outside the home; the family usually is the only place where he can exercise power, demand obedience to his authority" (99). It is surprising, however, that this SES difference did not also emerge for the effects of father-son conflict, as might be predicted.

A second factor may have contributed to the stronger association between midlife identity concerns and sons' emotional autonomy for blue-collar fathers than for white-collar and professional fathers. In contrast to white-collar and professional fathers, blue-collar fathers may perceive a greater difference between what they have achieved in their lives and what their sons could potentially attain in their adulthood, particularly with respect to occupational status and earnings. Seeing signs of their sons' increasing maturity and independence may cause all fathers to consider their adult accomplishments, since men are likely to base their definition of self in terms of individual achievement and success (Eisler and Ragsdale 1992), but may lead to a greater sense of disappointment among blue-collar fathers. Interestingly, Jacob's (1974) family interaction research suggests that adolescent sons may gain influence at the expense of their *father* in working-class families but at the expense of their *mother* in middle-class families. (See Ryff, Schmutte, and Lee, chapter 10 of this volume, for a discussion of the negative self-evaluations that may be experienced by women in older cohorts who watch their young adult daughters reach higher levels of educational and occupational attainment than they themselves have.)

Wave 1 data: Perceived increases of challenge/distance in the parent-adolescent relationship. Before moving on to longitudinal analyses, we conducted a final set of correlational analyses on the Wave 1 data (Silverberg 1986). Here we examined whether mothers' and fathers' perceptions of increased challenge/distance in three domains of the parent-child relationship (control, emotional support, and guidance) were related to parents' well-being and to their engagement in life/self questioning and reappraisal (midlife identity concerns). As can be seen in table 6.6, clear patterns of significant relations emerged for mother-daughter, father-son, and mother-son dyads. For example, mothers who reported increased challenge/distance in their relationship with their daughter compared with two years ago were those who reported more difficulties across three well-being areas. Specifically, mothers who perceive their daughters as becoming more disagreeable (control), less willing to come for or accept emotional support (emotional support), or less willing to come for or accept guidance and advice (guid-

TABLE 6.6. Correlations between Wave 1 Parent Well-Being
Variables and Perceived Increases in Challenge/Distance across
Three Domains of the Parent-Adolescent Relationship

Challenge/ Distance Domain	Absence of Midlife Concerns	Self- Esteem	Life Satisfaction	Lack of Psychological Symptoms
Mothers of daughters				
Control	−.33**	−.13	−.28*	−.35**
Emotional support	−.17†	−.06	−.26*	−.31**
Guidance	−.34**	−.20†	−.31**	−.40**
Mothers of sons				
Control	−.16	−.10	−.13	−.10
Emotional support	−.22*	−.05	−.18†	−.16
Guidance	−.31**	−.23*	−.30**	−.18†
Fathers of daughters				
Control	−.06	.01	−.11	.00
Emotional support	−.08	−.11	−.05	−.12
Guidance	−.18†	−.13	−.20†	−.08
Fathers of sons				
Control	−.20†	.02	−.13	.01
Emotional support	−.21†	−.13	−.29*	−.09
Guidance	−.45***	−.18†	−.32**	−.32**

Note: Ns range from 55 to 65.
†$p < .10$. *$p < .05$. **$p < .01$. ***$p < .001$.

ance) reported more intense midlife identity concerns, lower life satisfaction, and more psychological symptoms.

Those fathers who reported increased challenge/distance in the
guidance and emotional support domains vis-à-vis their sons seemed
to experience more intense midlife identity concerns and lower general
life satisfaction. There was little relation between any of the areas of
father well-being and perceptions of sons challenging the control domain of parenting (e.g., sons becoming more disagreeable). This is consistent with our finding discussed above that intensity of parent-child
conflict does not seem to be related to paternal well-being but is related
to maternal well-being. We also found that mothers' reports of increased challenge/distance in the guidance and emotional support domains in relation to their sons were related to mothers' reports of more
intense midlife identity concerns, lower life satisfaction, and (relative
to the guidance domain only) lower self-esteem.

In short, the measures of perceived change in the parent-child relationship were especially consistent correlates of parental well-being in mother-daughter, father-son, and mother-son dyads. They stood out, therefore, as some of the most promising predictor variables to examine in the longitudinal analyses of changes in parental well-being over time.

Longitudinal analyses. Recall that a second wave of data on parental sense of self and well-being was collected from the sample of mothers and fathers after a twelve-month interval. These data permitted an examination of whether signs of the transition to adolescence, quality of the parent-child relationship, and perceived increases in challenge/distance in the parent-child relationship (all assessed at Wave 1) actually predict *changes* in level of parental well-being and midlife concerns over time. To this end, a series of hierarchical regression analyses were conducted in which a Wave 1 adolescent or parent-child variable was used to predict a parent well-being variable at Wave 2 while controlling for scores on that same well-being variable as measured at Wave 1, that is, after first entering Wave 1 scores on the well-being variable. A separate equation was determined for each well-being variable in association with each adolescent/parent-child variable. As above, separate analyses were conducted for mother-son, mother-daughter, father-son, and father-daughter dyads. Because our previous analyses indicated that family SES and parents' level of work-role orientation are important moderating factors, separate analyses were conducted for working-class and middle-class mothers and fathers and for parents with "high" work-role orientation and "low" work-role orientation (based on a median split). Dividing the sample according to adolescent gender and by family SES or parent work-role orientation limited the sample size of each set of regression analyses (typical cell size: N = 25); thus, until replicated, the results presented here should be interpreted with some caution.

Overall, analyses indicated that the developmental and relational aspects of adolescence do seem to have some impact on parents' sense of self and well-being over time. The significant effects—though not especially strong or pervasive (i.e., apparent across all well-being areas or for all predictor variables)—did emerge among the subgroups of parents predicted to be the most susceptible. Tables 6.7–6.13 show the effects for which the increment in R^2 (associated with the Wave 1 predictor variable) is significant for one or both of the subsamples

TABLE 6.7. Regression of Wave 2 Parental Well-Being Variables on Wave 1 Indices of Adolescent Development, Quality of Parent-Child Relationship, and Perceived Increases of Distance/Challenge in the Parent-Adolescent Relationship: Significant Effects for Mothers of Sons

	Mothers with High Work-Role Orientation		Mothers with Low Work-Role Orientation	
	Beta	R^2 chg[a]	Beta	R^2 chg[a]
Absence of midlife concerns				
Conflict	.37	.13*		
Emotional autonomy	−.33	.10*	−.32	.10†
Control			−.43	.18**
Emotional support			−.35	.12*
Guidance			−.59	.34***
Self-esteem				
Heterosocial	.32	.10*	−.36	.12*
Conflict			−.29	.09†
Control			−.47	.21**
Guidance			−.42	.18**
Life satisfaction				
Conflict	.47	.17*		
Emotional autonomy			−.60	.36**
Control	−.44	.19*		
Emotional support			−.37	.14†
Guidance			−.39	.15†
Lack of psychological symptoms				
Pubertal			−.37	.14*
Control			−.37	.13*
Emotional support			−.36	.13*
Guidance			−.49	.24***

[a]Additional variance in 1986 parental well-being variables explained by 1985 predictors after controlling for 1985 scores on parental well-being variables. Ns range from 20 to 26.
†$p < .10$ (reported if part of a larger pattern). *$p < .05$. **$p < .01$. ***$p < .001$.

being compared. We find several interesting patterns of significant results, but a few stand out as most striking and consistent. The discussion here will focus on these findings.

First, when the sample is divided by parent's level of work-role orientation, it appears to be *low work-role orientation mothers of sons* who are most vulnerable to indicators of adolescence and to perceived in-

TABLE 6.8. Regression of Wave 2 Parental Well-Being Variables on Wave 1 Indices of Adolescent Development, Quality of Parent-Child Relationship, and Perceived Increases of Distance/Challenge in the Parent-Adolescent Relationship: Significant Effects for Mothers of Sons

	Mothers in Middle-Class Households		Mothers in Working-Class Households	
	Beta	R^2 chg[a]	Beta	R^2 chg[a]
Absence of midlife concerns				
Heterosocial	.31	.08**	−.41	.17*
Emotional autonomy			−.34	.11†
Guidance	−.20	.04†	−.41	.14†
Self-esteem				
Conflict	−.18	.03†		
Control	−.23	.05*		
Life satisfaction				
Control	−.37	.12*	−.45	.20*
Emotional support			−.54	.27**
Guidance			−.53	.25*
Lack of psychological symptoms				
Pubertal			−.30	.09†
Control			−.29	.08†
Emotional support			−.44	.19**
Guidance	−.31	.09*	−.40	.15*

[a]Additional variance in 1986 parental well-being variables explained by 1985 predictors after controlling for 1985 scores on parental well-being variables. Ns range from 18 to 32.
†$p < .10$ (reported if part of a larger pattern). *$p < .05$. **$p < .01$.

creases in challenge/distance vis-à-vis their youngster (see table 6.7). For these mothers, perceived increases in challenge/distance in the parent-child relationship in the domains of control and guidance (as measured at Wave 1) were especially good predictors of *increases* in midlife identity concerns and psychological symptoms and of *decreases* in self-esteem and life satisfaction. Sons' level of emotional autonomy, pubertal maturation, and heterosocial involvement also predicted diminished maternal well-being among the low work-role orientation mothers, but these effects were more restricted. Among mothers with a relatively weak orientation toward their paid-work role, then, perceptions of increased challenge/distance in the mother-son relationship—as evidenced, for example, in more frequent occasions of sons' argu-

TABLE 6.9. Regression of Wave 2 Parental Well-Being Variables on Wave 1 Indices of Adolescent Development, Quality of Parent-Child Relationship, and Perceived Increases of Distance/Challenge in the Parent-Adolescent Relationship: Significant Effects for Fathers of Sons

	Fathers in Middle-Class Households		Fathers in Working-Class Households	
	Beta	R^2 chg[a]	Beta	R^2 chg[a]
Absence of midlife concerns				
Emotional autonomy			−.25	.05†
Guidance	.21	.04†		
Self-esteem				
Emotional support	.25	.06*		
Life satisfaction				
Heterosocial	.39	.15**		
Emotional autonomy	.29	.07†		
Guidance			−.44	.12+

[a]Additional variance in 1986 parental well-being variables explained by 1985 predictors after controlling for 1985 scores on parental well-being variables. Ns range from 18 to 32.
†$p < .10$ (reported if part of a larger pattern). *$p < .05$. **$p < .01$.

ments about rules and of sons' devaluing maternal opinion—appear to lead to diminished well-being and heightened life/self questioning and reappraisal. Perceptions of a loss in control over youngsters' behavior have been documented by other researchers (Anderson, Hetherington, and Clingempeel 1989; Papini and Sebby 1987); the present analyses suggest that such perceptions have poor, but perhaps only temporary, mental health consequences for low work-orientation mothers.

When the sample of mothers of sons is divided by family SES (which shows only a modest though significant correlation with mother's work-role orientation: $r = .19$, $p < .05$), it is, as predicted, mothers living in working-class households who show a more consistent pattern of diminished well-being in the face of realignments in the parent-child relationship (see table 6.8); the social class difference in pattern of effects is not as clear as the difference according to work-role orientation, however.

These longitudinal findings bring fairly compelling confirmation to the idea (suggested in our Wave 1 analyses) that without a strong basis

TABLE 6.10. Regression of Wave 2 Parental Well-Being Variables
on Wave 1 Indices of Adolescent Development, Quality
of Parent-Child Relationship, and Perceived Increases
of Distance/Challenge in the Parent-Adolescent Relationship:
Significant Effects for Mothers of Daughters

	Mothers with High Work-Role Orientation		Mothers with Low Work-Role Orientation	
	Beta	R^2 chg[a]	Beta	R^2 chg[a]
Absence of midlife concerns				
Heterosocial	.35	.12†	.38	.14*
Self-esteem				
Control	−.59	.35***		
Emotional support	−.41	.17*		
Guidance	−.36	.13*		
Life satisfaction				
Emotional autonomy			−.49	.20*
Guidance			−.40	.16†
Lack of psychological symptoms				
Heterosocial	.44	.19**		

[a]Additional variance in 1986 parental well-being variables explained by 1985 predictors after controlling for 1985 scores on parental well-being variables. Ns range from 15 to 29.
†p < .10 (reported if part of a larger pattern). *p < .05. **p < .01. ***p < .001.

outside of the family for their sense of self and satisfactions, mothers
may have difficulty handling the occasional challenges of their sons'
maturity and the realignments in the parent-child relationship that
tend to emerge during the adolescent years. Why might this be more
true for mothers of sons than for mothers of daughters? First, it is
possible that the challenges of a son's maturity at early adolescence are
experienced as more potent. Research by Steinberg (1981) and Hill
(1988) suggests that although mothers may experience a temporary
increase in conflict with sons and daughters during early adolescence,
only sons appear to gain in influence in family decision making at the
expense of their mother at this time. It is also possible that the greater
degree of emotional closeness apparent in mother-daughter dyads
(Steinberg 1987b; Youniss and Smollar 1985) serves as a buffer to
changes in the parent-child relationship. In the absence of this level
of emotional closeness, changes in the parent-child relationship when
instigated by sons may be experienced as unsettling to low work-role

TABLE 6.11. Regression of Wave 2 Parental Well-Being Variables on Wave 1 Indices of Adolescent Development, Quality of Parent-Child Relationship, and Perceived Increases of Distance/Challenge in the Parent-Adolescent Relationship: Significant Effects for Mothers of Daughters

	Mothers in Middle-Class Households		Mothers in Working-Class Households	
	Beta	R^2 chg[a]	Beta	R^2 chg[a]
Absence of midlife concerns				
Heterosocial			.45	.17**
Control	−.24	.05†	.51	.14*
Self-esteem				
Conflict			.24	.05†
Control	−.33	.11**	−.25	.06†
Life satisfaction				
Conflict			.48	.22*
Lack of psychological symptoms				
Heterosocial	.34	.11**		

[a]Additional variance in 1986 parental well-being variables explained by 1985 predictors after controlling for 1985 scores on parental well-being variables. Ns range from 18 to 34.
†$p < .10$ (reported if part of a larger pattern). *$p < .05$. **$p < .01$.

TABLE 6.12. Regression of Wave 2 Parental Well-Being Variables on Wave 1 Indices of Adolescent Development, Quality of Parent-Child Relationship, and Perceived Increases of Distance/Challenge in the Parent-Adolescent Relationship: Significant Effects for Fathers of Daughters

	Fathers with High Work-Role Orientation		Fathers with Low Work-Role Orientation	
	Beta	R^2 chg[a]	Beta	R^2 chg[a]
Absence of midlife concerns				
Control			−.30	.09*
Emotional support			−.27	.07*

[a]Additional variance in 1986 parental well-being variables explained by 1985 predictors after controlling for 1985 scores on parental well-being variables. Ns range from 22 to 26.
†$p < .10$ (reported if part of a larger pattern). *$p < .05$.

TABLE 6.13. Regression of Wave 2 Parental Well-Being Variables
on Wave 1 Indices of Adolescent Development, Quality
of Parent-Child Relationship, and Perceived Increases
of Distance/Challenge in the Parent-Adolescent Relationship:
Significant Effects for Fathers of Daughters

	Fathers in Middle-Class Households		Fathers in Working-Class Households	
	Beta	R^2 chg^a	Beta	R^2 chg^a
Absence of midlife concerns				
Conflict	.17	.03†		
Control	−.25	.06**		
Self-esteem				
Emotional autonomy	.27	.07*		
Lack of psychological symptoms				
Emotional autonomy			−.45	.19†

^{a}Additional variance in 1986 parental well-being variables explained by 1985 predictors after controlling for 1985 scores on parental well-being variables. Ns range from 17 to 33.
†$p < .10$ (reported if part of a larger pattern). *$p < .05$. **$p < .01$.

orientation mothers' sense of self and well-being. One might predict as
well that increased distance/challenge in the mother-son relationship
would be especially unsettling for low work-orientation mothers when
it is accompanied by family interaction patterns in which sons align
with their fathers in devaluing (or in competition against) mothers.
This sort of coalition in family interactions was identified by Powers
and her colleagues in many families of "high-functioning" fourteen-
year-old sons (Powers et al. 1987).

Analyses of our Wave 1 data also suggested that some parents may
respond *favorably* to signs of their youngster's development at the transition to adolescence. And, indeed, the second striking pattern of results to emerge from the longitudinal analyses provides some confirmation of this idea. As can be seen in table 6.9, *middle-class fathers of
sons*—fathers who are employed in white-collar or professional/tech-
nical jobs—seem most likely to react favorably to their youngster's
development and to realignments in the parent-child relationship.
Whereas for other subsamples of parents, for example, mothers of
daughters, the developmental and relational changes of adolescence
predict a *mix* of increases and decreases in well-being (tables 6.10 and
6.11), among middle-class fathers of sons, increased emotional distance

in the parent-adolescent relationship and adolescent involvement in heterosocial activities predicts *increased* paternal well-being. In contrast, the analyses bring forth some tentative evidence that fathers employed in blue-collar occupations show decreases in well-being (life satisfaction) and increases in life/self questioning and reappraisal (midlife concerns) in the face of greater distance and emotional autonomy on the part of their sons.[3] This differential pattern was noted and interpreted in some detail above with regard to Wave 1 results. Overall it appears that blue-collar fathers may be more likely to feel threatened by these early signs of autonomy and independence on the part of their sons; early adolescent sons' increasing maturity and independence may not only provoke life/self reappraisal among blue-collar fathers but also instigate some feelings of disappointment in their own achievements. If these fathers value conformity and obedience in their children over independence and self-direction, as is suggested in other research (Kohn 1977), it is possible that they interpret early signs of emotional autonomy in their sons as disturbing challenges to their role as parent. On the other hand, fathers working in white-collar/professional jobs may have greater leeway to experience a vicarious sense of pride and well-being in response to signs of their sons' growing independence.

CONCLUSIONS AND DIRECTIONS FOR FUTURE RESEARCH

This research, although limited with respect to both its sample composition and size and its strong reliance on questionnaire measures, begins to raise some doubts about the claims that parents' mental health is inevitably "at risk" and that all parents will experience a personal crisis as a result of observing the signs and relationship changes marking their youngster's adolescence. Complicated, yet systematic individual differences in parental vulnerability as a function of parent gender, parent investment in paid work, and socioeconomic status were pervasive in the findings.

For some parents early adolescence does seem to be a stressful and/ or provocative time. In the face of even minor challenges, distancing, and signs of their youngster's expanding social world, some parents experience declines in their own sense of life satisfaction and self-esteem and increases in their tendency to engage in life/self questioning and reappraisal. The longitudinal data presented here suggest that mothers who have sons *and* who are low with respect to their investment in their paid work are most likely to fit this description. What can account for this finding? First, we know from other research that mothers tend to be more greatly affected than fathers by emotional strains and stresses in family relationships (Scott and Alwin 1989), perhaps because as women they ground their sense of self and psychological well-being to a large degree on the quality of their ongoing relationships (Baruch, Barnett, and Rivers 1983; Gilligan 1982; McGrath et al. 1990). We also know that, on the whole, realignments in parent-child relationships at early adolescence seem to be most potent in the mother-son dyad (Hill 1988; Powers et al. 1987, Steinberg 1981). Mothers of sons are not equally vulnerable to declines in mental health, however. Those who seem most vulnerable are those who do not have the supportive buffer of a strong investment in paid work. A psychological investment and satisfaction in work may support a mother's sense of competence and self-worth and thus may protect her against the potentially unsettling challenges that are sometimes a part of adolescence (Steinberg and Steinberg 1994).

For other parents, the defining aspects of early adolescence in their children seem to bring a time of increased satisfaction, well-being, and perhaps even pride. Fathers of sons—in particular, white-collar and professional fathers of sons—are among those most likely to fall into this group. Blue-collar fathers, as was discussed above, seem more likely to react negatively to early signs of autonomy and independence on the part of their sons. For most parents, however, the normative development and relational changes of adolescence seem to bring a mix of positive and negative emotions and reactions. In this sample, a mixed pattern was most readily observed among mothers of early adolescent daughters, which is quite consistent with research that suggests that mother-daughter relationships are often the most emotionally charged, in terms of *both* closeness and conflict (e.g., Youniss and Smollar 1985).

More than anything else, then, this research underscores the necessity of systematically exploring individual differences among parents at midlife. The notion that some parents are more susceptible to the impact of their youngster's maturation is consistent with Peck's (1968) theoretical work in which he proposed that because middle adulthood is a time of waning familial roles, healthy development during these years is dependent on the individual's ability to invest himself or herself in a variety of roles and relationships. Interestingly, the findings in the present research provide evidence to suggest that for some parents, relationships to roles in spheres outside of the family—to paid work—

can in fact serve as pivotal moderators of the parent's sensitivity or vulnerability to developmental and relational changes of their youngster's adolescence.

In this chapter, I have pointed out the potential benefits of parents of having a relatively strong work-role orientation during their child's transition into adolescence. It is important, however, for future research to examine the impact of children's development on parental mental health—and the role that work commitment plays in the process—during other periods of the family life cycle, because variations in work orientation may have different implications and consequences at different stages of the child's development. A strong work orientation during earlier phases of the child's development, for example, when time and energy demands on parents are greater, may be associated with more intense multiple role strain, conflict between work and parenting, and diminished parental well-being (see, however, Hoffman 1989 and Repetti, Matthews, and Waldron 1989). Future research efforts should also consider the potential moderating effects of parent commitments to *other* valued extrafamilial activities such as volunteer work, church involvement, and community affairs. Parents' psychological investment in these kinds of activities also may serve as a buffer to the normative challenges in the family at early adolescence that might otherwise be unsettling to sense of self and life satisfaction.

A strength of the present research is that it incorporated a longitudinal design. Although the longitudinal analyses revealed numerous significant and theoretically meaningful effects, some scholars might have expected the impact of adolescence to be stronger than was found here. There are several possible explanations for why the longitudinal effects were somewhat restricted. First, the gap between the two points of data collection was twelve months—an interval during which many factors can intervene. Second, and perhaps more telling, is that some parents may actively keep the positive aspects of their youngster and of the parent-adolescent relationship in mind in the face of occasional challenges, daily provocations, and signs of distancing. The mixed perceptions of a mother of a fifteen-year-old boy, who participated in a later interview phase of the research (see Steinberg and Steinberg 1994), provide a good illustration of a parent framing challenge within a larger context of positive appraisals: "I enjoy the boys a lot more now that they're older than when they were younger. But I think the problems are really more of a challenge [now]. . . . I find it a real challenge, but

I enjoy them more now that they're older. . . . We've always been real close, I mean, even when we were doing a lot of arguing, fighting, and carrying on . . . that was 8th and 9th grade."

Models of stress and coping (see Lazarus and Folkman 1984) would consider this ability to see change and challenge in perspective—the ability to reframe—a critical factor that may buffer parents from being especially vulnerable or sensitive during their children's early adolescence. Future research on parenting and parental mental health at adolescence should therefore examine the potential moderating role of cognitive coping strategies. Moreover, there is no doubt, as was mentioned above, that other intrapersonal factors, including the parent's belief system regarding what is normative behavior during the period of adolescence (Collins 1990) and the parent's personal characteristics (e.g., sense of control), might also serve as moderators and warrant further study as well.

The data discussed here are based on responses from parents who were in their thirties and forties in the mid-1980s. If the attitudes of these parents about parenting, about adolescence, and/or about work are distinctly cohort-particular (Rossi 1980), the present results may not adequately represent the experiences or feelings of parents from previous cohorts or those of future cohorts. It is critical to note as well that the data were collected from married parents, who have not experienced divorce, and their firstborn youngsters. This raises the question of whether the pattern of findings that emerged can be generalized to parents living in other family structures and to parents' well-being vis-à-vis their relationship with later-born children. It is possible, for example, that single mothers of daughters—especially those who have developed a very close, positive relationship with their daughters and who have enlisted their daughters as emotional confidantes (Hetherington 1989; Wallerstein 1985; Wallerstein and Blakeslee 1989; Weiss 1979)—experience a greater sense of loss as they detect signs of their daughter's maturation and emotional independence (see Anderson et al. 1989).

The influence of adolescents on parents as developing adults most certainly involves a dynamic interplay of intrapersonal, familial, and extrafamilial factors. The processes involved seem subtle and complex enough that a combination of interview, questionnaire, and observational data would be required to capture fully the meaning of this period for parents and their well-being. Future research endeavors in this area would benefit, therefore, from a multimethod approach to data collection and from a focus on parents living in a variety of family structures, communities, and cultures.

NOTES

1. Analyses revealed that level of parenting-role orientation is neither a strong nor a systematic moderating factor in the present study. The very few significant interactions that did emerge do not account for a sizable proportion of the variance in parental well-being or form any interpretable pattern. The plan for the regression analyses is therefore described here with reference to work-role orientation only.

2. The direction of the signs associated with these slopes is negative because all four parent well-being scales were scored so that higher scores indicate positive adaptation.

3. The longitudinal analyses point to family SES, based on father's occupational status, as a more powerful moderator than father's level of work-role orientation; the correlation between SES and father work-role orientation, however, was significant though modest in strength: $r = .19$, $p < .05$.

REFERENCES

Adelmann, P., T. Antonucci, S. Crohan, and L. Coleman. 1990. A causal analysis of employment and health in midlife women. *Women and Health* 16:5–20.

Anderson, E., E. M. Hetherington, and W. Clingempeel. 1989. Transformations in family relations at puberty: Effects of family context. *Journal of Early Adolescence* 9:310–334.

Anderson, S., C. Russell, and W. Schumm. 1983. Perceived marital quality and family life-cycle categories: A further analysis. *Journal of Marriage and the Family* 45:127–139.

Ballenski, C., and A. Cook. 1982. Mothers' perceptions of their competence in managing selected parenting tasks. *Family Relations* 31:489–494.

Barnett, R., and G. Baruch. 1978. Women in the middle years: A critique of research and theory. *Psychology of Women Quarterly* 3:187–197.

Bart, P. 1971. Depression in middle-aged women. In V. Gornick and B. Moran, eds., *Women in sexist society: Studies in power and powerlessness*, pp. 163–186. New York: Basic Books.

Baruch, G., R. Barnett, and C. Rivers. 1983. *Lifeprints.* New York: McGraw-Hill.

Bassoff, E. 1987. Mothering adolescent daughters: A psychodynamic perspective. *Journal of Counseling and Development:* 65:471–474.

Benedek, T. 1959. Parenthood as a developmental phase: A contribution to the libido theory. *Journal of the American Psychoanalytic Association* 7:389–417.

Biddle, B., and E. Thomas, eds. 1979. *Role theory: Concepts and research.* New York: Krieger.

Birnbaum, J. 1975. Life patterns and self-esteem in gifted family-oriented and career-committed women. In M. Mednick, S. Tanger, and L. Hoffman, eds. *Women and achievement: Social and motivational analyses*, pp. 396–419. New York: Hemisphere-Halstead.

Blos, P. 1967. The second individuation process of adolescence. *Psychoanalytic Study of the Child* 15:162–186.

———. 1979. *The adolescent passage.* New York: International Universities Press.

Boxer, A., B. Solomon, D. Offer, A. Petersen, and F. Halprin. 1984. Parents' perceptions of young adolescents. In R. Cohen, B. Cohler, and S. Weissman, eds., *Parenthood: A psychodynamic perspective,* pp. 64–84. New York: Guilford.

Breytspraak, L. 1984. *The development of self in later life.* Boston: Little, Brown.

Campbell, A., P. Converse, and W. L. Rodgers. 1976. *The quality of American life: Perceptions, evaluations, and satisfactions.* New York: Russell Sage Foundation.

Chiriboga, D. 1989. Mental health at the midpoint: Crisis, challenge, or relief? In S. Hunter and M. Sundel, eds., *Midlife myths: Issues, findings, and practice implications,* pp. 116–144. Newbury Park, Calif.: Sage.

Cohen, R., and H. Balikov. 1974. On the impact of adolescence upon parents. In S. Feinstein and P. Giovacchini, eds. *Adolescent psychiatry,* 3:217–236. New York: Basic Books.

Colarusso, C., and R. Nemiroff. 1982. The father in midlife: Crisis and the growth of paternal identity. In S. Cath, A. Gurwitt, and J. Ross, eds., *Father and child: Developmental and clinical perspectives,* pp. 315–327. Boston: Little, Brown.

Coleman, L., and T. Antonucci. 1983. Impact of work, on women at midlife. *Developmental Psychology* 19:290–295.

Collins, W. A. 1990. Parent-child relationships in the transition to adolescence: Continuity and change in interaction, affect, and cognition. In R. Montemayor, G. Adams, and T. Gullotta, eds., *From childhood to adolescence: A transitional period?* pp. 85–106. Newbury Park, Calif.: Sage.

Eisler, R., and K. Ragsdale. 1992. Masculine gender role and midlife transition in men. In V. Van Hasselt and M. Hersen, eds., *Handbook of social development: A lifespan perspective,* pp. 455–471. New York: Plenum.

Farrell, M., and S. Rosenberg. 1981a. *Men at midlife.* Dover, Mass.: Auburn House.

———. 1981b. Parent-child relations at middle age. In C. Getty and W. Humphreys, eds., *Understanding the family: Stress and change in American family life* pp. 57–76. New York: Appleton-Century-Crofts.

Flannery, D. 1991. The impact of puberty on parent-adolescent relations: An observational study of the relationship between affect and engagement in interactions, parent-adolescent conflict, and adolescent problem behavior. Ph.D. diss., Ohio State University.

Freud, A. 1958. Adolescence. *Psychoanalytic Study of the Child* 13:255–278.

Garbarino, J., N. Burston, S. Raber, R. Russell, and A. Crouter. 1978. The social maps of children approaching adolescence. *Journal of Youth and Adolescence* 7: 417–428.

Gilligan, C. 1982. Adult development and women's development: Arrangements for a marriage. In J. Z. Giele, ed., *Women in the middle years: Current knowledge and directions for future research and policy,* pp. 89–114. New York: Wiley.

Glenn, N. 1975. Psychological well-being in the post-parental stage: Some evidence from national surveys. *Journal of Marriage and the Family* 37:105–110.

Gould, R. L. 1972. The phases of adult life: A study in developmental psychology. *American Journal of Psychiatry* 6:16–20.

Greenberger, E., and W. Goldberg. 1989. Work, parenting, and the socialization of children. *Developmental Psychology* 25:22–35.

Hetherington, E. M. 1989. Coping with family transitions: Winners, losers, and survivors. *Child Development* 60:1–14.

Hill, J. P. 1980. The family. In M. Johnson, ed., *Toward adolescence: The middle school years* (Seventy-ninth yearbook of the National Society for the Study of Education, pp. 32–55). Chicago: University of Chicago Press.

———. 1988. Adapting to menarche: Familial control and conflict. In M. Gunnar and W. A. Collins, eds., *Development during the transition to adolescence: Minnesota symposium on child development,* 21:43–77. Hillsdale, N.J.: Erlbaum.

Hill, J., and G. Holmbeck. 1986. Attachment and autonomy during adolescence. In G. Whitehurst, ed., *Annals of child development,* 3:145–189. Greenwich, Conn.: JAI.

———. 1987. Familial adaptation to biological change during adolescence. In R. Lerner and T. Foch, eds., *Biological-psychological interactions in early adolescence,* pp. 207–223. Hillsdale, N.J.: Erlbaum.

Hoffman, L. 1989. Effects of maternal employment in the two-parent family. *American Psychologist* 44:283–292.

Hoffman, L., and J. Manis. 1978. Influences of children on marital interaction and parental satisfactions and dissatisfactions. In R. Lerner and G. Spanier, eds., *Child influences on marital and family interactions,* pp. 165–213. New York: Academic Press.

Jacob, T. 1974. Patterns of family conflict and dominance as a function of child age and social class. *Developmental Psychology* 10:1–12.

Josselson, R. 1980. Ego development in adolescence. In J. Adelson, ed., *Handbook of adolescent psychology,* pp. 188–210. New York: Wiley.

Julian, T., P. McKenry, and M. McKelvey. 1991. Mediators of relationship stress between middle-aged fathers and their adolescent children. *Journal of Genetic Psychology* 152:381–386.

Keniston, K. 1963. Scales for the measurement of identity. Unpublished manuscript, Yale University School of Medicine.

Kenny, M. 1987. The extent and function of parent attachment among first-year college students. *Journal of Youth and Adolescence* 16:17–29.

Kidwell, J., J. Fischer, R. Dunham, and M. Baranowski. 1983. Parents and adolescents: Push and pull of change. In H. McCubbin and C. Figley, eds., *Stress in the family: Coping with normative transitions,* pp. 74–89. New York: Bruner/Mazel.

Kohn, M. 1977. *Class and conformity: A study of values.* Chicago: University of Chicago Press.

La Sorsa, V., and I. Fodor. 1990. Adolescent daughter/midlife mother dyad. *Psychology of Women Quarterly* 14:593–606.

Lazarus, R., and S. Folkman. 1984. *Stress, appraisal, and coping.* New York: Springer.

Lidz, T. 1969. The adolescent in his family. In G. Caplan and S. Lebovici, eds., *Adolescence: Psychosocial perspectives,* pp. 105–112. New York: Basic Books.

Maret, E., and B. Findlay. 1984. The distribution of household labor among women in dual-earner marriages. *Journal of Marriage and the Family* 46:357–364.

McCall, G., and J. Simmons. 1978. *Identities and interactions.* New York: Free Press.

McGrath, E., G. Keita, B. Strickland, and N. Russo. 1990. *Women and depression: Risk factors and treatment issues.* Washington, D.C.: American Psychological Association.

Montemayor, R. 1986. Family variation in storm and stress. *Journal of Adolescent Research* 1:15–31.

Neugarten, B. 1977. Personality and aging. In J. Birren and K. W. Schaie, eds., *Handbook of the psychology of aging,* pp. 626–649. New York: Van Nostrand Reinhold.

Oliver, R. 1977. The "empty nest syndrome" as a focus of depression: A cognitive treatment model based on rational emotive therapy. *Psychotherapy* 14:87–94.

Papini, D., and R. Sebby. 1987. Adolescent pubertal status and affective family relationships: A multivariate assessment. *Journal of Youth and Adolescence* 16:1–15.

Pasley, K., and V. Gecas. 1984. Stresses and satisfaction in the parenting role. *Personnel and Guidance Journal* 2:400–404.

Pearlin, L., and M. Lieberman. 1979. Social sources of emotional distress. In R. Simmons, ed., *Research in community and mental health,* 1:217–248. Greenwich, Conn.: JAI.

Peck, R. 1968. Psychological developments in the second half of life. In B. Neugarten, ed., *Middle age and aging,* pp. 88–92. Chicago: University of Chicago Press.

Powell, B. 1977. The empty nest, employment, and psychiatric symptoms in college-educated women. *Psychology of Women Quarterly* 2:35–43.

Powers, S., W. Beardslee, A. Jacobson, and G. Noam. April 1987. Family influences on the development of adolescent coping processes. Paper presented at the biennial meeting of the Society for Research in Child Development, Baltimore.

Radloff, L. 1977. The CES-D scale: A self-report depression scale for research in the general population. *Applied Psychological Measurement* 1:385–401.

Repetti, R. L., K. A. Matthews, and I. Waldron. 1989. Employment and women's health: Effects of paid employment on women's mental and physical health. *American Psychologist* 44:1394–1401.

Richardson, R., N. Galambos, J. Schulenberg, and A. Petersen. 1984. Young adolescents' perceptions of the family environment. *Journal of Early Adolescence* 4:131–153.

Robin, A., and J. Weiss. 1980. Criterion-related validity of behavioral and self-report measures of problem-solving communication skills in distressed and non-distressed parent-adolescent dyads. *Behavioral Assessment* 2:339–352.

Rollins, B. 1989. Marital quality at midlife. In S. Hunter and M. Sundel, eds., *Midlife myths: Issues, findings, and practice implications*, pp. 184–194. Newbury Park, Calif.: Sage.

Rosenberg, M. 1965. *Society and the adolescent self-image.* Princeton: N.J.: Princeton University Press.

Rossi, A. 1980. Aging and parenthood in the middle years. In P. Baltes and O. Brim, eds., *Life-span development and behavior*, 3:137–205. New York: Academic Press.

Rubin, L. 1976. *Worlds of pain: Life in the working-class family.* New York: Basic Books.

———. 1979. *Women of a certain age: The midlife search for self.* New York: Harper and Row.

Ryan, R., and J. Lynch. 1989. Emotional autonomy versus detachment: Revisiting the vicissitudes of adolescence and young adulthood. *Child Development* 60: 340–356.

Scott, J., and D. Alwin. 1989. Gender differences in parental strain: Parental role or gender role. *Journal of Family Issues* 10:482–503.

Sheehy, G. 1976. *Passages: Predictable crises of adult life.* New York: Dutton.

Silverberg, S. 1986. Psychological well-being of parents with early adolescent children. Ph.D. diss., University of Wisconsin, Madison.

Silverberg, S., and L. Steinberg. 1987. Adolescent autonomy, parent-adolescent conflict, and parental well-being. *Journal of Youth and Adolescence* 16:293–312.

———. 1990. Psychological well-being of parents with early adolescent children. *Developmental Psychology* 26:658–666.

Silverberg, S., D. Tennenbaum, and T. Jacob. 1992. Adolescence and family interaction. In V. Van Hasselt and M. Hersen, eds., *Handbook of social development: A lifespan perspective*, pp. 347–370. New York: Plenum.

Small, S., G. Eastman, and S. Cornelius. 1988. Adolescent autonomy and parental stress. *Journal of Youth and Adolescence* 17:377–392.

Smith, B. 1976. Adolescent and parent: Interaction between developmental stages. *Center Quarterly Focus.* St. Paul: University of Minnesota Center for Youth Development and Research.

Smollar, J., and J. Youniss. 1989. Transformations in adolescents' perceptions of parents. *International Journal of Behavioural Development* 12:71–84.

Steinberg, L. 1981. Transformations in family relations at puberty. *Developmental Psychology* 17:833–840.

———. 1987a. The impact of puberty on family relations: Effects of pubertal status and pubertal timing. *Developmental Psychology* 23:451–460.

———. 1987b. Special issue: Sex differences in family relations at adolescence. *Journal of Youth and Adolescence* 16 (3).

———. 1988. Reciprocal relation between parent-child distance and pubertal maturation. *Developmental Psychology* 24:122–128.

———. 1990. Autonomy, conflict, and harmony in the family relationship. In S.

Feldman and G. Elliot, eds., *At the threshold: The developing adolescent,* pp. 255–276. Cambridge: Harvard University Press.

Steinberg, L., J. Elmen, and N. Mounts. 1989. Authoritative parenting, psychosocial maturity, and academic success among adolescents. *Child Development* 60: 1424–1436.

Steinberg, L., and S. B. Silverberg. 1986. The vicissitudes of autonomy in early adolescence. *Child Development* 57:841–851.

———. 1987. Influences on marital satisfaction during the middle stages of the family life cycle. *Journal of Marriage and the Family* 49:751–760.

Steinberg, L., and W. Steinberg. 1994. *Crossing paths.* New York: Simon and Schuster.

Sullivan, K., and A. Sullivan. 1980. Adolescent-parent separation. *Developmental Psychology* 16:93–99.

Thoits, P. 1983. Multiple identities and psychological well-being: A reformulation and test of the social isolation hypothesis. *American Sociological Review* 48:174–187.

Turner, B. F., and C. B. Turner. 1982. Mental health in the adult years. In T. Field, A. Huston, H. Quay, L. Troll, and G. Finley, eds., *Review of human development,* pp. 456–470. New York: Wiley.

Vaillant, G. 1977. *Adaptation to life.* Boston: Little, Brown.

Veroff, J., and S. Feld. 1970. *Marriage and work in America.* New York: Van Nostrand Reinhold.

Wallerstein, J. 1985. The overburdened child: Some long-term consequences of divorce. *Social Work,* 30:116–123.

Wallerstein, J., and S. Blakeslee. 1989. *Second chances: Men, women, and children a decade after divorce.* New York: Ticknor and Fields.

Weiss, R. 1979. Growing up a little faster: The experience of growing up in a single-parent household. *Journal of Social Issues* 35:97–111.

Youniss, J., and J. Smollar. 1985. *Adolescent relations with mothers, fathers, and friends.* Chicago: The University of Chicago Press.

SEVEN

Reproductive Transitions: The Experience of Mothers and Daughters

Julia A. Graber and Jeanne Brooks-Gunn

The period of adolescence poses unique challenges for adolescents and their parents as both work through the process of redefining roles and expectations in the family environment. These adaptations in the family have been identified as a source of increased conflict between adolescents and their parents; however, at the same time, warmth, closeness, and general cohesion are not necessarily diminished in family relations, with these factors playing an important role in the individual's navigation of the adolescent decade (Collins 1990; 1980, 1987; Paikoff and Brooks-Gunn 1991).

Reproductive transitions have been important landmarks for defining the developmental transitions at either end of adolescence. That is, entry into puberty and pubertal development have defined the early adolescent transition, and starting a family of one's own or pregnancy is one transition that has characterized young adulthood (and midlife, given recent trends for pregnancy in some groups of women). In between these events, for most adolescents, is the entry into sexual activity. At the same time that adolescents are experiencing reproductive transitions, their mothers are also either in or approaching their own reproductive transition, menopause. Coupled with an interest in the literature on changing family relations during adolescence has been an interest in how pubertal development intersects with these changes. (See Paikoff and Brooks-Gunn 1991 for a review of this literature.)

The authors were supported by a grant from the National Institute of Child Health and Human Development (NICHD) during the writing of this paper. Studies conducted under the Adolescent Study Program were supported by grants from the W. T. Grant Foundation and NICHD. The authors also wish to acknowledge the influence of Michelle P. Warren, the co-director of the Adolescent Study Program, and Karen Matthews, Judith Rodin, Nancy Adler, Joyce Bromberger, Judy Cameron, Ralph Horowitz, Bruce McEwen, Anne Petersen, Marielle Rebuffe-Scrive, and Elizabeth Susman, members of the Reproductive Transitions Working Group of the John D. and Catherine T. MacArthur Foundation Research Network on Health-Promoting and Disease-Preventing Behaviors, in some of the ideas presented.

More generally, most reproductive transitions have been associated with changes in some aspect of parent-child relationships, often with emphasis on mother-daughter relationships.

We take the approach, as do other authors in this volume (e.g., Silverberg), that adolescent transitions and the life experiences of their parents are interconnected and interactive in their influence on both the adolescents and their parents. The correspondences between reproductive transitions may be particularly salient in the lives of mothers and daughters. Specifically, reproductive transitions across the life span are potentially linked in at least two ways. First, puberty and menopause may be linked in the manner already described, with both mothers and daughters experiencing reproductive transitions at the same time; the psychological experience of each individual's transition may affect her perception of the other's transition. A second link between these transitions is the fact that they involve the same reproductive system physiologically.

The focus in this chapter is on the role of reproductive transitions in the lives of women with specific interest in mother-daughter relationship changes around puberty, sexuality, pregnancy, and menopause. The links between reproductive transitions have engendered interest in understanding women's health and how reproductive transitions, stress, and adjustment are interrelated to one another and to subsequent health outcomes.

Based on a growing body of cross-disciplinary research in developmental and health psychology, it is likely that the nature of reproductive transitions may be a key factor in predicting mental and physical health outcomes. In particular, experiences of stress during periods of physiological change may be qualitatively different and have different effects on girls' and women's health than during a time of stability. This hypothesis is based on the assertions that (1) stress encompasses a broad range of environmental influences on the individual, (2) stress affects health, both physical and mental, (3) large individual differences exist in responsivity to stress and, hence, the ultimate health outcomes of the stress, (4) reproductive transitions are unique developmental periods when the physiological system is especially vulnerable to stress, (5) stress actually affects the physiological system differently during these periods, and (6) the most significant changes in health outcomes are likely to occur because of the accumulation of stress during a reproductive transition. In combination, evidence points to periods of reproductive transition as being crucial times when the nature of those experiences is likely to predict individual differences in subsequent mental and physical health outcomes.

Estrogen influences have been found on many physiologic systems of the body, including cardiovascular lipids, bone accretions, fat deposition, as well as affective and cognitive function across the life span (Adler and Matthews 1994), and especially during reproductive transitions such as puberty, pregnancy, and menopause. In addition, due to the interactive nature of the endocrine system, bidirectional effects are likely to exist between stress and reproductive hormones, that is, stress affects the production of reproductive hormones, as seen in elongation of the follicular phase of the menstrual cycle in response to psychological stressors. Commensurately, reproductive hormones affect the magnitude of cardiovascular and neuroendocrine responses to stress. For example, blood pressure responses to stress are higher in men than women but postmenopausal women exhibit higher blood pressure than same-age premenopausal women (Matthews 1989).

In addition, reproductive transitions are not merely experienced at a biological level but are also intrapsychic and social events. This is true of puberty, sexuality, pregnancy, and menopause. All have meaning to the individual as well as meaning in a social context, eliciting behavioral responses from others and indicating changes in roles. Such reconstructions of the sense of self and the self in social domains are likely to result in multiple changes during periods when the physiological system itself is more vulnerable to these accumulated stressors.

Our focus will be primarily on the social, biological, and psychological correlates of the pubertal transition, with an emphasis on mother-daughter relationships during puberty and subsequent reproductive transitions. Each of these transitions exists in the context of the physiological and psychological mutuality of mother-daughter reproductive transitions. Within the examination of the pubertal transition, the roles of mother-daughter conflict, cohesion, and discourse in mother-daugther relationships will be discussed. The initiation of sexual behavior and adolescent pregnancy will each be addressed, and we will highlight potential areas for future investigation of how adolescent and maternal roles are transformed by these transitions.

MODELS AND ISSUES IN THE STUDY OF REPRODUCTIVE TRANSITIONS

In this section, we present six models for studying reproductive transitions and brief examples of how these models apply to specific transitions, most often puberty, as the emphasis on transitions has been a focal point in research on adolescence (Graber, Brooks-Gunn, and Petersen in press). In addition, we describe the studies and issues that make up the program of research on which we will draw for the present discussion.

Models employed for studying reproductive transitions generally take into consideration the biological nature of the change as it interacts with psychological and social transitions either causally linked to or in combination with the biological transition. Six models are relevant for discussion. The first centers on the biological nature of the transition and its influence on related psychological and social developmental processes. In particular, changes in mother-daughter relationships at puberty may be due to changes in increased emotionality of the adolescent associated with pubertal hormone increases (Buchanan, Eccles, and Becker 1992) or may be related to psychological and social changes that puberty signals to the adolescent and her environmental context (Brooks-Gunn and Reiter 1990). Such interactions are also likely at other transitions, as in the case of pregnancy and menopause. At these times, hormonal systems may affect moods and behavior directly or via indirect paths. In either model, social context also factors into relational changes at the time of transition.

A second model focuses on the social context of the transition with less attention given to biological processes that may interact with social factors. Instead, emphasis is on identifying changing roles and responsibilities commensurate with the transition. The reproductive changes made in adolescence and the transition to adulthood—puberty, sexuality, pregnancy—are associated with changing status from childhood to adulthood, along with different social expectations in school, family, and peer domains. For example, teachers exhibit different grading practices between more and less pubertally advanced adolescents (Eccles et al. 1993), and parents of more physically mature girls are often more accepting of their dating behaviors than parents of same-age girls who are less mature (Stattin and Magnusson 1990).

A third approach focuses on self-definitional or intrapsychic changes that are associated with the reproductive transition. In this case, the individual herself associates a specific meaning to making the transition. In line with the aforementioned examples, more physically developed adolescents are more likely to expect to be treated as adults (Hill and Lynch 1983; Simmons and Blyth 1987). Other transitions also involve self-definitional change; pregnancy involves the transition into viewing oneself as a parent in addition to the other roles the adolescent or woman may already have incorporated into her sense of self (Deutsch et al. 1988; Ruble et al. 1990).

Cumulative events models draw on the previous models but note that intrapsychic, social role and context, and biological changes are often happening at the same time and hence have a cumulative effect on the outcome (Simmons & Blyth 1987). The importance of experiencing simultaneous or cumulative events during puberty without having time to cope with each successive change has been linked to the development of depressive affect and depression in girls (Brooks-Gunn 1991; Petersen, Sarigiani, and Kennedy 1991). Cumulative models have not been applied as often to other reproductive transitions, but it is this hypothesis, as discussed above, that suggests that the reproductive transition is a time of increased vulnerability to multiple stressors. It has also been demonstrated that stressors accumulate during these transitions.

An important corollary is that the timing of the transition influences how the reproductive transition is experienced. Timing refers to whether the individual experiences the event at about the same time, earlier, or later than other girls or women her age. Timing has been a pervasive theme across most transitions studied. It has been predictive of adjustment outcomes of puberty, onset of sexual behavior, pregnancy, and menopause (e.g., Bromberger and Matthews 1994; Brooks-Gunn and Chase-Lansdale 1995; Graber et al. 1994). Timing effects themselves may be demonstrated biologically, psychologically, and socially, with most of the research identifying the effects of experiencing the transition off-time from a social perspective (Neugarten 1979; Rossi 1977). Interestingly, it is the experience of each transition—puberty, sexuality, pregnancy, and menopause—earlier than one's peers that has most often been associated with negative outcomes for girls and women and potentially their families.

Finally, more recent interest in family systems (as exemplified by much of the work in this volume) has highlighted the intersection of the lives of adolescent girls and their mothers, examining the joint biological and intrapsychic changes, the new social contexts and roles occurring for each individual, and how adolescents' reproductive transitions impact on the lives of mothers and parents, in general. In this case, much of the research has been in the area of the pregnancy transition, especially in the context of teen childbearing (Brooks-Gunn and

Chase-Landsdale 1995), along with a few studies examining puberty and menopause conjointly (Paikoff, Brooks-Gunn, and Carlton-Ford 1991).

Although these frameworks are easily applied to all reproductive transitions, most research on these models has been on the pubertal transition (and, to a lesser extent, menopause). The body of literature on the pubertal transition has been conducted on white, middle- to upper middle-class adolescents and their families; thus, it is difficult to consider issues of diversity or generalizability across the range of adolescent experiences. Context of a transition plays a role mostly vis-à-vis individual level (e.g., timing of and/or preparation for pubertal events) and family level factors (e.g., relationships, conflict), rather than larger contexts such as neighborhoods, workplaces, and so forth. (See Brooks-Gunn and Warren 1985; Caspi, Lynam, Moffitt, and Silva 1993; Eccles et al. 1993; Stattin and Magnusson 1990; and Simmons and Blyth 1987 for exceptions in studies of puberty, especially in the study of school and peer contexts.) In addition, this work has typically not been intergenerational and instead focuses on the outcome of one person at a time—either the girl as she goes through puberty or the adult woman (usually a mother) as she goes through menopause. Much less studied is the intersection of mother and daughter lives in relation to reproduction. The effects of pubertal changes (biological, psychological, and social) on the mother or the effects of menopausal changes (again, biological, psychological, and social) on the daughter have rarely been studied. (See Ryff and Seltzer, chapter 1 of this volume, for a more general discussion of this issue in the study of midlife parental experiences.) Related gaps in the literature include determining how pubertal changes, in terms of biological, social, and psychological changes, influence parents and parenting more generally; the reciprocal question of how parents experience the multiple dimensions of pubertal development; and how menopausal changes, also in terms of its biological, social, and psychological aspects, influence daughters.

While we subscribe to a more contextually rich and truly generational approach, the literature base is so sparse that we have chosen to present examples from our own collaborative research projects that mainly address adolescent outcomes. These examples are our initial investigations of mother-daughter relationships in the context of reproductive transitions and will be linked to suggestions for the direction of future research. We will discuss mother-daughter relationships mainly in the context of the daughter's pubertal transition with brief discussions of relationship changes around sexuality and pregnancy.

Puberty is the universal reproductive transition of adolescence, most commonly used as the signifier that the individual is moving out of late childhood and into adolescence. Pubertal development consists of a series of interrelated processes including maturation of the reproductive organs, growth spurt in height and weight as well as changes in composition and distribution of fat and muscle mass, development of the circulatory and respiratory systems resulting in increased endurance and strength, and, finally, changes in the central nervous system and endocrine systems that regulate and initiate the other pubertal changes. Most girls will begin pubertal development around ten years of age with breast budding followed shortly by the appearance of pubic hair (Marshall and Tanner 1969). It takes four to five years for a girl to traverse the main developmental landmarks of puberty, with most girls reaching menarche around twelve and a half years of age, fairly late in the developmental progression (Brooks-Gunn and Reiter 1990). Notably, substantial variations exist in the timing of maturation such that reaching menarche anywhere between age nine and a half to fifteen and a half is considered well within normal range; hence, variations fall within biological constraints.[1]

Interest and issues in mother-daughter relationships during the pubertal transition span a range of perspectives as noted in the models outlined above. The specific questions of interest to us have come out of the Adolescent Study Program. Since the inception of this program twelve years ago, a series of studies of the biological and psychosocial aspects of adolescent development in girls has been conducted. The specific studies of relevance here are the Late Adolescence Study, the Early Adolescence Study, and the Mother-Daughter Interactions Study. The Adolescent Study Program began with a large cross-sectional study of girls in grades five through twelve. Girls were drawn from private schools in a major metropolitan area and were from white, middle- to upper middle-class, well-educated families. Girls and their mothers filled out questionnaires on a variety of measures tapping their feelings and behaviors. The Early Adolescence and Late Adolescence Studies were both more intensive longitudinal examinations of girls who participated in the initial cross-sectional study.

The Late Adolescence Study is a longitudinal investigation of adolescent development in girls who were in grades seven, eight, and nine in the initial cross-sectional study. The primary focus of this investigation was the development of adjustment and psychopathology through midadolescence, late adolescence, and into young adulthood.

The Early Adolescence Study is a longitudinal study of development in adolescent girls who were in grades four, five, and six in the initial cross-sectional study. Girls were seen annually for four consecutive years and with a final follow-up assessment two years later. This study focused intensely on the biological changes of puberty and the links to psychosocial development during the early adolescent period.

The Mother-Daughter Interactions Study was designed as an intensive examination of conflict resolution in mother-daughter discourse and the association between different patterns of conflictual interactions to pubertal and psychosocial development (Brooks-Gunn and Zahaykevich 1989). This study did not draw on the same population of girls as the adolescence studies but was conducted under the aegis of the Adolescent Study Program, incorporating similar measures and concepts. Ninety seventh and ninth graders and their mothers participated in this study. The sample was predominantly white and middle class. Fourteen percent of the mothers were separated or divorced at the time of the study. Mothers and daughters completed a battery of questionnaires to assess their psychosocial functioning. Dyads were then videotaped as they engaged in twenty-minute discussion sessions about two self-selected, real-life conflicts. Measures covered the domains of pubertal development, family relations, self-image and affective state, and ego development. Interactional changes around the pubertal transition were considered cross-sectionally.

Objectives

Using these three investigations, we consider several aspects of mother-daughter relationships during adolescence. Our first focus is on the experience of conflict in this relationship and its correlates for adolescent development. In contrast to conflictual mother-daughter relations, the role of cohesion and warmth in mother-daughter relationships is also examined, identifying the daughter and mother perceptions of cohesion and the links between these perceptions and adjustment. Discourse between mothers and daughters is the final aspect of mother-daughter relationships at puberty to be considered. The investigation of discourse addresses the nature of changes in autonomy and reciprocity in the adolescent's relationship with her mother. Discourse is examined in relation to daughter's pubertal status and to adjustment. Future directions for research on reproductive transitions are also presented with a focus on the impact of transitions other than puberty, such as adolescent sexuality and pregnancy.

THE EXPERIENCE OF MOTHER-DAUGHTER CONFLICT

Much of the literature on mother-daughter relationships has focused on conflict in the early adolescent years. As such, we begin with an overview of the role of conflict during the adolescent transition identifying the theoretical basis and nature of changes in family conflict at this time. Specifically, conflict has been studied in terms of the perceptions of conflict on the part of both mothers and daughters and the links between these perceptions and adjustment outcomes for daughters and, to a lesser extent, the outcomes of mothers. In keeping with our interest in models for studying transitions that incorporate multiple facets of the transition (biological, social, and psychological) along with the intersection of lives, we also discuss work on the links between mother's menopause and daughter's puberty in predicting familial conflict and adjustment outcomes for daughters. Also building from the more interactive models, we examine bidirectional associations between familial relationships and the timing of pubertal development.

Family relationships in families with adolescent offspring have typically been studied under the rubric of the stressful nature of the transition for the adolescent. Although other conceptual frameworks are appropriate and have been applied to studying family relationships at this time (e.g., family systems, psychodynamic, transactional approaches), most of the research has focused on the transitional quality of the early adolescence experience. Consequently, we frame our initial remarks around how the adolescent and her family experience the transition toward adolescence as well as how interactions and family life might be altered during this life phase.

The transition to adolescence has been characterized as stormy and stressful since at least the time of G. Stanley Hall (1904), the father of adolescent psychology. Much of the early research on adolescence conducted in the 1960s and 1970s focused on testing this commonly accepted premise. Two of the most popular topics of study were whether storm and stress really were characteristic of almost all young teenagers and whether one's self-image changed dramatically during the transition to adolescence. Somewhat surprisingly, most of the initial research did not focus on either the biological or social changes that accompany the adolescent transition as possible mediators of tumultuous behavior or alterations in self-images (Brooks-Gunn 1990; Brooks-Gunn and Reiter 1990). Generally, these seminal, early studies did not substantiate either the belief in universal storm or a dramatic, discontinuous change in self-image during adolescence (Offer 1987).

The initial characterization of storm and stress really encompasses two overlapping but not exactly identical dimensions. The stress experienced by the young adolescent is defined here in terms of the potentially stressful life events that characterize the transition from childhood to adolescence and leads to alterations in mood and affect via cumulative event models as presented earlier (e.g., Simmons and Blyth 1987).

In common parlance, storminess refers to moodiness, rapid shifts in moods, and outbursts of often short-lived negative behavior. Pubertal changes are usually mentioned as the most likely culprit, with hormones as the prime candidate of pubertal change to be nominated as the underlying cause of mood perturbations—given the deference paid to "raging hormones" in explanations for young adolescents' behavior (Buchanan, Eccles, and Becker 1992). Indirect pathways have been postulated; such pathways propose that hormonal changes of puberty lead to increased moodiness or lability, which subsequently exacerbates parent-child interactions and relationships. Evidence that hormonal changes do influence moods and reactivity lends support to this hypothesis (Buchanan, Eccles, and Becker 1992; Olweus et al. 1988). For example, we have found an increase in depressive symptomatology and aggressive feelings and behavior at the time that the hormonal system is producing the fastest rise in gonadal hormones (Warren and Brooks-Gunn 1989). Whether such feelings and behavior contribute to interactive behavior has not been studied, although Susman and her colleagues (Susman et al. 1987) found effects of hormonal status on aggressive affect but not on actual behavior in parent-child interactions (Inoff-Germain et al. 1988). In looking at biological effects on parent-child interactions (or interactions between the adolescent and any other person more generally), not only do the behaviors or arousal systems affected need to be specified (and models tested), but the possibility of reciprocal effects between family interactions and biological changes must also be considered.

As indicated previously, puberty may also influence relationships via the social stimulus value of the development of secondary sexual characteristics. As the external signs of development signal the incipient reproductive and social maturity of the child, an event laden with meaning for both parent and child, parent-child interactions may be influenced by both adolescent and parent responses to puberty.

At the same time, since rapid rises in hormones occur at precisely the time that multiple social changes are encountered, comparisons of relative effects of biological and social changes on moodiness and affective behaviors must be considered as an interactive system that accounts for rises in certain behaviors from about age ten to age fifteen (Brooks-Gunn, Graber, and Paikoff 1994). Indeed, ample evidence indicates that certain behaviors do increase at this time; these include depressive symptomatology, eating problems, aggressive behavior, as well as clinical forms of these problems with increases in depressive and eating problems being more common in adolescent girls.

Perhaps the most colloquial use of storm and stress, however, arises in terms of adult-adolescent interchanges. Parental interchanges with young adolescents are almost always portrayed as conflictual (Steinberg 1990). Personal experiences lend face validity to the characterization of conflict and strife, often impeding the study of parent-child relationships at this age. At the very least, belief in the pervasiveness of conflict has hindered the search for mechanisms underlying conflict when it occurs. Conflict has become reified vis-à-vis interactions between parents and young adolescents.

What does the research to date tell us about changes in relationships during the first half of adolescence? Conceptual models stress the transformations from unilateral authority to mutuality, from a more vertical to a somewhat more horizontal relationship. Renegotiation models however, have not been applied to the young adolescent or to the pubertal years directly, being used instead for older adolescents.

The indices that have been used to study parent-child interactions at this time include time spent with parents, changing perceptions of relationships, emotional distance, and yielding to parents in decision making. All four decrease from early to middle adolescence. The most prevalent index of family relations has been conflict. Conflict seems to be higher in early adolescence, although the frequency of conflict is similar in early and middle adolescence (Montemayor and Hanson 1985). But little comparative work exists that looks at late childhood through late adolescence.

Smetana (1988b) describes these conflicts as "mild bickering, disagreements, and conflicts over everyday issues and emotional stress during early adolescence" (79). Parents and children both report that their most frequent disagreements occur over rules and regulations regarding dress codes, dating, grades, and other personal management issues (as has been the case since the late 1920s; see Montemayor 1983). During midadolescence, Montemayor (1982) reported that parent-adolescent conflicts occurred approximately twice per week in a sample of sixty-four tenth-grade girls—a high rate when compared with conflict in marital couples who are not distressed (Montemayor 1986). Adolescents tend to report that conflicts occur more frequently than do parents. The conflict is not intense and does not necessarily presage a diminution of a strong bond between parents and children. Although mild, both parents and children agree that these conflicts are significant.

In studies of the cognitive understanding of changing social roles, Smetana (1988a,b) finds that teenagers and parents disagree as to the legitimacy of parental authority in many situations. Teenagers tend to classify more situations as involving personal choice, and parents categorize more situations as involving social conventions. Although these findings do not address role change in relation to pubertal change per se, the greatest shift toward personal choice categorizations by children occurs in early adolescence. Parent-child disagreements are largest in the middle school years. It is important that many of the seventh and eighth graders understand, but reject, their parents' perspective for issues in which they believe personal jurisdiction is legitimate.

Of particular interest is evidence that conflict is more frequent in the mother-daughter dyad than in other family dyads (Hill 1988; Montemayor 1983; Smetana 1988b). For this dyad, conflict peaks after midpuberty and only slowly tapers off until the transition out of the home (Papini, Datan, and McCluskey-Fawcett 1988; Steinberg 1987). Collins (1988, 1990) notes that transitional periods, in this case the reproductive transition of puberty, are time when families are less likely to share similar views about the family, for such transitions usually indicate role change on the part of at least one family member.

Drawing from the Late Adolescence Study of the Adolescent Study Program, our group conducted investigations of the role of conflict in the adolescent daughter-mother relationship. First, comparisons of mothers' and daughters' perceptions of the family environment were investigated to determine if mothers and daughters shared similar views of their family relations (Paikoff, Carlton-Ford, and Brooks-Gunn 1993).

In the present analyses, 161 girls in ninth, tenth, or eleventh grade (or the midadolescent assessment point) were examined. Perceptions of family relations were measured using the Conflict and the Cohesiveness subscales of the Family Environment Scale (FES; Moos 1974), which were completed by both daughters and mothers. (Findings for cohesion will be presented in the next section.) The true-false format of the FES was altered to a four-point, Likert-type scale as has been done in other studies of family relations (e.g., Plomin et al. 1988).

Adjustment of daughters and mothers was assessed via reports of depressive affect and eating problems. The Center for Epidemiological Studies Depression Scale (CES-D; Radloff 1977) was administered to girls and mothers because it is a well-validated and reliable measure of depressive affect with adolescents and young adults (Radloff 1991). Dieting and bulimic behaviors were measured by the respective subscales of the EAT-26, an abbreviated version of the Eating Attitudes Test (EAT; Garner and Garfinkel 1979).

Do Mothers and Daughters Have Similar Perceptions of Family Conflict?

The first consideration was to determine the extent of similarity in the perceptions of family conflict held by adolescent girls and their mothers. In general in this study, mothers and daughters differed as to their ratings of family climate. Whereas mother and daughter reports of conflict were significantly associated, with $r = .51$ (sharing about 25 percent of variance), daughters rated conflict higher than did mothers (Paikoff, Carlton-Ford, and Brooks-Gunn 1993). The moderate level of shared variance indicates that substantial differences in perceptions of family conflict clearly exist. Higher scores on the part of daughters may indicate that conflict is more salient to daughters, who are in the midst of working out autonomy issues. Alternatively, daughters may be rating the family climate more (or less) realistically than are the mothers. Observation studies coupled with self-reports would address this issue.

An opposing view holds that reports of family climate are only perceptions, and therefore realism or accuracy is a misguided notion. That mothers and daughters perceive the family climate somewhat differently is an important observation in itself. Such perceptions make up the dynamic family system, which is composed of the multitude of sometimes divergent beliefs and expectations held by various family members.

Are Perceptions of Conflict Linked to Daughter Adjustment?

A related objective was to understand whether differing perceptions of the family environment were linked to the emotional well-being of the daughter as indexed by depressive affect and dieting behaviors. It was hypothesized that disparate perceptions either in absolute value or dependent on direction may result in poorer adjustment outcomes for adolescents.

Interestingly, in initial examinations of correlations among scores, neither the mother's nor the daughter's perceptions of conflict were correlated with adolescent adjustment. Instead, the *discrepancy* as indicated by the absolute value of the difference between mother and daughter ratings of conflict was correlated with depressive symptomatology. Even though significant, the size of the correlation was small ($r = .15$). No associations between perceptions of conflict and dieting were found.

We suspect that such discrepancies are highlighting underlying tension in the family about how conflict is defined and possibly how different family members approach it. Discrepancies may indicate denial or a low level of awareness of conflict on the part of one member of the dyad (given that conflict had to do with *family* conflict, not *dyadic* conflict; high conflict scores could indicate high conflict among all family members or high conflict among only a few family members). However, it is not the case that discrepancies were due only to mothers reporting high conflict (perhaps with their spouses) that was being masked from the daughter. (See Carlton-Ford, Paikoff, and Brooks-Gunn 1991 for a discussion of the analytic procedures for calculating and comparing discrepancy scores.)

Typically, such results would be interpreted as demonstrating that family conflict contributed to poor outcomes of the adolescent without taking the next step to assess whether these effects might be reciprocal. That is, families with more depressed daughters may over time become more conflictual. Preliminary analyses incorporating a prior time of measurement two years earlier (i.e., using cross-lagged panel analyses) suggest that effects may be bidirectional, in that families with more depressed daughters in middle school do in fact experience (or report) more conflict in high school (Carlton-Ford et al. 1992).

Furthermore, this study examined the effect of maternal working status on daughter depression and perceptions of family environment. To test the effect of additional maternal factors in daughter adjustment, hierarchical regressions were run for each indicator of adjustment (e.g., depressive affect, dieting). Models first accounted for overall family functioning as indexed by the sum of the mother and daughter reports of conflict, then either tested the influence of the discrepancy between mother and daughter reports or the absolute value of the discrepancy, finally testing the effect of maternal employment status on daughter adjustment. (See Paikoff, Carlton-Ford, and Brooks-Gunn 1993 for a complete description of the models tested.)

In combined models, maternal employment was a stronger correlate of daughter depressive affect than divergent perceptions of conflict. Daughters of mothers who worked outside the home reported significantly higher depressive affect than girls whose mothers did not work (Paikoff, Carlton-Ford, and Brooks-Gunn 1993). This finding is surprising given that others report positive or no effects of maternal employment on midadolescent girls (Hoffman 1989; Richards and Duckett 1991). As mothers in this sample held fairly prestigious occupations, this finding may have been a result of diminished time mothers spent with or attended to their daughters. Such associations require further investigation, controlling for level of maternal employment and time spent with child along with role satisfaction on the part of the mother.

The influence of conflict on maternal adjustment has also been assessed, although not as extensively as the effect on daughters. Examination of this question indicated that neither maternal nor daughter perceptions of family conflict were related to a variety of indices of maternal adjustment (Paikoff, Brooks-Gunn, and Carlton-Ford 1991). Links between discrepant perceptions of conflict and maternal adjustment were not studied in the present investigation, although such questions could be addressed, especially in relation to issues of the mother's role satisfaction as she attempts to devote time to both a career and her adolescent daughter. Related to this question is the issue of how reproductive transitions of both adolescent and mother may be influencing their reports on the family environment, specifically, conflict in the family.

Do Pubertal and Menopausal Transitions Have Effects on Both Mother and Daughter Adjustment?

We have extended these analyses by adding reproductive transitions into the equation. We expected that the timing of daughter's maturation might influence family climate, given previous research. Since this sample was about sixteen years of age, the late maturers would be completing their secondary sexual development. If, as Hill (1988) suggested, conflict peaks around the time of peak pubertal development, then more conflict might be expected for the late-maturing girls. Of course, given that the sample was sixteen years of age at the high school assessment point, it was also possible that puberty effects might have dissipated. Effects might be most pronounced for early-maturing girls whose families may be less prepared for commensurate changes in adolescent roles and sense of self.

Psychodynamic theorists have talked about the mother's difficulty in accepting her daughter's reproductive maturity, when her own reproductive years are coming to an end. Taking seriously the notion that the changes in family conflict and other aspects of family climate are due to the parent as well as the teenager, the mother's reproductive status was also examined. It is possible that a greater proximity between daughters' onset of menarche and mothers' menopause would result in heightened conflict between mothers and daughters and, perhaps, in lowered levels of maternal well-being.

The interaction between mother and daughter reproductive status may also be understood under the framework of timing of reproductive transitions. The combination of maternal and daughter reproductive changes to produce "on-time" versus "off-time" parenting (Neugarten 1979; Rossi 1977) would be germane to an understanding of maternal well-being, with off-time parenting perhaps having negative consequences. In a recent survey, Rossi (personal communication 1994) found that only 35 percent of married women in their fifties had a child living at home, whereas 81 percent of women in their forties had one or more children residing with them. In the Late Adolescence Study, mothers who had experienced menopause might be considered off-time, as they are in their fifties and still have at least one child living at home. Alternatively, elements of self-definition and role change may be salient given that this sample was highly professional and that childbearing was likely delayed in many families, with the result of an older normative age of having a teenage daughter; in this case, the older mothers may not perceive themselves to be off-time.

Analysis of Covariance, or ANCOVA (2 × 3, controlling for maternal age), was used to test the effect of mother's reproductive status (menstruating versus not menstruating) and daughter's menarcheal timing (early, on time, late) on mother and daughter reports of family functioning. A significant effect for daughter's pubertal timing was found for maternal perceptions of family conflict ($F[2, 137] = 3.18$, $p < .05$). Specifically, mothers of late-maturing girls reported more family conflict than did those of early-maturing girls, although late-maturing girls, themselves, did not perceive increased family conflict (Paikoff, Brooks-Gunn, and Carlton-Ford 1991). These findings concur with the notion of a "temporary perturbation" as put forth by Hill (1988). Notably, this is the only study to look at girls late enough in the maturation process to demonstrate increased conflict for late maturers.

The same models (2 × 3 ANCOVAs) were used to predict daughter and mother well-being as indexed by depressive affect, dieting behaviors, and bulimic symptoms. Maternal reproductive status was associated with daughter's dieting behavior, via an interaction with daughter's menarcheal timing ($F[2, 134] = 3.65$, $p < .05$), and demonstrated a trend for association with mother's own dieting behavior ($p < .10$). Postmenopausal women had the tendency to engage in more dieting behaviors than premenopausal women. In follow-up tests of the interaction effect on daughters' dieting, the highest dieting scores were reported by early-maturing girls whose mothers were postmenopausal; much lower scores were seen for early-maturing girls whose mothers were premenopausal. Maternal menopausal status did not influence the dieting scores of on-time and late-maturing girls. This association did not disappear when analyses controlled for daughter or mother ponderal index (weight for height), ruling out weight as the mediating mechanism.

Perhaps girls whose mothers are postmenstrual are more conscious of possible weight gain (due to maternal concerns over this issue) and thus the girls engage in more dieting behavior. The mothers themselves may urge the girls to diet, more in response to their own weight gain (which often occurs after menopause); this would occur for early-maturing girls since they are more likely than the later maturers of the same age (M age = 16.03, SD = 1.00) to have the rounded contours of a woman.

However, no associations of maternal reproductive status on family climate were found. Our primary hypothesis, then, was not substantiated. What is interesting, however, is that reproductive status of the mother played a role in dieting behavior and body concerns, the arena in which changes are taking place for the adolescent.

In reflecting on our own studies and the majority of research examining the role of conflict in mother-daughter relationships at the time of puberty, all have similar constraints. Most research has been conducted on white, middle- and upper middle-class, two-parent families. (Although exceptions exist, as exemplified by the work of Hetherington [1989] on family relations during divorce and remarriage.) In most of these families, mothers were in their twenties when children were born. Hence, what is known about mothers and daughter at this phase in their respective lives is based on a very limited segment of the population. Whether effects such as those reported linking mother's assessment of family environment to daughter dieting and depressive affect would be found in mothers and daughters from different ethnic, racial, or income backgrounds is unclear. Mothers who are younger or single have different constraints on their own roles and different contexts for their own development and that of their daughters. Future research on conflict (and affective family environment, in general) must incorporate a more diverse subject pool of families in order to reflect accurately and generalize to more of the population of families.

In addition, research on mother-daughter relations and the influence on adjustment and well-being is also limited by several assessment issues. Whereas in the Late Adolescence Study mothers and daughters completed the same measures of family functioning and adjustment (at least for depressive affect and eating concerns), comparable measures for adults and adolescents are not available for all constructs that may be of interest in this research area. This has been a challenge for developmental research in general because children of different ages have different response abilities and because the constructs themselves may change with development, thus making it unclear whether the same construct is still being measured. Another factor in the assessment of family influences on well-being is that the indicators of adjustment have been limited. In our own research, we have frequently focused on depressive affect and eating problems; hence, the findings reflect an emphasis on unhealthy adjustment rather than positive aspects of adjustment. This issue may be particularly salient in the subsequent discussion of family cohesion, as cohesion might be more predictive of healthy rather than unhealthy development.

The Role of Family Conflict in the Timing of Pubertal Development

In the investigation of links between pubertal processes and family relations, we have also studied more complex or bidirectional models of physical and psychological associations. Variations in pubertal timing—specifically, age at menarche—have been associated with several antecedents, both genetic and environmental. Recent research has considered a broader range of environmental stressors and their influence on the development of the reproductive system (Moffitt et al. 1992; Steinberg 1989). Surbey (1990), in analysis of retrospective reports of stressful events and family structure, found that young women who grew up in father-absent homes had earlier ages of menarche than other women and that in two-parent households greater numbers of stressful life events were also associated with earlier ages at menarche. Subsequent prospective examinations of the links between stress and timing of maturation indicated that family conflict was also predictive of earlier ages at menarche (Moffitt et al. 1992). Prior research was not able to control for responses of others (e.g., parents) to physical signs of development which may act as cues that precipitate behavior change.

In our investigation (Graber, Brooks-Gunn, and Warren 1995) conducted using the Early Adolescence Study, the following possible antecedents were considered: hereditary transmission, absence or presence of the father in the household, family warmth and acceptance as well as conflict, and stressful life events. Models were also investigated that examined the role of psychological adjustment, specifically depressive affect, in place of the family relational component. In addition, we tested whether effects would still be maintained after controlling for external signs of pubertal development (i.e., breast development, weight, and weight for height).

The subsample of seventy-five girls who were premenarcheal at the first time of measurement was drawn from larger sample of the Early Adolescence Study for the purposes of assessing the effects of stress on pubertal development. As the girls were premenarcheal, age at menarche was obtained from subsequent times of measurement, specifically, from the assessment in which it was first reported. Breast development was based on Tanner staging of development.

The potential correlates were drawn from daughter reports, with the exception of maternal age at menarche, which mothers reported and which was used as a proxy for hereditary transmission, although it includes environmental influences. Other measures included self-reported life events on a checklist format and depressive affect as measured by the Youth Self-Report (YSR; Achenbach and Edelbrock 1986).

In this study, girls completed the Family Relations Scale of the Self-Image Questionnaire for Young Adolescents (SIQYA; Petersen, Schulenberg, Abramowitz, Offer, and Jarcho 1984). Because the Family Relations Scale measures multiple aspects of family functioning, the twelve items were factor analyzed to create two subscales, which tapped (a) parental approval and warmth and (b) conflict with parents.

In hierarchical regression models (outlined above), the model significantly predicted age at menarche ($F[7, 52] = 7.39, p < .0001, R^2 = .31$). The strongest psychosocial predictors of age at menarche were the affective measures of the family (change in $R^2 = .15, p < .01$) such that more warmth and less conflict were associated with later ages at menarche. The model that examined psychological stress as indexed by depressive affect, rather than family relations, was also significant. As expected, breast development and weight were predictive of age at menarche. But family relations continued to predict age at menarche, even after accounting for the influence of breast development or weight (the external signs of development). Weight for height, presence of an adult male in the home, and stressful events were not predictive of age at menarche.

The complex interactions of biological and psychosocial development demonstrated here may account to some extent for the inter- and intra-individual variation observed in pubertal development. Additionally, the association of family affective environment with timing of maturation, along with the existing literature on maturational timing effects on subsequent psychological adjustment, is the beginning for demonstrating the interactive nature of early adolescent development and for teasing apart developmental processes, in general. Our results are similar to those reported by Moffitt and her colleagues (1992). In our research (and that of others), family conflict and/or paternal absence seems to be associated with earlier puberty. Our study is the only one with longitudinal measures of family conflict *and* puberty, allowing us to control for initial pubertal status.

Although very few girls in our study did not live with their biological father, findings in other projects suggest that family structure may be an important factor (Moffitt et al. 1992; Surbey 1990). Although mechanisms for such effects are still unclear, several possibilities exist. Biological explanations have focused on animal models that have found that the presence of related males suppresses reproductive functioning, whereas exposure to unrelated males stimulates functioning, presumably as a population control against inbreeding. An alternative hypothesis is that different family structures themselves can be a stressor. Certainly, research on divorce and remarriage patterns would fit this model for some girls and their mothers. This particular scenario has strong implications for the mother-daughter dyad, for the resulting situation involves not only a key change in the mother's life (e.g., divorce or death of partner resulting in father absence for the daughter) but also acceleration of the pubertal process, itself altering their relationship at a time when it is already in flux. As yet, studies on mechanisms for effects and studies that follow these relationships through the periods of change still need to be conducted.

THE EXPERIENCE OF MOTHER-DAUGHTER COHESION

Despite the tendency to focus on negative changes in parent-adolescent relationships, the literature has also described positive dimensions of relational changes. Whereas the study of positive family relations has been less extensive than the literature on conflict, we will present analyses assessing the nature and influence of family cohesion that have been conducted in the Late Adolescence Study. These analyses parallel the analysis of conflict previously described and hence will be covered more briefly. Specifically, cohesion has been studied in terms of both mothers' and daughters' perceptions of cohesion and the links between these perceptions and adjustment outcomes for daughters and, to a lesser extent, the outcomes of mothers. Again, as we are interested in models for studying transitions that incorporate multiple facets of the transition (biological, social, and psychological) along with the intersection of daughters' and mothers' lives, we also present findings on the links between mother's menopause and daughter's puberty in predicting perceptions of cohesion and adjustment outcomes for daughters.

Probably only a minority of all families with adolescents experience a marked deterioration in parent-child relationships (Steinberg 1990), which suggests that conflicts or, more specific, the processes by which conflicts are resolved contribute in positive ways to adolescent development. This may occur through greater individuation in the context of a warm parental relationship (Cooper 1988; Hill 1988; Steinberg 1990). As such, family warmth and cohesion may reflect somewhat different family relational processes.

Again, different perceptions of family closeness and cohesion are likely to be held by differing members of the family (Rossi and Rossi 1990). Similar analytic strategies were employed to examine the role of cohesion in mother-daughter relationships as were applied to conflict. First, the extent of similarity or agreement in perceptions within the dyad was assessed, followed by testing the effect of perceptions on adolescent and mother well-being.

Do Mothers and Daughters Have Similar Perceptions of Family Cohesion?

As indicated, mothers and daughters differed in their ratings of family environment. Both had higher overall scores for cohesion than for conflict, thus providing supporting data for the premise that conflict and warm affective bonds coexist in most families (Paikoff, Carlton-Ford, and Brooks-Gunn 1993). Aggregate scores for cohesion were more similar across dyad pairs than were scores for conflict, that is, mother and daughter reports of cohesion were not significantly different. The correlation between mother and daughter reports, however, was in the moderate range ($r = .48$), indicating that mothers and daughters within families do not rate cohesion the same.

Such reports are comparable with those of Rossi and Rossi (1990). In examination of the four adolescent-parent dyads, they report that mothers rated cohesion higher than fathers and that daughters rated cohesion higher than sons, which resulted in the mother-daughter dyad reporting the highest rates of cohesion. It is possible that women use a different response set when assessing cohesion than do men; as such, their scores are inherently more likely to be similar on this dimension than on other dimensions or between other dyads.

Are Perceptions of Cohesion Linked to Daughter Adjustment?

Again, analyses were conducted to test whether differing perceptions of family cohesion related to the emotional well-being of the daughter as indexed by depressive affect and dieting behaviors. It was hypothesized that disparate perceptions either in absolute value or dependent on direction may result in poorer adjustment outcomes for adolescents.

In contrast to findings for conflict, discrepant perceptions of cohesion were not associated with depressive symptoms; however, the absolute value of the discrepancy in family cohesion was significantly correlated ($r = .24$, $p < .01$) with daughter dieting. Hierarchical regression models were used to test for the effects of either the difference score in perceptions of cohesion or the absolute value of the difference score after controlling for overall family cohesion. These analyses did not diminish the association between discrepancy scores and daughter dieting. Mothers' reports of cohesion (Attie and Brooks-Gunn 1989) as well as discrepancy scores were correlated with daughter eating problems, whereas daughter's reports were not (Carlton-Ford et al. 1992).

In general, mothers' positive feelings about the family environment were associated with higher body image for daughters. Mother reports of poor cohesion in the family were also associated with increased disturbances in the eating habits of the daughter (e.g., dieting and bulimic symptoms).

These results are in line with those found in samples of adolescent girls with eating disorders and their families. The clinical literature focuses on enmeshment and warmth. Families of girls with eating disorders may exhibit less warmth and more distant parental behavior. (See reviews by Attie, Brooks-Gunn, and Petersen 1990; Attie and Brooks-Gunn 1995). Some observers have suggested that family conflict is suppressed to maintain a perception of control within the family. But the absence of conflict, coupled with low warmth, might also indicate the absence of any meaningful interaction.

Comparable analyses for maternal adjustment found that effects were limited to the mother's own reports of cohesion, that is, a daughter's perceptions of the family were not linked to mothers' adjustment (Paikoff, Brooks-Gunn, and Carlton-Ford 1991). Instead, mother's feelings of family cohesion were related both to her depressive affect and to her body image, with better feelings about family warmth correlating with better adjustment (i.e., lower depressive affect, more positive body image.).

Do Pubertal and Menopausal Transitions Have Effects on Both Mother and Daughter Perceptions of the Family?

Paralleling the analyses for conflict, daughter's menarcheal timing and mother's menstrual status were examined in relation to family cohesion. No association was found between either mother's or daughter's reproductive transition and their perceptions of family cohesion (Paikoff et al. 1991). Effects of reproductive status on adjustment were discussed previously.

Overall, links between cohesion and transitional processes were not extensive with the exception of associations with dieting behavior. Certainly, one consideration for interpreting these findings is that, in general, reports of family cohesion by both mothers and daughters were quite high in this sample. As already suggested, women may be predisposed to define relationships as close, dissociating negative aspects (e.g., conflict) from the sense of cohesion, at least in part. In fact, correlations between reports of cohesion and conflict were −.56 for daughters and −.40 for mothers, suggesting more dissociation between the two domains on the part of the mother. Another constraint in these analyses is that cohesion may be more strongly associated with positive aspects of daughter and mother development and adjustment rather than the presence or absence of depressive affect or eating problems. Such factors have not been analyzed as yet.

The Experience of Mother-Daughter Discourse

Interactions between mothers and daughters are one of the venues in which adolescent girls begin to assert the new images they have of themselves and in which they attempt to have these new roles recognized. Through the study of adolescent and mother discourse, it is possible to ascertain how important others who will help shape the outcome of the transition actually respond to the adolescent's changes in self and role at the time of reproductive transitions.

Taking the perspective that self-definitional changes are due in part to the meaning of pubertal changes, reorganization of self-definitions may be based on bodily changes and the social role alterations that accompany them. However, the pubertal changes themselves may not be a comfortable topic for girls to discuss with family members, even mothers. The early studies in this area (Brooks-Gunn 1987; Brooks-Gunn et al. 1994) reported a variety of emotional responses to puberty, specifically menarche. The general pattern noted across these investigations is a shifting of communication from the family to the peer environment with the transition into adolescence. Although almost all girls learn about pubertal changes, in particular menarche, from their mothers, they tend not to discuss their feelings with her, turning instead to girlfriends, with girls engaging in few discussions about puberty with their fathers (Brooks-Gunn and Ruble 1982). In some cases, girls perceive their mothers and fathers as insensitive to the concerns about body changes. For example, fifth- and sixth-grade girls perceive their parents' comments about breast development as teasing (Brooks-Gunn et al. 1994). Anecdotal evidence indicates that parents do not see their comments in the same light.

Rather than directly via discussions about pubertal development, the self-definitional changes resulting from pubertal development presumably stimulate other, often conflictual discussions between mothers and daughters. From a psychodynamic perspective, such interactions stem from both the parents' need to recognize the separateness of their daughters and the daughters' need to be more autonomous (Blos 1979; Brooks-Gunn and Zahaykevich 1989; Hill 1988).

The Mother-Daughter Interactions Study was conducted for the purpose of understanding these issues. This study is particularly relevant to the nature of interactions between mothers and daughters during early adolescence and speaks to psychodynamic approaches to understanding mother-daughter conflict. The psychological correlates (e.g., depressive affect) of each member of the dyad were studied in relation to the behavior exhibited in a conflict resolution task. In addition, this study tested whether the nature of interactions differed depending on the maturational level of the daughter (i.e., pre- or post-menarcheal).

Separation-Individuation in Mother-Daughter Interactions

In examination of discussions about conflictual situations in this sample, mothers clearly exhibited differing levels of acceptance of their daughters' assertion of increased independence (Brooks-Gunn and Zahaykevich 1989; Graber, Zahaykevich, and Brooks-Gunn under review). Some mothers had difficulty accepting their daughters' legitimate requests in discussions and were less likely to provide models of negotiation and legitimation than were other mothers. Less accepting maternal behaviors influenced daughters' emotional well-being such that girls whose mothers were less likely to accept their arguments and claims as legitimate had lower ego development scores, as well as higher anxiety and depressive affect (Brooks-Gunn and Zahaykevich 1989). Daughters of mothers who project their feelings (and claims) onto their daughters were also more likely to show poorer psychological functioning than were daughters whose mothers did not use projection during discussions about disagreements.

As separation-individuation, in the psychodynamic sense, is a two-way street, mothers can either facilitate or block their daughters' moves toward more autonomous functioning. In this sense, the *process* by which conflicts are negotiated in families is more important than the frequency, severity, or content of conflict (Grotevant and Cooper 1985; Hauser et al. 1984).

Role of Puberty in Separation-Individuation Processes

Of additional interest is the role of puberty in signaling the initiation of a change in mother-daughter interchanges. Examinations of this question indicated that pubertal development appeared to be a transition point in interactions. Changes based on daughter's menarcheal status occurred in both the content of the conflicts most frequently reported by mothers and daughters and the type of dyadic interaction (Brooks-Gunn and Zahaykevich 1989; Graber, Zahaykevich, and Brooks-Gunn under review). Younger girls and their mothers argued about clothes and appearance more often than did older girls and their mothers. More important, premenarcheal girls exhibited more active opposition to their mothers during the conflict resolution task, whereas postmenarcheal girls, especially those in ninth grade, were more likely to move from more aggressive to more passive modes of resisting maternal control (Brooks-Gunn and Zahaykevich 1989; Graber, Zahaykevich, and Brooks-Gunn under review). Mothers also attempted more covert means of control with premenarcheal than postmenarcheal daughters.

These findings suggest that relationships do change at the time of puberty. Changes may be interpreted as increased bids for autonomy by daughters, bids that are met by some parental resistance. Individual differences in interaction patterns are critical to examine, as they allow for an understanding of the ways in which families facilitate girls' movement to more autonomous functioning and more advanced ego development. These initial results highlight the continual changes and renegotiations that occur in mother-daughter relationships during adolescence. How these behavioral patterns relate to the psychological well-being of the adolescent girls is still under investigation.

Summary of Pubertal Transition Studies

Clearly, the pubertal transition is a period of change and, at least initially, one of conflict for mothers and daughters. This transition has demonstrated influence on both the girls experiencing it at well as their mothers, but the girl's experience has been better studied. Maternal characteristics influence how mothers interact with their daughters as well as with daughters' outcome (e.g., Paikoff, Carlton-Ford, and Brooks-Gunn 1993). How the girl's puberty influences her mother's adjustment and role change requires further investigation. (See Silverberg, this volume, for discussion of parental satisfaction and young adolescence, more generally.) Of interest was the sparsity of effects of mother-daughter relationship variables on mothers. Lack of effects may be due to a variety of unexplored causes, such as the limitations of self-report measures to tap increases in distance and challenge in the dyadic relationship and family, more globally. Potentially, mother's well-being may not be as affected by the relationship changes as is daughter's well-being. This would be in sharp contrast to the hypothesis that separation is a difficult developmental task and that autonomy issues often are enacted in the context of mother-daughter interactions. Because of the centrality of puberty to the adolescent, the challenges of early adolescence may have primary impact on the adolescent herself, with the mother being more capable to reflect objectively rather than internally on the redefinition of roles. Given that mothers (and daughers) continue to report closeness in the relationship, the conflict may be less salient.

Alternatively, puberty may not be the reproductive transition of the daughter that proves the most stressful for the mother. Later-occurring adolescent transitions such as becoming sexually active, pregnant, or a young mother may be more relevant to the mother-daughter relationship and to the mother's realignment or new definition of self in response to the daughter's transition. A further consideration is the spacing of these transitions. Mothers and daughters may experience more individual and dyadic upheaval if the daughter makes several of these transitions in rapid succession before role integration and coping have occurred. As yet, these issues have rarely been addressed directly.

FUTURE DIRECTIONS IN THE STUDY OF REPRODUCTIVE TRANSITIONS

In this section, we highlight aspects of mother-daughter relationships that may be associated with or be influenced by adolescent sexuality and adolescent pregnancy. As research in these areas is sparse, our focus is on identifying areas for future investigation and providing exemplars of existing work. We will briefly present some recent findings from the Late Adolescence Study to highlight particular points.

Mother-Daughter Relationships in the Context of Adolescent Sexuality

Several issues arise between mothers and daughters with respect to the adolescent's sexuality. Our discussion draws on the models we have previously presented for the study of reproductive transitions. Rather than reviewing the adolescent literature in this area to the same extent to which we considered the pubertal transition, our hope is instead to identify topics for further research in the context of the intersection of mother and daughter lives.

Very little research has investigated the effect of daughter's initiation of sexual behavior on mother's well-being or the effect mother's sexuality has on her daughter's emerging sexual self. Whereas pubertal development is an age-normative experience for early adolescents that is acknowledged as inevitable even if potentially tumultuous in the minds of parents, peers, and often the self, the transition into sexual behavior rarely engenders the same sense of resignation on the part of parents.

Most adolescents will begin sexual activity in the form of dating and kissing early in adolescence, and approximately 75 percent of African American and 50 percent of white girls will have had intercourse by age eighteen (Brooks-Gunn and Furstenberg 1989; Moore, Nord, and Peterson 1989). In the most recent follow-up of the Late Adolescence Study when participants were young adults (M age $= 22.3$), young women reported retrospectively the age at which they first had intercourse. In our sample of white, middle- to upper middle-class adolescents, the mean age for first having intercourse was 17.5 years of age ($SD = 2.13$), which is comparable with the aforementioned ages for first intercourse found in larger survey studies.

Across studies it is clear that the sexual transition may in fact be normative for many if not most adolescents, yet parental responses to it are often in sharp opposition to this notion. Given polarization between the reality of the adolescent's world and parental beliefs and expectations, mother-daughter relationships may involve significant change around this transition. Unfortunately, the young women and their mothers who participated in the Late Adolescence Study were not contacted around the time that the daughters began to have intercourse; hence, it was not possible to investigate changes in relationships around this transition.

Much of the literature on sexual behavior in adolescence focuses on the importance of the peer group in the development of the sexual self (Brooks-Gunn and Furstenberg 1989; Hofferth and Hayes 1987); notably, beliefs in the influence of peers on sexual behavior are probably much stronger than the actual documented influence of peers. Peers are thought to affect decisions to engage in or initiate sex and the timing of this decision, as well as to influence the process of self-definition as a sexual being—occurring whether or not the adolescent has engaged in intercourse or other sexual activities with another person. Despite prevailing beliefs, the family still affects the development of attitudes about sexual behavior and the timing and consequences of engaging in sexual behavior during adolescence.

Family communication about sexual behavior has not been extensively measured. Although the topic is usually viewed as uncomfortable to discuss for both parents and adolescents (Hofferth and Hayes 1987), approximately two-thirds of midadolescent girls report having discussed intercourse with their parents (Dawson 1986). Paralleling findings for puberty that mother-daughter communication has a positive effect on daughter's feelings about puberty (e.g., Brooks-Gunn and Ruble 1982), mother-daughter communication about sex was associated with later onset of intercourse (Kahn, Smith, and Roberts 1984). (Effects of communication were not uniform across other family dyads.) Even though mothers and daughters may be reluctant to discuss sex openly, feelings of closeness and supportiveness in family relationships in general have also been linked to later ages of intercourse. Poor communication with parents has not only been linked to earlier initiation of intercourse but to engagement in drinking and smoking—behaviors also viewed as undesirable for adolescents (Jessor and Jessor 1977). Thus, the quality of mother-daughter relationships influences the timing of this transition and potentially several other aspects of it.

Mothers undoubtedly influence adolescent sexual behavior not only via communication about it but also via their own sexual behavior. While very little research addresses how mothers set norms for behavior through their own behavior, recent ethnographic studies of urban economically disadvantaged families suggest that maternal sexual behavior might be particularly salient for single mothers who themselves are dating (Burton, Allison, and Obeidallah 1995). Single mothers of adolescent girls were often teen parents and as such may be, on average, only fifteen years older than their daughters. Burton and her colleagues refer to these families as "age-condensed" and note that differentiation of roles is often blurred. The blurring of roles may lead to daughters and mothers discussing dating and conduct with boyfriends more as peers than as parent and child. In fact, some daughters and mothers reported dating the same men (although not at the same time). In these situations, both the mother's and the daughter's behaviors will presumably have reciprocal influences. This type of mother-daughter relationship is only one of many types in the range of family constellations. Yet, it exemplifies the need for more thorough investigation of diverse family relationships and roles in understanding sexual behavior of adolescents (and mothers).

The context in which the mother herself became sexually active also comes into play in predicting the subsequent behavior of her daughter. Most notable, mothers who became pregnant at an early age (and hence engaged in sex at a young age) have daughters who also become pregnant at an early age (Furstenberg, Levine, and Brooks-Gunn 1990). These mothers may implicitly model behavior via their prior behaviors or may feel that an earlier timing of this transition is not inherently a problem.

Religious and moral beliefs about contraception, abortion, and marriage are additional sources of norms and models for behavior imparted by mothers to daughters. Girls' reports of adherence to religious beliefs have been linked to later ages of initiation of intercourse (Devaney and Hubley 1981); however, conservative religious beliefs about contraception have been linked to lower use of contraception in those youth who have sex despite religious beliefs (Fisher, Byrne, and White 1983). It is not known how daughter sexual behavior influences mother well-being in the context of mother's belief system. For some families, differing beliefs or adherence to beliefs is a potential source of conflict.

Process-oriented research on how mothers influence behavior or respond to their daughter's behavior would be particularly profitable. In the Mother-Daughter Interactions Study discussed previously, ninth-grade girls and their mothers reported that dating and staying out late were common sources of conflict (Brooks-Gunn and Zahaykevich 1989; Graber, Zahaykevich, and Brooks-Gunn under review). Clearly, mothers are feeling the need to supervise and restrict daughters' potential sexual situations. This is in contrast to daughters seeking more autonomy and freedom.

Historically, parents have been more restrictive with adolescent girls than with adolescent boys, presumably because of traditional gender stereotypes about the appropriateness of sexual behavior for girls and boys and the salience to girls of becoming pregnant (Fine 1988; Hill and Lynch 1983). The interaction of mother's and daughter's gender roles is likely to be a factor in the extent of conflict they experience over the competing demands of supervision versus autonomy. In fact, it may be middle- and upper-class mothers who have broken out of traditional gender roles who experience the most internal conflict over their daughter's sexuality as they find themselves trying to enforce traditional roles with their daughters.

Finally, perhaps the least studied disturbance in the family and the one most likely to have the strongest effects on daughters and mothers is sexual abuse in the family. Rates of nonvoluntary sexual behavior and incest, specifically, vary widely depending on the nature of the abuse and source of the data. Across survey studies, Finkelhor (1991) reports that anywhere from 6 to 62 percent of women have experienced sexual abuse in childhood, with two-thirds of these incidents occurring with a family member. Peak ages for experiencing abuse are from nine to twelve. Familial risk factors linked to sexual abuse include parental absence, family conflict, living in homes with stepparents, and/or having poor family relationships (Finkelhor 1991; Moore, Nord, and Peterson 1989). The abuser is most often male, and daughters are most often the abused. Sexual abuse is strongly associated with subsequent sexual behavior as well as a range of poor adjustment outcomes for girls.

Sexual abuse in the family is likely to have far-reaching influences on both the abused girl and her mother. Psychoanalytic and feminist perspectives on the treatment of abused girls have emphasized the role of the mother in the abusive situation (McIntyre 1981). The mother's knowledge of the abuse or inability to protect the daughter from being abused was thought to be a critical factor in daughter outcome (Meiselman 1978). Mothers were often characterized as complacent in situations where the mother may have been unwilling to confront the abuser for fear of losing him or out of fear of physical retaliation. Blame-oriented views of mothers often portrayed them as "unresponsive" wives who relegated their daughters to fulfilling the sexual role in the mother's relationship (Jones 1979). In studies of girls in treatment, blame on the mother for the abuse—with little attention to the abuser or his relationship with the mother—was a recurrent theme (Cammaert 1988).

Notably, these scenarios have been identified in only a small number of abusive situations (Cammaert 1988). More often, mothers may not be aware of the abusive situation, experiencing guilt and anger when they do become aware of it. The abuse is likely to disrupt severely the daughter's and the mother's relationship with the abuser; the strain to the mother's coping abilities may actually render her less effective at helping her adolescent daughter deal with the abuse. In fact, the abuser is often physically and emotionally abusive in his relationship with the mother as well as the daughter (Sgroi 1982). The full extent of parallel and interactive effects of sexual abuse on the mother-daughter relationship is poorly understood. However, as the experience of childood sexual abuse is considered a predictor of several clinical disorders (including depression, eating disorders, and personality disorders), how mothers and daughters contend with it probably plays an important role in the long-term effects of abuse on both individuals.

These issues represent a few directions for investigating the impact of adolescent sexuality on the lives of mothers and daughters. As this area is not well-studied, especially from the approach of understanding interactive effects of the transition on daughters and mothers, many issues could have been presented.

Mother-Daughter Relationships in the Context of Adolescent Pregnancy

An obviously related topic to the transition into sexuality is that of pregnancy, the next reproductive transition experienced by most women. While pregnancy results in redefining roles on the parts of both mothers (now grandmothers) and daughters (now mothers) in general (Rossi and Rossi 1990), the case of adolescent pregnancy poses unique challenges to mother-daughter relationships. Intergenerational approaches have been more common in the study of teen pregnancy than in the study of the sexual transition (e.g., Burton and Bengtson 1985; Chase-Lansdale, Brooks-Gunn, and Zamsky 1994; Furstenberg, Brooks-Gunn, and Morgan 1987; Merriwether-de Vries, Burton, and Eggeletion, in press). Hence, the following discussion is brief but highlights potential areas for expansion of these studies. (See Brooks-Gunn and Chase-Lansdale 1995 and Burton and Bengtson 1985 for reviews of this literature.)

Recent years have seen a marked increase in the number of adolescent pregnancies (about 25 percent of girls become pregnant during adolescence) and the number of single adolescent girls choosing to carry to term and raise their babies. Pregnancy and parenthood in adolescence is perceived differently as a function of community norms (Brooks-Gunn and Chase-Lansdale 1995). As such, mother-daughter relationships will be influenced dependent on those norms and expectations for acceptance of new roles within the community. As with the timing of any reproductive transition, the definition of the transition as off-time is dependent on the referent group, such as national norms or one's peers. In some cases, early pregnancy may not be seen as negative by the adolescent's mother, or more likely, negative responses to the pregnancy are resolved by the time the baby arrives. The increase in the past few decades in the percentage of adolescent girls who keep their babies (92 percent of African American girls and 54 percent of white girls, Furstenberg 1991) is due, in part, to the willingness of the (grand)mothers to help care for their daughter's child or children.

Whereas the aforementioned factors are salient to how the timing of the adolescent daughter's pregnancy is defined, also of interest is how the mother's transition to being a grandmother is defined. That is, what does it mean for a woman to become a grandmother in the early years of midlife (in her thirties or forties)? Again, whether the mother's transition is defined by herself or others as off-time is dependent on community norms. In addition, if these mothers have children of their own still living at home (usually at least the adolescent mother), they are not merely redefining themselves as grandmothers but also must balance several maternal roles. This attempt at balance may be a source of conflict between the mother and daughter as the mother attempts to continue to provide parenting to her adolescent daughter as well as the daughter's infant. Hence, these mothers may be especially taxed by their daughter's reproductive transition, working through issues of autonomy and infant care simultaneously. When the demands of parenting are coupled with the fact that women of this age most often work outside the home and have significant personal relationships with a spouse or partner—roles that must also be juggled—cumulative effect models may be most appropriate for predicting maternal outcome of the adoelscent's transition.

To date, research has examined several effects of adolescent pregnancy and the commensurate life changes on young grandmothers (Baydar and Brooks-Gunn 1994; Burton and Bengston 1985; Furstenberg, Brooks-Gunn, and Morgan 1987). The accumulation of conflicting roles for these women is exemplified in age-condensed families as described by Burton and her colleagues (Burton, Allison, and Obeidallah 1995; Merriwether-de Vries, Burton, and Eggeletion in press). They note that in these situations, neither mother nor daughter may engage in role-appropriate behavior; in some cases, mothers and daughters who were closely spaced in age behaved more like siblings, relying on the next older generation to perform "mothering" duties.

Overall, this literature is perhaps the most interactive in its approach to understanding changes in the family system; examinations have included relational influences on the well-being of the adolescent mother, her child, and her mother as well as the influence of intergenerational relations on parenting behaviors. Outcomes for a specific generation are often moderated by contextual factors. For example, several studies have questioned whether it is good for the teen mother to reside with her mother after the baby is born. Rather than coresidence providing additional supports, it may increase conflict instead. In fact, coresidence appears to be stressful for some adolescent mothers and their mothers (Chase-Lansdale, Brooks-Gunn, and Zamsky 1994). When teen mothers were older adolescents (over sixteen years of age), with a presumably greater need for autonomy, coresidence led to more conflict and to more negative parenting practices in relation to the new infant on the part of both "mothers." In contrast, coresidence led to more positive parenting of the infant when the adolescent mother was young and presumably less prepared to reside independently. In general, more closeness was reported in families who did not coreside (Chase-Lansdale, Brooks-Gunn, and Zamsky 1994).

In examinations of the quality of relationships between adolescent mothers and their mothers, adolescents who scored higher on autonomy with their mothers were more emotionally supportive, positive, and facilitative with their children (Wakschlag, Chase-Lansdale, and Brooks-Gunn in press). They also were more interactive with their own mothers. Adolescent mothers who scored low on autonomy were more withdrawn from their mothers.

As indicated, the study of adolescent pregnancy has been truly multigenerational in its attempts to understand the impact of this transition on each generation involved. These studies have also been exemplars, as they measure and account for the influence of diverse contextual factors on the multigenerational family. Comparison of changes in intergenerational relationships around the birth of a child between families experiencing the transition off-time versus in a normative progression may also be of value. For example, mothers usually become more involved in their daughter's life after the birth of a child even when this transition is made in young adulthood rather than in adolescence (Fischer 1986).

Interestingly, much of the research on the pregnancy transition has focused on adolescents who become pregnant, give birth, and keep their babies, often examining low-income, disdvantaged families. The sample of the Late Adolescence Study provides a distinct contrast to the experiences of girls who give birth and raise children as adolescents. In the most recent follow-up of this sample, when the participants were about twenty-two years of age, young women were asked about their reproductive history. To reiterate, this study consisted of girls from middle-class to upper middle-class white families originally seen in young adolescence (M age $= 14.3$), midadolescence (M age $= 16.0$), and, as just noted, young adulthood.

In young adulthood, 15 percent (N $= 24$) of the young women indicated that they had been pregnant. All pregnancies occurred between 16 and 24 years of age, with the mean age of pregnancy being 20.2 ($SD = 2.26$). What is interesting about this information is that only one woman reported having a child: two reported miscarriage and the remaining young women had abortions. Thus, for this sample of young women, most unplanned pregnancies occurred in the college years rather than during high school. Also, almost exclusively, these young women choose not to continue the pregnancy. This is likely due to the fact that young women in college perceive greater opportunities in their lives and may be less willing to have an unplanned child when they are still in school. In fact, at the young adult assessment, these women were also asked to indicate when they expected to make certain key adult transitions. Most expected to have their first child around the age of thirty, about two years after getting married and about six years after starting their first full-time job (Graber and Brooks-Gunn in press).

Because young women in the Late Adolescence Study reported pregnancies almost exclusively during the college years, it was possible to examine the psychosocial precursors to these pregnancies. Using information from the midadolescent assessment, we examined whether getting pregnant in the college years was associated with adolescent mental health, family relations, and sexual experiences. One-way analysis of variance was used to test for differences between girls who did and did not go on to get pregnant in later adolescence. Few differences were found between these two groups in midadolescence for measures of adjustment or mental health. Girls who later became pregnant were more perfectionistic than other girls ($F[1, 122] = 4.94, p < .05$). Interestingly, by young adulthood, the young women who had been pregnant had higher scores than other young women on a measure of depressed affect, with $F(1, 155) = 5.45, p < .05$ on the CES-D (M age $= 17.87$ versus M age $= 13.10$, respectively).

More precursors to pregnancy were found in the area of family relations as measured by the FES. Girls who would later get pregnant had, in midadolescence, lower family cohesion ($F[1, 113] = 10.59, p < .01$), more family conflict ($F[1, 109] = 4.02, p < .05$), and a more controlling family environment ($F[1, 111] = 5.28, p < .05$) than girls who did not go on to become pregnant. In young adulthood, family conflict was assessed separately for mothers and fathers using the Relationship with Mother and the Relationship with Father scales assessing conflictual independence (Hoffman 1984). Conflict with father in young adulthood was associated with prior pregnancy such that young women who had been pregnant had more conflict with their fathers than young women who had not as yet been pregnant ($F[1, 144] = 8.89, p < .01$). Conflict with mother in young adulthood was not associated with pregnancy history. In addition, neither mothers' feelings about the family environment or mothers' depressive affect was related to whether or not their daughters subsequently became pregnant.

The associations between pubertal development and both prior sexual behavior and becoming pregnant were also examined. In young adulthood, women reported retrospectively their age at menarche, which was used as a comparison of the timing of pubertal development among the young women, and as indicated above, they also reported their age at first intercourse. It has been suggested that girls who go through puberty earlier than their peers engage in sexual behaviors at an earlier age. Adolescent girls who are younger when they begin having sex may be less likely to use contraception and hence might be more likely to have an unplanned pregnancy. As would be expected, age at first intercourse differed significantly between young women who had been pregnant (M age $=$ 16.0) and those who had not been pregnant (M age $=$ 17.8) with $F(1, 138) = 14.5$, $p < .001$. These two groups did not differ on their ages at menarche. Furthermore, age at first intercourse was not significantly correlated with age at menarche. Because these adolescent girls began to have intercourse much later than their pubertal development—about four and a half years between these two events for most girls—the effects of earlier maturation may have been suppressed in this sample by contextual factors that promoted delaying intercourse. In contrast, girls who had sexual intercourse for the first time at an earlier age were more likely to become pregnant at a younger age than did their peers.

Overall, our analyses suggest that pregnancy is a problem for some young women from middle- and upper middle-class backgrounds. Such young women choose to terminate the pregnancy rather than alter their education and career paths. Interestingly, these young women would have more resources for caring for a child (at least financial and educational resources) than most single women who decide to continue their pregnancies and have children in their late teens and in young adulthood. But it is exactly these women who do not want to have a child before completing their educational plans. Whereas the present sample is unusual in comparison with the majority of unmarried women who become pregnant, this study provides an interesting prospective examination of predictors of pregnancy in a group of adolescents and young women whose pregnancies have been relatively unstudied. The present investigation identifies a potential course of events in which family relationships, defined by lower cohesion, higher conflict, and higher control, precedes late-adolescent pregnancy, which in turn leads to increased depressive affect. How poor family relations predispose young women to become pregnant earlier than their peers is undetermined. Young women may become depressed while trying to cope with the strain of pregnancy (and potentially the subsequent abortion), especially in the absence of a supportive family environment. Poorer family relations appear to be confined to the relationship between father and daughter rather than with mother. As yet the processes that link these events have not been ascertained but merit further study with adolescents and young women who give birth and keep their children as well as with young women who terminate their pregnancies.

Conclusion

Returning to our initial hypothesis that reproductive transitions are periods of potential vulnerability for the experience of stress and the translation of that stress into longer-term health outcomes, evidence indicates that potential effects may exist in each of the transitions discussed—puberty, sexuality, pregnancy, and menopause. Each reproductive transition is in some sense shared by mothers and daughters in as much as the progression of one member of the dyad through the transition influences and is influenced by the response of the other member.

Developmental study has necessitated a focus on continuity and change over the course of the life span. Reproductive transitions may be discontinuous periods that set individuals on different mental and physical health trajectories. As we have tried to demonstrate, the navigation of a reproductive transition is influenced by numerous individual and contextual factors. This is also true for nearly all transitions, although this perspective has been most often applied to the study of adolescence. (For exemplars, see Graber, Brooks-Gunn, and Petersen in press.)

One challenge to studies of reproductive transitions will be to understand better the nature of individual differences in response to the transition and how different contexts interact with these differences. For several of the reproductive transitions, research has been limited to how a particular segment of the population makes the transition and the effect this has on their families (or how the families influence the transition). Once we understand how these processes are similar and different for other groups of adolescent girls and their mothers, better predictions can be made about whose transitional experience is likely to have negative health outcomes. Notably, studies have not examined the interconnection of the transitions themselves; that is, if the pubertal transition has negative effects on an adolescent and her mother, will the daughter's pregnancy also produce negative effects on both members of the dyad? If consistent responses to the challenge of navigating a reproductive transition are exhibited by a dyad or consistently by one member of a dyad, then stress during reproductive transitions could be intensified and accumulate over the life course. Studies of conflict and autonomy around puberty often assume that once mothers and daughters come to terms with the effects of puberty on each of their lives and on their relationship, the dyad experiences improvements in the relationship. But, will the same process begin again with the advent of sexual behavior or pregnancy? As studies of intergenerational developmental processes progress, identifying consistency and change will become increasingly complex but hopefully more enlightening.

NOTE

1. Several factors are known to influence the timing of puberty (Brooks-Gunn 1988; Graber, Brooks-Gunn, and Warren 1995). Both intense exercise and restricted food intake can result in delaying pubertal development (Warren 1980), but even then, menarche usually occurs by seventeen or eighteen years of age.

REFERENCES

Achenbach, T. M., and C. S. Edelbrock. 1986. *Youth self-report profile for girls aged 11–18.* Burlington: University of Vermont.

Adler, N., and K. A. Matthews. 1994. Health psychology: Why do some people get sick and some stay well? *Annual Review of Psychology* 45:229–259.

Attie, I., and J. Brooks-Gunn. 1989. The development of eating problems in adolescent girls: A longitudinal study. *Developmental Psychology* 25 (1):70–79.

———. 1995. The development of eating regulation across the lifespan. In D. Cicchetti and D. J. Cohen, eds., *Developmental psychopathology* 2:332–368. New York: Wiley.

Attie, I., J. Brooks-Gunn, and A. C. Petersen. 1990. The emergence of eating problems: A developmental perspective. In M. Lewis and S. Miller, eds., *Handbook of developmental psychopathology,* pp. 409–420. New York: Plenum.

Baydar, N., and J. Brooks-Gunn. 1994. Profiles of America's grandmothers: Those who provide care for their grandchildren and those who do not. Unpublished manuscript.

Blos, P. 1979. The second individuation process. In P. Blos, ed., *The adolescent passage: Developmental issues at adolescence,* pp. 141–170. New York: International University Press.

Bromberger, J. T., and K. A. Matthews. May 1994. Does stress accelerate the cessation of menses in middle-aged women? Paper presented at the symposium "Methods and Models for Studying Stress during Reproductive Transitions," at the APA conference, "Psychosocial and Behavioral Factors in Women's Health: Creating an Agenda for the twenty-first Century," Washington, D.C.

Brooks-Gunn, J. 1987. Pubertal processes: Their relevance for psychological research. In V. B. Van Hasselt and M. Hersen, eds., *The handbook of adolescent psychology,* pp. 111–130. New York: Pergamon.

———. 1988. Antecedents and consequences of variations in girls' maturational timing. *Journal of Adolescent Health Care* 9 (5):365–373.

———. 1990. Overcoming barriers to adolescent research on pubertal and reproductive development. *Journal of Youth and Adolescence* 19 (5):425–440.

———. 1991. How stressful is the transition to adolescence in girls? In M. E. Colten and S. Gore, eds., *Adolescent stress: Causes and consequences,* pp. 131–149. Hawthorne, N.Y.: Aldine de Gruyter.

Brooks-Gunn, J., and P. L. Chase-Lansdale. 1995. Adolescent parenthood. In M. Bornstein, ed., *Handbook of parenting* 3:113–149. Mahwah, N.J.: Erlbaum.

Brooks-Gunn, J., and F. F. Furstenberg Jr. 1989. Adolescent sexual behavior. *American Psychologist* 44 (2):249–257.

Brooks-Gunn, J., J. A. Graber, and R. L. Paikoff. 1994. Studying links between hormones and negative affect: Models and measures. *Journal of Research on Adolescence* 4 (4):469–486.

Brooks-Gunn, J., D. Newman, C. Holderness, and M. P. Warren. 1994. The experience of breast development and girls' stories about the purchase of a bra. *Journal of Youth and Adolescence* 23 (5):539–565.

Brooks-Gunn, J., and E. O. Reiter. 1990. The role of pubertal processes in the early adolescent transition. In S. Feldman and G. Elliott, eds., *At the threshold: The developing adolescent,* pp. 16–53. Cambridge: Harvard University Press.

Brooks-Gunn, J., and D. N. Ruble. 1982. The development of menstrual-related beliefs and behaviors during early adolescence. *Child Development* 53:1567–1577.

Brooks-Gunn, J., and M. P. Warren. 1985. The effects of delayed menarche in different contexts: Dance and nondance students. *Journal of Youth and Adolescence* 14 (4):285–300.

Brooks-Gunn, J., and M. Zahaykevich. 1989. Parent-child relationships in early adolescence: A developmental perspective. In K. Kreppner and R. M. Lerner, eds., *Family systems and life-span development.* Hillsdale, N.J.: Erlbaum.

Buchanan, C. M., J. S. Eccles, and J. B. Becker. 1992. Are adolescents the victims of raging hormones: Evidence for activational effects of hormones on moods and behavior at adolescence. *Psychological Bulletin* 111:62–107.

Burton, L. M., K. Allison, and D. Obeidallah. 1995. Social context and adolescence:

Perspectives on development among inner-city African American teens. In L. Crockett and A. Crouter, eds., *Pathways through adolescence: Individual development in relation to social context.* Mahwah, N.J.: Erlbaum.

Burton, L. M., and V. L. Bengtson. 1985. Black grandmothers: Issues of time and continuity of roles. In V. L. Bengtson and J. Robertson, eds., *Grandparenthood.* Beverly Hills, Calif.: Sage.

Cammaert, L. A. 1988. Nonoffending mothers: A new conceptualization. In L. E. A. Walker, ed., *Handbook on sexual abuse of children,* pp. 309–325. New York: Springer.

Carlton-Ford, S., R. L. Paikoff, and J. Brooks-Gunn. 1991. Methodological issues in the study of divergent views of the family. In R. L. Paikoff, ed., *New directions for child development.* Vol. 51, *Shared views in the family during adolescence,* pp. 87–102. San Francisco: Jossey-Bass.

Carlton-Ford, S., R. L. Paikoff, J. Oakely, A. Sharer, and J. Brooks-Gunn. 1992. Adolescent depressive affect and daughter's and mother's reports of family cohesion and conflict. Unpublished manuscript.

Caspi, A., D. Lynam, T. E. Moffitt, and P. A. Silva. 1993. Unraveling girls' delinquency: Biological, dispositional, and contextual contributions to adolescent misbehavior. *Developmental Psychology* 29:19–30.

Chase-Lansdale, P. L., J. Brooks-Gunn, and E. S. Zamsky. 1994. Young multigenerational families in poverty: Quality of mothering and grandmothering. *Child Development* 65:373–393.

Collins, W. A. 1988. Research on the transition to adolescence: Continuity in the study of developmental processes. In M. R. Gunnar and W. A. Collins, eds., *Development during transition to adolescence: Minnesota symposia on child psychology* 21:1–15. Hillsdale, N.J.: Erlbaum.

———. 1990. Parent-child relationships in the transition to adolescence: Continuity and change in interaction, affect, and cognition. In R. Montemayor, G. Adams, and T. Gullotta, eds., *Advances in adolescent development.* Vol. 2. *The transition from childhood to adolescence,* pp. 85–106. Newbury Park, Calif.: Sage.

Cooper, C. R. 1988. Commentary: The role of conflict in adolescent-parent relationships. In M. R. Gunnar and W. A. Collins, eds., *Development during transition to adolescence: Minnesota symposia on child psychology* 21:181–187. Hillsdale, N.J.: Erlbaum.

Dawson, D. A. 1986. The effects of sex education on adolescent behavior. *Family Planning Perspectives* 18:162–170.

Deutsch, F. M., D. N. Ruble, A. Fleming, J. Brooks-Gunn, and C. Stangor. 1988. Information-seeking and self-definition during the transition to motherhood. *Journal of Personality and Social Psychology* 55 (3):420–431.

Devaney, B. L., and K. S. Hubley. 1981. *The determinants of adolescent pregnancy and childrearing.* Final report to the National Institute of Child Health and Human Development. Washington, D.C.: Mathematica Policy Research.

Eccles, J. S., C. Midgley, A. Wigfield, C. M. Buchanan, D. Reuman, C. Flanagan, and D. MacIver. 1993. Development during adolescence: The impact of stage-environment fit in young adolescents' experiences in schools and in families. *American Psychologist* 48:90–101.

Fine, M. 1988. Sexuality, schooling, and adolescent females: The missing discourse of desire. *Harvard Educational Review* 58:29–53.

Finkelhor, D. 1991. Child sexual abuse. In M. L. Rosenberg and M. A. Fenley, eds., *Violence in America: A public health approach*, pp. 79–94. New York: Oxford University Press.

Fischer, L. R. 1986. *Linked lives: Adult daughters and their mothers.* New York: Harper and Row.

Fisher, W., D. Byrne, and L. White. 1983. Emotional barriers to contraception. In D. Byrne and W. Fisher, eds., *Adolescents, sex, and contraception*, pp. 207–239. Hillsdale, N.J.: Erlbaum.

Furstenberg, F. F., Jr. 1991. As the pendulum swings: Teenage childbearing and social concern. *Family Relations* 40:127–138.

Furstenberg, F. F., Jr., J. Brooks-Gunn, and P. Morgan. 1987. *Adolescent mothers in later life.* New York: Cambridge University Press.

Furstenberg, F. F., Jr., J. A. Levine, and J. Brooks-Gunn. 1990. The daughters of teenage mothers: Patterns of early childbearing in two generations. *Family Planning Perspectives* 22 (2):54–61.

Garner, D. M., and P. E. Garfinkel. 1979. The Eating Attitudes Test: An index of the symptoms of anorexia nervosa. *Psychological Medicine* 9:1–7.

Graber, J. A., and J. Brooks-Gunn. In press. Expectations for and precursors of leaving home in young women. In J. A. Graber and J. S. Dubas, eds., *New directions for child development: Leaving home*, ser. ed. W. Damon. San Francisco: Jossey-Bass.

Graber, J. A., J. Brooks-Gunn, R. L. Paikoff, and M. P. Warren. 1994. Prediction of eating problems: An 8-year study of adolescent girls. *Developmental Psychology* 30 (6):823–834.

Graber, J. A., J. Brooks-Gunn, and A. C. Petersen, eds. In press. *Transitions through adolescence: Interpersonal domains and context.* Mahwah, N.J.: Erlbaum.

Graber, J. A., J. Brooks-Gunn, and M. P. Warren. 1995. The antecedents of menarcheal age. *Child Development* 66:346–359.

Graber, J. A., M. Zahaykevich, and J. Brooks-Gunn. 1995. Changing relations during adolescence: Mothers and daughters. Unpublished manuscript.

Grotevant, H. D., and C. R. Cooper. 1985. Patterns of interaction in family relationships and the development of identity exploration in adolescence. *Child Development* 56:415–428.

Hall, G. S. 1904. *Adolescence: Its psychology and its relations to physiology, anthropology, sociology, sex, crime, religion, and education.* New York: Appleton.

Hauser, S. T., S. I. Powers, G. G. Noam, A. M. Jacobson, B. Weiss, and D. J. Follansbee. 1984. Familial contexts of adolescent ego development. *Child Development* 55:195–213.

Hetherington, E. M. 1989. Coping with family transitions: Winners, losers, and survivors. *Child Development* 60:1–14.

Hill, J. P. 1980. The family. In M. Johnson, ed., *Toward adolescence: The middle school years. The seventy-ninth yearbook of the National Society for the Study of Education*, pp. 32–55. Chicago: University of Chicago Press.

———. 1987. Research on adolescents and their families: Past and prospect. In C. E. Irwin, ed., *Adolescent social behavior and health.* Vol. 37, *New directions for child development*, pp. 13–31. San Francisco, Calif.: Jossey-Bass.

———. 1988. Adapting to menarche: Familial control and conflict. In M. R. Gunnar and W. A. Collins, eds., *Development during transition to adolescence: Minnesota symposia on child psychology*, 21:43–77. Hillsdale, N.J.: Erlbaum.

Hill, J. P., and M. E. Lynch. 1983. The intensification of gender-related role expectations during early adolescence. In J. Brooks-Gunn and A. C. Petersen, eds., *Girls at puberty: Biological and psychosocial perspectives*, pp. 201–228. New York: Plenum.

Hofferth, S. L., and C. D. Hayes, eds. 1987. *Risking the future: Adolescent sexuality, pregnancy, and childbearing.* Vol. 2. Washington, D.C.: National Academy of Sciences Press.

Hoffman, J. A. 1984. Psychological separation of late adolescents from their parents. *Journal of Counseling Psychology* 31:170–178.

Hoffman, L. W. 1989. Effects of maternal employment in the two-parent family. *American Psychologist* 44:283–292.

Inoff-Germain, G., G. S. Arnold, E. D. Nottelmann, E. J. Susman, G. B. Cutler, and G. P. Chrousos. 1988. Relations between hormone levels and observational measures of aggressive behavior of young adolescents in family interactions. *Developmental Psychology* 24 (1):129–139.

Jessor, R., and S. L. Jessor. 1977. *Problem behavior and psychosocial development: A longitudinal study of youth.* New York: Academic Press.

Jones, P.S. 1979. Treating sexually abused children. *Child Abuse and Neglect* 3:285–290.

Kahn, J., K. Smith, and E. Roberts. 1984. *Familial communication and adolescent sexual behavior.* Final report to the Office of Adolescent Pregnancy Programs. Cambridge, Mass.: American Institutes for Research.

Marshall, W. A., and J. M. Tanner. 1969. Variations in the pattern of pubertal changes in girls. *Archives of Disease in Childhood* 44:291–303.

Matthews, K. A. 1989. Interactive effects of behavior and reproductive hormones on sex differences in risk for coronary heart disease. *Health Psychology* 8:373–387.

McIntyre, K. 1981. Role of mothers in father-daughter incest: A feminist analysis. *Social Work* 26:462–466.

Meiselman, K. 1978. *Incest: A psychological study of causes and effects with treatment recommendations.* San Francisco: Jossey-Bass.

Merriwether-de Vries, C., L. M. Burton, and L. Eggeletion. In press. Early parenting and intergenerational family relationships within African-American families. In J. A. Graber, J. Brooks-Gunn, and A. C. Petersen, eds., *Transitions through adolescence: Interpersonal domains and context.* Mahwah, N.J.: Erlbaum.

Moffitt, T. E., A. Caspi, J. Belsky, and P. A. Silva. 1992. Childhood experience and the onset of menarche: A test of a sociobiological model. *Child Development* 63:47–58.

Moore, K. A., C. W. Nord, and J. L. Peterson. 1989. Nonvoluntary sexual activity among adolescents. *Family Planning Perspectives* 21:110–114.

Moos, R. H. 1974. *Family Environment Scale.* New York: Consulting Psychologists Press.

Montemayor, R. 1982. The relationship between parent-adolescent conflict and the amount of time adolescents spend alone and with parents and peers. *Child Development* 53:1512–1519.

———. 1983. Parents and adolescents in conflict: All families some of the time and some families most of the time. *Journal of Early Adolescence* 3:83–103.

———. 1986. Family variation in parent-adolescent storm and stress. *Journal of Adolescent Research* 1:15–31.

Montemayor, R., and E. Hanson. 1985. A naturalistic view of conflict between adolescents and their parents and siblings. *Journal of Early Adolescence* 5:23–30.

Neugarten, B. L. 1979. Time, age, and life cycle. *American Journal of Psychiatry* 136: 887–894.

Offer, D. 1987. In defense of adolescents. *Journal of the American Medical Association* 257:3407–3408.

Olweus, D., A. Mattsson, D. Schalling, and H. Low. 1988. Circulating testosterone levels and aggression in adolescent males: A causal analysis. *Psychosomatic Medicine* 50:261–272.

Paikoff, R. L., and J. Brooks-Gunn. 1991. Do parent-child relationships change during puberty? *Psychological Bulletin* 110 (1):47–66.

Paikoff, R. L., J. Brooks-Gunn, and S. Carlton-Ford. 1991. Effect of reproductive status changes upon family functioning and well-being of mothers and daughters. *Journal of Early Adolescence* 11 (2):201–220.

Paikoff, R. L., S. Carlton-Ford, and J. Brooks-Gunn. 1993. Mother-daughter dyads view the family: Associations between divergent perceptions and daughter well-being. *Journal of Youth and Adolescence* 22 (5):473–492.

Papini, D. R., N. Datan, and K. A. McCluskey-Fawcett. 1988. An observational study of affective and assertive family interactions during adolescence. *Journal of Youth and Adolescence* 17:477–482.

Petersen, A. C., P. A. Sarigiani, and R. E. Kennedy. 1991. Adolescent depression: Why more girls? *Journal of Youth and Adolescence* 20:247–271.

Petersen, A. C., J. E. Schulenberg, R. H. Abramowitz, D. Offer, and H. D. Jarcho. 1984. A Self-Image Questionnaire for Young Adolescents (SIQYA): Reliability and validity studies. *Journal of Youth and Adolescence* 13:93–111.

Plomin, R., G. E. McClearn, N. L. Pedersen, J. R. Nesselroade, and C. S. Bergeman.

1988. Genetic influence on childhood family environment perceived retrospectively from the last half of the life span. *Developmental Psychology* 24:738–745.

Radloff, L. S. 1977. The CES-D scale: A self-report depression scale for research in the general population. *Applied Psychological Measurement* 1:385–401.

———. 1991. The use of the Center of Epidemiologic Studies Depression Scale in adolescents and young adults. *Journal of Youth and Adolescence* 20:149–166.

Richard, M. H., and E. Duckett. 1991. Maternal employment and adolescents. In J. V. Lerner and N. L. Galambos, eds., *Employed mothers and their children*, pp. 85–130. New York: Garland.

Rossi, A. S. 1977. A biosocial perspective on parenting. *Daedalus* 106:1–31.

Rossi, A. S., and P. H. Rossi. 1990. *Of human bonding*. New York: Aldine de Gruyter.

Ruble, D. N., J. Brooks-Gunn, A. S. Fleming, G. Fitzmaurice, C. Stangor, and F. Deutsch. 1990. Transition to motherhood and the self: Measurement, stability, and change. *Journal of Personality and Social Psychology* 58:450–463.

Sgroi, S. 1982. *Handbook of clinical interventions in child sexual abuse*. Lexington, Mass.: Lexington Books.

Simmons, R. G., and D. A. Blyth. 1987. *Moving into adolescence: The impact of pubertal change and school context*. New York: Aldine.

Smetana, J. G. 1988a. Adolescents' and parents' conceptions of parental authority. *Child Development* 59:321–335.

———. 1988b. Concepts of self and social convention: Adolescents' and parents' reasoning about hypothetical and actual family conflicts. In M. R. Gunnar and W. A. Collins, eds., *Development during transition to adolescence: Minnesota symposia on child psychology*, 21:79–122. Hillsdale, N.J.: Erlbaum.

Stattin, H., and D. Magnusson. 1990. *Paths through life*. Vol. 2, *Pubertal maturation in female development*. Hillsdale, N.J.: Erlbaum.

Steinberg, L. 1987. Impact of puberty on family relations: Effects of pubertal status and pubertal timing. *Developmental Psychology* 23:451–460.

———. 1989. Pubertal maturation and parent-adolescent distance: An evolutionary perspective. In G. R. Adams, R. Montemayor, and T. P. Gullotta, eds., *Biology of adolescent behavior and development*, pp. 71–97. Newbury Park, Calif.: Sage.

———. 1990. Autonomy, conflict, and harmony in the family relationship. In S. Feldman and G. Elliott, eds., *At the threshold: The developing adolescent*, pp. 255–276. Cambridge: Harvard University Press.

Surbey, M. K. 1990. Family composition, stress, and the timing of human menarche. In T. E. Ziegler and F. B. Bercovitch, eds., *Socioendocrinology of primate reproduction*, pp. 11–32. New York: Wiley.

Susman, E. J., G. E. Inoff-Germain, E. D. Nottelmann, G. B. Cutler, Jr., D. L. Loriaux, and G. P. Chrousos. 1987. Hormones, emotional dispositions, and aggressive attributes in early adolescents. *Child Development* 58:1114–1134.

Wakschlag, L. S., P. L. Chase-Lansdale, and J. Brooks-Gunn. In press. Not just

"Ghosts in the Nursery": Contemporaneous intergenerational relationships and parenting in young African American families. *Child Development.*

Warren, M. P. 1980. The effects of exercise on pubertal progression and reproductive function in girls. *Journal of Clinical Endocrinology and Metabolism* 51:1150–1157.

Warren, M. P., and J. Brooks-Gunn. 1989. Mood and behavior at adolescence: Evidence for hormonal factors. *Journal of Clinical Endocrinology and Metabolism* 69 (1):77–83.

Mothers' Parental Efficacy at Midlife in a Black and Latina Sample: Effects of Adolescent Change across a School Transition

LaRue Allen, J. Lawrence Aber, Edward Seidman,
Jill Denner, and Christina Mitchell

Theories regarding the course of human development through adulthood have focused largely on the issues and themes that dominate the lives of white middle-class males. Giele (1982) suggests that different segments of the population may experience adulthood in different ways. For example, researchers who investigate stages of adult development focus on the midlife crisis as a hallmark event. But those who study the lives of lower-class research participants, whose simple jobs, limited education, and narrow network of social contacts limit the amount of choice in their lives, find that stage theories are not descriptive or predictive for their samples. In contrast, high-status individuals who enjoy jobs that offer opportunities to develop autonomous selves appear to live lives that are more accurately described by theories with distinct stages and patterns of behavior differentially associated with each stage.

Research on the course of midlife development also suggests that, in addition to social class, both gender and ethnicity may influence the life course for adults. For women, for example, relationships may be more central in determining the course of their lives than for men. Both Giele (1982) and Miller (1976) have questioned whether the pivotal male midlife values of mastery and achievement are germane to the study of women as adults. Questions such as these point to the need for examination of midlife development among women and minorities of different social classes to discern whether the course of midlife development varies across groups.

In the hierarchy of relationships, women's relationships with their children are among the most central to their lives. At midlife, the na-

This research was supported in part by grants from the National Institute of Mental Health (MH43084) and the Carnegie Corporation (B4850) awarded to Edward Seidman, J. Lawrence Aber, LaRue Allen, and Christina Mitchell. We are grateful to the parents, youth, and schools whose cooperation made this study possible.

ture of this central relationship changes radically (Collins 1990). Children become adolescents and actively work on figuring out who they will be as adults. These changes are affected by the parents and the parenting culture, in turn having an effect on parents and the parenting culture (Bell 1979). Yet for all the diversity in the United States population, we know that research on changes in parent-child relationships has not yet attended to variations in relationship changes across families of different racial/ethnic backgrounds or of different family structures; rather, researchers have relied almost exclusively on data from white, two-parent, middle-class families (Collins 1990).

Although researchers such as Richard Q. Bell have raised our consciousness about the importance of conceptualizing research on parent-adolescent relationships with a bidirectional focus, what usually occurs is examination of only the effects of parents on adolescents. In this chapter, we use data collected, in part, for the study of the effect of parent behaviors on youth to examine the flow of causality in the other direction. The data are particularly suited to their new role because they are longitudinal, allowing us to look at the effect of change in youth on two specific aspects of parent well-being: efficacy in interactions with the outside world and efficacy in interactions with child and family.

The data for this examination are from the Adolescent Pathways Project (APP), a longitudinal study of the developmental trajectories of low-income, ethnically diverse, urban adolescents (Seidman 1991). In addition to the survey of 1,432 youth from three eastern seaboard cities, across three waves (a fourth wave of data collection is in progress), the project also included two-hour individual interviews with parents that were designed to provide additional information to help define the progress of youth toward various developmental outcomes. Parent Study data were collected contemporaneous with the second wave of youth data, thus permitting an analysis of the effects of changes in youth from wave 1 to wave 2 on selected aspects of parents' well-being.

A significant change in the lives of youth is the transition from elementary to junior high or middle school. For many, a school transition occurs during early adolescence, a time of rapid biological and interpersonal change (Brooks-Gunn and Petersen 1983). This is often the first time a young person has made the change from the small, personal environment of a typical elementary school to a larger, more impersonal one involving multiple teachers who are less involved in their students' lives. The transition is often a difficult one, placing youth who do not successfully negotiate it at increased risk for long-term negative developmental outcomes. This may be especially true for poor, minority urban youth who are experiencing a greater number of environmental stressors, though little empirical research on school transitions involving poor minority youth has been reported.

Some investigations have found that esteem declines across the transition (e.g., Simmons, Rosenberg, and Rosenberg 1973), others have found this effect only for females (e.g., Simmons et al. 1987), and still others have failed to replicate this decrement in self-esteem (e.g., Hirsch and Rapkin 1987), leading Eccles and Midgeley (1989) to conclude that the results regarding the impact of the school transition on self-esteem are mixed. However, other aspects of the self-system that have been investigated in the transition literature have shown more consistent results. For example, academic performance has invariably been shown to decline across the transition (Petersen and Crockett 1985) for both boys and girls (Simmons and Blyth 1987). The decline for black youth has been reported to be particularly precipitous (Simmons and Blyth 1987).

In one of the few additional studies to involve a large, ethnically diverse urban sample, Seidman et al. (1985), analyzing data from the Adolescent Pathways Project, found extensive negative effects in the transition to junior high school, across blacks, whites, and Latinos. Declines in self-esteem, class preparation, and grade point average (GPA) were common across race/ethnic groups and across males and females. The school transition was also perceived to be associated with changes in the school and peer contexts. Daily hassles within school increased, while social support and extracurricular involvement decreased. Daily hassles with peers decreased, and peer values were perceived as more antisocial. These context changes were also robust across race/ethnicity and gender groups.

The dramatic impact of this transition to junior high school provides us with an opportunity to test a model of the effects of these school transition–associated changes on the efficacy of black and Latino parents. Among mothers of youths' experiencing the transition from elementary to junior high school, we are interested in the direct effects of this transition on mothers' sense of efficacy. Our hypothesis is that family background characteristics as well as characteristics of the mothers themselves have both direct effects on mothers' efficacy and moderating effects on the impact of transition risk on efficacy. We are also interested in whether race/ethnicity and child's gender are best conceptualized as direct effects or as moderators of the impact of transition risk on efficacy. The specifics of how we address our questions will be presented in a later section. We now turn to an examination of the predictor variables in our model, which, in addition to transition risk, are conceptually relevant to our prediction of two dimensions of mothers' sense of efficacy.

RESOURCES: DIRECT AND MODERATING EFFECTS
Family Demographic Resources

Our family demographic resources include race/ethnicity, youth gender, parent age, parent education, and parent marital status. Examining the effects of youth transitions on racial and ethnic minority parents requires that we examine what is known about the climate or culture of minority families that may influence youth and adolescent interactions.

Race/ethnicity. Black and Latino families in the United States are distinguished from the white majority by having to negotiate both the majority and their own minority culture. While no single black or Latino family type exists, both differ from the white families most often represented in research (De Alva 1988). For example, among both, the idea of family is not limited to the immediate family but often includes a network of relatives and friends that make up an extended family (Hendricks 1974; Stack 1974). These larger families may provide multiple sources of support and influence for the parent-child relationship.

Studies on Latino families emphasize the importance of multiple relatives in the parent-child relationship. Two concepts important in Latino family life are *familism* (attachment to the family, or children's respect for authority) and *fatalism* (belief in the adaptation to life's circumstances) (Rogler and Cooney 1986; Sabogal et al. 1987). For example, Puerto Rican families, the second largest Latino group in the United States, are found to place a great deal of importance on interpersonal relations with family and others (Sjostrom 1988), living with or close to extended family members. Thus interaction or involvement with one's child and family may moderate the impact of a negative family event such as symptoms of transition stress in their adolescents.

The literature provided some limited suggestions of the nature of the differences between black and Latino families. In a sample of low-income urban mothers, after giving birth, Latinas reported less social

304

support, lower self-esteem, and more punitive or demanding attitudes toward their children than did blacks (Wasserman et al. 1990). Another difference between family life among blacks versus Latinos, cited by Dore and Dumois (1990), is the more highly defined family roles among Latinos, with mothers responsible for childrearing functions in a role with high social value.

Differences between black and Latino youth on important developmental outcomes have also been reported. For example, black adolescents have higher rates of suicide than do Latinos; both have higher rates than whites (Department of Health and Human Services 1992). Also, among black, white, and Puerto Rican youth in grades nine to twelve, career aspirations varied. For males, whites were lowest in aspirations, followed by blacks, then Puerto Ricans. Among females, blacks are often found to have the highest levels of aspiration (Dillard and Perrin 1980). Findings such as these suggest either causal or correlational relationships to the culture of their families of origin.

Gender. Regarding the role of child's gender, research suggests that gender-related role expectations in adolescence are associated with increased monitoring of girls and decreased monitoring of boys in white (Hill and Lynch 1983; Ianni 1989), black (Jarrett 1990), and Latino families (De Alva 1988; Vazquez-Nuttall and Romero-Garcia 1989). Some studies suggest that parent-child relationships are characterized by the control of sons' expression of emotion and daughters' whereabouts (Block 1978), while others suggest that parents are more controlling of children of their own sex (Maccoby and Martin 1983). When parents are controlling but not warm, girls are more socially competent than boys, whereas boys are more competent than girls in the absence of control (Cooper, Grotevant, and Condon 1983). Latino mothers may encourage their daughters to work and become educated and, at the same time, maintain traditional notions of gender in interpersonal relations (Comas-Diaz 1987; Jarrett 1990; Pessar 1990, 1991). These gender distinctions may influence the relationship between youth transition risk and its effects on parents.

Parent age. Parent's age is positively associated with a white mother's level of education and employment status and her ability to provide supportive, consistent parenting. Older low-income black mothers are found to be less punitive and more positive about parenting their infants than are younger or adolescent parents (Reis 1989). Similarly,

Rauh, Wasserman, and Brunelli (1990) found a negative relationship between parent age and parent report of strictness and aggravation with their infants in a low-income black and Latino sample. Because of these findings, age is included as a control variable without specific predictions attached to its relationship with the outcomes.

Parent education. Maccoby (1980) cites socioeconomic status as one of the most powerful yet least understood influences on parenting style. Low levels of education, a proxy for low social class, are associated with more emphasis on obedience than on the free expression of a child's personality. Parents with less education are likely to be more controlling, authoritarian, and show less warmth toward their children. Furthermore, these patterns appear to generalize across societies in other countries and across blacks and whites in the United States. These findings take on even more importance given that, in 1981, only 45 percent of all Latinos completed four years of high school or more, compared with 53.2 percent of all blacks and 70.3 percent of the total population (Davis, Haub, and Willette 1988).

Marital status. Poor, single parents, in less supportive communities as well as in economically distressed marriages, are at risk for psychological symptoms and dissatisfaction with parenting (McLoyd 1990). As of 1985, 46 percent of black women between the ages of thirty-five and forty-four were in intact marriages (Glick 1988). In 1988, 53 percent of Puerto Rican and at least 40 percent of Dominican children did not live in households with a married couple (Gurak 1988). Because of the need to work outside the home, single-parent households invest less time and money in their children. This lack of resources may be the causal mechanism for the poorer developmental outcomes frequently found among poor children.

Maternal Engagement

In addition to descriptors of the socioeconomic context of these families, maternal behaviors both inside and outside the home may influence the relationship of youth risk to dimensions of parents' midlife status. We are focusing on three distinct parental behaviors that may serve this function: involvement with child and family, involvement with work, and parenting style.

Involvement. Findings from white middle-class samples suggest that the relationship between an adolescent's development and parents' well-being is influenced by parents' involvement in relationships outside the home (Silverberg and Steinberg 1990). For parents with a relatively strong orientation toward work, for example, the relationship between indices of increased youth maturity and parents' well-being were positive. For those with a weak orientation to work, the reverse was true—indices of increased youth maturity were negatively associated with parents' well-being.

In black and Latino families where family connectedness is a lifelong value, nonfamily involvement may not be as important in moderating the impact of child change on parent well-being. Black and Latino families are more likely to maintain ties with extended relatives throughout the life course and may depend less on outside involvement for a sense of competence and rely more instead on involvement with their children and families.

Parenting style. An important dimension of parent-child interaction for all is parenting style and its effects on youth. In a review of parent influences on socialization of children, Rollins and Thomas (1979) indicate that two dimensions of parental influence have been repeatedly cited as important over the last several decades of research: parental control and parental support. These dimensions are combined in Baumrind's (1971) typology of parenting styles, which have been related to child behavioral outcomes in research with mainstream populations.

Baumrind described parents with different combinations of reliance on control and support in their childrearing as authoritative, authoritarian, or permissive. Authoritative parents are those who direct their children, but with reason, explaining the reasons for their demands and discipline efforts. These parents direct with reason by choice but are willing to use more overt power moves when necessary. Authoritative parents produce children who are both independent and socially responsible.

Permissive parents, high on support but low on control, are accepting of all their child's impulses, make few demands, and use reasoning but without overt power moves. In Baumrind's research, children with permissive parents are neither independent nor socially responsible.

Authoritarian parents, high on control but low on warmth, do not typically use reason, place great value on obedience, and are sometimes rejecting of their children. Children of authoritarian parents demonstrate little independence and score only moderately on measures of social responsibility. Authoritarian parenting has been linked to low academic achievement in both black and white youth (Dornbusch et al. 1987; Johnson, Shulman, and Collins 1991). Studies of minority parents have focused almost exclusively on poor families, with concern about the effects of poverty-related stress on family functioning. Studies suggest that promoting survival techniques is a primary concern for many poor black parents (Gibbs 1990; Jarrett 1990), sometimes involving strict discipline (Spencer 1990) or corporal punishment for young children and warnings about negative consequences for older children (Jarrett 1990). Economic distress and the environmental stress associated with it contribute to a parenting style that is typically more restrictive than that among middle-class whites and perhaps Latinos (Garbarino and Sherman 1980; McLoyd 1990). Given the positive relationships between authoritative parenting and child outcomes in the developmental literature, authoritative parenting is expected to influence the impact of transition risk on a mother's sense of efficacy.

Outcome Measures

Our outcome measures involve two dimensions of parental efficacy. A sense of personal efficacy is a significant contributor to a woman's sense of well-being (Giele 1982). A sense of parenting efficacy has been related, among parents of younger children, to parents' involvement in children's education, which in turn affects children's accomplishments (Swick 1988). Whitbeck (1987) found that perceptions of parent efficacy predicted self-esteem in white middle-class adolescents. We, in turn, wonder how changes in youth across the school transition affect parents' own reports of self-efficacy, both in interaction with their child and family and in interaction with those outside the home. An ecological perspective (Bronfenbrenner 1979) supports the prediction that interactions involving the youth and family could well have effects on parents' efficacy beyond the parent-youth/family microsystem. We are interested, in summary, in the predictors of parent efficacy within the home, as well as beyond. We hypothesize that parental resources, in terms of both salient demographic resources (race/ethnicity, child's age, parent's age, parent's education, and marital status) and engagement resources (involvement with work, involvement with child and family, and authoritative parenting style), manifest a direct relationship to parent efficacy. Above and beyond the direct relationship of a parent's resources, transition risk will relate to efficacy such that the higher the risk, the lower the parent's efficacy. The most important hypothesis, however, is that family demographic resources and maternal engagement resources moderate transition risk in the prediction of efficacy. Under conditions of increasing risk, greater resources will lead to increased efficacy. The effect of resources on efficacy will be strongest for low-risk families.

Whether the relationships among these constructs and the specific hypotheses remain similar across gender and race/ethnicity is debatable. Our separate examination of the model within these groups is designed to provide the most sensitive test available of whether these constructs have direct or indirect effects on efficacy.

METHODS

The Young Cohort of the Youth Study of the APP consisted of 904 poor youth sampled from three eastern seaboard cities. For the current investigation, only black and Latino youth participating in waves 1 and 2 and whose parents participated in the Parent Study are included (for further details, see Seidman 1991). Before turning to a description of Parent Study youth, we describe school and youth participant selection procedures for the entire Young Cohort of the APP.

Youth Study

School selection. Our objective was to obtain the cooperation of elementary schools with predominantly black, Latino, or white students and with a minimum of 60 percent to 80 percent of the student body eligible for a reduced and/or free lunch. Within schools, all students in the grade prior to the transition to an intermediate or junior high school were recruited, that is, fifth or sixth graders. The grade structure of the Baltimore schools was kindergarten through fifth, then sixth through eighth grades; in Washington, it was kindergarten through sixth and then seventh through eighth grades. To avoid confounding grade sequence with city, schools with both grade structures were sampled in New York City. In the pretransition year, our youth came from twenty-five elementary schools across the three cities. In the transition year, youth had moved to forty intermediate or junior high schools.

Student recruitment. In the pretransition year, we met with teachers, principals, Parent-Teacher Organization leaders, and others to spark interest and investment in the project, thus increasing the chances that larger numbers of children would participate. Study participants were recruited in each classroom of the highest grade of each targeted school. All students in attendance were introduced to the study by the teacher and/or a staff member of the project. Students were given a description of the study and a consent form and asked to have a parent or guardian read the description, sign the consent form, and return it to the school. Study documents sent to parents were available in both English and Spanish because of the large percentages of parents in Washington and New York who were more comfortable reading Spanish.

A reminder notice and an extra consent form were sent home after a week or so. To encourage return of forms, pizza parties and other rewards suggested by school personnel were used as incentives. Prizes were awarded to the classroom in each school that had the largest percentage of parental consent forms returned, whether or not consent to participate was given. On the first day of data collection, students with signed parental consent forms were again presented with a description of the project and asked to sign their own consent form before participating. In wave 2, we recruited only the youth in wave 1 for whom we had signed consent forms from both parent and student.

Participation and representativeness. In wave 1, we collected data from 863 adolescents. The percentage who agreed to participate averaged 38 percent across classrooms: 24 percent in Baltimore, 36 percent in New York, and 57 percent in Washington. For the New York subsample, 76 percent of our New York respondents, we compared standardized achievement scores in reading and mathematics for participating youth to those of all youth in the same grade and school. Participants did not differ significantly from nonparticipants on these measures (Seidman 1991).

Sample description. Youth ranged in age from nine to fifteen ($M = 11.4$, $SD = .93$) at the time of the wave 1 data collection; 54 percent were female, 30 percent black, 19 percent white, 41 percent Latino, and 10 percent other (primarily Asians and biracial youth). The black youth were both African and Caribbean American, the whites were primarily Greek- and Italian-American, and the Latinos were predominantly Dominican and Puerto Rican. The Washington sample was largely black, with a small percentage of Latinos and no whites. The

Baltimore sample had a mix of black and white students, and the New York sample included Latinos as well as blacks and whites. These patterns of diversity reflect, in general, the ethnic composition of each city. Finally, 39 percent of these youth lived in census tracts where between 20 percent and 39 percent of the nonelderly residents fell below the official poverty line, and an additional 20 percent lived in tracts where 40 percent or more were below the poverty line (known as "concentrated" poverty areas).

Retention/attrition. Wave 2 included 74 percent of the youth interviewed for wave 1 (Seidman et al. 1994). We conducted analyses to examine differences between youth retained for both waves and those included only in wave 1. We found no differences in gender, nor were there interactions between gender by race/ethnicity. However, retention did differ by race/ethnicity, with whites retained to a significantly greater degree than Latinos ($p < .05$) and blacks ($p < .001$) and Latinos to a significantly greater degree than blacks ($p < .001$). The proportion of black youth in wave 2 (28 percent), however, was nearly equivalent to that in wave 1 (30 percent).

Data collection procedures. Data were collected in group settings at schools by APP staff, a racially/ethnically diverse group of graduate and undergraduate research assistants, and one of the study's principal investigators. Instructions and questions were read aloud to the group, while staff members circulated to answer students' questions and "spot-check" youth responses to measures whose directions were more complicated.

Parent Study Youth

For the analyses that follow, only data from black and Latino youth whose female parent or parent-figure had been interviewed in the Parent Study (see below) were included. Whites were not included because the number that met our selection criteria was too small and unrepresentative to produce stable estimates of regression coefficients.

Fifty-four youth were black; 106 were Latino. The black youth were slightly older ($X = 13.1$, $SD = .83$) than the Latinos ($X = 12.75$, $SD = .73$) ($p = .001$) at the time of the second youth assessment. Overall, 59 percent of study youth lived in tracts where between 20 percent and 39 percent fell below the poverty level, and an additional 26 percent lived in tracts where 40 percent or more fell below the poverty level. However, this subsample comes from poorer neighborhoods than does our full Young Cohort because the white youth from working-poor families were excluded.

Measures. The development of our transition risk index was based on Seidman and his colleagues' (1994) work on the impact of school transitions in early adolescence on the self-system and social context of urban youth. We chose measures of the youths' self-system and social context most responsive to changes in youth across the transition from elementary to junior high school.

To create the transition risk index, scores for the measures of self-esteem, class preparation, GPA, school hassles, school social support, and school involvement from wave 1 (pretransition) and wave 2 (posttransition) were standardized within gender and racial/ethnic subgroups. For each variable, the youth's score at wave 1 was subtracted from his/her score at wave 2 to create a measure of change. These measures of change were then summed to create the transition risk index ($\bar{X} = 15.57$, $SD = 2.84$).

Self-esteem was assessed with the five-item general self-worth subscale of the Self-Perception Profile for Adolescents (Harter 1987). Using a "structured alternative format," youth were asked to choose between two opposite items (e.g., "Some teenagers are very happy being the way they are" versus "Some teenagers wish they were different") and then to indicate if the statement was "sort of true" or "really true" for them. Items were scored on a four-point scale. Internal consistency for this scale was .71 (.73 for wave 2). Class preparation was measured by averaging the scores on four four-point, self-report items, such as "In general, do you: come to class prepared, or turn in neat, tidy homework?" (alpha = .73 [.79]). Grade point average was self-reported: F or unsatisfactory (1), D or needs improvement (2), C or satisfactory (3), B or good (4), and A or excellent (5). School records of GPA were not available; however, self-reported GPA correlated .29 ($p < .0001$) and .25 ($p < .0001$) with scores of standardized tests from mathematics and reading achievement, respectively.

The Daily Hassles scale was developed specifically for administration to inner-city adolescents (Seidman et al. 1994), based on the earlier work of Rowlison and Felner (1988) and Kanner et al. (1981). Several subscales were suggested by principal axis factor analysis with varimax rotation. The School Hassles subscale consisted of four typical daily events (e.g., pressure to do well in school). For each, the youth checked whether the event "happened in the past month" and, if it had, rated how much of a hassle it was, on a four-point scale ranging from "not at all a hassle" to "a very big hassle" (alpha = .70 [.79]).

School social support came from a modification of the Social Support Rating Scale developed by Cauce, Felner, and Primavera (1982). The school subscale was composed of six items assessing emotional support; instrumental support; and satisfaction with the relationship with two groups of people, teachers and principals/assistant principals (alpha = .70 [.74]). School involvement came from a measure also developed specifically for this study (Seidman et al. 1994). Youth were asked how often they engage in several activities "at your school" (e.g., student government). Each item was rated on a six-point scale ranging from "never or almost never" to "almost every day." A principal axis factor analysis with varimax rotation yielded an eight-item school involvement subscale (alpha = .61 [.69]).

PARENT STUDY

Sampling

Our objective was to recruit the parents of one-third of the Young Cohort youth and to interview them within three or four months of the wave 2 interviews. We recruited parents through their youth to assure the youth that we were not planning to disclose any information that they had given us to their parents. At schools where wave 2 interviewing had already been completed, interviewers made special trips to meet with students, give them a recruitment flyer for their parents, and promise them five dollars if they brought back a response from their parents, whether it was yes or no. At other schools, parent study flyers were handed out in conjunction with wave 2 interviewing. In all cases, interviewers returned to schools at specific times to pick up parent responses and give youth their rewards.

Procedure

A sample of 246 parents of primary caregivers of the Young Cohort participants was interviewed approximately fourteen months after the first wave of Youth Survey data was collected. Interviewers were residents of parents' neighborhoods in most cases. Two advanced graduate students who were residents of parents' communities also served as interviewers. All were trained in two five-hour sessions, then supervised weekly, in sessions that included review of tapes of their interviews. Interviews were conducted in parents' homes, local diners, li-

313

braries, and other community facilities that were convenient and comfortable locations for parents.

Interviewers administered an intensive, semistructured interview in sessions lasting one and one-half to two hours. Parents chose whether they wanted the interview to be conducted in Spanish or English. Parents were paid twenty dollars on completion of the interview. Ninety-three percent of all respondents were females, and 95 percent of these were the youth's biological mother. Because of the disproportionately large number of female parents, male parental respondents were eliminated from the sample for the following analyses.

Because of the small, unrepresentative nature of the white (N = 32) and Asian or mixed race (N = 12) sample, only the 213 responses from parents of black and Latino children were retained. Of those interviews, 176 were from parents of youth who had been interviewed in both youth data waves. From these, we used the 160 respondents who were female caregivers, dropping the sixteen fathers because they were too small a group for separate analyses. The final sample consisted of 54 black and 106 Latina mothers.

Measures

The means and standard deviations for each variable within race/ethnicity and gender are presented in table 8.1.

Family demographic resources. Parent education was measured on a seven-point scale from "finished less than the 7th grade" to "graduate or professional degree" ($\bar{X} = 3.07$, $SD = 1.55$). The two groups were significantly different in level of education, 3.89 and 2.63 for blacks and Latinas, respectively ($p < .001$). Parent marital status is coded as either having a partner (married, living with someone) or not (single, divorced) ($\bar{X} = 1.28$, $SD = 1.46$). The mean age for black (39.4) and Latina (38.45) mothers was not significantly different (overall $\bar{X} = 38.78$, $SD = 6.74$).

Maternal engagement resources. Maternal engagement resources consists of three constructs: parent involvement with child and family, parent involvement with work, and parenting style.

Parent involvement with child and family was part of a six-item measure developed for this project to determine the parent's frequency of involvement with family and others. A principal components analysis using varimax rotation revealed two factors measuring close (fam-

Table 8.1. Means (Standard Deviations) of the Predictor and Criterion Variables by Child's Gender and Ethnicity

Predictor Variables	Black X̄ Mean (SD)	Latino X̄ Mean (SD)	Girl X̄ Mean (SD)	Boy X̄ Mean (SD)
Family demographic resources				
Parent's age	39.42	38.45	38.66	38.95
	(8.30)	(5.82)	(6.45)	(7.23)
Parent's education	3.89	2.63***	3.05	3.08
	(1.22)	(1.53)	(1.65)	(1.38)
Marital status	1.19	1.52	1.25	1.32
	(1.36)	(1.52)	(1.44)	(1.50)
Maternal engagement				
Involvement with work	1.98	1.55**	1.58	1.86
	(1.32)	(1.08)	(1.09)	(1.29)
Involvement with child				
and family	.05	−.15*	1.04	.03
	(.55)	(.59)	(.58)	(.57)
Parenting style	.24	.26	.26	.25
	(.43)	(.44)	(.44)	(.43)
Youth risk				
Transition risk	16.50	15.10**	15.66	15.43
	(2.59)	(2.85)	(2.69)	(3.09)
Criterion variables				
Child-family efficacy	3.07	2.93	2.96	3.02
	(.48)	(.38)*	(.45)	(.37)
Efficacy outside family	3.01	2.87	2.92	2.92
	(.40)	(.34)*	(.37)	(.37)

$*p < .05.$ $**p = .01.$ $***p < .001.$

ily) and distant (institution) relations, which accounted for 51 percent of the total variance. Four items, rated on a four-point scale, loaded on the child and family involvement component and reflected how often the respondent is engaged in activities with her child and family. The four items were unit-weighted and combined to create the scale. A sample item is "In the past month, how often have you engaged in activities with your family (e.g., rented or watched a movie, visited a friend, went for a drive, took a walk)?" (alpha = .59) ($\bar{X} = -.09$, $SD = .58$).

Parent involvement with work was derived from a measure on which mothers could endorse one or more forms of attachment to the labor force (e.g., "Last week, was this person: working full-time/with a job, but on vacation, temporarily ill, or on strike/looking for work. . . ."). Involvement with work was initially coded on a nine-point scale, with categories ranging from "on welfare and not looking for work" to "working full- and part-time." Responses were then collapsed into four categories, reflecting least to most involvement with work ($\bar{X} = 1.69$, $SD = 1.18$).

For parenting style, we began with responses to our twelve-item adaptation of Rickel and Biasatti's (1982) modification of Block's Child Rearing Practices Report. Statements describing childrearing practices were rated on a five-point scale (almost never to almost always to, for example, "I talk it over and reason with my child when s/he misbehaves"), indicating the degree to which each item describes the respondent's own practices. A principal components analysis using varimax rotation confirmed the two-factor structure of the original measure, accounting for 40 percent of the total variance. Internal consistency, computed using Cronbach's alpha, was .69 for the restrictiveness scale (six items) and .64 for the nurturance scale (six items). Scores on these two scales were used to create a dichotomous variable—authoritative versus nonauthoritative parents. Authoritative parents were those who scored above the median on both nurturance and restrictiveness. The authoritative parents (N = 41) were given a score of one. All others were scored zero ($\bar{X} = .25$, $SD = .44$).

Criterion variables. Efficacy was measured from responses to seventeen items, developed by the researchers, presenting situations of potential conflict or challenge. Parents responded on a five-point scale indicating how hard to how easy it was for them to cope with the situation described (e.g., "Your child asks you to talk to his/her teacher about a bad grade. Meeting with that teacher is. . . ."). A principal components analysis using varimax rotation suggested three components—Efficacy with child and family, efficacy with authorities, and efficacy with institutions—which accounted for 45 percent of the total variance.

After unit-weighting items to create the three scales, we found a high intercorrelation ($r = .51$) between efficacy with authorities and efficacy with institutions. Scores on these two scales were therefore combined to create a scale reflecting efficacy outside the family. The internal consistency coefficient for items involving efficacy with child and family was .78 ($\bar{X} = 2.98$, $SD = 1.83$); reliability for items involving efficacy outside the family was .80 ($\bar{X}$ = 2.92, SD = .37). One item (getting a refund at the store) did not load onto either of these scales.

RESULTS

The intercorrelation matrix for all variables is presented in table 8.2. To address the hypothesized relationships, for each of the parent criterion variables—efficacy with child and family and efficacy outside the family—we conducted a four-step hierarchical multiple regression. In the first and second blocks, family demographic resources (parent's education, parent's age, child's gender, child's ethnicity) and maternal engagement resources (involvement with child, involvement with work, parenting style) were entered to assess their potential direct effects. Next, the transition risk index was entered to test the primary hypothesis that changes in the child and her microsystem transactions over the transition to junior high school influence parental efficacy, above and beyond the direct effects of demographic and maternal engagement resources. The moderating effects of the demographic resource and maternal engagement variables on transition risk were examined by entering these interaction terms into the regression equation last. Because of power constraints, tests for interactions between risk and demographic resource variables and between risk and maternal engagement variables were conducted separately.[1]

As suggested above, we performed regression analyses for the total sample and for subgroups of youth by gender and by race/ethnicity, with the focus on our hypotheses regarding the main effects of family demographic and maternal engagement resources and their interactions with transition risk. Results involving these effects will be highlighted. Because of the difficulty detecting interaction effects in field studies (Krantz and Shinn 1992; McClelland and Judd 1993), significance level for interactions was set at $p < .10$; significance level for the main effects was set at $p < .05$.

In all equations predicting efficacy outside the family, neither the risk variable nor its interactions with family demographic or parent behavior variables contributed significant amounts of variance. This was true for analysis of the sample as a whole as well as for the subgroup analyses. Thus the hypotheses regarding both main effects and interactions involving transition risk in predicting efficacy outside the family were not confirmed.

For efficacy with child and family, the full equations for the total and female child samples were significant, as were they for the interac-

TABLE 8.2. Correlations among Predictor and Outcome Variables

	Child's Gender	Child's Ethnicity	Parent's Age	Parent's Education	Involvement with Work	Involvement with Child	Parenting Style	Transition Risk	Efficacy outside Family	Child-Family Efficacy
Child's gender										
Child's ethnicity	.04									
Parent's age	.02	−.07								
Parent's education	.02	−.39**	−.10							
Involvement with work	.12	−.17*	.09	−.01						
Involvement with child	.01	.16*	−.14	.17*	.10					
Parenting style	−.01	.02	.06	−.03	−.17*	−.05				
Transition risk	−.04	−.24**	.04	.16	.01	.06	−.05			
Efficacy outside family	−.00	−.17*	−.10	.22**	−.05	.24**	.15	−.03		
Child-family efficacy	.07	−.16*	−.16**	.16*	−.15	.14	.15	−.04	.54**	

*p < .05. **p < .01.

TABLE 8.3. Summary of Hierarchical Multiple Regression Analysis of Child-Family Efficacy: Whole Sample

Steps	Step Statistics			Final Equation Statistics	
	Adj R^2	Total F	ΔR^2	b(SEb)	Beta
1. Family demographic resources	.05	2.82	.07*		
Child's gender				.11 (.07)	.13
Child's ethnicity				−.16 (.08)	−.17†
Parent's age				−.05 (.04)	−.11
Parent's education				.02 (.02)	.09
2. Maternal engagement resources	.07	2.69	.05†		
Involvement with work				−.06 (.03)	−.16†
Involvement with child				.03 (.04)	.08
Parenting style				.12 (.08)	.13
3. Transition risk	.07	2.44	.01	−.15 (.07)	−.36*
4. Interaction of transition risk and maternal engagement resources	.12	2.82	.06*		
Transition risk × involvement with work				.03 (.03)	.15
Transition risk × involvement with child				−.04 (.04)	−.11
Transition risk × parenting style				.24 (.08)	.30**

†$p < .10$. *$p < .05$. **$p < .01$.

tions of transition risk and maternal engagement resources. In the interaction of transition risk and family demographic resources, the full equation was significant for only the black child sample. Analyses with maternal engagement resources as moderator are highlighted before the analyses of family demographic resource variables as moderated by transition risk.

Transition Risk × Maternal Engagement Resources

For the whole sample (see table 8.3), the full equation was significant ($F[11, 136] = 2.81$, $p < .01$). The only direct effects evidenced were with step 1, which contributed an increment of 7 percent in variance ($p < .05$). Race/ethnicity was most responsible for this effect

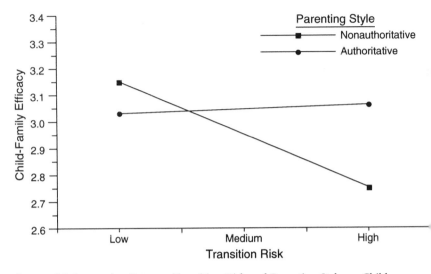

FIGURE 8.1. Interaction Between Transition Risk and Parenting Style on Child-Family Efficacy for the Whole Sample.

($b = -.16$), with blacks more likely to be efficacious. Although transition risk did not add significant variance to the prediction of child and family efficacy on entry in the third step, it appeared to have been suppressed by interactions tested in the next step, since it was significant in the final equation. In the final step, R^2 change for transition risk $\times$ maternal engagement resources was significant, accounting for a 6 percent increment in variance. The interaction between transition risk and parenting style ($b = .24$) is primarily responsible for the significant fourth step. The plot of the interaction in figure 8.1 shows that authoritative parents showed little change in efficacy across varying levels of youths' transition risk. Nonauthoritative parents, however, were highest in efficacy in the least challenging situation, that involving low risk. Conversely, these parents were lowest in efficacy under conditions of high risk, those that we hypothesize to be the most challenging. A parallel set of hierarchical regression analyses was performed separately within female and male youth. Only the equation for females was significant ($F[10, 80] = 3.34$, $p < .01$, see table 8.4). The results for female youth were similar to those for the whole sample, with the exception that the female equation statistics did not reveal a direct effect for transition risk ($b = -.06$, NS) on entry or in the final equa-

TABLE 8.4. Summary of Hierarchical Multiple Regression Analysis of Child-Family Efficacy: Mothers of Girls

Steps	Adj R^2	Total F	ΔR^2	b(SEb)	Beta
		Step Statistics		Final Equation Statistics	
1. Family demographic resources	.09	33.85	.11*		
Child's age				−.21 (.11)	−.23*
Parent's age				−.07 (.06)	−.16
Parent's education				.04 (.03)	.14
2. Maternal engagement resources	.09	2.49	.03		
Involvement with work				−.02 (.04)	−.05
Involvement with child				.00 (.04)	.00
Parenting style				.16 (.10)	.15
3. Transition risk	.09	2.34	.01	−.06 (.09)	−.13
4. Interaction of transition risk and maternal engagement resources	.21	3.34	.13**		
Transition risk × involvement with work				−.07 (.04)	−.24
Transition risk × involvement with child				−.07 (.04)	−.15
Transition risk × parenting style				.27 (.09)	.35**

†$p < .10$. *$p < .05$. **$p < .01$.

tion. Nevertheless, the transition risk by maternal engagement resources interaction contributed a 13 percent increment in variance, accounted for again primarily by transition risk × parenting style ($b = .27$, $p < .01$). As can be seen in figure 8.2, the interaction was accounted for by the differences between authoritative and nonauthoritative parental styles at high levels of risk. Authoritative parents manifested increasing efficacy as risk increased, whereas nonauthoritative parents decreased in efficacy as risk increased. In comparing figures 8.1 and 8.2, it is suggested that for authoritative parents of females, in contrast to males, efficacy was positively affected under conditions of increased transition risk.

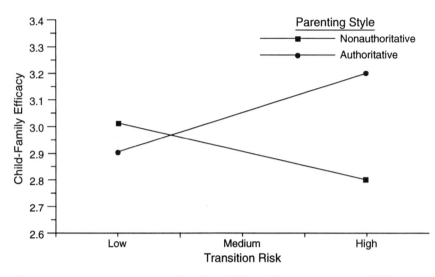

FIGURE 8.2. Interaction Between Transition Risk and Parenting Style on Child-Family Efficacy for Mothers of Girls.

Transition Risk × Family Demographic Resources

For the analyses testing the moderation of transition risk by family demographic resources, the only significant equation of the five tested was for the black subsample ($R^2_{adj} = .44$, $F[10, 37] = 2.88$, $p < .01$; see table 8.5). A direct effect in step 2 contributed an increment of 17 percent of the variance; it was accounted for largely by involvement with work ($b = -.32$, $p < .01$). The step statistics indicated that the significance of the risk hypothesis had been suppressed by interactions tested in the final step, because transition risk did yield a significant direct relationship ($b = .66$, $p < .01$) in the full equation. The interaction block added a significant 18 percent increment in variance. This step was accounted for primarily by transition risk × parent education. For mothers with low education, the relationship between risk and efficacy was strongly negative. For mothers with high levels of education, the relationship between risk and efficacy was strongly positive (see figure 8.3).

DISCUSSION

Our research has demonstrated that the influence of youth change over the transition to junior high school on black and Latina mothers' sense of efficacy varies depending on mothers' access to certain re-

TABLE 8.5. Summary of Hierarchical Multiple Regression Analysis of Child-Family Efficacy: Mothers of Black Children

Steps	Step Statistics			Final Equation Statistics	
	Adj R^2	Total F	ΔR^2	b(SEb)	Beta
1. Family demographic resources	−.01	.87	.06		
Child's gender				−.09 (.13)	−.09
Parent's age				−.16 (.08)	−.30†
Parent's education				−.06 (.05)	−.15
2. Maternal engagement resources	.11	1.20	.17*		
Involvement with work				−.12 (.05)	−.32*
Involvement with child				.06 (.06)	.14
Parenting style				.28 (.16)	.26†
3. Transition risk	.13	1.99	.03	.66 (.23)	1.41**
4. Interaction of transition risk and maternal engagement resources	.29	2.88	.18*		
Transition risk × child's gender				.09 (.14)	.11
Transition risk × parent's age				−.04 (.08)	.09
Transition risk × parent's education				−.18 (.05)	−1.71**

†$p < .10$. *$p < .05$. **$p < .01$.

sources. We hypothesized that the effects of transition risk on efficacy would be moderated by family demographic and/or maternal engagement resources. This hypothesis received partial confirmation for the whole sample, for mothers of female youth, and for blacks.

For the whole sample and for female youth, the effects of risk were moderated, largely by parenting style, with nonauthoritative parents least effective under conditions of high risk, whereas efficacy for authoritative parents was largely unchanged with changing risk. In the same interaction among mothers of female youth, efficacy for nonauthoritative parents still decreased, but efficacy for authoritative parents actually increased with high risk.

For mothers of black youth, transition risk was moderated largely

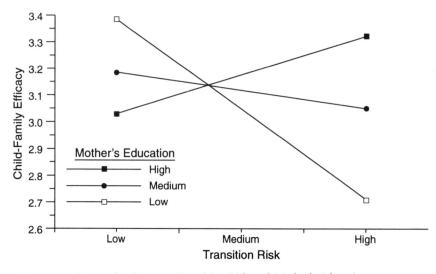

FIGURE 8.3. Interaction Between Transition Risk and Mother's Education on Child-Family Efficacy for Black Mothers.

by parent education—a family demographic resource. At low levels of education, mothers showed highest levels of efficacy under conditions of low risk. At high levels of education, mothers showed the highest levels of efficacy under conditions of highest risk. This group also showed a direct effect for involvement with work, with high involvement related to lower efficacy.

None of our models predicting efficacy outside the family accounted for statistically significant amounts of variance. That the youth's transition did not affect parental efficacy outside the home may imply that changes within the family do not necessarily have repercussions on mothers' ability to cope with situations outside the family. Indeed, in the context of the midlife existence of these urban minority women, perhaps their children's school events are relatively modest blips on their ecological radar screens. That is, although these events may well affect how mothers cope with their child, they may pale in comparison with the larger life issues that these women confront. Prior work on spillover of stress effects from home to the outside world of work (e.g., Bolger et al. 1989) have not included low-income and minority women to any great degree. Our findings suggest that the home-to-work spillover hypothesis should be explicitly tested with measures and methods designed to address the issue among these groups.

There were also no main effects of transition risk in the step statistics in the prediction of efficacy with child and family. For the whole sample and for mothers of black youth, the effect of transition risk appears to have been initially suppressed by its interaction with parenting style for females and with parent's education for blacks.

Parenting style has been associated with adolescent adjustment in school performance and psychosocial adjustment in an ethnically diverse sample (Steinberg et al. 1991). The findings in this study suggest that parenting style may have significant psychological benefits for the whole sample of mothers. Authoritative parents, whose style is a combination of high nurturance and high control, report a relatively high level of efficacy with their children across low to high levels of risk. This finding is consistent with other studies which suggest that authoritative parents are likely to be involved with and receptive to their child's needs (Baumrind 1971; Maccoby and Martin 1983), but it has implications for addressing the question of whether this involvement is beneficial for the parent as well. Nonauthoritative parents report less efficacy with the more transition risk that their child experienced. Authoritarian and permissive parents, the two styles of parenting combined in the nonauthoritative category, are less warm—or responsive—to a decrease in child's self-esteem and performance in school. It appears that the ability of nonauthoritative parents to cope with changes in their child's life is most taxed when the child's situation is most challenging to them—when the youth is at highest risk.

Although authoritative parents would be expected to be more responsive to children who are more at risk, this appears to be the case primarily for mothers of girls. Parenting style was found to moderate the effects of transition risk on parental efficacy for these mothers. Authoritative parents of girls responded to a high level of transition risk with a high report of efficacy, which suggests not only a greater sense of well-being for the parent but also a higher level of responsivity to the youth. Nonauthoritative parents responded to their daughter's reported high risk in the opposite manner, which indicates that these parenting styles may decrease the potential for positive coping for both parent and youth.

Comparing these findings with the nonsignificant relationship between parenting style and risk for mothers of boys depicted in figure 8.4, it appears that authoritative mothers feel more competent in the face of their daughter's increased risk than they do when sons face similar risk. A comparison of figures 8.3 and 8.4 reveals a pattern con-

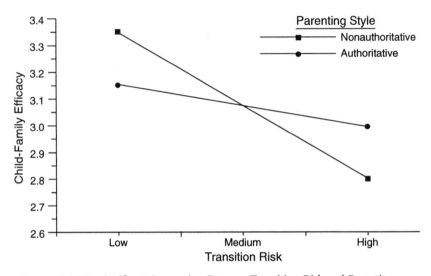

FIGURE 8.4. Nonsignificant Interaction Between Transition Risk and Parenting Style on Child-Family Efficacy for Mothers of Boys.

sistent with previous studies that suggest gender differences in parent-adolescent relationships (Cooper, Grotevant, and Condon 1983; Jarrett 1990). While the absolute value of mother's efficacy with sons is higher than her efficacy with daughters, none of these mothers feel competent about their interactions with their son when son's risk increases. This pattern may be related in origin to findings in studies of white middle-class families which show that boys become less communicative with mothers as they enter into adolescence (Cooper, Grotevant, and Condon 1983). If mothers are more in touch with their daughters, parenting style may play more of a role in determining a mother's ability to cope with changes experienced by a daughter than changes experienced by a son. In the Latino family literature, for example, the value placed on mothering and the strong mother-daughter bond are described for Puerto Rican families (Comas-Diaz 1987; Vazquez-Nuttal and Romero-Garcia 1989).

Mother's education was also found to moderate transition risk in predicting mothers' sense of efficacy. While education did not predict parental efficacy in the total sample, it was found to moderate the effects of transition risk in the subgroup of mothers of black youth. For blacks, the most educated mothers report the least efficacy when their

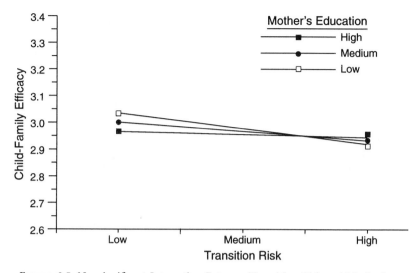

FIGURE 8.5. Nonsignificant Interaction Between Transition Risk and Mother's Education on Child-Family Efficacy for Latina Mothers.

child is at low risk and the most efficacy when their child is at the greatest risk. Parents with the lowest levels of education demonstrate the opposite relationship, reporting the least efficacy when the youth is at highest risk. This finding is consistent with studies which suggest that education is a factor in black and white mothers' sense of child-rearing efficacy, responsivity, and psychological health (Coleman et al. 1987; Simmons, Black, and Zhou 1991; Stevens 1988). These relationships were not significant for parents of Latino children, who reported less efficacy when their child was at higher risk, regardless of level of education (see figure 8.5), although other findings suggest a relationship between education and efficacy outside the home, at least for a Puerto Rican subgroup of Latina mothers (Soto and Shaver 1982). In our sample, Latinas are lower in both education and involvement with work, both proxies for the socioeconomic resources that may permit the educated black mothers the greater exposure to contact with the outside world that increases their ability to deal with challenges. These better-resourced black mothers are also likely to have more time and other resources to devote to efficacious interactions with their child.

Within the black subgroup, certain parent characteristics or behaviors predicted parental efficacy. Parent's involvement with work was positively associated with efficacy. This finding is consistent with previous findings which suggest that parental resources outside the home are positively related to parent well-being for black and white women (Coleman et al. 1987; Silverberg and Steinberg 1990). The fact that the finding is confined to black mothers may reflect the higher proportions of black than Latina mothers in the work force in this sample.

What can we conclude from these findings, which suggest that the effect of children's changes on their mothers' well-being are moderated by other aspects of mothers' lives? First, the child's transition does affect mother's efficacy within the family. This provides further evidence for the importance of parent-child relations for mother's well-being (Miller 1976), but only within the domain of the family. The child's influence on the parent is all the more remarkable in light of the other potential hardships experienced by mothers in poor families, in relatively poor neighborhoods (McLoyd 1990).

Second, the finding that authoritative parenting may have positive implications for the parent's coping ability and the parent-child relationship adds to the literature on the positive effects of authoritative parenting on the child, but its importance is realized here only under conditions of greatest challenge. Third, the finding that education plays a role in determining black mothers' coping response to child risk is consistent with findings on white parents from a range of socioeconomic backgrounds which suggest that more educated parents are more responsive (Simons et al. 1991). For authoritative and higher-education mothers, increased adolescent transition risk is associated with increased child and family efficacy. For nonauthoritative and lower-education mothers, increased transition risk is associated with decreasing child and family efficacy. It appears that mothers with more resources to draw on face the challenge of youth transition differently. These resources seem to be activated only when problems surface to a certain level, since situations of low risk do not provoke the same high levels of efficacy. These findings are consistent with the framework presented by Allen and Britt (1983), emphasizing the importance of conceptualizing resources, particularly for poor populations, as more than just economic. Their tripartite economic, social, and personal resource model is compatible with our findings and suggests a fruitful avenue for further exploration of the multiple ways in which developmental trajectories vary, even among those who are uniformly without economic resources.

In light of the association of low efficacy and psychological problems such as depression, a high-risk adolescent transition may have a more negative effect on mothers who are lower in education or who have a nonauthoritarian parenting style. Future research on midlife development among the groups studied here might benefit from further examination of how mothers with lower levels of social and economic resources cope over a longer term.

These findings have implications for developmental theory and for preventive interventions. The impact of transition risk on parent well-being appears to be moderated most often by parenting style, which is a factor potentially amenable to change. Similarly, the finding that education moderates the effects of transition risk on parental efficacy or well-being adds support to the argument that we need to provide increased opportunities for access to education and other resources.

Studies of parenting style in minority families have consisted of descriptions of the degree to which their styles compare with the typologies generated from research involving white middle-class families. Future research that begins by looking at the interactions of these mothers and youth and tries to define parenting behaviors from their perspective might increase our ability to understand why authoritative parenting is associated with the greatest sense of efficacy within the family. The most important clue that we can contribute from the current investigation is that the ability to cope with transition risk depends on access to certain personal and social resources, in our case, education and parenting style. A major limitation of this study is that it tests hypotheses about the effect of changes in children's lives on parent efficacy with data that were not designed for that purpose. Another is that our measures of parental well-being were restricted to only one domain—efficacy. Nonetheless, both the longitudinal youth design and the existence of measures of efficacy in two domains provide a reasonably strong foundation from which to explore the effects of youth on parents in a sample of minority mothers, a group that is not widely represented in the literature. The findings from this study provide information about how changes in youth's school experiences and self-system predict mother's well-being, measured by her report of efficacy within her family. The effect of this transition on the mother has been found to vary by mother's education and her parenting style, as well as by the gender and racial/ethnic group of the child. Research that includes other indices of well-being is suggested, especially measures of psychological well-being such as depression. Research with larger samples that can be stratified on these variables would allow us to test their relative contribution. Samples that allow examination of youth-parent effects within subgroups of the Latino population who differ, for example, in levels of acculturation or in immigration history, and within blacks, where African Americans and Caribbean Americans have different experiences in the labor force, for instance, would increase our understanding of how generalizable various causal scenarios actually are.

Given the stressful contexts in which many of these families exist (Greene 1990; McAdoo 1978), we might also predict that parents' efficacy can be more precisely predicted by including contextual variables in our models in future efforts. Denner (1993) recently found that high-risk neighborhoods had a moderating influence on how restrictive mothers were in their interactions with both male and female youth. Other dimensions of neighborhood and family contexts should be explored to capture both the stresses and the buffers that mothers derive from their contexts in order to function efficaciously. This study has demonstrated that changes in low-income, minority youth affect aspects of their midlife mothers' functioning. The conditions under which these relationships vary remain to be more fully explored.

NOTE

1. Additional analyses including parent marital status as a predictor were performed; patterns from these results were the same as those reported here. Therefore, this variable was eliminated from the remaining regression equations in view of the relatively small sample size relative to the number of predictor variables.

REFERENCES

Allen, L., and D. W. Britt. 1983. Social class, mental health, mental illness: The impact of resources and feedback. In R. D. Felner, L. A. Jason, J. N. Moritsugu, and S. S. Farber, eds., *Preventive Psychology*, pp. 149–161. New York: Pergamon.

Baumrind, D. 1971. Current patterns of parental authority. *Developmental Psychology*, monograph, 4 (1, p. 2):1–103.

Bell, R. Q. 1979. Parent, child, and reciprocal influences. *American Psychologist* 34 (10):821–826.

Block, J. H. 1978. Another look at sex differentiation in the socialization behaviors of mothers and fathers. In J. Sherman and F. L. Denmark, eds., *The Psychology of Women: Future Direction of Research*, pp. 29–89. New York: Psychological Dimensions.

Bolger, N., A. DeLongis, R. C. Kessler, and E. Wethington. 1989. The contagion of stress across multiple roles. *Journal of Marriage and the Family* 51:175–183.

Bronfenbrenner, U. 1979. *The ecology of human development: Experiments by nature and design.* Cambridge: Harvard University Press.

Brooks-Gunn, J., and A. C. Petersen, eds. 1983. *Girls at puberty: Biological and psychosocial perspectives.* New York: Plenum.

Cauce, A., R. D. Felner, and J. Primavera. 1982. Social support in high-risk adolescents: Structural components and adaptive impact. *American Journal of Community Psychology* 10:417–428.

Coleman, L. M., T. C. Antonucci, P. K. Adelmann, and S. E. Crohan. 1987. Social roles in the lives of middle-aged and older black women. *Journal of Marriage and the Family* 49 (4):761–771.

Collins, A. W. 1990. Parent-child relationships in the transition to adolescence: Continuity and change in interaction, affect, and cognition. In R. Montemayor, G. R. Adams, and T. P. Gullotta, eds., *From childhood to adolescence: A transitional period?*, pp. 85–106. Newbury Park, Calif.: Sage.

Comas-Diaz, L. 1987. Feminist therapy with mainland Puerto Rican women. *Psychology of Women Quarterly* 11:461–474.

Cooper, C. R., H. D. Grotevant, and S. M. Condon. 1983. Individuality and connectedness in the family as a context for adolescent identity formation and role taking skill. In H. D. Grotevant and C. R. Cooper, eds., *Adolescent Development in the Family: New Directions in Child Development*, pp. 43–59. San Francisco: Josey-Bass.

Davis, C., C. Haub, and J. L. Willette. 1988. U.S. Hispanics: Changing the face of America. In E. Acosta-Belen and B. R. Sjostrom, eds., *The Hispanic experience in the United States: Contemporary issues and perspectives*, pp. 3–55. New York: Praeger.

De Alva, J. J. K. 1988. Telling Hispanics apart: Latino socio-cultural diversity. In E. Acosta-Belen and B. R. Sjostrom, eds., *The Hispanic experience in the United States: Contemporary issues and perspectives*, pp. 107–136. New York: Praeger.

Denner, J. 1993. Restrictive parenting: Parent, child, and contextual influences. Unpublished manuscript.

Department of Health and Human Services. 1992.

Dillard, J. M., and D. W. Perrin. 1980. Puerto Rican, black, and Anglo adolescents' career aspirations, expectations, and maturity. *Vocational Guidance Quarterly* 28:313–321.

Dore, M. M., and A. O. Dumois. 1990. Cultural differences in the meaning of adolescent pregnancy. *Families in Society* 71 (2):93–101.

Dornbusch, S. M., P. L. Ritter, H. Leiderman, D. F. Roberts, and M. J. Fraleigh. 1987. The relation of parenting style to adolescent school performance. *Child Development* 58:1244–1257.

Eccles, J. S., and C. Midgeley. 1989. Stage/environment fit: Developmentally appropriate classrooms for young adolescents. In R. E. Ames and C. Ames, eds., *Research on motivation in education*, 3:139–186. New York: Academic Press.

Garbarino, J., and D. Sherman. 1980. High-risk neighborhoods and high-risk families: The human ecology of child maltreatment. *Child Development* 56 (2):415–428.

Gibbs, J. T. 1990. Developing intervention models for black families: Linking theory and research. In H. E. Cheatham and J. B. Stewart, eds., *Black families: Interdisciplinary perspectives,* pp. 325–351. New Brunswick, N.J.: Transaction.

Giele, J. Z. 1982. *Women in the middle years: Current knowledge and directions for research and policy.* New York: Wiley.

Glick, P. C. 1988. Demographic pictures of black families. In H. P. McAdoo, ed., *Black families,* 2d ed., pp. 111–132. Newbury Park, Calif.: Sage.

Greene, B. 1990. Sturdy bridges: The role of African-American mothers in the socialization of African-American children. *Women and Therapy,* 10:205–225.

Grotevant, H. D., and C. R. Cooper. 1985. Patterns of interaction in family relationships and the development of identity exploration in adolescence. *Child Development* 56 (2):415–428.

Gurak, D. T. 1988. New York Hispanics: A demographic overview. In E. Acosta-Belen and B. R. Sjostrom, eds., *The Hispanic experience in the United States: Contemporary issues and perspectives,* pp. 57–78. New York: Praeger.

Harter, S. 1987. The perceived competence scale for adolescents. Unpublished manuscript, University of Denver.

Hendricks, G. 1974. *The Dominican diaspora.* New York: Teachers College Press.

Hill, J. P., and M. E. Lynch. 1983. The intensification of gender-related role expectation during early adolescence. In J. Brooks-Gunn and A. C. Petersen, eds., *Girls at puberty: Biological and psychosocial perspectives,* pp. 201–228.

Hirsch, B. J., and B. D. Rapkin. 1987. The transition to junior high school: A longitudinal study of self-esteem, psychological symptomology, school life, and social support. *Child Development* 58:1235–1243.

Ianni, F. 1989. *The search for structure: A report on American youth today.* New York: Free Press.

Jarrett, R. 1990. *A comparative examination of socialization patterns among low income African Americans, Chicanos, Puerto Ricans, and whites: A review of the ethnographic literature.* Report to the Social Science Research Council.

Johnson, B. M., S. Shulman, and W. A. Collins. 1991. Systemic patterns of parenting as reported by adolescents: Developmental differences and implications for psychosocial outcomes. *Journal of Adolescent Research* 6 (2):235–252.

Kanner, A. D., J. C. Coyne, C. Schaefer, and R. S. Lazarus. 1981. Comparison of two modes of stress measurement: Daily hassles, uplifts, and major life events to health status. *Journal of Behavioral Medicine* 4:1–39.

Krantz, D. H., and M. Shinn. 1992. Important interaction effects are hard to detect. Unpublished article.

Maccoby, E. E. 1980. *Social development: Psychological growth and the parent-child relationship.* New York: Harcourt Brace Jovanovich.

Maccoby, E. E., and J. A. Martin. 1983. Socialization in the context of the family:

Parent-child interaction. In P. H. Mussen, ed., *Handbook of child psychology.* Vol. 4, *Socialization, personality, and social development,* ser. ed. E. M. Hetherington. New York: Wiley.

McAdoo, H. P. 1978. Minority families. In J. H. Stevens and M. Matthews, eds., *Mother/Child, Father/Child Relationships.* Washington, D.C.: National Association for the Education of Young Children.

McClelland, G. H., and C. M. Judd. 1993. Statistical difficulties of detecting interactions and moderator effects. *Psychological Bulletin* 114:376–389.

McLoyd, V. C. 1990. The impact of economic hardship on black families and children: Psychological distress, parenting, and socioemotional development. *Child Development* 61:311–346.

Miller, J. B. 1976. *Toward a new psychology of women.* Boston: Beacon.

Pessar, P. R. 1990. International migration: The role of households and social networks. In R. W. Palmer, ed., *In search of a better life: Perspectives on migration from the Caribbean.* New York: Praeger.

———. 1991. *Between two islands: Dominican international migration.* Berkeley: University of California Press.

Petersen, A. C., and L. Crockett. 1985. Pubertal timing and grade effects on adjustment. *Journal of Youth and Adolescence* 14:191–206.

Rauh, V. A., G. A. Wasserman, and S. A. Brunelli. 1990. Determinants of maternal child-rearing attitudes. *Journal of the American Academy of Child and Adolescent Psychiatry* 29 (3):375–381.

Reis, J. 1989. A comparison of young, teenage, older teenage, and adult mothers on determinants of parenting. *Journal of Psychology* 123 (2):141–151.

Rickel, A. N., and L. L. Biasatti. 1982. Modification of the Block child rearing practices report. *Journal of Clinical Psychology* 38 (1):129–134.

Rogler, L. H., and R. S. Cooney. 1986. *Puerto Rican families in New York City: Intergenerational processes.* Maplewood, N.J.: Waterfront.

Rollins, B. C., and D. L. Thomas. 1979. Parental support, power, and control techniques in the socialization of children. In W. R. Burr, R. Hill, F. I. Nye, and I. L. Reiss, eds., *Contemporary theories about the family* 1:317–364. New York: Free Press.

Rowlison, R., and R. D. Felner. 1988. Major life events, hassles, and adaptation in adolescence: Confounding in the conceptualization and measurement of life stress and adjustment revisited. *Journal of Personality and Social Psychology* 55: 432–444.

Sabogal, F., G. Marin, R. Otero-Sabogal, B. V. Marin, and E. J. Perez-Stable. 1987. Hispanic familism and acculturation: What changes and what doesn't? *Hispanic Journal of Behavioral Sciences* 9 (4):397–412.

Seidman, E. 1991. Growing up the hard way: Pathways of urban adolescents. *American Journal of Community Psychology* 19:173–205.

Seidman, E., L. Allen, J. L. Aber, C. Mitchell, and J. Feinman. 1994. The impact of school transitions in early adolescence on the self-system and social context of poor urban youth, *Child Development* 65 pp. 507–522.

Seidman, E., L. Allen, J. Feinman, C. Mitchell, J. L. Aber, K. Comtois, J. Golz, R. Miller, B. Ortiz-Torres, and G. Roper. 1995. Development and validation of adolescent perceived microsystem scales: Social support, daily hassles and involvement. *American Journal of Community Psychology.*

Silverberg, S. B., and L. Steinberg. 1990. Psychological well-being of parents with early adolescent children. *Developmental Psychology* 26 (4):658–666.

Simmons, R. G., A. Black, and Y. Zhou. 1991. African-American versus white children and the transition to junior high school. *American Journal of Education* 99:481–520.

Simmons, R. G., and D. A. Blyth. 1987. *Moving into adolescence: The impact of pubertal change and school context.* New York: Aldine de Gruyter.

Simmons, R. G., R. Burgeson, S. L. Carlton-Ford, and D. A. Blyth. 1987. The impact of cumulative change in early adolescence. *Child Development* 58: 1220–1234.

Simmons, R. G., F. Rosenberg, and M. Rosenberg. 1973. Disturbance in the self-image at adolescence. *American Sociological Review* 38:553–568.

Simons, R. L., L. B. Whitbeck, R. D. Conger, and W. Chyi-In. 1991. Intergenerational transmission of harsh parenting. *Developmental Psychology* 27 (1):159–171.

Sjostrom, B. R. 1988. Culture contact and value orientations: The Puerto Rican experience. In E. Acosta-Belen and B. R. Sjostrom, eds., *The Hispanic experience in the United States: Contemporary issues and perspectives,* pp. 73–186. New York: Praeger.

Soto, E., and P. Shaver. 1982. Sex-role traditionalism, assertiveness, and symptoms of Puerto Rican women living in the United States. *Hispanic Journal of Behavioral Sciences* 4 (1):1–19.

Spencer, M. B. 1990. Development of minority children: An introduction. *Child Development* 61:267–269.

Stack, C. B. 1974. *All our kin: Strategies for survival in a black community.* New York: Harper and Row.

Steinberg, L., N. S. Mounts, S. D. Lamborn, and S. M. Dornbusch. 1991. Authoritative parenting and adolescent adjustment across varied ecological niches. *Journal of Research on Adolescence* 1:19–36.

Stevens, J. H. 1988. Social support, locus of control, and parenting in three low-income groups of mothers: Black teenagers, black adults, and white adults. *Child Development* 59 (3):635–642.

Swick, K. J. 1988. Parental efficacy and involvement: Influences on children. *Childhood Education* 64:37–42.

Vazquez-Nuttall, E., and I. Romero-Garcia. 1989. From home to school: Puerto Rican girls learn to be students in the United States. In C. T. Garcia Coll and M. de Lourdes Mattei, eds., *The psychosocial development of Puerto Rican women,* pp. 60–83. New York: Praeger.

Wasserman, G. A., V. A. Rauh, S. A. Brunelli, and M. Garcia-Castro. 1990. Psychosocial attributes and life experiences of disadvantaged minority mothers: Age and ethnic variations. *Child Development* 61 (2):566–580.

Whitbeck, L. B. 1987. Modeling efficacy: The effect of perceived parental efficacy on the self efficacy of early adolescents. *Journal of Youth and Adolescence* 7 (2): 165–177.

The Prediction of Parental Psychological Functioning: Influences of African American Adolescent Perceptions and Experiences of Context

Margaret Beale Spencer, Dena Phillips Swanson,

and Alvin Glymph

Like the study of normative development for African American youths generally (see Spencer 1995), minority adult developmental processes have been inadequately addressed from a life-course or adult perspective. Jones's edited volume (1989) is one of very few texts that focuses on aging among African Americans. Midlife parenting for African Americans has generally been ignored except for a focus on psychopathology of family relations and inadequacy of parenting efforts. One of many areas ripe for exploration is the mutual influence of African American parents and their adolescent children on each other's development within their very specific cultural context.

Independent of ethnicity, social class, and race, middle adulthood is marked by particular psychosocial tasks (Erikson 1963; Tamir and Antonucci 1981), the most important of which is the childrearing role. Erikson suggests that midlife parenting—stage seven of his epigenetic model—requires a resolution of the generativity versus stagnation crisis. According to Erikson, this developmental task involves people's ability to turn their efforts outward; the goal is to assist younger individuals along and to take an interest in more global social concerns (Vander Zander 1985).

For visible minorities, these developmental tasks are particularly complex and difficult. Many midlife parenting adults have problems and needs that are specific to low-resource families. These tasks are further confounded for parents in the throes of rearing adolescents of color who themselves are plagued with unique ethnicity-linked experiences—generally unaddressed in the adolescent literature—associated with the content of the normative adolescent developmental crisis. Even without the adjustments associated with ethnicity, economic problems in themselves have a significant impact on the ability to parent effectively during middle adulthood. And minority parents share with all parents the specific psychohistorical problems associated with rearing adolescents in a rapidly changing society.

The context for individual development, along with parental provisions of nurturance and support, is in the community. Awareness that development does not occur within a vacuum but in a context of environmental influence has a long history (e.g., Barker and Wright 1971; Bronfenbrenner 1979; Garbarino 1982). The neighborhood as an important setting for exploring developmental processes and family functioning, however, has only recently come under consideration for serious policy-relevant study. There has also been a long-standing recognition of the disadvantaged status of African Americans and an equally large assortment of explanations for the group's disproportionate social location in the lower strata of the social system. But, again, the effects of living in a race-divided society on individual group member's developmental processes and subsequent opportunities have become a focus of interest among researchers only more recently.

As noted by Tienda (1991), the rise in urban underserviced neighborhoods, chronically impoverished communities, families under stress, and the common phenomenon of African American male joblessness continue to characterize the fragile infrastructure of many American urban centers. Chestang (1972) was prescient in his basic premise that character formation for African American youth takes place in a hostile environment. He suggested that American culture and social policies are fraught with discrepancies in what is wanted and expected from minority group members; while independence, social responsibility, and competence are espoused as desirable for the long run, the built-in obstacles to achieving those outcomes are many. Furthermore, Kochman (1992) suggests that African American communities are characterized by "environmental racism"—adverse environmental conditions that pose barriers to social and emotional as well as health status. He suggests that because African American neighborhoods are beset with crowding problems, hazardous waste facilities, and other high-risk environmental conditions, these surroundings contribute to an increased level of stress and inadequate coping, a diminished sense of community and psychological mutuality, and resulting behavior problems.

Too frequently, however, behavior problems have represented the starting place for research (for example, the traditional "violence initiatives") as opposed to strategies that explore more interactive and transactional influences on untoward outcomes *and* resiliency. It is not enough to look at behavior. It is also essential to examine the manner in which people make meaning of their experiences. This process is influenced by normative developmental tasks that are required of everyone (Havighurst 1953), shared cultural and global-level understandings and expectations such as sex-role orientation, and, for African Americans, specific understandings, prospects, and constraints associated with visibility and institutionalized class/caste-based biases.

One important setting in which "meaning making" takes place is the home; meanings are worked out as parents and children interact with each other. This interaction is at the heart of the emergence of resiliency among African American youth in a high-risk environment. Although seldom acknowledged, resiliency characterizes the urban experience for many lower-income and minority parents and youth. Our data suggest that African American youth resiliency is associated with particular parental psychosocial characteristics (Spencer 1983). Socialization efforts that include cultural identity features (e.g., ability to transmit cultural information concerning a group's history, strengths, and societal situation) are associated with parents who rear children who have Afrocentric or group-appreciating cultural values. Youth who demonstrate group-accepting cultural values have been associated with greater resiliency and intellectual competence (Spencer 1983, 1990).

Needed, then, is a contextualized understanding of the mutual development of African American adolescents and parents whose lives unfold in communities typified by the experience of high risk. Although the reciprocal influence of adolescents on their midlife parents has not been explored for African Americans, there is a body of literature that examines such influences in nonminority families. In the following section of this paper, that literature will be reviewed, followed by a review of the literature on the perceptions and experiences of African American youths. This literature creates an initial framework for exploring the influences of those adolescent perceptions and experiences on midlife parenting efforts among African American adults. Finally, data will be presented from the first phase of a longitudinal study of 549 African American early adolescents and their parents.

REVIEW OF LITERATURE
Adolescent Effects on Parental Well-Being: Literature
on Nonminority Families

Although the available work does not explore the issues of adolescent effects on parental well-being for minorities, there is a literature that examines issues linked to gender and social class concerns. In fact,

Silverberg offers a full review of her work in this volume; however, a few studies are excerpted here because they raise important issues of special salience to our work. One study by Silverberg and Steinberg (1990) focused on whether parents' reports of life reappraisal and a low sense of well-being are related to pubertal, social, and cognitive signs of their child's transition into adolescence. For their study of 129 adolescent-parent pairs, they hypothesized that stronger unfavorable relations between the signs of adolescent status and parental well-being would exist both for parents with relatively strong orientation toward the parenting role and for parents with a relatively weak orientation toward their role as paid worker. Findings indicated an association between signs of adolescent development in children and parental reports of self or life concerns that varied as a function of parents' investment in paid work. Higher levels of child dating behavior and mixed-sex group activities were associated with more intense midlife concerns, lower life satisfaction, or more frequent psychological symptoms for parents who were invested, even if not strongly, in a paid work role. However, strong work-role orientation did not protect mothers of daughters as it did other parents. Among parents who were strongly invested in their paid-work role, physical and social indicators of children's transition into adolescence appeared to be either unrelated or favorably related to well-being.

Another related set of findings from the same data (Koski and Steinberg 1990) also suggested the linkage between parenting satisfaction and child's gender. The researchers explored a hypothesized relationship between maternal characteristics of psychological well-being and child's gender. They additionally hypothesized that the relationship between mother's midlife crisis score and parental satisfaction would be more closely associated if the child was a female, but that hypothesis was not supported.

Steinberg and Silverberg (1987) theorized that the biological, cognitive, and social changes of early adolescence somehow destabilize the family system and have an indirect negative impact on the marital dyad. The data suggested that factors in the parent-child relationship may play important roles in their influence on marital satisfaction within same-sex, but not within opposite-sex, parent-child dyads.

From the same dataset, Silverberg and Steinberg (1987) explored whether parents' reports of midlife identity concerns, life satisfaction, self-esteem, and psychological symptoms are related to the level of parent-adolescent conflict in the family and to their child's level of emotional autonomy. Among other findings, results suggested that fathers' sense of self and well-being was unrelated to the level of conflict they experienced with sons or daughters but was related to the emotional autonomy of sons.

The analysis by Steinberg (1987) examined whether and in what ways puberty may distance adolescents from their parents. The analysis was also designed to examine whether the distancing effects of puberty are related to pubertal timing, pubertal status, or chronological age. Steinberg hypothesized that pubertal maturation, independent of chronological age, is associated with diminished parent-child closeness, increased parent-child conflict, and increased adolescent autonomy. Pubertal status scores were based on visible signs of secondary sex characteristics. Adolescents' pubertal status scores were also used to assign the child to pubertal timing groups. Findings varied by gender; for example, with sons, pubertal status was not related to either mothers' or fathers' reports of closeness. Pubertal timing did not relate to fathers' reports of closeness, but mothers reported less cohesion with late-maturing youth. Neither pubertal status nor pubertal timing was related to mothers' reports of conflict with sons, and the relationship for fathers' reports did not reach significance. However, fathers tended to report more conflict with late-maturing sons. Neither mothers' nor fathers' reports of autonomy in the midpubertal boys described their homes as less authoritarian. Fathers of physically mature sons described the households as more permissive.

With respect to daughters, mothers and fathers reported less cohesion with physically mature daughters. Fathers' reports of calm communication did not vary with daughters' pubertal status; however, mothers' reports were negatively related to pubertal status. Fathers' reports of conflict with daughters were unrelated to pubertal status or timing. Mothers' reports of intensity of conflict with daughters did not reach significance. Both mothers' and fathers' reports concerning autonomy in the parent-child relationship were related to daughters' pubertal timing or status. Parents of physically mature girls reported less authoritarianism than other parents. The set of findings suggest specific mother-daughter and father-son tensions.

Together, these findings suggest patterned sex differences in the relationship between specific adolescent-linked developments and the psychological well-being of fathers and mothers with either sons or daughters. They indicate, for example, paternal "impatience" with a late-maturing son. In general they are important in that they delineate other effects on the quality of parent-child relationships, such as parental involvement, quality of paid work experience, and level of parental life satisfaction. The finding that parent-child relationships play a causal role in marital satisfaction within same-sex but not within opposite-sex parent-child dyads is compelling. Sex differences in marital satisfaction during middle adulthood for women were linked to women's concern about midlife identity issues. The finding of a lack of a relationship between the impact of child autonomy and patterned sense of self and well-being has ramifications for child development and family relations. Similarly, the finding that mother's life satisfaction was decreased when experiencing more intense conflict with sons has significant consequences for the importance of family intactness for cross-gender childrearing efforts.

The father-son crisis was explored by Levi, Stierlin, and Savard (1972) in a five-year longitudinal study of troubled adolescents and their families. Over a period of three and one-half years, adolescents were referred to the authors by the school system for psychotherapy, usually because of underachievement. The parents of the eleven target adolescents (fifteen to sixteen years old) were interviewed in outpatient conjoint family therapy. An additional fifteen families were seen in therapy as comparisons.

Levi, Stierlin, and Savard concluded that the middle-aged father goes through a normative crisis in which he will likely doubt the value of his work efforts and the meaning of his marriage. They hypothesized that he must grieve long-time aspirations, now clearly beyond his reach, and reassess the meaning of success. In the authors' observations of the families of troubled adolescents, the fathers were unable either to grieve successfully or to find a satisfying new course of action. If the father cannot do this, he may envy and disparage his son or over-identify with him in trying to relive through him what he feels he has missed. Levi and colleagues suggest that if the father has established a clear definition of his own values, he will likely disagree with his son's different modes and values and engage in open conflict (the "loving fight"). On a displaced level, it may represent the final stage in the Oedipal competition between father and son. On an ego level, the "fight" provides grounds for self-definition and differentiation. The father who has a real sense of his own worth and integrity can afford to lose the battle, at least partially; he can allow the son to differ from him without the difference being a threat to his sense of integrity.

In the group of adolescents studied, however, Levi, Stierlin, and

Savard saw abrupt bitter separations, failures of differentiation between father and son, and long-standing alienation between them. All fathers in these eleven families emerged as frustrated, unhappy men. They were unable or unwilling to engage their sons in a "loving fight" from which differentiation and mutual respect could grow. The authors could not generalize about why in some families one sibling was chosen as bearer of special pathology and in some more than one child was affected. They noted that where there were two or more male children, in parallel with envy of one son, the fathers tended to feel close to a son who was near in age to the index child and to idealize that other son. In relation to their daughters, depressed fathers did not seem to become resigned but instead became intrusive "rescuers."

Sometimes, instead of a conflict over content, over how to live best, the "annihilating fight" ensued, involving verbal assault. In such a fight the victim cannot survive and still retain his self-respect. This was usually followed by a resignation and withdrawal on the part of the father. As interpreted by Levi, Stierlin, and Savard, the masked depression of resigning fathers typically emerged as envy.

The set of findings was consistent with traditional theorizing about ego identity processes during middle adulthood. If current identity processes are unable to be resolved, difficulties in interaction with others result (see Erikson 1963). Thus, although the findings and clinical observations are not unexpected, the empirical data support the clinical assumption that interpersonal problems are intimately linked to self-differentiating processes independent of where an individual is developmentally.

It would appear from LaSorsa and Fodor (1990) that mothers and adolescent daughters do not fare much better. They examined the developmental tasks and dyadic issues of adolescent daughters and their midlife mothers from a psychodynamic perspective. Drawing on their review of psychoanalytic and life-span literature, they suggest that both mother and daughter are experiencing a life-cycle crisis of separation and self-definition. The database comes from their own clinical experience and four focused interviews with majority middle-class, mother-daughter pairs. LaSorsa and Fodor examined the adolescent daughter's development according to classical psychoanalytic theory, Erikson's stages of identity, and a more recent perspective, the "self in relation" model, which emphasizes attachment and connection rather than separation. The mother's separation process and midlife search for self are also examined in relation to the daughter's development. The authors posit that the development of the adolescent daughter can negatively affect mother's self-esteem and cause conflict. The dimensions of competition and rebellion were also proposed as being tied into separation and self-definition for both members of the dyad. The authors proposed developing a dyadic interactional model with a cognitive-developmental or life-cycle perspective. Although specified for non-minorities, hypotheses concerning parental satisfaction and child gender are not novel (see Koski and Steinberg 1990); in fact, gender-specific patterns of findings are clearly evident in the literature (e.g., Steinberg 1987; Silverberg and Steinberg 1987).

In general, data from these studies represent the experiences of non-minority parents and their adolescent youths and are suggestive. They indicate different cross-gender effects on parents. Variables such as parental depression and life satisfaction appear to be important constructs independent of family economy, given that both high-resource and low-resource parents encounter multiple stresses in the rearing of their youth. Less well understood for low-resource parents is the potential exacerbating impact of the actual neighborhood characteristics as perceived by their adolescents and as characterized by the census. An additional question to be raised is the added effect of low-resource neighborhoods, underserviced communities, and chronically hostile environments on normal family tensions and the normative life-course experiences of children and their midlife parents.

African American Youths' Perceptions and Experiences of Psychological Well-Being

While there is a dearth of research on the perceptions and experiences of African American youth, studies by Chestang (1972), Fordham and Ogbu (1986), Spencer (1990, 1995), and Spencer and Dornbusch (1990) provide interesting perspectives. African American adolescents are exposed to the same level of violence, aggression, and gratuitous sex in the media as all American youth. They are unique in that they (a) are objects of well-publicized stereotypes for expectations of violence, psychopathology, and aggression, (b) generally attend resource-weak schools, (c) are often taught by teachers who actually do not prefer teaching in minority communities, (d) have few role models available for guidance, mentoring relationships, and support, (e) as suggested by Chestang (1972), share with their parents the experience of societal inconsistency (i.e., personal injustices experienced from which there is no legal protection), (f) have a high probability of developing under conditions of intergenerationally experienced chronic impoverishment, and (g) have little evidence that academic motivation and performance, especially for males, are linked to productive life-course experiences in the work force (and thus, according to Fordham and Ogbu [1986], too often may equate an academic orientation with "acting white"). These unique, context-linked experiences have implications for the type and quality of parenting required for the manifestation of resilience during adolescence. Unfortunately, very little is known about parent-youth relationships for African Americans specifically (Spencer 1990, 1995), although the problem of inadequate research scholarship is evident for minority parents and youths generally (see Spencer and Dornbusch 1990). The extant literature that explores the psychological well-being of parents with adolescents in general is sparse, although it raises interesting questions concerning the effect of the period of adolescence and of particular adolescent characteristics on parental well-being. Except for issues of chronic poverty, early childbearing, and female headship, other parental characteristics are seldom included when considering parental influences on child outcomes or vice versa. Although assumptions about youths' ego processes have been consistently focused on in the psychological literature, except for a priori assumptions of psychopathology and deviancy (see Kardiner and Ovesey 1951), more differentiating analysis of minority parent psychological characteristics is usually found in the literature, especially that on adult development. But a book by Jones (1989) offers hope. Specifically, although cultural identity processes have been consistently exploited for children, cultural identity processes among adults are not addressed directly in the literature. However, it is hypothesized that adults would exhibit attitudes more reflective of their cumulative experiences and the nature of their contexts.

The racial identity model proposed by Parham and Helms (1985) was originally conceptualized to facilitate an understanding of a racial identity metamorphosis (i.e., conversion from Negro to black) within the context of the social movement of the late 1960s and early 1970s (Cross 1971). Although in his work Cross did not address the formation of racial identity from childhood through adulthood, the impact of social and personal contextual experiences throughout the life course appear both inherent and relevant. In response to Cross's theorizing, the relationship between racial (cultural) identity and self-esteem among African American college students attending predominantly white institutions was assessed by Parham and Helms (1985). With global self-esteem as the dependent variable, they found that low self-esteem was associated with preencounter (Eurocentric) and immersion ("reactive" Afrocentricity) attitudes. For this college-age adult population, Parham and Helms suggest that one explanation for students' low self-esteem during the immersion (which theoretically assesses reactive attitudes toward nonblacks) has a specific source: according to this perspective, African Americans' reactive cultural beliefs about non-blacks are due to attempts to overcompensate for previous negative feelings toward their race.

However, the global self-esteem score is less conducive to understanding positive self-appraisals in a culturally different environment. Another explanation suggests the lack of cultural continuity and connectedness African American adults experience in many predominately white communities or the experiences of college students on majority white compuses. Their experiences highlight the significance of contextual and environmental influences on identity processes.

Research findings on children's and adolescents' identity processes suggest an important enculturating role for parents, which also suggests the ambivalence of African American parents concerning issues of race, ethnicity, and color (see Spencer 1983, 1990). In fact, even in the face of continued social biases concerning race, African American parental teaching strategies stress the equality of all people versus a program of socialization, which places specific value on one's own group above others. In addition, 91 percent of parents interviewed indicated that their childrearing strategies would not change if their child were white (Spencer 1983). The findings were replicated in a follow-up study of African American parents that indicated a lack of difference in expected number of years of completed schooling irrespective of socioeconomic status. The findings suggest that low-resource families value the importance of schooling, although they may have less information about how to transform high-achieving values into reality (Spencer 1990). This counterintuitive finding that parental educational values for children are independent of social class is seldom addressed. The study also reported more conventional findings, such as the presence of economic resources and educational attainment of family members across generations is more often associated with reports of children's manifest competence and less prevalence of behavioral problems and symptoms (Spencer 1990, 118).

The research on minority youth and families tends to focus on availability and quality of resources and community characteristics and problems as important influences both on the psychological well-being of individuals and on family dynamics. The demographic characteristics of the family, characteristics of neighborhoods, and youths' perceptions of contexts are seen as important areas of assessment.

In the following section of this paper, research is presented that explores the effects of three groups of variables on parental characteristics: background demographic and family measures, neighborhood (census tract) characteristics, and child-perceived context measures. The parental attributes predicted include parental psychological well-being (e.g., life satisfaction and depression) measures, cultural identity processes, and measures relevant to family economy (e.g., sources of support reported to be available and extent of low levels of family support).

THE STUDY

The research presented comes from a large longitudinal effort: Promotion of Academic Competence Project (Project PAC) (Spencer 1989). The larger project explores multiple interactive influences on the transition into and out of adolescence. We offer a set of analyses that tests specific components of the much broader theoretical framework that integrates a phenomenological perspective with ecological systems theory (Spencer 1995; Markstrom-Adams and Spencer 1993). The current data analysis examines parental well-being characteristics as predicted by family background, neighborhood characteristics, and measures of child-perceived context characteristics. For adolescents, perception of context becomes especially important as unavoidable cognitive maturation sharpens their awareness of context characteristics, especially those features having to do with physical threat and the potential of experiencing physical harm. Ongoing work and analyses suggest that males, not unexpectedly, experience the social context in very different ways that are associated with specific, negative, black male experiences. The exceptional experiences of African American males are linked to sex-role needs that are associated with societal expectations for male instrumentality (see Cunningham 1994) and for experienced hostility (see Chestang 1972; Glymph 1994). For this reason, analyses were run separately to understand the unique predictive relationships for sons and daughters with their parents (i.e., usually mothers).

Subjects

Data are presented from the first year of a longitudinal study of 394 adolescent males and 168 females who are students in sixth, seventh, or eighth grade at public middle schools in a large southeastern American city (Spencer 1989). The majority African American sample was randomly selected from four middle school populations. For the four schools, signed consent rates for participation by school ranged between 55 and 80 percent. For three of the four schools, 80 to 90 percent of the students received free or reduced lunch support. For the fourth school, approximately 70 percent of the students received free or reduced lunch. From the parental self-reported family income information, it was determined that 58 percent of the subjects' families met federal poverty guidelines (i.e., for a family size of four, the criterion for poverty was an annual family income of $13,950).

Procedures and Measures

As part of their participation in the larger longitudinal study that explores the development of competence and resilience of mainly African American boys, male and female subjects participated in one-on-one interviews and, in addition, were seen in small groups at their respective schools; they completed survey instruments during three sessions. In an in-home, one-on-one format, parents completed the adult version of the same rating instrument in addition to completing an extensive in-home interview.

All in-home parental interviewers were same-race examiners. The majority of the small-group testers were the same race as the participants. All testers were well-trained graduate, undergraduate, or older adult interviewers who were hired specifically as adolescent interviewers. The in-home interviewers were local mental health professionals who had earned at least one degree in mental health (including pastoral counseling) or were in fact practicing ministers. All parental interviewers were familiar and comfortable with working in African American, lower-income homes and communities. For the first year, the parental participation rate (i.e., those parents of participating families who, in fact, actually took part in an in-home interview) was approximately 80 percent. As indicated, the majority of parental respondents were women.

Background measures. Mother's education was assessed using highest level of completed education and was coded as the number of years of education (e.g., high school diploma was coded as twelve, college degree was coded as sixteen). Based on initial analyses, gender was treated as a moderator variable (see Baron and Kenney 1986). Specifically, as indicated elsewhere (Spencer et al. 1993), like ethnicity, gender has been routinely critiqued as an important factor in development. The role of gender was carefully described in physical and physiological terms by Wingard (1987); its idiosyncrasies (e.g., changes in achievement patterns for girls entering adolescence), empirically demonstrated by Hare and Castenell (1985); its relationship to parental characteristics, behaviors, and beliefs, delineated by Allen (1985), Clark (1983), and Spencer (1983, 1990); and its temporal patterns in many areas (e.g., years of schooling achieved, employment attained), comparatively illustrated with females by Gibbs (1988). Previous findings (Spencer and Glymph 1993) suggest that for this inner-city sample, gender may be a moderator given the unique patterned findings for African American adolescent and young adult males. Accordingly, the sample was split by gender for the testing of research questions as suggested by Baron and Kenney (1986).

Means and standard deviations for each measure (i.e., family background, neighborhood, parental characteristic, and adolescent's perception of context) by gender were obtained and are presented in table 9.1. Female headship was included as a dichotomous measure, with subjects reporting living with their mother without a male caregiver (female headship) coded as one and living with their mother and a male caregiver or living with their father without their mother coded as zero. Family income was assessed using parents' self-reported family income; these figures were then transformed into an index based on family size and federal poverty guidelines. The reported family income was divided by the criterion income for poverty for that family size. An index of 1.0 indicated that the family was living at poverty level; an index of less than 1.0 indicated that the family was living below poverty level. Major life events is a summary score based on subjects' responses to forty-seven questions concerning life events that may have occurred during the prior year (e.g., suspended from school, began to date, brother or sister died). The major life events score is the total number of events that subjects considered to have had a *negative* effect on them.

Neighborhood (census) measures. Neighborhood background measures were assessed using 1980 census tract data. A principal compo-

TABLE 9.1. Means and Standard Deviations for Background, Neighborhood, and Parental Measures

Measure	Males (N = 394)		Females (N = 168)	
	M	SD	M	SD
Background measures				
Mother's education	11.48	2.26	11.73	2.72
Female headship[a]	.47	.50	.40	.49
Family income[b]	1.05	.89	1.24	1.08
Major life events	3.78	3.40	4.32*	3.30
Neighborhood (census) measures				
Neighborhood poverty/female headship	2.35***	.81	2.12	1.01
Neighborhood high SES	−1.13	.57	−1.05	.64
Neighborhood ethnic diversity	−.42	.38	−.36	.43
Neighborhood crowding	.59	1.03	.45	1.10
Neighborhood joblessness	1.79	1.16	1.70	1.29
Parental measures				
Life dissatisfaction	110.52	8.70	110.11	10.76
Depression	13.37	5.30	12.75	3.93
Inadequacy of family support	8.68	2.75	8.39	2.77
Sources of support	35.71	10.30	35.37	9.80
Race identity: preencounter	17.96	4.03	28.32	5.70
Race identity: encounter	20.68	3.15	20.10	3.62
Race identity: immersion	28.97	4.86	28.22	5.70
Race identity: internalization	20.63	3.30	20.99	2.93
Child-perceived context measures				
Violent context	.05	1.46	−.10	1.54
Family conflict	−.02	1.39	.05	1.55
Weapons context	.13***	1.27	−.29	1.45
Fear of people (school/neighborhood)	−.01	1.23	.02	1.19
Police bias	.09**	1.21	−.19	1.19

[a]Female headship (1 = yes, 0 = no).
[b]Family income adjusted for size of family and poverty level.
*p < 10. **p < .05. ***p < .01.

nents analysis of thirty-five census tract variables revealed five factors: (1) poverty, female headship, race (African American), (2) high socioeconomic status (SES), (3) ethnic diversity, (4) crowding and age structure, and (5) joblessness. Factors were transformed to indices that represented standard deviation units away from the average of a nationally representative sample of neighborhoods.

Parental measures. The inadequacy of family support is a summed score (maximum score of twenty, with a higher score indicating less support) of the number of areas of support that the parent believed they lacked (e.g., emotional, household, transportation, or financial). Scores on a life satisfaction measure were reversed for arriving at a life dissatisfaction measure. It represents a summed score based on thirty-eight items (maximum score of 190, a higher score indicating more dissatisfaction) that measures dissatifaction with life and as indicated by such factors as adequacy of schools, recreational facilities, quality of stores, family, and friends (Bowman and Viveros-Long 1981; Conte and Salamon 1982). Depression was measured with the Beck Depression Inventory (BDI) (Beck 1987). The BDI is a 21–item, self-administered questionnaire designed to measure the severity of depression in adults. Each item represents a symptom or attitude description that the subject rated on a scale from zero to three based on how they had been feeling during the past week. Higher total scores indicate a more severe depressed mood.

Child-perceived context measures were developed from items selected from the year 1 survey instruments that dealt with the child's perceptions of family, school and neighborhood (e.g., Are you afraid of the people in your neighborhood?). A principal components analysis of sixty items revealed five context factors: violent context (Cronbach's alpha = .69); family conflict (alpha = .70); weapons context (alpha = .68); fear (alpha = .65); and police bias (alpha = .65). Summary scores for each factor were calculated by summing the z-scores of the raw scores of the items that loaded on the factors.

Demographic Characteristics

Marital status. Approximately one-third of the sample were married (32 percent); the others were either divorced (24 percent), separated (15 percent), widowed (6 percent), single (20 percent) or lived with a boyfriend or girlfriend (3 percent).

Parental age. Parental age ranged from sixty-plus years down to twenty-plus years; 10.6 percent were older than fifty, another 19.6 percent were between forty and fifty years. However, almost 70 percent were either in their twenties or thirties. As noted, the majority of parents were younger than generally expected. However, *chronological* youthfulness of parents may not necessarily shield parents from the midlife crisis often associated with adolescent parenting. Specifically, although mid-life parenting for "younger" parents may occur at a time different from other "on-time" birth cohort members, younger "off-time" parents would be expected to cope with the same traditional midlife parenting difficulties generally associated with the parenting of adolescents.

Parental education. Twenty-six percent of the sample had received some post–high school training. Of those remaining, 4 percent had received schooling up to between only kindergarten and sixth grade, 12 percent completed seventh through ninth grade, 58 percent had received between ten to twelve years of schooling for a total of 74 percent of the entire sample.

Parental occupation. Approximately one-half the occupations reported for mothers were in the lowest four ranking categories of the census listing of workers' occupational classification. Almost seventy percent of fathers' occupations fell within the lowest four categories.

Current total family income. Consistent with the sampling plan, the sample was unusually impoverished. A total of 61 percent of our adolescents came from families with incomes at or less than $15,000. Twenty percent reported incomes between $16,000 and $25,000. The remaining 19 percent reported incomes of $26,000 and above. By adjusting family income as a function of number of people in the household, we found that, overall, the sample was 2.5 standard deviations *above* the national mean for poverty.

Perceptions of economy. The parents also indicated the stability of their economic situation by responding to the following: (a) How stable is your family's current economic situation generally? and (b) Indicate the security of your current job. Relative to economic stability, 21.5 percent indicated either "no" or "little stability"; 57 percent indicated "economic stability" (which for some, of course, could mean stable "unemployment"); 21 percent indicated "very stable" or "extreme economic stability." When asked about current job security, 30 percent indicated either "no stability" or "little stability," another 57 percent indicated "job stability," and 24 percent labeled their current job as "very stable" or "extremely stable."

Sources of household income. Five options for sources of household income were investigated: parental job, child support, AFDC payments, child's job, and "other." Parents were asked to indicate primary, secondary, and tertiary sources of household income. Relative to a primary source of family income, 65 percent indicated parental job as the primary source of household income; another 5 percent, child support; 22 percent, AFDC payments; and 8 percent, "other."

Significant Differences for Family Economy Based on Demographic Characteristics

Marital status and economic characteristics. It was not unexpected that our sample's economic situation differed as a function of marital status. Significant differences in the sources of economic support available $(F[2, 333] = 7.38, p < .001)$ were apparent between married, unmarried, and those living with a boyfriend or girlfriend; as evident from figure 9.1, Neuman-Keuls tests indicated significant differences between families headed by two as opposed to one parent. Similarly, there are significant differences for the adequacy of support obtained from family $(F[2, 404] = 7.75, p < .001)$; a comparison of means suggests that dual-parenting adults obtain more support, and cohabitating adults most frequently report the least or most inadequate levels of support.

Questions having to do with the degree of stability of family economy and job security were consistent with the family income variable. For example, significant differences existed between groups representing the least stable family economy statuses and those groups reporting more family economic stability as a function of how much support was obtained from family: $F(4, 414) = 5.76, p < .001$. Means comparison tests suggest that those reporting a low stability of family economic status said they obtained significantly less in family support than others who indicated very stable or extremely stable family economic situations; similarly, those reporting a moderate amount of family stability said they received lower levels of family support than those indicating either extreme or very stable family economic situations. The pattern is the same for job security and amount of support obtained from

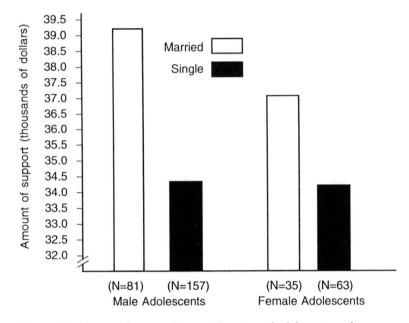

FIGURE 9.1. Amount of support by marital status and adolescent gender.

family members: $F(4, 412) = 6.93$, $p < .0001$. Those reporting the least job security had lower mean scores for support obtained from families. In fact, means comparison tests (Neuman-Keuls) show that those indicating very secure job situations reported significantly higher mean levels of support from family members than those with jobs of moderate, low, or no stability; in addition, those saying they had extremely stable job situations obtained significantly higher reports for amount of support from family than others who indicated either moderate or low levels of security for current employment.

Mother's educational level, family economics, life experiences, and depression. Families where mothers had more education (i.e., twelve-plus years) reported more sources of support ($t[323] = -3.30$, $p < .01$); as indicated by figure 9.2, however, the pattern differed somewhat by adolescent's gender. On the other hand, mothers with less education noted significantly less support from family ($t[395] = 2.76$, $p < .01$). Mothers with more education reported more adverse life experiences with the year ($t[391] = -2.21$, $p < .05$). However, life dissatisfaction did not differ with respect to mother's level of schooling. Finally, ma-

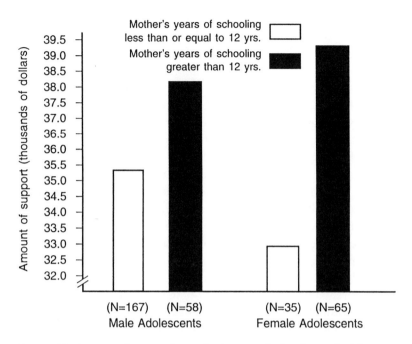

FIGURE 9.2. Amount of support by mother's years of schooling and adolescent gender.

ternal depression varied as a function of reported income. For the three income groups—low (<$15,000), moderate ($16,000–25,000), and high ($26,000+)—significant differences emerged ($F[2, 415] = 3.07$, $p < .05$). A means comparison test (Neuman-Keuls) indicated the counterintuitive finding that significantly higher depression scores were obtained for mothers with incomes greater than $15,000 when compared with mothers of moderate means. But the difference between the lowest income and the highest income groups was not significant.

Life experiences and dissatisfaction by mother's age. Older mothers (fifty years or older) reported the lowest level of significant life-course (negative) events having occurred in the last year when compared with both younger (forty-plus-year-olds) and the youngest mothers (i.e., twenties and thirties): $F(2, 404) = 5.07, p < .007$. On the other hand, the reverse relationship held by age for life dissatisfaction. Older mothers gave responses indicating a significantly lower level of life dissatisfaction ($F[2, 408] = 4.44, p < .02$); in fact, a means comparison test (Neuman-

Keuls) indicated that the level of life dissatisfaction was significantly lower both for older mothers and the most youthful mothers when compared with the "middle-years" mothers.

Overview of Data Analyses

As indicated in table 9.1, first, descriptive statistics were computed for family background measures, neighborhood (i.e., census-defined) measures, parental psychological functioning measures, and child-perceived context measures. Second, correlations among all measures were examined. Only correlations of explanatory importance will be reported, and due to space limitations, they will be incorporated directly into the discussion if warranted. Third, hierarchical least squares regression models were employed to analyze whether family background characteristics, neighborhood measures, and child-perceived context measures were related to any of the parental psychological functioning measures.

The parental psychological functioning variables were included because, consistent with other adult *human development* literature reviewed in this volume, it is not surprising that parental depression should be linked with the transition through adolescence for offspring. Some would argue from more of a pathology-assuming or deficit perspective concerning this population of low-income parents that depression should be a way of life. We include these variables because many parents and their children, although low in economic resources, show consistent resiliency and go on to lead productive lives in spite of race hostility (Chestang 1972) and economic inequities.

For each regression, background measures and grade were entered in the first step of the regression, which predicted the parental psychological functioning criterion measure. Grade was entered to adjust for possible cohort differences. At step two, neighborhood indicators, measured as census variables, were entered. In the third step, child-perceived context measures were entered. Significant findings at this step suggest that the child's perceptions of the neighborhood (e.g., violent context, family conflict, weapons context, fear [at school and home], and police bias) are related to parental psychological functioning (i.e., the inadequacy of support from family, number of sources of support, life dissatisfaction, cultural identity, and maternal depression) after controlling for effects of background measures. The specific sequence of the predictors represents specific conceptual concerns and the broader theoretical framework that formed the basis for the re-

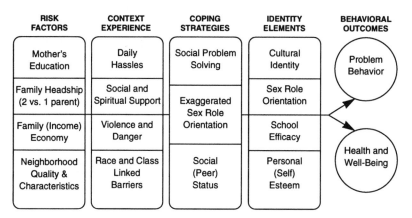

FIGURE 9.3. A phenomenological variant of ecological systems theory (Spencer 1995).

search design (Spencer 1995; see figure 9.3). Background measures for the family (e.g., mother's education and family structure, income, and major life events) represent very proximal, perpetually salient variables of importance. Similarly, the adolescent's age is unchanging in relevance. Accordingly, for each regression background measures were entered first. The family variables when considered together across families appear more enduring than census-level neighbrohood characteristics. It appeared important, then, to enter them second. The child-perceived context measures were entered last since it was assumed that the first two sets of measures (i.e., family background and neighborhood-level census measures) are linked to specific youth experiences (i.e., child-perceived context measures). The child's neighborhood experiences appear linked to actual family status and more macrolevel (census-level) conditions of neighborhood. The third regression equation, then, contains the three sets of measures for predicting psychological characteristics.

Before reporting the results of the regression analyses, we present descriptive statistics, particularly for the child-perceived context measures, for few studies adequately explore the mediating effect of *context* as linked to patterned findings for families generally and especially for those who have few resources. Thus, as indicated elsewhere (Spencer 1995; Spencer et al. 1993; Markstrom-Adams and Spencer 1993) and as illustrated in figure 9.4 in a mediational form, alternative mediating models afford a better interpretation of context both as experienced

357

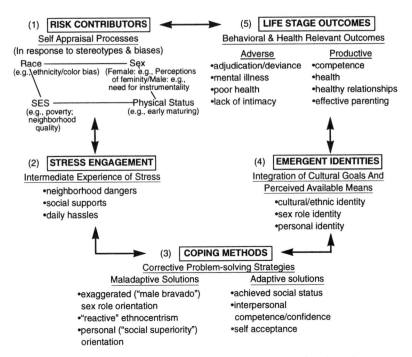

FIGURE 9.4. Mediational model: Phenomenological variant of ecological systems theory.

and as perceived by adolescents. Figure 9.4 illustrates the hypothesized connection between risk factors and the actual context experience. Specific context experiences and appraisals require particular coping strategies for survival, which invariably become patterned as identity elements over time. Finally, the stability of manifest identifications given ongoing adverse circumstances become predictive of behavioral outcomes. As suggested elsewhere (Spencer et al. 1993; Spencer 1995), the pattern of outcomes reciprocally exacerbates risk factors (which makes it easier for behavioral theorists *to blame the victim*).

Descriptive Statistics for the Child-Perceived Context Measures

As illustrated in figures 9.3 and 9.4 and described more fully elsewhere (Spencer et al. 1993; Spencer 1995), the project emanates from a theoretical framework that assumes a stable linkage between youths' psychosocial processes and context characteristics (see Figure 9.3). In fact, context struggles such as adolescents' risk experienced are linked

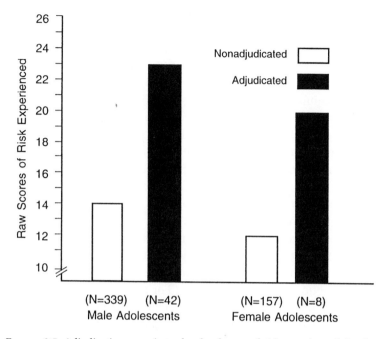

FIGURE 9.5. Adjudication experience by the degree of risk experienced (in the neighborhood).

to actual adjudication encounters as described in figure 9.5. Similarly, the ways in which adolescents (a) perceive and then relate to their context, (b) are enveloped by family background characteristics, and (c) are surrounded by more macrolevel neighborhood characteristics (as measured at the level of the census) are hypothesized to be important predictors of parental psychological functioning and social attributes (e.g., depression, life dissatisfaction, sources of support, the adequacy of family supports, and parental cultural identity). The cultural socialization methods used by African American parents have implications for youth competence and effective coping (Spencer 1983, 1990) and would appear linked to parental cultural identity processes.

Table 9.1 listed five child-perceived context measures: violent context, family conflict, weapons availability in context, fearfulness (i.e., fear of people in school and neighborhood), and police bias. Each measure represents a tranformed z-score; thus, the overall mean for each measure is zero. Findings listed in table 9.1. suggest significant sex differences for the child-perceived context factors of weapons context and police bias; in each case, male adolescents' rates are significantly higher.

The trend is in keeping with findings from the same dataset, which suggest that, for males, the level of violence and aggression experienced is linked to a particular sex role–related method of coping—machoism (Cunningham 1994; Spencer 1995; Swanson and Cunningham 1993; Spencer, Cunningham, and Swanson 1995). The issue is relevant for overall competence since machoism in black youths is related to Eurocentric cultural identity and underachievement (Swanson and Cunningham 1993). It would appear that the perception of the context as violent is linked to a specific mode of coping, that is, machoism, which is further correlated with the lack of academic competence and a culturally own-group–rejecting (i.e., Eurocentric identity). The other child-perceived context measures also have interesting links to family background variables.

Intercorrelation matrices that report Pearson product moment correlation coefficients for males (see table 9.2) and females (see table 9.3) suggest that the family background measures are correlated with the child's perception of context measures. For males, the violent context measure is significantly correlated with maternal education. Similarly, the fact of female headship is also significantly linked to the violent context measure. The data are consistent for females (see table 9.3). Girls' reports of a violent context are significantly correlated with low family income, few completed years of schooling for mothers, and female headship. Generally, irrespective of gender, the findings are consistent with the problem of low-resource neighborhoods. Single parenting and low levels of completed education are related to a life of poverty and few resources: that includes inadequate resources for obtaining a better quality of housing. Low-resource neighborhoods may be associated with the use of more violent methods of coping with an often impervious social system (Chestang 1972).

The family conflict measure of context suggests an interesting sex difference: table 9.2 indicates that family conflict as a youth-perceived context measure is unrelated to family demographics for males, although, for females, family conflict is significantly correlated with family income (see table 9.3); unexpectedly, more conflict is reported by females in families with higher family income. The difference might suggest that families with greater economic resources prefer a closer monitoring style that may result in greater inter- and intra-individual generational family conflict.

For both males and females, family background measures are not correlated with either context measure: fearfulness (being afraid of

TABLE 9.2. Intercorrelations among Neighborhood and Family Background Measures (males)

	Violent Context	Family Conflict	Weapons Context	Fear	Police Bias	Family Income	Mother's Education	Female Headship	Grade
Neighborhood									
Violent context	...	.13* (355)	.36*** (359)	.06 (358)	.10† (359)	−.11† (302)	−.18** (279)	.13** (363)	.01 (363)
Family conflict		...	.17** (352)	.21*** (351)	.08 (352)	−.06** (299)	−.05 (276)	−.07 (370)	−.08 (370)
Weapons context			...	.07 (358)	.27*** (359)	−.02 (298)	−.03 (275)	−.08 (359)	.05 (359)
Fear of people (school/ neighborhood)				...	.05 (358)	−.04 (298)	−.06 (274)	−.01 (358)	−.16** (358)
Police bias					...	−.01 (298)	.01 (275)	−.01 (359)	.01 (359)
Family background									
Family income (1989)						...	.17** (282)	−.32*** (310)	.28*** (310)
Mother's education							...	−.00 (286)	.13* (286)
Female headship								...	.01 (394)
Grade									...

†$p < .10$. *$p < .05$. **$p < .01$. ***$p < .001$.

TABLE 9.3. Intercorrelations among Neighborhood and Family Background Measures (females)

	Violent Context	Family Conflict	Weapons Context	Fear	Police Bias	Family Income	Mother's Education	Female Headship	Grade
Neighborhood									
Violent context	...	.11 (160)	.45**** (159)	.08 (159)	.24** (158)	−.23** (127)	−.23** (124)	.16* (160)	.17* (160)
Family conflict		...	.16* (159)	.17* (159)	−.03 (158)	.23** (129)	−.02 (126)	−.02 (165)	.04 (165)
Weapons context			...	−.03 (159)	.27*** (158)	−.01 (126)	−.04 (123)	.00 (159)	.01 (159)
Fear of people (school/ neighborhood)				...	.02 (158)	−.03 (126)	.03 (123)	.13† (159)	−.04 (159)
Police bias					...	.18* (125)	.17† (122)	.01 (158)	.12 (158)
Family background									
Family income (1989)						...	.40*** (125)	−.40*** (129)	.07 (129)
Mother's education							...	−.14 (126)	.09 (126)
Female headship								...	−.02 (168)
Grade									...

†*p* < .10. **p* < .05. ***p* < .01. ****p* < .001.

people in school or neighborhood) or the availability of weapons in the context (refer to tables 9.2 and 9.3). For males, no significant correlations exist between the violent context score and parental characteristics except for a slight trend for inadequate family support reports by parents and violent context. The data are more revealing for females: daughters report a more violent context. The reporting by sons of family conflict and parental dissatisfaction is negative and counterintuitive: more family conflict with less life dissatisfaction. However, daughters' reporting of family conflict is moderately correlated with parental depression. Independent of gender, there appears to be no direct correlation between the child-perceived context score, weapons in context, and parental characteristics. A report of fearfulness by boys is significantly correlated with Eurocentric parental cultural identity scores (i.e., the valuing of Euro-American culture and the denigration of African American culture). Since most students attend school and live in predominating African American communities, significant "other group" preference scores for parents may suggest a parallel reactive parental belief that identifies other African Americans as the major source of their children's fearfulness.

The pattern of relationships was different for girls. A report of fearfulness by daughters is significantly correlated with parental scores of proactive Afrocentric cultural identity that represent a celebration of African American history and culture concurrent with an appreciation of other cultural traditions; additionally, girls' reports of fearfulness at school and in the neighborhood are significantly correlated with parental reports of inadequate levels of family support. The reporting of police bias as a child-perceived context score by males has a parallel relationship with parental cultural identity scores: sons' reports of police bias were significantly correlated with a parental transitional identity score that indicated a transition from a Eurocentric score toward a more group (African American) acceptance score. In addition, for males, reports of police bias are significantly correlated with a pattern of reactive Afrocentric cultural identity for parents: reactive Afrocentric cultural identity scores suggest an affinity for one's own cultural niche and a denigration of other cultural groups. Although this identity pattern is related to lower achievement and greater psychopathology for adolescents (see Swanson and Cunningham 1993; Spencer et al. 1993), the implications of this parental cultural identity status for efficacy of parenting efforts generally and adult developmental tasks specifically are not known.

The patterned relationships between child-perceived police bias and parental characteristics vary somewhat for daughters. The reports of police bias by daughters, like the pattern for sons, are significantly correlated with parental scores for proactive cultural identity (i.e., own cultural group celebration along with other cultural group acceptance). In addition, daughters' reports of police bias as a context score are significantly correlated with greater parental depression. The findings suggest a different psychological response by parents to their adolescents' perceptions of context as a function of the child's gender. The finding of less parental depression associated with daughters' reports of police bias suggests that it may be "reassuring" to parents to know that police are showing "extra vigilance" in their communities. On the other hand, the finding for male adolescents suggested that police bias is associated with a particular parental identity response, reactive Afrocentricity. Thus reports by their sons of police bias may generate a specific parental psychosocial identity response that reactively responds to nonminority culture as less valued: that is, only the African American culture is deemed to be valued and acceptable.

This research focuses on specific parental characteristics such as sources of social support and the inadequacy of family support because low-resource parents often require more support in the rearing of competent youth, particularly given the high-risk nature of low-resource communities. Parental life dissatisfaction and depression have important implications for adult mental health and the psychological resources available for the rearing of psychologically and physically healthy offspring.

The research also considers parental cultural identity processes that appear important to childrearing practices (Spencer 1983, 1990) in that they influence the method and content of socialization strategies employed (Bowman and Howard 1985). The culturally relevant products of such strategies play a role in child competence and coping (Spencer, Dobbs, and Swanson 1988). Significant correlational findings suggest interesting gender-linked relationships between adolescents' perceptions of context and parental characteristics and psychological functioning.

Prediction of Maternal Psychological Functioning: Findings for Males

Prediction of maternal mental health: Depression and life satisfaction. For each regression, run separately by gender, background measures and grade were entered in the first step for predicting the criterion measure (i.e., parental psychological well-being). Grade was entered to adjust for possible cohort differences. In the second step, neighborhood (census) measures were entered to explain the additional economically relevant issues that consistently confront parents. Finally, at step three, the child's perception of context measures is entered after the first two groups are controlled for, because, although important, this group is viewed as linked to the first two sets (i.e., family background and neighborhood as defined by census measures).

In predicting maternal depression, hierarchical regression models were used to analyze the effects of background, census-defined neighborhood factors, and child-perceived context measures for assessing parental psychological functioning. As suggested by table 9.4, a significant amount of the variance (10 percent) in maternal depression is accounted for by the neighborhood measures at step two, but family background measures are not significant predictors at step one. Specifically, for an unusually impoverished African American sample, rearing male children in a high-SES and more ethnically diverse neighborhood is a significant predictor of maternal depression. At step three, overall, there were no significant changes when the child-perceived context measures were entered; the findings suggest that what predicts parental psychological distress (i.e., depression) concerning male adolescents is being poor in high-SES communities that also have ethnic diversity. Data reported in table 9.1 listed significant gender differences in the neighborhood measure—poverty/female headship: males more often lived in impoverished neighborhoods. The regression findings suggest that parenting efforts in low-resource families residing in more diverse and economically enriched neighborhoods might be psychologically more challenging for parents than generally assumed (i.e., perhaps being unable to keep up with their children's desires, given the influences of peer pressure and exposure to more affluent neighbors).

As indicated from table 9.5, at step one, background measures accounted for only 2 percent of the variance in mother's life dissatisfaction. Low reporting of negative major life events is the lone and counterintuitive significant predictor at step one for parental life dissatisfaction: fewer life-course events with more life dissatisfaction. At step two, the F change increased significantly to 4 percent: having fewer high-SES neighbors, less ethnic diversity, and less crowding were the significant contributors. At step three, when the neighborhood measures were added, the child-perceived context measure, family conflict,

TABLE 9.4. Regressions of Parental Depression on Background, Neighborhood, and Child-Perceived Context Measures (males)

Step/Predictor Variables	Adjusted R^2	F Change	Beta
1. Background measures	.01	1.43	
Grade			−.03
Mother's education			−.10
Female headship			.04
Family income			−.07
Major life events			−.05
2. Neighborhood (census) measures	.10***	6.31***	
Grade			−.05
Mother's education			−.07
Female headship			.02
Family income			−.10
Major life events			.02
Neighborhood poverty/female headship			.04
Neighborhood high SES			.25**
Neighborhood ethnic diversity			.30**
Neighborhood crowding			.08
Neighborhood joblessness			.12
3. Child-perceived context measures	.10***	1.15	
Grade			.03
Mother's education			−.08
Female headship			.04
Family income			−.10
Major life events			.04
Neighborhood poverty/female headship			.04
Neighborhood high SES			.24**
Neighborhood ethnic diversity			.31**
Neighborhood crowding			.09
Neighborhood joblessness			.12
Violent context			−.08
Family conflict			.02
Weapons context			.05
Fear of people			.09
Turf wars			−.08

*$p < .10$. **$p < .05$. ***$p < .01$.

TABLE 9.5. Regressions of Parental Life Dissatisfaction
on Background, Neighborhood, and Child-Perceived
Context Measures (males)

Step/Predictor Variables	Adjusted R^2	F Change	Beta
1. Background measures	.02+	1.88+	
Grade			.05
Mother's education			−.04
Female headship			.01
Family income			−.12+
Major life events			−.12*
2. Neighborhood (census) measures	.04*	2.01*	
Grade			.04
Mother's education			−.04
Female headship			.04
Family income			−.13+
Major life events			−.10
Neighborhood poverty/female headship			−.14
Neighborhood high SES			−.19*
Neighborhood ethnic diversity			−.23*
Neighborhood crowding			−.18*
Neighborhood joblessness			−.10
3. Child-perceived context measures	.05*	1.91+	
Grade			.03
Mother's education			−.04
Female headship			.02
Family income			−.13+
Major life events			−.08
Neighborhood poverty/female headship			−.13
Neighborhood high SES			−.19*
Neighborhood ethnic diversity			−.22*
Neighborhood crowding			−.18*
Neighborhood joblessness			−.11
Violent context			.04
Family conflict			−.18**
Weapons context			.04
Fear of people			−.04
Police bias			.01

$*p < .10. **p < .05. ***p < .01.$

obtained a trend level F change: less family conflict with more parental dissatisfaction.

As indicated, similar to the depression data, at step two, maternal life dissatisfaction is significantly predicted by a low rate of high-SES neighbors ($p < .05$), low rates of ethnic diversity ($p < .05$), and low rates of neighborhood crowding ($p < .05$). At step three, when the child-perceived context variables are entered, the one significant change is the counter intuitive statistical contribution of low family conflict for maternal life dissatisfaction ($p < .01$); the overall adjusted R^2 is enhanced from .04 to .05.

Prediction of Economically-Relevant Measures as an Indication of Maternal Psychological Functioning

For low-resource families, one of the most important compromises to psychological functioning and parental efficacy may be knowing that you have options for social support and/or economic backup in time of extreme need. The intercorrelation, in fact, between the number of negative events and parental reported life dissatisfaction was significant for males ($r[302] = -.12$, $p < .05$) and females ($r[125] = .19$, $p < .05$). For females, more negative events are associated with more parental life dissatisfaction. For males, reports of fewer negative events are associated with more life dissatisfaction for mothers. The fact that the sign is not reversed for males suggests that negative events reported by males are perhaps qualitatively different from those reported by females and, possibly, contribute differently to parental life dissatisfaction. Further, statistics listed in table 9.1 suggest a trend for females to report a higher rate of negative life events than their male cohort.

Prediction of reported inadequate family support. For the variable "inadequate family support," the parental respondent is actually indicating that it is more often *not* true that "(a) If worried, there is someone I can turn to, (b) [could] get help with housework without paying, (c) If no car, could get help with transportation, and (d) If needed, could borrow a large sum of money." For the first equation, the regressions at step one indicate that family background measures significantly predict inadequate family support, which is an important component of economy-linked parental psychological functioning and well-being. The adjusted R^2 obtained was 9 percent, and the significant Beta weights were for two variables: low levels of family support is most often and significantly predicted both by female-headed families and by membership in low-income families. The addition of either the census-level neighborhood measures at step two or the child-perceived context measures at step three did not contribute to the prediction equation.

Prediction of sources of support available. At step one of the regression analysis, two background measures (i.e., mother's education and female headship) accounted for the overall significance, which obtained an adjusted R^2 of 4 percent: mothers with higher levels of education and who were less often single parents reported more sources of support. At steps two and three, entering either the neighborhood measures or the child-perceived context measures did not contribute to the overall adjusted R^2. Although only the family background variables appeared important for the prediction of economic-relevant dependent variables, the parental cultural identity characteristics appeared to be much more sensitive to children's reports of their context perceptions.

Prediction of parental cultural identity as an indication of psychological functioning. Previous research has shown that cultural socialization by parents tends to serve as a buffer for youth who experience significant stress and who are also expected to perform well in school. Assessing cultural identity is viewed as important for understanding more general adult ego functioning and particular aspects of adult psychological well-being. Parental *preencounter* or adult Eurocentric cultural identity (Euro-American cultural preference) has been traditionally hypothesized to be related to mental health (Kardiner and Ovesey 1951). A more *transitional* cultural identity suggests that some event or set of experiences may have occurred that initiated a change from a Eurocentric identification to an Afrocentric cultural orientation (see Cross 1971). The assumption made is that an event salient enough to introduce a "transitioning into another identity mode" should be disconcerting to one's well-being. An *immersion* cultural identity score represents the extent to which the parent's psychosocial identity is characterized by an unquestioning acceptance of one's own culture without a concomitant appreciation of other cultural patterns, values, and traditions. Finally, an *internalization* cultural identity suggests an appreciation of one's own cultural identity, behavioral patterns, and beliefs while also valuing the cultural contributions of others.

At step one, background measures obtained a significant adjusted R^2 accounting for 6 percent of the variance in the prediction of parental Eurocentric identity for males. The first equation indicates that it is actually mother's years of schooling (i.e., lower levels of parental education) that is associated with a more Eurocentric cultural identity.

At step two, when the neighborhood measures are included, although low parental education is important in the prediction of Eurocentric cultural identity, being *afraid* of people in the neighborhood and at school contributes significantly to parental Eurocentricity; and at step three there is a trend for parental Eurocentricity to be predicted by the lack of visible weapons in the environment.

For male adolescents, the overall adjusted R^2 at step one was not significant. Similarly, at step two, when the neighborhood measures are entered, living in neighborhoods with a greater prevalence of high-SES families tends to predict a transitional cultural identity with an overall adjusted R^2 of 4 percent ($p < .05$). Although a low level of achieved education and low ethnic diversity remained marginally significant at step two, it was the child-perceived context-measure *police bias* that was responsible for the overall significance level. That is, male adolescents' report of police bias ($p < .01$) was the one significant predictor of a movement from Eurocentric toward more reactive Afrocentric parental cultural identity, or transitional identity. On the other hand, it was not possible to predict parental proactive or reactive Afrocentricity from either family background measures or child-perceived context measures.

Prediction of Parental Psychological Functioning:
Findings for Females

Prediction of maternal mental health: life dissatisfaction and depression. For daughters, there were no significant predictors of maternal life dissatisfaction as a function of background, neighborhood, or daughter-reported perceived context characteristics. Given the smaller number of females in the sample and the large listing of measures, the lack of an effect may be due to this statistical problem.

On the other hand, regression findings suggest that background and neighborhood measures for females did not predict maternal depression, although at step three, the overall adjusted R^2 obtained trend level: 7 percent of the variance was accounted for, and the F change was significant. It was the daughter's report of family conflict and (absence of) police bias that obtained marginal significance ($p < .05$) for the prediction of maternal depression.

Prediction of economy-relevant measures on maternal psychological well-being. Low level of family support was defined as the frequency of situations such as a large sum of money being required or transportation being needed when the parent does not have a car. As noted, an inadequate level of family support appears to be compromising of psychological well-being. For females, as was the case for males, inadequate family support could be predicted. The predictive relationship was significant in that 9 percent of the variance was accounted for: maternal level of education obtained a significant beta weight. There was a trend for low levels of parental education to predict low levels of family support. Also different for females is the finding that at step two, the F change becomes trend level only with an adjusted R^2 of 6 percent; the important contributors include the daughter's reporting of high violence in the environment (trend level) and reports of being afraid both in the neighborhood and at school ($p < .05$). In other words, the daughter's reports about a violent context and being afraid in the neighborhood and at school are associated with the prediction of maternal reports of inadequate family support. (It might be important to explore whether the finding actually means that mothers *expect* more support when daughters report instances of violent contexts and fearfulness concerning school and neighborhood.)

With respect to prediction of sources of support, the findings indicate a trend level significance for the adjusted R^2 of 7 percent and 9 percent for steps two and three, respectively. No individual beta weight was significant at either step of the regression.

Prediction of parental cultural identity as an indication of parental psychological well-being. For females, it was not possible to predict maternal transitional, reactive, or proactive Afrocentric cultural identity for parents from either background measures or the daughter's perception of context. On the other hand, maternal Eurocentric cultural identity was predicted by background measures: adjusted R^2 was .07 ($p < .05$). Low levels of completed years of education ($p < .05$) and trend levels for lower numbers of major negative life events, little neighborhood diversity, and high neighborhood joblessness ($p < .10$) contributed to the overall significance level.

CONCLUSIONS

Although researchers who examine the lives of lower-income citizens generally and African American families specifically appear quite liberal in assigning blame to parents for problem outcomes and low academic performance of their youth, little information about midlife parenting is available on African American parents. Even less research is available on African American midlife adulthood issues as linked specifically to parenting efforts. One of the more salient midlife parenting tasks requires a resolution of the generativity versus stagnation crisis by turning efforts outward. It would appear that the findings suggest specific effects of African American youth on their parents' psychological well-being and thus the adults' efforts to be responsive parents. Another interpretation of the prediction model is that, in fact, it is the parents' psychological well-being that is linked to the quality of child characteristics and associated neighborhood and family outcomes. This perspective addresses the important buffering or interpretive role that, like all parents, minority mothers serve in childrearing.

In general, the parents' efforts to negotiate the normative adolescent crisis successfully are critical. The context is of special influence on adolescents' patterned behavior. That is to say, the ability of parenting adults at midlife to assist younger individuals and to take an active interest in more global social concerns requires a degree of psychological well-being. Apparent from the available research on nonminority parenting adults at midlife is that psychological well-being is related to adolescent effects on parental characteristics that are of importance to psychological health. Adolescent effects on adults must be analyzed in a more contextually sensitive manner.

As a first step in bridging the conceptual and empirical void, we examined traditional family demographic measures along with conceptually significant child-perceived context measures as potentially important influences on the psychological well-being of midlife parenting African American adults. Not unexpectedly, the predictive relationships varied widely by gender.

For male adolescents, child-perceived context measures associated with parental characteristics follow: (a) parental life dissatisfaction was associated with youth reports of low family conflict, (b) parental Eurocentric cultural identity was associated with youth reports of fearfulness at school and in the neighborhood and trend level for low weapons availability, and (c) parental transitional Afrocentric cultural identity was associated with youth reports of police bias. The finding for male youths that parental life dissatisfaction was associated with youth reports of low family conflict appears counterintuitive. However, it may be that male youths report less family conflict perhaps in empathy with parents perceived as already dissatisfied with life. The majority of youths in the study, with one exception, attended predominately own-race or monoracial schools. Parental beliefs concerning the undervaluing of their racial group may be connected to adolescent neighborhood- and school-linked adverse experiences that occur in a predominately black setting; parents don't feel support from other blacks. In essence, black parents may have Eurocentric beliefs as a consequence of observing their own youths' mishaps with other adolescents—who also happen to be African American.

Particularly salient was the lack of a relationship between parental economy-relevant measures and child-reported context measures. That is, both expected low family support and sources of support were significantly predicted by background measures such as female headship and low family income. On the other hand, the higher rates of parent-identified sources of support were significantly predicted by higher levels of maternal attainment of education and low rates of female headship. Thus, not surprisingly, measures of family economic concerns are predicted by parental characteristics (background measures) and more specific psychological well-being indicators that are related to the child's report of experiences in the context. However, the counterintuitive finding that parental life dissatisfaction is related to low family conflict (i.e., reports of parental and/or sibling conflict) was unexpected. The findings might suggest that adolescents underestimate family conflict when a parent is clearly unhappy or dissatisfied with life. Another interpretation might be that parental life dissatisfaction is linked with parental withdrawal from family involvement and thus a decrease in conflict associated with "active, involved" childrearing activities.

Similarly, given that sample youths more often attend majority African American schools and live in majority African American neighborhoods, it is not surprising that youths' reports of being afraid either in the neighborhood or at school are a significant predictor of parental Eurocentric cultural identity: that is, believing that more integrated settings containing whites and believing that whites themselves are preferred is a consistent sentiment given the reported context experiences of adolescents in the neighborhood and school. On the other hand, a transitional (encounter) cultural identity score assumes a parental movement from Eurocentricity to more Afrocentricity. The significant predictor in this case is the report of police bias, a measure that assesses the view that police officers treat African American minorities and poor people in offensive ways. Parents who may have been initially Euro-centric or white culture–valuing might move in a more Afrocentric direction (i.e., transitional cultural identity) in response to reports of youth-reported police hassles. Thus, the finding of parental transitional cultural identity as linked to the adolescents' untoward report of police bias suggests a basic change in parental cultural identity. Of course, another interpretation might be that parents' own evolving Afrocentric way of thinking or heightened "cultural consciousness" might also rep-resent youths' greater sensitivity to police and beliefs about their treat-ment or respect for the African American community.

Findings for the females' effects on parental psychological character-istics have both parallels and differences. For example, the prediction of parental depression for females is linked to the girls' reports of family conflict and negative police bias: greater adolescent-reported sibling and parental conflict is linked to the parental report of greater depres-sion and the finding that daughter-reported police bias is significantly predictive of low parental depression, the latter of which might appear counterintuitive. But it makes sense when considered in the context of neighborhood characteristics. Parents may believe, in fact, that when it comes to their daughters, greater police bias is good since the as-sumption might be that greater (although thought to be biased) police vigilance decreases parental worry and depression about their daugh-ters' well-being in low-resource neighborhoods. On the other hand, high parental depression or extreme worry may be due to what they view as underreporting or inadequate levels of reported attention or oversight of their daughters by the police given parental views about the neighborhood.

Unlike the data on boys, it was not possible to predict parental cul-tural identity from child-perceived context measures. For girls, moth-er's low education was the best predictor of parental Eurocentric cul-tural identity. However, since women are concerned about femininity issues (e.g., makeup, clothes, hairstyles—physical characteristics), the generally communicated stereotypic beliefs concerning beauty might be a source of stress for some black women, particularly during the adolescent-stage, secondary school experience. Another interpretation of the findings might be that perhaps less education obtained is related to Eurocentric beliefs about beauty, desirability, and other femininity-linked attributes that might have made the adolescent stage and schooling efforts more difficult. On the other hand, the youth-reported context variables did not predict economy-linked parental outcome measures for males, although for females, two female adolescent–reported perceived context measures did predict parent-reported low family support measures: violent context (trend level) and fearfulness in neighborhood and school. For girls, then, reports of fearfulness in neighborhood and school and exposure to violent context predicted lower rates of family support. For females, lower rates of family support may also suggest that parents may have responded to girls' reports of violent context and fearfulness by seeking *more* support from family members, although the requests would appear to have been generally unsuccessful.

In sum, although some parallels and differences exist between male and female adolescents' perceived context effects on parental psychological status, the data, in general, are consistent with findings for nonminority adolescents and midlife adult parents. Specific sex differences are evident, although there is a generalized effect. The role of context, as hypothesized, is obviously important when predicting parental well-being from adolescent reports. However, the sex differences and lack of actual measures on adolescent inference-making processes make definitive interpretations difficult since males and females obviously experience neighborhoods, family, and school settings in varying ways. But data on African American preschool and middle-childhood youth suggest that this sociocognitive interpretation is plausible during the middle-childhood years that just precede adolescence (Spencer, Cunningham, and Swanson 1995).

Although deficit-focused researchers have difficulty understanding how parents cope with chronic stress and few resources, this sample of parents endured in forceful ways. To illustrate, parental interview data indicated that 79 percent of the sample believed "I am a happy person" either always or most of the time, in spite of the fact that 49 percent noted that "current income is very adequate" either rarely or never. Similarly, 84 percent reported "my life is very meaningful" either always or most of the time. These parents were clearly "upbeat" and positive, although many would infer a dreadful or unhappy life for them. The "counterintuitive" findings suggest significant coping resiliency of parents. Other interview questions suggest several reasons for parental sustenance. Over 90 percent of parents responded that the role of *faith* in childrearing was either "very important" or "fairly important." Relative to adolescent responsiveness to parental values and faith, over 91 percent of the respondents noted that *faith* was either "very important" or "fairly important" in their children's lives. In addition, relative to parental connectedness to other institutions, 90 percent of parental respondents indicated the importance of church for childrearing. Other responses suggested that the noted supports were of particular salience during adolescence, because only 10 percent indicated that the period between seven and eleven years of age was important, although 35 percent indicated that the years between eleven and sixteen were the most difficult. Only 25 percent noted the period between seventeen and twenty-one years of age as most difficult.

Parents seemed to differentiate their perceptions about their adolescents' difficulties along gender lines. Over 60 percent of the parents noted that the major problem confronted by black male youths is exposure to drugs: neighborhoods have been besieged by drug dealers. The second most challenging problem facing black males, as reported by 31 percent of parental respondents, is community violence. And, 65 percent of these respondents believe that experiences today are much worse for black males than they were twenty years ago. The parents have learned, however, to lean on their own faith, church, and self for childrearing guidance: over 50 percent indicate that their own experiences represent "the #1 source for childrearing information." Their values concerning teaching children the great importance of maintaining a job (91 percent), paying bills (98 percent), providing for family (98 percent), getting more education (64 percent), family safety (98 percent), planning for future (87 percent), and maintaining loving relationships with family members (99 percent) overwhelmingly sound like traditional *family values* revered by most Americans. Particularly when attempting to rear adolescents, one would think that turning such values into practices, traditions, and desired outcomes should be much more stressful, although clearly not impossible, and doing so appears to be actively pursued.

In future studies, researchers should continue to examine context in a variety of ways. Given the importance of inference-making processes (i.e., both about people and contexts), it would be important to examine adolescent differences in such processes for determining whether the greater empathy of some youth would impact their inferred assumptions about their parents' psychological status and, perhaps, youths' own subsequent behavior.

One important shortcoming of our own dataset is that the majority of adult (parental) respondents (approximately 75 percent) were women, and most were mothers versus grandmothers. Having a larger sample of male respondents would have been helpful in looking for more cross-gender results. Although not presented here, an advantage of our dataset is its inclusion of multiple assessments of neighborhood context that include parental perceptions, police reports, and an independent drive-through method for evaluating neighborhood characteristics. Findings to date suggest different relationships of each "level" and adolescent mental health and achievement outcomes (see Spencer, McDermott and Burton in press). The findings indicate that adolescents demonstrate different reactions to different aspects of the context. For example, police reports of transgressions at the zone or block level may have different meanings for adolescents as a function of whether they have been aggressed in some way. Parental perceptions of neighborhood (e.g., the meaning of police vigilance) might be interpreted differently for a son versus a daughter: perhaps harassing of black male adolescents and potentially protective of female teens. Obviously, these differences in perceptions of neighborhood quality might be different between parents and their teens and, potentially, different from police reports. As evident from this study, census reports of community characteristics as linked to adolescent and parental variables are different from those expected. In sum, the data reported in the current study suggest a need to be more differentiating in analysis of context.

The findings suggest a first step in exploring adolescent effects on midlife parenting efforts. A study that more closely balanced the research design by parent gender would have been helpful. An advantage of the approach taken, however, was the inclusion of culturally specific identity variables that are especially important to minority parents who have the additional task of cultural socialization. Understanding parents' own cultural identity is of considerable consequence for better understanding their methods of cultural socialization of their youths. Previous data indicate that specific cultural identity patterns of minority youth are important for academic efficacy and stress reduction. This research provides a starting point to the understanding of the interactive effects on these processes because of particular adolescent-parental dyadic relationships.

REFERENCES

Allen, W. R. 1985. Race, income, and family dynamics: A study of adolescent male socialization processes and outcomes. In M. B. Spencer, G. K. Brookins, and W. R. Allen, eds., *Beginnings: The social and affective development of black children,* pp. 273–292. Hillsdale, N.J.: Erlbaum.

Barker, R. G., and H. F. Wright. 1971. *Midwest and its children: The psychological ecology of an American town.* Evanston, Ill. Row and Peterson.

Baron, R. M., and D. A. Kenney. 1986. The moderator-mediator variable distinction in social psychological research: Conceptual, strategic, and statistical considerations. *Journal of Personality and Social Psychology* 51 (6):1173–1182.

Beck, A. T. 1987. *Beck Depression Inventory Manual.* San Francisco: Psychological Corporation.

Bowman, H., and A. Viveros-Long. 1981. *Balancing jobs and family life.* Philadelphia: Temple University Press.

Bowman, P. J., and C. Howard. 1985. Race-related socialization, motivation, and academic achievement: A study of black youths in three-generation families. *Journal of the American Academy of Child Psychiatry* 24:134–141.

Bronfenbrenner, U. 1979. *The ecology of human development: Experiments by nature and design.* Cambridge: Harvard University Press.

Chestang, L. W. 1972. *Character development in a hostile environment.* Occasional Paper Series, no. 3, pp. 1–12. Chicago: Unviersity of Chicago Press.

Clark, Reginald. 1983. *Family life and school achievement: Why poor black children succeed or fail.* Chicago: University of Chicago Press.

Conte, V. A., and M. J. Salamon. 1982. An objective approach to the measurement and use of life satisfaction. *Measurement and Evaluation in Guidance* 15:194–200.

Cross, W. E. 1971. Negro to black conversion experience: Toward a psychology of black liberation. *Black World* 20:13–27.

Cunningham, M. 1994. Expressions of manhood: Predictors of educational achievement and African American adolescent males. Ph.D. diss., Emory University, Atlanta.

Erikson, E. H. 1963. *Childhood and society,* 2d ed. New York: Norton.

Fordham, S., and J. U. Ogbu. 1986. Black students' school success: Coping with the "burden of 'acting white.'" *Urban Review* 18 (3):176–206.

Garbarino, J. 1982. *Children and families in the social environment.* New York: Aldine.

Gibbs, Jewelle Taylor. 1988. *Young, black, and male in America: An endangered species.* Dover, Mass.: Auburn House.

Glymph, A. 1994. Assessing youths' perception of their neighborhood: Development of the student perception of neighborhood. Master's thesis, Emory University, Atlanta.

Hare, Bruce R., and L. A. Castenell. 1985. No place to run, no place to hide: Comparative status and future prospects of black boys. In M. B. Spencer, G. K. Brookins, and W. R. Allen, eds., *Beginnings: The social and affective development of black children.* Hillsdale, N.J.: Erlbaum.

Havighurst, R. J. 1953. *Human development and education.* New York: McKay.

Jones, R., ed. 1989. *Black adult development and aging.* Berkeley, Calif.: Cobb and Henry.

Kardiner, A., and L. Oversey. 1951. *The mark of oppression.* New York: Norton.

Kochman, T. J. 1992. The relationship between environmental characteristics and the psychological functioning of African American youth. Bachelor's with honors thesis, Emory University, Atlanta.

Koski, K., and L. Steinberg. 1990. Parenting satisfaction of mothers during midlife. *Journal of Youth and Adolescence* 19 (5):465–474.

LaSorsa, V. A., and I. G. Fodor. 1990. Adolescent daughter/midlife mother daughter dyad. *Psychology of Women Quarterly* 14:593–606.

Levi, L. D., H. Stierlin, and R. J. Savard. 1972. Fathers and sons: The interlocking crisis of integrity and identity. *Psychiatry* 35:48–56.

Markstrom-Adams, C., and M. B. Spencer. 1993. Interventions with minority cultures. In S. Archer, ed., *Interventions for adolescent identity development.* Beverly Hills, Calif.: Sage.

Parham, T. A., and J. E. Helms. 1985. Attitudes of racial identity and self-esteem of black students: An exploratory investigation. *Journal of College Student Personnel* 26 (2):143–147.

Silverberg, S. B., and L. Steinberg. 1987. Adolescent autonomy, parent-adolescent conflict, and parental well-being. *Journal of Youth and Adolescence* 16:293–312.

———. 1990. Psychological well-being of parents with early adolescent children. *Developmental Psychology* 26:658–666.

Spencer, M. B. 1983. Children's cultural values and parental child rearing strategies. *Developmental Review* 4:351–370.

———. 1989. Persistent poverty of African American male youth: A normative study of developmental transitions in high risk environments. Unpublished proposal submission to the Spencer Foundation, Emory University, Atlanta, Ga.

———. 1990. Parental values transmission. In J. B. Stewart and H. Cheatham, eds., *Interdisciplinary perspectives on black families,* pp. 111–130. New Brunswick, N.J.: Transactions Press.

———. 1995. Old issues and new theorizing about African American youth: A phenomenological variant of ecological systems theory. In R. L. Taylor, ed., *Black youth: Perspectives on their status in the United States,* pp. 31–52. Westport, Conn.: Praeger.

Spencer, M. B., S. P. Cole, D. Dupree, A. Glymph, and P. Pierre. 1993. Self-efficacy among urban African American early adolescents: Exploring issues of risk, vulnerability, and resilience. *Development and Psychopathology* 5:719–739.

Spencer, M. B., M. Cunningham, and D. P. Swanson. 1995. Identity as coping: Adolescent African American males' adaptive responses to high risk environments. In H. W. Harris, H. C. Blue, and E. E. H. Griffith, eds., *Identity processes among African American youth.* New Haven: Yale University Press.

Spencer, M. B., B. Dobbs, and D. P. Swanson. 1988. Afro-American adolescents: Adaptational processes and socioeconomic diversity in behavioral outcomes. *Journal of Adolescence* 11:117–137.

Spencer, M. B., and S. Dornbusch. 1990. American minority adolescents. In S. Feldman and G. Elliot, eds., *At the threshold: The developing adolescent,* pp. 123–146. Cambridge: Harvard University Press.

Spencer, M. B., and A. Glymph. 1993. The development of context: Violent behaviors in American youths' context. Paper presented at the meeting of the American Criminality Society, Phoenix, Ariz.

Spencer, M. B., P. McDermott, L. Burton, In press. An alternative approach for assessing neighborhood effects on early adolescent achievement and problem behavior. In J. Brooks-Gunn and G. Duncan, eds., *Neighborhood, poverty, and youth outcomes.*

Spencer, M. B., D. P. Swanson, and M. Cunningham. 1991. Ethnicity, ethnic identity, and competence formation: Adolescent transitions and cultural transformations. *Journal of Negro Education* 60 (3):366–387.

Steinberg, L. 1987. Impact of puberty on family relations: Effects of pubertal status and pubertal timing. *Developmental Psychology* 23:451–460.

Steinberg, L., and S. B. Silverberg. 1987. Influences on marital satisfaction during the middle stages of the family life cycle. *Journal of Marriage and the Family* 49:751–760.

Swanson, D. P., and M. Cunningham. 1993. African American males; coping strategies: Expressions of manhood. Paper presented at the Society for Research in Child Development meetings, March 21–25, New Orleans.

Tamir, L. M., and T. C. Antonucci. 1981. Self-perception, motivation, and social support through the family life course. *Journal of Marriage and the Family* 43: 151–160.

Tienda, M. 1991. Poor people and poor places: Deciphering neighborhood effects on poverty outcomes. In J. Huber, ed., *Macro-micro linkages in sociology,* pp. 244–262. Newberry, Calif.: Sage.

Vander Zanden, J. W. 1985. *Human development,* 3d ed. New York: Knopf.

Wingard, Deborah L. 1987. Social behavioral and biological factors influencing the sex differential in longevity. Background paper prepared for the National Institute on Aging (NIA).

V Parents and Children as Adults

How Children Turn Out: Implications for Parental Self-Evaluation

Carol D. Ryff, Pamela S. Schmutte, and Young Hyun Lee

Few would challenge the observation that raising children consumes much time and energy. From the moment parents hold their newborn until they witness the child's departure from the home, parents deal with a daily array of needs from the physical essentials of food, clothing, and shelter to the emotional essentials of love, guidance, and attention, to the challenges of direction and discipline, to the omnipresent requests for funds and transportation. Amid the demands of raising children, parents are continually confronted with evidence, from their own observations as well as others' feedback, about how these offspring are doing in life and, hence, how they themselves may be doing as parents.

As children grow into adulthood, these perceptions begin to crystallize into a sense of how they have "turned out." For some parents, watching children emerge as adults in their own right is a time of fulfillment and pride; for others, it may be a period of difficulty as they see grown children struggle with life's challenges, perhaps prompting regrets about their past as active parents.

The premise of this chapter is that a central issue of parenting in midlife is the task of evaluating how one's children have turned out, that is, what kinds of adults they have become. A further assumption is that the lives of these grown children constitute an important lens through which midlife adults judge themselves and their accomplishments in life. To explore these ideas, we present empirical research that examines how parents evaluate their children's achievements and adjustment and link these assessments of children to how parents evaluate themselves in midlife.

We begin the chapter with a description of the general rationale and objectives that guide our program of research. These topics are

This research was supported by the John D. and Catherine T. MacArthur Foundation Research Network on Successful Midlife Development. Pamela Schmutte received additional support from a National Science Foundation Graduate Research Fellowship.

elaborated in terms of prior empirical findings and relevant theoretical frameworks. Particular attention is given to the social psychological theories we employ to explicate the mechanisms by which the lives of grown children are linked with parents' self-evaluation. Following this conceptual overview, our research sample and methods are briefly described. We then present and discuss empirical findings from the research program and, in the final section, offer directions for future research on parental evaluations of grown children and of self.

RATIONALE AND PRIMARY RESEARCH OBJECTIVES

Our inquiry begins with certain fundamental questions. First, *why* study parents' views of how children turn out? The rationale follows, in part, from the observation that parents are deemed key players in how their children's lives unfold. Both conventional wisdom and social science contribute to this view. "How to parent" guides, featured prominently in local bookstores, attest to widespread beliefs that the behavior and attitudes of children are importantly molded by parents. In the research realm, long traditions of inquiry, from psychodynamic psychology (Freud 1955) to conceptions of ego development (Erikson 1959), to attachment theory (Bowlby 1951, 1969) have postulated that early interactions between parents and children have lasting consequences for the personal and social development of these offspring. More recently, parents' actual beliefs and practices have received detailed examination by developmentalists, again, with emphasis on the consequences of parental thoughts and behaviors for children (Goodnow 1995; Goodnow and Collins 1990; McGillicuddy-DeLisi and Sigel 1995; Sigel, McGillicuddy-DeLisi and Goodnow 1992). Thus, parents are strongly implicated in their children's development. As such, it is relevant to investigate what they perceive as the "products" of their efforts.

A further rationale is that parents' assessments of how children turn out may be importantly linked to their own self-evaluations in midlife. For some, grown children constitute powerful statements about their successes or failings as parents. Erikson, originator of the generativity construct widely linked to the parental experience, states that "it is through reconsidering their children's adulthood successes and failures that they seek, retroactively, to validate the responsible caring they themselves provided in their years of active parenting" (Erikson, Erikson, and Kivnick 1986, 75). Thus, how children turn out may be a salient, even charged, issue for parents.

Another fundamental question is *when* to study how children turn out. Presumably, "turning out" is a continual process without explicit starting or stopping points. Parents may thus think about how children are doing at any and all phases of their children's lives. We propose that the transition to adulthood constitutes a particularly salient point to evaluate how grown children are doing. It is at this time that parents see their children in adult roles with adult responsibilities and hence have insight into each child's strengths and weaknesses. Also, at this time children are more similar to than different from their parents, with both occupying adult roles. Thus, in judging their children, parents may begin to apply standards similar to those they use for themselves. Given this reasoning, we targeted a sample of midlife parents, averaging around fifty-three years of age, who had children, averaging around twenty-seven years of age.

A third fundamental issue is *how* to study midlife evaluations of grown children. As an organizational guide to the overall research program, we distinguish between descriptive objectives and process objectives. With regard to the former, we first explored parents' goals for their children—that is, what they hoped for in the lives of these children. This descriptive question was expanded by assessing how parents actually evaluate their grown children across multiple life domains. Questions of process pertained to the ways in which the lives of grown children were linked with parent's evaluations of themselves in midlife. This issue required assessment of parental functioning as well as explication of the mechanisms that connect child outcomes and parental well-being. It was at this juncture that we drew on social psychological theory to clarify processes by which children's lives may impact parents' self-evaluations.

These descriptive and process objectives are elaborated below. Our discussion also involves select background issues, such as an interest in individual differences. We assume, for example, that parents may differ in what they want for and in how they evaluate their children, as a function of parental age, gender, socioeconomic status (SES), work status, or personality. Evaluations of children may also differ as a function of the child's age, gender, birth order, temperament, and so on. Among this array of possible differences, we target gender (of parent and child) as a dimension of individual variation in our hypotheses and analyses. We note that the contrast between mothers and fathers addresses a much-needed corrective to prior literature, where "parent" has frequently meant "mother."

A final issue lurking in the background of our inquiry is the important question of whether parents can be dispassionate observers of their children. It might be argued that because their ego investments are high, parents cannot afford to see children realistically. Developmentalists have addressed these questions (Goodnow and Collins 1990), and social psychologists have given extensive attention to the human propensity for "positive illusions" (Taylor 1989; Taylor and Brown 1988; Wood 1989). These literatures sensitize us to the possibility that parents may see children through rose-colored glasses, in part because it enhances their self-evaluations. We revisit such issues in the discussion of research findings.

Parental Goals for Grown Children

To understand how parents think their children have turned out, it is necessary to know what parents hoped for in the first place. Earlier research on parental goals covers diverse terrain, from studies of the broad influences of culture and class on parental goals (Kohn 1977; LeVine 1974, 1988) to historical changes in the qualities parents value in children (Alwin 1989, 1990), to investigations of specific personal and interpersonal qualities that parents wish to see their children develop (Goodnow and Collins 1990; Richman, Miller, and Solomon 1988), to research on how parents' goals for themselves and for their children regulate their behavioral interactions (Dix 1992). These studies demonstrate a wide array of goals present when children are young and parents are actively engaged in rearing them. Such goals involve children's inner psychological qualities (e.g., happiness), their interpersonal qualities (e.g., generosity, honesty), and their acquisition of economic capacities (e.g., a good job). Little is known about how parents evaluate their *grown* children according to these hopes. As stated by Goodnow and Collins, "The field displays a bias towards ideas about young children and early parenting, as if later phases were of less interest" (1990, 4).

To explore parental goals, we asked midlife parents to articulate, in their own words, the hopes and dreams they had for each of their grown children. We analyzed these open-ended reports from several vantage points, including the actual content of the parents' goals—the specific categories of hopes and dreams reported and whether parents' goals for grown children would differ from those obtained from parents of young children. We were, in addition, interested in whether mothers and fathers would differ in their expressed hopes and dreams for their children. Drawing on prior sex-role socialization findings (as summarized in Schmutte and Ryff 1994), mothers might, for example, be expected to have goals regarding their children's capacities to "get along," whereas fathers might emphasize goals of having their children "get ahead" in life.

These open-ended data were further employed as a validation check for the life domains in which parents were asked to provide structured evaluations of their children (see below). The essential question was whether parents' spontaneous reports about goals for their children fit with the a priori dimensions on which we asked parents to rate their children.

Parental Evaluations of Grown Children

Our assumption was that multiple indicators of "success" were required to assess how grown children had turned out. This premise emerges from the above literature, which points to numerous parental goals, as well as from socialization research (suggesting possibly different expectations for sons and daughters) and from formulations of the tasks of adult life, such as "to love and to work" (Smelser and Erikson 1980). Thus, our operationalization of how children turned out was multidimensional, covering broad aspects of their general adjustment and achievements in life.

With regard to adjustment, we examined parents' views of children's personal well-being, such as their happiness and self-confidence, as well as their interpersonal functioning, such as the quality of their relationships with others. Children's achievements were examined in two life domains: how much education each child had completed and his/her occupational status.

Earlier literature on sex-role socialization provided guidance as to how parents might evaluate children. Many societies differentially assign the needs to "get ahead" and "get along" to men and women (Bem 1974; Bakan 1966; Wiggins 1991). Such cultural mandates to practice sex-typical behaviors (Langlois and Downs 1980; Romer 1981; Sears, Maccoby, and Levin 1957) may, in turn, contribute to different abilities in men and women. Among parents, such beliefs may further influence judgments about sons and daughters. We expected that personal, and particularly interpersonal, adjustment would be viewed by parents as more important and rated more highly among adult daughters than sons, whereas achievement (educational and occupational attainment) would be deemed more important and rated more highly among adult sons than daughters.

Children's Lives and Parental Self-Evaluation

Parental self-evaluation was assessed with a multidimensional conception of psychological well-being derived from the literatures on lifespan development (e.g., Buhler and Massarik 1968; Erikson 1959; Jung 1933; Neugarten 1973), mental health (Jahoda 1958; Birren and Renner 1980), and clinical formulations of positive functioning (Allport 1961; Maslow 1968; Rogers 1961). Ryff (1985, 1989a; Ryff and Essex 1992a) identified points of convergence in the above theoretical perspectives and used these as the basis for operationalizing six key dimensions of well-being: self-acceptance, purpose in life, environmental mastery, autonomy, personal growth, and positive relations with others. Earlier studies have documented age and sex differences in these aspects of well-being (Ryff 1989b, 1991, 1995; Ryff and Keyes 1995) and have examined how various life experiences influence well-being (e.g., Heidrich and Ryff 1993; Ryff and Essex 1992a, 1992b; Ryff et al. 1994; Van Riper, Ryff, and Pridham 1992).

In this inquiry, we linked parents' views of how their children had turned out to their self-evaluations on these multiple components of psychological well-being. The general prediction was that parents would feel more positive about themselves if they perceived that their children had turned out well. Specifically, children's profiles of adjustment and achievement were hypothesized to be significant positive predictors of parents' basic regard for themselves and their past lives (self-acceptance), their sense of meaning and direction in life (purpose in life), and their sense of being able to manage the world around them (environmental mastery). Other aspects of well-being, such as autonomy, personal growth, positive relations with others, and depression were included in the assessment battery to examine the pervasiveness of links between children's lives and parents' mental health.

Mechanisms: Social Comparison and Attribution Processes

Developmentalists sometimes look outside their field for theories that enrich their investigations. For example, information-processing and attributional perspectives have been used to elaborate the sources and consequences of parents' ideas about childrearing (Goodnow 1988; Goodnow and Collins 1990). In this investigation, we looked to social psychology for insight about how the lives of grown children might affect the self-evaluations of their midlife parents. Theoretical guidance came from two research traditions: the study of social comparison processes, here applied to how parents think their children compare with themselves and with other people's children; and the study of attribution processes, here addressed as the extent to which parents see themselves as responsible for their children's lives.

Social comparison processes. Since the emergence of Festinger's (1954) social comparison theory, social psychologists have explored how comparisons with others influence self-evaluation (Suls and Wills 1991; Suls and Mullen 1982; Suls and Sanders 1977). Current research has refined and challenged many of the original propositions, such as the claim that individuals prefer to compare themselves with similar rather than dissimilar others (Kruglanski and Mayseless 1990) or the argument that comparisons are primarily about opinions and abilities. More recent work shows that social comparisons are relevant to all kinds of dimensions, including "status (whether ascribed or achieved), attractiveness, attainments, life-style, good or bad fortune, taste, and social sensitivity" (Kruglanski and Mayseless 1990, 204).

Renewed vitality in social comparison research also stems from the observation that individuals harbor goals other than accurate self-evaluation, as Festinger proposed, in making social comparisons (Wood 1989; Wood and Taylor 1991). Sometimes the goal is not unbiased self-knowledge but self-enhancement, in which people may have unrealistically positive views of themselves vis-à-vis others to make themselves feel good. Wood (1989) further emphasizes that the social environment is not an inactive backdrop from which people are free to select their comparisons. Sometimes the social environment *imposes* comparisons.

Families provide obvious contexts in which social comparisons are made, but surprisingly little research has examined comparison processes within the family. Many questions in the above literature are actually brought into sharp relief in family contexts. For example, comparisons with family members are imposed: how siblings compare with each other and how children and parents compare with each other are unavoidable features of family life. Further, these comparisons may well occur across multiple domains (e.g., ability, attractiveness, personality, and so forth). Issues of self-enhancement may also be salient in family comparisons: parents' views of children may be unrealistically positive, thereby allowing themselves to bask in the reflected glory of children's accomplishments.

Our assumption was that watching one's children grow into adulthood affords a particularly relevant context for the study of social comparisons. We hypothesized that parents' self-evaluations would be predicted not only by children's accomplishments and adjustment but also by parents' views of how these children compared with other people's children and with themselves. The direction of our prediction was grounded in the "American Dream"—we expected that parents would want their children to do well relative to others and to themselves. Thus, comparisons in which children were seen as doing better than others, or better than self, were expected to be significant, positive predictors of parental well-being.

Tesser's (1986, 1991) self-evaluation maintenance model proposes that comparisons with similar others will be more affectively charged than comparisons with dissimilar others. Using parent and child sex as a dimension of similarity, we predicted mothers' comparisons with daughters would be more salient for mothers' well-being, while fathers' comparisons with sons would have greater salience for fathers' well-being. That is, parental well-being was expected to be more strongly influenced by same-sex comparison dyads because of the greater similarity in such comparisons (Wheeler and Miyake 1992).

Attribution processes. A small but growing literature applies principles of attribution theory to study of parents' beliefs about the causes of their children's behavior (Goodnow 1988; Gretarsson and Gelfand 1988; Himelstein, Graham, and Weiner 1991). Researchers have addressed whether parents attribute their children's behavior to dispositional versus situational factors; the comparative importance parents give to childrearing practices versus child's disposition versus the environment as determinants of children's behavior; and whether parents explain their children's talent (academic success and failure) as due to inherited ability factors or to effort and schooling. Like much developmental research, this literature is primarily about young children.

Himelstein and colleagues (1991) examined the hedonic bias, a basic principle from attribution theory, to explain parental beliefs. The hedonic bias refers to the tendency to take personal credit for positive outcomes and avoid personal blame for negative outcomes. This pattern of attribution is believed to maximize self-worth and positive self-esteem. Applied to parenting, "One's children also might be considered to be 'successes' or 'failures,' and thus they represent positive or negative 'achievement outcomes' " (Himelstein, Graham, and Weiner 1991, 303). The investigators predicted that parents ascribe the characteristics and behaviors of their successful children to causes internal to themselves, such as childrearing practices, whereas the personalities and characteristics of failing children are ascribed to factors external to parents, including peers and schooling. These hypotheses, targeted on the differences between gifted and special education children, were empirically supported.

For our purposes, the key attributional question pertained to the extent to which parents viewed themselves as *responsible* for how their grown children had turned out (Ryff and Schmutte 1995). We predicted parents' sense of responsibility for children's lives would interact with their assessments of children's success. Consistent with the hedonic bias, parents of children viewed as successful were hypothesized to have a higher sense of responsibility for their children's outcomes, whereas parents of children viewed as unsuccessful were hypothesized to have low sense of responsibility. In addition, these responsibility ratings were predicted to explain additional variance in parents' well-being (net of parental assessments of how children had turned out). Parents of less successful children were expected to have higher well-being *if* they attributed low responsibility to themselves for the child outcomes.

As with the social comparison effects, we expected that the above patterns would be strongest in the same-sex, parent-child dyads. That is, mothers were expected to feel greater sense of responsibility for daughters, whereas fathers were predicted to show greater sense of responsibility for sons. The well-being of mothers and fathers was also hypothesized to be more strongly predicted by responsibility attributions for same-sex versus opposite-sex child evaluations.

EMPIRICAL TRANSLATION

This section summarizes the sample on which the research is based, gives a brief description of instruments used to assess key constructs, and provides an overview of findings. Greater detail on all such features of the research is available in the underlying empirical studies (Ryff et al. 1994; Ryff and Schmutte 1995; Schmutte and Ryff 1994).

TABLE 10.1. Demographic Characteristics of Parents

Characteristics	Total (N = 215)	Mothers (N = 114)	Fathers (N = 101)	t
Average age	53.7 (6.8)	53.1 (7.2)	54.3 (6.2)	NS
Marital status				
Married	78.1%	64.9%	93.1%	
Divorced	14.9	21.9	6.9	
Separated	1.4	2.6	—	
Widowed	5.6	10.5	—	
Education				
1. High school graduate or less	26.5%	31.6%	20.8%	
2. Some college	32.6	35.1	29.7	
3. College graduate	23.2	21.1	25.7	
4. Advanced degree	17.7	12.3	23.8	
Average education	2.3 (1.1)	2.1 (1.0)	2.5 (1.1)	2.70**
Income($):				
1. 0–10,999	3.3%	6.1%	—%	
2. 11,000–20,999	8.8	11.4	5.9	
3. 21,000–30,999	19.5	27.2	10.9	
4. 31,000–40,999	19.1	21.1	16.8	
5. 41,000–44,999	7.9	8.8	6.9	
6. 45,000 and above	41.4	25.4	59.4	
Average income	4.4 (1.5)	3.9 (1.5)	5.0 (1.3)	5.70**

Sample

Findings are reported for a probability sample of 215 midlife parents (114 mothers and 101 fathers, all from separate families). The sample was contacted through random-digit dialing of phone numbers in a midwestern county. Respondents were invited to participate in a study about parents and their adult children. Criteria for inclusion were that the respondent had to be under the age of sixty-five and have at least one child aged twenty-one or older. Participation included a face-to-face interview of approximately one hour in length and the completion of a self-administered survey. Of those who met the selection criteria, 70 percent agreed to participate in the study.

Demographic characteristics of the respondents are summarized in table 10.1. In terms of age, both mothers and fathers were, on average, in their early fifties, with no significant differences between the two. Nearly all fathers were married, while about two-thirds of mothers were married, with the rest divorced or separated and a few widowed. Fathers had significantly higher levels of education and income than mothers. The sample was primarily Protestant, Catholic, or nonreligious.

Data were obtained from parents about each of their children aged twenty-one and older. About one-fourth of the parents had only one adult child, about a third had two, and nearly a fifth had three or four or more children. The age range of these children was from 21 to 44 years, with an average of 27.6 years of age. Children were divided nearly equally between sons and daughters, and almost half of these children were married. With regard to proximity to parents, 11 percent lived at home, 37 percent lived within thirty minutes of their parents, 8 percent lived within an hour away, and 44 percent lived more than an hour away.

Measures

Parental goals were assessed with an open-ended question about the "hopes and dreams" parents had for each of their children as they were growing up. All remaining data were collected with structured assessments, which are described in the following five categories: children's adjustment, children's attainment, social comparison processes, attribution processes, and parents' psychological well-being. The first four were obtained from the face-to-face interviews, and the last, from the self-administered survey.

Children's adjustment. Parents were asked a series of questions about the personal and social adjustment of *each* of their children aged twenty-one or older. For personal adjustment, the objective was to obtain parents' views of positive and negative aspects of each child's functioning. Thus, adjustment items included ratings of how happy, satisfied with life, self-confident, down or discouraged, frustrated, tense, or anxious parents found each child. Two additional items pertained to whether parents thought the child was making the most of him/herself and the extent to which the child was living by sound values and morals.

Parents were also asked to assess how their grown children were doing socially. Here the questions asked whether each child was well-liked by others, was a caring friend to others, was fun to be with, and had developed lasting relationships with others. Parents were also asked to assess the extent to which each child had had problems or difficulties in close relationships with others.

To simplify the analyses and look at overall adjustment compared with overall attainment, parental ratings of children's personal adjustment were combined with their ratings of children's social adjustment.[1] The correlation between the two scales was .59. The internal consistency (coefficient alpha) of the overall adjustment index was .86. The scale range for children's adjustment was from thirteen to fifty-two.

Children's attainment. Two aspects of children's attainment were obtained. First, parents were asked to indicate the highest level of education that had been completed by each child. Second, parents were asked about each child's occupational attainment. This included responses to three questions about the child's work, his/her principal activities and duties, and the kind of business or industry the work is in. Responses to these questions were then coded according to an eight-point scale derived from modifications of Featherman and Stevens's (1982) index of occupational status. The categories ranged from unemployed/homemaker (1) to high-status professional (8). These two indices of attainment were also highly correlated ($r = .77$) and thus were combined as a single indicator of children's attainment. The scale range for children's attainment was from two to seventeen.

Social comparisons. Two forms of social comparisons were investigated as possible influences on how midlife parents felt about themselves vis-à-vis their children. The first addressed how parents felt their children compared with the grown children of their siblings or friends. Specifically, we asked respondents, "How well would you say (name of child) has done with his/her education compared to these children?" Answers ranged from "A Lot Better" (5) to "A Lot Worse" (1). Similar questions were then asked about the domains of occupational or work pursuits, personal adjustment (i.e., making the most of him/herself, happiness, self-confidence, frustration), and social adjustment (i.e., being well liked, dealing well with relationship problems). Scores for attainment comparisons ranged from two to ten; scores for adjustment comparisons ranged from six to thirty.

To assess how parents personally compared with each child, parents were asked, "Think back to when you were about the same age as (name of child). Try to recall where you were living and what you were doing. How do you think he/she compares with you when you were that age on the following things?" Parents then rated each child as to whether he/she had done "A Lot Better" (5) to "A Lot Worse" (1) than themselves (at the same age) in the domains of education, occupational or work pursuits, personal adjustment (i.e., happiness, self-confidence, frustration), and social adjustment (i.e., being well liked, dealing well with relationship problems). Score ranges for personal comparisons were the same as those for other comparisons (see above).

Attributions. Parents were asked three categories of questions regarding their sense of responsibility for their children's lives: how much they were involved in the child's life, across multiple domains (educational and occupational achievements, personal life, social relations); to what extent they viewed themselves as a role model for the child, again across multiple life domains; and how much they took credit or responsibility for how well (or poorly) the child had done across the different life domains. Answers ranged from "A Great Deal" (5) to "Not at All" (1). Scores for attainment and adjustment attributions ranged from six to thirty.

Parental well-being. Parents completed a self-report inventory designed to measure six dimensions of psychological well-being (Ryff 1989b, 1991, in press). Each dimension was operationalized with a fourteen-item scale divided between positively and negatively phrased items. Prior work with longer scales demonstrated high internal consistency, high test-retest reliability, and that the scales correlated positively with earlier measures of positive functioning (e.g., life satisfaction, affect balance, and self-esteem) and negatively with measures of depression and external control (Ryff 1989b). Confirmatory factor analysis (with a reduced set of items) from a national probability sample supported a six-factor dimensional structure (Ryff and Keyes 1995). Each scale had a score range of fourteen to eighty-four.

Depression was also assessed using the CES-D scale (Radloff 1977), which is a twenty-item, self-report scale designed to assess depressive symptomatology in the general population. This measure was chosen because it measures current levels of symptomatology with an emphasis on depressed mood or affect, has few somatically based items, and has demonstrated reliability and validity. Twenty statements of pathology (e.g., "I felt sad") are rated on a four-point scale of frequency for the "past week." Concordance with other depression measures, dis-

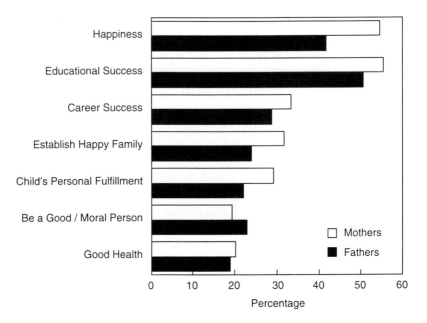

FIGURE 10.1. Parents' Hopes and Dreams for Their Children.

criminant validity, and utility as a screening scale have been demonstrated (Radloff 1977). Scores ranged from zero to sixty.

RESEARCH FINDINGS
What Goals Do Parents Have for Their Children?

Figure 10.1 provides a frequency distribution of mothers' and fathers' responses to the question about the "hopes and dreams" they had for each of their children. Happiness and educational success were the two most frequently occurring responses for both mothers and fathers, followed by an emphasis on career success, having a happy family, personal fulfillment, being a good/moral person, and having good health. No significant differences were found between mothers and fathers in these answers (assessed by multivariate analysis of variance in which separate answer categories represented the dependent variables, scored dichotomously). That is, the findings provided no evidence that mothers emphasized primarily "getting along" capacities of children or that fathers emphasized primarily "getting ahead" capacities.

These qualitative findings show that parents' hopes and dreams converged with earlier studies (LeVine 1988; Richman, Miller, and

TABLE 10.2. Mean Level Differences between Mothers' and Fathers'
Ratings of Their Children

| | Parent | | |
| | Mothers (N = 114) | Fathers (N = 101) | |
Variable	Mean (SD)	Mean (SD)	t
Ratings of children			
Adjustment	43.0 (4.7)	43.4 (4.6)	NS
Personal comparison	19.6 (3.5)	18.8 (2.6)	NS
Other comparison	21.1 (3.3)	21.6 (3.3)	NS
Importance	9.5 (0.8)	9.2 (1.0)	2.13*
Responsibility	21.4 (3.1)	20.3 (3.3)	2.44*
Attainment	8.1 (3.3)	8.7 (2.9)	NS
Personal comparison	7.3 (1.8)	6.5 (1.6)	3.32*
Other comparison	7.2 (1.6)	7.4 (1.4)	NS
Importance	9.0 (1.1)	9.0 (0.9)	NS
Responsibility	21.0 (3.6)	20.6 (3.5)	NS

*$p < .05$.

Solomon 1988) where parental goals involved children's inner psychological qualities, their interpersonal qualities, and their economic capacities. The same themes were evident in the present findings in terms
of parents' wishes that their children be happy, have happy families,
and have educational and career success. Wanting children to be personally fulfilled was a new goal evident in these data. Further, parents'
self-generated hopes and dreams revealed strong fit with the life domains in which detailed evaluations of children were made (see below).
That is, our structured ratings of children's personal and social adjustment, along with their educational and occupational attainments, paralleled the domains spontaneously endorsed by parents as important
to them.

How Do Parents Evaluate Their Children?

Differences between mothers and fathers in ratings of their children's adjustment and attainment, as well as subevaluations within
these domains, are summarized in table 10.2. Three significant differences were obtained between mothers' and fathers' ratings of their children. Mothers attached greater importance to having well-adjusted
children than did fathers, and mothers also reported a greater sense
of responsibility for their children's adjustment than did fathers. With
regard to comparison ratings, mothers scored significantly higher than

TABLE 10.3. Mean Level Differences between Mothers' and Fathers'
Ratings of Themselves

| | Parent | | |
Variable	Mothers (N = 114) Mean (SD)	Fathers (N = 101) Mean (SD)	t
Ratings of self			
Environmental mastery	66.6 (11.6)	66.9 (10.3)	NS
Personal growth	72.1 (7.5)	68.8 (8.3)	3.06*
Purpose in life	69.1 (9.5)	69.1 (9.7)	NS
Personal acceptance	65.8 (12.0)	66.9 (11.6)	NS
Depression	8.6 (9.2)	7.5 (7.7)	NS
Autonomy	64.6 (10.4)	64.7 (9.8)	NS
Positive relations with others	69.9 (9.8)	65.1 (11.56)	3.21*

*p < .05.

fathers on personal comparisons in the attainment realm. Higher scores meant that mothers more than fathers felt that their children had done better than themselves in educational and occupational pursuits.

When the above differences were reexamined with a focus on sex of child (Schmutte and Ryff 1994), no significant differences were obtained. That is, mothers and fathers did not rate their daughters as more interpersonally skilled than their sons, nor were sons viewed as more successful than daughters in the attainment domain. Parents also did not assign differential importance to these domains for daughters and sons. Thus, predictions derived from sex-role socialization research received only partial support. Mothers, as hypothesized, attached more importance to the adjustment of their children than did fathers, and they felt more responsible for this domain of children's lives. However, parents did not emphasize the adjustment realm to a greater degree among daughters than sons.

Table 10.3 provides parental differences in mental health. Mothers scored significantly higher than fathers on self-ratings of personal growth and positive relations with others. These findings replicate previous patterns of sex differences obtained on these measures (Ryff 1989b, 1995; Ryff, Lee, and Na 1995).

Children's Lives and Parents' Well-Being

Guiding predictions for the hierarchical regression analyses were that parents' well-being would be significantly and positively predicted by children's adjustment and attainment profiles. (The directional prediction for depression was negative.) Net of these effects, parents' comparisons with their children were also hypothesized to influence their self-evaluations, with parents of children who had done better than other people's children or better than themselves expected to have higher profiles of well-being. Comparisons with daughters were predicted to have greater influence on mothers' well-being, while comparisons with sons were hypothesized to have greater influence on fathers' well-being.

The analyses of parental attribution processes led to predicted interactions between parents' responsibility assessments and their evaluations of children's success. Consistent with the hedonic bias, we believed that parents would report higher levels of responsibility for children's lives *if* they viewed their children as successful. Parents of children viewed as less successful were hypothesized to have lower perceptions of responsibility. When linked to parental well-being, interactions were again predicted: parents of less successful children were predicted to have higher well-being *if* they attributed low responsibility to themselves for children's outcomes.

The following findings are organized according to the two broad categories of child outcomes: adjustment and attainment. Within each, the findings are further divided between analyses focused on social comparisons and those employing attributional/responsibility indicators as the moderating mechanism. For ease of presentation, regression results and interaction analyses are presented graphically. Detailed tables of numerical values (e.g., slopes, betas) are available in the original studies (Ryff et al. 1994; Ryff and Schmutte 1995; Schmutte and Ryff 1994).

Children's adjustment. Figure 10.2 summarizes the results from a series of regression analyses in which children's adjustment was used to predict parents' well-being. Along the abscissa are the dependent variables. The ordinate indicates the variance explained for each outcome. First entered into the equation were control variables (parental age, education, number of children). The figure illustrates the variance explained

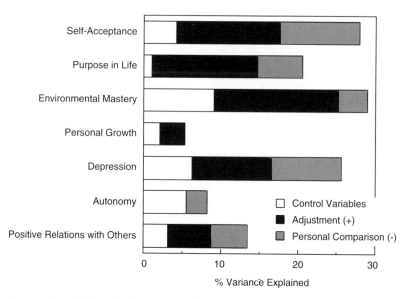

FIGURE 10.2. Children's Adjustment and Personal Comparisons as Predictors of Parental Well-Being.

by these sociodemographic background factors. Following the control variables, the remaining predictor variables are displayed in the graph *only if they had significant beta coefficients and contributed a significant increment in variance explained.* Children's adjustment ratings were entered in the second step. Comparison ratings—or responsibility ratings, depending on the analysis—were entered as the third variable to test their effects, net of the controls and children's adjustment, on parents' well-being.

For parents with more than one adult child, ratings were averaged across children within each family. Additional analyses were conducted where the child rather than the parent was the unit of analysis, thereby obviating the need for family averages. The general pattern of effects paralleled the results presented here. When investigating differences between sons and daughters, analyses are based on the child as the unit of analysis.

As hypothesized, parents' ratings of their children's adjustment significantly predicted (net of the control variables) multiple aspects of their own parental well-being. In fact, all aspects of positive functioning except autonomy had significant variance explained by child ratings (see figure 10.2). Increments to explained variance were particularly strong, accounting for 10 percent to 16 percent of the variance, for ratings of self-acceptance, purpose in life, environmental mastery, and depression. The direction of these predictive effects was positive (negative for depression). Thus, parents who perceived that their children were well-adjusted rated themselves higher on the well-being indicators and lower on depression. No significant differences were obtained between mothers and fathers, as assessed with interaction terms between the adjustment variable and parental sex.

Parents had reported detailed evaluations of 291 sons and 251 daughters. In separate analyses (employing the child as the unit of analysis), we examined whether parents' well-being was differentially predicted by daughters' versus sons' adjustment. To sharpen tests of the prediction that parents would emphasize the "getting along" capacities of daughters more than sons, we decomposed the adjustment measure into its personal and interpersonal subdimensions (Schmutte and Ryff 1994). Analyses revealed that the personal and interpersonal adjustment of both sons and daughters added significant increments to variance explained in multiple aspects of parents' well-being. However, it was the adjustment (personal and interpersonal) of *sons*, rather than daughters, that explained greater variance in parental well-being. In particular, significant gender interactions indicated strong links between sons' interpersonal adjustment and parents' self-acceptance, autonomy, and depression, whereas only weak links existed between daughters' interpersonal adjustment and parents' well-being.

SOCIAL COMPARISONS. Figure 10.2 also shows that parents' ratings of how their children compared with themselves in the adjustment domain added further significant increments in variance explained for all the dependent measures except personal growth. Strongest effects were obtained for parents' ratings of their self-acceptance and depression, where 9 to 10 percent of additional variance was explained. Here, the direction of effects was contrary to what had been predicted. Parents who perceived that their children were better adjusted than they had been in early adulthood had significantly *lower* levels of current well-being. No differences were obtained between mothers and fathers.

When the above analyses were repeated with the measure of "other comparison" (i.e., parents' assessments of how their children's adjustment compared with the adjustment of their friends' or siblings' children), no significant increments to variance explained were obtained.

Thus, only parents' views of how they themselves compared with children were tied to ratings of their psychological well-being.

Because of the greater similarity in same-sex dyads, we had predicted that mothers' well-being would be more strongly tied to social comparisons with daughters, whereas fathers' well-being would be more strongly tied to social comparisons with sons. Partial support was obtained for these predictions—mothers who perceived their daughters' personal adjustment as better than their own had lower levels of self-acceptance and a trend toward higher depression, whereas sons' personal adjustment was only weakly associated with these aspects of maternal well-being (Schmutte and Ryff 1994). On the paternal side, no significant interactions of child sex with the comparison ratings were obtained.

PARENTAL RESPONSIBILITY. Preliminary mean level analyses examined whether parents' responsibility ratings for their children's adjustment would vary as a function of whether they viewed such children as well- or poorly adjusted. Median-split procedures were used to distinguish between children rated high versus low on adjustment (cases at the median were omitted). As predicted, parents of children rated low on adjustment had significantly lower responsibility scores than parents of children rated high on adjustment (Ryff and Schmutte 1995).

To examine the influence of attributional processes on parents' well-being, the above regression models were repeated with responsibility ratings, rather than comparison ratings, included in the third step in the equation. The results of these analyses are represented in figure 10.3. As predicted, parents' sense of responsibility for their children was a significant positive predictor of multiple aspects of well-being. These effects were, however, obtained for outcomes different from those evident in the social comparison analyses. For example, greatest variance was explained in parents' sense of personal growth, an outcome showing no effects in the social comparison analyses. Thus, feelings of responsibility for children's lives appeared to be an important link to parents' self-evaluations, with effects particularly evident for assessments of their own continued development and having quality relations with others.

The hedonic bias led to predicted interaction effects in these analyses. Three significant interactions were obtained and are illustrated in figure 10.4. For parents of children viewed as successful (i.e., highly adjusted), parents' levels of well-being, specifically, environmental

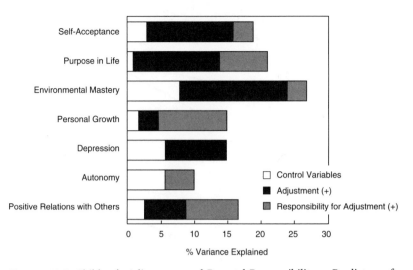

Figure 10.3. Children's Adjustment and Parental Responsibility as Predictors of Parental Well-Being.

mastery, purpose in life, and depression, did not vary substantially as a function of whether they saw themselves as having high or low responsibility for children's lives. However, *if* children were viewed as unsuccessful (e.g., low on adjustment), parents who saw themselves as having low responsibility reported *lower* ratings of well-being (higher for depression) than parents who saw themselves as having high responsibility. Thus, contrary to the hedonic bias, parents with low sense of responsibility appeared to feel *worse*, not better, about themselves.

Analyses of parental responsibility ratings by sex of child did not support our predictions that mothers' well-being would be more strongly linked with the adjustment of daughters (Ryff and Schmutte 1995). Significant sex-by-responsibility interactions were observed for mothers' self-acceptance, environmental mastery, purpose in life, and depression, but it was for ratings of *sons* that mothers had lower well-being if they perceived themselves as having exercised little responsibility. Mothers' sense of responsibility for daughters' adjustment appeared to have no bearing on their own self-evaluations.

These patterns were reversed for fathers, but only for one outcome. Fathers who reported little responsibility for *daughters' adjustment* had lower levels of personal growth than fathers with a higher sense of responsibility. Fathers' sense of responsibility for sons' adjustment had little association with paternal well-being.

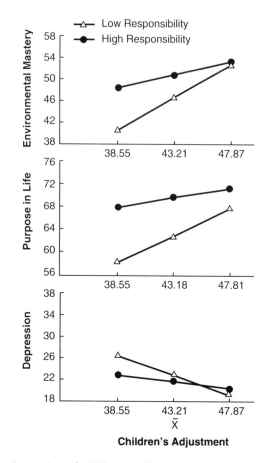

FIGURE 10.4. Interaction of Children's Adjustment with Parental Responsibility.

Children's attainment. Figure 10.5 summarizes the results of the series of regression analyses in which children's educational and occupational attainments were used to predict parents' well-being. Overall, the figure reveals fewer significant linkages between children's attainment and parental well-being. Significant increments to explained variance were obtained only for measures of self-acceptance, purpose in life, personal growth, and positive relations with others, with small effects (R^2 increments = 3 percent to 5 percent). As predicted, the directionality of these effects was positive—parents of children with higher levels of attainment reported higher well-being. No differences were obtained between mothers and fathers as assessed with interactions of children's attainment and parent sex.

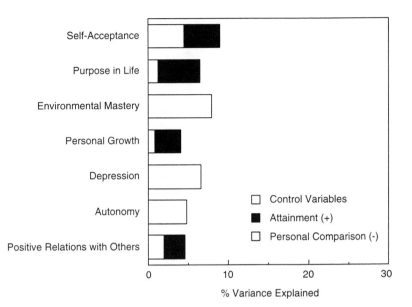

FIGURE 10.5. Children's Attainment and Personal Comparisons as Predictors of Parental Well-Being.

When the above analyses were conducted with the child as the unit of analysis, we found, as predicted, that sons' attainment contributed significant (but small) increments to variance explained in parents' self-acceptance, environmental mastery, and purpose in life. Daughters' attainment did not explain significant variance in parental well-being.

SOCIAL COMPARISONS. Parents' ratings of how their children's attainment compared with their own young adult attainment added no significant increments to variance explained for any measure of well-being. When these models were reexamined with measures of how children's attainment compared with that of other children, there were again no significant increments to variance explained.

Significant interactions were, however, obtained between mothers and fathers in ratings of these "other comparisons" (see figure 10.6). When parents compared their children's attainment with that of their friends' or siblings' children, fathers showed higher levels of autonomy and positive relations with others as they perceived their children had attained more than these other children, whereas mothers showed a

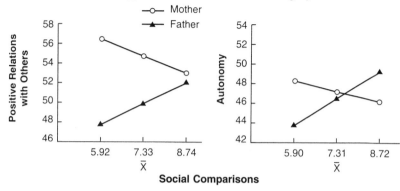

FIGURE 10.6. Interaction of Social Comparison with Other Children's Attainment and Parent Gender.

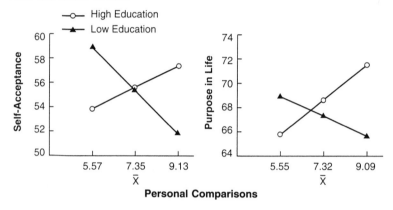

FIGURE 10.7. Interaction of Mothers' Personal Comparison on Attainment and Maternal Education.

negative directional pattern—as they perceived their children's attainment as better than others' children, their self-ratings of positive relations with others and autonomy declined.

These patterns were further clarified by analyses regarding interactions of *parents' own attainment* (indicated by their education) with their assessments of children's attainment. Such analyses were conducted separately for mothers and fathers because the two had been shown to have significantly different levels of educational attainment. Significant effects were obtained only for mothers and are illustrated in figure 10.7. For self-acceptance, it was found that mothers with higher levels of education showed ever higher levels of well-being as they perceived that their children's attainment was better than their own. Mothers with lower levels of education showed ever lower levels

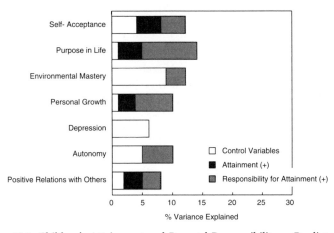

FIGURE 10.8. Children's Attainment and Parental Responsibility as Predictors of Parental Well-Being.

of purpose in life and self-acceptance as they perceived their children's attainment was higher than their own.

The analysis of same- and cross-sex parent-child dyads revealed partial support for the similarity predictions for mothers. Here it was found that mothers' attainment comparisons with daughters, but not sons, added significant increments to variance explained in mothers' self-acceptance, environmental mastery, autonomy, and depression. The direction of all effects was consistent—mothers who perceived that their daughters had done better than themselves in the attainment domain had *lower* well-being. For fathers, attainment comparisons with sons or daughters did not explain any variance in their ratings of themselves.

PARENTAL RESPONSIBILITY. Preliminary analyses addressed whether parents' responsibility ratings would vary depending on whether children were viewed as high versus low on educational and occupational attainment. We found a marginal effect in which parents of children with low attainment profiles had lower responsibility ratings than parents of children with high attainment profiles ($p < .09$, Ryff and Schmutte 1995).

Figure 10.8 summarizes the pattern of findings when the above regression models were repeated with measures of parents' sense of responsibility for their children's educational and occupational attainment. These responsibility ratings revealed multiple significant main effects on parents' well-being. For all outcomes except depression and positive relations with others, significant variance was explained, net of children's actual attainment, by parents' sense of responsibility for their children's attainment. The direction of all effects was positive. Thus, parents who perceived that they had been involved in and responsible for their children's attainment had higher levels of multiple aspects of psychological well-being. Strongest effects were evident for parents' sense of purpose in life, personal growth, and autonomy. Mothers and fathers did not differ in the above pattern of effects. Also, contrary to predictions from the hedonic bias, there were no significant interactions between children's attainment levels and parents' sense of responsibility.

Analyses of differences between sons and daughters revealed that mothers' purpose in life was significantly and positively linked with their ratings of responsibility for sons' attainment success, but not for daughters. For fathers, no significant sex-by-responsibility interactions were obtained.

SUMMARY AND DISCUSSION

Four themes will be used to summarize and interpret the findings: (1) the influence of children's lives on parental well-being, (2) the social psychological mechanisms of linkage (social comparisons and attributions), (3) the differences between sons and daughters, and (4) issues of self-serving bias and directional effects in the study of children's lives and parental well-being.

The Adjustment and Attainment of Grown Children: Implications for Parents

As described earlier, qualitative analyses of parents' hopes and dreams for their children converged with those in prior literature, which emphasized children's inner qualities (e.g., happiness), their interpersonal lives (e.g., have happy family), and their attainment capacities (e.g., educational and career success). These self-generated goals underscored the relevance of the two key domains, adjustment and attainment, in which parents provided structured evaluations of each child. Parents thus gave detailed assessments of their children in the areas that they themselves deemed important.

The actual ratings of grown children's adjustment and attainment revealed that mothers and fathers had largely similar views of how their children had "turned out." Mothers, however, gave greater importance to and felt more responsible for their children's adjustment than did fathers. Mothers' ratings of their own mental health also showed significantly higher scores than fathers on the measure of positive relations with others. Thus, the findings provide some support, from the parental perspective, for the view that tasks of "getting along" and "getting ahead" in life are differentially assigned according to gender (Bem 1974; Bakan 1966; Hogan, Jones, and Cheek 1985; Wiggins 1991; Parsons and Bales 1955). Parents, however, did not report differential success stories for daughters and sons. That is, the predicted gender differences applied primarily to parents' views of themselves and their own parenting rather than differential evaluations of daughters and sons.

The linkage of parents' ratings of children with their own psychological well-being revealed extensive support for the prediction that parents' self-evaluations were strongly tied with assessments of how children had turned out. Weaker effects were evident in the attainment domain—children's educational and occupational achievements significantly predicted multiple outcomes, but the increments in variance explained were small (3 percent to 5 percent). Children's adjustment, however, added substantial increments to variance explained (10 percent to 16 percent) for parents' ratings of their self-acceptance, purpose in life, environmental mastery, and depression. In fact, of the multiple dimensions of parental well-being considered, only autonomy was not significantly predicted by ratings of children's adjustment.

The predominance of children's adjustment over their attainment is curious in light of the qualitative reports, in which parents gave comparable emphasis to children's happiness and educational success. Thus, the obtained differences do not seem attributable to the attainment domain having less importance to parents. An alternate explanation is methodological: parents were asked to report only their child's educational and occupational levels, not to *evaluate* how the child was doing in these realms, as was done for the adjustment ratings. Had more evaluative ratings been obtained in the attainment realm (e.g., "How *well* has your child done educationally?"), stronger predictive effects may have been evident. The fact that nonevaluative attainment ratings emerged as significant predictors of multiple aspects of parental well-being underscores the likely importance of the attainment domain.

Consistent with the guiding hypotheses, the direction of effects for both children's adjustment and attainment was positive—parents felt better about themselves and their lives (self-acceptance) and had greater sense of directedness (purpose in life), enhanced perceptions of their capacity to manage a complex world (environmental mastery), and lower profiles of depression when they saw their children as doing well. However, given the correlational nature of these data, it is possible that parents' well-being may influence how they construe their children. The question of directional influence is examined in conjunction with the issue of parental bias in the final section of this discussion.

Mechanisms of Linkage: Social Comparisons and Attributions

We hypothesized that parents' evaluations of themselves would be influenced not only by their assessments of how children had turned out but also by their views of how these children compared with others (children of their friends and siblings) and themselves. The direction of the prediction followed the American Dream: parents were expected to feel better about themselves if they had children who had done as well or better than others and themselves. Personal comparisons did, in fact, emerge as significant predictors of parents' well-being, net of children's adjustment and attainment, but the direction of these effects was reverse of our prediction. Parents who perceived their children were doing better than they themselves had done in young adulthood had lower profiles of well-being.

These negative effects were restricted largely to the adjustment realm, which may admittedly be distant from visions of upward mobility embodied in the American Dream. That is, while parents may want children to get ahead in life, have good jobs, and gain economic security (even beyond their own achievements), they may not be equally enthusiastic about having children who are more self-confident, happy, or interpersonally skilled than themselves. It is worth noting that the direction of these latter effects is consistent with prior research and theory on social comparison processes (Suls and Wills 1991; Suls and Mullen 1982; Suls and Sanders 1977; Tesser 1991), in which negative consequences for self-esteem have been documented when individuals perceive others to be better than themselves. Our assumption that family relationships constitute possible exceptions to these prior findings was not supported.

In the attainment realm, interaction effects provided some support for social comparison hypotheses. Fathers, for example, had higher levels of autonomy and positive relations with others when they viewed their children's attainment as better than the attainment of their friends' or siblings' children. And mothers with higher levels of education had a greater sense of purpose in life and higher self-acceptance when their children's educational and occupational attainment exceeded their own. Overall, however, mothers saw themselves as comparing less favorably with both sons and daughters in the attainment realm (mean level analyses), a finding probably linked to differences in the mothers' career opportunities compared with their children.

Turning to attribution processes, the findings point to new issues raised by the application of attribution theory to family research. Consistent with earlier studies, we found that parents who viewed their children as less "successful" in overall adjustment and attainment also reported lower levels of responsibility for these children. This attribution was hypothesized to protect parental self-evaluation by enabling parents to avoid blame for negative outcomes. Tests of the purported hedonic bias revealed the opposite effects: parents of children viewed as less successful who also saw themselves as having low parental responsibility actually had *lower* levels of environmental mastery and purpose in life and higher levels of depression than parents with higher levels of responsibility.

Two points bear on the interpretation of these data. First, our measure of parental responsibility did not include an assessment of other influences (e.g., peers, schools, child disposition) external to the parent. Thus, we cannot address the extent to which parents of less successful children might attribute the child outcomes to external influences (e.g., peers, teachers) or to the child's own disposition. What the findings do suggest, however, is that parents who feel they exercised little responsibility for their children's lives do not appear to get themselves "off the hook." Parents with the lowest well-being were, in fact, those who saw their children as less successful *and* saw themselves as having exercised little responsibility.

The second point is that application of attributional perspectives to family life requires consideration of the *normative expectations* surrounding family roles and responsibilities. Normatively speaking, children represent realms of inescapable responsibility—parents who were not actively involved in their children's lives may sense that they *should* have been. The failure to exercise parental responsibility is thus a violation of parental role prescriptions. This, combined with the observation that one's child has not done well, might be expected to have negative consequences for parental self-assessment. It is a disappointment about the lack of success in one's offspring, compounded by a recollection that one was not sufficiently involved in, a role model for, or responsible for these children. We underscore that this interaction pattern was obtained *only* in the domain of children's adjustment. In the attainment realm, parental responsibility ratings were strong, positive predictors of all aspects of well-being, and none were qualified by significant interactions.

Viewed together, these findings show that the application of social psychological theory enriches understanding of how children's lives influence parental self-evaluation. They demonstrate that parents' well-being is importantly linked not only to assessments of how children have turned out but also to how these children compare with parents themselves and to the extent to which they see themselves as responsible for their children. Thus, the avenues by which parents make sense of and are affected by children's lives require insights provided by social psychology, a realm of theory that is rarely considered but uniquely suited to probing subtleties of family life.

Daughters versus sons and parental well-being. Our interest in differences between sons and daughters drew on the sex-role socialization literature. We hypothesized that parents would report greater "getting ahead" success in adult sons and greater "getting along" success in adult daughters. We also predicted that parents' own well-being would be predicted by the interpersonal success of daughters and the attainment success of sons. Finally, because of higher similarity in same-sex dyads, we predicted that fathers' well-being would be more strongly linked with social comparisons with sons, whereas mothers' well-being would be more strongly tied to social comparisons with daughters. Parental responsibility ratings were also predicted to show stronger linkage to well-being in same-sex, parent-child dyads.

Sons and daughters were not, however, seen by parents to have "turned out" with differential strengths. Mean level analyses of their adjustment and attainment indicated no "getting along" advantages for daughters or "getting ahead" strengths for sons. These similarities may reflect social change, that is, these sons and daughters represent a cohort that has enjoyed opportunities in multiple domains, as evidenced by their comparable levels of educational and occupational attainment. Research on contemporary parents further shows more similarities than differences between ratings of sons and daughters than were reported by parents of earlier eras (Intons-Peterson 1985; Aberle and Nagle 1952).

Despite these similarities, gender differences were prominent when ratings of children were linked with parental well-being. Sons' attainment success was found to account for more variance in parental outcomes, as predicted. In the adjustment realm, however, it was again sons who explained greatest variance in parental well-being. Interaction effects further clarified that parents' self-acceptance, autonomy, and depression were strongly linked to sons' interpersonal adjustment, whereas weak associations were obtained for daughters. This unexpected finding may be explained, paradoxically, by the fact that interpersonal success is less "expected" from sons than daughters. Prior social psychological research has shown that disconfirmation of expectations has greater affective consequences than confirmation (Carlsmith and Aronson 1963). That parents saw their sons as comparable with their daughters (mean level analyses) in the interpersonal realm may thus reflect a positive disconfirmation of expectations, with accompanying consequences for well-being. This disconfirmation interpretation should have been matched with parallel findings for daughters in the attainment realm (i.e., daughters' attainment should have been more strongly tied to parental well-being), which was not the case. We speculate that had attainment ratings been more evaluative in nature ("How *well* has your daughter done occupationally?"), the results may have shown greater positive disconfirmation effects for daughters.

Support for the same-sex comparison effects was evident for mothers. Mothers' comparisons with daughters' attainment, but not sons', contributed significant increments in maternal ratings of self-acceptance, environmental mastery, autonomy, and depression. The direction of all effects was negative (positive for depression)—mothers who perceived that their daughters had done better than themselves in getting an education and in achieving occupational success had lower well-being. Similar but less pervasive effects were found for the adjustment domain—mothers who perceived their daughters' adjustment as better than their own had lower self-acceptance and a trend toward higher depression.

These findings, particularly the attainment effects, may be related to differences in career opportunities for mother and daughter cohorts. Such differences are underscored by the finding that fathers had significantly higher education and income levels than did mothers, whereas sons and daughters have comparable levels of attainment in education and occupation. Thus, these mothers may have watched

413

their daughters grow into adulthood in an era quite different from their own early adulthood. While increased opportunities for women represent positive social change, such advances may leave older cohorts of women regretful about their own missed opportunities and, hence, vulnerable to negative self-evaluations when comparing themselves with their daughters. This interpretation is strengthened by the finding that mothers with higher levels of education showed more positive well-being as they perceived their children to have attained more than themselves.

On the paternal side, little support was found for the prediction that comparisons with sons would have greater predictive influence on the well-being of fathers. Attainment comparisons, with sons or daughters, did not explain any variance in fathers' ratings of themselves. Comparisons in the interpersonal and adjustment domains revealed significant effects, but here it was comparisons with daughters, not sons, that explained more paternal variance. A possible explanation invokes theories of individual development at midlife. Jung (1933) and Neugarten and Gutmann (1968) have described gender crossovers at midlife, whereby men begin to identify with their nurturant qualities and women begin to identify with their agentic or assertive qualities. Thus, for midlife men, self-evaluations in the interpersonal domain may be especially salient. The midlife push for self-evaluation coupled with possibly low levels of perceived competence in newly important life domains may make fathers (and mothers, in the attainment domain) vulnerable to unfavorable social comparisons.

Parents' assessments of responsibility for their children's adjustment and attainment revealed differences between sons and daughters, but here it was the cross-sex dyads that were most prominent. Mothers who saw themselves as having exercised little responsibility for sons' adjustment had lower well-being (self-acceptance, environmental mastery, purpose in life, higher depression), while regression slopes for daughters were not significantly different from zero. For fathers, it was the sense of low responsibility for daughters' adjustment that was significantly linked with lower levels of personal growth. Only one interaction effect was obtained in the attainment domain: for mothers, the perception that they exercised low responsibility for sons was associated with lower purpose in life, whereas daughters' attainment was not significantly related to this outcome.

We note that the same-sex dyadic predictions received greater support in the analyses of parents' personal comparisons with their chil-

414

dren, whereas cross-sex effects were more prominent in analyses of parents' responsibility ratings. Thus, as Tesser (1986, 1991) suggests, high similarity in comparisons between parent and child, particularly between mothers and daughters, appears to be an important influence on maternal self-evaluation. In the attributional realm, however, it is mothers' sense of responsibility for son's adjustment that is most strongly linked with their own well-being. Presumably, adjustment is the maternal domain (i.e., mothers saw themselves as holding greater responsibility for adjustment, and they rated their own relations with others as better than did fathers). Because of this sexual division, mothers may see sons as the more critical test of their maternal involvement in personal and interpersonal matters, and hence, it is responsibility ratings for sons' adjustment that are most strongly tied to mothers' well-being.

In summary, we observed similarities in how parents evaluated daughters' and sons' life success. Sons' lives, however, were better predictors of parental well-being, particularly in terms of sons' interpersonal and personal adjustment. Social comparisons with daughters, in turn, showed strong predictive effects, especially for mothers' well-being. For responsibility ratings, it was again assessments of sons that were most influential for mothers' well-being. The overall pattern of findings brought to the fore issues of social change, such as discrepant opportunities between the mother and daughter cohorts, as well as issues of individual development, suggesting heightened salience of certain domains of personal comparison for midlife parents.

Self-enhancement biases and questions of directional influence. We acknowledged at the outset that in the background of our inquiry looms the possibility that parents are biased reporters of how their children have turned out. Such bias may well be expected, given the extensive effort required to raise children and the pervasive view that parents play important roles in their children's development. Our data suggest, however, that parents do not see their children as perfect products— parental ratings of children across the domains of assessment were not uniformly high. It is, in fact, the range of variability among parental ratings of children that renders them powerful predictors in the preceding regression analyses.

Further evidence against self-enhancement biases (Taylor 1989; Taylor and Brown 1988; Wood 1989) pertains to parents' ratings of how they personally compared with their children across various life domains. Our data indicated that parents generally viewed both sons and daughters as having *exceeded* their own young adult accomplishments across all three life domains. That is, mean scores across these comparison items gave advantage to children (see Schmutte and Ryff 1994). The fact that these comparisons were, in turn, *negative* predictors of parents' own well-being further contradicts claims of self-enhancement bias. Similarly, the responsibility analyses did not support the predicted hedonic bias, whereby parents of unsuccessful children would feel better about themselves if they saw themselves as having little responsibility for their children's lives. Instead, we found that parents with lowest well-being were those who reported less successful children *and* viewed themselves as having exercised little parental responsibility. Overall, these patterns suggest that parents' views of children constitute a realm of honest, if painful, life appraisal.

In an effort to obtain additional evidence to validate the accuracy of these parental reports, we collected data (within a year of the initial data collection) from spouses of the parent respondents (see Ryff et al. 1994). This sample consisted of 139 spouses, which represented an 81 percent response rate among married respondents. Telephone interviews were conducted with these spouses, using shortened but parallel forms of the measures employed with the target parents. Spouses were interviewed about a maximum of two children per family (selected to maintain a balance of sons and daughters and to maximize variability in the ratings of children, based on data collected earlier from target parents).

These data showed very high parent/spouse intercorrelations for reports of the same children's education ($r = .80$ to $.93$), personal adjustment ($r = .54$ to $.61$), and social relations ($r = .55$ to $.62$). These coefficients were contrasted with parent/spouse correlations for reports for *different* children: the latter were all nonsignificant and close to zero. Agreement between parents in assessments of same children was also contrasted with intercorrelations between spouses' own levels of psychological well-being ($r = .03$ to $.31$). Thus, parents were quite discrepant in their views about their own well-being, although they indicated strong convergence in how they assessed their children.

Such findings address not only the validity of parents' reports about their children but also questions of directional influence between parents' rating of children and their ratings of themselves. Our guiding conceptual model suggests that parents' views of how children turn out influence their own psychological well-being, but it is also possible that parents' well-being influences how they construe the lives of their children. Parents with positive views of themselves may tend to see their children as healthy and happy, whereas parents with negative self-assessments may focus on the limitations of their children. Time-ordered data, beyond the scope of the present project, are ultimately necessary to resolve such questions, but our findings do offer points of clarification. As noted above, the data point to high convergence between spouses in how children are evaluated, even though there is limited correspondence between spouses' own levels of well-being. Such data are inconsistent with the view that it is parents' well-being that "drives" how they construe their children. We found instead that spouses with discrepant levels of well-being reported similar evaluations of children. In addition, our regression analyses for sons and daughters showed that the relationship between children's functioning and parental well-being *differed* as a function of child gender (Schmutte and Ryff 1994). Were the reverse causality operative (i.e., parental well-being determines child ratings), we would not observe differential predictive effects of children's success ratings on parental well-being. Finally, we note that our proposed model of causal directionality is consistent with a recent metanalysis (Richters 1992), which showed no evidence of distortion in depressed mothers' assessments of their children.

Future Directions

This program of research has addressed how midlife parents think their grown children have turned out and have related these assessments to their views of themselves. Overall, the findings show that self-evaluations in the middle years of adulthood are strongly linked to perceptions of adult children, particularly children's personal and social adjustment. Parental well-being is also linked with parents' views of how they compare with their children and their assessments of the degree to which they have been involved in and responsible for children's lives. These social psychological mechanisms illuminate how parents' mental health is tied to the products of their parental efforts.

The research agenda is usefully expanded in several directions. Issues that warrant further investigation include the variability of children within families and whether parents' well-being is tied more strongly to particular children (e.g., the "bad apple" hypothesis). How specific child characteristics (e.g., age, birth order, personality) influence the linkage between children's life outcomes and parental self-evaluation is also of interest. Variability ensuing from macrolevel influences would be profitably examined via social class differences in what parents expect from grown children and in how they evaluate their accomplishments and are influenced by their lives. Earlier research has examined childrearing practices from a class perspective (e.g., Kohn 1977), but the present agenda would broaden the inquiry to encompass questions of whether parents at different locations in the social structure are differentially influenced by how their children turn out. Cultural contrasts, especially with contexts where mothers are assigned primary responsibility for the educational achievements of children (e.g., Japan, Korea), would also illuminate variations in the linkage of children's life outcomes with parental well-being.

Because the evaluation of self and other is unavoidably subjective, this line of inquiry is also fruitfully augmented with input from grown children. That is, how do they evaluate themselves, their parents, and the quality of parenting they received? What is their assessment on how their own lives compare with those of their parents, and how do they construe the extent of parental involvement in their own growth and development? These questions lead directly to explorations of the fit between children's and parents' constructions of themselves, each other, and their interconnections. Shared versus discrepant realities, in turn, are usefully examined in terms of their consequences for the psychological well-being of both children and parents.

Finally, all the above issues would be sharpened by longitudinal tracking of specific events and transitions that punctuate the lives of parents and children. The assumption is that parents' evaluations of children and of themselves are brought into high relief during times of change in children's lives (e.g., when children themselves become parents, when they experience occupational advancements or setbacks). Similarly, events in the lives of parents (e.g., retirement, death of their own parents) may prompt heightened awareness of how grown children influence their lives. In short, parents' and children's views of each other and of themselves are perhaps most informative when anchored in the substantive experiences of their separate and interconnected lives.

NOTE

1. Parents also provided ratings of the importance they attached to their children's adjustment and attainment (two importance items were asked for each domain). These items revealed mean level differences between mothers and fathers

418

(see table 10.2), but they had no significant influence in any of the regression analyses. The probable reason for the latter was a skewed distribution—parents uniformly endorsed high importance.

REFERENCES

Aberle, D. F., and K. D. Nagle. 1952. Middle-class father's occupational role and attitudes toward children. *American Journal of Orthopsychiatry* 22:366–378.

Allport, G. W. 1961. *Pattern and growth in personality.* New York: Holt, Rinehart, and Winston.

Alwin, D. F. 1989. Changes in qualities valued in children in the United States, 1964 to 1984. *Social Science Research* 18:195–236.

———. 1990. Historical changes in parental orientations to children. In N. Mandell, ed., *Sociological studies in child development.* Vol. 3. Greenwich, Conn.: JAI.

Bakan, D. 1966. *The duality of human existence: Isolation and communion in Western man.* Boston: Beacon.

Bem, S. L. 1974. The measurement of psychological androgyny. *Journal of Clinical and Consulting Psychology* 42:155–162.

Birren, J. E., and V. J. Renner. 1980. Concepts of mental health and aging. In J. E. Birren and R. B. Sloane, eds., *Handbook of mental health and aging,* pp. 3–33. Englewood Cliffs, N.J.: Prentice-Hall.

Bowlby, J. 1951. *Maternal care and mental health.* Geneva: World Health Organization.

———. 1969. *Attachment and loss.* Vol. 1. New York: Basic.

Buhler, C., and F. Massarik, eds. 1968. *The course of human life.* New York: Springer.

Carlsmith, J. M., and E. Aronson. 1963. Some hedonistic consequences of the confirmation and disconfirmation of expectancies. *Journal of Abnormal and Social Psychology* 66:151–156.

Dix, T. 1992. Parenting on behalf of the child: Empathic goals in the regulation of responsive parenting. In I. E. Sigel, A. V. McGillicuddy-DeLisi, and J. J. Goodnow, eds., *Parental belief systems: The psychological consequences for children,* 2d ed., pp. 319–346. Hillsdale, N.J.: Lawrence Erlbaum.

Erikson, E. 1959. Identity and the life cycle. *Psychological Bulletin* 95:542–575.

Erikson, E. H., J. M. Erikson, and H. Q. Kivnick. 1986. *Vital involvement in old age.* New York: W. W. Norton.

Featherman, D. L., and G. Stevens. 1982. A revised socioeconomic index of occupational status: Application in analysis of sex differences in attainment. In R. M. Hauser, D. Mechanic, A. O. Holler, and T. Hauser, eds., *Social structure and behavior,* pp. 141–181. New York: Academic.

Festinger, L. 1954. A theory of social comparison processes. *Human Relations* 7: 117–140.

Freud, S. [1905] 1955. Three essays on the theory of sexuality. In J. Strachey, ed., *The standard edition of the complete psychological works of Sigmund Freud,* 7: 125–145. London: Hogarth.

Goodnow, J. 1988. Parents' ideas, actions, and feelings: Models and methods from developmental and social psychology. *Child Development* 59:286–320.

Goodnow, J. J. 1995. Parents' knowledge and expectations. In M. H. Bornstein, ed., *Handbook of parenting.* Vol. 3, *Status and social conditions of parenting,* pp. 305–332. Mahwah, N.J.: Lawrence Erlbaum.

Goodnow, J. J., and W. A. Collins. 1990. *Development according to parents: The nature, sources, and consequences of parents' ideas.* Hillsdale, N.J.: Lawrence Erlbaum.

Gretarsson, S., and D. Gelfand. 1988. Mothers' attributions regarding children's social behavior and personality characteristics. *Developmental Psychology* 24: 264–269.

Heidrich, S., and C. D. Ryff. 1993. The role of social comparisons processes in the psychological adaptation of elderly adults. *Journal of Gerontology* 48:P127–P136.

Himelstein, S., S. Graham, and B. Weiner. 1991. An attributional analysis of maternal beliefs about the importance of child-rearing practices. *Child Development* 62:301–310.

Hogan, R., W. Jones, and J. M. Cheek. 1985. Socioanalytic theory: An alternative to armadillo psychology. In R. B. Schlenker, ed., *The self and social life,* pp. 175–198. New York: McGraw-Hill.

Intons-Peterson, M. J. 1985. Father's expectations and aspirations for their children. *Sex Roles* 12 (7/8):877–895.

Jahoda, M. 1958. *Current concepts of positive mental health.* New York: Basic.

Jung, C. G. 1933. *Modern man in search of a soul.* Trans. W. S. Dell and C. F. Baynes. New York: Harcourt, Brace, and World.

Kohn, M. L. 1977. *Class and conformity: A study in values.* 2d ed. Chicago: University of Chicago Press.

Kruglanski, A. W., and O. Mayseless. 1990. Classic and current social comparison research: Expanding the perspective. *Psychological Bulletin* 108:195–208.

Langlois, J. H., and A. C. Downs. 1980. Mothers, fathers, and peers as socialization agents of sex-typed play behaviors in young children. *Child Development* 51: 1217–1247.

LeVine, R. A. 1974. Parental goals: A cross-cultural view. *Teachers College* 76 (2): 226–239.

———. 1988. Human parental care: Universal goals, cultural strategies, individual behavior. In R. A. LeVine, P. M. Miller and M. M. West, eds., *Parental behavior in diverse societies,* pp. 5–12. San Francisco: Jossey-Bass.

Maslow, A. H. 1968. *Toward a psychology of being.* 2d ed. New York: Van Nostrand.

McGillicuddy-De Lisi, A. V., and I. E. Sigel. 1995. Parental beliefs. In M. H. Bornstein, ed., *Handbook of parenting.* Vol. 3: *Status and social conditions of parenting,* pp. 333–358. Mahwah, N.J.: Lawrence Erlbaum.

Neugarten, B. L. 1973. Personality change in late life: A developmental perspective. In C. Eisdorfer and M. P. Lawton, eds., *The psychology of adult development and aging,* pp. 311–335. Washington, D. C.: American Psychological Association.

Neugarten, B. L., and D. L. Gutmann. 1968. Age-sex role and personality in middle age: A thematic apperception study. In B. L. Neugarten, ed., *Middle age and aging*, pp. 58–71. Chicago: University of Chicago Press.

Parsons, T., and R. F. Bales. 1955. *Family, socialization, and interaction process*. New York: Free Press.

Radloff, L. 1977. The CES-D scale: A self-report depression scale for research in the general population. *Applied Psychological Measurement* 1:385–401.

Richman, A. L., P. M. Miller, and M. J. Solomon. 1988. The socialization of infants in suburban Boston. In R. A. LeVine, P. M. Miller, and M. M. West, eds., *Parental behavior in diverse societies*, pp. 65–74. San Francisco: Jossey-Bass.

Richters, J. E. 1992. Depressed mothers as informants about their children: A critical review of the evidence of distortion. *Psychological Bulletin* 112:485–499.

Rogers, C. R. 1961. *On becoming a person*. Boston: Houghton Mifflin.

Romer, N. 1981. *The sex-role cycle: Socialization from infancy to old age*. New York: McGraw-Hill.

Ryff, C. D. 1985. Adult personality development and the motivation for personal growth. In D. Kleiber and M. Maehr, eds., *Advances in motivation and achievement*. Vol. 4, *Motivation and adulthood*, pp. 55–92. Greenwich, Conn.: JAI.

———. 1989a. Beyond Ponce de Leon and life satisfaction: New directions in quest of successful aging. *International Journal of Behavioral Development* 12:35–55.

———. 1989b. Happiness is everything, or is it? Explorations on the meaning of psychological well-being. *Journal of Personality and Social Psychology* 57:1069–1081.

———. 1991. Possible selves in adulthood and old age: A tale of shifting horizons. *Psychology and Aging* 6:286–295.

———. 1995. Psychological well-being in adult life. *Current Directions in Psychological Science* 4:99–104.

Ryff, C. D., and M. J. Essex. 1992a. Psychological well-being in adulthood and old age: Descriptive markers and explanatory processes. In K. W. Schaie and M. P. Lawton, eds., *Annual Review of Gerontology and Geriatrics* 11:144–171. New York: Springer.

———. 1992b. The interpretation of life experience and well-being: The sample case of relocation. *Psychology and Aging* 7:507–517.

Ryff, C. D., and C. L. M. Keyes. 1995. The structure of psychological well-being revisited. *Journal of Personality and Social Psychology* 69:719–727.

Ryff, C. D., Y. H. Lee, M. J. Essex, and P. S. Schmutte. 1994. My children and me: Mid-life evaluations of grown children and of self. *Psychology and Aging* 9:195–205.

Ryff, C. D., Y. H. Lee, and K. C. Na. 1995. Through the lens of culture: Psychological well-being at midlife. Unpublished manuscript, University of Wisconsin-Madison.

Ryff, C. D., and P. S. Schmutte. 1995. Parental responsibility for the lives of grown children. Unpublished manuscript, University of Wisconsin-Madison.

Schmutte, P. S., and C. D. Ryff. 1994. Success, social comparison, and self-assessment: Parents' midlife evaluations of sons, daughters, and selves. *Journal of Adult Development* 1:109–126.

Sears, R. R., E. E. Maccoby, and H. Levin. 1957. *Patterns of child rearing.* Evanston: Row, Peterson.

Sigel, I. E., A. V. McGillicuddy-DeLisi, and J. J. Goodnow, eds. 1992. *Parental belief systems: The psychological consequences for children.* 2d ed. Hillsdale, N.J.: Lawrence Erlbaum.

Smelser, N. J., and E. H. Erikson. 1980. *Themes of work and love in adulthood.* Cambridge: Harvard University Press.

Suls, J., and B. Mullen. 1982. From the cradle to the grave: Comparison and self-evaluation across the life span. In J. Suls, ed., *Psychological perspectives on the self,* 1:97–125. Hillsdale, N.J.: Lawrence Erlbaum.

Suls, J., and G. S. Sanders. 1977. Self-evaluation through social comparison: A developmental analysis. In J. M. Suls and R. L. Miller, eds., *Social comparison processes: Theoretical and empirical perspectives,* pp. 171–197. Washington, D.C.: Hemisphere.

Suls, J., and T. A. Wills. 1991. *Social comparison: Contemporary theory and research.* Hillsdale, N.J.: Lawrence Erlbaum.

Taylor, S. E. 1989. *Positive illusions: Creative self-deception and the healthy mind.* New York: Basic.

Taylor, S. E., and J. D. Brown. 1988. Illusion and well-being: A social psychological perspective on mental health. *Psychological Bulletin* 103:193–210.

Tesser, A. 1986. Some effects of self-evaluation maintenance on cognition and action. In R. Sorrentino and E. T. Higgins, eds., *Handbook of motivation and cognition,* pp. 435–464. New York: Guilford.

———. 1991. Emotion in social comparison and reflection processes. In J. Suls and T. A. Wills, eds., *Social comparison: Contemporary theory and research,* pp. 115–145. Hillsdale, N.J.: Lawrence Erlbaum.

Van Riper, M., C. D. Ryff, and K. Pridham. 1992. Parental and family well-being in families of children with down syndrome: A comparative study. *Research in Nursing and Health* 15:227–235.

Wheeler, L., and K. Miyake. 1992. Social comparison in everyday life. *Journal of Personality and Social Psychology* 62:760–773.

Wiggins, J. S. 1991. Agency and communion as conceptual coordinates for the understanding and measurement of interpersonal behavior. In W. M. Gove and D. Cicchetti, eds., *Thinking clearly about psychology.* Vol. 2, *Personality and psychopathology.* Minneapolis: University of Minnesota Press.

Wood, J. V. 1989. Theory and research concerning social comparisons of personal attributes. *Psychological Bulletin* 106:231–248.

Wood, J. V., and K. L. Taylor. 1991. Serving self-relevant goals through social comparison. In J. Suls and T. A. Wills, eds., *Social comparison: Contemporary theory and research,* pp. 23–50. Hillsdale, N.J.: Lawrence Erlbaum.

ELEVEN

The Returning Adult Child and Parental Experience at Midlife

William S. Aquilino

Change in parental experience as children move from adolescence to young adulthood is a neglected area of research in midlife adult development. There has been little research describing the impact of children's transitions into adult roles on parents' life experiences and well-being. In this chapter I focus on one category of young adult transitions: the home-leaving process and, specifically, the propensity of adult children to return to the nest and the effects of such returns on parents.

How might parents' lives be affected by the home-leaving process? Empirical literature on parenthood and adult well-being suggests that having children in the home has negative consequences for parents of any age (Glenn and Weaver 1979; Goetting 1986; McLanahan and Adams 1987; Lee 1988; Umberson and Gove 1989; White, Booth, and Edwards 1986; White and Edwards 1990). Raising children has been associated with lower happiness and life satisfaction and higher levels of psychological distress, for both men and women (McLanahan and Adams 1987). The transition to empty nest, in contrast, has been linked to an upturn in parents' psychological well-being (Glenn 1975; McLanahan and Adams 1989; Menaghan 1983; Umberson and Gove 1989) and in marital happiness (White and Edwards 1990). Most parents look forward to their years without children in the home, and few empty-nest–stage parents savor the prospect of an adult child's return (Aldous 1987; Clemens and Axelson 1985; Hoffman and Manis 1978).

In studying the home-leaving process and its implications for parents, I take the position that movements into and out of the home by

This research was supported by a MacArthur Foundation grant to Professor Larry Bumpass. The National Survey of Families and Households was funded by a grant (HD21009) from the Center for Population Research of the National Institute for Child Health and Human Development. The survey was designed and carried out at the Center for Demography and Ecology at the University of Wisconsin-Madison under the direction of Larry Bumpass and James Sweet. The fieldwork was done by the Institute for Survey Research at Temple University.

adult offspring reflect a critical aspect in the lifelong development of the parent-child relationship: change in children's autonomy and dependency vis-à-vis parents over the life course of the relationship. The changing nature of young adult children's dependency and autonomy should have major implications for parent-child relations and for parental experiences when parent and adult child coreside (Ward and Spitze 1992).

This chapter addresses three general questions concerning young adult children's propensity to return home:

(1) What is the prevalence of returning home in a current cohort of young adults?

(2) Under what circumstances are returns to the parental home most likely among young adults who have left home at least once? This involves developing a multivariate predictive model for returns to the nest among young adults.

(3) What factors influence parental satisfaction with having a coresident "returned" adult child, and what factors influence the quality of parent-child interaction after an adult child has returned home?

Data from the 1987–88 National Survey of Families and Households (NSFH) will be presented throughout the chapter (see Sweet, Bumpass, and Call 1988 for a full description of the dataset). The NSFH collected and detailed family life interviews from 13,017 respondents drawn through a multistage area probability sample of the coterminous United States. Personal interviews averaging 102 minutes in length were conducted from March 1987 to May 1988. One respondent per household was randomly selected from residents aged nineteen or over. Data have been weighted to reflect sampling probabilities, nonresponse, and the age, sex, and race structure of the U.S. adult population. Analyses of home-leaving and returning behavior are based on the subsample of nineteen- to thirty-four-year-old NSFH primary respondents who had left home at least once (N = 4,922). The four hundred respondents in this age group who had never left home are excluded from analysis.

PREVALENCE OF RETURNING HOME IN YOUNG ADULTHOOD

Although parent–adult child coresidence is generally considered a "nonnormative" event in parenthood, it is quite astounding how prevalent a nonnormative event it is. Nearly half (45 percent) of NSFH parents of forty-five to fifty-four years of age who have children aged

TABLE 11.1. Weighted Percentages of Young Adults Ever Returning
Home, among NSFH Respondents Aged 19–34
Who Had Left Home at Least Once

	Total Sample (N = 4,922)	Men (N = 2,009)	Women (N = 2,913)
Total ever returned	42.4%	46.2%	38.9%
Age category			
19–24	44.3	52.0	37.4
25–29	42.9	45.4	40.7
30–34	40.2	41.8	38.7
Race/ethnicity			
Black	42.9	49.3	38.5
White	43.4	47.5	39.6
Chicano	36.6	32.1	42.0
Other	33.6	39.4	28.9
Age at first home leaving			
12–17	47.2	55.0	40.4
18–21	43.7	46.6	41.0
22–25	23.4	26.4	19.7
26 or older	18.6	14.1	22.1

nineteen or older have an adult child living at home (Aquilino 1990; Marks, chapter 2, this volume). Census data show that parent–adult child coresidence increased modestly during the 1980s (Glick and Lin 1986). From the child's perspective, NSFH data show that three out of four nineteen- to thirty-four-year-olds in a recent cohort had lived in a parental household for some time after turning nineteen.

What is the likelihood that young adult children will return home after leaving to be on their own? The weighted estimates in table 11.1 are based on the 4,922 respondents who had left home at least once. The tabulations rely on responses to two questions: (1) How old were you the first time you left home to be on your own for four months or more? (2) Did you ever move back home for four months or more, other than for school vacations?

As shown in table 11.1, among those nineteen to thirty-four who left home at least once, slightly over 42 percent have returned home to live with parents at some time. Returns to the nest are more common among men than women. The propensity to return home appears to have increased among men over the last fifteen years, with men aged nineteen to twenty-four years much more likely to report a return than those thirty to thirty-four years old. Over half of this youngest cohort of men had returned home after leaving. This is an underestimate for this cohort since some of the younger cohort members will return at some future time. There appears to be little cohort trend among women.

One implication of these estimates is that parents with two or more children are more likely than not to have at least one adult child return home after leaving. If we had life history data on the home-leaving careers of all adult children of the parents in the NSFH, we would undoubtedly see that having an "emancipated" child move back in is a quite normative experience for parents with multiple children. As Marks (chapter 2, this volume) points out, relatively few midlife parents may fit into the socially expectable or "ideal" pattern of having all children leave home once and for good.

Using the subsample of those twenty-five to thirty-four years old who were not currently living at home, I also computed the average length of time between first home leaving and first return, the amount of time spent at home before leaving again, and the proportion who returned more than once (see table 11.2). A large number of returns occur quickly—40 percent of adult children who returned did so within about a year or less of their first home leaving, and nearly 60 percent, within two years. Overall, 90 percent of first returns occurred within five years after leaving home. Given that the median age of first home leaving is about eighteen, the bulk of such returns occur in children's early to to midtwenties.

Spells of living with parents after returning are also relatively short. About one-quarter stay less than one year, and fully two-thirds remain with parents less than two years; 90 percent of these spells after first return home are less than four years in duration. Although these returning adults may leave home again fairly soon, it still may not be their final home leaving. Fully twenty-five percent of returnees returned a second time (or, a little over ten percent of young adults in the NSFH had returned home more than once).

These NSFH estimates reinforce the notion that children's home leaving is often not a single event in either their lives or in their parents' lives. Home leaving is best construed as a *process* of separation for many children. For the majority of parents, the launching and empty-nest phases of the family life cycle play out over many years—from the first home leaving of one of their children to the last home leaving of the

Table 11.2. Length of Interval before Returning, Length of Spells Living with Parents after Returning, and Probability of Multiple Returns, among NSFH Respondents Aged 25–34 Returning Home at Least Once

	Total Sample (N = 1,444)	Men (N = 616)	Women (N = 828)
Length of interval between home leaving and first return			
Less than 1 year	13.5%	12.2%	14.9%
1 year	26.3	25.0	27.5
2 years	19.5	20.1	18.9
3 years	11.7	11.3	12.2
4 years	13.0	14.6	11.4
5 years	6.0	6.6	5.3
6 years or more	10.0	10.2	9.9
Length of spell living with parents after first return			
Less than 1 year	26.3%	26.5%	26.0%
1 year	39.2	35.6	42.6
2 years	16.3	17.5	15.1
3 years	7.2	7.7	6.8
4 years or more	10.9	12.7	9.3
Percentage of returnees who returned more than once	25.4%	25.8%	25.1%

last of their children. For parents with three children spaced two to three years apart, for example, this phase of the life cycle could easily span a decade or more, with multiple transitions to empty nest during the period.

These findings have implications for interpreting the extensive body of cross-sectional research that compares empty-nest parents to parents with coresident children. The cross-sectional approach gives the impression, unwittingly, that the empty nest transition is quite abrupt, with positive effects on parental well-being immediately following the last child's departure. Cross-sectional comparisons thus do not present an accurate picture of parental experience during the early adult phases of their children's lives. They do not reflect the sometimes frequent comings and goings of children or parents' level of involvement with children when they live elsewhere.

PREDICTING ADULT CHILDREN'S RETURNS TO THE NEST

Under what conditions are adult children most likely to return to the nest? My approach to answering this question reflects a life-course perspective on family development (Elder 1977; Elder, Caspi, and Burton 1988; Elder, Caspi, and Downy 1986). This framework emphasizes the linkages between the intra-individual development of family members and change in family relationships.

The life-course perspective applied to family change emphasizes the interdependence of family members' life histories. Individual life-course transitions reverberate through a network of interwoven and interdependent lives, similar to the concept of life-event webs described by Pruchno, Blow, and Smyer in 1984. A key concept is that interactions between life careers occur across generations in the family, so that voluntary transitions or life decisions of one family member create sometimes involuntary changes for others in the family (Hagestad 1981, 1984). Children's decisions concerning home leaving, for example, move parents, voluntarily or not, into the launching and empty-nest phases of the family life cycle.

In applying this framework to the propensity of adult children to return home, I focus on the individual transitions and life trajectories of both children and parents. Specifically, I hypothesized that the likelihood of returning home is a function of: (1) *young adult transitions* in the areas of marriage and cohabitation, parenthood, work, schooling, military service, and timing of home leaving; and (2) *parental factors*, focusing on parents' marital transitions and decisions concerning custody of their children. These aspects of parents' life histories determine the variety of living situations and family structures that children will experience while growing up. Both sets of predictors reflect the implications of transitions in one generation in the family for other generations and are thus a good example of the interdependency of life trajectories within the family.

Empirical Literature and Hypotheses

Young adult transitions. Findings on returning home among young adults (DaVanzo and Goldscheider 1990) show that transitions involving marriage, school, employment, military service, and parenthood have significant effects on the odds of a return. Research on home leaving consistently shows that marriage is the single strongest influence on children's movement out of the parental home (Aquilino 1990;

DaVanzo and Goldscheider 1990; Goldscheider and Goldscheider 1987), whereas adult children's separation and divorce has been associated with increased parent-child coresidence (Aquilino 1991a). Although marriage effects on home leaving have been studied extensively, cohabitation has been all but ignored in this literature. The NSFH provides detailed life history data on cohabitation, with dates of transitions into and out of cohabiting relationships. I predicted that transitions into and out of cohabiting unions would have the same impact on the likelihood of returns as marriage and marital dissolution: getting married or beginning a cohabitation should reduce the probability of returns; marital dissolution or ending a cohabiting relationship should raise the probability of returns.

Leaving school or ending military service should increase the probability of returns, since many young adults may need a temporary place to stay during periods between the major transitions of young adulthood (DaVanzo and Goldscheider 1990), such as the period between the end of schooling and the beginning of occupational career. These are among the most common reasons adults give for returning home and were mentioned by 29 percent of NSFH respondents who had ever returned home.

DaVanzo and Goldscheider (1990) found that employment transitions had less impact than marriage and other normative transitions of young adulthood. However, both getting a job or losing a job were associated with a greater chance of a return home. I predicted that employment transitions in general would tend to increase the probability of returns.

The transition to parenthood was predicted to have a negative impact on the probability of returning home. Becoming an unmarried parent has been shown to reduce the likelihood of returns and of parent–adult child coresidence in general (DaVanzo and Goldscheider 1990; Ward, Logan, and Spitze 1992), compared to unmarried adults who are nonparents. Although DaVanzo and Goldscheider (1990) also found that becoming a parent after marriage increased the likelihood of a return, relatively few adults return home while currently married.

I hypothesized that age at first home leaving would be negatively related to the probability of returns. Early home leaving should be associated with a higher likelihood of returning, because children who leave home at young ages may not be prepared to handle the challenge of adult roles and responsibilities.

TABLE 11.3. Definitions for a Categorical Variable Reflecting
Childhood Family Structure

Definition	N cases	%
Intact: lived with both biological parents from birth through age seventeen or until leaving home for the first time (this was the omitted category in regression analyses)	3,240	66.1
Single-parent from birth: born to a single parent and lived in a single-parent household through-out childhood	105	2.1
Intact, then single-parent: lived in single-parent house-hold after parents' marital disruption but never lived with a stepparent or adoptive parent or in a nonparental situation	524	10.7
Stepparent: lived in stepparent household but never with an adoptive parent or in a nonparental situation; three-quarters of these respondents had also lived in a single-parent household before acquiring a stepparent	549	11.2
Adoptive: lived with adoptive parents, regardless of other family types experienced	88	1.8
Nonparental: lived apart from both parents for at least a portion of childhood; the majority of these chil-dren had also lived in single-parent or step-parent families	396	8.1

Childhood family structure. Extant research on home leaving shows that childhood family structure has a substantial impact on both the timing of first home leaving and the pathway out of the parental home. Expo-sure to single-parent families, stepparent families, adoptive families, and nonparental living situations (defined in table 11.3) leads to chil-dren's earlier home leaving (Aquilino 1991a; Mitchell, Wister, and Burch 1989; White and Booth 1985), increases the probability of an early transition to residential independence, and decreases the likeli-hood of leaving to attend school (Aquilino 1991a). Among the nonin-tact family types, adoption and nonparental living arrangements exert the strongest influence on home leaving.

The impact of single-parent family experience on home leaving var-ies according to the stability of childhood family structure (Aquilino 1991a). NSFH data show that remaining in a single-parent home after family disruption significantly increased the chances of early emancipation. The home-leaving patterns of children who lived in a stable single-parent family from birth did not differ from children in intact families.

My expectation was that childhood family structure would have the same effects on the probability of returning home as it has on the timing of first home leaving. Children who experienced single-parent, stepparent, and adoptive families would be less likely to return home as young adults than children who lived with both biological parents only. Further, children who had ever experienced nonparental living situations, such as living with relatives, foster parents, or in institutions, would be less likely to return to a parental home than children from intact families.

Analysis

Logistic regression was used to model first returns to the parental household (subsequent returns were not considered). The dependent variable was coded one if the respondent had returned home within a specified time frame, and zero, otherwise. Independent variables included the occurrence of young adult role transitions, age at home leaving, childhood family structure, and family socioeconomic status (SES) during childhood.

Three separate models were fit: the first predicted returns within one year of home leaving; the second, within two to three years; and the third, within four to five years of home leaving. The analysis was broken into these narrow time frames to allow for valid comparisons on the adult role transitions variables between young adults who had returned home and those who had not. Dummy variables were constructed indicating whether transitions involving marriage, cohabitation, parenthood, employment, education, and military service had occurred (1) within the specified time frame in each model, and (2) causally before the first return (see table 11.4 for the list of dummy variables). For returnees, transitions were counted only if they occurred before their first return, a fairly short period of time for most adults who return home, often less than two years. This restriction obviously did not apply to young adults who never returned. For accurate comparison, then, I needed to define time frames for the occurrence of events that would be roughly equivalent in length between returnees and nonreturnees.

In addition to adult role transitions, predictors in the model in-

TABLE 11.4. Weighted Percentages of Young Adults Returning
Home, by Transitions of Young Adulthood: NSFH Respondents
Aged 19–34 Who Had Left Home at Least Once

Transitions	% Returning within 1 Year (N = 4,562)	% Returning within 2–3 Years (N = 3,645)[a]	% Returning within 4–5 Years (N = 2,767)[b]
Married	8.4	8.3	3.9
Separated or divorced	35.3	30.0	16.0
Became a parent	10.9	9.1	3.8
Began cohabiting	16.7	15.8	7.8
Stopped cohabiting	29.9	25.7	17.0
Began working	21.0	19.2	16.5
Stopped working	16.9	15.3	6.9
Began postsecondary school	20.6	18.0	10.8
Ended postsecondary school	28.8	17.9	19.0
Left military	35.9	29.9	30.5
TOTAL RETURNED	19.2	16.1	11.7

[a]Respondents who returned within one year are excluded from this column.
[b]Respondents who returned within three years are excluded from this column.

cluded childhood family structure; age at first home leaving; current
age, sex, and race of respondent; and two indicators of family SES:
mother's education and whether the family ever received public assistance while the child was growing up. Six mutually exclusive categories
of family structure were constructed: intact (the omitted category),
single-parent from birth, single-parent after marital dissolution, stepparent, adoptive, and nonparental living situations (see table 11.3 for
definitions). Several independent variables had no net effects on returns and were dropped from the models: number of siblings (family
size), birth order, ever lived with step- or half-siblings, and mother-
child age difference.

Results

Predictions concerning role transitions were generally supported in
all three models (see table 11.5). Change in marital status had large
and highly significant effects across all three models in the expected
direction. Marriage decreased the likelihood of returns, while separa-

Table 11.5. Logit Models Predicting Returns to the Parental Home: NSFH Respondents Aged 19–34 (standard errors in parentheses)

Independent	Likelihood of Returning within 1 Year (N = 4,562)	Likelihood of Returning within 2–3 Years (N = 3,645)[a]	Likelihood of Returning within 4–5 Years (N = 2,767)[b]
Transitions			
Got married	−1.20 (.13)***	−.89 (.15)***	−1.50 (.27)***
Separated/divorced	1.54 (.24)***	1.01 (.18)***	.75 (.22)***
Began cohabiting	−.40 (.15)**	−.10 (.15)	−.70 (.28)*
Stopped cohabiting	.58 (.21)**	.51 (.19)**	.51 (.27)†
Began school	−.42 (.10)***	−.04 (.13)	−.85 (.20)***
Ended school	.90 (.10)***	.12 (.12)	1.15 (.18)***
Left military	—	.66 (.23)**	1.65 (.25)***
Began working	−.01 (.09)	.28 (.11)*	.11 (.16)
Stopped working	.03 (.14)	.07 (.15)	−.43 (.23)†
Became a parent	−.37 (.15)*	−.61 (.14)***	−.98 (.27)***
Age at first home leaving	−.11 (.02)***	−.04 (.02)†	−.11 (.04)**
Childhood family structure (vs. intact)			
Single-family only	−.61 (.35)†	.16 (.35)	−.59 (.68)
Single-family after marital dissolution	−.24 (.13)†	−.17 (.17)	−.02 (.21)
Stepfamily	−.30 (.13)*	.05 (.15)	−.31 (.23)
Adopted	−.10 (.27)	−.65 (.40)	−.05 (.43)
Nonparental situation	−.90 (.19)***	−.41 (.20)*	−1.02 (.32)**
Sex (female)	−.04 (.08)	−.26 (.10)**	−.16 (.13)
Race (vs. white/other)			
Black	−.04 (.13)	−.04 (.16)	.50 (.20)*
Chicano	−.37 (.19)†	−.04 (.21)	−.04 (.33)
Age of respondent	−.06 (.01)***	−.03 (.01)*	−.06 (.02)***
Mother's education	−.02 (.02)	−.01 (.02)	.01 (.02)
Mother's education missing	−.02 (.02)	−.47 (.21)*	−.22 (.27)
Family ever received public assistance	.19 (.13)	.16 (.15)	−.57 (.25)*

[a]Respondents who returned within one year are excluded from these analyses.
[b]Respondents who returned within three years are excluded from these analyses.
†p = .06. *p < .05. **p < .01. ***p < .001.

tion and divorce greatly increased its likelihood. Similar results were obtained for the initiation and ending of cohabiting relationships, although the size of the effects is smaller than for change in marital status.

The effects of beginning a union may reflect American cultural norms that young couples live independently of parents and establish their own nuclear family. The effects for ending a union suggest that, for many young adults, the parental home remains a haven during hard times, given the often heightened emotional and financial difficulties after a parting.

As expected, leaving school and ending military service strongly increased the chances of returning. Also, those who began postsecondary school were less likely to return in all three time frames. These findings point to young adults' use of the parental home as a temporary way station in making the transition from student or soldier to work and family roles. Returns in these circumstances do not necessarily represent a retreat from the march toward independence.

As hypothesized, the transition to parenthood was associated with a decreased likelihood of returning to the nest. The return of sons and daughters with their own dependent children marks a much greater disruption of parents' lifestyle and living arrangements than the return of an adult child alone. For parents, it can mean moving from the empty nest to heading a three-generation household, a drastic change that many parents might resist.

Few significant effects were found for employment transitions. Contrary to expectations, losing a job was not associated with an increased probability of returning. There was some indication (in model 2) that starting a job is positively related to returning. This is consistent with DaVanzo and Goldscheider's (1990) findings that some young adults use the parental home for support when making employment transitions.

As expected, age at home leaving was negatively associated with the probability of returns in all three models, suggesting that many children leave home before they have the means to establish and maintain an independent lifestyle. Inspection of the raw data (see table 11.1) shows a demarcation line quite clearly—those who left home at age twenty-one or sooner were about twice as likely to return home as those who left at age twenty-two or older.

Hypotheses concerning childhood family structure were supported in model 1 only. Adults who experienced single-parent families or step-parent families while growing up had a lower probability of returning within one year of home leaving than adults who grew up with both biological parents. Contrary to expectations, the same effect was found for both types of single-parent experience (single-parent from birth and single-parent after marital disruption). Single parents have fewer economic resources to share with adult children (see Marks, chapter 2, this volume), creating a disincentive for children to return home. Prior research (Goldscheider and Goldscheider 1989; White and Booth 1985) suggests that the negative impact of parental remarriage (or having a stepparent) on the probability of returns is due to the more difficult (or strained) parent-child relationships in remarried families. When a stepparent lives in the household, both the parent and child generations expect young adult children to establish early residential independence (Goldscheider and Goldscheider 1989).

By far the strongest family structure effects were found for those who experienced nonparental living situations, that is, who lived apart from both parents at any point while growing up. Strong negative effects of separation from both parents were found in all three models. About two-thirds of the respondents in this category were living in a nonparental situation at the time they left home to be on their own. Thus, many of these young adults essentially had no parental home to return to, or at least may have felt that way. Other than nonparental effects, family structure had little impact in the second and third time frames. It's possible that the impact of childhood experiences wanes over time.

Women were generally less likely to return than men, although the negative coefficient for sex was significant in model 2 only. Race/ethnicity effects were minimal. Blacks were significantly more likely to return than whites/others in model 3 only. Age of respondent was associated with a decreased likelihood of returning in all three models. This reflects cohort differences in propensity to return, with young cohorts more likely to return than older cohorts, which is consistent with a growing literature reporting increases in parent–adult child coresidence since the 1970s (Glick and Lin 1986; Heer, Hodge, and Felson 1985; DaVanzo and Goldscheider 1990).

Conclusions. The multivariate results provide strong support for a life-course perspective that emphasizes linkages among the life trajectories of family members. Parents' risk of having an adult child return home and thus parents' transitions into and out of the empty nest are strongly related to children's progress through the transition to adulthood. The parental home appears to serve as a "normal base of operations" for young adults as they negotiate the transitions of early adulthood that eventually lead to full independence (DaVanzo and Goldscheider 1990). For many young adults, the parental home is a haven when role transitions have failed, such as the breakup of marital and cohabiting relationships.

The main import of these analyses is that parental experience at midlife is tied to the life course of their children, even after they have left home. Children's transitions confront parents with decisions on how much support they can or should give to young adult offspring. Sons and daughters who have been living in "quasi-autonomous" situations while attending college or serving in the military often require additional financial and housing support from parents before making the transition to fully independent living. The breakup of marital and cohabiting relationships may deposit at parents' door young adults in need of both emotional and financial support. Obviously, refilling the nest represents only one form of parental support; parents can extend considerable economic and emotional support to children living elsewhere. Coresidence is, nonetheless, the form of support with the most drastic implications for parents' everyday experience and lifestyle.

IMPACT OF RETURNED ADULT CHILDREN ON PARENTS

The core question in this phase of the analysis was, What factors determine the nature of parental experiences with returned adult children? Given that midlife parents have a returned adult child living in their household, under what conditions does this living arrangement have more positive rather than more negative effects.

The life-course perspective on family development, described earlier in this chapter, guided my approach to these questions. The central challenge of this approach was to identify linkages between children's intraindividual development, on the one hand, and the quality of parent-child relations and parental experience, on the other (Collins and Russell 1991). I propose that this linkage is mediated in part by parents' expectations for their children's development during the young adult years. Parents' expectations for children's development in young adulthood will shape their experiences with adult children during periods of coresidence.

This theoretical framework is similar to the parental expectancies model described by Collins (1992). Throughout childhood and adolescence, according to Collins, children frequently violate parents' behavioral expectancies. Parents must continually modify old expectancies to accommodate children's physical, social, and cognitive development. When typical patterns of parent-child interaction are interrupted by behavior inconsistent with parental expectancies, conflict and emotional arousal occur. Thus, parental expectations and their violation should have a significant impact on the quality of parent-child interaction and on parental experiences. Parental expectations may be most challenged during times of rapid developmental change in children, for example, during the transition to adolescence or the transition to adulthood. This formulation fits well with the life-course framework in addressing the linkages between children's developmental change, parents' adaptations to children's intraindividual development, and parental experiences.

What expectations do parents have concerning the development of young adult children? Although the NSFH provides no data on this, it's likely that parental expectancies center on the life-course changes and role transitions typical of the early adult years (Greene and Boxer 1986; Ward and Spitze 1992). These include home leaving, decisions to leave or enter school or military service, career choice and labor market entry, entry into marriage and cohabiting relationships, the transition to parenthood, and establishing economic independence. Progress through these "normative" young adult transitions should entail a gradual increase in independence from parents and thus represent a continuation of the growing emotional autonomy that is one of the prime developmental tasks of adolescence (Steinberg 1987; Steinberg and Silverberg 1986; Silverberg and Steinberg 1987). This is consistent with the literature on filial maturity (Nydegger 1991), which suggests that a critical transition in adult intergenerational relations is the movement of adult children away from reliance on parental support and care and movement toward acceptance of the role of provider of support and care to aging (and possibly increasingly dependent) parents. From the perspective of parents, I would argue, young adult development should bring about a gradual weaning from parental support and guidance and the eventual establishment of a fully independent lifestyle.

Schnaiberg and Goldenberg (1989) offered a conceptualization of the "incompletely launched young adult" phenomenon that emphasizes such parental expectancies. Their model suggests that young adults' unanticipated economic dependence on parents (due to failure to launch careers) deviates from parental expectations. Returning home after failing to fulfill parental expectations for autonomy fosters anger on the part of both child and parent, resulting in heightened parent-child conflict. At this stage of children's life course, mothers and fathers may measure their success as parents by the ability of their children to demonstrate increasing autonomy.

The central hypothesis flowing from this model is that relations between parents and returned adult children—and parental satisfaction with the coresident living arrangement—will be influenced by the degree to which the returned adult children evidence renewed dependency on parents. Increasing dependency in young adulthood violates parental expectations concerning the life course of their children (Ward and Spitze 1992) and should lead to less parental satisfaction and more conflicted parent-child relations.

Specific Hypotheses

Predictors in the model of parental experience with returned adult children are displayed in table 11.6. Specific hypotheses were derived for four categories of predictors related to dependency: the child's movement toward autonomy, child's economic dependency, health of child and parent, and child's self-esteem.

Child's movement toward autonomy. Young adults who return home will vary in their degree of dependency on parents. Not all returns will be perceived by parents as implying the child's failure to establish an independent lifestyle. One question parents may consider is whether an adult child has a legitimate reason for returning. For example, young adults who return home after completing a college degree will less likely be viewed as returning to long-term dependency on parents than returnees who drop out of school. Some returns could themselves be viewed as an essential step on the road to full autonomy, for example, adult children who return home so that they can afford to enroll in college or other career preparation programs. Parents may have quite different perceptions of children who return after marital dissolution or those whose income or employment status did not allow them to maintain an independent lifestyle. In these cases, the return home is more likely to be viewed as a failure to achieve autonomy.

The general hypothesis was that parents' experiences with returned adult children would be more positive if children's current role status suggested movement toward autonomy rather than renewed dependency on parents. Specifically, I predicted that (a) parental experiences

TABLE 11.6. Means and Standard Deviations for Independent
Variables in a Model Predicting Parental Experiences
with Returned Adult Children (N = 242)

Independent Variables	Mean	SD
Child education (years of school completed)	12.83	2.24
Child enrolled in college	.20	.40
Child marital status (vs. never married)		
Currently married	.12	.33
Separated or divorced	.16	.37
Child's parent status (vs. nonparent)		
Own minor children in household	.21	.41
Minor children living elsewhere	.09	.28
Child financial dependency (average over five items tapping extent to which parent pays for child's food, clothing, health care, transportation, and entertainment; coded 1 = none, 2 = some, 3 = most)	1.69	.62
Child pays monthly room and board	.35	.48
Child earnings income in past year (dollars)	9,183.00	11,366.00
Child health (1 = very poor to 5 = excellent)	4.20	.71
Parent health (1 = very poor to 5 = excellent)	3.96	.82
Child self-esteem (sum over three items coded from 1 = strongly disagree to 5 = strongly agree: I feel that I'm a person of worth, at least on an equal plane with others; on the whole I am satisfied with myself; I am able to do things as well as other people)	12.20	1.65
Parent education (years of school completed)	12.08	3.13
Parent unmarried (separated, divorced, or widowed)	.40	.49
Child age	24.24	3.94
Child race (proportion black)	.19	.39
Child sex (proportion male)	.59	.49

with returned adult children would be positively related to educational attainment and to current college enrollment; (b) parents will report more negative experiences with separated or divorced children than with never-married children, because the former are more likely to be perceived as role failures; and (c) children who are unemployed will have a negative impact on parental experiences, compared with employed children.

Additionally, it's likely that the return of sons and daughters who are single parents represents a greater retreat from autonomy than the return of adult children who are not parents. Returning adult sons or daughters who also bring minor children into the home place a greater burden on parents' time, energy, and financial resources than do adult offspring who return alone. The transition to a three-generation household entails a much greater disruption of parents' lives than a return to a two-generation household. Thus, bringing grandchildren into the home should have a negative impact on parental experiences.

I am using the child's current role status in these models instead of the circumstances that obtained at the time she or he moved back home. Since many had been living at home for several years, I assumed that parents would be much more affected by what the child is currently doing than by events that occurred two, three, or four years earlier. To model the effect of the circumstances of the return on parental well-being, one would need to interview parents within the first year after the return, at a minimum.

Child economic dependency. Young adults who have returned home will differ in the degree of economic dependency on parents. To what extent must parents pay for the child's other necessities, such as food, clothing, and transportation? Do "returned" children contribute to household finances through room and board payments and bring extra income into the household? I hypothesized that children's economic dependency would be negatively related to parental experiences. Specifically, the more basic necessities paid for by parents, the more negative parental experiences would be. Additionally, children's room and board payments and children's income should be positively related to parental experience, and parental financial transfers to children for expenses other than daily living costs should be negatively related to parental experiences.

Health of parent and child. Physical health is another aspect of dependency included in these models. The return of adult children in poor health would appear to place more of a burden on parents than the return of healthier children; thus one would expect a positive relationship between returning children's health and parental satisfaction with coresidence. Parents' health should have the opposite effect. Parents in poorer health might benefit greatly from the return of a young adult child who could provide care, help with housework or transportation, and bring additional income to the household. Thus, I expected parents' health to be negatively associated with parental satisfaction and the quality of parent-child relations.

Child's self-esteem. Low self-esteem may be linked to parents' perceptions of greater dependency because children may seem less ready for assuming adult roles and responsibilities. Children with feelings of low self-worth or low confidence in their own abilities may need more emotional support from parents. It may be easier for parents of children with high self-esteem to imagine their children becoming fully independent. I predicted that the child's self-esteem would be positively related to parental experiences with returned adult children.

Additional hypotheses: Parental expectations for midlife development. Schnaiberg and Goldenberg (1989) maintained that the norms of individual development for midlife parents have changed, with parents expecting more opportunities for self-development and autonomy after children are grown. Adult children's continued presence in the household may deny parents these anticipated opportunities. The NSFH provides no direct measure of parental expectations for development at midlife or after the transition to empty nest. The Schnaiberg and Goldenberg model suggests, however, that the more education parents have, the higher their expectations for self-development will be. To the extent that this is true, parental education should be negatively related to parental experiences. Also, more educated parents may have higher expectations for children's autonomy (Kohn 1977; Silverberg and Steinberg 1987) and may desire a more rapid transition to residential independence (Goldscheider and Goldscheider 1989).

The desire to have an empty nest and thus more time to focus on self and spouse may be more characteristic of older parents than of younger parents. I expected therefore that parental age would be negatively related to parental experiences in the coresident living arrangement.

It's likely that separated, divorced, and widowed parents have more precarious financial situations than married parents. Therefore the return of adult children may be more financially burdensome for unmarried parents than for currently married parents. I expected therefore that parents' marital dissolution would have a negative effect on satisfaction with the adult child's return.

Finally, Menaghan's (1989) "normative expectedness" role theory implies that the older the returned child, the more nonnormative the living arrangement is for parents. The older the child, the more parents' expectations for child autonomy are violated. Thus, child's age should be negatively related to parental experiences. In prior research, however, age did not have negative impact on parental reactions to adult-child coresidence (Aquilino 1991b). Research by Suitor and Pillemer (1987, 1988) with elderly parents and middle-aged coresident children found few negative effects of older adult children on parents.

Data. Among the NSFH respondents aged nineteen to thirty-four, 308 were living in a parental household after returning home. In addition to the primary interview with these young adults, one parent was randomly selected and asked to complete a self-administered questionnaire concerning his or her relationship with this adult child, assessment of coresidence, and social and economic background. Of the 308 eligible parents, 242 completed the questionnaire (172 mothers and 70 fathers).

The average age of the returned adult children was twenty-four years, and of parents, fifty-one years; eighty-six of the parents were between the ages of forty and sixty-four. About 60 percent of the children were nineteen to twenty-four years of age, and about 40 percent, twenty-five to thirty-four. Surprisingly, 12 percent of the children were currently married, and in nearly all cases, the spouses also coresided; 16 percent of the children were previously married. About one in five of the returnees had their own children also living in the household. while 9 percent had children living elsewhere. Twenty percent were enrolled in college; 10 percent had bachelor's degrees; 33 percent, high school diplomas; and 16 percent had dropped out of high school. Means and standard deviations for all independent variables in the multivariate model are displayed in table 11.6.

Descriptive Results

Distributions on the dependent variables for parental experience are shown in table 11.7. These include parents' satisfaction with the coresident living arrangement; two measures of parent-child conflict, namely, frequency of open disagreements and frequency of open hostilities; and two measures of positive social interaction between parent and child: frequency of enjoyable time with the child, and frequency of shared activities. These variables are measured from the perspective of parents. My goal in choosing dependent variables was to focus on

TABLE 11.7. Sex-of-Parent Effects on Dependent Variables in Regression Analyses

Item Wording	Total (N = 242)	Mothers (N = 172)	Fathers (N = 70)	F for 1-Way ANOVA
Parental satisfaction with coresidence	5.90	5.96	5.75	.99
Taking things altogether, how does having (child) living here work out for you? (coded from 1 = very poorly to 7 = very well)	(1.41)	(1.43)	(1.37)	
Average frequency of open disagreements	1.55	1.56	1.52	.21
Concerning dress, boy/girlfriend, friends, staying out late, work, house-work, sex, substance use, money, and getting along with family members (averaged over ten categories coded 1 = never to 6 = almost every day; alpha = .82)	(0.63)	(0.65)	(0.59)	
Frequency of open hostilities	0.68	0.69	0.65	.07
During the past 30 days, how often did you argue or fight or have a lot of difficulty dealing with him/her? (coded from 0 = never to 5 = almost every day)	(0.98)	(1.02)	(0.88)	
Frequency of enjoyable time together	2.91	3.03	2.60	3.79†
During the past 30 days, how often did you have an especially enjoyable time with him/her? (coded from 0 = never to 5 = almost every day)	(1.49)	(1.49)	(1.44)	
Average frequency of shared activities	3.23	3.31	3.05	1.85
Leisure activities away from home, working on a project or playing together at home, and having private talks (averaged over three items coded from 1 = never or rarely to 6 = almost every day; alpha = .69)	(1.29)	(1.27)	(1.30)	

Note: The numbers in parentheses are standard deviations.

†$p < .06$.

indicators that directly measured the parenting experience with this particular coresident child, that is, satisfaction with having this child living in the home and conflict and social interaction with this coresident child. More general measures of psychological well-being, such as depression, optimism, hopefulness, and self-concept, might also be relevant indicators of parental experience but are beyond the scope of this chapter (these are good candidates for future research).

Univariate analysis of variance found new significant differences on the dependent measures between mothers and fathers. Only one marginally significant sex-of-parent effect was evident ($p < .06$): mothers reported a higher frequency of enjoyable time with returned adult children than did fathers.

Two of the dependent variables are averaged over multiple items. Both had acceptable levels of interitem reliability: Cronbach's alpha was .82 for open disagreements, averaged over ten items, and .69 for shared activities, averaged over three items.

Decidedly positive ratings on coresidence satisfaction were obtained from parents. Slightly over half the parents chose seven on the seven-point scale, indicating that the living arrangement worked out very well for them; slightly over one-quarter chose a five or six, indicating some degree of dissatisfaction; and 20 percent gave a rating of four or below, suggesting a great deal of dissatisfaction with the child's return.

Three-quarters of both mothers and fathers reported open disagreements with the returned child over the past year. By far the most frequent source of diagreement was the child's help around the house (58 percent), followed by money (39 percent) and getting along with other family members (39 percent). About one-quarter reported disagreements over dress, friends, staying out late, drinking and drug use, or work. Few reported disagreements about sex (8 percent).

About 45 percent reported at least some fighting or hostility with the child over the past thirty days, while only 13 percent reported open hostilities once a week or more. In contrast, nearly all parents (96 percent) reported at least one especially enjoyable time with the child over the past thirty days, and more than half reported enjoyable times once a week or more. Most parents also reported high levels of shared activities with these adult children. About 60 percent had private talks with the child at least once a week, whereas only 8 percent never or rarely had such talks. Seven in ten parents reported at least occasional leisure activities away from home with the child, and about a third went out together once a week or more. Slightly higher percentages were reported for shared leisure activities at home. These data suggest that, in the majority of cases, the returned adult children are not just using the parental home as a cheap and convenient place to eat and sleep. Instead, there appears to be a great deal of positive integration between the lives of parent and child, with some conflict as well. Parents and returned adult children are quite involved in each other's lives.

The Multivariate Model

The LISREL VII software package was used to estimate a maximum likelihood regression model for the five dependent variables (see table 11.8). Equations for the five dependent variables were fit simultaneously, and disturbance terms of the equations were allowed to be correlated. No causal order was specified among the dependent measures. Models were fit for mothers and fathers separately as two groups. In the initial analyses, the hypothesis of completely invariant regression coefficients for mothers and fathers was tested. In subsequent models, regression parameters were estimated for mothers and fathers separately when LISREL modification indices indicated that the model's goodness of fit would be significantly improved by freeing a parameter.

Invariant model for mothers and fathers. The first step involved fitting a completely invariant regression model for mothers and fathers (in LISREL terms, the gamma matrix was constrained to be equal between the two groups). This proved a poor fit to the data ($X^2 = 172.2$, $d.f. = 90$, $p < .001$). The next step involved allowing certain parameters to be estimated separately for mothers and fathers if this significantly improved the goodness of fit of the model. In the final model ($X^2 = 90.5$, $d.f. = 80$, $p = .20$), ten parameters were freely estimated for mothers and fathers, and eighty parameters were constrained to be equal between the two groups. Overall, this indicates a very high degree of invariance between the models for mothers and fathers. The models for parental satisfaction and for the two conflict variables were nearly completely invariant, with just one of fifty-four parameters significantly different between mothers and fathers. The equation for frequency of enjoyable times was the least invariant, with seven of eighteen parameters freely estimated for the two groups.

Predictors were dropped from the models if they had no significant effects of any of the five dependent variables. Variables dropped included children's employment status, parents' lump sum financial transfers to children, and parents' age.

TABLE 11.8. Regression Model for Dependent Variables, as Reported by Parents of Returned Adult Children: Coefficients Are Maximum Likelihood Estimates from LISREL VII (standard errors in parentheses)

Independent Variables	Parent's Satisfaction with Coresidence	Frequency of Open Disagreements	Frequency of Open Hostilities		Frequency of Enjoyable Times	Frequency of Shared Activities
					Dependent Variables	
Child educational attainment	.06 (.04)	−.06 (.02)**	−.07 (.03)*	M	.00 (.05)	−.01 (.04)
				F	.31 (.07)***	
Child currently in college	.80 (.24)**	−.22 (.11)*	−.40 (.16)*	M	1.15 (.31)***	.42 (.23)†
				F	.14 (.33)	
Child marital status (vs. never married)						
Currently married	.03 (.31)	.07 (.14)	.18 (.20)	M	.57 (.32)†	−.35 (.29)
Previously married	−.57 (.28)*	.12 (.13)	.48 (.19)**	F	.11 (.29)	.02 (.26)
Child's parent status (vs. nonparent)						
Coresident minor children	−.23 (.28)	−.20 (.13)	−.09 (.22)	M	−.01 (.30)	.43 (.27)
			−.63 (.21)**	F		
Children elsewhere	.96 (.34)**	−.19 (.15)	−.51 (.23)*	M	.69 (.40)†	.12 (.32)
				F	−.63 (.23)**	

	(1)	(2)	(3)	(4)	(5)
Financial dependency	−.30 (.19)	.34 (.09)***	.52 (.12)***	−.03 (.19)	.12 (.17)
Pays room/board	.28 (.20)	.19 (.09)*	.17 (.14)	.21 (.21)	.39 (.19)*
Child income (log)	−.06 (.03)*	.01 (.01)	−.02 (.02)	M .01 (.04) / F .15 (.05)**	−.06 (.03)*
Income missing	.06 (.21)	−.02 (.10)	.15 (.14)	−.33 (.22)	.29 (.19)
Child health	.31 (.12)*	−.06 (.06)	.06 (.08)	.19 (.13)	M .06 (.13) / F .64 (.18)***
Parent health	.24 (.11)*	−.13 (.05)*	−.19 (.07)**	.00 (.11)	.06 (.10)
Child self-esteem	.18 (.05)**	−.06 (.02)*	−.07 (.04)†	−.03 (.06)	−.03 (.05)
Parent education	−.08 (.03)*	.01 (.01)	−.02 (.02)	M −.04 (.04) / F −.22 (.05)***	−.04 (.03)
Parent unmarried	−.55 (.19)*	.08 (.09)	.19 (.13)	−.27 (.20)	−.34 (.18)*
Child age	−.01 (.03)	−.03 (.01)*	−.07 (.02)**	.03 (.03)	−.02 (.03)
Child race (black)	.40 (.24)†	−.02 (.11)	−.23 (.16)	M .83 (.28)** / F −1.33 (.37)***	.34 (.22)
Child sex (male)	−.08 (.20)	.04 (.09)	−.02 (.13)	M −.61 (.24)* / F .51 (.31)†	M −.45 (.21)* / F .84 (.30)*
R^2 (Mothers)	.21	.21	.22	.21	.18
(Fathers)	.30	.27	.41	.41	.24

Notes: Where one coefficient is given, the parameters in the models for mothers and fathers were constrained to be equal; separate coefficients are given when parameters were freely estimated for mothers and fathers. In the table, M indicates the coefficient for mothers, and F, the coefficient for fathers. Chi-square for goodness of fit for this model is 90.5, with 80 degrees of freedom ($p = .20$). N = 172 mothers; N = 70 fathers.

†$p < .10$. *$p < .05$. **$p < .01$. ***$p < .001$.

Hypotheses concerning the returned child's movement toward autonomy were partially supported. The most consistent effects were found for education. Children's attainment of education was associated with fewer disagreements, less open hostility, and, for fathers, a greater frequency of enjoyable time with the child. Children's college enrollment had consistent effects across all five dependent variables. The returned child's enrollment in college led to greater parental satisfaction with coresidence, less parent-child conflict, and higher levels of positive social interaction (stronger effects for mothers on social interaction). The effects for enrollment suggest that parents are highly affected by the adult child's progress toward independence. It's likely that parents view education as a means toward better jobs and better wages in the future. Thus, parents are willing to provide high levels of support if children are using that support to better their life chances. Also, returning home to attend school may be seen by parents as a legitimate reason for coresidence, since college might otherwise be unaffordable.

Returned children's marital dissolution was related to parental experiences in the expected direction. Compared with never married returnees, returning after separation or divorce was associated with less parental satisfaction and increased open hostility between parent and child. The findings for currently married children were surprising, because almost all these children had their spouse also living with them. There was little evidence of any negative impact, and enjoyable time with the child was somewhat higher, compared with never married returnees. Married returnees represent a very highly selected group; NSFH data show that only 1.5 percent of married adult children nineteen to thirty-four years of age live in a parental household. Parents may allow such returns only if they expect to get along well with their son- or daughter-in-law as well as with their adult child or in cases where the return would benefit parents as well as children.

The returned child's parental status was not related to parents' experience in the expected manner. Parents who headed three-generation households (who had minor grandchildren living with them) did not report lower satisfaction with coresidence, and fathers reported significantly *less* conflict with the returned adult children than parents in two-generation households. These findings are not consistent with results of earlier research with a different set of NSFH parents (Aquilino and Supple 1991). In slightly over one-third of these cases, the returning adult child was not a single parent but was married and living with spouse. In these situations, where entire "intact" families move into a parent's household, it may be that the childcare burden on the grandparental generation (the parents of the returned adults) is less than when a single parent moves back home. A larger sample of coresident households is needed to tease out the interactions between returned children's parental status and marital status.

The effects of having minor children living elsewhere were generally positive. Parents of returned adult children who were noncustodial parents, compared with returnees who were nonparents, reported more satisfaction and less open hostility. The effects on frequency of enjoyable time differed for mothers and fathers: if the adult child had minor children living elsewhere, mothers reported more enjoyable time, and fathers, less. In 90 percent of these cases the returnees are men (about 20 percent of the men in the sample had minor children elsewhere). It is not clear why this situation has positive implications for parents. One possibility is that coresidence increases the amount of contact these parents have with their grandchildren.

Contrary to expectations, employment status was not related to any of the dependent variables in the model. This occurred most likely because there are several variables in the model that account for the influence of the economic relationship between children and parents. The actual flow of resources between parent and child may be more important than job status.

Children's economic dependency. Financial dependency on parents was measured by the degree to which parents paid for the child's expenses in five areas: food, clothing, transportation, health care, and entertainment. The returned child's degree of financial dependency strongly increased parent-child conflict, both in frequency of open disagreements and frequency of open hostility. Similarly, children's room and board payments had a positive effect on parent-child social interaction. Interestingly, room and board payments were also related to higher levels of open disagreement. It's possible that the payments themselves are a contentious issue in some families, if children need to be coerced or cajoled into contributing to family income. It also may be that adult children who pay room and board feel they should have more of a say in decision making or more of a right not to be the subject of parental criticism since they are behaving more like equals in the family.

Unexpected results were obtained for returned children's income. There was no evidence that children's earnings had a beneficial impact on parental experiences. After controlling for room and board payments and parents' payments for the child's daily expenses, children's income had either no effects or negative effects. Higher income was related to lower parental satisfaction and a lower frequency of shared activities (although fathers reported more enjoyable time with higher-income children). Higher earnings may enable adult children to lead a more independent lifestyle and be more involved in activities away from home. From parents' perspective, adult children with high incomes may have less legitimate reasons to live at home, for they would appear to have the means for maintaining an independent lifestyle. The dummy variable indicating parental lump sum financial transfers, that is, gifts and loans to the child for things other than daily living expenses, was not related to any of the five dependent variables and was dropped from the final model.

Health. Predictions concerning child health were supported. Returned children's health was positively related to parent's satisfaction with the living arrangement and, for fathers, positively related to shared social activities. Adult children's health problems may create more of a burden for parents and decrease children's ability to help with housework or contribute economically. This is consistent with the general hypothesis that parental experiences are influenced by adult children's dependency.

The findings for parents' health were directly opposite to the predicted effects. Parents in poorer health reported less satisfaction and more conflict with returned adult children than parents in good health. This suggests quite clearly that parents are not benefiting greatly from the child's return: coresidence is meeting adult children's needs more so than parents' needs (Aquilino 1990; Ward, Logan, and Spitze 1992).

Child's self-esteem. The self-esteem hypotheses were supported. The returned child's self-esteem was positively related to parents' satisfaction with the living arrangement and negatively related to levels of parent-child conflict. Adult children with low self-esteem may appear more dependent than children with higher self-esteem. From a parental perspective, low self-esteem is likely associated with increased difficulty in making the expected transitions of young adulthood and prolonged dependency on parental emotional support.

Parents' education, marital status, and age. Effects for parental education were in the expected direction. More educated parents were less satisfied with the coresident living arrangement; more educated fathers reported significantly less enjoyable time with their returned sons and daughters. This is consistent with expected social class differences in parental response to adult child coresidence. Education may be linked to heightened parental expectations for adult children's independence and greater parental desires for self-development in midlife.

Results for parents' marital status were also consistent with expectations. Unmarried parents reported considerably less satisfaction with returned adult children and less positive social interaction. This reinforces the idea that coresident adult children place some burden on parental resources and that unmarried parents may feel the strain more than would married parents. Again, coresidence appears to meet the needs of adult children more than those of parents.

The hypothesized effects of parents' age were not supported. Parental age had no significant effects on the dependent variables and was dropped from the model. Nothing indicates that older parents were less sanguine about returned coresident children than younger parents.

Child's age, sex, and race. Children's age per se did not have a great impact on parental experiences with returned adult children. The sole significant finding was less open hostility between older returnees and their parents. This does not support normativeness expectedness role theory, which holds that the more nonnormative the role configuration, the more negative the effects on well-being. Having children over age twenty-five still at home would be a much less expectable parental role than having a nineteen or twenty-year-old at home. Nevertheless, children's age has no negative effects. Young adult children's progress toward establishing autonomy is much more important than chronological age in influencing parental experiences.

The returned child's sex was related only to parent-child social interaction. For both dependent variables, strong differences between mothers' and fathers' coefficients show that positive social interaction was higher in same-sex pairs—mothers reported more enjoyable time and more shared activities with daughters than with sons, and fathers reported more with sons than with daughters. Race effects were found on only one variable, and the effects differed by sex of parent. Black mothers reported more enjoyable time with returned offspring than did white mothers; conversely, black fathers reported *less* enjoyable time with these adult children than did white fathers.

Conclusions

The model decribed above (table 11.8) furnishes strong evidence that midlife parental experience is tied to adult children's intraindividual development. Specifically, parents' experiences with adult children who return to the nest are linked closely to children's progress through the normative role transitions of early adulthood and to the changing nature of children's autonomy and dependency in relation to parents. This is consistent with the view that young adults' return to dependency violates parental expectations for their children's development and leads to lower parental satisfaction and more strain in parent-child relations.

The findings of this research fit well with literature on parent-child relations in adolescence, where there has been growing recognition that children's ontogenetic development drives change in parent-adolescent relationships (Collins 1992; Collins and Russell 1991). In particular, research by Larry Steinberg and Susan Silverberg on puberty and family relationships provides a good empirical example of this framework (Silverberg, chapter 6, this volume; Silverberg and Steinberg 1987; Steinberg 1981, 1987; Steinberg and Silverberg 1987). They demonstrated, for example, that the physical changes associated with the onset of puberty lead to increasing conflict between adolescent and mother and that pubertal maturation increases the emotional distance between adolescent and parent. Parents' experience of midlife identity concerns rises as adolescent emotional autonomy increases during puberty, whereas marital satisfaction is negatively influenced by increasing emotional distance in parent-adolescent relations. In short, research on adolescents illustrates quite well how the *physical* transitions of children impact parent-child interaction and how change in parent-child interaction influences parental well-being at midlife. The research described in this chapter carries the argument one step further, suggesting that adult children's transitions and intraindividual change, their changing levels of autonomy and dependency vis-à-vis parents, continue to shape the parent-child relationship during the launching and empty-nest phases of the life cycle.

The impact of adult children's autonomy and dependency in young adulthood contrasts in one important respect with the findings of Steinberg and Silverberg for parents of adolescents. In research on adolescence, children's emerging emotional autonomy is associated with greater parent-child conflict, parents' midlife crisis, and negative effects on parental well-being. In contrast, the model of parental experiences described in this chapter suggests that as children move into young adulthood, parental well-being and the parent-child relationship will *benefit* from children's increasing autonomy. This implies that a transformation in parents' orientation toward children's autonomy takes place between children's adolescence and early adulthood. Parents move from viewing autonomy as a threat to parental status or authority, in the case of younger adolescents, to a view of children's autonomy as a manifestation of parental success when children have reached adulthood. More research is needed to chart the timing of this transformation and the circumstances that bring it about.

DIRECTIONS FOR FUTURE RESEARCH

In this chapter I have focused on a highly selected subsample of parents and adult children: those coresiding in a parental household after an adult child has returned to the nest. But the central theme here—that change in adult children's autonomy and dependency has strong implications for the well-being of midlife parents—is relevant to the study of parent–adult child relations in general, not just to coresident pairs. I would like to see much more research on how the life course of children over age eighteen continues to impact the quality of life for parents at midlife and beyond. In particular, we need to chart how adult children's transitions into and out of intimate relationships, employment and education transitions, and movement toward economic independence affect the lives of parents, whether or not parents and children coreside. Well-being at midlife is surely tied to the demands adult children make on parents' economic and emotional resources, to parents' level of involvement in children's lives, and to the beliefs parents hold about adult children's progress toward autonomy and beliefs about their own success as parents.

One of the weaknesses of the analyses presented in this chapter is that the NSFH provides no direct measure of parental expectations for their young adult children. Research on midlife parents and young adult children would benefit greatly from an expanded data collection agenda. We need datasets that measure not only relationship quality and interaction patterns but also (1) parental expectations for young adult development, that is, how parents expect or desire the life course of their adult offspring to proceed; (2) whether parents have different expectations for different children and the extent to which expectations vary systematically according to the child's sex and birth order, family size, and so forth; and (3) the actual life-course trajectories of all adult children in the family. Research on coresidence would benefit greatly from longitudinal designs which measure, before the home-leaving process begins, the extent to which parents anticipate adult children returning to the nest, and which predict how parents' prior attitudes toward having coresident adult children affect their experiences after a child returns. Additionally, we need research that monitors what parents desire in terms of their own self-development in midlife and what behavior on the part of their adult children might be necessary to achieve those goals.

Similarly, a target for future research is measuring the expectations of young adult children concerning a return to the nest. How do young adults size up their rights to use the parental home as a base of support, and under what conditions would they anticipate a return home? What are adult children's beliefs concerning parental responsibilities to provide support, and how do these beliefs change over time and with experience? We know very little about how decisions to leave or return home are negotiated between parents and children, especially when older and younger generations have differing perspectives on the appropriateness of these transitions.

Research on the demographics of the empty-nest and launching phase of the parental life course also would benefit from a new approach to data collection. What's needed is a nationally representative dataset that provides a complete life history on the launching and empty-nest stages of the life cycle, taken from the parent's perspective. These data would enable researchers to chart the timing of parents' transitions into and out of the empty nest and to relate nest emptying and nest refilling to other midlife transitions and to changes in adult well-being. This is certainly a daunting data collection task, involving a history of the comings and goings of children from birth of the first child to parents' postretirement years. Such a history does not exist in any national dataset, as far as I know. Available cross-sectional data do not adequately tell the story of how the process of children's home leaving plays out in the lives of parents.

Summary

Children's impact on adult well-being at midlife does not vanish with their first departure from the parental home. Young adult children's needs for support will vary with their progress in making the transition to adulthood. For a great many parents (and a majority of those with two or more children), support will include allowing a formerly emancipated adult child to take up residence again in the parental home. The risk to parents of having an adult child return home is primarily a function of children's role transitions in early adulthood. Entering postsecondary school and beginning marital or cohabiting unions decreases the likelihood of returns; leaving school or military service, marital dissolution, and ending cohabiting relationships increases the likelihood of returns. Young adult children use the parental home as a fallback base of support as they move toward full adult autonomy. This is a good example of linkages among the life trajectories of family members. After adult children have returned home, parental experiences are highly related to children's dependency. Negative experiences are most likely when adult children's role status suggests that they are not moving toward autonomy and when children remain economically dependent, have low self-esteem, and poorer health. One explanation for these effects is that parents' expectations for the development of their young adult children are violated by a return to dependency, leading to greater parent-child conflict and lower parental satisfaction.

REFERENCES

Aldous, Joan. 1987. New views on the family of the elderly and near-elderly. *Journal of Marriage and the Family* 49:227–234.

Aquilino, William S. 1990. The likelihood of parent–adult child coresidence: Effects of family structure and parental characteristics. *Journal of Marriage and the Family* 52:405–419.

———. 1991a. Family structure and home-leaving: A further specification of the relationship. *Journal of Marriage and the Family* 53:999–1010.

———. 1991b. Predicting parents' experiences with coresident adult children. *Journal of Family Issues* 12:323–342.

Aquilino, William S., and Khalil Supple. 1991. Parent-child relations and parents' satisfaction with living arrangements when adult children live at home. *Journal of Marriage and the Family* 53:13–27.

Clemens, A., and Lee Axelson. 1985. The not-so-empty nest: The return of the fledgling adult. *Family Relations* 34:259–264.

Collins, W. A. 1992. Parents' cognitions and developmental changes in relationships during adolescence. In I. Sigel, A. McGillicuddy-DeLisi, and J. Goodnow, eds., *Parental belief systems: The consequences for children*, pp. 175–197. Hillsdale, N.J.: Lawrence Erlbaum.

Collins, W. A., and G. Russell. 1991. Mother-child and father-child relationships in middle childhood and adolescence: A developmental analysis. *Developmental Review* 11:99–136.

DaVanzo, Julie, and Frances K. Goldscheider. 1990. Coming home again: Returns to the parental home of young adults. *Population Studies* 44:241–255.

Elder, Glen. 1977. Family history and the life course. *Journal of Family History* 2: 279–304.

Elder, Glen, Avshalom Caspi, and Linda Burton. 1988. Adolescent transitions in developmental perspective: Sociological and historical insights. In M. Gunnar and A. Collins, eds., *Development during the transition to adolescence*. Hillsdale, N.J.: Lawrence Erlbaum.

Elder, Glen, Avshalom Caspi, and Geraldine Downey. 1986. Problem behavior and family relationships: Life course and intergenerational themes. In A. Sorenson, F. Weinert, and L. Sherrod, eds., *Human development and the life course: Multidisciplinary perspectives*. Hillsdale, N.J.: Lawrence Erlbaum.

Glenn, N. 1975. Psychological well-being in the postparental stage: Some evidence from national surveys. *Journal of Marriage and the Family* 37:105–110.

Glenn, N., and C. Weaver. 1979. A note on family situation and global happiness. *Social Forces* 57:960–967.

Glick, Paul C., and Sung-ling Lin. 1986. More young adults are living with their parents: Who are they? *Journal of Marriage and the Family* 48:105–112.

Goetting, A. 1986. Parental satisfaction: A review of research. *Journal of Family Issues* 7:83–109.

Goldscheider, Calvin, and Frances K. Goldscheider. 1987. Moving out and marriage: What do young adults expect? *American Sociological Review* 52:278–285.

Goldscheider, Frances K., and Calvin Goldscheider. 1989. Family structure and conflict: Nest-leaving expectations of young adults and their parents. *Journal of Marriage and the Family* 51:87–97.

Greene, Anita, and Andrew Boxer. 1986. Daughters and sons as young adults: Restructuring the ties that bind. In N. Datan, A. Greene, and H. Reese, eds., *Life-span developmental psychology: Intergenerational relations*. Hillsdale, N.J.: Lawrence Erlbaum.

Hagestad, G. 1981. Problems and promises in the social psychology of intergenerational relations. In R. Fogel, E. Hatfield, S. Kiesler, and E. Shanas, eds., *Aging: Stability and change in the family*. New York: Academic.

———. 1984. The continuous bond: A dynamic, multigenerational perspective on parent-child relations between adults. In M. Perlmutter, ed., *Parent-child interaction and parent-child relations in child development*. Hillsdale, N.J.: Lawrence Erlbaum.

Heer, David M., Robert W. Hodge, and Marcus Felson. 1985. The cluttered nest: Evidence that young adults are more likely to live at home now than in the recent past. *Sociology and Social Research* 69:436–441.

Hoffman, L., and J. Manis. 1978. Influence of children on marital interaction and parental satisfactions and dissatisfactions. In G. Spanier and R. Lerner, eds., *Child influences on marital and family interaction: A life-span perspective,* pp. 165–213. New York: Academic.

Kohn, Melvin L. 1977. *Class and conformity.* 2d ed. Chicago: University of Chicago Press.

Lee, G. 1988. Marital satisfaction in later life: The effects of nonmarital roles. *Journal of Marriage and the Family* 50:775–783.

McLanahan, S., and J. Adams. 1987. Parenthood and psychological well-being. *Annual Review of Sociology* 13:237–257.

———. 1989. The effects of children on adults' psychological well-being: 1957–1976. *Social Forces* 68:124–146.

Menaghan, E. 1983. Marital stress and family transitions: A path analysis. *Journal of Marriage and the Family* 45:371–386.

———. 1989. Psychological well-being among parents and nonparents. *Journal of Family Issues* 10:547–565.

Mitchell, Barbara A., Andrew Wister, and Thomas Burch. 1989. The family environment and leaving the parental home. *Journal of Marriage and the Family* 51: 605–613.

Nydegger, Corinne N. 1991. The development of paternal and filial maturity. In Karl Pillemer and Kathleen McCartney, eds., *Parent-child relations throughout life.* Hillsdale, N.J.: Lawrence Erlbaum.

Pruchno, Rachel, A., F. C. Blow, and M. A. Smyer. 1984. Life events and interdependent lives: Implications for research and intervention. *Human Development* 27: 31–41.

Schnaiberg, A., and S. Goldenberg. 1989. From empty nest to crowded nest: The dynamics of incompletely launched young adults. *Social Problems* 36:251–269.

Silverberg, S., and L. Steinberg. 1987. Adolescent autonomy, parent-adolescent conflict, and parental well-being. *Journal of Youth and Adolescence* 16:293–312.

Steinberg, L. 1981. Transformations in family relations at puberty. *Developmental Psychology* 17:833–840.

———. 1987. Impact of puberty on family relations: Effects of pubertal status and pubertal timing. *Developmental Psychology* 23:451–460.

Steinberg, L., and S. Silverberg. 1986. The vicissitudes of autonomy in early adolescence. *Child Development* 57:841–851.

Steinberg, L., and S. Silverberg. 1987. Influences on marital satisfaction during the middle stages of the family life cycle. *Journal of Marriage and the Family* 49: 751–760.

Suitor, J. Jill, and Karl Pillemer. 1987. The presence of adult children: A source of stress for elderly couples' marriages? *Journal of Marriage and the Family* 49: 717–725.

———. 1988. Explaining intergenerational conflict when adult children and elderly parents live together. *Journal of Marriage and the Family* 50:1037–1047.

Sweet, James A., Larry L. Bumpass, and Vaughn Call. 1988. The design and content of the National Survey of Families and Households. Working Paper NSFH-1, Center for Demography and Ecology, University of Wisconsin-Madison.

Umberson, D., and W. Gove. 1989. Parenthood and psychological well-being: Theory, measurement, and stage in the family life course. *Journal of Family Issues* 10:440–462.

Ward, R., J. Logan, and G. Spitze. 1992. The influence of parent and child needs on coresidence in middle and later life. *Journal of Marriage and the Family* 54: 209–221.

Ward, R., and G. Spitze. 1992. Consequences of parent–adult child coresidence: A review and research agenda. *Journal of Family Issues* 13:553–572.

White, Lynn K., and Alan Booth. 1985. The quality and stability of remarriages: The role of stepchildren. *American Sociological Review* 50:689–698.

White, Lynn K., Alan Booth, and J. Edwards. 1986. Children and marital happiness: Why the negative correlation? *Journal of Family Issues* 7:131–147.

White, Lynn K., and J. Edwards. 1990. Emptying the nest and parental well-being: An analysis of national panel data. *American Sociological Review* 55:235–242.

TWELVE

Midlife and Later-Life Parenting of Adult Children with Mental Retardation

Marsha Mailick Seltzer, Marty Wyngaarden Krauss,

Seung Chol Choi, and Jinkuk Hong

INTRODUCTION

The study of families is drawn from two primary domains of research. The first body of research emanates from studies of families experiencing *atypical,* unexpected, and nonnormative stress (e.g., Cole and Reiss 1993; Hill 1970). This tradition seeks to understand how acute or prolonged periods of stress affect family members and family functioning. Studies of this type ordinarily test the hypothesis that families who experience intense or chronic stress are affected negatively and have more familial and personal problems than unaffected families.

The second body of research investigates how families negotiate the *typical* developmental stages of family life (Carter and McGoldrick 1980; Olson et al. 1983). These stages include (1) young couples without children, (2) childbearing families and families with children in the preschool years, (3) families with school-age children, (4) families with adolescents in the home, (5) launching families, (6) empty-nest families, and (7) families in retirement. A major focus of study within this line of research is on the transitions from one stage to another. It is argued that transition points are frequently characterized by higher levels of familial and interpersonal stress and by disequilibrium in family roles, functions, and expectations of behavior (Olson et al. 1983).

In this chapter, we focus on parents who have a child with mental retardation to illustrate the intersection of these two lines of research. One purpose of this chapter is to examine the extent to which mothers who have a child with mental retardation differ in physical, psychologi-

An earlier version of this chapter was prepared for the Workshop on Mid-Life Parenting sponsored by the John D. and Catherine T. MacArthur Foundation, Chicago, Illinois, 16–17 October 1992. This chapter was prepared with support from the National Institute on Aging (AG08768) and the Graduate School of the University of Wisconsin—Madison. The authors gratefully acknowledge the contributions of Barbara Larson and Dotty Robison, who coordinated the data collection, and Jan S. Greenberg, who commented on an earlier version.

cal, and social well-being from selected reference groups, including other types of family caregivers and other women their age. These comparisons, which are in the tradition of family stress research, are intended to gauge the impact of lifelong caregiving for a child with a disability.

The second purpose of this chapter is to investigate the extent to which families with a child with retardation experience the stages of the family life course differently as compared with families whose children do not have a chronic illness or disability. This line of inquiry is in the tradition of research on family development. The specific stage of the family life course we examine is the launching stage, often considered the beginning of midlife parenting. The launching stage is generally defined as starting when the first child leaves home and ending when the last child moves away. For families who have a child with mental retardation, the probability of "postponed" or delayed launching is high. Indeed, many adults with retardation will live at home until the parents are not able to sustain this residential arrangement. Across the life course, fully 85 percent of persons with mental retardation live with or under the supervision of their parents (Fujiura, Garza, and Braddock 1992). Although there is a decrease in parent-child coresidence associated with the child's advancing age (Meyers, Borthwick, and Eyman 1985), this living arrangement remains very common until the parent becomes disabled or dies (Seltzer 1985). Thus, having a child with mental retardation is, in many families, a lifelong parenting challenge. A central question addressed in this chapter, therefore, is how postponement of the launching stage affects parental well-being and the parent-child relationship during the midlife and the later-life stages of parenting.

As Cook and Cohler (1986) noted, few adult roles other than parenthood last for such a long period of time and from time to time involve major readjustments in the demands and definition of the role. In most families, these readjustments are provoked by transitions in the family life cycle, as manifested by changes in the children as they grow up, leave home, and become independent adults. In contrast, parents of a child with retardation may experience a different family life cycle, characterized by extended coresident parenting. One consequence of this altered pattern of parenting may be a greater degree of constancy in their parent-child relationships because the son or daughter is less likely to experience the milestones that ordinarily provoke major readjustments in the parent role (such as departure from the home, marriage, becoming a parent). When we view these families through the lens of the child with retardation, one aspect of family life is cast in relief, namely, the altered family life cycle. Although, in this respect the parenting challenge faced by mothers and fathers of children with mental retardation is markedly different from that faced by other parents, much is also normative or typical about these families' lives. Most also have nondisabled children and experience a variety of "expected" stressors typical of most families. Little is known, however, about how these families respond to the normative or frequently experienced stressors that occur during midlife and old age. Our focus on the consequences of both normative and nonnormative stressor events provides insights into patterns of vulnerability and resilience of these mothers during the midlife and later years of parenting.

REVIEW OF PAST RESEARCH

Although most literature on family development has examined family responses to normative and predictable transitions, most research on family stress has focused on the effects of unanticipated and unwanted events (Mederer and Hill 1983). In fact, family development follows from both the normative and the nonnormative events in the lives of family members, although the developmental course of family life following nonnormative events has received comparatively little attention (Seltzer and Ryff 1994). The study of families with a child with mental retardation provides a framework for integrating research on family development with research on family stress.

Most studies of families with a child with retardation have emanated from a family stress perspective. These comparative studies examined the extent to which families who have a child with retardation differ from families who do not have children with lifelong disabilities with respect to a variety of aspects of parental well-being and family functioning. Overall, the results suggest that parents who have a child with mental retardation experience some stress associated with their child's disability (Crnic, Friedrich, and Greenberg 1983) but that psychopathology is not the ordinary consequence (Ramey, Krauss, and Simeonsson 1989). In fact, recent research reveals that families with a member with retardation exhibit variability comparable with the general population in various aspects of family functioning (e.g., Frey, Greenberg, and Fewell 1989; Kazak and Marvin 1984; Shonkoff et al. 1992). There is, therefore, a great deal of interest in articulating *how, why,* and *when* the presence of a child with retardation affects the family and its functioning in ways that distinguish these families from others without such nonnormative characteristics.

Other studies have emanated from the family development perspective and have examined the stages of the family life course that are characteristic of families with a child with mental retardation. Blacher (1984), for example, describes the stages of parents' adjustment to their infant's diagnosis of mental retardation with terms that parallel Kubler-Ross's (1969) categorization of stages of reactions to death and dying. First, the parents experience a crisis in response to the diagnosis, followed by a period of emotional disorganization. Finally, the parents reach the stage of emotional reorganization. The duration of these processes varies considerably across affected families, and some evidence indicates a periodic recurrence of emotional distress throughout the life course (Birenbaum 1971; Wikler 1986).

Turnbull, Summers, and Brotherson (1986) note that families with a child with severe disabilities have *two* family life cycles to negotiate: the passage through the normative family stages as experienced by the mother and father in their relationship with each other and with their other (nondisabled) children, and the modification of the timing and duration of these stages in their relationship with their child with mental retardation. Thus, the family may be "on cycle" with respect to some of its members and "off cycle" with respect to others.

Farber (1959) argued that because the child with mental retardation does not typically assume adult roles (such as being married or socially and financially independent), there is an arrest in the family life cycle. He concluded that families become "frozen" at the developmental level of the child with retardation, whose functioning mirrors that of a much younger child despite advancing chronological age.

Drawing on both family life-course and family stress perspectives, Wikler (1986) found that stress in families increases during periods of family transitions from one stage to another. For example, she noted that when normal chronological (e.g., turning sixteen) or developmental (e.g., leaving home) milestones are not experienced by the child with retardation in a way similar to that experienced by most children, families report a renewed period of stress. This phenomenon was attributed to the need to adjust to a new set of life challenges (prolongation of developmental periods) as well as the negative effects of social comparisons with families whose nondisabled children experience and handle these transactions more smoothly.

One stage of the family life course that is particularly problematic for parents who have a child with mental retardation is the launching stage. During this stage, parents of nondisabled adolescents and young adults struggle with the challenges of the emerging independence of their children, as signaled by achieving milestones such as obtaining a driver's license, going to college, finding a first job, getting married, or having children (Silverberg, chapter 6, this volume). In contrast, parents of a young adult with retardation struggle with their disappointment that their child is *not* experiencing these milestones.

One characteristic of midlife parenting is that the parents must "come to grips with" how their adult children have turned out with respect to both personal adjustment and social and occupational attainment (Ryff, Schmutte, and Lee, chapter 10, this volume). Older parents of nondisabled adults must reconcile their hopes and dreams for what the child might have become with his or her actual achievements, valuing the adult child for failures as well as successes. In contrast, parents of a child with retardation understood since the child's diagnosis that this child's attainment would be limited. Past research has found that parents of adults with mild retardation feel that their child has turned out *better* than they had expected earlier in the child's life (Wolraich, Siperstein, and Reed 1992). Thus, while many parents of nondisabled adults, in evaluating how their children have turned out, often have to make a downward adjustment from their unrealistically high hopes and dreams, parents of adults with mild retardation often have to make an upward adjustment from their overly negative concerns and fears. Nevertheless, parents of adults with retardation have a great deal of difficulty in relinquishing the parent-as-provider/protector role.

For many families with a child with retardation, the launching stage is never completed because of the parents' decisions that their child will reside at home until they are no longer able to provide care. Others do foresee the end of coresident parenting, although wide variation exists as to both the time at which an adult with retardation is expected to move away from home and the circumstances envisioned for his or her postcoresident lifestyle.

Although the phenomenon of coresidence between adult *non*disabled children and their parents has received considerable attention during the past few years (Aquilino 1990, and chapter 11, this volume), the challenges facing a parent of a coresident adult child with mental retardation are quite different from those in ordinary coresidence. When the coresident child has mental retardation, there is often a continuing dependency on the parents for personal care, supervision, financial support, and social support (Krauss, Seltzer, and Goodman 1992), which is ordinarily not characteristic of aging parent–adult child coresidence.

The most nonnormative challenge facing parents who have a coresident child with retardation concerns the need to plan for the future security of the child. Research on these families has indicated that parents worry about the child's future throughout the life course (Birenbaum 1971; Turnbull, Brotherson, and Summers 1985). However, most express a strong present, rather than future, orientation in their coping strategies, which does not facilitate the task of long-range planning (Freedman and Freedman 1994; Turnbull, Summers, and Brotherson 1986). The available evidence indicates that only about one-third of parents make concrete future plans for their child with retardation beyond the time of parental care and supervision (Heller and Factor 1991; Krauss and Seltzer 1993).

Mederer and Hill (1983), in their synthesis of theories of family development, family stress, and critical transitions, note that the central question is, How do families change in response to changing individual and family needs and changing expectations from the external environment? Our research on midlife and later-life parenting of a child with mental retardation provides a vehicle for addressing this integrative question.

STUDY DESCRIPTION

Our research is based on an ongoing longitudinal study of 461 families in which the mother was age fifty-five or older and had a son or daughter with mental retardation who lived at home with her at the time of entry into the study. All families volunteered to participate in the study. Half lived in Massachusetts and half in Wisconsin.

Each family is studied eight times over a twelve-year period. At each point of data collection, the mother is interviewed in her home and completes a set of standardized self-administered measures. In addition, the father (if living) and siblings complete similar self-administered questionnaires, and the adult with retardation is interviewed. Both qualitative and quantitative data are collected from each member of the family. Our overall goal is to chart the course of constancy and change in these families at a time of life when changes are increasingly likely. In specific, many changes in the marital status, employment status, and health of the parents are expected to occur during the study period, and some adults with retardation are expected to move away from home. Investigation of the antecedents and consequences of these normative and nonnormative transitions constitutes the central focus of our research. (See Seltzer and Krauss 1989; Seltzer et al. 1991; Krauss, Seltzer, and Goodman 1992; and Seltzer, Krauss, and Tsunematsu 1993 for additional details about study methods and findings.)

The sample used in the analyses presented in this chapter consisted of 387 mothers of adults with retardation who continued to live at home at the second data collection period.[1] These mothers ranged in age from fifty-seven to eighty-six years (mean = 66.8). Almost two-thirds (63.3 percent) were married. Fewer than one-third (30.5 percent) were widows, and only a small percentage (6.2 percent) were either divorced, separated, or single. On average, the mothers had 3.9 children, including the child with retardation. In only 8 percent of the families was the child with retardation the only child. About one-fourth of the mothers (27.5 percent) were currently employed outside of the home. Two-thirds of the mothers (67.7 percent) had no education beyond high school. The average family income in 1990–91 was $28,129.

Their sons (45.7 percent) and daughters (54.3 percent) with retardation ranged in age from seventeen to sixty-eight years (mean = 34.5). Most had mild or moderate retardation (78.8 percent), with fewer classified as having severe or profound retardation (21.2 percent). Most were in excellent (43.7 percent) or good (44.2 percent) health, as described by their mothers. Nearly all (91 percent) left home on weekdays for a job or a day program such as a sheltered workshop, which provided regular respite for the mothers.

The measures in the present analyses include characteristics of the mother and her son or daughter with retardation, indices of maternal well-being, and measures of the mother's feelings about parenting. All these data were collected from the mothers either via interview or self-administered questionnaires and are described in table 12.1.

FINDINGS

The analyses we present in this chapter emanate from the two domains of family research described earlier: research on family stress and research on family development. Based on the family stress perspective, we begin our analysis with comparisons of the mothers in our sample with other types of family caregivers and with age peers who do not have family caregiving responsibilities. Our purpose in conducting these comparisons is to gauge the impact on the mother's

TABLE 12.1. Key Variables and Measures

Variables	Measures
Characteristics of the mothers	
Marital status	1 = married, 0 = not married
Employment status	1 = employed, 0 = not employed
Health status	3 = excellent, 2 = good, 1 = fair, 0 = poor
Characteristics of the adults with retardation	
Level of retardation	3 = mild, 2 = moderate, 1 = severe, 0 = profound
Functional abilities (revised Barthel Index; Mahoney and Barthel 1965)	31 items (range = 0–93), alpha = .94, mean = 60.95
Behavior problems (ICAP; Bruininks et al. 1986)	8 items (range = 0–8), mean = 1.84
Maternal well-being	
Depression (CES-D; Radloff 1977)	20 items (range = 0–60), 16+ signifies clinical depression, alpha = .85, mean = 9.58
Life satisfaction (Philadelphia Geriatric Center; Lawton 1972)	17 items (range = 0–17), alpha = .81, mean = 12.16
Social support (Antonucci 1986)	Size of network, mean = 7.95
Feelings about parenting	
Burden (Zarit, Reever, and Bach-Peterson 1980)	29 items (range = 0–58), alpha = .80, mean = 29.46
Stress (QRS-F; Friedrich, Greenberg, and Crnic 1983)	52 items (range = 0–52), alpha = .91, mean = 15.82
Quality of the parent-child relationship (Bengtson and Black 1973)	15 items (range = 0–90), alpha = .91, mean = 74.34

physical, social, and psychological well-being of parenting a child with retardation. Next, we extend these comparisons to determine whether the mothers in our sample are uniquely vulnerable to "ordinary" stressful life events that occur in midlife and in later life, as compared with age peers who are mothers but whose children have no disabilities or chronic health problems.

In the last set of analyses, we turn to the developmental challenges facing these families. We examine whether mothers in late midlife differ from those in later life in their personal well-being and feelings about parenting. In that continued coresident parenting becomes increasingly nonnormative as the mother ages, this comparison may reveal how aging influences a mother's appraisal of active parenting. We then examine how the stages of the family life course unfold in these families. Following from this perspective, we examine differences between families who have begun the process of launching their child with retardation and families who have not yet taken steps to end the active parenting years. This investigation raises questions regarding the extent to which *placement* of an adult son or daughter with retardation is a process that is parallel to or distinct from *launching* nondisabled young adult children.

Comparison with Reference Groups

Our first question addresses the extent to which the mothers in our sample differ in well-being from other types of family caregivers and from age peers without family caregiving responsibilities. In light of prior research on the effects of chronic family stress, our hypothesis was that the mothers of the adults with retardation would manifest poorer physical, social, and psychological well-being than did the reference groups.

The reasons for this hypothesis were as follows. First, the literature shows that family caregiving takes a toll on the caregiver (Hoyert and Seltzer 1992) as a result of the physical demands, psychological stresses, and interpersonal losses that accompany this role. Thus, the mothers in our sample may be at greater risk for poor physical, social, and psychological well-being than are noncaregiving age peers. Second, as duration of caregiving has been found to be negatively associated with well-being (George and Gwyther 1984; Townsend and Noelker 1987) and because caring for an adult with retardation extends for a considerably longer time than other types of family caregiving,[2] we expect the mothers in our sample to have poorer outcomes than the caregiving reference groups. Although some controversy exists in the literature on this issue (Townsend et al. 1989), we hypothesized that the extremely long duration of caregiving experienced by the mothers in our sample would take a greater toll on them than on those with a shorter duration of caregiving responsibility, such as caregivers for the elderly and parents of a young child with retardation. Additionally, caring for

TABLE 12.2. Comparison of Well-Being of Sample Members
with Selected Reference Groups

Indicators	Present Study	Family Caregivers	Older Non-caregivers
Health (% in good or excellent health)	71	67[a]	60[b]
Depression (mean CES-D score)	10	16–17[c]	10[d]
Life satisfaction (mean Philadelphia Geriatric Center score)	12	8[e]	13[e]
Caregiving burden (mean Zarit Burden Score)	29	31[f]	—
Caregiving stress (mean QRS scale)	16	19[g]	—
Size of social support network (mean using Convoy Model)	8	—	9[h]

[a]Stone, Cafferata, and Sangl 1987
[b]Bumpass and Sweet 1987
[c]Pruchno and Resch 1989; Pruchno, Michaels, and Potashnik 1990
[d]Gatz and Hurwicz 1990
[e]Gallagher et al. 1985
[f]Zarit, Reever, and Bach-Peterson 1980
[g]Friedrich, Greenberg, and Crnic 1983
[h]Antonucci and Akiyama 1987

an elderly relative has become a normative role, especially for women (Brody 1985), but caring for a child with a disability remains a nonnormative role, which might increase the toll extracted by this family responsibility. Finally, the literature suggests that older parents are negatively affected by the health and social problems of their adult children (Greenberg and Becker 1988; Pillemer and Suitor 1991), although the effects on older parents of having the specific problem of a coresident adult child with mental retardation have not yet been investigated.

Table 12.2 presents data comparing the women in our sample with other groups of family caregivers and with noncaregiving age peers. On all six measures of maternal well-being, the mothers in our sample were functioning as well as or superior to the reference groups. In specific, fully 71 percent of the mothers in our sample rated their health as either good or excellent, a higher percentage than either family caregivers for the elderly (Stone, Cafferata, and Sangl 1987) or noncaregiving women their age drawn from the National Survey of Families and Households (Bumpass and Sweet 1987). Regarding depressive symptoms, the mothers of adults with retardation had scores that were virtually identical to a large sample of noncaregiving women their age (Gatz and Hurwicz 1990) and considerably lower than two large samples of caregivers for the elderly (Pruchno, Michaels, and Potashnik 1990; Pruchno and Resch 1989). A similar pattern was found with respect to life satisfaction, with the mothers in our sample comparable in life satisfaction to the general population of older persons and reporting better morale than caregivers for elderly relatives (Gallagher et al. 1985). The mothers in our sample were slightly less burdened by caregiving than were caregivers for the elderly (Zarit, Reever, and Bach-Peterson 1980) and less stressed than parents of young children with retardation (Friedrich, Greenberg, and Crnic 1983). Finally, the mothers of the adults with retardation had social support networks nearly as large as the networks of their noncaregiving age peers (Antonucci and Akiyama 1987).

These findings suggest that the nonnormative experience of providing decades of care for a son or daughter with mental retardation does not result in nonnormative outcomes, at least with respect to six commonly used measures of social, psychological, and physical well-being. Three explanations for these unexpected findings are offered. First, a *self-selection* process may exist regarding which families decide to rear their children with retardation at home and which families place their son or daughter elsewhere. However, self-selection may not be fully explanatory because, as noted earlier, most children with retardation live at home until the parents are not able to provide care.

Second, after many years of nonnormative parenting, these parents may have *accommodated* to their extra parenting responsibilities. As one mother explained: "Having a retarded child is a terrible tragedy, but I wouldn't trade him for any normal child. If one can get beyond the grief and sorrow about what he has lost, *and that takes some doing*, experiencing life through his eyes and sharing a life with him so filled with joy and innocence has been an extraordinary path to take. I wouldn't have missed it for the world." This explanation—accommodation to the demands of nonnormative parenting as time passes—is consistent with the adaptational hypothesis advanced by Townsend et al. (1989), who found that over a fourteen-month period, the majority of their noncoresiding sample of caregivers for the elderly manifested *improved* caregiving effectiveness and no increase in depression. Similar results were reported by Zarit, Todd, and Zarit (1986), who found that caregivers for the elderly were able to improve their ability to cope with the problem behaviors manifested by the care recipients, even though these behaviors became more extreme over time. Chiriboga, Yee, and Weiler (1992) studied the stress responses of adult children who provide care to parents with Alzheimer's disease and found that the longer the time since the parent's diagnosis, the less the burden.

A third explanation for the favorable well-being of our sample as compared with the reference groups is that the mothers may be *deriving benefit* from their relationship with their adult child or from the role of long-term coresident parent. Many told us that they feel that this role has given them a continued purpose in life and that they are proud of their success in meeting the challenge of parenting a child with a disability. One mother noted that "this experience has made me a better person. It's been a profound experience—and a great equalizer. It gave direction to my life and gave me something to work for. It also became a positive for others. In helping my daughter find a niche in the world, I also inadvertently helped other families to do the same for their children." This statement is consistent with the research of Krause, Herzog, and Baker (1992), who found that the provision of informal help *by* older people is associated with lower rates of depressive symptomatology.

For any one or a combination of these reasons, the mothers in our sample are, on balance, a well-functioning group of midlife and older women who perceive that their health is quite good and who appear to have weathered the nonnormative storm of having a child with retardation and rearing him or her into adulthood. Their surprisingly high level of personal well-being suggests that this example of nonnormative stress does not necessarily result in deleterious outcomes and may, in fact, have unexpected benefits.

Coping with the "Ordinary" Stresses of Midlife and Later Life

The next question we examined was the extent to which the mothers in our sample have faced other stressors that are commonly experienced by midlife and older women. While we have conceptualized our sample as mothers of unlaunched adults with retardation, in other respects their lives continue as they would have without a child with a disability. Our focus on the child with retardation should not obscure the range of normative and *other* nonnormative experiences they have had.

Past research indicates that persons who experience negative life events are at increased risk for psychological distress (Cohen and Wills 1985). Although clinical depression is not common, persons who expe-

470

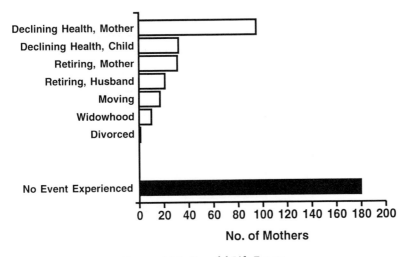

FIGURE 12.1. Stressful Life Events.

rience such events may have an elevated level of depressive symptoms, at least in the short run (Pearlin 1989). We examined the extent to which the mothers in our sample are at risk for depressive symptoms following stressful life events and compared their response with that of noncaregiving women their age who also experienced these stressful life events.

Data regarding the prevalence of the negative life events experienced by the mothers in our sample are presented in figure 12.1. During a recent eighteen-month period, nearly half the mothers (45.0 percent) had experienced at least one of seven stressful life events that might affect a mother's ability to continue as active coresident parent. These seven events were declining health in the mother, declining health in her son or daughter with retardation, retirement of the mother, retirement of her husband, moving from one home to another, widowhood, and divorce. The most common event was declining health (experienced by ninety-five mothers), and the least common was getting divorced (experienced by only one mother during this time period). These data confirm that many midlife and older mothers who have a son or daughter with retardation experience stressful life events which are increasingly common at this time of life and which have been associated with negative outcomes in past research (Pearlin 1989).

As expected, mothers who experience at least one stressful life event had a significantly higher level of depressive symptoms than mothers

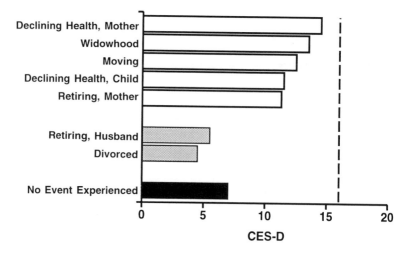

FIGURE 12.2. Depression Scores.

who experienced no negative life events during the past eighteen months (11.42 versus 8.08, $t = 3.98$, $p < .001$). The mean Center for Epidemiological Studies Depression Scale (CES-D) scores of mothers who experienced each of the life events are presented in figure 12.2. Excluding maternal divorce, all but one of these events were associated with significantly elevated levels of depression (at the $p < .001$ level). The exception was having one's husband retire from paid employment, which was associated with a significantly *lower* level of depressive symptoms, possibly because of the extra help a retired father could provide in the care of the son or daughter with retardation. The events most strongly associated with depression were declining health in the mother (mean = 14.05) and being widowed (mean = 13.08). However, it is noteworthy that the average score for those who had experienced even these very stressful events remained below the clinical cutoff of sixteen on the CES-D (Radloff 1977).

An important question that would help to interpret these data is whether mothers of adults with retardation are at greater risk of depressive symptoms following a stressful life event than are mothers their age who do not have a child with a disability. It might be the case that mothers of the adults with retardation, who have put so much physical and emotional energy into the care of this child, are less resilient than other mothers their age and are more likely to have elevated depression scores in response to *other* stressful life events. Alternatively, the reactions of the mothers of the adults with retardation to a stressful life experience may be similar to those of other mothers their age who do not have a child with a disability. Such a finding would be consistent with the surprisingly favorable physical, social, and psychological well-being of the mothers in our sample.

To address this question, we contrasted the mothers of adults with retardation in our sample with a similarly recruited sample of women their age (N = 128) on whom comparable data were available. Mothers in both samples were between the ages of fifty-five and eighty-five and had at least one child. In the comparison sample, however, none had either a child with a disability or a chronic illness or a coresident child, nor did any provide care to an impaired family member. More than half the comparison sample (60.16 percent) experienced a recent[3] stressful life event.

The two samples were compared with respect to demographic characteristics. Although marital or employment status did not differ, the comparison sample was significantly older (mean = 68.3 versus 66.8), better educated (73.4 percent had more than a high school education versus 30.7 percent), and wealthier (mean = $35,145 annual family income versus $28,129) than the mothers of adults with retardation. These three variables were thus used as covariates in subsquent analyses.

To examine whether the mothers of the adults with retardation who experienced stressful life events manifested a higher rate of depressive symptoms than comparison group mothers exposed to similar stressful life events, a two-way analysis of covariance was conducted. The two independent variables were (1) whether the mother had experienced at least one recent stressful life event, and (2) whether the mother had a child with retardation (i.e., was a member of the comparison sample). The dependent variable was the mother's depressive symptoms score. The covariates were maternal age, level of education, and family income.

As shown in table 12.3, there was a significant main effect for the life events variable, with higher depression scores evident for women who experienced a stressful life event ($F = 11.87$, $p < .001$). However, the main effect for the group variable was not significant. Although mothers of adults with retardation who experienced stressful life events had higher depression scores than the other three groups, the interac-

TABLE 12.3. Analysis of Covariance of Depression Scores
between Mothers with and without a Recent Stressful Life Event

Group of Mothers	No Event	At Least 1 Event
Mothers of adults with mental retardation	8.08	11.42
Comparison group	7.90	8.42

Notes: The covariates were maternal age, level of education, and family income. F(event) = 11.87, $p < .001$. F(group) = 0.05, NS. F(interaction) = 2.40, NS.

tion effect was not significant. Thus, we concluded that these mothers respond to stressful life events *similarly* to their age peers who have not had a nonnormative parenting history.

These findings have several implications. First, the prevalence of other stressful events in the lives of midlife and older women with ongoing nonnormative parenting responsibilities is notable. In an eighteen-month period, about half the mothers of the adults with retardation experienced at least one major event found in previous research to be stressful, a frequency nearly as high as their age peers who had no caregiving responsibilities. Clearly, their child's retardation and ongoing need for support is only one of a host of stresses experienced at this stage of life.

It was noteworthy that mothers of adults with retardation were not significantly more likely than their age peers to react to stressful life events with an elevated level of depressive symptoms. These findings are consistent with the perspective that the mothers have adapted well to the role of parenting a child with special needs and that at this stage of life they are not uniquely vulnerable to stressful life events. In fact, rather than being a source of stress, the adult with retardation is often a source of support to the mother as she copes with *other* stressful life events. One mother in our study, when describing her husband's final illness and recent death, commented on the support provided to her by her daughter with retardation: "We have been a comfort to each other. If I hadn't had her with me, I couldn't have gotten through my husband's illness."

Developmental Considerations in the Conceptualization of Midlife Parenting

The next line of inquiry we pursued pertained to how the stage of midlife parenting is experienced by families whose active parenting responsibilities extend far beyond the ordinary launching stage. Two factors make midlife parenting a prolonged stage for the mothers in our sample: the continued coresidence of the adult with the parents, and the continued functional dependency of the adult on the parents. Thus, both objectively and functionally, launching remains an uncompleted stage for these families.

Both everyday experience as well as empirical research suggest that the beginning of the launching stage is associated with increased parental stress (Silverberg, chapter 6, this volume), whereas its completion is marked by improved parental well-being and increased marital satisfaction (McLanahan and Adams 1987; Umberson, chapter 13, this volume). Based on Turnbull, Summers, and Brotherson's (1986) identification of *two* family life cycles, parents who have a child with mental retardation may experience the fluctuations in personal well-being associated with the launching of their nondisabled children at the same time that their retained active parenting responsibility for their child with retardation thwarts the completion of this stage of the family life cycle.

Given the constancy of coresidence in our sample, we aimed to identify sources of variability *within* the midlife parenting experience rather than to compare midlife parenting with an earlier or a later stage of the family life course. We examined two sources of variability within this stage: the mother's chronological age, and whether concrete plans had been made for the adult with retardation to leave the parental home at a future date, signifying the beginning of the launching stage. An examination of the mother's chronological age provides a lens on individual development, whereas investigation of the beginning of the launching stage provides a lens on family development, both in the context of midlife parenting.

We began by dividing our sample into two groups: late midlife (maternal age fifty-five to sixty-four, N = 168), and old age (maternal age sixty-five or older, N = 219). We hypothesized that the late midlife mothers would manifest superior general well-being and would have more favorable feelings about parenting their child with retardation than would the older mothers. One reason for this hypothesis was that midlife mothers are less "off-time" in their active parenting role than older mothers. Assuming the validity of Farber's (1959) characterization of families as being "frozen" in their life cycle, midlife mothers who continue to have active parenting responsibilities would be less atypical than older mothers, for whom the discrepancy between what

TABLE 12.4. Comparison of Midlife and Older Mothers

Variable	55–64 Years (N = 168)	65+ Years (N = 219)	t	p
Characteristics				
Mother				
Is married	0.78	0.52	5.56	<.001
Is employed	0.42	0.13	6.51	<.001
Health status	1.95	1.74	2.49	.013
Family income ($)	32,434.00	24,826.00	5.58	<.001
Child				
Level of retardation	2.06	2.15	−0.97	.335
Functional abilities	60.34	61.42	−1.06	.290
Number of				
behavior problems	2.00	1.72	1.60	.111
General maternal well-being				
Life satisfaction	12.43	11.42	2.61	.009
Depression	8.70	10.28	−1.85	.065
Feelings about parenting				
Burden	29.41	29.50	−0.12	.901
Stress	15.80	15.83	−0.03	.976
Quality of the mother-				
child relationship	74.00	74.61	−0.59	.553

they might have expected of their lives and what they actually provide to their children is more dramatic.

Confirming this line of reasoning, Sweet and Bumpass (1987) provide data to show that it is relatively common in our society for mothers in their fifties to have a child living at home. At the age of fifty-five, fully 35 percent of ever married mothers in the United States had a child living at home in 1980. With advancing maternal age, however, the likelihood of coresidence decreases in the general population, with only eighteen percent of mothers age sixty-five years having a coresident child. Thus, because older mothers of adults with retardation (i.e., those sixty-five or older) have fewer age peers who share their life circumstances, we expected they would have poorer general well-being and more negative feelings about parenting.

As shown in table 12.4, the older mothers indeed had objectively more difficult lives than the midlife mothers, although the children of the two groups were very similar in level of retardation, functional abilities, and behavior problems. Specifically, only about half the older mothers (52 percent) were married, as compared with more than three-fourths of the midlife mothers (78 percent). Their family incomes were considerably lower (about $25,000 as compared with about $32,000), in part because the older mothers were less likely to work outside of the home (13 percent versus 42 percent). Furthermore, the older mothers rated their health more negatively than did the midlife mothers. Similarly, the older mothers were significantly less satisfied with their lives than the midlife mothers, and there was a trend toward more depression in the older mothers.

On the basis of these differences in both the objective conditions of the lives of the older mothers and in their more negative general well-being, we hypothesized that older mothers would have more negative feelings about parenting than the midlife mothers. However, the older and midlife mothers were virtually identical in their responses to the parenting measures. They scored less than one point apart on measures of subjective burden of parenting, parenting stress, and relationship quality with their child with retardation. Thus, the age-related trends in the objective circumstances of their lives and in the general well-being were not reflected in their feelings about parenting. These data suggest that maternal age is not a useful marker of a mother's feelings about parenting her child with retardation during the prolonged period of continued active parenting.

Another perspective on the within-stage variability associated with the midlife stage of parenting a coresident child is based on the mother's expectations regarding the end of this period of family life. Some of the mothers in our sample (N = 124) have added their son's or daughter's name to a waiting list for residential placement in a setting such as a group home or a supported apartment, but the majority (N = 263) have not taken this step. Waiting lists are maintained by county and state mental retardation agencies and by private residential programs. Although it is relatively easy for a parent to add her child's name to the list, there is great variability in the significance of the waiting list for the mothers who have taken this step. Based on the qualitative data we collected, we learned that some mothers were impatiently awaiting a vacant spot in a group home or supported apartment for their son or daughter, whereas others were reluctantly accepting the inevitability of this transition. A few had acquiesced to their social workers' recommendation to place the child's name on the waiting list and had no serious intention of accepting a spot if one were to become available. Nevertheless, we viewed the waiting list as a behavioral indicator of a mother's willingness to relinquish the active parenting role and begin the launching stage for her family, even if this step would not be taken until some time in the future.

We hypothesized that mothers who have added their child's name to a waiting list for out-of-home placement would have more negative feelings about parenting than their counterparts who had not taken this step. Specifically, we hypothesized that the initiation of the launching stage would be associated with poorer general maternal well-being and more negative feelings about parenting, consistent with the literature on the stresses of the beginning of the launching stage (Silverberg, chapter 6, this volume) and past research that has demonstrated that transition periods are accompanied by disequilibrium within the family (McCullough 1980).

As shown in table 12.5, there was considerable similarity in the characteristics of the mothers whose child's name had been placed on a waiting list and those who had not made this decision. About two-thirds of both groups were married, and about one-fourth were still employed outside of the home. Family income averaged between $25,000 and $30,000, and there was no difference between the groups in maternal health status. Although the children of both groups of mothers had comparable levels of retardation and functional skills, those on the waiting list manifested significantly more behavior problems than those not on the list.

Despite the comparability of most of the *objective* circumstances of their lives, the mothers who had added their child's name to a residential waiting list were significantly less satisfied with their lives, had significantly higher depression scores, and had more negative feelings about parenting than those who had not used this option. Specifically, the waiting list mothers were significantly more burdened by parenting, had more parenting stress, and had a poorer relationship with their child than the mothers who had not made plans for their child to move away from home. It is possible that these differences were at least partially the result of the increased level of behavior problems in adults on the waiting list as compared with those not on a waiting list. While the causal direction of the relationship between parental well-being and use of the waiting list cannot be determined from these cross-sectional data, the findings presented in table 12.5 are consistent with past research that indicated that the initiation of the launching stage would be experienced negatively.

It is instructive to contrast the findings of the chronological age

TABLE 12.5. Comparison of Mothers with and without Future Plans

Variable	No Waiting List (N = 263)	Waiting List (N = 124)	t	p
Characteristics				
Mother				
Is married	0.63	0.62	0.11	.910
Is employed	0.26	0.24	0.60	.549
Health status	1.86	1.78	0.86	.389
Family income ($)	29,062.00	26,150.00	1.94	.053
Age (years)	66.45	67.48	−1.47	.141
Child				
Level of retardation	2.09	2.16	−0.70	.483
Functional abilities	61.00	60.84	0.14	.885
Number of behavior problems	1.71	2.12	−2.22	.027
Age	35.03	33.63	1.71	.070
General maternal well-being				
Life satisfaction	12.55	11.31	2.89	.004
Depression	8.97	10.89	−2.11	.036
Feelings about parenting				
Burden	28.62	31.23	−3.78	<.001
Stress	14.79	17.99	−3.41	<.001
Quality of the mother-child relationship	75.01	72.90	2.16	.032

comparisons and the waiting list comparisons. Although maternal aging was associated with a poorer quality of life, objectively speaking, there was no similar pattern of objective differences in the lives of mothers who had used the waiting list to plan for the beginning of the launching stage, as compared with those who had not. Regarding general well-being, both older chronological age and the initiation of the launching period were associated with less satisfaction with life and more depression in the mothers.

Finally, no relation existed between a mother's age and her feelings about parenting, but a mother's feelings about parenting were very sensitive to the initiation of the launching stage. Consistent with the general literature on the beginning of the launching stage, the dominant response was negative. Specifically, the burden and stress associated with parenting was perceived to be more severe, and the quality of the mother-child relationship was judged more negatively by mothers who placed their child's name on the waiting list. This pattern could be due, in part, to the differences in the level of behavior problems in the two groups of adults with retardation.

To examine whether beginning the launching stage (as signified by using the waiting list) was predictive of the mother's feelings about parenting once background characteristics and general maternal well-being were controlled, we conducted three hierarchical multiple regression analyses (see table 12.6). The dependent variables in these regression models were feelings about parenting: the burden of parenting, the stress associated with parenting, and the quality of the parent-child relationship, respectively. The characteristics of the mother and of the child were entered first as control variables, followed by the two measures of the mother's general well-being (life satisfaction and depression). Finally, the waiting list variable was entered. These models estimate the unique variance in a mother's feelings about parenting associated with use of the waiting list, an indicator of the beginning of the launching stage, net of maternal and child characteristics and general maternal well-being.

In total, 36 percent of the variance in a mother's feelings of burden associated with parenting was accounted for by the set of independent variables. Subjective burden was higher in mothers who were younger, had a child with more behavior problems, were less satisfied with their lives, and had more depressive symptoms. Once these variables were controlled, the waiting list variable remained a significant predictor of subjective burden, although it explained only an additional 1 percent of the variance in this dependent variable. Those who used the waiting list were more burdened.

A similar pattern was found in the regression of stress associated with parenting. Fully 62 percent of the variance in stress was accounted for in this model. The characteristics of the child were strong predictors of parenting stress, with mothers of more severely impaired older sons and daughters and of children who had more behavior problems being more likely to be stressed by parenting. Life satisfaction was also a significant predictor (in the expected direction). Controlling for all these variables, the waiting list variable remained a significant predictor, accounting for an additional 1 percent of the variance in the dependent variable. Again, the use of the waiting list was associated with more stress.

TABLE 12.6. Regressions of Feelings about Parenting

Characteristics	Burden beta[a]	Burden R^2	Stress beta[a]	Stress R^2	Relationship Quality beta[a]	Relationship Quality R^2
Mother						
Is married	−.041		.008		−.063	
Is employed	.025		.008		.057	
Health status	−.002		.052		−.134*	
Family income	.008		.077		.105	
Age	−.127*		−.028		−.005	
		.06		.04		.03
Child						
Level of Mental Retardation	.024		−.167***		.043	
Functional abilities	−.008		−.318***		.107	
Number of behavior problems	.284***		.276***		−.257***	
Age	.064		.115*		.047	
		.19***		.41***		.14***
General maternal well-being						
Life satisfaction	−.322***		−.445***		.171*	
Depression	.162**		.115		.045	
		.35***		.61***		.16*
Waiting list	.099*		.110**		−.061	
		.36*		.62**		.16

[a]The betas shown are derived from the final equation.

*$p < .05$. **$p < .01$. ***$p < .001$.

The waiting list variable was not a significant predictor of relationship quality. Only 16 percent of the variance in this dependent variable was accounted for, with the strongest predictor being number of behavior problems.

In accounting for these findings, two explanations must be considered. First, it is possible that mothers who have more negative feelings about parenting are more likey to use the waiting list option. Thus, using the waiting list may be a *product of* their more negative feelings about parenting. Alternatively, the knowledge that the end of the period of active parenting is near may *produce* feelings of strain and detachment in the parent-child relationship. The available cross-sectional data do not permit such longitudinal interpretations. For these mothers, however, the initiation of the launching stage is associated with more strained relations with their now adult child, consistent with the literature on the beginning of the launching stage in families with nondisabled adolescents (Silverberg, this volume).

It is not known, however, whether the *completion* of the launching stage (i.e., placement) will be experienced by these mothers in ways similar to the general population, namely, by an increase in personal and marital well-being. For mothers of adults with retardation, the completion of the launching stage denotes the end of their most significant role in adulthood, for which they sacrificed a great deal and to which they had to adjust despite great grief. In addition, the launching of an adult child with retardation has a very different meaning than the launching of a nondisabled child. In the case of a son or daughter with retardation, the mother is usually not launching a child to an independent life. Rather, she is launching her child to a life of at least partial dependency on other people. Most of the mothers in our study voiced concerns that these other people would not be as available, sensitive, or understanding of the son's or daughter's needs as she is. Thus, from the mother's perspective, launching signifies an expected decline in the quality of the son's or daughter's life.

A mother who recently completed the launching stage by placing her daughter out of the home stated: "Two months ago I placed my daughter Sally in a group home. I suppose this was a positive action. My health was deteriorating because Sally had regressed so much that it was very difficult for me to handle. I was afraid that I would be a victim of a stroke or a heart attack, and then the rest of my children would have two problems to deal with. I also knew that after my death, Sally would eventually have to move somewhere. And so, to make it easier, I thought it best to do it now. I worry about her care and hope that she will adjust well. She still aches to go home. I am very sad. I would rather see her dead." This example illustrates how the stages of the family life course may warrant reinterpretation in families with a child with mental retardation. When family transitions that ordinarily bring happiness bring sadness or anxiety instead, these transitions are postponed or avoided as long as possible.

DISCUSSION AND AVENUES FOR FUTURE RESEARCH

This chapter focused on a specific population of women who, as parents of adults with mental retardation, are commonly presumed to have atypical and potentially problematic parenting careers. As noted earlier, it has long been argued that the birth and rearing of a child with mental retardation thrusts parents and families into uncharted and rocky territory, resulting in an "arrest" in the family life cycle (Farber 1959) and placing other members of the family at risk for personal, psychological, and social maladaptation (Crnic, Friedrich, and Greenberg 1983). Our research—and that of others (Ramey, Krauss, and Simeonsson 1989)—does not support these common assumptions. Rather, the results raise important questions about the long-term effects of "marker" events (such as mental retardation in the family). Our findings suggest the need to articulate modifications to the typical family life cycle to account for the elongation of the parenting career in families and the need to lessen the weight given to the stressfulness of mental retardation in light of the multitude of other normative stressors to which these families are vulnerable.

That mental retardation in the family produces unique, difficult, and durable differences in parenting careers and family life patterns is well supported in the empirical literature (Wikler 1986) and in parental narratives (Featherstone 1980). What has been insufficiently studied, however, is the interplay between parental adaptive mechanisms and the challenges of mental retardation. Our study provides evidence that, over time, the challenges of parenting a child with mental retardation become part of the fabric of family life. While it is commonly found that there is an assaultive quality to the early parenting period, in which the diagnostic news and subsequent realization of permanent disability of the child are confronted, this period is replaced by adaptation and increased well-being. For families participating in our research, their decades of experience as parents of a child with retardation may render the "fact" of retardation much less predictive of their well-being at this stage of life in comparison with a host of other factors that affect the well-being of mothers without a child with retardation. Thus, our findings that mothers in the late midlife stage of parenting are more similar to than different from their age peers with respect to self-reported health status, depressive symptoms, life satisfaction, and social support networks may well reflect a degree of equilibration in their lives, such that indices of their current well-being appear to be unrelated to the "marker" event of parenting a child with retardation.

We also noted that because coresidence with parents is the norm rather than the exception for adults with mental retardation, the traditional sequence of stages postulated by family life-cycle theorists requires reconceptualization. Parents of children with mental retardation may either never fully complete the "launching stage" before their death (i.e., the son or daughter remains at home throughout the parents' lifetime) or may experience a launching stage that spans several decades (i.e., from the time the first child in the family leaves until the child with mental retardation moves away during the parents' elder years or before their death).

It may be appropriate to posit an additional life stage for families of children with mental retardation (or other types of lifelong impairments that result in extended parental caregiving), a stage that is characterized by companionship, mutual interdependence, and gradual emancipation of the adult with mental retardation from the proximal zone of influence of the parents. Indeed, the last stage of the life cycle, the "family in retirement" stage, may never be experienced or may be dramatically curtailed in duration. Our continuing study of the families in the present sample will be useful in determining the nature and course of family life after the launching stage is completed (i.e., post-placement).

Our research suggests that for many families, the possibility of launching is a subtle undercurrent in family life throughout the adulthood of the son or daughter with retardation. We also found that when the probability of home leaving increases (as signaled by the placement of the child's name on a waiting list for residential services), there is a concurrent elevation in parental distress. Although the causal relations between parental distress and placement probability cannot be disentangled in our present analyses, the co-occurrence of these phenomena warrants continued investigation. These findings suggest that the beginning of the launching stage is accompanied by considerable turmoil for the mother. Thus, there may be a U-shaped pattern of family distress, in which high levels of distress are experienced at the onset and the completion of active caregiving for a family member with lifelong or chronic needs.

NOTES

1. Of the initial sample, thirteen were not included in this analysis because the mother was either too ill to be interviewed or had died or because the child with retardation had died. In another fifteen families, the adult with retardation had moved out of the home. Thirty-six families declined to participate in this interview. The remaining eleven families either moved out of state or could not be located.

2. Stone, Cafferata, and Sangl (1987) estimated that the average period of caregiving for an elderly relative was about five years, whereas caring for an adult with retardation can easily last five decades.

3. In the comparison sample, the life events variable was coded one if any of the events occurred during the previous two years, whereas for the sample of mothers of adults with retardation, the period was eighteen months.

REFERENCES

Antonucci, T. C. 1986. Measuring social support networks: Hierarchical mapping techniques. *Generations* 10:10–12.

Antonucci, T. C., and H. Akiyama. 1987. Social networks in adult life and a preliminary examination of the Convoy Model. *Journal of Gerontology* 42:S19–S27.

Aquilino, W. S. 1990. The likelihood of parent–adult child coresidence: Effects of family structure and parental characteristics. *Journal of Marriage and the Family* 52:405–419.

Bengtson, V. L., and K. D. Black. 1973. Solidarity between parents and children: Four perspectives on theory development. Paper presented to the theory development workshop. National Council on Family Relations, Toronto.

Birenbaum, A. 1971. The mentally retarded child in the home and the family life cycle. *Journal of Health and Social Behavior* 12:55–65.

Blacher, J. 1984. Sequential stages of parental adjustment to the birth of a child with handicaps: Fact or artifact? *Mental Retardation* 22:55–68.

Brody, E. M. 1985. Parent care as a normative family stress. *Gerontologist* 29:19–29.

Bruininks, R. H., B. K. Hill, R. F. Weatherman, and R. W. Woodcock. 1986. *Inventory for Client and Agency Planning (ICAP).* Allen, Tex: DLM Teaching Resources.

Bumpass, L., and J. Sweet. 1987. *A national survey of families and households.* Madison: Center for Demography and Ecology, University of Wisconsin.

Carter, E. A., and M. McGoldrick. 1980. *The family life cycle: A framework for family therapy.* New York: Gardner.

Chiriboga, D. A., B. W. K. Yee, and P. G. Weiler. 1992. Stress and coping in the context of caring. In L. Montada, S. Filippi, and M. J. Lerner, eds., *Life crisis and experiences of loss in adulthood.* Hillsdale, N.J.: Lawrence Erlbaum.

Cohen, S., and T. A. Wills. 1985. Stress, social support, and the buffering hypothesis. *Psychological Bulletin* 98:310–357.

Cole, R. E., and D. Reiss, eds. 1993. *How do families cope with chronic illness?* Hillsdale, N.J.: Lawrence Erlbaum.

Cook, J. A., and B. J. Cohler. 1986. Reciprocal socialization and the care of offspring with cancer and schizophrenia. In N. Datan, A. L. Greene, and H. W. Reese, eds., *Life-span developmental psychology: Intergenerational relations.* Hillsdale, N.J.: Lawrence Erlbaum.

Crnic, K. A., W. N. Friedrich, and M. T. Greenberg. 1983. Adaptation of families with mentally retarded children: A model of stress, coping, and family ecology. *American Journal of Mental Deficiency* 88:125–138.

Farber, B. 1959. Effects of a severely mentally retarded child on family integration. *Monographs of the Society for Research in Child Development* 24 (2, ser. no. 71).

Featherstone, H. 1980. *A difference in the family: Life with a disabled child.* New York: Basic.

Freedman, R. I., and D. N. Freedman. 1994. Planning for now and the future: Social, legal, and financial concerns. In M. Seltzer, M. Krauss, and M. Janicki, eds., *Life course perspectives on adulthood and aging,* pp. 167–184. Washington, D.C.: American Association on Mental Retardation.

Frey, K. S., M. T. Greenberg, and R. R. Fewell. 1989. Stress and coping among parents of handicapped children: A multidimensional approach. *American Journal on Mental Retardation* 94:240–249.

Friedrich, W. N., M. T. Greenberg, and K. Crnic. 1983. A short-form of the Questionnaire on Resources and Stress. *American Journal of Mental Deficiency* 88:41–48.

Fujiura, G. T., J. Garza, and D. Braddock. 1992. *National survey of family support services in developmental disabilities.* Chicago: University of Illinois. Mimeographed.

Gallagher, D., M. Rappaport, A. Benedict, S. Lovett, D. Silven, and H. Kramer. 1985. *Reliability of selected interview and self-report measures with family caregivers.* Paper presented at the 38th Annual Meeting of the Gerontological Society of America, New Orleans, LA.

Gatz, M., and M. L. Hurwicz. 1990. Are old people more depressed? Cross-sectional data on Center for Epidemiological Studies Depression Scale factors. *Psychology and Aging* 5:284–290.

George, L. K., and L. P. Gwyther. 1984. *The dynamics of caregiver burden: Changes in caregiver well-being over time.* Paper presented to the annual meeting of the Gerontological Society of America, San Antonio, Tex.

Greenberg, J., and M. Becker. 1988. Aging parents as family resources. *Gerontologist* 28:786–791.

Heller, T., and A. Factor. 1991. Permanency planning for adults with mental retardation living with family caregivers. *American Journal on Mental Retardation* 96:163–176.

Hill, R. 1970. *Family development in three generations.* Cambridge: Schenkman.

Hoyert, D. L., and M. M. Seltzer. 1992. Factors related to the well-being and life activities of family caregivers. *Family Relations* 41:74–81.

Kazak, A., and R. Marvin. 1984. Differences, difficulties, and adaptation: Stress and social networks in families with a handicapped child. *Family Relations* 33:67–77.

Krause, N., A. R. Herzog, and E. Baker. 1992. Providing support to others and well-being in later life. *Journal of Gerontology* 47:P300–P312.

Krauss, M. W., and M. M. Seltzer. 1993. Current well-being and future plans of older caregiving mothers. *Irish Journal of Psychology* 14:47–64.

Krauss, M. W., M. M. Seltzer, and S. J. Goodman. 1992. Social support networks of adults with mental retardation who live at home. *American Journal on Mental Retardation* 96:432–441.

Kubler-Ross, E. 1969. *On Death and Dying*. New York: Macmillan.

Lawton, M. P. 1972. The dimensions of morale. In D. Kent, R. Kastenbaum, and S. Sherwood, eds., *Research, planning, and action for the elderly*. New York: Behavioral Publications.

Mahoney, F. I., and D. W. Barthel. 1965. Functional evaluation: The Barthel Index. *Maryland State Medical Journal* 14:61–65.

McCullough, P. 1980. Launching children and moving on. In E. A. Carter and M. McGoldrick, eds., *The family life cycle: A framework for family therapy*. New York: Gardner.

McLanahan, S., and J. Adams. 1987. Parenthood and psychological well-being. *Annual Review of Sociology* 13:237–257.

Mederer, H., and R. Hill. 1983. Critical transitions over the family life span: Theory and research. In H. I. McCubbin, M. B. Sussman, and J. M. Patterson, eds., *Social stress and the family: Advances and developments in family stress theory and research*. New York: Haworth.

Meyers, C. D., S. A. Borthwick, and R. Eyman. 1985. Place of residence by age, ethnicity, and level of retardation of the mentally retarded/developmentally disabled population of California. *American Journal of Mental Deficiency* 90:266–270.

Olson, D. H., H. Barnes, A. Larsen, M. Muxen, and M. Wilson. 1983. *Families: What makes them work*. Beverly Hills, Calif.: Sage.

Pearlin, L. 1989. The sociological study of stress. *Journal of Health and Social Behavior* 30:241–256.

Pillemer, K., and J. J. Suitor. 1991. Will I ever escape my child's problems? Effects of adult children's problems on elderly parents. *Journal of Marriage and the Family* 53:585–594.

Pruchno, R. A., J. E. Michaels, and S. L. Potashnik. 1990. Predictors of institutionalization among Alzheimer disease victims with caregiving spouses. *Journal of Gerontology* 45:S259–S266.

Pruchno, R. A., and N. C. Resch. 1989. Husbands and wives as caregivers: Antecedents of depression and burden. *Gerontologist* 29:159–165.

Radloff, L. 1977. The CES-D scale: A self-report depression scale for research in the general population. *Applied Psychological Measurement* 1:385–401.

Ramey, S. L., Krauss, M. W., and R. J. Simeonsson. 1989. Research on families: Current assessment and future opportunities. *American Journal on Mental Retardation* 94:ii–vi.

Seltzer, G. B., A. Begun, M. M. Seltzer, and M. W. Krauss. 1991. The impacts of siblings in the lives of adults with mental retardation and their aging mothers. *Family Relations* 40:310–317.

Seltzer, M. M. 1985. Informal supports for aging mentally retarded persons. *American Journal of Mental Deficiency* 90:259–265.

Seltzer, M. M., and M. W. Krauss. 1989. Aging parents with mentally retarded children: Family risk factors and sources of support. *American Journal on Mental Retardation* 94:303–312.

Seltzer, M. M., M. W. Krauss, and N. Tsunematsu. 1993. Adults with Down Syndrome and their aging families: Diagnostic group differences. *American Journal on Mental Retardation* 97:496–508.

Seltzer, M. M., and C. D. Ryff. 1994. Parenting across the lifespan: The normative and nonnormative cases. In D. L. Featherman, R. Lerner, and M. Perlmutter, eds., *Life-span development and behavior.* Vol. 12. Hillsdale, N.J.: Lawrence Erlbaum.

Shonkoff, J. P., P. Hauser-Cram, M. W. Krauss, and C. C. Upshur. 1992. Development of infants with disabilities and their families. *Monographs of the Society for Research in Child Development* 57 (ser. no. 230).

Stone, R., G. L. Cafferata, and J. Sangl. 1987. Caregivers of the frail elderly: The genetic approach. *Gerontology* 27:616–626.

Sweet, J. A., and L. Bumpass. 1987. *American families and households.* New York: Russell Sage Foundation.

Townsend, A., and L. Noelker. 1987. The impact of family relationships on perceived caregiving effectiveness. In T. Brubaker, ed., *Aging, health, and family: Long term care.* Newbury Park, Calif.: Sage.

Townsend, A., L. Noelker, G. Deimling, and D. Bass. 1989. Longitudinal impact of interhousehold caregiving stressors. *Psychology and Aging* 4:393–401.

Turnbull, A. P., M. J. Brotherson, and J. A. Summers. 1985. The impact of deinstitutionalization on families: A family system approach. In R. H. Bruininks and K. C. Laken, eds., *Living and learning in the least restrictive environment.* Baltimore: Brookes.

Turnbull, A. P., J. A. Summers, and M. J. Brotherson. 1986. Family life cycle: Theoretical and empirical implications and future directions for families with mentally retarded members. In J. J. Gallagher and P. M. Vietze, eds., *Families of handicapped persons: Research, programs, and policy issues.* Baltimore: Brookes.

Wikler, L. 1986. Periodic stresses in families of children with mental retardation. *American Journal of Mental Deficiency* 90:703–706.

Wolraich, M. L., G. N. Siperstein, and D. Reed. 1992. *The outcomes of mentally retarded adults raised at home with the benefits of PL 94-142.* Paper presented at the 25th Annual Meeting of the Gatlinburg Conference on Research and Theory in Mental Retardation and Developmental Disabilities, Gatlinburg, Tenn.

Zarit, S. H., K. E. Reever, and J. Bach-Peterson. 1980. Relatives of impaired elderly: Correlates of feelings of burden. *Gerontologist* 20:649–655.

Zarit, S. H., P. A. Todd, and J. M. Zarit. 1986. Subjective burden of husbands and wives as caregivers: A longitudinal study. *Gerontologist* 26:260–266.

VI Parent-Child Relations in Midlife

Demographic Position and Stressful Midlife Events: Effects on the Quality of Parent-Child Relationships

Debra Umberson

In the first part of this chapter I review what we know about the quality of parent-child relationships and the impact of relationship quality on parents' well-being. Two questions organize this review: What sociological factors affect the quality of relationships with children, and how does the quality of parent-child relationships affect parents' well-being? The latter part of the chapter addresses a specific concern of midlife parents: How do common stressful life events of middle adulthood affect individuals' relationships with their children? Do relationships with children become stronger and more supportive in times of parental need, or do children feel burdened and critical of parents in crisis? A number of stressful life events are common in midlife. I will consider how one of the most common events of midlife—the death of a parent—affects individuals' relationships with their own adult children.

In previous work, I defined relationship quality in terms of relationship "content": "Relational content is multi-faceted and includes both positive and negative elements. Positive relational content refers to the positive interactions and satisfactions associated with the relationship. Negative relational content refers to the conflicts, demands, and strains associated with the relationship" (Umberson 1989, 999). Is the quality of parent-child relationships an important issue? Parents easily answer this question; positive relationships with children can make parents feel accomplished and satisfied, whereas strained relationships can undermine parents' confidence and well-being. Empirical research supports parents' observations: strained and conflicted relationships with children seem to contribute to psychological distress among parents,

I thank Meichu Chen and Toni Terling for their assistance on this project and the attendees of the Workshop on Mid-Life Parenting for their comments on this chapter. This research was supported in part by a First Independent Research Support and Transition Award from the National Institute on Aging (NIA AGO8554, Debra Umberson, principal investigator) and NIA Grant #AGO5562 (James S. House, principal investigator).

and supportive relationships with children appear to enhance parents' well-being. The quality of parent-child relationships is associated with parents' well-being throughout the life course—even after children become adults and leave the parental home (Mutran and Reitzes 1984; Quinn 1983; Umberson 1992a).

THEORETICAL ORIENTATION

When I refer to sociological factors that affect the quality of intergenerational relationships, my primary focus is on sociodemographic characteristics of parents and how those characteristics affect relationship quality, a focus guided by theoretical work on social structure and personality developed by Sheldon Stryker (1981) and others (e.g., House 1977; Mutran and Reitzes 1984; Umberson 1992a). This theoretical orientation suggests that sociodemographic position represents much more than descriptive characteristics of individuals; rather, one's position in the social structure has profound implications for one's life experiences. Social position, as determined by such stratification variables as sex, race, and socioeconomic status, is associated with different opportunities, constraints, and demands: "These elements of social context then shape the individual's life experiences—including the nature of one's relationships which, in turn, have an effect on one's psychological state" (Umberson 1992a, 665).

Whether one is male or female, African American or white, rich or poor determine the types of structural opportunities and constraints an individual will face throughout the life course. In regard to parenting, gender can serve as a specific example. Structural contingencies associated with motherhood encourage and coerce women's responsibility for children and childrearing tasks. For instance, structural constraints associated with employment and availability of child care promote greater maternal than paternal involvement in childrearing (Chodorow 1978; Epstein 1988). In turn, parenting is an experience very different for men from that for women—resulting in a different kind of relationship with children.

Throughout this chapter, I adopt the structuralist approach. Although other factors, such as parents' personality characteristics, may affect the quality of relationships with children, I emphasize the power of parents' structural position to influence the quality of parent-child relationships. This view is dynamic in that as structural position changes, the quality of relationships with children may also be affected. For example, shifting from the married to the divorced status may introduce new constraints and demands that, in turn, affect the quality of relationships with children.

I emphasize several key constructs that require some elaboration: *midlife parenting, quality of relationships,* and *parental well-being.* These terms can be defined in a number of different ways, and the way they are defined may importantly affect research conclusions.

Midlife Parenting

Although parent's age can be used as a proxy variable for midlife parenting, this approach does not tell us much about the structural contingencies associated with parenting. I adopt the strategy of defining midlife parents in terms of stage in the family life course. The most straightforward family life-stage approach is to sort parents into those with minor children only, those with both minor and adult children, and those with adult children only. This approach would roughly distinguish between parents involved in active daily parenting of dependent children, parents who have more equal and independent relationships with adult children, and parents who are involved in both types of situations. An additional layer of elaboration would be to establish whether these children live in the parent's home or elsewhere. I adopt a family life-course model primarily for conceptual reasons. Position in the family life course tells us a great deal about the individual's current parenting experiences. The structural contingencies associated with parenting differ very much depending on the age and living arrangements of one's child, and these contingencies shape the qualitative experience of parenting.

The family life-course model allows us to distinguish between young, mid-, and later-life parents, but it oversimplifies matters to suggest that these divisions constitute clear conceptual divisions. One must ask, When does the transition from early to midlife parenthood occur, and when does the transition from midlife to later-life parenthood occur? There is no magic moment at which a parent can celebrate these transitions. Rather we must view these transitions as prolonged and existing along a continuum. The shift into midlife parenting is correlated with increasing independence of children, and certainly the movement of children out of the parental home is a critical step in this process. The shift from midlife to later-life parenting is even more difficult to pin down but may be associated with such factors as decline in health of parents or the birth of grandchildren. While family life course may be roughly operationalized in terms of age and living arrangements of children, age of parent should also be taken into account as an indicator of position along the family life-course continuum. I consider both factors in my later analyses. The previous research I review, however, generally divides parents into two groups: parents with minor children, and parents with adult children.

Quality of Relationships

As noted earlier, it is important to consider both positive and negative features of relationships to have a broad understanding of the quality of those relationships. It is possible for a parent both to experience a high level of conflict in relationships with children and to feel a lot of love from those children. However, previous research suggests that the negative aspects of parent–adult child relations have more impact on the well-being of parents than do the positive aspects (Umberson 1992a; see also Rook 1984). The positive and negative dimensions of relationships may also differentially affect different indicators of parental well-being. For example, demands from children may be conducive to psychological distress but at the same time contribute to a parent's sense of being needed and having purpose in life (Umberson and Gove 1989). In other words, demands from children may have some negative *and* positive effects for parents' well-being. This latter point suggests the need to consider a range of measures of parents' well-being.

Well-Being

Well-being is also a multidimensional concept. Most generally speaking, it includes both physical and psychological well-being. Psychological well-being may include affective well-being (for example, anxiety and happiness), psychiatric symptoms (e.g., depression), and a sense of meaningfulness or purpose (Ryff 1989; Umberson and Gove 1989). Physical well-being is reflected in physical health status, health behaviors, and mortality rates. Parenthood has been studied in relation to all these possible outcomes, and the effects differ in important ways depending on the nature of the dependent variable and position in the family life course (Umberson and Gove 1989). Most research on the effects of parenting has focused on psychological distress (e.g., depression) or psychological well-being (e.g., happiness, satisfaction) as the primary outcome variable. But the focus on only one outcome obfuscates our overall understanding of how children affect parents at various stages in the family life course. This chapter, as well as most of the other chapters in this volume, considers how parenting affects a range of well-being indicators.

PREVIOUS RESEARCH ON INTERGENERATIONAL RELATIONSHIP QUALITY

Most previous research on the impact of children on parents does not focus specifically on the quality of parent-child relationships. However, almost all research on the effects of parenthood implicitly suggests that the quality and, consequently, the costs and rewards of parenting are not the same for all parents.

The Family Life Course

The costs and rewards of parenting seem to be especially influenced by stage in the family life course. Parenting of an infant, a toddler, an adolescent, or the thirty-six-year-old child who has her own young children represents a wide range of experiences and social dynamics. It is often suggested that the quality of parent-child relationships changes over the family life course—with the situation improving only after one's children leave the parental home. In fact, several studies show that there is a psychological boost for parents, especially mothers, once children become adults and leave the parental home (Glenn 1975; Harkins 1978).

Although a few studies suggest that having minor children may benefit parents' health behaviors (Umberson 1987) and reduce parents' mortality rates (Kobrin and Hendershot 1977), the vast majority of studies emphasize that parenting of young children is characterized by demands and strains that are conducive to dissatisfaction, unhappiness, and psychological distress (McLanahan and Adams 1987). In contrast, the literature on families of later life strongly emphasizes that relationships with adult children are positive for parents. Several basic themes exist in the research on families of later life: parents and adult children maintain regular contact with each other (Bengtson et al. 1985; Rossi and Rossi 1990); there is a high level of positive sentiment between the generations (Bengtson, Mangen, and Landry 1984) as well a fairly even exchange of support and services (see reviews by Brubaker 1990; Mancini and Blieszner 1989); parents and adult children share many attitudes and values (Glass, Bengtson, and Dunham 1986); and even the provision of help to adult children may be rewarding to parents (Spitze et al. 1994).

The picture generated by a review of families of later life is a rosy one indeed. The primary feature of intergenerational relationships that is cast as potentially negative is the psychologically costly role that adult children may play in providing care to parents who become ill or disabled in later life (Mancini and Blieszner 1989). But even here there is some good news—*most* adult children do not have a disabled parent, and the fact that children often provide care to parents who need care may be good news to parents. A recent study of individuals in the general population leads Spitze and her colleagues to conclude that "helping parents at the low levels found in the general population may cause some distress, especially for men, but *only* when buffering conditions are not present" (1994, S115; emphasis mine). Even the recent studies on adult children who return to the parental home indicate that relationships between parents and their coresidential adult children are not generally problematic (Aquilino and Supple 1991).

If anything, it appears that research on parenting of minor children may overemphasize the negative (Goldsteen and Ross 1989; Umberson and Gove 1989), whereas research on parents' relationships with adult children may overemphasize the positive. One thing that is strongly implied by all these studies taken together is that the quality of parent-child relationships seems to change over the family life course and that it only improves with time.

Variation in the Quality of Parent-Child Relationships

Although the literature suggests that parenting of adult children may be more positive than parenting of minor children, there is considerable variation in the experience of being a parent *within* both stages of parenting. Previous research suggests several possible causes of variation in the quality of parent-child relationships.

Relationships with minor children. It is important to consider briefly the predictors of relationship quality for parents of minor children, because these factors have important implications for intergenerational relationships as children and parents grow older. While most studies indicate that young children are conducive to psychological distress among parents, the degree to which this is the case is influenced by a complex interplay of social and economic factors (Ambert 1992). This impact depends on such factors as having an adequate income (Ross and Huber 1985) and housework and child-care supports (Ross and Mirowsky 1988).

In a previous study using a nationally representative sample, I analyzed sociodemographic predictors of the quality of relationships between parents and their minor children (Umberson 1989). In that study, the positive content of relationships was ascertained with a scale made up of three questions concerning (1) satisfaction with being a parent, (2) happiness with the way children had turned out so far, and (3) how well parents felt they got along with their children. The negative content of relationships was ascertained with a question about the degree to which parents felt their children placed demands on them.[1] Several sociodemographic factors were associated with the reported quality of relationships with minor children. These associations are generally what one would expect based on the structuralist perspective. For example, a great deal of evidence indicates that mothers are primarily responsible for childrearing and that parenthood results in greater costs for women than men. The results on relationship quality corroborated these views in that mothers reported substantially more demands from minor children than did fathers. Younger mothers reported more demands than older mothers, and mothers reported more demands from children when they had more children. The level of demands felt by fathers was not influenced by these factors—probably because fathers play a more minor role in childrearing, a role that is little influenced by the daily imperatives of parenting. I found few race differences in perceived quality of relationships with minor children. African American mothers reported fewer demands from minor children than did other mothers, which may occur because African American mothers are more likely to parent in supportive kinship networks (Stack 1974) or because they define demands from children according to a different standard.

Views on the positive aspects of relationships with minor children were also affected by sociodemographic factors. Compared with divorced parents, married mothers and fathers reported more positive relationships with their minor children. Older parents also viewed relationships with minor children in more positive terms than did younger parents—regardless of age of the minor child. This may occur because older parents have more financial and personal resources that facilitate positive relationships with young children (Goetting 1986).

Overall, the positive features of relationships with minor children are associated with enhanced psychological well-being of parents, whereas the demands of parenting are associated with reduced levels of psychological well-being. Although some studies suggest that the daily strains and psychological costs of parenting may be reduced when children become adults and leave the parental home (e.g., Glenn 1975), the same social structural factors that affect relationships with minor children have implications for the quality of relationships with adult children. This happens in at least two ways: (1) carry-over effects from relationships with preadult children (e.g., remaining strains associated with an early divorce), and (2) effects of the parent's current structural position.

Relationships with older children. The quality of intergenerational relationships is as variable in middle and later adulthood as it is when children are young. In a recent study, I examined sociodemographic variation in the quality of relationships between parents and their children aged sixteen and older (Umberson 1992a). In this study, quality of relationships was indicated by three measures: (1) the amount of social support provided by children to parents as measured by two questions—about how much children listen to parents, and how much children make parents feel loved and cared for; (2) the degree of relationship strain, indicated by the extent to which children place demands on and are critical of parents; and (3) the overall level of dissatisfaction with being a parent, indicated by parents' satisfaction with being a parent, how happy they are with the way their children turned out, and how often they feel bothered or upset as a parent.

A measure of frequency of contact with nonresidential children aged sixteen and older was also considered. Scales were coded so that higher scores indicate higher levels of the construct being measured (see the appendix for complete wording of these questions). The data for this study were from a 1986 national survey of 3,618 individuals aged twenty-four and older in the contiguous United States (House 1986).[2] Results for this study were obtained by regressing the quality of relationship measures on whether parents had a coresidential child under the age of eighteen or a coresidential child aged eighteen or older and on demographic characteristics of parents including sex, race, age, marital status, education, and income.

Gender. As noted earlier, young children do their part to enforce gender expectations about who is responsible for childrearing by placing significantly more demands on mothers than fathers (Umberson 1989). Ryff, Schmutte, and Lee (chapter 10, this volume) find that mothers feel more responsible than fathers for their children's overall level of adjustment (see also Scott and Alwin 1989). After children reach the age of maturity and leave the parental home, it appears that they continue to be more involved with mothers than fathers (Rossi and Rossi 1990). Results from my previous work suggest that these different roles of mothers and fathers across the life course may result in a different quality of relationship with older children. I found that mothers visit and talk with their adult children more often than do fathers, that children provide more social support to their mothers than their fathers, and that mothers report less overall dissatisfaction with their older children. It appears that mothers' greater investment in parenting of minor children—even with the attendant demands—may contribute to closer and more positive relationships between children and their mothers in middle and later adulthood.

Age of parent. Parent's age is a particularly important variable in that it indicates the parent's position along the continuum from early to midlife to later-life parenting. My research evidence suggests that relationships with adult children improve as parents age: age of parent is positively associated with frequency of contact with children and social support from children and inversely associated with strain and dissatisfaction with children (Umberson 1992a). Relationships with adult children might improve as parents age for several reasons (see a discussion by Rossi and Rossi 1990). Children may make a greater effort to support and visit with older parents. Older parents are more likely to be retired and have the time and interest to develop relationships with their adult children. And, as parents age and grandchildren are born, issues of generativity may become more important and rewarding to parents. It may be that older parents have more financial or personal resources (e.g., maturity) that enhance relationships with children and happen to be correlated with parents' age. It may also be that, as parents age, they lower their expectations and evaluate relationships more positively even though there is no real difference in the objective quality of those relationships. Finally, there is the possibility of cohort effects, with older cohorts using different subjective criteria to evaluate relationships with their children.

It is clearly important to consider age of parent, as an indicator of parents' position along the family life-course continuum—even when the sample of parents consists entirely of individuals who have older children. I have plotted the mean scores on the quality of relationship measures according to gender and age of parents to illustrate

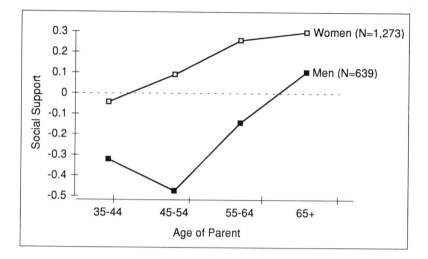

FIGURE 13.1. Mean scores on social support from children aged sixteen and older. Data from Americans' Changing Lives (House 1986). See the appendix for measures used to construct this scale.

how age is associated with parent-child relationship quality. These plots show how a monolithic view of midlife parenting may be misleading, as relationships with adult children appear to differ substantially across age cohorts.[3]

Figure 13.1 shows mean scores on social support from children separately for men and women of different age cohorts. You can see that social support from children is successively greater in older age cohorts among women. This general pattern also holds for men with the exception of slightly lower levels of social support from children among men aged forty-five to fifty-four. It is noteworthy that women report more social support from adult children than do men in all age cohorts.[4]

Figure 13.1 raises the question of whether there might be some generational crossover so that children provide more support to parents in older age cohorts because of greater parental need and, correspondingly, whether parents in older age cohorts provide less social support to their children, a question on which table 13.1 sheds some light.[5] This table gives information on parents' reports of whether the adult child or the parent provides more social support to the other. About half the parents report a fairly equal exchange of social support with their adult children, 39 percent report that they provide more of the support, and a mere 10 percent report that their children provide more

TABLE 13.1. Social Support between Parents and Children

Parents' Reports	N	Percentage	Mean Age of Parent
Parent provides more	694	39	57.08
Exchange about equal	912	51	65.20
Child provides more	184	10	72.39

Source: Americans' Changing Lives, 1989 survey.

Notes: This measure was not obtained in the 1986 survey. Respondents were asked, "Right now, would you say you provide more support, advice, and help to your child(ren), is it about equal, or does he/she (they) provide more to you?" The measure was reported for only those respondents who have at least one child aged sixteen or older.

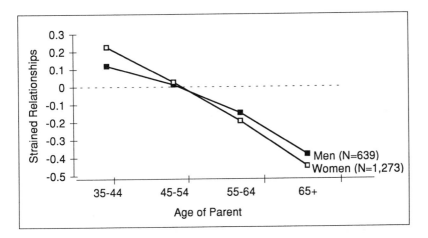

FIGURE 13.2. Mean scores on relationship strain with children aged sixteen and older. Data from Americans' Changing Lives (House 1986). See the appendix for measures used to construct this scale.

support. This table also shows the mean age of those reporting for each category. Individuals reporting a fairly equal exchange are about eight years older on average than those parents who are doing more of the supsport provision. And those parents who report that they receive more social support than they give are about seven years older than those parents reporting an equal exchange. So there is indirect evidence that some role reversal may exist in the provision and receipt of social support among the very oldest parents and their children.

Figure 13.2 indicates the degree of strain in relationships with older children. There appears to be improvement for successive age cohorts of men and women, with less strain reported in older age cohorts. The

Debra Umberson

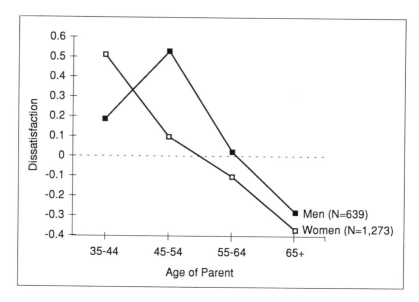

FIGURE 13.3. Mean scores on parental dissatisfaction. Data from Americans' Changing Lives (House 1986). See the appendix for measures used to construct this scale.

difference between men and women is not as great as with social support. Parental dissatisfaction follows a similar pattern, as shown in figure 13.3. Finally, we look at frequency of contact with nonresidential children in figure 13.4. Here we see that men and women are similar in reports of how often they visit with nonresidential adult children, especially in the two oldest cohorts. There is also less variation across age cohorts, compared with variation on the social support, strain, and dissatisfaction measures.

Divorce. Whether the parent was divorced or not is one of the most important factors influencing the quality of adult child–parent relationships. Divorced parents report more strain, less social support, and more dissatisfaction with adult children (Umberson 1992a). As discussed earlier, divorced parents with minor children also experience more strained relationships with children, so it may be that this simply carries over into later life for divorced parents (see also Cooney and Uhlenberg 1990). If divorce occurs after children leave the parental home, other factors may contribute to strained relationships between parents and their adult children—for example, feelings of betrayal

504

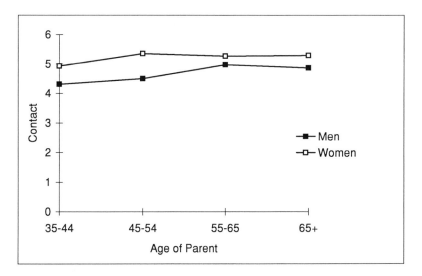

FIGURE 13.4. Mean scores on frequency of contact with nonresidential children aged sixteen and older. Data from Americans' Changing Lives (House 1986). See the appendix for wording of this measure.

and torn allegiances. Parents may also remarry, introducing new strains into relationships with children (Brubaker 1990; Cooney and Uhlenberg 1990). Daniel Meyer (chapter 3, this volume) emphasizes the economic strain associated with being a single parent, suggesting yet another reason that divorced parents may experience more parental dissatisfaction and strain.

These patterns become clearer in the graphic presentation of mean scores on the relationship quality measures presented separately by marital status. Figure 13.5 shows social support provided by adult children to divorced, widowed, and married parents. The figure suggests that divorced women receive less social support than married women in all age cohorts except that of thirty-five to forty-four years of age, perhaps because women in this age group are more recently divorced and are focusing more on relationships with their children in the relatively new absence of a marital partner. Married women in successive age cohorts report steadily higher levels of social support from adult children. Widowed women are fairly similar to married women with one important exception: widowed women forty-five to fifty-four years old report higher levels of social support than do married or divorced women. It is only in the older age cohorts that reports of widowed

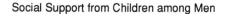
Social Support from Children among Men

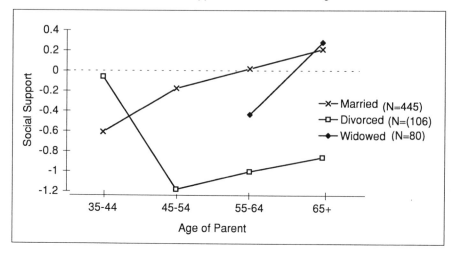

Social Support from Children among Women

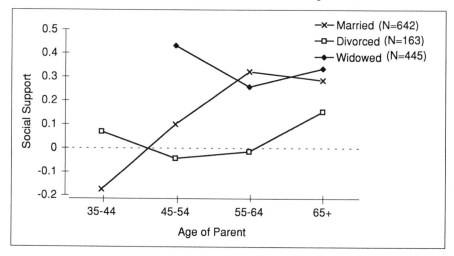

FIGURE 13.5. Mean scores on social support from children aged sixteen and older. Data from Americans' Changing Lives (House 1986). See the appendix for measures used to construct this scale.

and married women largely converge. These higher levels of support may occur because widowhood, due to parental need, elicits an increase in support from adult children earlier in the life course. Married men exhibit steadily higher levels of social support in older cohorts, whereas divorced men report drastically lower levels of support, with one exception: the thirty-four-year-old to forty-four-year-old cohort. These may be more recently divorced men who feel a greater urgency about staying involved with children and who have not disengaged from their children as much as men who have been divorced for longer periods of time (Furstenberg, Morgan, and Allison 1987).

Figure 13.6 presents mean scores on relationship strain by marital status and age. Recall that strain reflects ongoing demands in relationships with children that may differ for men and women. In the youngest age cohort, divorced men experience more strain than do married men, possibly because many recently divorced men initially attempt to remain involved with children under difficult circumstances or because the separation from children produces greater parental role strain, perhaps due to a sense of role failure (Cooney and Uhlenberg 1990; Umberson and Williams 1993). There is less difference between divorced and married men in older age cohorts, with married men reporting lower levels of strain.

The youngest divorced and married women are fairly similar in reported levels of strain with adult children. However, the situation appears to be better for older age cohorts of married women than for divorced women.

The parental dissatisfaction index refers more to overall assessments of the parenting experience than to day-to-day issues of parenting. Figure 13.7 suggests that divorced parents are generally more dissatisfied with their parenting role than are their married counterparts. This is true for both men and women, but the gap between the married and the divorced is greater for men. Figure 13.8 on frequency of contact with nonresidential children indicates that little variation exists across age cohorts of women and that marital status seems to have little to do with how often women are in contact with their children. Among men, however, the divorced appear to see their nonresidential adult children less often than do married men, with the exception of the youngest age cohort.

In sum, the divorced status of parents is associated with more strain and dissatisfaction with parenting and less support from children. Numerous studies document the difficulties associated with parenting in

Strained Relationships with Children among Men

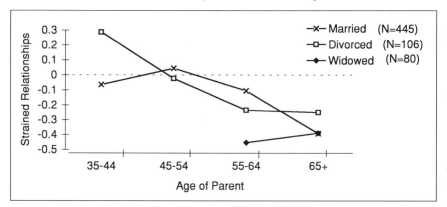

Strained Relationships with Children among Women

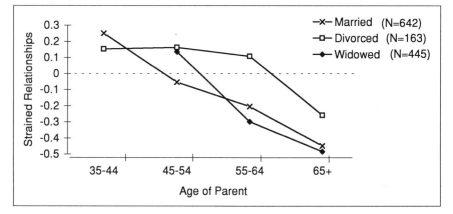

FIGURE 13.6. Mean scores on relationship strain with children aged sixteen and older. Data from Americans' Changing Lives (House 1986). See the appendix for measures used to construct this scale.

the divorced status; economic difficulties and other structural barriers make it harder for parents to maintain relationships with their children (Arendell 1986; Cooney and Uhlenberg 1990; Umberson and Williams 1993). These difficulties appear to affect relationships with both minor and adult children.

Coresidential children. How do coresidential children under the age of eighteen affect relationships with nonresidential adult children? Having

Parental Dissatisfaction among Men

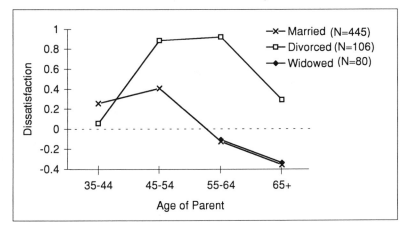

Parental Dissatisfaction among Women

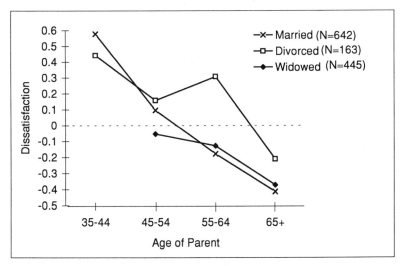

FIGURE 13.7. Mean scores on parental dissatisfaction. Data from Americans' Changing Lives (House 1986). See the appendix for measures used to construct this scale.

Contact with Nonresidential Children among Women

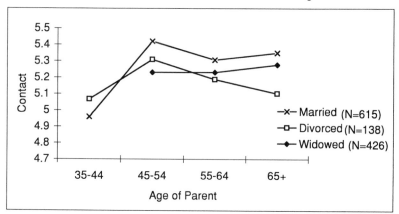

Contact with Nonresidential Children among Men

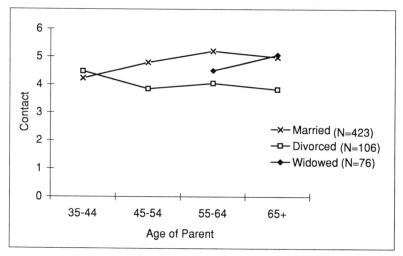

FIGURE 13.8. Mean scores on frequency of contact with nonresidential children aged sixteen and older. Data from Americans' Changing Lives (House 1986). See the appendix for wording of this measure.

nonresidential adult children and at least one minor child still at home may be the quintessential situation for what we typically think of as midlife parents: an almost empty nest. Parents who still have coresidential minor children may continue to face the daily obligations of parenting, and these obligations and associated demands may interfere with relationships with older, nonresidential children. My previous research shows that parents who have adult children living away from home *and* at least one minor child still in the parental home do not visit with their older, nonresidential children as often as parents who have a completely empty nest (Umberson 1992a). This is not too surprising, as younger children impose constraints on parents' time. In addition, parents who still have young children in the home report higher levels of strain with their *non*residential adult children. This may occur, in part, because parents who have minor children probably also have younger adult children than the typically older, fully post-empty-nest parent, and strain with parents is higher in younger age cohorts.

How does the coresidence of children aged eighteen and older affect relationships with parents? Coresidential adult children are truly a mid-life phenomenon for parents; Nadine Marks (chapter 2, this volume) shows that those parents most likely to have a coresidential adult child are in the age range of forty-five to fifty-four. In a previous study, Aquilino and Supple (1991) found that parents whose adult children return to live in the parental home are generally satisfied with this situation. However, my findings suggest a more difficult situation may present itself if we ask about both positive and negative qualities of the relationship. I found that parents who have adult children that include a coresidential child over the age of seventeen report receiving more social support from their adult children than parents of adult children who all live separately from the parents. Unfortunately, in these data, parents were asked to evaluate relationships with all their children generally rather than with one specific child. Therefore, I cannot determine if the parent receives more social support from the coresidential child or from other adult children living elsewhere. In either case, this finding is positive for parents, indicating that those parents who have an adult at home are receiving more support from adult children than parents for whom all adult children have left the parental home.

On the other hand, parents with coresidential adult children report more strain and parental dissatisfaction than parents whose children live elsewhere. Again, I cannot determine if the strain and dissatisfaction pertains specifically to the child at home or to relationships with their adult children generally. But, again, it is important either way: having a coresidential child may impose some strains and problems on intergenerational relationships. It seems that coresidential adult children may be a mixed blessing—reflecting greater intensity of inter-generational relationships in both social support and strains experienced. This may occur, in part, because of difficulties in making the transition from active to "hands-off" parenting. These findings emphasize the importance of considering both positive and negative aspects of parent-child relationships.

Race. There is some evidence that kinship ties are stronger among African Americans than whites partly in response to social structural strains faced by African Americans (Stack 1974; Sussman 1985). For example, socioeconomic strain, poverty, and single parenthood are more common among African Americans (Zinn and Eitzen 1990). In my previous research, I found that African American parents report their adult children provide less social support to them than other parents report (Umberson 1992a). African American parents also report more parental dissatisfaction. These results may occur because parenting, especially of minor children, has been a more stressful experience—due to economic strain and racism—for African Americans and there may be some carryover of this strain into relationships with adult children. On the other hand, African American adult children report that their mothers provide them with substantially *more* social support than other children report receiving from their mothers. Both findings may reflect the demographic trend toward African American women playing the primary role in rearing their grandchildren (Burton 1985; Burton and Dilworth-Anderson 1991), a situation that may lead to some African American women feeling dissatisfied with their adult children who provided these grandchildren and, at the same time, to the adult children's sense that their mothers are very supportive.

Socioeconomic status. Many authors report that parents' socioeconomic status (SES) influences the nature of relationships with their children, with parents of lower SES being closer to their adult children (Treas and Bengtson 1987). I find some support for this argument in that parents of higher SES report receiving less social support from their children and experiencing more strain and higher levels of parental dissatisfaction with adult children. This may occur, in part, because parents with more money have given their children more throughout the life course, and their privileged children may be more demanding and feel less compelled to provide various kinds of support to what they perceive as self-sufficient parents. Parents of higher SES may also have higher expectations for their children that lead them to evaluate their children as less supportive according to this standard. There is some evidence that families of lower socioeconomic status may be closer and rely more on one another (Rossi and Rossi 1990; Treas and Bengtson 1987), perhaps because of greater structural need. This context of need may also contribute to lower-SES parents' more positive perceptions of their children. Parents' educational levels influence relationships with children in a different way. Controlling for income, parents' education was associated only with the amount of social support they received from children: more educated parents report receiving more social support from their children.

IMPACT OF RELATIONSHIP QUALITY ON PARENTS' WELL-BEING

How important is the quality of parent–adult child relationships to parents? Both the support and strains experienced in relationships with adult children are important to parents' psychological distress levels (Umberson 1992a). Strain and dissatisfaction in relationships with children are conducive to psychological distress, whereas social support provided by children is associated with diminished levels of distress. Fortunately, most parents report fairly positive relationships with adult children. Unfortunately, strained relationships have more impact on distress levels than do supportive relationships (Rook 1984; Umberson 1992a). This may occur because people weight negative experiences more heavily than positive ones, making the negative experiences more salient to the individual (see Rook 1984).

I argued earlier that it is important to consider the effects of relationship quality on a range of dependent variables. I have, to this point, considered only how relationship quality affects parents' psychological distress levels, presenting findings from an analysis of cross-sectional data to address this issue. I have conducted an additional analysis for this chapter to consider whether the quality of relationships between parents and older children is associated with parents' physical health status and alcohol consumption, as well as psychological distress, using longitudinal data.

The Issue of Causal Order

Any finding of an association between relationship quality and parents' well-being raises questions about causal ordering. For example, does parental dissatisfaction undermine parents' well-being, or do psychologically unstable parents evaluate relationships with their children more negatively? This issue cannot be resolved with cross-sectional data. In the subsequent analysis, I approach this problem in two ways. First, I argue for theoretically driven hypotheses about the link between relationship quality and well-being. The structuralist framework suggests that the quality of relationships with children is shaped by the structural circumstances of parents and that relational quality has a causal effect on parents' well-being (see House, Umberson, and Landis 1988). Second, my proposed analysis considers how relationships at one point in time affect parents' well-being at a later point in time, and I control for parents' well-being at the earlier time.

Psychological Distress, Health, and Alcohol Consumption

This new analysis uses the same data as used in my previous study on intergenerational relationships and psychological distress, with the addition of a 1989 reinterview with 2,867 of the original 3,618 respondents who were interviewed in 1986. The present analysis is based on the 1,858 respondents in the 1989 interviews who had at least one child aged sixteen or older. Quality of relationships with children is measured as in the previous study. These measures of social support, strain, parental dissatisfaction, and frequency of contact may be reviewed in the appendix.

The three well-being outcomes—psychological distress, physical health status, and alcohol consumption—were chosen because they represent various ways of expressing distress. Psychological distress is measured with an eleven-item version of the Center for Epidemiological Studies Depression Scale (CES-D), which consists of the following items, for which respondents were asked how often they felt that way in the previous week: "I felt depressed," "everything I did was an effort," "my sleep was restless," "I was happy," "I felt lonely," "I did not feel like eating, my appetite was poor," "I felt sad," "I felt that people disliked me," and "I could not get going" (1986 $\alpha = .89$, 1989 $\alpha = .82$). The CES-D scale is widely used in community surveys as a measure of psychological distress (Radloff 1977).

Physical health status is measured with a single question: "How would you rate your health at the present time? Would you say it is excellent, very good, good, fair, or poor?" Social epidemiologists have found that self-reported physical health is a valid measure of physical health status (Idler and Angel 1990). In fact, it seems that people are better at rating their health than are doctors. Self-reported health is more strongly associated with subsequent mortality than are physician

514

TABLE 13.2. OLS Estimates for the Effects of Time 1 Relationships with Children on Parents' Well-Being at Time 2

Relationship Measure	CES-D	Health	Alcohol
Social support from child(ren)	.017	.009	.763
	(.025)	(.026)	(.701)
Relationship strain with child(ren)	.050**	−.015	1.450**
	(.024)	(.025)	(.660)
Parental dissatisfaction	.066***	−.067**	−.910
	(.025)	(.025)	(.673)
Frequency of contact	−.002	−.007	−.524*
	(.011)	(.012)	(.311)
Coresidential child 18+	.059	.031	.089
	(.049)	(.051)	(1.345)
Coresidential child <18	.132*	.026	−.167
	(.072)	(.075)	(2.000)
Intercept	.196	1.373	12.877
	(.192)	(.210)	(5.311)
R^2	.287	.372	.255
N	1,858	1,858	1,858

Notes: Numbers in parentheses are standard errors. Control variables include age, sex, race, education, income, marital status, and the time 1 value for the dependent variable. Data are from Americans' Changing Lives, two-wave panel survey. See the appendix for wording of questions and items used to construct scales.

$^*p \leq .10.$ $^{**}p \leq .05.$ $^{***}p \leq .01.$

reports of physical health status (Idler and Angel 1990). Alcohol consumption is a common expression of distress, particularly among men, as compared with women (Horwitz and White 1991); consumption is measured by multiplying the number of days per month that respondents drink by the number of drinks that they typically consume on those days. Scores on alcohol consumption range from zero to six hundred. All dependent variables are coded so that higher scores indicate higher levels of the construct being measured.

I consider whether the quality of relationships with children aged sixteen and older is associated with parents' well-being by regressing the well-being variable on the relationship quality measures, the demographic characteristics of parents, and the time 1 value of the well-being variable. These results are presented in table 13.2.

Social support from children in 1986 is not associated with any of the indicators of subsequent parental well-being. However, relationship strain is associated with an increase in parents' psychological distress and alcohol consumption, and parental dissatisfaction is associated with an increase in distress and a decline in physical health status. Greater frequency of contact with children is associated with a decrease in alcohol consumption over time. Having adult children in the parental home is not associated with any of the well-being measures, but having coresidential minor children is associated with an increase in psychological distress among parents.

In sum, it appears that several aspects of midlife parent-child relationships have important effects on parents' well-being. The negative content of parent-child relationships seems to be more important than the positive content in predicting parents' well-being. As argued earlier, this probably occurs because the negative aspects of relationships are more salient to individuals than are the positive aspects.

MIDLIFE EVENTS AND THEIR IMPACT ON PARENT-CHILD RELATIONS

The middle adult years are characterized by a number of common life events. Many of these life events concern change in family structure and dynamics that may affect the quality of relationships with older children. The life event, as well as relationships with children, may lead to change in midlife parents' well-being. In this part of the chapter, I examine in detail a common stressful event of midlife: the death of one's own parent. I chose this particular event for several reasons. First, this life event may be the most common of one's middle years (Winsborough, Bumpass, and Aquilino 1991; see also chapter 2 by Marks, this volume). Second, this particular event disrupts family structure in various ways—by disrupting the parent-child dyad and, if there is a surviving parent, by leading to widowhood of that parent. Finally, fairly strong evidence indicates that the death of a parent is a stressful life event, one associated with an increase in psychological distress and alcohol consumption as well as a decline in physical health status among adults (Umberson and Chen 1994).

We also have several reasons to believe that the death of a parent would affect bereaved individuals' relationships with their own children. Stressful life events are often associated with change in social relations—sometimes in a positive direction, sometimes in a negative direction (Ferraro, Mutran, and Barres; 1984). Moss and Moss (1983–84) suggest a number of ways that the death of a parent in adulthood might affect relationships with one's adult children. They posit an increased focus on generativity that leads bereaved individuals to place more emphasis on relationships with their own children; or the death might affect the "family system as a whole," either by eliciting support from children or by introducing new strains and conflicts into relationships with children.

As we have seen, the quality of relationships with adult children is strongly associated with parents' well-being. Midlife events that alter the quality of relationships with children have implications for parental well-being, at a time when the individual may already be experiencing distress as a result of the life event. Under these circumstances, the parent-child relationship might exacerbate the parent's distress or serve to alleviate some of the distress associated with the event. I conducted an analysis to consider how a parent's death affects the quality of respondents' relationships with their children aged sixteen and older. The measures of relationship quality are those presented in the Appendix: social support from children, strain in relationships, parental dissatisfaction, and frequency of contact with nonresidential children.

This analysis is unique in that I have information from parents on the quality of relationships with their children both before and after the midlife respondent experienced the death of his or her own parent. These data allow me to compare the quality of intergenerational relationships before and after the life event and in comparison with a nonbereaved control group. This is the same two-wave panel survey used in the analysis presented in the last section of this chapter. In the three-year period between interviews, 207 adults experienced the death of a biological parent. Of these individuals, 184 had children of their own, and 143 had at least one child age sixteen or older. The comparison group of nonbereaved individuals includes those persons who have at least one living biological parent and at least one child sixteen or older (N = 1,274). Bereavement was coded zero for those individuals who did not experience the death of a parent and one for individuals who had experienced the death of a parent during this time. Length of time bereaved was measured in number of months since the death. Individuals were bereaved for a period between one and thirty-one months, with a mean of fifteen months.

I first tested the possibility that the quality of adults' relationships with a parent might change as a consequence of the death of the other parent. This was accomplished by regressing the time 2 relationship measures on bereavement, time bereaved, demographic characteristics of parents, and a control for the time 1 value of the relationship measure. Table 13.3 shows that the death of a parent is associated with an

TABLE 13.3. OLS Estimates for the Effects of Filial Bereavement
on Relationships with Children

	Social Support	Strain	Parental Dissatisfaction	Frequency of Contact
Bereaved (1 = yes)	.394*	.214	.046	.500*
	(.218)	(.224)	(.219)	(.275)
Time bereaved (months)	−.055*	−.015	.002	−.086*
	(.031)	(.032)	(.031)	(.040)
Quadratic of time	.002*	.000	.000	.002*
	(.000)	(.000)	(.000)	(.001)
Intercept	−.775	1.242	.502*	1.247
	(.295)	(.306)	(.290)	(.412)
R^2	.304	.250	.408	.353
N	614	614	626	444

Notes: Numbers in parentheses are standard errors. Control variables include age, race, sex, education, income, marital status, and the time 1 value for the dependent variable. Data are from Americans' Changing Lives, two-wave panel survey. See the appendix for wording of questions and items used to construct scales.

*$p < .10$.

increase in social support from children and in frequency of contact with nonresidential children; it also indicates that social support and frequency of contact with adult children decline over time following bereavement. These findings suggest that adult children may rally to a parent's side following this midlife event, but the rally may be most active in the first few months following the death. Of course, it is important to remember that the period immediately following the death may be the time when the midlife parent is in greatest need. It is noteworthy that the measures tapping into negative aspects of parent-child relationships were not affected by parental death—so while positive content may increase following the life event, negative content may be relatively unaffected.

Thus, the quality of parent-child relationships appears to be affected by the midlife event of filial bereavement. But how do parents perceive these changes in relationships, and what are the underlying dynamics that lead to increases in support and strain with children? I have recently collected two additional sources of data that illuminate these processes. I conducted in-depth interviews with 72 people, and mail questionnaires were completed by an additional 119 individuals who experienced the death of a parent within the previous three years. These individuals—recruited through the local newspaper in Austin,

Texas—were asked a number of questions about their experiences around losing a parent, including how relationships with their own children had been affected by the loss.

Paralleling the national survey, the questionnaire data revealed that increased strain in relationships with children was much less common following a parent's death than were increased support and closeness. We asked respondents who have children whether they felt that change in relationships with children was attributable to the death of the respondent's parent. Only 10 percent (N = 13) of those who completed questionnaires reported increased strain or conflict in relationships with their children as a result of the death. Data from the in-depth interviews and open-ended questions in the questionnaire shed some light on why relationships with children sometimes become more strained following this type of loss. The loss was made more difficult for some respondents because they were also dealing with life strains associated with parenting. These strains would, in and of themselves, be conducive to parents' distress. They also reduced the parents' strength to cope with the bereavement experience. Taken together, the strains associated with parenting and bereavement sometimes contributed to increased strain in relationships with children. For example, a thirty-six-year-old mother with two daughters, one under eighteen years old and one over, stated: "My youngest daughter has had severe emotional problems coupled with drug and alcohol abuse. . . . It was hard to help her when I was so sad." The forty-nine-year-old mother of a son of twenty-seven said: "[My son's] attitude—coldness, uncaring—at the funeral and increasing since then led to a breakdown in our relationship."

Much more often, however, as in the national data, questionnaire respondents reported that they felt closer to their children as a result of the loss. Fifty-one percent (N = 40) of respondents with children reported that they spent more time with at least one of their children because of the loss, and 66 percent (N = 53) felt that a child made it easier for them to deal with the loss. The most recurrent theme pertaining to parent-child relationships in the in-depth interviews and open-ended responses in the questionnaire data was that parents became closer to a child because of their shared loss and grief: "[My younger son] really experienced a lot of grief, and he and I have been able to talk about that and to share our feelings. . . . [That has been] helpful to both of us" (fifty-three-year-old mother of twenty-six-year-old son). And another mother (age forty-five) noted: "I think my daughter [over eighteen years old] and I are closer because she and I both realize the significant loss. And I have told my daughter how important it is to discuss things that bother you—with your parents. Don't wait until they are gone—then have regrets!"

Some respondents began to reevaluate their parenting roles—placing a higher priority on their children—in ways that could enhance the quality of relationships with their children: "My family is my #1 priority now. Before, I was juggling job and family. Now there is no contest" (forty-six-year-old mother of two daughters and one son all over eighteen). And, "My father's death has helped me to deal with problem areas in my relationships with [my daughters]. . . . [I] felt the need to heal any old wounds" (forty-five-year-old mother of two daughters over eighteen).

Notably, mothers were much more likely than fathers to talk about how the death had affected relationships with their children. This fits with all the previously reviewed research showing that mothers tend to be more involved than fathers with their children—whether their children are adults or very young. This greater degree of involvement may make mothers more aware of—and perhaps more concerned with—changes in the quality of parent-child relationships.

The death of a parent is an important developmental milestone for many midlife adults, often leading to a review of the relationship with the deceased parent and with their own children. The midlife event of losing a parent often affects the nature of relationships between midlife parents and their own children. More often than not, these changes are viewed as positive by the midlife parent.

Why Do Midlife Adults Remain Involved with Aging Parents?

It appears that adults tend to remain involved with parents throughout the life course and that involvement may intensify somewhat following a stressful life event. Do midlife adults remain involved with older parents out of sense of duty or because they reap some reward from that involvement? Our in-depth interviews offer some insights into the reasons for adults' continuing involvement with parents. In general, most of our respondents seem to remain involved with their parents because they want to remain involved. These individuals are maintaining a lifelong tie with someone they care about, and they often express the importance of their parent as source of support, love, and friendship. One thirty-six-year-old man spoke of his mother as the one person in the world that no matter what I did . . . always . . . wished the best for me . . . the most important person in my life. . . . It was almost impossible to conceive of a world without her." And, a woman of twenty-eight stated, "She was always there for me when I had trouble."

In our qualitative analysis, we identified several reasons that midlife adults may gradually increase the degree of involvement with parents. One reason seemed to be that many adults, as they grew older and matured, began to appreciate their parent more than they had in the past: "I developed a much closer bond with my mother because going through womanhood and then marriage and childbirth served to draw us closer together because I could be more sympathetic with her trials and tribulations" (forty-one-year-old female). Another women (of forty-two) noted: "I started seeing . . . how good my dad was. I mean, he would do anything for me." It is not just children who grow older and begin to appreciate the other generation; many respondents also talked about changes that occurred in their parent over time—changes that sometimes resulted in the parent developing a greater appreciation for the adult child: "The older he got, I think he started realizing he couldn't make all of his four children's lives perfect, so he kind of gave up a little bit. . . . He seemed to turn into a happier person" (thirty-eight-year-old female). And a man of thirty-one indicated: "We never tended to be close. It wasn't until later that my dad came around in his emotional composition."

Parenthood of the respondent often facilitated greater closeness between the generations, providing a reason for increasing intergenerational involvement: "The primary objective [of moving next door to my parents] was to have my daughter be there so she could know them" (forty-one-year-old female); and, "Once I had my son, [my father] just idolized him and it was reciprocal too. So that brought us closer," noted a forty-six-year-old man. Some adults became more involved with a parent as the parent developed new needs: "When my dad was sick we bonded together and pulled together" (twenty-seven-year-old male). Similarly, when respondents were in need of support, they often found it in relationships with parents: "If it wasn't for my mom, I would not have gotten through [the divorce]" (thirty-four-year-old female). Even when involvement with parents was based on parental need and carried some degree of burden, most respondents indicated that they remained involved with their parent because they wanted to. On average, however, intergenerational involvement tended to be based less on need than on mutual friendship and support.

DIRECTIONS FOR FUTURE RESEARCH

The review of previous research and new analyses in this chapter raise some questions and suggest a number of important directions for future research.

Midlife Events

The data reported in this chapter indicate that relationships with children aged sixteen and older may become more supportive and that children may visit with their parents more often following the death of the parent's parent. These findings suggest that children over the age of sixteen may serve a supportive role to parents following a stressful midlife event. A number of possible life events are common to the middle adult years: children may leave or return to live in the parental home (Aquilino, chapter 11, this volume); children may divorce (Marks, chapter 2, this volume); a parent may become widowed (Umberson, Wortman, and Kessler 1992) or divorced (Brubaker 1990); or a parent's health or economic crisis (Fischer 1985; Mancini and Blieszner 1989) might modify the quality of relationships between parents and children. Future research should explore the role that children do or do not play in assisting their parents following midlife events. Although the present results suggest that children may rise to the occasion when parents experience a death in the family, other life events may not elicit such a reaction. Some events may be more likely to introduce strain into relationships with children. For example, divorce of the child or parent may alienate the two generations.

Divorce may be an especially important concern in that so many midlife parents had a divorce earlier in life or have a divorce after their children become adults (Brubaker 1990). As figure 13.7 shows, parental dissatisfaction is especially pronounced among the divorced. In turn, parental dissatisfaction is strongly associated with psychological distress. This may be an even greater problem for divorced fathers than mothers (Cooney and Uhlenberg 1990; Umberson and Williams 1993). Divorced fathers report much more strain and dissatisfaction in relationships with children than do other fathers or mothers, and they are at higher risk for psychological distress and alcohol abuse—outcomes that could benefit from more positive relationships with children. Many major life events occur in midlife. The impact of these life events on family relationships (and the impact of family relationships on the occurrence and nature of life events) represents an important area for additional research.

Measuring Quality of Relationships

Both the positive and negative dimensions of parent-child relationships seem to affect parents' well-being, although the negative aspects of relationships may have stronger effects on parents' well-being. These findings indicate the importance of attempting to measure the positive as well as the negative dimensions of relationships. Some epistemological issues should be addressed in future research.

For example, figure 13.1 suggests that parents receive more social support from children as the parent ages. And previous research on race indicates that African American mothers receive less social support from their children than do other mothers. But these conclusions assume that social support means the same thing to all individuals. It may well be that there are sociocultural differences in expectations about children so that African American and white mothers and individuals in different age cohorts define social support differently. For example, "a great deal" of social support from children may mean one phone call a week for white mothers. But, due to sociocultural differences in familial expectations, one phone call a week might indicate minimal social support to African American mothers. A useful direction for future research on midlife parenting is to consider the meaning of parent-child relationships to parents in different sociodemographic groups. The meaning a specific parent attaches to various aspects of parent-child relationships not only influences how questions about relationship quality are answered but may also suggest new and important questions about relationship quality. We might find too that the impact of relationship quality on well-being depends on the parent's understanding of what relationship quality means.

Change in Quality of Relationships over the Life Course

A primary finding of this chapter is that relationship quality seems to improve with age. This is indicated by the strong association of age of parent with parents' perceptions about the quality of relationships with their children. But other possible explanations exist for this association. As indicated above, the way that parents define quality may change with age. For example, parents' expectations about what constitutes adequate social support from children may diminish as parents age so that they are more likely to report high levels of social support from children even though the actual level of social support changes very little. This explanation corresponds to several authors' observations that life satisfaction is higher in older age cohorts; these authors suggest that individuals may lower their expectations about what constitutes life satisfaction as they grow older and become more realistic about life's possibilities (e.g., Veroff, Kulka, and Douvan 1981; Gove, Ortega, and Style 1989).

Another possible explanation is that, rather than real improvement in relationships with children over time, cohorts differ in perceptions of relationships with children or in the amount of social support that children actually provide to parents. For example, compared with younger generations, the cultural milieu of older age cohorts may have more strongly inculcated values into children about the degree to which children should be supportive of parents (Goldscheider and Waite 1991). Qualitative research on the meaning of relationship quality may be an important step in ascertaining whether such cohort differences exist. Ideally, longitudinal data should be used to chart change in intergenerational relationship quality over time.

Longitudinal Data

A number of chapters in this book, including this one, have analyzed longitudinal data in an attempt to consider the causal ordering of parent-child relationship issues and parents' well-being. Longitudinal data is quickly becoming the approach of choice for such research questions, but its use does not fully resolve most issues of causal ordering. For example, in the later analyses of this chapter, a mere three years has elapsed between data collections. This is adequate for considering how the impact of an intervening life event such as the death of a parent may lead to change in the quality of intergenerational relationships. However, is three years an adequate period of time to determine if time 1 relationship quality affects time 2 parental well-being? If parental well-being has the potential to affect perceptions of relationship quality—and surely it does—then three years may not be an adequate interval of time. Research on parents of mentally retarded children (Seltzer, Krauss, Choi, and Hong, chapter 12, this volume) suggests that the characteristics of children may begin to have effects on parents very early in the family life course (see also Ambert 1992). LaRue Allen et al.'s chapter on parents in poor urban areas suggests how the socio-cultural context of early parent-child relationships may affect midlife parents' perceptions of relationships with their children.

There is almost certainly some reciprocity between parents' well-being and the quality of parent-child relationships. This issue of reciprocity needs to be more fully considered. While future research should include longitudinal designs, the limits of such designs must be recognized and other innovative approaches to examining the link of midlife parenting and well-being should be developed.

Dependent Variables

Research on midlife and later-life parents has traditionally emphasized the effects of parent-child relationships on parents' psychological well-being. The findings reported in this chapter suggest that the quality of parent-child relationships may have important consequences for parents' alcohol consumption, physical health status, and psychological distress levels. As the chapters in this volume illustrate, midlife parenting experiences may affect a number of different dimensions of parental well-being. Future research should consider how various aspects of parent-child relationships affect a range of well-being measures.

It may be especially important to consider how midlife parenting affects physical health status. As parents age, physical health decline is of increasing concern. Children may affect parental health in a variety of ways that should be considered. First, the quality of intergenerational relationships may be conducive to psychological well-being, which in turn, affects physical health status or health behaviors. Second, children may serve the role of health regulator for parents, encouraging them to engage in health-protective behaviors such as regular doctor visits and healthy diets and to avoid risky health behaviors like alcohol consumption (Umberson 1987, 1992b). Because women generally engage in more self-monitoring than do men and, among the married, wives serve important health-regulating functions for men (Umberson 1992b), adult children may be the only people who monitor and respond to older men's health functioning, especially if these men are divorced or widowed. This possible role of children is seen in data reported in this chapter showing that frequency of contact with adult children is associated with a subsequent decline in alcohol consumption among men.

CONCLUSION

Parents' and children's life spans overlap more now than at any previous point in history (Treas and Bengtson 1987). It is quite difficult to determine when a parent becomes or ceases to be a midlife parent. It could easily be argued that one does not become a later-life parent—that is, an "old" parent—unless one becomes physically or psychologically impaired to the extent that the child provides more support to the parent than the parent provides the child. However, many parents never reach this point. As we saw, only 10 percent of parents in a recent national sample reported that their children provide more support to them than do they to the child. And this particular sample included an oversample of elderly individuals. Perhaps it is more useful to adopt a life-span approach that considers parents in specific parenting situations—for example, living with or apart from adult or minor children—but also heavily emphasizes how relationships between parents and older children continue to change across the life span.

NOTES

1. Results were obtained by regressing the quality of relationship measures on race, sex, marital status, income, age, education of parents, and living arrangements of children.

2. This is a national probability sample of persons living in noninstitutionalized housing in the contiguous United States. Data are based on a stratified, multi-stage area probability sample. Blacks and persons aged sixty and older were sampled at twice the rate of whites and persons aged forty to fifty-nine. The response rate was 67 percent. For additional information, see Umberson 1992a.

3. The data used in the multivariate analyses previously summarized in this section (see also Umberson 1992a) are the same data that were used to construct the following graphs. These graphs present simple plots of age of respondent with various measures of relationship quality. Although these graphs do not take into account statistical controls for other variables, the basic associations of respondent age with relationship quality follow the same pattern as that found in the multivariate analyses. To avoid confounding parent's age with age of child, however, these graphs exclude those respondents who have any children under the age of eighteen and include only those with at least one child aged eighteen or over living separately from the parent. Significance tests for group differences in relationship quality are not provided in figures for tests of significance (see Umberson 1992a).

4. These cross-sectional reports on age should not be interpreted as indicating that relationship quality changes as individuals age. The association of age and

relationship quality could be due to cohort effects or a number of other reasons reviewed above. Longitudinal data are needed to document change over time. The present findings are used merely to illustrate trends in the measures of relationship quality across age cohorts.

5. This question was not asked in the 1986 survey but was included in a re-interview survey in 1989. The data presented in table 13.1 are from the 1989 interviews. The 1989 survey is described at greater length later in this chapter.

References

Ambert, Anne-Marie. 1992. *The effect of children on parents*. New York: Haworth.

Aquilino, W. S., and K. R. Supple. 1991. Parent-child relations and parent's satisfaction with living arrangements when adult children live at home. *Journal of Marriage and the Family* 53:13–27.

Arendell, Terry. 1986. *Mothers and divorce: Legal, economic, and social dilemmas.* Berkeley: University of California Press.

Bengtson, Vern L., N. E. Cutler, D. J. Mangen, and V. W. Marshall. 1985. Generations, cohorts, and relations between age groups. In R. H. Binstock and E. Shanas, eds., *Handbook of aging and the social sciences,* pp. 304–338. New York: Van Nostrand Reinhold.

Bengtson, Vern L., D. J. Mangen, and P. H. Landry Jr. 1984. The multigenerational family: Concepts and findings. In V. Garms-Homolova, E. Hoering, and D. Schaeffer, eds., *Intergenerational relations,* pp. 63–73. New York: Hagrefe.

Brubaker, Timothy H. 1990. Families in later life: A burgeoning research area. *Journal of Marriage and the Family* 52:959–981.

Burton, Linda M. 1985. Black grandmothers: Issues of timing and meaning in roles." In Vern L. Bengtson and J. Robertson, eds., *Grandparenthood: Research and policy perspectives,* pp. 61–77. Beverly Hills, Calif.: Sage.

Burton, Linda M., and P. Dilworth-Anderson. 1991. The intergenerational family roles of aged black Americans. *Marriage and Family Review* 16:311–330.

Chodorow, Nancy. 1978. *The reproduction of mothering: Psychoanalysis and the sociology of gender.* Berkeley: University of California Press.

Cooney, T. M., and P. Uhlenberg. 1990. The role of divorce in men's relations with their adult children after mid-life. *Journal of Marriage and the Family* 52:677–688.

Epstein, Cynthia Fuchs. 1988. *Deception distinctions: Sex, gender, and the social order.* New Haven: Yale University Press.

Ferraro, Kenneth F., Elizabeth Mutran, and Charles M. Barresi. 1984. Widowhood, health, and friendship support in later life. *Journal of Health and Social Behavior* 25:245–259.

Fischer, Lucy R. 1985. "Elderly parents and the caregiving role: An asymmetrical transition." In Warren A. Peterson and Jill Quadagno, eds., *Social bonds in later life,* pp. 105–114. Beverly Hills, Calif.: Sage.

Furstenberg, Frank, Jr., S. P. Morgan, and P. D. Allison, 1987. Paternal participation and children's well-being after marital dissolution. *American Sociological Review* 52:695–701.

Glass, Jennifer, Vern L. Bengtson, and Charlotte C. Dunham. 1986. Attitude similarity in three-generation families: Socialization, status inheritance, or reciprocal influence. *American Sociological Review* 51:685–698.

Glenn, Norval D. 1975. Psychological well-being in the postparental stage: Some evidence from national surveys. *Journal of Marriage and the Family* 37:105–110.

Goetting, Anne. 1986. Parental satisfaction: A review. *Journal of Family Issues* 7 (1): 83–109.

Goldscheider, Francis K., and Linda J. Waite. 1991. *New families, no families? The transformation of the American Home.* Berkeley: University of California Press.

Goldsteen, K., and C. E. Ross. 1989. The perceived burden of children." *Journal of Family Issues* 10 (4):504–526.

Gove, Walter R., Suzanne T. Ortega, and Carolyn Briggs Style. 1989. The maturational and role perspectives on aging and self through the adult years: An empirical evaluation. *American Journal of Sociology* 94 (5):1117–1145.

Harkins, Elizabeth. 1978. Effects of empty nest transition on self-report of psychological and physical well-being. *Journal of Marriage and the Family* 40:549–556.

Horwitz, Allan V., and Helene R. White. 1991. Becoming married, depression, and alcohol problems among young adults. *Journal of Health and Social Behavior* 32:221–237.

House, James S. 1977. The three faces of social psychology. *Sociometry* 40:161–177.

———. 1986. Americans' changing lives: Wave I [Computer File]. Ann Arbor, Mich.: Survey Research Center [producer], 1989. Ann Arbor, Mich.: Inter-University Consortium for Political and Social Research [distributor], 1990.

House, J. S., D. Umberson, and K. Landis. 1988. Structures and processes of social support. *Annual Review of Sociology* 14:293–318. Palo Alto, Calif.: Annual Reviews.

Idler, Ellen L., and Ronald J. Angel. 1990. Self-rated health and mortality in the NHANES-I Epidemiologic Follow-up Study. *American Journal of Public Health* 80:446–452.

Kobrin, F., and G. Hendershot. 1977. Do family ties reduce mortality? Evidence from the United States, 1966–1968. *Journal of Marriage and the Family* 39:737–745.

Mancini, J. A., and R. Blieszner. 1989. Aging parents and adult children: Research themes in intergenerational relations. *Journal of Marriage and the Family* 51: 275–290.

McLanahan, Sara, and Julia Adams. 1987. Parenthood and psychological well-being. In *Annual Review of Sociology,* 13:237–257. Palo Alto, Calif.: Annual Reviews.

Moss, Miriam S., and Sydney Z. Moss. 1983–84. The impact of parental death on middle aged children. *Omega* 14:65–75.

Mutran, Elizabeth, and Donald C. Reitzes. 1984. Intergenerational support activities and well-being among the elderly: A convergence of exchange and symbolic interaction perspectives. *American Sociological Review* 49:117–130.

Quinn, W. H. 1983. "Personal and family adjustment in later life. *Journal of Marriage and the Family* 45:57–73.

Radloff, Lenore S. 1977. The CES-D scale: A self-report depression scale for research in the general population. *Applied Psychological Measurement* 1:385–401.

Rook, K. S. 1984. The negative side of social interaction: Impact on psychological well-being. *Journal of Personality and Social Psychology* 46:1097–1108.

Ross, Catherine E., and Joan Huber. 1985. Hardship and depression. *Journal of Health and Social Behavior* 26:312–327.

Ross, Catherine E., and John Mirowsky. 1988. Child care and emotional adjustment to wives' employment. *Journal of Health and Social Behavior* 29:127–138.

Rossi, A. S., and P. H. Rossi. 1990. *Of human bonding: Parent-child relations across the life course.* New York: Aldine de Gruyter.

Ryff, Carol D. 1989. Happiness is everything, or is it? Explorations on the meaning of psychological well-being. *Journal of Personality and Social Psychology* 57 (6): 1069–1081.

Scott, J., and D. F. Alwin. 1989. Gender differences in parental strain: Parental role or gender role. *Journal of Family Issues* 10 (4):482–503.

Spitze, G., J. R. Logan, G. Joseph, and E. Lee. 1994. Middle generation roles and the well-being of men and women. *Journal of Gerontology* 49 (3):S107–S116.

Stack, C. B. 1974. *All our kin: Strategies for survival in a black community.* New York: Harper and Row.

Stryker, S. 1981. Symbolic interactionism: Themes and variations. In M. Rosenberg and R. H. Turner, eds., *Social psychology: Sociological perspectives,* pp. 3–29. New York: Basic.

Sussman, M. B. 1985. The family life of old people. In R. H. Binstock and E. Shanas, eds., *Handbook of aging and the social sciences,* pp. 415–440. New York: Van Nostrand Reinhold.

Treas, J., and Vern L. Bengtson. 1987. The family in later years. In M. B. Sussman and S. K. Steinmetz, eds., *Handbook of marriage and the family,* pp. 625–648. New York: Plenum.

Umberson, Debra. 1987. Family status and health behaviors: Social control as a dimension of social integration. *Journal of Health and Social Behavior* 28 (3): 306–39.

———. 1989. Relationships with children: Explaining parents' psychological well-being. *Journal of Marriage and the Family* 51:999–1012.

———. 1992a. Relationships between adult children and their parents: Psychological consequences for both generations. *Journal of Marriage and the Family* 54 (3):664–674.

———. 1992b. Gender, marital status, and the social control of health behavior. *Social Science and Medicine* 34 (8):907–917.

Umberson, Debra, and Meichu Chen. 1994. Effects of a parent's death on adult children: Relationship salience and reaction to loss. *American Sociological Review* 59:152–169.

Umberson, Debra, and W. R. Gove. 1989. Parenthood and psychological well-being: Theory, measurement, and stage in the family life course. *Journal of Family Issues* 10:440–462.

Umberson, Debra, and Christine L. Williams. 1993. Divorced fathers: Parental role strain and psychological distress. *Journal of Family Issues* 14 (3):378–400.

Umberson, Debra, Camille B. Wortman, and Ronald C. Kessler. 1992. Widowhood and depression: Explaining long-term gender differences in vulnerability. *Journal of Health and Social Behavior* 33:10–24.

Veroff, Joseph, Richard A. Kulka, and Elizabeth Douvan. 1981. *Mental health in America: Patterns of help-seeking from 1957 to 1976.* New York: Basic.

Winsborough, H. H., L. L. Bumpass, and William S. Aquilino. 1991. The death of parents and the transition to old age. Unpublished manuscript, University of Wisconsin-Madison.

Zinn, M. B., and D. Eitzen. 1990. *Diversity in families.* New York: HarperCollins.

APPENDIX: MEASURES OF RELATIONSHIP QUALITY

Social support (alpha = .72):

1. How much (does your [son/daughter]/do your children) make you feel loved and cared for? Would you say a great deal, quite a bit, some, a little, or not at all?

2. How much (is [he/she]/are they) willing to listen when you need to talk about your worries or problems? Would you say a great deal, quite a bit, some, a little, or not at all?

Relationship strain (alpha = .56):

1. How much do you feel (he makes/she makes/they make) too many demands on you? Would you say a great deal, quite a bit, some, a little, or not at all?

2. How much (is he/is she/are they) critical of you or what you do? Would you say a great deal, quite a bit, some, a little, or not at all?

Parental dissatisfaction (alpha = .64):

1. At this point in your life, how satisfied are you with being a parent? Are you completely satisfied, very satisfied, somewhat satisfied, not very satisfied, or not at all satisfied?

2. How often do you feel bothered or upset as a parent? Almost always, often, sometimes, rarely, or never?

3. How happy are you with the way your (son has/daughter has/children have) turned out to this point? Very happy, quite happy, somewhat happy, not too happy, or not at all happy?

Frequency of contact:

1. Think of your (son/daughter/children) who (does/do) not live with you and who (is/are) sixteen or older. In the past twelve months, how often did you have contact with (him/her/at least one of them) either in person, by phone, or by mail? Would you say more than once a week, once a week, two or three times a month, about once a month, less than once a month, or never?

Midlife: The Prime of Fathers

Corinne N. Nydegger and Linda S. Mitteness

Many of the issues addressed by the Fatherhood Project over the past years are pertinent to that ill-defined period called midlife. The goals of this research have been to describe the parallel role development of fathers through midlife into late life and of children from young adulthood to their middle age, as well as to identify some of the major influences on the experiences of both generations. Using data from these studies, we will address four related issues here: (1) the father's role in midlife and late life, (2) paternal and filial maturing, (3) sons versus daughters, and (4) resource-ful fathers.

THE FATHERHOOD PROJECT

The Fatherhood Project studies emphasized family roles as experienced and interpreted by fathers and children themselves. This approach, called *emic* by anthropologists, does more than document the subjective perceptions and feelings of individuals; it shows how they are culturally organized and given meaning—literally, the phenomenology of culture.

In contrast to structural role analysis on the one hand and case study on the other, the intent has been to conduct middle-level analyses of the reciprocal roles of father and adult child, to describe their distinctive features and their meaning to those family members. To this end, we posed deliberately "naïve" questions, such as, What does it mean to be the father to an adult son or daughter? What issues are salient to such children? What difference does gender make in adult relations? Although an eclectic mix of methods was used to obtain data, we relied most heavily on lengthy, semistructured taped interviews that allowed for a variety of analyses.

One important set of analyses was the derivation of implicit theories in which "everyday" concepts and evaluations of parents and children

Corinne N. Nydegger gratefully acknowledges the support of NIMH (MH29657) and NIA (AG00097, AG03871, and AG07778).

are embedded. Such theories have been variously called *folk models* or *emic paradigms* by anthropologists, and others use terms such as *beliefs* (Stolz 1967), *everyday philosophy* (e.g., Gubrium 1988) and *naïve psychology* (Heider 1958). The term *implicit theory* emphasizes the fact that all the elements in these theories are seldom fully in respondents' consciousness but must be derived by the investigator from wide-ranging discussions.

Implicit theories are sets of integrated values, assumptions, and putative causal relations. They are shared, that is, they are cultural, not merely idiosyncratic. And they represent the cognitive bases used by people to anticipate and explain the behavior of others.

Samples

The data discussed here are drawn primarily from two studies in the Fatherhood Project. The first research involved over 250 men aged forty-five to eighty years, randomly selected within the greater San Francisco Bay area. They were college-educated and largely advantaged middle-class: all fall within the three highest positions on the Hollingshead (1957) scale of occupational prestige, ranging from minor civil service jobs to high-level professional and managerial positions, the majority being businessmen. They had traditional marriages, with few wives working while their children were young, and all had been functioning members of their first families, at least until their children were in their teens.

Thus, in terms of family, these men represent the most stable portion of middle-class fathers; they also include the last cohort whose members could take "traditional" gender roles for granted (Lewis 1986). Most important for the focus here, the majority of these fathers were successful, and the resources they can provide are by no means negligible, even in retirement. Therefore, because the sample is not representative of the general population, it enables us to examine family relations free of the common problems posed by generational mobility and financial strain.

A subsequent study drew a random sample from the pool of local adult children of the previously interviewed fathers: one child per family, sixty-two sons and sixty-two daughters, ranging in age from their twenties to their fifties (mean thirty-two years). Sixty percent of these children were married. Further research involved special subsamples to examine reciprocal work-family influences and parent-child relations in family firms.

The Fatherhood Project research explicitly rejected the traditional indexing of all parent-child relations in the family by one of the relationships. To capture the full experience, we obtained data from the fathers about relations with all their children. The results fully justify that decision: dyadic father-child relations are so varied within families that one can predict from one dyad to the next only in extreme cases. However, this variability also pinpoints critical influences on paternal role performance.

FAMILY ROLE RESEARCH

Most family researchers these days go about their work with but passing reference to role theory (a notable exception is Nye 1976). In part this is undoubtedly due to the very real and difficult problems posed by expressive roles. But in larger part it is due to the emphasis on ties of affection as the sine qua non of family membership. This emphasis is so pronounced that it is unusual to find an outcome defined in terms other than some version of quality of relations, family solidarity, or the like. Even frequency of contact, ubiquitous in gerontology, has been studied so well because it was considered an index of affectional ties. Only in regard to caregiving of elderly parents have other aspects of the relationship, such as sheer obligation, even been raised—and this largely in response to criticism by Jarrett (1985) and others.

In short, family role discussions have been subject to a persistent confusion between role performance and interpersonal relations. Unquestionably, parent and child roles in our society involve affection norms (although we have not subjected the putative strength of these norms to scrutiny), but such norms do not exhaust the role. Over a decade ago this problem was emphasized:

> Americans have a culturally unique view of kinship as a set of interpersonal relationships rather than formal relations (Schneider 1968). In line with this perspective . . . gerontologists have solidly documented supportive kin behavior and positive bonds . . . the spectrum of tender, loving care. Acrimony is seldom mentioned. . . .
>
> Anthropologists, on the other hand, have been less concerned with qualities of relations as such unless they reflect significant features of the kinship structure. In anthropological discussions, controls and strategies figure promi-

535

nently, along with competition and hostility: a kind of kin cold war. . . . It would be beneficial if we looked at each others' questions more often. (Nydegger 1983, 30)

This unique family perspective has numerous consequences for the kind of questions posed by midlife research: (1) U.S. studies cannot readily be meshed with anthropological studies to form a continuous cross-cultural corpus, thus depriving us all of insights and valuable research opportunities; (2) one finds little encouragement to examine the substantive content of family roles other than affection (always excepting our fascination with marital roles); (3) the neglect of life-course or developmental aspects of these roles is reinforced: the strength of affectional ties between parents and adult children leads us to assume that the roles themselves are stable in adulthood as well; (4) there is an unwarranted assumption that the parental generation is relatively resourceless and powerless; and (5) although we need to assess the rapid changes in current family functioning, we have less data than we assume on traditional roles of fathers to use as a comparative base.

Role Functions

The first task of the Fatherhood Project was to specify the substance of the role of father and its changes over the lifetime. Implicit and explicit functions in the role of father to infants and young children have been exhaustively studied in more recent years—authority, caretaking, socialization, and so forth (e.g., Marsiglio 1993–94). Customary behavior in the role appears to be changing, although specific features are subject to current debate. However, most discussions focus on the relative distribution of functions between mothers and fathers or the relative importance attributed to various functions (such as fathers now valuing nurturance more). There seems little question about the overall substantive content (i.e., the function repertoire) of the role. Fathers have not ceased to exert authority, for example, even if they now more often share nurturant responsibility with mothers. It is these broadly defined functions of the father's role that come to mind when we use the term *father*, and do so with widespread academic and lay consensus.

Clarity, however, pertains only to fathers of young children. Once children have left the parental home, the professional literature provides few pointers to what the role of father is or should be. More often than not, once children are adult the terms *father* and *mother* are replaced by the amorphous *family relations*. In this vein, some early role-loss enthusiasts went so far as to include parenthood as one of the roles lost in later life. Most reject this position, although all agree that the dense repertoire content of father to a three-year-old is much reduced over time, and in that sense, the role is attenuated. Does this imply it gradually empties, thus qualifying as one of Rosow's "tenuous" roles (Rosow 1976)? What is left of this role that typically stretches over another fifty years?

The end of parents' lives provides information in regard to two features: assistance and affection. Gerontology has amassed a huge amount of data on children's (mostly daughters') caretaking of infirm parents, and has documented financial transfers between parents and children, especially at times of crisis in either generation. The Rossi and Rossi (1990) study of kin obligations is a good example of the latter kind of research, providing unusually broad coverage of the adult life span. And, as noted earlier, the affective ties between generations have been intensively studied, to general agreement that these ties are typically satisfying and important, especially for parents. These researches, however, fill in only a few portions of the large blank space of parent and adult child roles.

Role Measures

Preliminary discussions with fathers, along with Nye's (1976) analysis, had provided a list of functions meaningful in young adulthood and had also indicated that gender of child needed to be taken into account. Discussions further showed that most men hold implicit theories of fathers' effect on children by age and sex. For example, about half believe that fathers' parenting becomes most important just before and during adolescence (especially for sons), with mothers being regarded as most influential at earlier ages.

Based on these suggestions, one technique to assess the respondents' perceptions of the role "losses" of fathers was to have them rank the functions they regard as relevant, in relation first to preadolescent children and then to children the current age of their own eldest children. To emphasize contrasts, sons and daughters were ranked separately, and the men performed the same task for mothers. This crude task was intended as only one approach, and its very shortcomings proved

TABLE 14.1. Age Ranges at Which Paternal Functions
Are Lost and Gained

Child's Age (years)	Functions Lost		Functions Gained		Stable Functions
	Sons	Daughters	Sons	Daughters	
15–18	Caregiver				Model
19–22		Caregiver		Counselor	Caregiver E
23–26	Authority Protector		Counselor		(emotional support)
27–30	Provider Teacher	Authority Protector Provider	Friend		
31–34		Teacher	Companion	Friend	
35+				Companion	

Note: Function levels based on median rankings of functions per age group.

useful, for it provoked the men to discussion of role changes in their own families and across generations and forced us to take notice of alternative meanings of some functions.

The overall trend of these functions can be summed up in one word: convergence. Various patterns of parenting preadolescent children emerged: some men see little difference between their parenting and that of their wives; others sharply differentiated responsibilities. Most reported overlapping functions. The older cohorts tend to report the more traditional distinct patterns, but this trend is not as pronounced as expected. Perhaps experience as a grandparent or educational level may account for this. But, given the frequency of this same pattern in the youngest cohorts and the results of more recent research (e.g., Marsiglio 1991), it is just as likely that sweeping family role changes have been exaggerated.

Regardless of early patterns, children's maturing is accompanied by reduction of functions for both parents; their roles converge, but not until children reach their thirties.[1] The broad picture emerging from these data is unambiguous: those functions that disappear from the repertoire (i.e., medians approach or reach zero) are those implying children's subordination and dependence. But the age at loss is surprising. As shown in table 14.1, only Caregiver disappears during the late teens; Authority, Protector, and Provider persist through the twenties, and Teacher remains viable into the early thirties. Fathers certainly regard few of their role functions as finished until their children are fully adult and settled in life.

However, the pattern of reduction significantly differs by child's gender, which is consequential in family relations, particularly after marriage: supervisory functions are retained longer for daughters, as shown, and Provider and especially Protector are ranked as more important for daughters than for sons as long as they remain in the role repertoire.

Two functions remain stable across age: Model and the alternative interpretation Caregiver E (giver of emotional support), which are status-neutral and ranked at a middle level of importance. Those functions exhibiting dramatic gains over time (age at highest median shown in table 14.1) are the clearly egalitarian Friend, Counselor, and Companion (although the latter is salient only to men with local children). In regard to adult children, it is the highest ranked function, that of Friend, that is selected by virtually all fathers as their most important defining function, followed by Counselor, Model, and, for some, Companion and (Care)giver of emotional support.[2]

Is this role loss or emptying? We would argue against such an interpretation. Confronted by the necessary reduction of functions in the father's role as his children grow into adulthood, the notion of role loss was probably inevitable, as was the middle-aged housewife's empty-nest syndrome, so recently put to rest. The reality of fathering is a process of negotiated change: the status unequal, supervisory functions are gradually performed less and less often and at the same time are reformulated again and again in ways appropriate to the child's maturing. In time, they cease to be performed at all. The parent role is unique in that it demonstrates success by no longer being needed—at least, in its early form. It must be divested of many of its no longer appropriate functions and must, literally, be transformed. In effect, the role itself matures along with the children. The mentor role is the only one that comes to mind with a similar course. Two processes are involved: role transformation and function latency.

Role transforming. Cohler (1983) emphasized the necessity for change in relations in later life: "Too often it is assumed that family relationships which are satisfying and appropriate within young and middle adulthood will also be appropriate in later life" (37). This is just as true of functions in the role repertoire. No paternal function that is performed over the span of a child's growth into adulthood can remain unchanged. Even those functions that are dropped persist too long to escape a series of major changes. For example, authority over a twenty-year-old cannot be exercised as it had been when the child was nine; to do so would be highly inappropriate. Indeed, recommendations for parental changes in performing just this one function form the bulk of popular parenting literature.

In another example, respondents' comments about Caregiver forced us to differentiate between the literal caregiving only appropriate to children through their teens and that transformed version of Caregiver E applicable to adult children—emotional support. Gender exerts a constant influence as well: providing in regard to a daughter and a son will be performed in very different ways, and fathers expect to do more for daughters. Also it differs greatly from the function in childhood: little tact is required in providing money to a ten-year-old or in refusing a teenager's request, but a great deal of tact is demanded of a father refusing to bankroll a child's business venture or new house.

The major change as children move toward adulthood is in control and subordination, as mentioned. But it is not until children are in their thirties that the new role picture stabilizes. During this lengthy, gradual shift toward an egalitarian adult relationship, *all* functions are either transformed or must be dropped from the repertoire. Thus, Authority soon disappears, but a function such as Teacher gradually diminishes to yield to Counselor, whereas Caregiving in childhood is transformed into its appropriate adult form. The process is one of continual transformation, influenced by the unique attributes characterizing each father-child dyad, as well as patterned expectations based on age and gender of children.

Latent functions. The stance of role research, regardless of theoretical perspective, tends to be active, concerned with performance. This is not surprising, since the predominant purpose of role analysis has been to explain regularities of behavior, not to explain inaction (save when the latter is considered to be an act of restraint because of inhibitory norms). Nevertheless, much of the behavioral repertoire of certain roles is typically enacted only now and then; these behaviors are latent most of the time. For example, caretaking/nursing of a spouse is performed only when cued by the spouse's illness, thus, it may never be enacted. But we continue to regard this behavior as an essential, if latent, function of the spouse role. Turner (1970) early pointed out that kinship is a "reservoir of persons," hence of latent relationships, and Riley (1983) emphasized the family's latent resources; network theory also implies a view of social contacts as latent social resources (Boissevain 1974). Latency is such a common feature of roles that we take it for granted, focusing on specific functions only when they are activated.

So it is with most of the functions that parents no longer cite as part of their role repertoire. These functions remain latent, ready to be performed at need. The financial obligations so often documented are obviously the latent, adult version of the providing function: Rossi and Rossi (1990) noted that "higher obligations are expressed toward descendants than ascendants in the kindred" (206). Renewed protection can be depended on when children are threatened or need help, as can caregiving in times of illness or crisis. For the men in our advantaged sample, a child's first move into real estate or the stock market is likely to elicit resurgent teaching behavior. Even authority may recur, as reported by annoyed daughters returning to parental homes following divorce.

Sometimes reactivation of latent functions causes discomfort, even provoking intergenerational squabbling reminiscent of disputes with adolescents. The reasons are not hard to find. Contrary to the popular myth, "The assumption that the lifelong status and role of parent is paramount in the self-identity of older adults is one that deserves scrutiny rather than complacent acceptance" (Eisenhandler 1992, 254). And qualitative studies of healthy, community-dwelling elderly contradict this assumption (Blieszner and Mancini 1987; Eisenhandler 1992). Rather, the majority of parents to adult children feel they have done their job as parents and have gone on to develop their own lives; they prefer less active involvement and enjoy the newfound liberty to structure their relationships in an adult fashion to suit their own desires (Aldous 1987; Hess and Waring 1978; Troll 1988; Wellman 1990). Even though they stand ready to help children, if help involves disruptions of their lives, such as coresidence, it also is likely to arouse discomfort.

In addition, it is all too easy for parents and children to regress to earlier patterns of behavior, as if the child is still a subordinate, thus undoing in one stroke all the work of previous negotiations. This may be likely to occur when the parent feels the child's problems reflect faults in his or her own parenting. In the emphatic judgment of one of our respondents, "If a father has been a good parent, he wouldn't have a thirty-year-old [son] who can't even support himself!" Circumstances do influence the degree to which parents blame their children or themselves, but not to the exclusion of such gut responses.

Problems such as these may or may not occur, but they are inherent in mid- and late-life parental roles. For the point we want to make here is that the role of father to adult children can usefully be thought of not as an empty but as a largely latent role: a father is most like a lifelong friend, but one who is *also* his child's primary resource or guarantor, that is, he stands ready when needed to perform his early functions again, now transformed to age-appropriate form.

THE GOAL: ROLE MATURITY

Long-term family roles are the most visible shapers of our adult lives. And those with whom our lives are involved interact with us in the contexts of these roles. Thus, the roles are subject to strong pressures to change, from alterations in the individual, from interpersonal relations, and from the external conditions that are the context of role performance. At crisis points these pressures are the stuff of drama as well as research. But the constant, small changes—the slowly altering roles of coworker, friend, family member—are absorbed without note and seldom examined (Matthews 1986). Often it is only after the fact, as we look back over the years to when the role was young, that we realize how much has altered. Although some change is always idiosyncratic, in many roles, patterned change is routine.

The Role Course

In dealing with long-term roles that typify the adult years, it is useful to think of these roles as having a life course of their own—the *role course* (Nydegger 1986a). Few roles are static over a long span of time, and they can be classified according to the nature of their characteristic changes. For example, one type is the limiting case of the stable role, in which change is neither expected nor desired: the lay religious functionary and the ward boss are examples of desired role stability. At the other extreme is the *sequencing* role, with predictable transitions in an orderly pattern, as in the bureaucratic career ladder. *Transforming* roles may exhibit qualitative changes, even patterned ones, but they show no inherent necessity or orderly sequence, as in friendship changes resulting from changed circumstance, such as relocation or marriage.

Most pertinent here, some roles *develop* over time, exhibiting gradual, qualitative modifications that are predictable, desired, and unidirectional toward a particular goal state. This is clearly the implicit theory of parental and child roles that Fatherhood Project respondents had in mind. In their perspective, the midlife period of parenthood is not static, nor is the role of the maturing child.

Paternal Maturity

Fathering is an interactive process, characterized by uneven development and lasting more than half a father's lifetime. When children are young, paternal goals are clear and the role largely preshaped; the role develops primarily in response to the child's growth and skill acquisition. But as children develop toward maturity, both father's and child's roles must also develop and mature in tandem to accommodate the changing balance of independence and dependence. These roles are negotiated and renegotiated during a decades-long process with only slight help from fuzzy cultural guidelines and a general consensus on the goal: friendship plus parental guarantees.

The process is not simple: paternal functions are relinquished or transformed, children take on new responsibilities, somehow the father and child must move from a control and dependence relationship to one of essential equality. And this must be accomplished within the complexity of emotionally charged and entangled lives that is the family. But accomplished it must be, for the cultural expectation of development is very clear: for example, Hagestad (1986) quotes a mother, asked whether there had been changes in her relationship with a twenty-five-year-old daughter: "No! And that's the problem!" (685). Such comments were also commonplace among the men in the Fatherhood Project. Respondents not only can specify a general timetable for children's maturational events based on role synchrony (Nydegger 1986b) but are also insightful as to the processes involved.

Dimensions of Maturing

Previously (Nydegger 1991), the two major conceptions of adult maturing were assessed as to their utility in expanding Blenkner's (1965) classic discussion of filial maturity. Briefly, these are an ideal state model (predominantly psychoanalytic, reviewed by Kiefer 1988) and an empirical, competence model (especially Heath's [1965]). Neither offers much help in clarifying the notion of maturity in filial or parenting roles, and Blenkner's brief discussion is insightful but limited in use by its extraneous Eriksonian task and crisis framework. It was the Fatherhood Project respondents who proved most useful, detailing a grounded implicit theory of filial maturity matched by a parallel theory of paternal development.

Two dimensions or processes appear to be critical in these developments, as they may be to all intimate roles. "One is distancing, the other comprehending. As the first pulls parent and child apart, the second tends to draw them together; development in these roles is the result of balancing these forces at each stage of life" (Nydegger 1991, 101).

Distancing. Children's distancing is a well-established necessity in emotional emancipation from parents, most notable in adolescence (Colarusso and Nemiroff 1981; Erikson 1963). In the respondents' view, this process is expected to continue, to establish that psychological separation essential for the child's personal growth and also for the objectivity necessary to see the parent as a person, not only as "parent." In time, this objectivity is expected to be reflexive: thus, in reverse, children then can see themselves in the role of "child," not only as individuals.

A parallel development characterizes fathers: "And the father must also distance himself from his children, for his life is not defined solely by the parental role; he must look forward to an altered relationship and reduced involvement" (Nydegger 1991, 105). If all goes well, father and child finally reach their goal: they relate to each other as mature adults.

Comprehending. Considerable objectivity is a precondition of comprehension. For children, it typically is a slow process, beginning most often in the twenties. But respondents emphasized the gradualness of deepening understanding as they themselves matured, entered into career, marriage, and their own parenthood. Parenthetically, the last is commonly cited as being the most enlightening about parents. The final phase of this development is reached when children comprehend their parents' world and how it shaped parents' opinions and limited their options.

This level of comprehension is difficult to achieve and not expected before the forties (when sons often discover they resemble their fathers much more than they had realized). But, once gained, comprehension serves to reduce conflict with parents, especially fathers. For insofar as past social trends tend to be perceived as historical processes beyond individual control, knowledge of the sociohistorical context of a father's life gives the child the option of excusing attitudes the child deplores (Nydegger, Mitteness, and O'Neil 1983).

The parallel development for fathers is considered essential to good parenting of children at all ages. One major function of fathers is to teach and counsel, to socialize their children. But they must try to socialize to the child's world and an unknown future. Just as one aspect of a father's own filial maturity in midlife is comprehending his now old parents within their social history, so his paternal maturity is evidenced in his willingness to comprehend his children's distinctive social world. We expect a great deal from middle-aged fathers!

But we cannot expect perfection, and asymmetry is evident. A father may come to rationalize and excuse his own father's shortcomings in time: "Although his parents' world impinged and constrained, he lived in it as a child, not as an adult: It is not *his* world" (Nydegger, Mitteness, and O'Neil 1983, 544). But the same father is more likely to misperceive social changes in his children's generation as personal faults, the willful rejection of his own values. And these are very much a part of his own world. Accusations of wrongheadedness alternate with empathy for years before reaching stability of comprehension—or incomprehension.

Sons versus Daughters

Insofar as gender has been shown to be critical in determining parental patterns of belief and behavior in early childhood and adolescence, we should expect gender to remain an important determinant of adult children's relations with parents. To date, it has been so documented repeatedly in regard to old, and especially ill, parents. And attention to the middle years has produced various hypotheses, though little data (e.g., Gutmann 1987; Hess and Waring 1978).

Certainly the Fatherhood Project concluded, in agreement with its respondents' assertions, that being a father to a son and to a daughter are profoundly different experiences. Despite apparent convergence once children have reached full maturity, the distinctive relations established early persist throughout life. These differences, however, are not always obvious, for they are seldom matters of "How much?" but most often responses to "How?" or "In what way?" That is, they are predominantly *qualitative*.

Quality of Differences

Fathers' ratings of the quality of their current relationship with each child are strongly correlated with problems experienced with that child (Nydegger and Mitteness 1991), but gender shows no significant differences in the sheer number or severity of these problems. When the kinds of problems are examined, however, those presented by sons and daughters show virtually no overlap. Even the youngest cohort of fathers (now in their fifties) reported the classic "sugar 'n spice" versus "puppy dog tail" gender stereotypes as the bases for distinctive problems: "Briefly, sons are harder to control, more assertive and defiant in testing limits and pushing for independence; proving their masculinity can lead to serious trouble. Daughters are more sensitive and emotionally labile, but less defiant and easier to control, in part because they mature earlier than boys; but maturation entails worry about early pregnancy" (Nydegger and Mitteness 1991, 254).

Fathers make little attempt to justify or explain these perceived gender differences; it is simply part of the world as it is, a fact in these men's social landscapes and personal experiences. Fathers are aware of current trends toward redefining gender expectations and, with some distinct exceptions, are cautiously supportive. But most who become truly engaged with this movement are those who have been influenced via the difficulties experienced by their daughters or granddaughters.[3]

These beliefs about gender exert an important influence on men's parenting, permeating their attitudes and priorities. For example, they are the bases of those differences in functions earlier noted: fathers see their primary function for sons as fostering independence and a secure future, whereas daughters, believed to be more vulnerable, must be better provided for and protected for a longer time. Adult children attribute even more importance to gender than do their fathers: in families with both boys and girls, almost two-thirds reported dissimilar treatment specifically because of gender.

A Shared World

One point that emerged in discussions of gender differences is critical in shaping the lifelong relations between children and their fathers. It is a point deserving focused study: in anthropological perspective, it is "sharing a world." It is both a source and a consequence of gender differences.

Fathers not only socialize sons into their male world but also share it with them. They find it easy to understand sons, easy to develop shared interests and empathy. To the contrary, daughters have a different perspective and inhabit a different, female world. (The following discussions are based on fathers' relations with traditional daughters; nontraditional daughters will be dealt with separately.) Fathers find it more difficult to understand their daughters and to find interests in common. The children agree that, in both adolescence and adulthood, fathers understood sons better than daughters.

For fathers and sons, this sense of sharing a world and a distinctively male perspective grows stronger as sons enter their careers, establish their own families, and move through adulthood. This is a cognitive, not emotional, issue. Therefore, regardless of the quality of relations, it provides a commonality of experience between sons and fathers that is not available to daughters.

Father-Son Relations

Relations between fathers and sons are more complex than those between fathers and daughters. They involve more dimensions, must accommodate to greater changes over time, and are plagued by inherent, sustained tensions. Typically, fathers were more negative about sons (more dissatisfied, critical, worried, and so forth), and sons, more critical of fathers, but as noted, they also understood sons better than daughters. The most salient issue raised by respondents in defining good father-son relations is *respect:* "Fathers hope for their sons' respect and sons want to earn the respect of their fathers. But each wants to gain it on his own terms, that is, to be respected on the basis of his own values, not the other's. Attaining this goal is a slow, lengthy process, with tension typically unresolved until the son is well into his 30's" (Nydegger and Mitteness 1991, 258).

The thorniest issue is sons' independence. From the father's perspective, it is his duty to guide his son safely into independence.[4] Sons push for unfettered autonomy, while fathers apply brakes and try to correct erratic steering. In this advantaged sample, however, independence presupposes a sound economic basis for a son's future—a lengthy process—therefore, legal adulthood is irrelevant to fathers as a developmental milestone, but college graduation is a major one. Moreover, most fathers maintain some level of oversight of a son's early career, availing themselves of opportunities to advise and counsel.

Balancing between help and intrusion, on one hand, and between maintaining privacy and rejection, on the other, is a tightrope act for both fathers and sons (Nydegger and Mitteness 1988). The common tensions of young adulthood recede by the late twenties or so, and relations steadily improve. Sons no longer feel they must prove themselves, and fathers have fulfilled their major obligation, even if not altogether satisfied with the result. Relaxation from responsibility allows fathers the freedom to accept and respect sons on their own, now adult terms and to express affection. As sons settle into careers, they better understand their fathers' problems and achievements. With their own marriages and parenthood, they can better comprehend their fathers' perspectives and can excuse many attitudes as remnants of an earlier social world. Sons too are now free to accord their fathers respect and affection.

Father-Daughter Relations

Fathers have the least complex, most relaxed relations with traditional daughters, that is, those whose lives are much like their mothers': job (rather than career), marriage and children, return to work optional. In these dyads, good relations are generally established by early adulthood, and the salient characteristic is affection; each wants the other's love. A favorable bias toward daughters appears throughout the data. Fathers, apparently feeling less responsible for daughters' socialization, are less critical of daughters and readier to excuse their mistakes. Freed of the responsibility of critical oversight, fathers relax and enjoy their daughters.

But fathers and traditional daughters inhabit different social worlds. Fathers tend to regard daughters as delightful but mysterious creatures; daughters are equally likely to find fathers hard to understand. Although proving no hindrance to affection, comprehension is necessarily constrained: the most common complaint of daughters is that they are misunderstood and are not close to their fathers. Thus the relationship remains in many ways immature (as I have defined it here), despite real mutual affection.

Fathers and Children-in-Law

The key issue governing fathers' relations to daughters is their perceived vulnerability. Predictably, tension arises when their protection is most seriously challenged—a daughter's marriage (or long-term involvement). This is the most frequently cited source of tension be-

TABLE 14.2. Blame for Child's Divorce

Who Blamed	Sons (N = 45)	Daughters (N = 44)
Child	18%	2%
Spouse	33	34
Both	4	18
No fault	27	45
No opinion	18	0
TOTAL	100%	100%

Source: After table 5.2 in Nydegger 1986c, 103.

tween married children and their fathers. As noted, daughters elicit less dissatisfaction than do sons, but it is more focused: the primary complaint about a daughter has to do with her marriage. In regard to sons, marriage is surpassed by concerns about their lack of achievement in young adulthood, but with age, marriage also gains prominence. However, gender differences remain: "Marriage is the *only* complaint that does not decrease with age. . . . However, it never looms so large for sons as it does for daughters" (Nydegger 1986c, 102).

Fathers shrugged off most dissatisfactions with children and in-laws as inevitable frictions in family life. But for roughly 20 percent, they cause serious strains: of these, 37 percent blame daughters-in-law, and 54 percent, sons-in-law. Two basic problems are involved: divorce and disapproval of a child's spouse. Blame for divorce clearly illustrates the favoritism toward daughters. As table 14.2 shows, when blame is assigned, the child's spouse rather than the child is most often found at fault. But sons are blamed far more often than are daughters, who, at worst, share blame with their former husbands.

The reasons for disapproval of children-in-law are far more revealing than their sheer frequency: sons-in-law typically pose a different *kind* of problem than do daughters-in-law. Of the various reasons given, the dominant one for sons-in-law is that they are hurtful to daughters in some way (emotionally abusive, adulterous, shiftless and poor providers, and so on). Fifty percent of the complaints against sons-in-law fall into this category and obviously reflect concerns that they are not adequately performing fathers' earlier protecting and providing functions.[5]

In contrast, daughters-in-law are disliked more often for personal qualities than for poor family performance. In the latter case (38 percent), however, the problem is not that they harm the sons but that they harm the parents themselves by pulling the sons away from their own families toward the wives' families.

Married children agree that sons-in-law are the typical locus of strain and assign blame for this problem more often to fathers than mothers. But they also point out another source of difficulty fathers had glossed over: the father's new wife. "Informants were eloquent about the disruption of family bonds due to [fathers'] remarriage and drew an exact parallel to parental complaints about daughters-in-law" (Nydegger 1986c, 107). Thus, the son-in-law is the most obvious and modal source of tension. But the most serious threat, although less frequently encountered, is caused by wives alienating their husbands from their families. This latter threat is posed both by daughters-in-law and by late second wives.[6]

Nontraditional Daughters

Current trends in women's lives are altering relations between fathers and their daughters. As daughters more often move into occupational worlds dominated by men and plan careers instead of, or along with, marriage and children, their relations with fathers come to resemble more closely those typical of fathers and sons. For example, fathers' responsibilities expand to include socializing these daughters to the male world of work, easing their career entry, and overseeing their progress. As with sons, their now shared work world promotes commonality and mutual comprehension, facilitating closeness and appreciation.

However, these daughters lose their immunity from criticism. A career-oriented daughter may benefit from her father's tutoring but is also subject to his criticism and blame for failure: their relationship now is likely to exhibit the same tensions characterizing father-son relations. The relations being correspondingly more complex, they also achieve a higher level of role maturity. Thus, fathers and nontraditional daughters are able to attain a fuller understanding and respect for each other and their achievements than is typical between fathers and traditional daughters[7] (Nydegger and Mitteness 1991).

RESOURCE-FUL FATHERS

The advantaged status of the Fatherhood Project sample provided an opportunity to examine that factor variously referred to as affluence, social class, high status, and so forth, in adult families. Early studies of young families showed that fathers' authority increased with social class (e.g., Kohn 1963); Robert Coles reminded us that affluent, upper middle-class suburban families encourage self-esteem and facilitate their children's school achievements (1977); many high-status professions are traditionally handed down the generations; dynastic families wield enormous influence over their members. But despite our everyday knowledge of the importance of money and power in domestic relations, there has been surprisingly little interest in their influence on relations between fathers and children once they reached adulthood.

Similarly, gerontology has paid scant attention to the well-off elderly. In part this is due to the problem orientation of the field: since income is one of the best predictors of life satisfaction, the wealthy have been dismissed as not having problems and hence of little interest, even, perhaps, as not deserving study. Certainly, they are the only group not routinely oversampled.

But another research bias is also at work: assumptions about mainstream cultural homogeneity exert a strong influence not only on what we study but on how we study it as well. For example, we expect ethnicity to produce qualitatively distinct family relations; but we expect social class or income to produce only quantitative differences—a matter of more or less along the same dimensions. Consequently, within mainstream samples, we typically limit questions to dimensions appropriate for all class levels: thus, we guarantee that only more or less differences *can* emerge. These results, in turn, reinforce our assumptions of amount-only class differences. This loop bypasses the question of qualitative differences entirely.

Social Mobility and Fathers' Image

The image of the middle-aged and older father that emerges from gerontological and popular literature of the last several decades is predominantly one of social ineffectiveness and personal weakness. The older father is repeatedly portrayed as nearing or already in retirement, out of touch with the world, relatively uninvolved with his children, and as socially dependent on his increasingly assertive wife. It is assumed that he can no longer contribute instrumentally to the family and especially to his upwardly mobile children: he cannot offer assistance, as does his wife, who can help domestically when needed, and he cannot share his children's interests. His children feel obligations toward him, but there is little basis for esteem. He is a "rocking chair" father (Reichard, Livson, and Petersen 1962). Warnings, such as

Streib's (1977), that even among the very old are men who continue to be fully capable and contribute to their families, have made only modest dents in this image.

Anthropologists will recognize this classic picture of paternal loss of competence and relevance caused by major disjunctions in the socioeconomic worlds of adjacent generations. From warriors stripped of their weapons or nomads of their herds, to the introduction of Western education, the effects of conquest and modernization on the father's role are strikingly the same. And these men are fathers in their forties, not their seventies.

Social mobility in the United States, especially when coupled with assimilation, is another classic instance of this process: the father can provide little of value to children who have outstripped him socially and financially; he cannot share their lives, may not even understand or approve of their aspirations. As Dowd (1975) pointed out, such a father lacks the currency of exchange and is structurally dependent. But this is *not* the result of age. It is a consequence of the social change and mobility that have characterized mainstream United States for generations. Thus, the weak father image represents not the older father but simply the father of socially mobile children.

Resource-ful Fathers

The Fatherhood Project data emphatically contradict the weak father image and do so for fathers at *all* age levels. The effects of advantage are evident throughout most of the sample, but for emphasis, we can concentrate on a subsample of over a third (38 percent) of these fathers who are high-status: professionals and businessmen with assets identifying them as very well off and whose status involves accomplishment as well as income.

One of our cherished beliefs about highly achieving fathers is that they attain their success at the expense of their families. Although competitive time pressures while children are growing up frequently are reported, most children of the high-status subsample do not agree with this negative assessment of their fathers. Rather, it is the successful men who take their responsibilities, especially that of socialization, most seriously. And they do not rely on formal schooling alone.

Instead of being ignored, their children receive a great deal of this focused attention, with fathers often going to considerable lengths to ensure that their children receive what they regard as appropriate social and occupational training. In an extreme example, a surgeon even incurred administrative wrath by bringing his eleven-year-old son into the operating room to observe him at work. (Being himself a third-generation doctor, this father was leaving as little as possible to chance.)

Sometimes this is outright control and domination by typically forceful, self-assured fathers, and it has caused dramatic rebellion and permanent estrangement. But most children who are no longer "young" (which they define as precareer) feel they ultimately benefited from such early exposure, even if they resented paternal pressure at the time. It is the sample's low-level, white-collar fathers who are most likely to state with pride that they never brought work home and never talked shop with their families—and whose adult children are least likely to be sure exactly what their fathers' work involves and report the least mutual comprehension.

The importance and value (in sheer utilitarian terms) of fathers who can command significant resources increases with children's maturity. These are not just financial resources, for the networks of these high-status men are extensive: fathers can help children (and children-in-law) to facilitate college entry, open job opportunities across a wide range of occupations, make credit available for business ventures, access informal power structures, and so forth. Their expertise is also valuable in buying real estate, stocks, or coping with the Internal Revenue Service. One son, working on the East Coast, has for years phoned his semiretired stockbroker father weekly for tips in managing his own portfolio. Moreover, as children grow older, they develop their own networks, which, in turn, can be tapped by fathers to their advantage (which is a very satisfying validation to children).

The significance here is that the functional involvement of these fathers in their children's lives remains important and grows ever more important as children mature. For example, among these men, the providing function does not become latent, awaiting a child's need. Rather, it continues to develop, along with the children, gradually transformed into egalitarian, mutual helpfulness.

Adult sons of these affluent fathers do not feel compelled to upward mobility; their aspirations (and fathers' concerns) are foremost to maintain the level already established. In consequence, fathers and children are likely to share the same social world and have interests in common regardless of specific occupation; many personal networks of fathers and children show considerable overlap. Their relations are strongly influenced by this mutuality of assistance, interests, and networks. Age and generational influences are minimized, encouraging relations more companionate and partnerlike than any except for those children actually working with their fathers.

Earlier we pointed out some of the problems in comparing ethnographic data with U.S. studies. Here is another example. All too often in comparative gerontological discussions, what really happens is that the weak older man image (presumed typical in our society) is being compared with older men "typical" in other societies. But the deck is stacked: generally, those men in other societies are active older men, often in leadership positions. But they are no more typical of their societies than are the highly successful men we interviewed. It is these resource-ful men who are the appropriate group in such comparisons, and they do not suffer by it.

MIDLIFE: FATHERS' PRIME

Conceptions of the "middle years" are being gradually revised. Once adulthood was seen as an undifferentiated plateau, essentially unaltered until the declines of old age. Midlife does not, after all, generate the high drama of adolescent rebellion, nor does it possess youth's exciting career options. Nevertheless, challenges to this view became fashionable, portraying midlife as a time of personal travail: first mothers' empty-nest desolation, then male menopause and its angst. At the same time, the traditional view of static, "given" roles shifted toward an interactive conception (e.g., Goffman 1959, 1967; Strauss 1978). Now the assumption of stability in long-term roles is giving way to conceptions of these roles as flexible and adaptable (Chappell and Orbach 1986; Matthews 1986; Nydegger 1991).

It is clear from the materials presented here that the father's role is quintessentially adaptable. At the midlife of men in stable families, the father's role is less dense than when children were young, but it certainly has not been emptied. However, the role typically now enters a period of relative stability after its history of constant change.

The role of adult child is also highly adaptable. As earlier noted, achieving filial maturity and stability in the role is a lengthy, complex, interactive process, seldom fully completed until sons are in their forties. At this point, the sons are also midlife fathers and working, in turn, toward their own paternal maturity. No doubt there is an interplay between these developments, speeding progress for some, hindering it for others. But for those many men for whom all has gone well, midlife is a period of goal attainment in both generational roles.

From the point of view of the father's role, this is the climax of its most active phase. Fathers can now begin to catch their breath and relax. In the words of one of our respondents, a sixty-year-old father: "You could say my work is finished. I'm still a father, of course, but now it's more visiting with the family, the grandchildren. . . . I don't feel that pressure any more, that watching over, pushing John to finish his degree. It's great now! We [sons] talk, even argue, but it's with each other, as friends. If they don't agree with me, it's OK, I don't have to worry about it." This sense of an ending to the active, dense phase of the role is echoed by many older parents (Blieszner and Mancini 1987; Eisenhandler 1992; Hess and Waring 1978; Nydegger 1991).

In most fathers' lives, midlife ushers in this phase. In brief summary of this period: fathers' supervisory functions are sharply reduced as children mature; the role becomes characterized by egalitarian functions, particularly friendship. The time of greatest change in functions, the crossover from predominantly subordinate to mainly egalitarian does not occur until children's late twenties—typically the father's midlife—and is not stabilized until their thirties. After that, the maturing process slowly continues for both fathers and children, facilitating and in turn facilitated by mutual comprehension and respect.

Much has been made of parent-child relations during times of dependency—children when young, parents when aged. The Fatherhood Project data suggest that achieving independence without rejection is also the critical issue in maturing of relations during that lengthy period between children's youth and fathers' old age. A child's independence is the goal of fatherhood: fostering it the basis of years of socialization, providing the competencies to attain it is accepted by fathers as their major responsibility. When all goes well, fathers' midlife is the period of culmination of these efforts, of validating success in the role.

Fathers' importance to their adult children has been neglected in the literature, perhaps as part of the general neglect of the middle years. But midlife appears to be a time for father's salience to rise—at least among advantaged men such as our respondents. Almost two-thirds of the fathers reported their relative influence increasing as children matured, perhaps in part because their value as a resource peaks at this time for most children. The fathers also provided an overview of relations with children that improved from the late teens through adulthood.

Nor is this a generation-biased view. Their children agreed that fathers make significant gains as children grow into adulthood. As expected and shown in table 14.3, children, especially daughters, reported

TABLE 14.3. Closest Parent in Childhood and Adulthood

	Childhood		Adulthood	
	Son (N = 61)	Daughter (N = 59)	Son (N = 55)	Daughter (N = 55)
Mother	59%	76%	24%	60%
Same	15	7	47	31
Father	26	17	29	9

Source: Nydegger and Mitteness 1991, 257.

being closest to mothers when young. By the time these children are adult, however, a significant shift had been made toward equal closeness, this change being most pronounced for sons.[8] And they overwhelmingly reported that their fathers' approval was currently important to them (sons 91 percent, daughters 85 percent). These are some of the satisfying consequences of successful filial and paternal maturing.

If we plot a hypothetical curve of success rather than activity for the role of father, it approaches its zenith in midlife, to improve much more gradually thereafter as children's life experiences engender deeper understanding. Fathers at this time have established adult relations with their children, the goal of their fathering; they have achieved filial maturity as well. Their influence and importance to their children probably are at their peak. And children, especially sons, feel closer to fathers now than ever before. Rather than the end, midlife is the prime of fathers.

NOTES

1. Only age of child is a determinant of the role changes discussed here; age/cohort of father is not significant.

2. One of the few studies of late-life parental roles also noted that respondents "view their children more as age peers and friends than as subordinates" (Blieszner and Mancini 1987, 178).

3. Gerontologists have noted that nothing focuses one's attention on problems of the aged more effectively than one's own parent's need for home care and so forth. The implication of Fatherhood Project data is that the road to men's involvement in redefining gender roles is through their daughters' experiences.

4. The reverse problem of dependency in adult sons (but not daughters) is unanticipated and more troubling, as also reported by Greenberg and Becker (1988).

5. Not surprisingly, the son-in-law employed in his wife's family firm is in the most vulnerable position.

6. A comparative framework of residence/kinship suggests that a second factor

is divided loyalty, caused by the de facto asymmetry of kin behavior at odds with our normatively bilateral kinship system (Nydegger 1986c).

7. It will be fascinating to see if a parallel developmental pattern emerges in nontraditional mothers' relations with adult sons.

8. Recent research supports this differential importance of fathers to adult sons (Barnett, Marshall, and Pleck 1992; Rossi and Rossi 1990).

References

Aldous, J. 1987. New views on the family life of the elderly and the near-elderly. *Journal of Marriage and the Family* 49:227–234.

Barnett, R., N. Marshall, and J. Pleck. 1992. Adult son–parent relationships and their association with sons' psychological distress. *Journal of Family Issues* 13: 505–525.

Blenkner, M. 1965. Social work and family relationships in later life with some thoughts on filial maturity. In E. Shanas and G. Streib, eds., *Social structure and the family: Generational relations*, pp. 46–59. Englewood Cliffs, N.J.: Prentice-Hall.

Blieszner, R., and J. Mancini. 1987. Enduring ties: Older adults' parental role responsibilities. *Family Relations* 36:176–180.

Boissevain, J. 1974. *Friends of friends*. New York: St. Martin's.

Chappell, N., and H. Orbach. 1986. Socialization in old age: A Meadian perspective. In V. Marshall, ed., *Later life*, pp. 75–106. Beverly Hills, Calif.: Sage.

Cohler, B. 1983. Autonomy and interdependence in the family of adulthood: A psychological perspective. *Gerontologist* 23:33–39.

Colarusso, C., and R. Nemiroff. 1981. Adult development. New York: Plenum.

Coles, R. 1977. *Privileged ones*. Vol. 5, *Children in crisis*. Boston: Little, Brown.

Dowd, J. 1975. Aging as exchange: A preface to theory. *Journal of Gerontology* 30: 584–594.

Eisenhandler, S. 1992. Lifelong roles and cameo appearances. *Journal of Aging Studies* 6:243–257.

Erikson, E. 1963. *Childhood and society*. New York: Norton.

Goffman, E. 1959. *The presentation of self in everyday life*. Garden City, New York: Doubleday.

———. 1967. *Interaction ritual*. Garden City, New York: Doubleday.

Greenberg, J., and M. Becker. 1988. Aging parents as family resources. *Gerontologist* 28:786–791.

Gubrium, J. 1988. *Analyzing field reality*. Newbury Park, Calif.: Sage.

Gutmann, D. 1987. *Reclaimed powers: Toward a new psychology of men and women in later life*. New York: Basic.

Hagestad, G. 1986. Dimensions of time and the family. *American Behavioral Scientist* 29:679–694.

Heath, D. 1965. *Explorations of maturity*. New York: Appleton-Century-Crofts.

Heider, F. 1958. *The psychology of interpersonal relations*. New York: Wiley.

Hess, B., and J. Waring. 1978. Parent and child in late life: Rethinking the relationship. In R. Lerner and G. Spanier, eds., *Child influences on marital and family interaction*, pp. 241–273. New York: Academic.

Hollingshead, A. 1957. Two-factor index of social position. New Haven, Conn.: 1965 Yale Station. Mimeographed.

Jarrett, W. 1985. Caregiving within kinship systems: Is affection really necessary? *Gerontologist* 25:5–10.

Kiefer, C. 1988. *The mantle of maturity*. Albany, New York: State University of New York Press.

Kohn, M. 1963. Social class and parent-child relationships. *American Journal of Sociology* 68:471–480.

Lewis, R. 1986. Men's changing roles in marriage and the family. In R. Lewis and M. Sussman, eds., *Men's changing roles in the family*, pp. 1–10. New York: Haworth.

Marsiglio, W. 1991. Paternal engagement activities with minor children. *Journal of Marriage and the Family* 53:973–986.

———, ed. (1993–94). *Fatherhood*. 2 vols. *Journal of Family Issues* 14 (4); 15 (1).

Matthews, S. 1986. *Friendship through the life course*. Beverly Hills, Calif.: Sage.

Nydegger, C. 1983. Family ties of the aged in cross-cultural perspective. *Gerontologist* 23:26–32.

———. 1986a. Age and life-course transitions. In C. Fry and J. Keith, eds., *New methods for old age research*, pp. 131–161. South Hadley, Mass.: Bergin and Garvey.

———. 1986b. Timetables and implicit theory. *American Behavioral Scientist* 29: 710–729.

———. 1986c. Asymmetrical kin and the problematic son-in-law. In N. Datan, A. Greene, and H. Reese, eds., *Life-span developmental psychology: Intergenerational relations*, pp. 99–123. Hillsdale, N.J.: Lawrence Erlbaum.

———. 1991. The development of paternal and filial maturity. In K. Pillemer and K. McCartney, eds., *Parent-child relations throughout life*, pp. 93–112. Hillsdale, N.J.: Lawrence Erlbaum.

Nydegger, C., and L. Mitteness. 1988. Etiquette and ritual in family conversation. *American Behavioral Scientist* 31:702–717.

———. 1991. Fathers and their adult sons and daughters. *Marriage and Family Review* 16:249–266.

Nydegger, C., L. Mitteness, and J. O'Neil. 1983. Experiencing social generations: Phenomenal dimensions. *Research on Aging* 5:527–546.

Nye, F. 1976. *Role structure and analysis of the family*. Beverly Hills, Calif.: Sage.

Reichard, S., F. Livson, and P. Petersen. 1962. *Aging and personality*. New York: Wiley.

Riley, M. 1983. The family in an aging society: A matrix of latent relationships. *Journal of Family Issues* 4:439–454.

Rosow, I. 1976. Status and role change through the life span. In R. Binstock and

E. Shanas, eds., *Handbook of aging and the social sciences,* pp. 457–482. New York: Van Nostrand.

Rossi, A., and P. Rossi. 1990. *Of human bonding.* New York: Aldine de Gruyter.

Schneider, D. 1968. *American kinship: A cultural account.* Englewood Cliffs, N.J.: Prentice-Hall.

Stolz, L. 1967. *Influences on parent behavior.* Stanford: Stanford University Press.

Strauss, A. 1978. *Negotiations.* San Francisco: Jossey-Bass.

Streib, G. 1977. Bureaucracies and families. In E. Shanas and M. Sussman, eds., *Family, bureaucracy, and the elderly,* pp. 204–214. Durham, N.C.: Duke University Press.

Troll, L. 1988. New thoughts on old families. *Gerontologist* 28:586–591.

Turner, R. 1970. *Family interaction.* New York: Wiley.

Wellman, B. 1990. The place of kinfolk in personal community networks. *Marriage and Family Review* 15:195–228.

Child Life Events, Parent-Child Disagreements, and Parent Well-Being: Model Development and Testing

Rachel A. Pruchno, Norah D. Peters, and Christopher J. Burant

The lives of children and their parents have the capacity to intersect for decades (Aldous 1978; Hagestad 1986; Johnson and Bursk 1977; Litwak 1960; Moss, Moss and Moles 1985; Rosow 1970; Troll, Miller, and Atchley 1979; Veroff, Douvan, and Kulka 1981). In a theoretical framework posited by Pruchno, Blow, and Smyer (1984), it was suggested that family members form a network of interdependent lives in which change in one life begets change in many others. These connected lives, portrayed as a web, can both change and be changed by one another. Unfortunately, within the realm of gerontology as well as child psychology, the tradition has been to examine the ways in which parents act as sources of stress and burden for their offspring (e.g., Blenkner 1965; Brody 1985; Cicirelli 1983; Shanas 1979), or to examine the ways in which parental style affects offspring (Bell 1979), neglecting study of the effects that children's problems and actions can have on the well-being of their parents.

The discussion that follows will diverge from the traditional unidirectional focus on effects that parents have on their children and examine instead the effects that children can have on the well-being of their parents. It will also concentrate on parent-child relationships during a relatively neglected period—the middle years. The middle years is that period of time during which children are teenagers or young adults and when parents are not yet in need of support from their children. Unfortunately, researchers have investigated adult development and well-being at midlife independently from the study of adolescent development and parent-adolescent relationships. It will be suggested that because the adolescent and young adult years represent a period of time during which many changes occur in the lives of the child— changes that are physiological as well as social—and because family

Research based on data collected at the Philadelphia Geriatric Center as part of the Program Project "Caregiving and Mental Health: A Multifaceted Approach" (PO1 MH 43371) funded by the National Institute of Mental Health.

members' lives are interdependent, parents too experience change during these years.

The lives of middle-aged parents and their young adult children will be examined in the context of multigenerational living. Conservative estimates indicate that at any one point in time, between 8 percent and 10 percent of all families in the United States live in multigenerational households (Beck and Beck 1984). Marks (chapter 2, this volume) reports that between 35.1 percent and 91.7 percent of middle-aged parents have children living in their households, with frequency of joint household decreasing as age of the parent increases. However, the height of having adult children living at home occurs when the parent is between the ages of forty-five and fifty-four. During this same age range, approximately 15 percent of people report ever having had a parent live with them, and by age sixty-four, almost a third of midlife parents have experienced some period of parental coresidence.

Brody (1990), in her excellent review of caregiving research, comments that every study of caregiving has found that the strains on the caregiver are much greater when the disabled older person lives in the caregiver's household than when the older person lives separately. Although one should not assume that simply living under the same roof creates the increased level of stress, it is undeniable that shared households widen the arena for potential interpersonal conflicts. Contrasting caregiving stress in households consisting of one, two, and three generations, Brody and her colleagues (1988) found that when households included both the caregiver's children and her disabled elderly parent, caregivers reported significantly poorer mental health. Caregivers in three-generation households were more likely than those in two-generation households to view their mothers as critical of their husbands and children. Similar findings regarding the vulnerability of caregivers in three-generation households have been reported by Noelker and Poulshock (1982). It is in this spirit that relationships between midlife parents and their children are investigated in the context of multigenerational households.

Although the vast majority of adolescents feel fairly close to their parents and experience no dramatic changes in relationships with their parents, family discord does increase somewhat during the adolescent years. Most parents and adolescents report quarreling or bickering on a regular basis (Montemayor 1986). Typically, however, these disagreements are neither intense nor do they weaken the feelings that parents and children have for each other. Smetana (1988) has characterized the relationship between parents and adolescents as one involving "mild bickering, disagreements, and conflicts over everyday issues and emotional stress during early adolescence." Others report that parents and adolescents typically quarrel over day-to-day issues such as chores, curfew, appearance, and interpersonal issues (Hill et al. 1985). These day-to-day quarrels are generally mild, lacking the intense hostility, aggression, and emotion that are most often used to define conflict, leading Hall (1987) to discuss parent-child disagreements rather than conflict. Nonetheless, both parents and children agree that the disagreements are significant.

In this chapter, studies in which parental well-being is treated as the dependent variable and characteristics of child as the independent variables will be reviewed with an eye toward developing a theoretical model in which parental well-being is predicted as a function of negative life events as experienced by adolescent and young adult children as well as by the extent of disagreement between children and their parents. We suggest that a true understanding of family dynamics requires that data be collected from multiple family members and analyzed at the level of the family. The theoretical model will then be tested using data collected from 171 three-generation families whose members live together. Diversity among families will be examined by assessing the adequacy of the model controlling for age and gender of child and socioeconomic status of the family. Finally, the usefulness of the model will be tested for caregiving and noncaregiving families.

THEORETICAL FOUNDATIONS

It is because the parent-child relationship is a centrally important source of social integration that the strains and rewards of the relationship have the power to affect the psychological functioning of both parents and children. Brooks-Gunn and Zahaykevich (1989) suggest that certain critical points in the life phase presage an increase in behavioral changes. Entry into school, puberty, exit from school, pregnancy, parenthood—all may result in an active construction or reconstruction of self-definitions (Connell and Furman 1984; Deutsch et al. 1988; Ruble 1983). Since individuals facing or experiencing an important life event or transitional life phase are embedded in relational systems, persons in these systems may be affected by and react to an important life event even if that event is not being directly experienced by them.

Several explanations have been offered and are reviewed by Silverberg (chapter 6, this volume) to explain the relationship between change in the lives of adolescents and change in the well-being of their parents. Three theoretical models with very different bases provide support for the phenomenon that adolescent development and realignments in the parent-child relationship during adolescence are likely to provoke or intensify midlife concerns, reappraisals, and dissatisfactions among parents.

From a psychoanalytic perspective, because parents identify strongly with their children and view their children's accomplishments and difficulties as signs of their own success or failure, parents may use their children's lives as a way of working out solutions to important issues in their own lives. As such, since adolescents are frequently involved in extensive self-examination, so too are their parents (Baruch, Barnett, and Rivers 1983; Farrell and Rosenberg 1981; Kidwell et al. 1983; Smith 1976; Vaillant 1977). Parents identify with their children and are thereby provoked to reassess themselves in light of the developmental tasks and challenges of their youngsters (Benedek 1959). Furthermore, Farrell and Rosenberg (1981) contend that because middle-aged parents identify with and see their inner selves reflected in their children, as members of the younger generation distance themselves from their parents and search for their own identities, their parents may become defensive or ambivalent about themselves and may engage in a period of questioning or ambivalence about themselves, their values, and their lives.

An explanation for why parents of adolescents may experience change in their lives also comes from the perspective of role theory. As suggested by Silverberg (chapter 6, this volume), according to role theory, the self is the sense of identity that comes from playing one's roles (Breytspraak 1984). A positive sense of self and life satisfaction are based on continued performance of roles to which an individual is committed and considers valuable. As children move into adolescent years, several dimensions of the parenting role begin to change. As authority diminishes, parents strain to redefine basic assumptions about the self, find new outlets, and alter ways of relating to their children. Thus, it is the search for new roles that causes parents to reevaluate their sense of themselves.

Still another explanation for why parental well-being may be challenged by the exigencies of adolescence is offered by stress theory (Pearlin and Lieberman 1979). From this perspective, Silverberg (chapter 6, this volume) suggests, transformations in the parent-adolescent relationship cause stress to the parent. Parents may perceive disagreements and conflict as a challenge or threat to control or as a general stressor within the context of family life. This conflict, in turn, may cause parents to feel less competent in the parental role or less about themselves in general.

SPECIAL PARENTING SITUATIONS

Although mainstream studies of families have not focused on the effects that children have on their parents, the body of empirical literature that focuses on families in which a child suffers from a chronic disability has addressed the ways in which children affect the well-being of their parents. Mash and Johnson (1983), reviewing literature on parents of children with physical and mental disorders, conclude that mothers of children with such diverse conditions as hyperactivity, cerebral palsy, epilepsy, and developmental delays have interactions with children that are more stressful and less rewarding than do mothers of healthy children. Parental difficulties may begin with the birth of the disabled child: Fortier and Wanlass (1984) provide evidence that the initial diagnosis of the disability had a seriously negative impact on the family. Olshansky (1962) and Wikler, Wasow, and Hatfield (1981) identified feelings of chronic grief and mourning in families of retarded children. Countless other studies have documented the trials and tribulations experienced by parents of disabled children (Beckman-Bell 1981; Byrne and Cunningham 1985; Kazak and Marvin 1984; McKinney and Peterson 1987; Noh et al. 1989; Schilling, Shinkle, and Kirkham 1985; Slater and Wikler 1986; Sherman and Cocozza 1984; Spink 1976; Tavormina et al. 1981; Waisbren 1980).

These findings are not limited to families with young children. Rather, Pillemer and Suitor (1991) found that parents whose adult children were mentally or physically ill reported higher levels of depression, even when controlling for parents' health, age, gender, and living arrangements. Similarly, Greenberg and Becker (1988), based on interviews with both members of elderly married couples, found that parents reported stress and worry as a result of their childrens' problems with physical and emotional health and alcohol abuse.

Not all research, however, has found parenting a chronically disabled child to be associated with poorer levels of psychological well-being. Seltzer and Krauss (1989), for example, found that the well-being of mothers over the age of fifty-five whose mentally retarded adult children lived at home compared quite favorably with samples of their age peers and samples of other caregivers. Despite the long duration of their caregiving roles and the unique characteristics of their children, many of the mothers appeared to be resilient, optimistic, and able to function well in multiple roles. Similarly, findings reported by Gowen et al. (1989) and Harris and McHale (1989) indicate that mothers of mentally retarded children and mothers of nonretarded children did not differ on measures of maternal depression and feelings of parenting competence.

A separate line of research reviewed by Gubman and Tessler (1987) suggests that behaviors exhibited by mentally ill offspring can cause high levels of distress for families. Cook (1988; Cook and Cohler 1986) reports that parents with adult schizophrenic children experience feelings of hopelessness and despair, concern for the child's future, and anger at disruptive behavior. Mothers in particular experienced high levels of anxiety, depression, and emotional strain.

DIRECT VERSUS INDIRECT EFFECTS: DEVELOPMENT OF A THEORETICAL MODEL

That parent's mental health should be dependent on events occurring in the life of the child as well as on the parent-child relationship seems clear. What remains to be examined is whether the child's problems and parent-child relationships have direct or indirect effects on the well-being of the parents. Pillemer and Suitor (1991) suggest that children's problems may have both direct as well as indirect effects on parents. A mechanism proposed by these investigators is social interactions, whereby troubled children's behaviors may create conflict between parents and children, which could then lead to increased parental distress. Compelling evidence for such a relationship comes from research that has shown that the amount of parent-child conflict is related to distress in middle-aged parents (Hall 1987; Silverberg and Steinberg 1987). In studies of the elderly and their children, Aldous, Klaus, and Klein (1985) found that number of disagreements was a major predictor of parents identifying one of their children as disappointing. Rook (1984) also reports that negative social interactions with children as well as others—and specifically conflict with them—led to diminished well-being among the elderly. Empirical evidence, based on research conducted by Pillemer and Suitor (1991), however, indicates that parents whose adult children experienced serious problems (emotional or mental problems, serious problems with physical health, drinking or alcohol problem, child had been under stress during the past year) reported greater depression, an effect that was direct, rather than one mediated by parent-child conflict, lack of provision of support by the child, or the child's level of dependency. Furthermore, children's problems emerged as a more important predictor of depression than did other variables that have often been associated with depression. Among women, for example, having a problem child was a more powerful predictor than was marital status or educational level.

Umberson (1989) and Goldsteen and Ross (1989) found that the content of parent-child relationships has a significant effect on psychological well-being and on parents' sense of burden. Umberson (1989) reports that parent-child relationship predicted parent well-being, with quality of parent-child relationship having a significant effect (independent of parent characteristics or family composition) on six measures of well-being. Parent-child relationship was inversely related to a sense of meaninglessness, agitation, and psychiatric symptoms and was positively related to positive affect, home life satisfaction, and life satisfaction. A similar relationship was reported by Pillemer and Suitor (1991).

Umberson (1989) also proposes that the content of parent-child relationships may mediate the impact of parenting on parents' well-being. Relational content is multifaceted and includes both positive and negative elements. Positive relational content refers to the positive interactions and satisfactions associated with the relationship. Negative relational content refers to the conflicts, demands, and strains associated with the relationship. More recent data from Umberson (1992) indicates that only the negative features of relationships with children are associated with parents' psychological distress. Strained relationships with adult children are associated with elevated levels of psychological distress among parents.

Based on the work of Brooks-Gunn and Zahaykevich (1989), it is proposed that when adolescents experience critical events that they themselves view as negative, such as an unwed pregnancy, involvement with drugs or alcohol, change of schools, personal injury or new major illness, and beginning a serious relationship, the psychological well-being of their parents should be affected. In addition, the extent of disagreement characterizing the relationship between parents and children should have an effect on parents' well-being.

The question at hand is the way in which events and extent of disagreement between children and parents affect the psychological well-

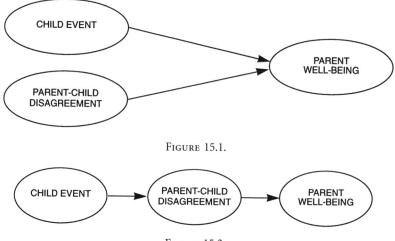

FIGURE 15.1.

FIGURE 15.2.

being of parents. Two competing theoretical models are proposed. The first, as depicted in figure 15.1, posits direct, independent effects from events and disagreements to parents' psychological well-being. The alternative model, depicted in figure 15.2, predicts that the experience of negative life events has direct effects on parent-child disagreements, which have direct effects on parents' psychological well-being, and that negative events as experienced by adolescents and young adults have indirect effects (through parent-child disagreements) on parents' psychological well-being.

SEPARATING EFFECTS AS EXPERIENCED BY MOTHERS AND FATHERS

The literature clearly suggests that mothers' relationships with their children are more intense than are fathers' relationships throughout the life cycle (Hagestad 1987; Rossi and Rossi 1990; Umberson 1989). Research by Montemayor (1982), Smetana (1989), and Steinberg (1987) indicates that mothers appear to experience more conflict with their adolescents (particularly daughters) than do fathers. Others, however, report that fathers are more involved with and sensitive to their adolescent sons than to their adolescent daughters (Richardson et al. 1984; Youniss and Ketterlinus 1987). At the same time, other studies have found no such differences (Crouter and Crowley 1990; Galambos and Almeida 1992; Montemayor and Brownlee 1987).

Studying parents with physically or emotionally disabled young children, Schilling, Shinkle, and Kirkham (1985) found that mothers experience more stress and greater reductions in physiological well-being than do fathers. More recently, studies have suggested that mothers and fathers have different perspectives on their experiences. Krauss (1993), for example, found that fathers of disabled toddlers reported more stress related to their child's temperament and their relationship to their child, whereas mothers reported more stress from the personal consequences of parenting. Differences between mothers and fathers regarding the most powerful predictors of child-related and parenting stress were also found, with fathers being more sensitive to the effects of family environment and mothers more affected by their personal support networks. Studies of middle-aged parents also show that children's psychological problems create more anxiety, depression, and emotional drain for mothers than for fathers (Cook 1988; Cook and Cohler 1986).

In terms of the quality of relationships between adolescents and their mothers and fathers or extent of disagreement in relationships between adolescents and their parents, Umberson (1989) reports that mothers and fathers do not significantly differ on overall quality of parent-child relationships. Furthermore, the quality of relationships between parents and children affected men and women in similar ways. In a later study, however, Umberson (1992) reports that compared with fathers, mothers experience less dissatisfaction in relationships with adult children.

Based on the above, it is proposed that predictors of well-being will vary for mothers and fathers. Both theoretical statements and empirical data suggest that it is important to consider psychological well-being of mother and father independently. Following this logic, it would be important to consider child-mother and child-father disagreement. The addition of these ideas to the two competing theoretical frameworks presented thus far is depicted schematically in figures 15.3 and 15.4.

DIVERSITY IN RELATIONSHIPS

In keeping with the goals of this book, it is expected that the theoretical model that best represents the data will vary in its ability to predict parental well-being based on characteristics of both parents and children. Characteristics to be examined include gender and age of child, socioeconomic status of the family, and whether the families are involved in caregiving activities for an elderly member.

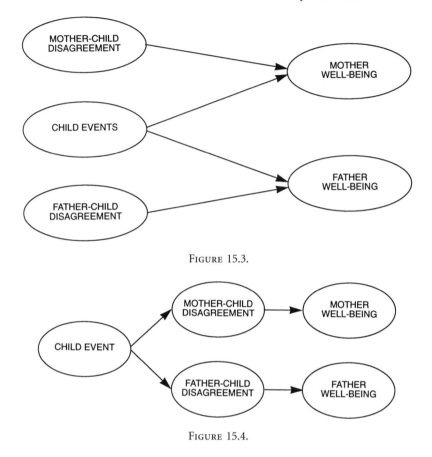

FIGURE 15.3.

FIGURE 15.4.

Gender of Third Generation

It is proposed that gender of the child will affect the nature of relationships between negative life events, parent-child disagreements, and parent well-being. Literature regarding the effects of gender of the child is reviewed by Brooks-Gunn and Zahaykevich (1989), who suggest that early adolescent events are more contradictory experiences for girls than for boys. The transition to an adult body and toward adult status highlights the contradictions in women's primary roles. Feminist theorists have argued that mothers and daughters tend to maintain a more fused relationship than mothers and sons, which makes it difficult and conflictual for daughters to assert their autonomy and separateness from their mothers (Bergman 1982; Chodorow 1978). Girls' relationships with parents, particularly their mothers, are more likely to be characterized by perceived and actual conflict than boys' relationships.

Silverberg and Steinberg (1987) posit that the effects of gender of the child on the relationships between events, disagreements, and parent well-being may interact with the effects of gender of parent. They relate predictions about the nature of these relationships from psychoanalytic, role, and stress theories. From the perspective of psychoanalytic theory, if the process of identification underlies the parent-child relationship, stronger relationships would be expected for same-sex dyads.

Role theory would predict that since mothers play a more central role than fathers in childbearing and have more opportunities to engage in conflictual interactions with their children (Montemayor 1986), they would experience more negative effects than fathers regardless of gender of the child. Mothers may also be more likely than fathers to base their sense of self and well-being on the quality of relationships with their children (Baruch, Barnett, and Rivers 1983; Gilligan 1982) and as such may be more sensitive or vulnerable to changes that challenge these relationships. Empirical findings from Silverberg and Steinberg (1987) are supportive of predictions that would derive from role theory. They found that fathers' sense of well-being was unrelated to level of conflict experienced with either sons or daughters, whereas mothers' sense of well-being was related to level of conflict with both sons and daughters.

Data supportive of predictions made by psychoanalytic theory are described by Silverberg (chapter 6, this volume). Similar to Sullivan and Sullivan (1980), who found that fathers more than mothers have difficulty adjusting to adolescent son's leaving home for college, Silverberg relates that fathers were more likely to report midlife identity concerns when they had sons who were more emotionally autonomous, that is, sons who have adopted less idealized images of their parents, have relinquished some of their childish dependencies on them, and have formed a more individuated sense of self. Mothers were more likely to report these feelings when they had daughters who were more emotionally autonomous. Mothers of daughters and fathers of sons reconsider own life choices, personal commitments, and life situation when they see their children developing into independent adults.

Silverberg also describes data supportive of the stress hypothesis, indicating that mothers, but not fathers, seem to be adversely affected by the intensity of conflict they experience with their children regarding day-to-day issues such as curfew, chores, free time, and style of clothes. That mothers seem to be so affected suggests that conflict may impact mothers directly, rather than through a mediating process.

Age

Two different research traditions have suggested that the extent of parent-child disagreements may be exacerbated in two very different periods of the family's life. Scholars of the adolescent years suggest that early adolescence is a time of great stress for parents and their children, whereas gerontologists and sociologists have indicated that stresses between young adults and their parents are greatest when young adults and their parents continue to live together beyond early adulthood. To address these concerns, therefore, the theoretical model must include age of the child.

According to Brooks-Gunn and Zahaykevich (1989), early adolescence is a life phase in which several important life events occur that seem to elicit self-definition alterations (Gunnar and Collins 1988; Lerner and Foch 1987). Parent-child relationships at this time are often characterized as conflictual or as becoming more distant (Hill et al. 1985; Steinberg 1987). Parents and adolescent children are thought to be transformed, as both renegotiate their relationship, moving toward more individuation from each other (Grotevant and Cooper 1986). Time spent with parents (Csikszentmihalyi and Larsen 1984; Youniss 1985), emotional closeness (Steinberg 1987), and yielding to parents in decision making (Hill 1980; Montemayor and Hanson 1985; Steinberg 1987) all decrease from early to middle adolescence.

Despite little systematic research of the relationship between parent-child relationships at early adolescence and parents' sense of self and well-being as middle-aged adults, research by Small et al. (1983) found that parental stress was higher among mothers and fathers of early adolescents than among those of preadolescent or middle-adolescent children. Furthermore, Montemayor (1986) found that approximately 20 percent of parents and adolescents had serious and continual difficulty with each other, while another 20 percent had intermittent relational problems. Conflict and arguments were the primary complaints of parents about the relationships they had with their adolescents. According to Richards, Bengtson, and Miller (1989), some studies indicate that both parents and children perceive improvement in their relationship as the children pass from adolescence to adulthood (Baruch and Barnett 1983; Green and Boxer 1985). These studies generally define adulthood as that period of time in which the child marries and has a family of his or her own.

From a very different perspective, Umberson (1992) found that parents who share a residence with a child over age eighteen report more strained relationships with their adult children and more dissatisfaction with the parental role than do parents of like-aged adult children who did not live with a child. Aquilino and Supple (1991), on the other hand, while postulating that presence of young adult children (ages nineteen to thirty-four) in the parent's household would be a source of stress for parents, found that this was not the case. Only seventeen percent of parents indicated considerable dissatisfaction with the adult child's presence in the household. They did find a slight tendency for a higher frequency of arguments with daughters; however, both mothers and fathers were more likely to spend enjoyable time with daughters than with sons. Coresidence did not lead inevitably to parental dissatisfaction with the living arrangement or to troubles in the parent-child relationship. Although parent-child relations were not dominated by conflict, conflict remained the strongest single predictor of parents' satisfaction with having their adult child living at home. For mothers, frequency of disagreements was less important than their intensity. For fathers, the occurrence of disagreements exerted a strong negative effect on satisfaction, whether or not they led to open hostilities with the child.

To address the effects that age of the child has on variables in the model, families with third-generation members in two age groups will be contrasted. These include families with adolescents under age nineteen and families with young adults ages nineteen and over. If the adolescent literature is supported, parent-child relationships would be most strained during the earlier years. If research conducted on adult children and their parents is supported, parent-child relationships would be most strained during the later years.

Socioeconomic Status

Based on research by Jacob (1974), Silverberg and Steinberg (1987) argued that socioeconomic status (SES) may serve as a moderator between parent-adolescent relationship and parent well-being. Because working-class parents value youngsters' conformity and obedience to a greater extent than do parents from middle-class families, the former may be more likely to perceive their youngsters' disagreements and arguments as a challenge or threat to their control as parents. From this, it is predicted that working-class people will be more adversely affected by conflict and distancing in the parent-child relationship than would middle-class parents. In their research, Silverberg and Steinberg (1987) found that blue-collar fathers reported lower levels of life satisfaction when they had higher levels of conflict with their daughters, yet the relationship did not reach statistical significance. Surprisingly, blue-collar fathers reported somewhat fewer psychological symptoms when they experience more intense conflicts with their daughters.

Empirical research by Silverberg (chapter 6, this volume) indicates that the relationship between sons' emotional autonomy and fathers' midlife identity concerns was stronger for blue-collar than for white-collar fathers. Her interpretation of the finding is that child's emotional autonomy may be viewed as a challenge to parental control, particularly by working-class fathers who generally place a greater value on their childrens' conformity and obedience and less value on their childrens' autonomy and independence (Kohn 1977). Furthermore, she suggests that although white-collar and professional fathers have outlets for exercising authority and control in their work outside the family, for the working-class man, few such rewards exist outside the home. Because the family is the one arena where working-class men can exercise power, obedience is more highly valued (Rubin 1976).

Caregiving versus Noncaregiving Families

Research regarding caregiving for an elderly relative, much of which derives from a stress paradigm, indicates that relationships among family members can become strained as a result of the caregiving experience (Brody 1989; Brody, Dempsey, and Pruchno 1990). A copious amount of literature has developed that documents the emotional strains experienced by primary caregivers, but little empirical work has been done on the effects that caregiving has on the other family members. Nonetheless, Brody (1989) has suggested that the demands of caregiving directly affect all individual members of the family as well as the family as a whole. The caregiving activities and emotional consequences have unique aspects that may strain the family to "an extraordinarily painful level." Brody contends that when an older person requires care, it is a family event, which leaves the family at risk for mental health problems.

Research on the ripple effects of caregiving has generally been based in one of two design perspectives. Either primary caregivers are asked to serve as reporter and describe the effects that caregiving has on other family members (e.g., Noelker and Poulshock 1982), or groups of secondary caregivers—husbands of caregivers, for example—have been interviewed and asked to report on their experience as a group (e.g., Kleban et al. 1989). There have been no prior attempts to gather information from multiple family members and then describe caregiving from the perspective of the family.

Given the paucity of empirical data regarding the effects of caregiving on multiple family members, it is difficult to generate specific hypotheses regarding the way in which the proposed theoretical model will vary as a function of caregiving status. Given that caregiving has the capacity to put stress on multiple family members, however, we expected that relationships between midlife parents and their children will be characterized by higher levels of disagreement than relationships between noncaregiving family members.

UNDERSTANDING FAMILIES

No matter which theoretical perspective one embraces, strong arguments can clearly be made for a change in the child's life having an impact on the parent's life. An understanding of the dynamics involved in these changes requires, however, that one pause and consider the issue of perception. It is contended that to understand a dyadic relationship, one must have perceptual information from both parties. As such, data collected solely from parents or solely from children result in incomplete knowledge about the family. Richards, Bengtson, and Miller (1989) maintain that perceptions are a crucial element of parent-child interactions and may vary by generational position. In a similar vein, Bengtson and Kuypers (1971) hypothesized that members of the older generations tend to perceive intergenerational relationships differently than do younger generations. They suggest a "generational stake" in perceptions whereby members of the older generation, because of their investment in younger generations, will focus on the positive aspects of their relationships and continuities between them. In contrast, members of the younger generation will tend to emphasize differences, distinctiveness, and distance. Exemplary of this is work by Montemayor (1982) and Smetana (1988), who find that conflicts between parents and adolescents are perceived as occurring more frequently by adolescents than by parents. As such, a comprehensive understanding of relationships within families calls for input from multiple reporters.

A true understanding of families requires that data not only be collected from multiple members of the family but also analyzed and integrated at the level of the family. Central to this goal is distinguishing between characteristics of individuals who happen to be members of a family and characteristics of families per se. In making the distinction between individuals and families, we can think about the kinds of characteristics which describe individuals and those which characterize families. Families can, for example be defined by their size, their stage of life cycle, or their social class (Ransom et al. 1990). Families can be defined according to an attribute of one member, so that we speak of "a family with an unemployed father" or a "family with an impaired person" (Ransom et al. 1990). Families can also be defined by a dyadic characteristic, such as "a family in which husband and wife have been married for twenty years." Finally, families can be described in terms of their norms, rules, and power structure.

On the other hand, families do not have opinions, attitudes, or beliefs. Rather, these characteristics represent individuals. As such, although it is appropriate either to describe the relationship between a husband's attitude and that of his wife and child or to develop typologies of families based on similarity or divergence of values, it is meaningless to describe an average family attitude.

Once the distinction between characteristics of individuals and characteristics of families has been made, the question becomes "can we gain information about families from individuals?" The answer is both yes and no. Thompson and Walker (1982), in their very elegant statement about family data, suggest that if the intention is to use an individual's report as either (1) an objective reality, implying that the report is independent of an individual's view, such as the number of family members, length of time a marriage has existed, or presence/absence of characteristics that can be corroborated by an outside observer, or (2) a subjective individual reality that is interpreted as one family member's perception of herself or himself, her or his family, or other family members, then data collected from one individual can provide information about the family. If, however, the intention is to use one family member's subjective perceptions to characterize the feelings of a whole family or to try to represent a family's objective reality beyond the confines of its physical and demographic characteristics, then gathering information from only one family member is insufficient (Pruchno 1989).

A further caveat, identified by Larsen and Olson (1990, 22) is that "just as it is dangerous to assume that one member can adequately represent the family's reality, it is equally problematic to conclude that the acquisition of several members' data can provide a more valid reality." Certainly, collecting data from multiple family members has the potential to result in a richer, more intricate description of what is going on within the family, yet the meaning and usefulness of these reports must be established at the theoretical rather than methodological level.

One of the most important issues with which a researcher must struggle when reports from multiple members of a family exist is the meaning of differences between these reports. Family researchers traditionally have embraced one of two perspectives. The first contends that reports are disparate because of individual bias or error. As such, individual discrepancies within families are explained away as the result of poor questions or inappropriate wording of questions (Wilkening and Morrison 1963). On the other hand, differences between family members may be interpreted as true differences. From this perspective, separate subjective realities characterize family members, and it is these differences that are reflected in the discrepant responses to questions.

We suggest here that both the differences as error and differences as true differences perspectives have validity for family research. If the aim of a study is to describe objective characteristics of the family, for example, family income or years of marriage, then disparate reports reflect error in measurement. If, on the other hand, the goal of the study is to describe the subjective characteristics of individuals, such as their attitudes or beliefs, then differences between reports reflect true, meaningful differences.

For purposes of testing the theoretical model described above, differences between reports made by family members regarding areas of disagreement are viewed as true, meaningful differences. It is assumed that individuals within families have different experiences regarding conflict and that each report is a true, valid representation of the reality of the individual. Occurrence of negative life events is reported only by the adolescent in the family. This decision reflects the belief that the people directly experiencing an event are the best reporters available. Finally, psychological well-being is reported separately by mother and father, because we assume that only an individual has the capacity to report on an inner psychological state.

THE PHILADELPHIA GERIATRIC CENTER PROJECT

Data for the following analyses were collected as part of the Program Project "Caregiving and Mental Health: A Multifaceted Approach" to the Philadelphia Geriatric Center. The focus of the grant was threefold: (1) to examine the longitudinal effects of caregiving, (2) to study the effects that marital status has on the caregiving experience, and (3) to investigate the effects that caregiving has on the lives of multiple members of multigenerational family members who are living together. To address the goals of the study, both caregiving as well as noncaregiving families were studied. The families who participated in the third component of the larger project are described in detail below.

Criteria for inclusion in the multigenerational component of the study were (1) the family elder (G1) must be sixty-five years of age or older and not married; (2) the middle generation (G2) must be a married daughter or daughter-in-law; and (3) the third generation (G3) must be a child of the G2 marriage and be between the ages of thirteen and twenty-five. When there were multiple children in the household who fulfilled study eligibility requirements, the middle generation daughter/daugher-in-law was asked to select that child whose life was "most affected" by the elder's presence in the household.

The sampling selection criteria enabled examination of the question of the ripple effects of caregiving on multiple family members. The analyses that follow are based on responses from 171 multigeneration families living in the largely urban Delaware Valley area. Respondents were volunteers recruited through newspaper announcements as well as through community organizations, including caregiver support groups, area agencies on aging, and religious institutions, resulting in a sample of convenience. For each eligible family, structured personal interviews were conducted individually with the daughter/daughter-in-law, her husband, and their child. Each interview lasted approximately one hour.

The sample was primarily white (93.0 percent) and included 124 daughters and 47 daughters-in-law (referred to below as "mothers"), most of whom lived with mothers or mothers-in-law (140) as opposed to fathers or fathers-in-law (31). The mothers who were interviewed ranged in age from 33 to 64 (mean age 48.0 years). Most (55.6 percent) were Catholic, while 36.3 percent were Protestant and 7.0 percent were Jewish. The women were highly educated, with 62.0 percent having more than a high school education.

The husbands of these women (referred to as "fathers") ranged in age from 32 to 75 (mean age 50.08). The majority (90.3 percent) were currently working. Using father's level of education as an indicator of socioeconomic status, we defined 53 families as lower SES and 112 families as upper SES.

The third generation ranged in age from 13 to 25 (mean age 18.63), with 59.1 percent being female. The majority of the third-generation respondents (74.3 percent) reported that they were currently in school, with a similar percentage reporting that they were currently working (66.1 percent). In 36.3 percent of the families, the target child was the only child within the specified age range living at home. Of the eighteen families having only boys, 56 percent of the mothers named the oldest son, 33 percent named the youngest, while only 11 percent indicated a middle child to participate in the study. For the twenty-four families having only daughters, 46 percent named the oldest daughter, while 46 percent named the youngest and 8 percent named a middle child. Families having both sons and daughters numbered sixty-eight. Of those families, 66 percent named a daughter as target child and 34 percent named a son. The child participating in the study was more likely to be the youngest (43.0 percent) than the oldest (38.5 percent) or a middle child (18.5 percent). Households of people in the sample ranged in size from 4 to 11 (mean 5.3) people. The three generations had been living together for a mean of 8.0 years (range 1 month to 59 years). In most cases (82.5 percent), the elder had moved into his/her adult child's household, whereas 8.8 percent of the joint households were formed when the younger generations moved into the elder's house and 5.3 percent of families had always lived together. The primary reason cited for joining households was decline in elder's physical and mental health.

The mean age of the elders was 80.0 (range 64 to 100 years). Independence of the elder was assessed based on the instrumental activities of daily living (IADL) questions of the Multilevel Assessment Instrument (Lawton et al. 1982). Eight abilities were measured, including housework, laundry, meal preparation, shopping for groceries, getting to places out of walking distance, using the telephone, managing money, and taking medications, each using a three-point scale (with a score of one indicating limited abilities and three indicating elder

TABLE 15.1. Third Generation Events

Events	Number of Occurrences	Number of Evaluations		
		Positive	Negative	Neutral
Breaking up with a boy/girlfriend	76	25	28	23
Having or fathering an unwed pregnancy	4	1	2	1
Becoming involved with drugs or alcohol	17	4	4	9
Changing to a different school	28	19	2	7
Having a personal injury or new major illness	35		35[a]	
Beginning a serious relationship	64	55	6	3

[a]The authors assumed all responses to have negative evaluations.

can do the task without any help). Scores on IADL ranged from eight to twenty-four, with higher scores indicating greater abilities. For the analyses that follow, caregiving families were defined as those in which the elder had IADL scores less than twenty. Using this definition, we consider 121 families to be caregiving families and 50 to be noncaregiving families.

MEASURES

The third generation reported whether each of the following events happened to them during the past year: breaking up with a boy/girlfriend; having or fathering an unwed pregnancy; becoming involved with drugs or alcohol; changing to a different school; having a personal injury or new major illness; and beginning a serious relationship. These events were selected because review of the literature indicated that they were especially stressful for those experiencing them. They also represent events that appear consistently on inventories of life events (Heisel et al. 1973; Johnson 1986; Johnson and McCutcheon 1980; McCubbin, Patterson, and Wilson 1982). For those events that did occur, the third-generation member reported whether he/she perceived each as having had a positive, negative, or neutral effect on their lives. The number of people experiencing each event as well as the evaluations of each event are included in table 15.1. A summary score was created that was a count of the events that each third-generation number experienced and evaluated as negative. We focused on negative rather than positively evaluated events because we expected that they would have a greater effect on parent's well-being. Scores ranged from 0 to 3 (mean score .468).

Extent of current level of disagreement between parents and the third-generation family member was assessed in fifteen areas: how money is spent, religious matters, friends, correct or proper behavior, aims, amount of time spent together, making major decisions, household tasks, career decisions, how free time is spent, education, dating, television, food, and relationships with other relatives. A six-point Likert scale (ranging from always agree [6] to always disagree [1]) was used to determine the extent to which parents and children agreed on each area. Level of disagreement was reported independently by mothers, fathers, and children.

Psychological well-being was operationalized as depression and measured using the twenty-item CES-D. The CES-D (Center for Epidemiologic Studies Depression Index) was developed by Radloff (1977) and has been widely used in the gerontological literature. Item responses, scored according to Radloff, included rarely (0), sometimes (1), occasionally (2), and most of the time (3), with a higher score indicating greater depression. Theoretically, scores could range from 0 to 60. Scores for the mothers ranged from 0 to 47 (mean score 11.3); scores for fathers ranged from 0 to 33 (mean score 7.1). Coefficient alpha for mothers' scores was .93; for fathers it was .86.

PRELIMINARY ANALYSES

Because both the third generation and their parents responded to the identical questions regarding areas of agreement/disagreement and the goal of the analyses was to maintain intrafamily comparisons, responses from mothers, fathers, and their children were analyzed using paired t-tests. Paired t-test analysis results are summarized in table 15.2. As indicated, these analyses revealed that mothers reported more agreement between themselves and their children than did children on religious matters, friends, how free time is spent, and dating, whereas children reported higher levels of agreement between themselves and their mothers on aims, goals, and things believed important and on household tasks. Fathers reported higher levels of agreement between their children and themselves than did their children on how money is spent, religious matters, and dating, whereas children reported

TABLE 15.2. Extent of Agreement between Mothers/Fathers
and Children (paired t-tests)

Topic	Mother	Child	Father	Child
How money is spent	4.42	4.26	4.35[a]	4.02
Religious matters	4.91[a]	4.66	4.95[a]	4.69
Friends	4.87[a]	4.69	4.84	4.87
Correct or proper behavior	4.65	4.62	4.60	4.55
Aims, goals, and things				
believed important	4.66	4.88[a]	4.66	4.97[a]
Amount of time spent together	4.63	4.69	4.54	4.59
Making major decisions	4.74	4.61	4.59	4.71
Household tasks	3.65	3.94[a]	3.80	4.06[a]
Career decisions	4.75	4.94	4.84	4.99
How free time is spent	4.23[a]	4.01	4.20	4.28
Education	5.01	5.13	4.90	5.17[a]
Dating	4.64[a]	4.28	4.71[a]	4.41
Television	4.52	4.48	4.37	4.52
Food	4.60	4.63	4.48	4.92[a]
Relationships with other relatives	4.81	4.89	4.91	5.00

[a]Significant at .05 level.

higher levels of agreement than did their fathers on aims, goals, and things believed important; household tasks; education; and food.

For the following structural path analyses, the sample size required that composite scores be created that would summarize the extent of disagreement between parent and child as reported separately by parents and children. As such, four composite scores were created that reflected disagreement across the fifteen areas as reported by (1) mother in relation to child (mother-teen disagree); (2) child in relation to mother (teen-mother diagree); (3) father in relation to child (father-teen disagree); and (4) child in relation to father (teen-father disagree). We created each summary score such that a lower score was indicative of greater disagreement between parent and third generation. Each summary scale had the theoretical range of 15 (disagree on all) to 90 (agree on all). Actual scores for teen-mother disagree ranged from 32 to 89 (mean 68.83); scores for teen-father disagree ranged from 36 to 89 (mean 69.5); scores for mother-teen disagree ranged from 39 to 90 (mean 69.1); and scores for father-teen disagree ranged from 33 to 90 (mean 68.5). Reliabilities ranged from .86 to .88.

Bivariate Correlations

Bivariate correlations among the model variables may be found in table 15.3. As can be seen, negative events experienced by the third-generation members were significantly related to teen-father disagreement, teen-mother disagreement, and mother-teen disagreement, with a greater frequency of events, in each case, being associated with more parent-child disagreement. Occurrence of events was not statistically associated with depression as reported by either mother or father. Father-teen disagreement was positively associated with teen-father disagreement, teen-mother disagreement, and mother-teen disagreement and negatively associated with father's depression (the more disagreement between father and child, the more depressed was father). Teen-father disagreement was positively associated with teen-mother disagreement and mother-teen disagreement and negatively associated with father's depression. Mother-teen disagreement was positively associated with teen-mother disagreement and negatively associated with mother's depression. An interesting pattern emerging from these data is the high correlation (.72) between teen's report of disagreement with mother and father and the much lower correlation between parent's report of disagreement between self and child (.38). Finally, father's depression was positively related to mother's depression.

Model Testing

The maximum likelihood procedure of AMOS (Arbuckle 1988) was used to fit the theoretical model depicted in figure 15.5. This model combined the predicted paths of both previously defined models. Similar to LISREL (Joreskog and Sorbom 1986), AMOS is a computer program that estimates structural equations. All analyses were calculated using covariance matrices. Although structural equation modeling techniques generally assume that measures are reliable (Rogosa 1979), this may not be the case when there are single indicators for a construct. For the analyses that follow, life events as reported by the third generation were assumed to have perfect reliability, that is, because these events are of major import, it was assumed that third-generation members would report them with great accuracy. The high correlations between father-teen disagreement and teen-father disagreement (.40) and between mother-teen disagreement and teen-mother disagreement (.44) led to creation of a single construct with two indicators for father-child disagreement as well as for mother-child disagreement. The terms

TABLE 15.3. Bivariate Correlations

	Child Events	Father-Teen Disagree	Teen-Father Disagree	Mother-Teen Disagree	Teen-Mother Disagree	Father Depression	Mother Depression
Child Events	1.00						
Father-Teen Disagree	−.04	1.00					
Teen-Father Disagree	−.30^b	.40^b	1.00				
Mother-Teen Disagree	−.21^b	.38^b	.40^b	1.00			
Teen-Mother Disagree	−.30^b	.31^b	.72^b	.44^b	1.00		
Father Depression	−.06	−.17^a	−.17^a	−.05	−.09	1.00	
Mother Depression	.14	−.10	−.13	−.42^b	−.14	.18^a	1.00

[a]Correlations significant at .05 level.
[b]Correlations significant at .01 level.

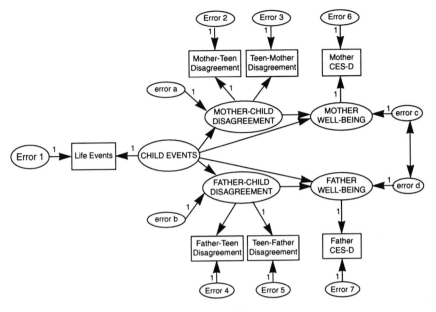

FIGURE 15.5.

father-child disagreement and *mother-child disagreement* will be used to refer to the theoretical construct created from the individual father-teen disagreement, teen-father disagreement, mother-teen disagreement, and teen-mother disagreement measured variables. The AMOS program estimated the reliability of father-teen, teen-father, mother-teen, and teen-mother disagreement. Finally, for the constructs of mother and father depression, the known reliabilities of the observed variables were used to remove 7 percent (mother) and 14 percent (father) of the variance as unreliable.

The initial model tested is depicted in figure 15.5. As indicated, this model simultaneously tested the direct and indirect effects of life events and parent-child disagreement on mother and father well-being. That model, with a chi-square of 134.44 ($d.f. = 10$, $p < .001$) provided a poor fit to the data. At this point, exploratory analyses were undertaken in which structural paths were modified, one at a time, based on modification indices as well as theory. Results indicating the change in model fit are depicted in table 15.4.

The first addition to the model was a covariance between the error terms associated with teen-mother disagreement and teen-

TABLE 15.4. Model Development

Step	(χ^2)	$(d.f.)$	$(\Delta\chi^2)$	$(\Delta d.f.)$	Bentler-Bonett	Bollen
1. Theoretical model	134.44	10	—	—	.49	.51
2. Add: Covariance between error terms of teen-mother disagree and teen-father disagree	63.58	9	70.86	1	.76	.79
3. Add: Father-child disagree → mother-child disagree	23.03	8	40.55	1	.91	.94
4. Remove: Child events → mother well-being	23.23	9	.20	1	.91	.94
5. Remove: Child events → mother-child disagree	24.19	10	.96	1	.91	.94
6. Remove: Child events → father well-being	26.95	11	2.76	1	.90	.94

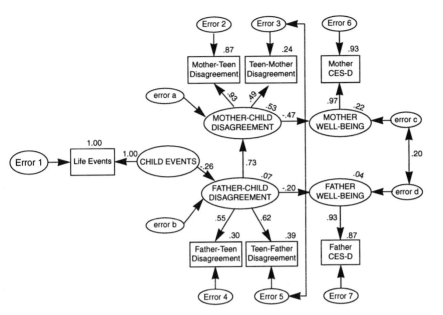

FIGURE 15.6. Final Model (Standardized Weights).

father disagreement. Next, a structural path between father-child disagreement and mother-child disagreement was added. Together, these modifications significantly improved the fit of the data. In steps four through six, insignificant paths between child events and mother well-being, child events and mother-teen disagreement, and child events and father well-being were removed. The final model, depicted in figure 15.6, provided a very good fit to the data (chi-square = 26.95, $d.f.$ = 11, p = .005). Evidence of the goodness of fit of the model to the data is provided by the chi-square to degrees of freedom ratio (2.45:1), Bentler-Bonett of .90, and Adjusted Goodness of Fit Index (AGFI) of .89. Carmines and McIver (1981) and Wheaton et al. (1977) suggest that a chi-square to degrees of freedom ratio in the range of 2:1 or 3:1 is indicative of an acceptable fit between the hypothetical model and the sample data; Bentler and Bonett (1980) use a value of .90; and Violato, Marini, and Hunter (1989) suggest an AGFI value of at least .82.

Conceptually, the final model is very different from either of the originally proposed models. It suggests that higher levels of parent-child disagreement lead to greater levels of depression for both mothers and fathers. The more negative events experienced by the third generation, the more disagreement there is between the third-generation members and their fathers. Negative events, however, do not affect the extent to which the third-generation members and their mothers disagree. Finally, the greater the extent to which the third generation and fathers disagree, the more likely the third generation and mothers are to disagree.

Examining the indirect as well as the direct paths leading to parent depression suggests that mother's level of depression (21.7 percent of which is predicted by the model variables) is predicted by extent of disagreement between father and child (through mother-child disagreement) and by child negative events (through father-child disagreement) in addition to the direct effect from mother-child disagreement. Father's depression (3.8 percent predicted by the model variables), on the other hand, is influenced directly by father-child disagreement and indirectly by child negative events (through father-child disagreement).

The importance of examining well-being of mother and father while maintaining the family as unit of analysis is well-demonstrated by these analyses. Not surprisingly, mother's and father's well-being are related to each other both directly as well as indirectly. Relationships between fathers and their children, for example, have direct effects on relationships between mothers and their children, which would be ignored if only one parent were the subject of study.

EXAMINATION OF THE USEFULNESS OF THE MODEL FOR DIVERSE SUBGROUPS

The usefulness of the model that was developed using the complete sample is now tested on four subgroups of families. First, because the literature suggests that gender of children affects family relationships, families in which the target child was a male are contrasted with families in which the target child was a female. Next, since a large body of literature exists, some of which demonstrates that the early adolescent years are especially difficult for parents, whereas other work indicates that living together with older adult children is stressful for parents, the age of the target child is examined as it affects relationships within the model. Socioeconomic status of the family is examined because previous studies have indicated that white-collar and blue-collar parents have very different relationships with their children. Finally, caregiving and noncaregiving families are contrasted given that stress theory would suggest that caregiving families may be at risk for problems within the family.

Each set of the tests followed the same four-step format. First, the structure of the model was tested on the subgroups with no constraints placed on the model. Next the regression weights for the subsets were forced to be identical. The third step forced the variances to be equal for all groups, and the final step forced the error variances and covariances to be equal. Because each subsequent step was nested in the previous step, the additional constraints placed on the models can be tested by comparing chi-square and degree of freedom values.

GENDER OF THIRD GENERATION

Comparison of mean values for all model variables using t-tests indicated no mean differences between families in which the third-generation member interviewed was male and those families in which the third-generation member was female. Bivariate correlations for families in which the third-generation member was female and those in which the third-generation member was male may be found in table 15.5. As indicated, relationships between model variables were generally stronger in families where the third-generation member was female. More specific, the more life events reported by the third-generation females, the more the disagreement between third-generation member and mother (as reported by both parties) and the more disagreement child reported between herself and her father. More events were also associated with higher levels of depression for mother. Mother's level of depression was associated with both mother's and third-generation member's report of disagreement and with child's report of disagreements with her father, with greater disagreement being associated with more depression. Father's level of depression was negatively associated with both father's and third generation's report of disagreement, with higher levels of disagreement being associated with more depression. For families where the third-generation member was male, only teen-mother disagreements were related to child events. Mother well-being was not related to any model variables.

The four-step test of the adequacy of the fit of the overall model for families in which the third-generation member was male and families in which the third-generation member was female indicated that the model provided an excellent fit for both types of families. Table 15.6 shows no significant differences in the goodness of fit of the model between the two types of families.

TABLE 15.5. Bivariate Correlations by Gender of Child

	Child Events	Father-Teen Disagree	Teen-Father Disagree	Mother-Teen Disagree	Teen-Mother Disagree	Father Depression	Mother Depression
Child Events	1.00	-.09	-.38[b]	-.24[a]	-.30[b]	-.05	.26[a]
Father-Teen Disagree	.02	1.00	.40[b]	.44[b]	.35[b]	-.24[a]	-.16
Teen-Father Disagree	-.18	.39[b]	1.00	.45[b]	.66[b]	-.29[b]	-.21[a]
Mother-Teen Disagree	-.15	.31[a]	.32[b]	1.00	.54[b]	-.10	-.53[b]
Teen-Mother Disagree	-.29[a]	.25[a]	.80[b]	.26[a]	1.00	-.18	-.29[b]
Father Depression	-.09	-.08	.02	.03	.04	1.00	.18
Mother Depression	-.01	-.02	-.02	-.25[a]	.07	.18	1.00

Note: Lower triangle values for families with male target child; upper triangle values for families with female target child.
[a]Significant at .05 level.
[b]Significant at .01 level.

TABLE 15.6. Test of Adequacy of Fit of Model for Families Where Third Generation is Male and Female

Model	Chi-Square	d.f.	Change in Chi-Square	Change in d.f.
No constraints	37.357	22	—	—
Equal regression weights	43.656	26	6.29	4
Equal variances	43.784	27	.13	1
Equal error variances and covariances	53.589	35	9.80	8

Age of Third Generation

Tests of model variable means for families in which the third-generation member was eighteen or under and those in which the third-generation member was nineteen or older revealed no significant differences between the two groups. The bivariate correlations, found in table 15.7, are also very similar for the two groups.

The four-step test of the adequacy of fit of the model (table 15.8) for families with older and younger third-generation members indicated that under conditions of no constraints, equal regression weights, equal variances, and equal error variances and covariances, the model provided a good fit for both groups.

Socioeconomic Status of Families

Tests of mean differences on all model variables indicated that low-SES mothers were more depressed than high-SES mothers ($t = -2.30$; $d.f. = 84.13$; $p < .05$) and that third-generation members from low-SES families reported more negative life events than third-generation members from high-SES families ($t = -2.74$; $d.f. = 89.60$; $p < .01$). Bivariate correlations for high- and low-SES families are included in table 15.9. In general, relationships between model variables were stronger for high-SES families than for low-SES families. For example, the relationships between father-teen disagreement and teen-father disagreement and between mother-teen and teen-mother disagreement were stronger for high-SES families than for low-SES families. Interestingly, level of depression as reported by mother and as reported by father were strongly related to each other for the high-SES families but not at all related in low-SES families. Furthermore, in low-SES families, child events were related to teen-father disagreement, mother-teen disagreement, teen-mother disagreement, and father depression; for high-

591

TABLE 15.7. Bivariate Correlations by Age of Third Generation

	Child Events	Father-Teen Disagree	Teen-Father Disagree	Mother-Teen Disagree	Teen-Mother Disagree	Father Depression	Mother Depression
Child Events	1.00	−.07	−.37[b]	−.33[b]	−.41[b]	.03	.25[a]
Father-Teen Disagree	−.02	1.00	.29[a]	.26[a]	.09	−.17	−.02
Teen-Father Disagree	−.24[a]	.49[b]	1.00	.44[b]	.63[b]	−.03	−.04
Mother-Teen Disagree	−.10	.49[b]	.36[b]	1.00	.39[b]	.05	−.26[a]
Teen-Mother Disagree	−.22[a]	.48[b]	.78[b]	.48[b]	1.00	.09	−.01
Father Depression	−.13	−.17	−.26[a]	−.12	−.21[a]	1.00	.12
Mother Depression	.06	−.17	−.20	−.55[b]	−.24[a]	.23[a]	1.00

Note: Lower triangle values for families with third generation aged eighteen or under; upper triangle values for families with third generation aged nineteen or older.

[a]Significant at .05 level.
[b]Significant at .01 level.

TABLE 15.8. Test of Adequacy of Fit of Model for Families with Third-Generation Members Aged 18 or Under and Families with Third-Generation Members Aged 19 or Older

Model	Chi-Square	d.f.	Change in Chi-Square	Change in d.f.
No constraints	42.753	22	—	—
Equal regression weights	47.164	26	4.41	4
Equal variances	47.296	27	.13	1
Equal error variances and covariances	59.018	35	11.72	8

SES families, child events was related only to teen-mother disagreement.

Testing the adequacy of fit of the overall model for families of high and low SES indicated that regression weights, variances, and error variances and covariances differed significantly between the two groups. These findings, detailed in table 15.10, suggest that the model does not provide a good fit when data are examined from families who vary on SES. Although small sample sizes prohibit accurate tests of the model, there was an especially poor fit for the lower-SES group, with results suggesting that paths were nonsignificant between child events and father-teen disagreement, father-teen disagreement and mother-teen disagreement, and father-teen disagreement and father well-being.

CAREGIVING AND NONCAREGIVING FAMILIES

Comparison of means for caregiving and noncaregiving families on model variables indicated that both mothers ($t = -2.98$; $d.f. = 102.21$; $p < .01$) and fathers ($t = -3.12$; $d.f. = 151.57$; $p < .01$) in caregiving families were more depressed than their counterparts in noncaregiving families. Bivariate correlations for caregiving and noncaregiving families may be found in table 15.11. In general, relationships between model variables are stronger for caregiving than for noncaregiving families. The relationships between life events and teen-father disagreement, mother-teen disagreement, teen-mother disagreement, and mother's depression are all significant for the caregiving families but nonsignificant for the noncaregiving families. For noncaregiving families only mother-teen disagreement predicts mother's well-being, whereas for caregiving families, in addition to mother-teen disagree-

TABLE 15.9. Bivariate Correlations by SES

	Child Events	Father-Teen Disagree	Teen-Father Disagree	Mother-Teen Disagree	Teen-Mother Disagree	Father Depression	Mother Depression
Child Events	1.00	.05	−.18	−.11	−.27^b	.06	.01
Father-Teen Disagree	−.14	1.00	.45^b	.49^b	.32^b	−.23^a	−.13
Teen-Father Disagree	−.45^b	.29^a	1.00	.48^b	.73^b	−.19^a	−.06
Mother-Teen Disagree	−.31^a	.19	.20	1.00	.49^b	−.26^b	−.39^b
Teen-Mother Disagree	−.41^b	.30^a	.72^b	.34^a	1.00	−.16	−.08
Father Depression	−.30^a	−.07	−.10	.33^a	.01	1.00	.27^b
Mother Depression	.22	−.04	−.19	−.44^b	−.24^b	.04	1.00

Note: Lower triangle values for families with low SES; upper triangle values for families with high SES.
[a]Significant at .05 level.
[b]Significant at .01 level.

TABLE 15.10. Test of Adequacy of Fit of Model for Families
with High and Low SES

Model	Chi-Square	d.f.	Change in Chi-Square	Change in d.f.
No constraints	34.10	22	—	—
Equal regression weights	47.53	26	13.43[a]	4
Equal variances	51.87	27	4.34[a]	1
Equal error variances and covariances	77.48	35	25.61[a]	8

[a]Differences significant at .05 level.

ment, child events and teen-mother disagreements predict mother's depression.

Results of the four-step test of adequacy of fit of the model for caregiving and noncaregiving families are detailed in table 15.12. As indicated, tests of no constraints, equal regression weights, and equal variances resulted in no significant differences between the two groups. The test for equal error variances and covariances, however, indicated statistically significant, although conceptually minor, differences in the fit of the model between the two groups.

DISCUSSION

These analyses failed to support either the theoretical model, which predicted that life events experienced by third-generation members would have direct effects on the well-being of their parents, or the model predicting that life events would have indirect effects on parental well-being as a result of their effects on parent-child relationships. Instead, the data reveal that a more complex set of relationships characterizes parents and their adolescent/young adult children. These findings will be reviewed, followed by a brief discussion of study limitations and suggestions for future research.

Collection of data from multiple family members enables more complete understanding of the way in which the lives of family members are changed by events occurring directly to third-generation members. Although levels of well-being as experienced by mother and father are correlated, they clearly have different predictors. The model derived from these data indicates that father's well-being is predicted directly from father-child disagreement and indirectly from life events experienced by the child. The more negative events experienced by the child,

TABLE 15.11. Bivariate Correlations for Caregiving and Noncaregiving Families

	Child Events	Father-Teen Disagree	Teen-Father Disagree	Mother-Teen Disagree	Teen-Mother Disagree	Father Depression	Mother Depression
Child Events	1.00	−.06	−.35[b]	−.29[b]	−.34[b]	−.05	.28[b]
Father-Teen Disagree	.04	1.00	.36[b]	.30[b]	.34[b]	−.18	−.09
Teen-Father Disagree	−.16	.50[b]	1.00	.36[b]	.77[b]	−.18	−.16
Mother-Teen Disagree	.01	.57[b]	.51[b]	1.00	.49[b]	−.05	−.40[b]
Teen-Mother Disagree	−.19	.22	.56[b]	.31[a]	1.00	−.11	−.21[a]
Father Depression	.04	−.29[a]	−.12	−.13	−.09	1.00	.17
Mother Depression	−.10	−.21	−.05	−.56[b]	.02	.06	1.00

Note: Lower triangle values for noncaregiving families; upper triangle values for caregiving families.
[a]Significant at .05 level.
[b]Significant at .01 level.

TABLE 15.12. Test of Adequacy of Fit of Model for Caregiving and Noncaregiving Families

Model	Chi-Square	d.f.	Change in Chi-Square	Change in d.f.
No constraints	29.468	22	—	—
Equal regression weights	35.117	26	5.64	4
Equal variances	35.645	27	.53	1
Equal error variances and covariances	72.776	35	37.13[a]	8

[a]Differences significant at .05 level.

the more disagreement there is between father and child. The more father and child disagree, the more depressed is the father. Mother's well-being, on the other hand, is predicted directly from mother-child disagreement and indirectly by life events and father-child disagreement. The more negative events experienced by the child, the more disagreement there is between child and father. The less the disagreement between father and child, the less disagreement there is between mother and child. And the less disagreement there is between mother and child, the less depressed is the mother.

These results, which find that mother's well-being varies as a function of father-child disagreement, child negative events, as well as mother-child disagreement, support hypotheses derived from role theory. Mothers generally play a more central role than fathers in child-rearing and are generally the glue that holds families together (Turner 1970). When there is trouble in the lives of family members, it is mother's well-being that suffers the most.

The lack of relationship between child events and mother-child disagreement may be explained by more closely examining the nature of the variables that make up parent-child disagreement. Parents and children reported on the extent of disagreement on such day-to-day topics as dating, household chores, food, and television. It is possible that when third-generation members experience negative events, their mothers are more likely than their fathers to be sympathetic about the situation, and that any minor disagreements characterizing their relationship (such as arguments about dating, household chores, television) are temporarily suspended. Once the difficult issues are dealt with, the normal family bickering continues. For fathers, on the other hand, the experience of major negative life events seems to exacerbate disagreements over day-to-day problems. It seems as though these negative life events have the capacity to stir up old fires between fathers and their children and lead to increased bickering about the small, day-to-day events.

The lack of effect of both gender of child and interaction of gender of parent and gender of child on the model fails to support the psychoanalytic theory. From these data, the lives of mothers of daughters and fathers of sons do not seem to be more fused than are the lives of mothers of sons and fathers of daughters. Similar findings have been reported by Crouter and Crowley (1990) and Galambos and Almeida (1992), yet stand in contrast to research findings which suggest that the mother-daughter dyad is more conflicted than other parent-adolescent combinations (Montemayor 1982; Smetana 1989).

The finding that the model fits regardless of age of the third-generation member must be tempered by limitations of the data. First, the relatively small sample size prohibited a fair test of the model differences as predicted by theory. Earlier work led to the hypothesis that families with very young adolescent children (families in which the target child was under the age of fourteen) and families in which the target child was postadolescence (over the age of twenty-five) should experience very different effects. It is possible that since sample size forced the sample to be split at age nineteen, the differences were minimized. Future research focusing on samples of young adolescents and young adults would provide a more appropriate test of the model.

When the sample was split on socioeconomic status, results indicate that the model did not provide a good fit to the data. Although the small sample size must temper generalization, results do provide provocative information. Mean differences on model variables, which included more frequent negative life events being reported by lower-class, third-generation members and higher levels of depression being reported by lower-class mothers, as well as correlations that were higher for higher-SES families than for lower-class families, combine to yield very different results for the two groups. Interestingly, the finding that both parent-child disagreement and mother-father depression were stronger for higher SES than lower suggests that family relationships are stronger for higher- than lower-socioeconomic status groups. The predicted relationships, in which working-class parents value children's conformity more so than do upper-class parents and are therefore more likely to perceive disagreements as a challenge to their sense of authority and well-being, were not borne out by the data.

The finding that mothers and fathers in caregiving families experienced higher levels of depression is consistent with stress theory. While the model fit equally well for caregiving and noncaregiving families, it is important to note that correlations between child events and mother-teen disagreement, teen-mother disagreement, teen-father disagreement, and mother's depression were all significant for caregiving families but not significant for noncaregiving families. These findings hint that people in caregiving families experience higher levels of stress because of their elder care responsibilities. They were also most likely to experience stress between the middle and the younger generation. Future research that examines more closely the stress experienced by family members as a function of relationships between generations would help to explain the inner workings of families.

Although the model developed in this chapter seems relatively robust, some caveats regarding generalizability must be acknowledged. First, the cross-sectional nature of the data prohibit statements regarding causality. Structural modeling techniques, in combination with theory, permit some confidence in directionality, but true understanding of cause-and-effect variables requires longitudinal data. Second, the relatively small sample size prohibited examining theoretically meaningful group effects (e.g., effects of SES). It also reduced the number of families experiencing each event. A large-scale study in which the effects of individual events could be examined would provide invaluable data from which policy statements could be derived. Such a study would enable individual effects as well as interactive effects to be examined. Third, although this study focused only on reports of life events as made by the third generation, a more complete understanding of the effect of life events on family members would include reports of events from multiple family members. Fourth, operationalization of well-being as including positive as well as negative dimensions would add to our understanding of the effects of life events on families. Fifth, if the goal is to understand parent's level of well-being as a function of events as experienced by children and extent of disagreement between parent and children, then all children in the family, rather than only one child, should be included in the study. Finally, generalization of results must be made with caution given that these data were collected from households containing three rather than two generations. An interesting follow-up study would contrast parent-child relationships in two- and three-generation households.

Nonetheless, these results do highlight the ripple effects that life events can have on family members. The webs that join the lives of family members to one another are intricate and complex and have a stronghold on the lives of family members. Adequate understanding of these effects requires that data be collected from multiple family members and analyzed using the family rather than the individual as the unit of analysis.

REFERENCES

Aldous, J. 1978. *Family careers: Developmental changes in families.* New York: Wiley.

Aldous, J., E. Klaus, and D. M. Klein. 1985. The understanding heart: Aging parents and their favorite child. *Child Development* 56:303–316.

Aquilino, W. S., and K. R. Supple. 1991. Parent-child relations and parent's satisfaction with living arrangements when adult children live at home. *Journal of Marriage and the Family* 53:13–27.

Arbuckle, J. 1988. *AMOS: Analysis of Moment Structures user's guide.* Temple University.

Baruch, G., and R. C. Barnett. 1983. Adult daughters' relationships with their mothers. *Journal of Marriage and the Family* 45:601–606.

Baruch, G., R. C. Barnett, and C. Rivers. 1983. *Lifeprints.* New York: McGraw-Hill.

Beck, S. H., and R. W. Beck. 1984. The formation of extended households during middle age. *Journal of Marriage and the Family* 46:277–288.

Beckman-Bell, P. 1981. Child-related stress in families of handicapped children. *Topics in Early Childhood Special Education* 1:43–53.

Bell, R. 1979. Parent-child and reciprocal influences. *American Psychologist* 34:821–826.

Benedek, T. 1959. Parenthood as a developmental phase: A contribution to the libido theory. *Journal of the American Psychoanalytic Association* 7:389–417.

Bengtson, V. L., and J. A. Kuypers. 1971. Generational differences and the developmental stake. *Aging and Human Development* 2:249–260.

Bentler, P. M., and D. G. Bonett. 1980. Significance tests and goodness of fit in the analysis of covariance structures. *Psychological Bulletin* 88:588–606.

Bergman, A. 1982. Considerations about the development of the girl during the separation-individuation process. In D. Mandell, ed., *Early female development: Current psychoanalytic views,* pp. 62–79. New York: Spectrum.

Blenkner, M. 1965. Social work and family in later life, with some thoughts on filial maturity. In E. Shanas and G. Streib, eds., *Social structure and the family: Generational relations,* pp. 46–59. Englewood Cliffs, N.J.: Prentice-Hall.

Breytspraak, L. 1984. *The development of self in later life.* Boston: Little, Brown.

Brody, E. M. 1985. Parent care as a normative family stress. *Gerontologist* 25:19–29.

———. 1989. The family at risk. In E. Light and B. Lebowitz, eds., *Alzheimer's disease treatment and family stress: Directions for research.* Washington, D.C.: NIMH.

———. 1990. *Women in the middle: Their parent-care years.* New York: Springer.

Brody, E. M., N. Dempsey, and R. A. Pruchno. 1990. Sons and daughters of the institutional aged: Mental health effects. *The Gerontologist* 20:212–219.

Brody, E. M., M. H. Kleban, C. Hoffman, and C. Schoonover. 1988. Adult daughters and parent care: A comparison of one-, two- and three-generation households. *Home Health Care Services Quarterly* 9:19–45.

Brooks-Gunn, J., and M. Zahaykevich. 1989. Parent-daughter relationships in early adolescence: A developmental perspective. In K. Kreppner and R. M. Lerner, eds., *Family systems and life span development,* pp. 233–246. Hillsdale, N.J.: Lawrence Erlbaum.

Byrne, E. A., and C. C. Cunningham. 1985. The effects of mentally handicapped children on families: A conceptual review. *Journal of Child Psychology and Psychiatry* 26:847–864.

Carmines, E. G., and J. P. McIver. 1981. Analyzing models with unobserved variables. In G. W. Bohrnstedt and E. F. Borgatta, eds., *Social Measurement: Current Issues.* Beverly Hills, Calif.: Sage.

Chodorow, N. 1978. *The reproduction of mothering: Psychoanalysis and sociology of gender.* Berkley, Calif.: University of California.

Cicirelli, V. G. 1983. Adult children's attachment and helping behavior to elderly parents: A path model. *Journal of Marriage and the Family* 45:815–825.

Connell, J. P., and W. Furman. 1984. The study of transitions: Conceptual and methodological considerations. In R. Emde and R. Harmon, eds., *Continuity and discontinuity in development,* pp. 183–193. New York: Plenum.

Cook, J. A. 1988. Who "mothers" the chronically mentally ill? *Family Relations* 37: 42–49.

Cook, J., and B. J. Cohler. 1986. Reciprocal socialization and the care of offspring with cancer and schizophrenia. In N. Datan, A. Greene, and H. Reese, eds., *Life-span developmental psychology: Intergenerational relations,* pp. 223–243. Hillsdale, N.J.: Lawrence Erlbaum.

Crouter, A. C., and M. S. Crowley. 1990. School-age children's time alone with fathers in single- and dual-earner families: Implications for the father-child relationship. *Journal of Early Adolescence* 10:296–312.

Csikszentmihalyi, M., and R. Larsen. 1984. *Being adolescent: Conflict and growth in the teenage years.* New York: Basic.

Deutsch, F. M., D. N. Ruble, A. Fleming, J. Brooks-Gunn, and C. Stangor. 1988. Information and maternal self-definition during the transition to motherhood. *Journal of Personality and Social Psychology* 55 (3):420–431.

Farrell, M., and S. Rosenberg. 1981. *Men at midlife.* Dover, Mass.: Auburn House.

Fortier, L. M., and R. L. Wanlass. 1984. Family crisis following the diagnosis of a handicapped child. *Family Relations* 33:13–24.

Galambos, N. L., and D. M. Almeida. 1992. Does parent-adolescent conflict increase in early adolescence? *Journal of Marriage and the Family* 54:737–747.

Gilligan, C. 1982. Adult development and women's development: Arrangements for a marriage. In J. Z. Giele, ed., *Women in the middle years: Current knowledge and directions for future research and policy,* pp. 89–114. New York: Wiley.

Goldsteen, K., and C. E. Ross. 1989. The perceived burden of children. *Journal of Family Issues* 10:504–526.

Gowen, J. W., N. Johnson-Martin, B. D. Goldman, and M. Appelbaum. 1989. Feelings of depression and parenting competence of mothers of handicapped and nonhandicapped infants: A longitudinal study. *American Journal of Mental Retardation* 94:259–271.

Greenberg, J., and M. Becker. 1988. Aging parents as family resources. *Gerontologist* 28:786–791.

Green, A. L., and A. M. Boxer. 1985. Daughters and sons as young adults: Restructuring the ties that bind. In N. Datan, A. Greene, and H. Reese, eds., *Life-span developmental psychology: Intergenerational relationships,* pp. 125–149. Hillsdale, N.J.: Lawrence Erlbaum.

Grotevant, H. D., and C. R. Cooper. 1986. Individuation in family relationships. *Human Development* 29:82–100.

Gubman, G. D., and R. C. Tessler. 1987. The impact of mental illness on families. *Journal of Family Issues* 8:226–245.

Gunnar, M., and W. A. Collins. 1988. *Transitions in adolescence: Minnesota symposium on child psychology.* Hillsdale, N.J.: Lawrence Erlbaum.

Hagestad, G. O. 1986. Dimensions of time and the family. *American Behavior Scientist* 29:679–694.

———. 1987. Parent-child relations in later life: Trends and gaps in past research. In J. B. Lancaster, J. Altmann, A. S. Rossi, and L. R. Sherrod, eds., *Parenting across the life span: Biosocial dimensions,* pp. 405–434. New York: Aldine de Gruyter.

Hall, J. A. 1987. Parent-adolescent conflict: An empirical review. *Adolescence* 22: 767–789.

Harris, V. S., and S. M. McHale. 1989. Family life problems, daily caregiving activities, and psychological well-being of mothers of mentally retarded children. *American Journal of Mental Retardation* 94:231–239.

Heisel, J. S., S. Ream, R. Raitz, M. Rappaport, and R. D. Coddington. 1973. The significance of life events as contributing factors in the diseases of children. *Journal of Pediatrics* 83:119–123.

Hill, J. P. 1980. The family. In M. Johnson, ed., *Toward adolescence: The middle school years.* Chicago: University of Chicago Press.

Hill, J. P., G. N. Holmbeck, L. Marlow, T. M. Green, and M. E. Lynch. 1985. Menarcheal status and parent-child relations in families of seventh-grade girls. *Journal of Youth and Adolescence* 14 (4):301–316.

Jacob, T. 1974. Patterns of family conflict and dominance as a function of child age and social class. *Developmental Psychology* 10:1–12.

Johnson, E. S., and B. Bursk. 1977. Relationships between the elderly and their adult children. *Gerontologist* 17:90–96.

Johnson, J. H. 1986. *Life events as stressors in childhood and adolescence.* Newbury Park, Calif.: Sage.

Johnson, J. H., and S. M. McCutcheon. 1980. Assessing life stress in older children and adolescents: Preliminary findings with the life events checklist. In I. G. Sarason and C. D. Spielberger, eds., *Stress and anxiety.* Washington, D.C.: Hemisphere.

Joreskog, K. G., and D. Sorbom. 1986. *LISREL VI: Analysis of linear structural relationships by maximum likelihood, instrumental variables, and least squares methods.* Chicago: National Educational Resources.

Kazak, A. E., and R. S. Marvin. 1984. Differences, difficulties, and adaptation: Stress and social networks in families with a handicapped child. *Family Relations* 84: 67–77.

Kidwell, J., J. Fischer, R. Dunham, and M. Baranowski. 1983. Parents and adolescents: Push and pull of change. In H. McCubbin and C. Figley, eds., *Stress in the family: Coping with normative transitions,* pp. 74–89. New York: Bruner/Mazel.

Kleban, M. H., E. M. Brody, C. B. Schoonover, and C. Hoffman. 1989. Family help to the elderly: Perceptions of sons-in-law regarding parent care. *Journal of Marriage and the Family* 51:303–312.

Kohn, M. 1977. *Class and conformity: A study of values.* Chicago: University of Chicago Press.

Krauss, M. W. 1993. Child-related and parenting stress: Similarities and differences between mothers and fathers of children with disabilities. *American Journal on Mental Retardation* 97:393–404.

Larsen, A., and D. Olson. 1990. Capturing the complexity of family systems: Integrating family theory, family scores, and family analysis. In T. W. Draper and A. C. Marcos, eds., *Family variables: Conception, measurement, and use,* pp. 19–47. Newbury Park, Calif.: Sage.

Lawton, M. P., M. Moss, M. Fulcomer, and M. H. Kleban. 1982. A research and service-oriented Multilevel Assessment Instrument. *Journal of Gerontology* 37: 91–99.

Lerner, R. M., and T. T. Foch. 1987. *Biological-psychosocial interactions in early adolescence: A life-span perspective.* Hillsdale, N.J.: Lawrence Erlbaum.

Litwak, E. 1960. Geographic mobility and extended family cohesion. *American Sociological Review* 25:385–394.

Mash, E. J., and C. Johnson. 1983. Parental perception of child behavior problems, parenting self-esteem, and mothers' reported stress in younger and older hyperactive and normal children. *Journal of Consulting and Clinical Psychology* 51: 86–99.

McCubbin, H. I., J. M. Patterson, and L. R. Wilson. 1982. Family inventory of life events and changes. In D. Olson, H. I. McCubbin, H. Barnes, and A. Larsen, eds., *Family inventories: Inventories used in a national survey of families across the family life cycle.* St. Paul, Minn. Working document.

McKinney, B., and R. A. Peterson. 1987. Predictors of stress in parents of developmentally disabled children. *Journal of Pediatric Psychology* 12:133–150.

Montemayor, R. 1982. The relationship between parent-adolescent conflict and the amount of time adolescents spend alone and with parents and peers. *Child Development* 53:1512–1519.

———. 1986. Family variation in parent-adolescent storm and stress. *Journal of Adolescent Research* 1 (1):15–31.

Montemayor, R., and J. R. Brownlee. 1987. Fathers, mothers, and adolescents: Gender-based differences in parental roles during adolescence. *Journal of Youth and Adolescence* 16:281–291.

Montemayor, R., and E. Hanson. 1985. A naturalistic view of conflict between adolescents and their parents and siblings. *Journal of Early Adolescence* 5:23–30.

Moss, M., S. Moss, and E. Moles. 1985. The quality of relationships between elderly parents and their out-of-town children. *Gerontologist* 25:134–140.

Noelker, L. S., and S. W. Poulshock. 1982. The effects on families of caring for impaired elderly in residence. Final report submitted to Administration on Aging. Washington, D.C.

Noh, S., J. E. Dumas, L. C. Wolf, and S. Fisman. 1989. Delineating sources of stress in parents of exceptional children. *Family Relations* 38:456–461.

Olshansky, S. 1962. Chronic sorrow: A response to having a mentally defective child. *Social Casework* 43:190–194.

Pillemer, K., and J. J. Suitor. 1991. "Will I ever escape my child's problems?" Effects of adult children's problems on elderly parents. *Journal of Marriage and the Family* 53:585–594.

Pruchno, R. A. 1989. Alzheimer's disease and families: Methodological advances. In E. Light and B. Lebowitz, eds., *Alzheimer's disease treatment and family stress: Directions for research*. Washington, D.C.: NIMH, Government Printing Office.

Pruchno, R. A., F. C. Blow, and M. A. Smyer. 1984. Life events and interdependent lives: Implications for research and intervention. *Human Development* 27:31–41.

Radloff, L. 1977. The CES-D scale: A self-report depression scale for research in the general population. *Applied Psychological Measurement* 1:385–401.

Ransom, D., L. Fisher, S. Phillips, R. Kokes, and R. Weiss. 1990. The logic of measurement in family research. In T. Draper and A. Marcos, eds., *Family variables: Conceptualization, measurement, and use*, pp. 48–63. Newbury Park, Calif.: Sage.

Richards, L. N., V. L. Bengtson, and R. B. Miller. 1989. The "generation in the middle": Perceptions of changes in adults' intergenerational relationships. In K. Kreppner and R. M. Lerner, eds., *Family systems and life-span development*. Hillsdale, N.J.: Lawrence Erlbaum.

Richardson, R. A., N. L. Galambos, J. E. Schulenberg, and A. C. Petersen. 1984. Young adolescents' perceptions of the family environment. *Journal of Early Adolescence* 4:131–153.

Rogosa, D. 1979. Causal models in longitudinal research: Rationale, formulation, and interpretation. In J. R. Nesselroade and P. B. Baltes, eds., *Longitudinal research in the study of behavior and development*. New York: Academic.

Rook, K. S. 1984. The negative side of social interaction: Impact on psychological well-being. *Journal of Personality and Social Psychology* 46:1097–1108.

Rosow, I. 1970. Old people: Their friends and neighbors. *American Behavioral Scientist* 14:59–69.

Rossi, A. S., and P. H. Rossi. 1990. *Of human bonding: Parent-child relations aross the life cycle*. New York: Aldine de Gruyter.

Rubin, L. 1976. *Worlds of pain: Life in the working class family*. New York: Basic.

Ruble, D. N. 1983. The development of social comparison processes and their role in achievement-related self-socialization. In E. T. Higgins, D. N. Ruble, and W. W. Hartup, eds., *Social cognition and social development: A sociocultural perspective*, pp. 134–157. New York: Cambridge University Press.

Schilling, R. F., S. P. Shinkle, and M. A. Kirkham. 1985. Coping with a handicapped child: Differences between mothers and fathers. *Social Science Medicine* 21:857–863.

Seltzer, M. M., and M. W. Krauss. 1989. Aging parents with adult mentally retarded children: Family risk factors and sources of support. *American Journal on Mental Retardation* 94:303–312.

Shanas, E. 1979. Social myth as hypothesis: The case of the family relations of old people. *Gerontologist* 19:3–9.

Sherman, B., and J. Cocozza. 1984. Stress in families of the developmentally disabled: A literature review of factors affecting the decision to seek out-of-home placements. *Family Relations* 33:95–103.

Silverberg, S. B., and L. Steinberg. 1987. Adolescent autonomy, parent-adolescent conflict, and parental well-being. *Journal of Youth and Adolescence* 16 (3):293–312.

Slater, M., and L. Wikler. 1986. "Normalized" family resources for families with a developmentally disabled child. *Social Work* 31:385–390.

Small, S. A., S. Cornelius, and G. Eastman. 1983. *Parenting adolescent children: A period of storm and stress?* Paper presented at a meeting of the American Psychological Association, Anaheim, Calif.

Smetana, J. G. 1988. Concepts of self and social convention: Adolescents' and parents' reasoning about hypothetical and actual family conflicts. In M. Gunnar and W. A. Collins, eds., *Development during transition to adolescence: Minnesota symposia on child psychology*, 21:79–122. Hillsdale, N.J.: Lawrence Erlbaum.

———. 1989. Adolescents' and parents' reasoning about actual family conflict. *Child Development* 60:1052–1067.

Smith, B. 1976. Adolescent and parent: Interaction between developmental stages. In *Center Quarterly Focus*. St. Paul: University of Minnesota Center for Youth Development and Research.

Spink, D. 1976. Crisis intervention for parents of the deaf child. *Health and Social Work* 1:140–160.

Steinberg, L. 1987. The impact of puberty on family relations: Effects of pubertal status and pubertal timing. *Developmental Psychology* 23:451–460.

Sullivan, K., and A. Sullivan. 1980. Adolescent-parent separation. *Developmental Psychology* 16:93–99.

Tavormina, J. B., T. J. Boll, N. J. Dunn, R. L. Luscomb, and J. R. Taylor. 1981. Psychosocial effects on parents of raising a physically handicapped child. *Journal of Abnormal Child Psychology* 9:121–131.

Thompson, L., and A. J. Walker. 1982. The dyad as the unit of analysis: Conceptual and methodological issues. *Journal of Marriage and the Family* 44:889–900.

Troll, L. E., S. J. Miller, and R. C. Atchley. 1979. *Families in later life.* Belmont, Calif.: Wadsworth.

Turner, R. H. 1970. *Family interaction.* New York: John Wiley.

Umberson, D. 1989. Relationships with children: Explaining parents' psychological well-being. *Journal of Marriage and the Family* 57:999–1012.

———. 1992. Relationships between adult children and their parents: Psychological consequences for both generations. *Journal of Marriage and the Family* 54 (3): 664–674.

Vaillant, G. 1977. *Adaptation to life.* Boston: Little, Brown.

Veroff, J., E. Douvan, and R. Kulka. 1981. *The inner American: A self-portrait from 1957 to 1976.* New York: Basic.

Violato, C., A. Marini, and W. Hunter. 1989. A confirmatory factor analysis of a four-factor model of attitudes toward computers: A study of preservice teachers. *Journal of Research on Computing in Education* 22:199–213.

Waisbren, S. 1980. Parent reactions after the birth of a developmentally disabled child. *American Journal of Mental Deficiency* 4:345–351.

Wheaton, B., B. Muthen, D. F. Alwin, and G. F. Summers. 1977. Assessing reliability and stability in panel models. In D. R. Heise, ed., *Sociological Methodology,* pp. 84–136. San Francisco: Jossey-Bass.

Wikler, L., M. Wasow, and E. Hatfield. 1981. Chronic sorrow revisited: Parent versus professional depiction of the adjustment of parents of mentally retarded children. *American Journal of Orthopsychiatry* 51:63–70.

Wilkening, E. A., and D. E. Morrison. 1963. A comparison of husband and wife responses concerning who makes family and home decisions. *Marriage and Family Living* 25:349–351.

Youniss, J. 1985. *Adolescent relations with mothers, fathers, and friends.* Chicago: University of Chicago Press.

Youniss, J., and R. A. Ketterlinus. 1987. Communication and connectedness in mother- and father-adolescent relationships. *Journal of Youth and Adolescence* 16:265–280.

SIXTEEN

Looking Back and Looking Ahead: Life-Course Unfolding of Parenthood

Rosemary Blieszner, Jay A. Mancini, and Lydia I. Marek

Parenting experiences in the middle years of adulthood not only affect psychological, financial, marital, and other aspects of well-being but also set the stage for parenting experiences later in life. Beginning with this premise and grounding our discussion in a broadly conceived life-course perspective that encompasses consideration of both psychological development and sociological structure (Bengtson and Allen 1993; Rodgers and White 1993; Rossi 1989), we define midlife parenting as a location on the parenting continuum that is associated not with parental age alone or with family life-cycle stage alone but rather with consideration of the intersection between individual development and family experience. Midlife parenting involves people who are old enough to have offspring who are teens or young adults, although they may also have offspring who are young children. For our purposes, the focus is on age of children or age of parents only indirectly; our primary concern is with midlife parenting as a successor to previous parenting and personal development experiences and as a precursor of late-life parenting and other old-age experiences. This definition of midlife parenting places the parent on a changing developmental trajectory and acknowledges the need to look both backward to earlier parent-child relationship experiences and forward to future ones to understand fully the effects of parenting on development.

We designed figure 16.1 to illustrate our conceptualization of parenthood over the life course, with an emphasis on middle and late adulthood. Looking first at the largest box, note that parenting occurs within the context of life-span development. This context entails personal development in biological, psychological, and social domains; the

The authors appreciate the assistance of Dan Sandifer, who conducted a literature review; Leigh Anne Faulconer, who produced the figure; and Carol D. Ryff, Marsha M. Seltzer, and two anonymous reviewers, who provided helpful guidance and editorial comments. Our study of aging parent–adult child relationship quality was supported by a grant from the AARP Andrus Foundation to Jay A. Mancini, principal investigator.

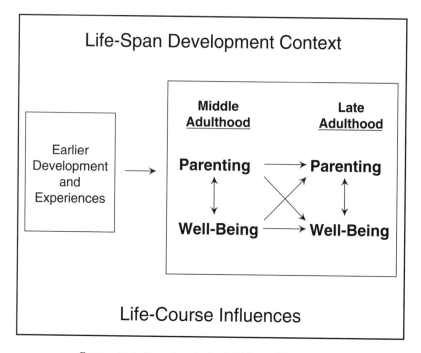

FIGURE 16.1. Parenting in the Middle and Later Years.

historical and environmental settings in which development takes place; and the life events and other factors that influence personal development (Baltes, Reese, and Lipsitt 1980). Parenting simultaneously takes place within a set of life-course influences, reflecting the socially constructed norms, expectations, opportunities, and constraints associated with members of different age strata, genders, racial ethnic groups, classes, and marital statuses (Hagestad and Neugarten 1985). Parenting in middle and late adulthood is also affected by an individual's earlier parenting involvement and other developmental events and experiences (the smallest box; see Rossi and Rossi 1990).

The medium-sized box that signifies parenting in middle and late adulthood conveys, via double-headed arrows, the notion of reciprocity between parenting experiences and psychological well-being for each age period. For discussions of midlife parenting and well-being (the vertical arrow on the left) see chapters in this volume by Allen, Aber, Seidman, Denner, and Mitchell (chapter 8); Aquilino (chapter 11); Graber and Brooks-Gunn (chapter 7); Pruchno, Peters, and Burant (chapter 15); Ryff, Schmutte, and Lee (chapter 10); Seltzer, Krauss,

Choi, and Hong (chapter 12); Silverberg (chapter 6); and Spencer, Swanson, and Glymph (chapter 9). For research on late-life parenting and well-being (the vertical arrow on the right), see work by Blieszner and Mancini (1987), Hess and Waring (1978), Mancini and Blieszner (1992), Mutran and Reitzes (1984), Pillemer and Suitor (1991a,b), Quinn (1983), Suitor and Pillemer (1987), and Umberson (1992). Note that the typical approach has been examination of the effects of aspects of parenting on well-being; left relatively unexplored are the effects of well-being on parenting.

The other arrows in the medium box (between middle adulthood and late adulthood) imply that parenting experiences and well-being status at midlife affect parenting and well-being in old age. Existing research on the parent-child relationship in the middle and later years does not address the transition from one parenting stage to the other very specifically or thoroughly. Apparently, few studies of middle-age antecedents of late-life parenting experiences have been conducted (but see Seltzer et al., chapter 12, this volume, for a unique example of such research).

Our task for this chapter is to start at the point that the other authors in this volume, who have examined the influence of child-related factors and life circumstances on midlife parents, have ended. That is, we explicitly acknowledge that parenting continues beyond the middle years of life by addressing the implications of midlife parenting and well-being for the transition to old-age parenting and well-being. We begin with a selective review of research on late-life parenting, into which we integrate examples of the links between midlife and late-life parenting from other chapters in this volume. We then proceed to a discussion of new directions for linking mid- and late-life parenting in terms of substantive topics and conceptual frameworks. Our conclusion reiterates the importance of expanding existing agendas in parenting research to conceptualize midlife parenting as a precursor of late-life parenting and to address late-life parenting from the perspective of its midlife antecedents. We also advocate development of new topics and questions for research on parenting when children are adults.

Research on Late-Life Parenting: Key Issues and Findings

In this section of the chapter we "look ahead" to the later years of the life span. An overview of existing research on parent-child relations when parents are elderly provides a basis for analyzing developmental trajectories from midlife to late-life parenting in light of the findings presented in some of the earlier chapters. We organized the literature review around three important topics that have received extensive research attention: parent and child roles and relationship quality, caregiving by adult children for aged parents, and intergenerational influences on development.

Parent-Child Relations in Later Life

Although it is clear that relationships between parents and their adult children change over the course of history and as both members of the parent-child dyad develop and grow older (Hagestad 1984; Hess and Waring 1978), the nature, mechanisms, and outcomes of such changes are not well understood. Among the major categories of research on aged parent–adult child relationships, however, are studies of role expectations, significance of the parental role, interaction patterns, and relationship quality (see Mancini and Blieszner 1989 for a broad review). We briefly discuss each domain in turn.

Role expectations. An important dimension of knowledge about parent-child relationships involves understanding role expectations. As shown by authors of other chapters in this volume, parents' expectations of their children and the extent to which children fulfill them affect parental well-being in the middle years of life. For example, Ryff, Schmutte, and Lee (chapter 10, this volume) reported a strong association between parental well-being and parental assessments of children's success in young adulthood. Aquilino (chapter 11, this volume) found that appropriate launching of children contributes to parental well-being, whereas continued or renewed dependency of adult children violates parental expectations and contributes to their dissatisfaction with the parenting role. The findings of Seltzer et al. (chapter 12, this volume) suggest that launching of disabled children can evoke concerns and distress, perhaps because mothers are ambivalent about the capabilities of such offspring to function autonomously.

In this section we point out that parental well-being in the later years of life is also related to parental expectations of offspring. Instead of focusing on adult-child success and autonomy, however, researchers of the later years have investigated well-being in relation to filial responsibility expectations. This shift in focus reflects the developmental transitions of both generations under typical circumstances. The findings of this line of research reveal that parents express the desire for affection, thoughtfulness, and communication from their adult children more than the wish for direct caregiving and residential proximity, although some parents do endorse the latter filial norms. Those who expect and receive high levels of filial support from their children are likely to be female, older, not married, of low income, and in poor health. Holding high filial responsibility expectations is inversely related to older parents' morale, probably because of discrepancies between parents' and children's views of appropriate levels of filial responsibility or failure of the offspring to live up to parental expectations. Morale seems to be enhanced when parents perceive that their children will fulfill their roles as responsible others in the event of a crisis that requires their help (Blieszner and Hamon 1992; Blieszner and Mancini 1987; Brody, Johnsen, and Fulcomer 1984; Hamon and Blieszner 1990; Mancini and Simon 1984; Marshall, Rosenthal, and Daciuk 1987; Seelbach 1984; Schlesinger, Tobin, and Kulys 1981).

In contrast to normative filial responsibility expectations and fulfillment, refilling of the empty nest represents a nonnormative transition in the adult child–parent role relationship. Economic and marital instability conditions in society result in some adult children being unable to afford to live independently of their parents (Aquilino, chapter 11, this volume; Suitor and Pillemer 1991; Ward and Spitze 1992). Their return to the parental home can occur at any time during the parents' middle or old-age years. When the once empty nest is refilled, the demands on parents increase and make their lives more complex than anticipated, probably with differential effects according to their life-stage circumstances. Where and how people reside gives some insight into issues of intergenerational dependence, independence, and interdependence. Expectations about the launching of adult children in midlife might represent precursors of expectations concerning filial responsibility in late life. For example, parents who view their children as successfully launched might hold expectations of filial duties different from those of parents whose children are deemed less successfully launched. Various reasons for leaving home, delaying the leaving process, or returning to the parental home (Aquilino, chapter 11, this volume) might also have differential implications for parents' filial responsibility expectations. In any event, living in a multigenerational household offers potential benefits such as mutual assistance between the generations as well as potential liabilities such as increased marital conflict between the older parents (Suitor and Pillemer 1987, 1991).

Role significance. In the middle years of life, the significance of the parenting role may begin to decline concurrently with children's movement toward autonomy. This shift in role significance affects parental well-being in accordance with the larger context of the parent's life. If the parent is focusing on a review of personal development, assessment of a child's maturation might signal an opportunity for self-evaluation, with either positive or negative outcomes (e.g., Ryff, Schmutte, and Lee chapter 10, this volume). Work is another key focal context of the middle years. Data on parents with a relatively strong orientation toward employment reveal a positive association between increased child maturity and parental well-being, whereas data for those with a relatively weak orientation toward employment show the reverse trend, a negative association between increased child maturity and parental well-being (Allen et al., chapter 8, this volume). A third context is the unanticipated resumption of the direct parenting role, as when a launched child returns to the parental home, which can reduce parental well-being (Aquilino, chapter 11, this volume). To take yet another example, in the context of parenting a child with mental retardation, the findings of Seltzer et al. (chapter 12, this volume) about the increase in parental distress occurring along with an increase in the probability of the child leaving home (and consonant decreased centrality of the parental role) signifies a decline in parental well-being, at least temporarily.

Taken together, these results exemplify the complexity of meaning attached to the changing centrality of the parental role in the middle years. How these shifts in role significance might affect parenting and well-being in the later years is not clear. Few investigators have asked elderly parents directly about the meaning of their late-life parenting role to them or the implications of transitions in the role over the years, although several have advocated this approach (including Umberson, chapter 13, this volume).

In one study of parental role significance in old age, qualitative data from focus-group settings revealed that the majority of elderly parent participants said they currently had a parenting role, but a majority also said that they did not need the role at the present stage of life (Blieszner and Mancini 1987). They enjoyed the feeling of being needed and loved by their children, and they were flattered when their children asked for advice. One even mentioned that parenthood continued to add interest to life. But these active retirees, living self-sufficient lives, did not rely on their children as major sources of identity or activity.

This attitude was further reflected in respondents' statements about continuity and change in the parental role, as they compared parenting in retirement with parenting when their children were young (Blieszner and Mancini 1987). Beyond the obviously enduring genetic connection, these older adults recognized a number of continuities in parenthood over the years. They spoke of love, interest in their children's activities and welfare, exchanges of assistance and advice, and for some, continued financial support to their children. In other words, biological and emotional ties were strong, and certain family responsibilities endured. Regarding perceived changes in parenting now as compared with when their children were young, respondents noted that they view their children more as age peers and friends than as subordinates. Although they did continue to feel some responsibility for the children, the character and intensity of that responsibility had changed, and they realized that they were no longer the chief influence in their children's lives. Thus the parents had more freedom and members of each generation led more independent lives than in the past. These results imply that the respondents successfully negotiated the transition in parental role salience from the middle to the later years of life.

Interaction patterns. Much of the aging parent–adult child research has focused on interaction, including frequency of contact and support patterns, in an effort to demonstrate that older people in the family are not isolated from their offspring and other kin. Research since the 1960s has shown repeatedly that most older adults who are parents have at least weekly contact with their children, either face-to-face or via telephone calls. Parents and their children spend time with each other for both task accomplishment and companionship, engaging in considerable mutual assistance between the generations. This exchange of support is both instrumental and psychological and includes help during illness, child care, listening to problems, offering advice, and many other services (Mancini and Blieszner 1989; Mutran and Reitzes 1984; Rossi and Rossi 1991). In general, intergenerational interaction patterns enhance relationship quality and psychological well-being (Cicirelli 1983; Levitt, Guacci, and Weber 1992), although problematic relationships between parents and adult children exist, as we discuss later. This general conclusion corresponds to results obtained in studies of parenting during middle adulthood (Umberson, chapter 13, this volume), suggesting some degree of continuity in the effects of parenting from middle to old age.

Relationship quality. In another stream of research, with relatively fewer studies than in the previous area, contact patterns have been contrasted with variables that assess relationship quality more directly. On average, the latter variables are more strongly related to the well-being of older parents than are the former (Quinn 1983). Similar results occur for middle-aged parents. For example, Umberson (chapter 13, this volume) found that relationship quality between parents and children aged sixteen years or older was predicted by the amount of social support children gave to parents, the degree of strain in the relationship, and parents' dissatisfaction with the parental role. Furthermore, negative features of the parent-child relationship are associated with lower levels of parental well-being for both middle-aged and older adults, but positive features are not necessarily connected to higher parental well-being (Umberson 1992, and chapter 13, this volume).

Apparently, the quality of the parent-child relationship in earlier stages of life affects the quality in later stages. This occurs through carry-over effects from relationships with preadult children (e.g., mothers, who typically invested more time in caring for young children than did fathers, received more social support and felt less dissatisfaction with parenting in middle age than did fathers) and contextual effects in current parenting circumstances (e.g., parents who had positive relationships with their children earlier in life have the time and interest in their retirement years to develop further their relationships with their children) (Umberson, chapter 13, this volume).

Our study of older parents' perceptions of their affiliations with adult children provides a specific example of research that assessed parent-child relationship quality directly, as well as its implications for parental well-being. The investigation was grounded in a conceptual framework that shows promise for understanding the parent-child relationship within the context of the full range of social relationships available to the older person. Whereas we focused on elderly parents, the results suggest additional aspects of midlife parenting that could be examined fruitfully to ascertain stable or changing dimensions of parent-child relationship quality across the adult years.

STUDY OVERVIEW. A six-stage modified compact sampling procedure was used to select community-dwelling study participants randomly. Of the 635 potential respondents identified, 494 (78 percent) completed the study. The sample compared favorably to both local and national census data on key demographic characteristics. All participants were of retirement age ($M = 73$ years) and had at least one living adult child. During face-to-face interviews, respondents answered questions in terms of one of their children.

The study was based on the social provisions theory of Robert Weiss (Mancini and Blieszner 1992; Weiss 1974). According to this theory, people have six key relationship needs that must be met if they are to achieve happiness and avoid loneliness and other forms of social distress. Two of the provisions in Weiss's framework, attachment and reliable alliance, are especially germane to the parent-child relationship in adulthood because of the longevity of the relationship and because of the changing needs that older parents may have as a result of health deficits and loss of the spouse. *Attachment* involves feelings of intimacy, peace, and security as found in relationships with spouses and very close family members and friends. *Reliable alliance* is knowing that one can count on receiving assistance in times of need, a function often provided by kin. Lack of the attachment provision leads to emotional isolation and profound loneliness; the absence of a sense of reliable alliance is experienced as vulnerability (Weiss 1974).

The concepts of attachment and reliable alliance provided guidance for identification of independent variables that theoretically signify parent-child relationship quality in adulthood: attachment is reflected in *companionate* and *task interaction* and in *affection*. Reliable alliance is provided through *instrumental* and *emotional support*. Availability of these social provisions influences *satisfaction with interaction*. We predicted that these indicators of relationship quality would affect *parents' psychological well-being*.

A second set of independent variables, reflecting the family context, consisted of the parents' *marital status* (denoting potential parental obligation, source of support, or level of dependency that can affect the intensity of the relationship with the child), *number of living children* (potential moderator of interaction and emotional intensity in a given relationship and of parental well-being, if the larger family constellation is a source of concern), and the parent's *residential proximity* to the adult child (practical dimension of access and interaction opportunity; any security that comes from ready access to a child may influence a parent's general view of life).

The third class of independent variables was situational, accounting for those dimensions that enable a person to experience life in particular ways or insure that life will be disadvantaged. We assessed parental health, age, sex, and socioeconomic status.

The dependent variable was the parent's psychological well-being. We used the multidimensional Philadelphia Geriatric Center Morale Scale as its indicator, including three domains: *attitude toward own aging, lonely dissatisfaction,* and *agitation* (Lawton 1975).

OVERVIEW OF RESULTS FOR PARENTING AND PSYCHOLOGICAL WELL-BEING. Multiple regression analyses for the three domains of psychological well-being revealed first that a positive attitude toward own aging was best explained by greater affection, higher satisfaction with interactions, and younger parents who were in better health. Second, less lonely dissatisfaction was associated with more affection, greater satisfaction with interactions, and better health. Third, a lower level of agitation was related to higher satisfaction with interactions, better health, and less instrumental and emotional support and was more typical of men than of women. Across the three regressions, only five variables were systematically related to the successful aging domains: affection, interaction satisfaction, instrumental and emotional support, age, and health.

PERSONAL SITUATION, FAMILY CONTEXT, AND WELL-BEING. People's estimation of their own health was the principal component in general feelings of well-being, a finding that confirms the results of many other studies in gerontology. One's level of health is a primary situational variable that enables involvement in social relationships of all kinds, including with an adult child. None of the family context variables related significantly to the well-being dimensions. Apparently, whether the older person is married, has only one or many children, or lives close to or far from the adult child has no direct association with the extent to which one feels good or bad about aging, lonely and dissatisfied, or agitated.

ATTACHMENT AND WELL-BEING. One indicator of attachment was contact with the adult child. In contrast to previous studies, we investigated a refined two-dimensional measure of type of contact, focusing on both task accomplishment and companionship. We anticipated that these variables would covary with well-being. Although the results showed that task interaction (but not companionship) was initially correlated with agitation and attitude toward own aging, this relationship did not hold in the regression analyses. Thus, the reasons for spending time together did not outweigh other relationship and situational factors in the model of well-being. The other indicator of attachment—affection—was related to feelings about one's own aging and to a sense of loneliness, however. Parents who reported more affection for their adult child were more positive about their own aging and less lonely compared with other parents. In addition, the parent's overall satisfaction with interaction covaried significantly with all the psychological well-being dimensions. Parents who were content with the amount and type of contact they had with the child were likely to feel positive about their own aging, to be less lonely or dissatisfied, and to be less agitated. Note that whereas the indicators of amount of time together were unrelated to well-being, the feelings about the time together, as reflected in affection and satisfaction with interactions, were related to all three aspects of well-being.

RELIABLE ALLIANCE AND WELL-BEING. Our indicator of reliable alliance was two forms of support. We found that greater levels of instrumental and emotional support occurred along with greater levels of agitation. Considered without paying attention to why support is given, this finding seems counterintuitive. But recognizing that support probably is designed to meet existing needs, we would expect adult children to give more support under conditions of greater need, as reflected in the measure of agitation.

STUDY CONCLUSION. All things considered, the findings indicate that the close relationship between parent and child is related to an aging parent's sense of well-being, especially as affection and contentment with the time spent together are examined in the context of feelings of loneliness and feelings about one's own aging. The results provide support for Weiss's (1974) theory that close relationships involve essential social provisions, the availability of which contributes to psychological well-being. Additional research is needed, however, on the extent to which the salience and availability of these indicators of social provisions remain stable or change as individuals move from middle to old age.

Summary of research on parent-child relations. Studies of parent-child roles when parents are elderly reveal that adult children respond to their parents' filial expectations, particularly when parents are in obvious need (e.g., widowed, in frail health). In turn, aged parents provide housing, money, and other assistance to adult children with marital or financial exigencies. Older adults who are in good health and have adequate resources view the parenting role largely in terms of independence, companionship, emotional support, and affection rather than focusing on continued authority over or responsibility for their adult children. For the most part, intergenerational interaction patterns enhance relationship quality and psychological well-being.

Caregiving to Aged Parents

Another dominant theme in research on late-life parent-child relations is caregiving (see Dwyer and Coward 1992). When parents become widowed, develop frail health, or suffer from conditions that impair their cognitive functioning, parent-child interactions often change from reciprocal give-and-take to those in which adult children provide direct and indirect care to needy parents. Investigators have focused on the types of assistance that adult children give their parents, structural variables and filial responsibility norms that affect caregiving, as well as the problems and, to a lesser extent, the benefits of caregiving.

Types of assistance. Adult children help their aging parents with a wide variety of tasks, depending on parental needs and family resources (Chappell 1990; Mancini and Blieszner 1989). Help with instrumental activities of daily living (IADLs) includes doing housework, preparing meals, shopping, assisting with financial matters, and providing transportation. These forms of assistance, relatively less demanding than others, are given to parents who are still able to live fairly independently. Increased parental frailty requires adult children to help with functional activities of daily living (ADLs) necessary for survival—mobility, eating, bathing, toileting. These tasks are more difficult and less appealing to perform; usually it is failure of ADL functioning, not IADL performance, that leads to institutional placement of the aged parent. Adult children also help their parents by providing emotional support and companionship, maintaining family traditions, negotiating bureaucracies, seeking information, and making decisions, regardless of the level of parental functioning. Another category of assistance is indirect. Adult children often provide management services to meet their parents' needs, coordinating and supervising help from professional and other informal care providers.

Structural predictors of caregiving. One child usually serves as primary caregiver for a needy parent, sometimes but not always identified on the basis of availability or skills (Mancini and Blieszner 1989). Typically, daughters provide more care and more intense, personal forms of care than sons contribute regardless of either gender's attitudes of obligation, available time, or resources such as education or employment status (Finley 1989; Montgomery 1992). Sons' reduced efforts relative to daughters' are deemed "sufficient" because in our male-dominated society, males' contributions are considered more valuable than are females' labors (Finley 1989). This gendered pattern of caregiving reflects continuity for women across the adult years, from being more involved than men in caring for children and teenagers (Umberson, chapter 13, this volume) to being more involved than men in caring for parents.

Married children give less assistance to parents than do unmarried ones and employed daughters provide less help than unemployed ones provide with personal care and cooking (but they do not differ in amount of errands, emotional support, and the like), presumably because of other demands on their time (Mancini and Blieszner 1989). Racial ethnic group and class have been less carefully studied than other structural predictors, which renders conclusions about their effects on parental caregiving unclear (Chappell 1990).

Filial responsibility norms for caregiving. Because legal or economic imperatives for helping aging parents are not strong in American culture, researchers have sought other explanations for adult children's sense of responsibility to care for their elderly parents. Some children might be prompted to help because of moral imperatives originating in the Judeo-Christian commandment to honor parents. Others (especially daughters) might be responding to lifelong socialization for caring roles, affection and attachment no doubt undergird the ministries of some offspring, and the norm of reciprocity or feelings of indebtedness motivate still others (Blieszner and Hamon 1992; Cicirelli 1983; Montgomery 1992).

Using paired data from a random sample of 144 parent-child dyads, Hamon and Blieszner (1990) analyzed intergenerational consensus on filial responsibility expectations. Overall, the data revealed a moderate level of agreement between pair members about the obligations of children to parents. The greatest divergence of opinion concerned financial assistance: 87 percent of the children agreed that they should provide monetary aid if their parents needed it, but only 41 percent of the parents thought their children should do so.

Burdens and benefits of caregiving. Providing care to disabled parents can have profound negative and positive effects on primary caregivers and on their family members. Looking first at stresses and burdens of caregiving, research shows that caregivers' daily routines and employment are disrupted, unexpected expenses are incurred, and many hours are spent on caregiving tasks. Caregivers experience physical and psychological strain and report increased conflict with and negative affect toward care recipients. Tasks that involve personal care and bodily contact are more burdensome than impersonal assistance; tasks that restrict caregivers' time or geographic location require greater coping than responsibilities that allow more personal freedom (Chappell 1990; Lewis 1990; Mancini and Blieszner 1989; Montgomery 1992).

Nevertheless, caregiving can provide satisfactions even as it yields stresses. For example, predictors of caregiving benefits were examined in a study based on the theory of hassles (minor irritations) and uplifts (small satisfactions) (Kinney and Stephens 1989). Care recipient characteristics were the stronger predictors of hassles, but caregiver characteristics were the stronger predictors of uplifts. Caregivers reported receiving uplifts as a result of aid and understanding from their networks and because of certain aspects of the care recipients' cognitive and behavioral functioning. Women experienced more uplifts related to the care recipients' cognitive functioning than did men. Younger caregivers who spent more time in caregiving activities reported more uplifts associated with the care recipients' behavior than did those who spent less time. Caregivers to less impaired individuals reported more uplifts associated with care recipients' cognitive functioning and behavior than those assisting more impaired persons. Unexpectedly, caregivers who reported more uplifts in terms of care recipients' ADL functioning and behavior also experienced more distress than others.

Investigators have also provided information on the types of rewards that caregivers report (e.g., Allen and Walker 1992; Hinrichsen, Hernandez, and Pollack 1992). These rewards fall into categories describing improved relationships between caregivers and care recipients, enhanced relationships among the various family members, caregivers' personal growth and satisfaction, greater awareness of the meaning of life and appreciation of reciprocity between generations, and increased gratitude for assistance received from professional health care providers.

Summary of research on caregiving. Adult children usually endorse filial responsibility norms that guide their responses to frail parents who need assistance with a variety of personal care and household management tasks. Unmarried and unemployed daughters are the most typical adult child helpers for aged parents, although married and employed daughters also manage to meet their perceived caregiving duties. Sons tend to perform managerial and intermittent tasks rather than providing hands-on, day-to-day assistance. Parental caregiving can be quite disruptive to the career, family life, personal freedom, physical health, and mental well-being of the helping adult child. Caregivers do, however, cite numerous personal and family benefits associated with providing assistance to their parents, probably reflecting strong family bonds, as discussed in the following section.

Intergenerational Influences

Although the earliest work on parent-child influences focused on the effects of parents on children, since the late 1960s scholars have acknowledged the reciprocal nature of intergenerational influence and have studied the effects of children on parents as well (see conceptual discussion and empirical examples in Kreppner and Lerner 1989b; Lerner and Spanier 1978b; Pillemer and McCartney 1991; Pruchno, Peters, and Burant, chapter 15, this volume; and Ryff, Schmutte, and Lee, chapter 10, this volume). Because the generations represent different stages of individual development and different cohorts, their interactions afford many opportunities for reciprocal influence and transmission of information and values both up and down the generational lines (Bengtson and Troll 1978; Hagestad 1984). Important categories of research on parent-child influence in the later years include identification of factors that affect intergenerational solidarity, or cohesion, and the problems of adult children that cause their parents distress.

Intergenerational solidarity. A research program designed to provide information about the bonds across three generations—about why family members seek and enjoy one another's company—has resulted in development and refinement of the theory of intergenerational solidarity and has spawned numerous studies of the antecedents and consequences of such family cohesion (Bengtson and Roberts 1991; Mangen, Bengtson, and Landry 1988). Intergenerational solidarity encompasses six essential components of interaction: associational (shared activities); affectual (positive sentiment); consensual (agreement on values, attitudes, and beliefs); functional (resource exchanges); normative (commitment to familial obligations); and structural (opportunities provided by residential proximity, family size, health). Rossi and Rossi (1990) hypothesized a causal ordering among the elements of solidarity, proposing that affectual and normative dimensions are most deeply rooted in early family life and set the stage for the evolution of associational and functional solidarity. Consensual solidarity is a function of differential educational attainment, religiosity, and political orientation between parents and children and emerges during the child's adolescent years. Structural solidarity occurs according to the circumstances of both generations in adulthood. Their three-generation study confirmed the predicted effects of early family life on later interaction patterns and the transmission of attitudes, skills, family cohesion, and the like from one generation to the next.

Events in the lives of any generation can effect a reorganization of solidarity. For example, Johnson (1988) evaluated changes in patterns of solidarity that emerged among divorcing adult children. Parents played an active role in easing strains resulting from their children's divorce and were particularly supportive in providing instrumental aid, especially early in the divorcing process. Postdivorce, the families fell into three types with respect to solidarity: divorced adult children who emphasized the primacy of the intergenerational bond and evidenced dependency on their parents; those who were more isolated from their parents and focused on independence from their support and influence; and those whose friendly, sociable, and somewhat distant relationships with their parents were part of a larger, loose-knit network and who did not expect or receive instrumental support. No doubt the effects of the divorce on the parents varies across these three conditions of postdivorce solidarity.

Parental distress. The assumption of bidirectional intergenerational influence has guided research on parent-child relations in early stages of the family life cycle more than it has affected studies of parent-child relations in adulthood. A persistent bias in the gerontology literature has been on the distress that parents who require care cause their adult children, with relatively less attention given to ways that adult children burden their older parents. Recent research is serving to correct this imbalance. One line of inquiry is the effects of adult children failing to launch themselves on time or refilling the parental empty nest, discussed above (see also Aquilino, chapter 11, this volume; Ward and Spitze 1992).

Another focus of investigation is the effect of adult children's problems on their parents' well-being (see Pruchno, Peters, and Burant, chapter 15; Ryff, Schmutte, and Lee, chapter 10; Seltzer et al., chapter 12, all this volume). Researchers have found that grown offspring's troubles with physical or mental health or stressful events such as divorce are associated with strained parent-child relations and parental depression (Cicirelli 1983; Pillemer and Suitor 1991a,b; Umberson 1992). These effects vary by gender of the parent, with mothers reporting more distress than fathers in relation to parent-child disagreements or negative events in the child's life (Pruchno, Peters, and Burant, chapter 15, this volume). Serious problems may interfere with adult children's ability to help and support their parents. In the extreme case of violence against elderly persons, studies show that adult children who abuse their parents tend to have serious personal problems (Pillemer and Suitor 1991a).

Summary of research on intergenerational influences. Intergenerational solidarity denotes family cohesion in terms of shared activities, positive sentiment, agreement of values and beliefs, reciprocal assistance, and commitment to family obligations. Structural factors such as family size or geographic proximity and life events occurring for members of any generation affect interaction patterns and thus influence intergenerational solidarity. Just as caring for an aged parent can be burdensome to adult children, problems of adult children can cause distress in their parents and interfere with family cohesion.

Overall Summary of Late-Life Parenting Research

The overview of research presented above highlights some of the most important areas of inquiry on late-life parenting. Several themes emerge from this literature. Most elderly people and their adult children enjoy compatible relationships that seem to enhance older parents' psychological well-being, although some problematic relationships exist. The two generations engage in a wide range of activities together, most notably various forms of instrumental and emotional support, communication, and reciprocal influence. Their interaction patterns are affected by the personal developmental needs and life events of each generational partner.

These observations reflect the current state of knowledge about parenting in the later years and its effects on older adults' personal well-being. Recognizing that the patterns of association described for parent-child relations, caregiving, and intergenerational influences in the later years are long-term leads to consideration of the antecedent, midlife conditions that affect these and other aspects of late-life parenting and foster or hinder well-being in old age.

Linking Midlife and Late-Life Parenting: New Research Directions

In this section of the chapter we "look back" to the middle years of the life span and search for midlife antecedents of late-life parenting and well-being in order to address the processes represented by the arrows between the middle and later years in figure 16.1. Of course, the ideal situation would be to base our discussion on a wealth of longitudinal data that traces parenting and well-being throughout adulthood. Although such a database does not exist, Rossi and Rossi (1990) argued persuasively for the benefits of carefully crafted retrospective questions that explore perceptions and effects of earlier family experiences (see also Whitbeck, Simons, and Conger 1991). Rossi and Rossi focused on the implications of family of origin upbringing for current family functioning, but it should also be possible to employ similar techniques to ascertain aging parents' perceptions of more recent midlife influences on their current parenting situation and its outcomes. Experimental simulation of developmental processes (Baltes, Reese, and Nesselroade 1977; Ryff and Heincke 1983) is another potentially useful technique for such purposes. Thus, lack of time and resources to conduct prospective longitudinal research should not limit attempts to investigate the transition from mid- to late-life parenting.

Before proceeding to examples of new research directions, we wish to point out that the current literature on parent-child relations in adulthood does not represent a comprehensive exploration of diversity in parenting as experienced by members of different gender, racial ethnic, class, subculture, marital status, and sexual orientation groups (see examples in this volume by Allen et al., chapter 8; Meyer, chapter 3; and Spencer, Swanson, and Glymph, chapter 9). Understanding the implications of these demographic characteristics requires exploring their socially and culturally constructed meanings, not merely reporting sex, race, or other differences or "controlling" for them in the analyses (see Rossi and Rossi 1990). Thus we emphasize that all extensions of previous research must incorporate attention to population diversity in the study design and interpretation of results.

We turn now to consideration of new research directions and useful conceptual frameworks that should permit exploration of the unfolding of parenthood across the adult years. Keeping in mind the research thrusts summarized above—parent-child relations, caregiving, and intergenerational influence—we explore ways of building on previous approaches to accomplish a developmental perspective on parenting over the life course, rather than continuing to rely on studies of discrete stages as if each one is disconnected from earlier and later development.

Extension of Prior Research Agendas

For each of the research areas described above and many other topics, the central questions are, How did parent-child interactions during the parents' middle-age years lead to the interactions they have in old age? What characteristics of the child, the parent, the larger sociocultural system, and the historical period influenced the outcomes observed during the parents' later years? The challenge confronting researchers of parenthood and well-being is to find ways of applying these general questions to specific research foci. A useful approach might be to integrate new conceptual tools into traditional research topics. Our discussion in this section provides some suggestions to illustrate such a process. Important considerations that are theoretically relevant to the study of parenting transitions across the life course include identification of the generational context of the parent and child actors, analysis of the contribution of the topic under study to parental development, determination of the role of filial and parental maturity in the focal research domain, assessment of intergenerational transmission of the aspect of parenting being examined, and measurement of parental role centrality with respect to the selected research subject.

Generational context. In the course of conducting new research, scholars should give attention to examining the generational context of parents and their children (Hagestad 1984; Rossi and Rossi 1990). That is, because no necessary connection exists between age cohort membership and generational position, it is important to consider the developmental stages of parents and children. For example, differential developmental tasks and challenges (e.g., the concerns of generativity in the middle years and integrity in the later years as proposed by Erikson 1963; see Antonovsky and Sagy 1990 and Ryff and Heincke 1983) suggest differential implications for late-life parenting and well-being of having parented teens or young adults at earlier (e.g., age forty-five) versus later (e.g., age sixty-five) stages of the life span. Furthermore, variation in generational position leads to expectations of differential implications of being the oldest generation in the family versus simultaneously holding both parent and offspring roles, regardless of chronological age or level of maturity. This approach also implies the need to examine theoretically relevant historical events that occurred when elderly parents were middle-aged and to explore how they might have affected parenting then and set the stage of current parenting.

Applying these ideas to popular parenting research topics—the quality of aging parent–adult child relations, for example—suggests that researchers should gather information about not just the frequency of contact or resource exchange but also the extent to which the interaction is affected by generational position and developmental maturity. Do midlife adults who are also children of their elderly parents relate to their offspring differently from midlife parents whose own parents are deceased? Do parent-child relations of midlife parents who score high on generativity differ from those of midlife parents who score low? Are high generativity scores in midlife related to satisfactory parent-child relations in late life? Reciprocally, are high-quality parent-child relations in the middle years of adulthood associated with personal well-being in the later years? With respect to historical circumstances, did economic conditions or social policies affect the ability of either generation to socialize with or provide assistance to the other member of the parent-child dyad? If such events affected parent-child interactions, were the effects long-standing such that they endure into old age? Research that addresses questions such as these, thus accounting for the effects of developmental maturity, generational position, and historical context in conjunction with parenting, would serve to broaden the current database.

Contributions of parenting to adult development. Focusing on the earliest years of the parent-child relationship, Newman and Newman (1988) observed that parenthood affords opportunities for cognitive and emotional development because of the unpredictable nature of the child's physical characteristics, temperament, and life choices on the one hand and the parents' expanded capacity for caring on the other. Among the aspects of potential cognitive growth are a probabilistic view of the future, formulation of a philosophy of life, a more highly differentiated view of individual strengths and weaknesses, a capacity to hold two or more opposing ideas in mind at the same time, and the ability to function at various levels of abstraction. Examples of potential emotional growth areas include depth of commitment, new channels of expressing affection, balancing self and others' needs, enhanced feelings of value and well-being, empathy, and greater effectiveness in accepting and expressing one's own emotions as a result of assisting children to understand and express theirs appropriately. Koumans (1987), a psychiatrist, addressed possible areas of personality development resulting from parenthood. For example, a parent might benefit from reviewing and gaining insight about past conflicts and resolutions in light of the child's attempts to resolve the child's issues. Also, in an open parent-child relationship, the child can serve as a model of alternative possibilities and a collaborator in the development of the parent's parenting skills.

No doubt parent-child interactions in the middle and later years of life are affected by the extent to which parents reacted early on to these opportunities to develop cognitive and emotional competencies and to enhance their self-understanding and by the way they interpret current opportunities to expand in these domains. These issues could be fruitfully incorporated into expanded work on parent-child relations, such as research on parents' reactions to children who bring them disappointments or distress. Building on studies that have identified correlates and predictors of morale in such situations, future investigations should delve into the complex implications of children's problems on parents' cognitive, affective, and personality development. This approach could also be employed in studies of the effects of children's accomplishments on parental psychological development and well-being (cf. in this volume Pruchno, Peters, and Burant, chapter 15; Ryff, Schmutte, and Lee chapter 10).

Filial and parental maturity. Acknowledging that development is socially organized, Nydegger (1991) described the attainment of maturity as an ongoing process for both adult children and aging parents as they enact their respective roles in relation to each other. Because these roles endure for so long, it is reasonable to expect changes in them over time, based on the intersection of personal development and changes in the larger social context. Adult children are challenged to acquire filial maturity—accomplished through filial distancing, or becoming emotionally independent of parents—balanced with filial comprehending, or understanding parents as persons with their own viewpoints and needs. Reciprocally, parents are challenged to acquire parental maturity—encompassing parallel tasks of distancing, or encouraging children to become independent—and comprehending, or socializing children for the future. Several impulses toward accomplishment of these maturities occur, including socially defined role expectations (discussed earlier; in this volume cf. Ryff, Schmutte, and Lee, chapter 10), responses to changes in relevant others (e.g., coping with the refilling of the empty nest; cf. Aquilino, chapter 11, this volume), and personal maturing such as described by Erikson (1963).

Successful acquisition of these maturities enables adult children to adopt the filial role, which means being dependable for and depended on by their parents, and enables parents to maintain loving relationships with their emancipated children and assess their own youth realistically (Nydegger 1991). A particularly apt target of research on the processes and consequences of filial and parental maturity is caregiving to frail parents. If the transition from midlife to late-life parenting includes changes in the intensity and direction of aid, what is the role of the child's level of filial maturity on her or his provision of services, and what is the role of the parent's level of parental maturity on her or his acceptance of assistance? Linking these two domains of research adds another set of explanatory variables to the array currently in use.

Intergenerational transmission. As mentioned earlier, extensive research has been conducted on affective, behavioral, and structural predictors of intergenerational solidarity. An important question in that line of research concerns intergenerational transmission of values and behaviors associated with family solidarity. Nydegger (1991) postulated that those who achieve filial maturity might find it easier to attain parental maturity later in life than those who are less successful at meeting the adult child challenge. Moreover, those who are enacting the filial role by caring for their aged parents are not only preparing themselves for the future but also modeling filial maturity for the younger generation of family members, thereby helping to ensure that their own needs will be met when they are old (Levitt, Guacci, and Weber 1992; Spitze and Logan 1989). These suppositions about the transition from filial to parental maturity and the transmission of filial maturity norms provide yet another basis for extending previous research by elaborating the theory of intergenerational solidarity.

Parental role centrality. The question of the centrality of the parental role in the lives of older people, mentioned above in the discussion of key research issues, has not been explored adequately. Often researchers seem to assume that as children and parents pass through the adult years, the parent-child relationship pales in comparison with full-blown work and marital roles. Yet, as we have already shown, the literature indicates that older people interact regularly with their offspring and that these relationships include extensive reciprocal exchange of instrumental and affectional services. Nevertheless, certain elderly adults will rate parenting as a more significant component of their lives than others. Thus, when asking questions about various domains of mid- or late-life parenting, one must also assess the centrality of the parental role and whether that degree of centrality has changed over time.

Summary. The quest for midlife antecedents of late-life parenting and well-being is quite challenging, particularly because researchers of midlife parenting and of late-life parenting typically have investigated non-corresponding sets of variables and have not conducted longitudinal studies. It is thus difficult, if not impossible, to compare studies across stages of adulthood, find evidence concerning stability and change in aspects of parenting, or pinpoint earlier predictors of later outcomes. We have identified, then, four domains of conceptualizing about developmental aspects of parenting and have suggested that they could be integrated into typical research topics to gain a sense of influences on the transition from mid- to late-life parenting. Furthermore, researchers interested in this pursuit can be guided by conceptual frameworks that lend themselves well to the developmental issues running through this discussion. Thus we turn to application of prevalent family studies theories to our family gerontology topics.

Conceptual Frameworks for Research on Parenting over the Life Course

Addressing questions about the links between midlife and late-life parenting requires broad multidisciplinary perspectives that take into account the influences of individual development, dyadic and network relationships, cultural and subcultural membership, the larger society, and the historical period (cf. Kreppner and Lerner 1989a; Lerner and Spanier 1978a; Rossi 1989). In this section we briefly review several conceptual frameworks that hold promise for integrating these levels of influence and developing more informative research on parenting transitions throughout adulthood: life-course and family development perspectives, symbolic interactionism, and exchange and resource theory. These approaches, having a long history of attending to individual and family change and role-related issues, are excellent for delineating the many dimensions and effects of interaction over time.

Life course and family development. The life-course and family development perspectives are concerned with change in individuals and families over time. The life-course perspective encompasses five important themes: a focus on multiple temporal contexts of development (personal biographical, generational, and historical time); on diverse social contexts in which development takes place; on change and continuity as the dialectics of development; on heterogeneity of structures and processes associated with development; and on integration of concepts from disciplines such as biology, psychology, sociology, history, and economics (Bengtson and Allen 1993). Family development theory examines norms, roles, stages of the family cycle, transitions between stages, the timing of transitions, and processes through which the transitions take place (Rodgers and White 1993). Both perspectives incorporate multiple levels of analysis, from individual to dyadic to group to institutional.

The life-course and family development frameworks provide a basis for investigators of parenthood transitions to develop propositions about many changes and influences among personal, parent-child, family, and societal aspects of the topics reviewed previously. For example, an important research perspective concerns the reciprocal influences between individual development and close relationships in the family (cf. Lerner and Spanier 1978a). General research questions are, How does developmental well-being in middle and late adulthood affect the quality of the parent-child relationship at each period? Moreover, how does individual well-being in the middle years affect late-life parenting experiences, and how do midlife parenting experiences affect late-life personal well-being? On the one hand, these questions pertain to research on the contributions of parenting to adult development as hypothesized by Newman and Newman (1988). For instance, what is the association between perceived skill at parenting adult children and feelings of mastery and competence in the later years? Asking this question leads to a new approach to the topic of parent-child interaction patterns, one that goes beyond cataloging types or amounts of contact and looks instead at the quality of the contact and the skill with which the role is enacted.

On the other hand, the general questions above can also be applied to research on dyadic and family relations: To what extent do middle-aged adults interpret their parenting experiences in terms of their parents' success in aging? In other words, do people perceive that their current family experiences affect their future happiness? If so, then the quality of the parent-child relationship in the middle years, depending on the centrality of the parental role, is of paramount importance for well-being later on. Concerning interaction patterns, How much stability exists in parent-child contact, support, and assistance over the life course, and what difference does level of stability make for individual well-being and relationship quality over the life course? Looking at intergenerational solidarity and intergenerational transmission, How does dealing with the aging of one's parents affect one's own parenting abilities? This suggests the need to examine not only caregiving tasks, for example, but also middle-aged persons' perceptions of their parents' reactions to such help, in comparison with the parents' own reactions. Another key question is, Does the relationship between an adult child and older parent have an effect on how the grandchild will treat the parent in the future? Researchers seem to assume an affirmative answer but typically have not asked children or youth to describe the implications for them of their parents' caring for their grandparents. Thinking about developmental aspects of parent-child relationships in this manner suggests the need to interview members of multiple generations in the family within a given investigation, a procedure that has so far been rather uncommon.

Symbolic interaction theory. Symbolic interaction theory is concerned with the meanings that result from people enacting their respective roles. Individuals develop a concept of the self, associated feelings of self-esteem, and their role identities through social interaction. Interactions both shape and are shaped by the larger sociocultural context. Salience pertains to the prominence of a particular identity and becomes, along with positive self-esteem, a motivator for the effort that is put into a given role. Salience and identities go hand in hand in exploring the significance of a role. If a role is seen as meaningful, then it will be more prominent in one's life, which will be evidenced through behaviors that reflect the role (LaRossa and Reitzes 1993).

Using these symbolic interactionism principles to expand on previous research topics leads to other questions about parenting: What are the core characteristics of the parent role, what are its peripheral features, and do these perceptions change from middle to old age? How have adults made their decisions about the core dimensions of the parent role? What is the relationship between parental role salience and the energy placed on invoking the parental role—for instance, in the provision of emotional and instrumental support—in middle versus old age? To what degree does the parental role provide the rewards that help the parents feel valued and worthwhile, and to what extent do such rewards change over time?

Typically, people think about parental role norms with regard to the rearing of young children rather than when children gain maturity. Yet deeper understanding of mid- and late-life parenting requires that we pay attention to those prescriptions, even if we conclude that the norms are vague and require sharpening. Earlier we summarized research on role expectations and content in old age. Within that context, important additional research questions are, What norms pertain to the parental role and its importance in the middle years of life? What skills and competencies are expected of parents during those years? Is it expected that the intensity of emotions placed in the parental role wanes as time passes from middle to old age? How have past role experiences influenced present competence in the parental role in each stage of adulthood? As these examples illustrate, the tenets of symbolic interactionism can assist researchers in moving from separate descriptions of parenting at different stages to integrated conceptions of continuity and change in parenting over time by focusing on meanings and salience of roles.

Exchange and resource theory. Exchange and resource theory also highlights the development and experience of relationships, the patterns and dynamics of interaction, and the factors that mediate relationship stability. Key concepts include the rewards and costs that people gain and lose as they interact with others, the resources that people possess and others find desirable, the feelings of satisfaction that result from interaction, the fairness and equity that people expect and experience, the commitment that reflects interest in long-term relationship involvement, and the power and control that are vehicles for influencing others and gaining their compliance. *Comparison level* is a term used to represent people's evaluation of what they gain and give up in a relationship in terms of what they feel they deserve or what they can realistically expect. *Comparison level for alternatives* helps explain why people remain in a relationship or why they leave it; it is the minimal result a person will accept from a relationship after considering other choices (Sabatelli and Shehan 1993).

Again in keeping with topics reviewed previously, research questions about the parent-child relationship can be generated from the above exchange and resource concepts. With respect to the parental role, exchange and resource theory asks, To what degree is the centrality of the parental role influenced by what parents feel they gain from high involvement in the role? How aware are parents of the rewards and costs of the role? How does their level of satisfaction with the role reinforce future role enactment? To what degree are their expectations fulfilled by their parental experience? What are the essential aspects of the parent-child relationship that keep them committed to it? At what times do parents feel that their gains from the relationship are far outweighed by what it costs them? Does the commitment of personal energy change over time, and what determines that change? What place does power and control have in the perceived importance of the parent role? Finally, in what ways do the answers to these questions remain stable from middle to late adulthood, and in what ways do they change?

Summary. The life-course and family development, symbolic interactionism, and exchange and resource frameworks all permit exploration of dynamic aspects of parent-child relationships across middle and later adulthood at the same time as they have distinct foci. These perspectives provide conceptual bases for extending current research agendas in late-life parenting to enable identification of midlife antecedents of late-life conditions. We have posed numerous questions as a way of stimulating thinking about research directions to accomplish that goal. Implicit in those questions are variables and hypotheses that remain to be explored within the general context of life-span development and life-course influences.

CONCLUSION: UNDERSTANDING THE UNFOLDING OF PARENTHOOD

Existing research on parent-child relations when parents are old provides indirect insights into midlife antecedents of late-life parenting and well-being. Moving beyond oblique evidence to research specifically on the unfolding of parenthood from middle to late adulthood requires employment of new research approaches and relevant conceptual frameworks. Using figure 16.1 as a guide, we have demonstrated that looking backward and forward across an individual's life and across the generations suggests a wide array of potential research questions at the individual, the parent-child dyad, and the family levels of analysis. Based on this conceptualization, researchers can frame investigations that not only examine particular substantive topics but also simultaneously take into account principles of individual and family development. Such an approach should contribute significantly to advancing knowledge about parent-child relations as dynamic interactions with immediate and long-term effects on the participants' lives.

REFERENCES

Allen, K. R., and A. J. Walker. 1992. Attentive love: A feminist perspective on the caregiving of adult daughters. *Family Relations* 41:284–289.

Antonovsky, A., and S. Sagy. 1990. Confronting developmental tasks in the retirement transition. *Gerontologist* 30:362–368.

Baltes, P. B., H. W. Reese, and L. P. Lipsitt. 1980. Life-span developmental psychology. *Annual Review of Psychology* 31:65–110.

Baltes, P. B., H. W. Reese, and J. R. Nesselroade. 1977. *Life-span developmental psychology: Introduction to research methods.* Monterey, Calif.: Brooks/Cole.

Bengtson, V. L., and K. R. Allen. 1993. The life course perspective applied to families over time. In P. G. Boss, W. J. Doherty, R. LaRossa, W. R. Schumm, and S. K. Steinmetz, eds., *Sourcebook of family theories and methods,* pp. 469–499. New York: Plenum.

Bengtson, V. L., and R. E. L. Roberts. 1991. Intergenerational solidarity in aging families; An example of formal theory construction. *Journal of Marriage and the Family* 53:856–870.

Bengtson, V. L., and L. Troll. 1978. Youth and their parents: Feedback and intergenerational influence in socialization. In R. M. Lerner and G. B. Spanier, eds., *Child influences on marital and family interaction,* pp. 215–240. New York: Academic.

Blieszner, R., and R. R. Hamon. 1992. Filial responsibility: Attitudes, motivators, and behaviors. In J. W. Dwyer and R. T. Coward, eds., *Gender, families, and elder care,* pp. 105–119. Newbury Park, Calif.: Sage.

Blieszner, R., and J. A. Mancini. 1987. Enduring ties: Older adults' parental role and responsibilities. *Family Relations* 36:176–180.

Brody, E. M., P. T. Johnsen, and M. C. Fulcomer. 1984. What should adult children do for elderly parents? Opinions and preferences of three generations of women. *Journal of Gerontology* 39:736–746.

Chappell, N. L. 1990. Aging and social care. In R. H. Binstock and L. K. George, eds., *Handbook of aging and the social sciences,* 3d ed., pp. 438–454. San Diego: Academic.

Cicirelli, V. G. 1983. Adult children and their elderly parents. In T. H. Brubaker, ed., *Family relationships in later life,* pp. 31–46. Beverly Hills: Sage.

Dwyer, J. W., and R. T. Coward, eds. 1992. *Gender, families, and elder care.* Newbury Park, Calif.: Sage.

Erikson, E. H. 1963. *Childhood and society.* 2d ed. New York: Norton.

Finley, N. J. 1989. Theories of family labor as applied to gender differences in caregiving for elderly parents. *Journal of Marriage and the Family* 51:79–86.

Hagestad, G. O. 1984. The continuous bond: A dynamic, multigenerational perspective on parent-child relations between adults. In M. Perlmutter, ed., *Parent-child interaction and parent-child relations in child development,* pp. 129–158. Hillsdale, N.J.: Lawrence Erlbaum.

Hagestad, G. O., and B. L. Neugarten. 1985. Age and the life course. In R. H. Binstock and E. Shanas, eds., *Handbook of aging and the social sciences,* 2d ed., pp. 35–61. New York: Van Nostrand Reinhold.

Hamon, R. R., and R. Blieszner. 1990. Filial responsibility expectations among adult child–older parent pairs. *Journal of Gerontology: Psychological Sciences* 45:P110–P112.

Hess, B. B., and J. M. Waring. 1978. Parent and child in later life: Rethinking the relationship. In R. M. Lerner and G. B. Spanier, eds., *Child influences on marital and family interaction,* pp. 241–273. New York: Academic.

Hinrichsen, G. A., N. A. Hernandez, and S. Pollack. 1992. Difficulties and rewards in family care of the depressed older adult. *Gerontologist* 32:486–492.

Johnson, C. L. 1988. Postdivorce reorganization of relationships between divorcing children and their parents. *Journal of Marriage and the Family* 50:221–231.

Kinney, J. M., and M. A. P. Stephens. 1989. Hassles and uplifts of giving care to a family member with dementia. *Psychology and Aging* 4:402–408.

Koumans, A. J. R. 1987. The effect of children on adult development. *International Journal of Family Psychiatry* 8:417–428.

Kreppner, K., and R. M. Lerner. 1989a. Family systems and life-span development: Issues and perspectives. In K. Kreppner and R. M. Lerner, eds., *Family systems and life-span development,* pp. 1–13. Hillsdale, N.J.: Lawrence Erlbaum.

——, eds. 1989b. *Family systems and life-span development.* Hillsdale, N.J.: Lawrence Erlbaum.

LaRossa, R., and D. C. Reitzes. 1993. Symbolic interactionism and family studies. In P. G. Boss, W. J. Doherty, R. LaRossa, W. R. Schumm, and S. K. Steinmetz, eds., *Sourcebook of family theories and methods,* pp. 135–163. New York: Plenum.

Lawton, M. P. 1975. The Philadelphia Geriatric Center Morale Scale: A revision. *Journal of Gerontology* 30:85–89.

Lerner, R. M., and G. B. Spanier. 1978a. A dynamic interactional view of child and family development. In R. M. Lerner and G. B. Spanier eds., *Child influences on marital and family interaction,* pp. 1–22. New York: Academic.

————, eds. 1978b. *Child influences on marital and family interaction.* New York: Academic.

Levitt, M. J., N. Guacci, and R. Weber. 1992. Intergenerational support, relationship quality, and well-being: A bicultural analysis. *Journal of Family Issues* 13:465–481.

Lewis, R. A. 1990. The adult child and older parents. In T. H. Brubaker, ed., *Family relationships in later life,* 2d ed., pp. 68–85. Newbury Park, Calif.: Sage.

Mancini, J. A., and R. Blieszner. 1989. Aging parents and adult children: Research themes in intergenerational relations. *Journal of Marriage and the Family* 51: 275–290.

————. 1992. Social provisions in adulthood: Concept and measurement in close relationships. *Journal of Gerontology: Psychological Sciences* 47:P14–P20.

Mancini, J. A., and J. Simon. 1984. Older adults' expectations of support from family and friends. *Journal of Applied Gerontology* 3:150–160.

Mangen, D. J., V. L. Bengtson, and P. H. Landry Jr. 1988. *Measurement of intergenerational relations.* Newbury Park, Calif.: Sage.

Marshall, V. W., C. J. Rosenthal, and J. Daciuk. 1987. Older parents' expectations for filial support. *Social Justice Review* 1:405–424.

Montgomery, R. J. V. 1992. Gender differences in patterns of child-parent caregiving relationships. In J. W. Dwyer and R. T. Coward, eds., *Gender, families, and elder care,* pp. 65–83. Newbury Park, Calif.: Sage.

Mutran, E., and D. G. Reitzes. 1984. Intergenerational support activities and well-being among the elderly: A convergence of exchange and symbolic interaction perspectives. *American Sociological Review* 49:117–130.

Newman, P. R., and B. M. Newman. 1988. Parenthood and adult development. *Marriage and Family Review* 3–4:313–337.

Nydegger, C. N. 1991. The development of paternal and filial maturity. In K. Pillemer and K. McCartney, eds., *Parent-child relations throughout life,* pp. 93–112. Hillsdale, N.J.: Lawrence Erlbaum.

Pillemer, K., and K. McCartney, eds. 1991. *Parent-child relations throughout life.* Hillsdale, N.J.: Lawrence Erlbaum.

Pillemer, K., and J. J. Suitor. 1991a. Relationships with children and distress in the elderly. In K. Pillemer and K. McCartney, eds., *Parent-child relations throughout life,* pp. 163–178. Hillsdale, N.J.: Lawrence Erlbaum.

————. 1991b. "Will I ever escape my child's problems?" Effects of adult children's problems on elderly parents. *Journal of Marriage and the Family* 53:585–594.

Quinn, W. H. 1983. Personal and family adjustment in later life. *Journal of Marriage and the Family* 45:57–73.

Rodgers, R. H., and J. M. White. 1993. Family development theory. In P. G. Boss, W. J. Doherty, R. LaRossa, W. R. Schumm, and S. K. Steinmetz, eds., *Sourcebook of family theories and methods,* pp. 225–254. New York: Plenum.

Rossi, A. S. 1989. A life-course approach to gender, aging, and intergenerational relations. In K. W. Schaie and C. Schooler, eds., *Social structure and aging: Psychological processes*, pp. 207–236. Hillsdale, N.J.: Lawrence Erlbaum.

Rossi, A. S., and P. H. Rossi. 1990. *Of human bonding: Parent-child relations across the life course.* New York: Aldine de Gruyter.

———. 1991. Normative obligations and parent-child help exchange across the life course. In K. Pillemer and K. McCartney, eds., *Parent-child relations throughout life*, pp. 201–223. Hillsdale, N.J.: Lawrence Erlbaum.

Ryff, C. D., and S. G. Heincke. 1983. Subjective organization of personality in adulthood and aging. *Journal of Personality and Social Psychology* 44:807–816.

Sabatelli, R. M., and C. L. Shehan. 1993. Exchange and resource theories. In P. G. Boss, W. J. Doherty, R. LaRossa, W. R. Schumm, and S. K. Steinmetz, eds., *Sourcebook of family theories and methods*, pp. 385–411. New York: Plenum.

Schlesinger, M. R., S. S. Tobin, and R. Kulys. 1981. The responsible child and parental well-being. *Journal of Gerontological Social Work* 3:3–16.

Seelbach, W. C. 1984. Filial responsibility and the care of aging family members. In W. H. Quinn and G. A. Hughston, eds., *Independent aging: Family and social system perspectives*, pp. 92–105. Rockville, Md.: Aspen.

Spitze, G., and J. Logan. 1989. Gender differences in family support: Is there a payoff? *Gerontologist* 29:108–113.

Suitor, J. J., and K. Pillemer. 1987. The presence of adult children: A source of stress for elderly couples' marriages? *Journal of Marriage and the Family* 49:717–725.

———. 1991. Family conflict when adult children and elderly parents share a home. In K. Pillemer and K. McCartney, eds., *Parent-child relations throughout life*, pp. 179–199. Hillsdale, N.J.: Lawrence Erlbaum.

Umberson, D. 1992. Relationships between adult children and their parents: Psychological consequences for both generations. *Journal of Marriage and the Family* 54:664–674.

Ward, R. A., and G. Spitze. 1992. Consequences of parent-adult child coresidence: A review and research agenda. *Journal of Family Issues* 13:553–572.

Weiss, R. S. 1974. The provisions of social relationships. In Z. Rubin, ed., *Doing unto others*, pp. 17–26. Englewood Cliffs, N.J.: Prentice-Hall.

Whitbeck, L. B., R. L. Simons, and R. D. Conger. 1991. The effects of early family relationships on contemporary relationships and assistance patterns between adult children and their parents. *Journal of Gerontology: Social Sciences* 46:S330–S337.

VII SUMMARY AND CONCLUSIONS

The Parental Experience in Midlife: Past, Present, and Future

Marsha Mailick Seltzer and Carol D. Ryff

This volume brings a life-span perspective to the study of parenting and focuses on an often-neglected stage of family life—midlife parenting. The purpose of the volume is to shine a spotlight on the midlife parenting experience. This work has been guided by two major themes: diversity and development.

Our starting point was the recognition that the midlife parenting stage encompasses an extraordinary range of circumstances and experiences that had not yet been described or investigated in the literature. Our focus on the *diversity of midlife parenting* was a decided departure from previous family development research. Specifically, as summarized by Seltzer, Krauss, Choi, and Hong (chapter 12), past research in the family development tradition hypothesized that there was a series of stages through which all families were expected to pass in uniform order. The implicit assumptions of family stage theories are that once-married, two-parent families are the norm, that children leave home at the expected time and do not return, and that children are healthy and that parental health problems do not emerge until the retirement years. In contrast, the perspective taken in this volume is that no single trajectory is characteristic of all or even most families during the middle years of parenthood. The influence of specific characteristics of family members—such as social class, gender, life events and transitions, and psychological functioning—warrant exposure in research on parenthood during the middle years. To this end, we invited scholars to examine the diversity of the midlife parenting experience. Consequently, the chapters in this volume examine the demographic, economic, social, and psychological diversity that is characteristic of midlife parenting.

A second theme of this volume is that *developmental changes are occurring in the lives of both parents and children* and that these are linked in interactive processes. Although most past research has emphasized how parents influence and socialize their children throughout childhood and adolescence, less attention has been paid to the influence of the developing adolescent or young adult child on the parent. Decades ago, Erik Erikson observed that development during the adult years stems in part from a concern for guiding and directing the next generation. How the process of parenting influences the well-being and self-conceptions of parents, however, has remained uncharted territory until very recently. In response to this gap, chapters were invited for this volume that present research on how parenting during the midlife period affects the parent, reversing the usual order of causation.

The questions raised in this volume are, therefore, new. None of the studies portrayed here were designed explicitly to investigate the diversity of midlife parenting and its developmental effects. Rather, our invitation to study the parental experience in midlife provided the contributors with an opportunity to revisit their data with new questions. This process yielded a rich array of findings and offers abundant avenues for future research.

The purpose of this final chapter is to summarize and integrate the findings presented throughout this volume. We begin with an examination of the demography of midlife parenting, highlighting the diversity characteristic of families during this stage of life. However, while we acknowledge this diversity, we also recognize the common challenges facing midlife parents, such as the biological maturation of their children and, later, the launching of young adult sons and daughters. The juxtaposition of the diversity of midlife parenting and the common challenges faced by parents during the midlife period sets the context within which adult development during this stage of life occurs.

The chapter then focuses on the sources of variability in the well-being of parents in midlife. Some parents experience economic hardship, conflict with their children, and personal stress, whereas others feel growing intimacy with their children, develop an adult-to-adult relationship with them, and enjoy the familial security and comfort afforded by their affluence. To account for this diversity in parental well-being, we examine four factors: social class, gender, life events, and social psychological interpretive mechanisms. The collective findings of the research presented in this volume suggest that it is variability with respect to these factors, rather than any overarching or uniform characteristics of the stage of midlife parenting per se, that accounts for how midlife parenting is experienced.

Midlife parenting is a precursor to the later years of a parent's life course and to the midlife of the younger generation. Questions arise as to the continuities and discontinuities in the parental experience. We consider several substantive areas in which the aging of parents may set in motion reformulations of the parental role and the parent-child relationship. Particular attention is given to possible shifts in the reciprocity dynamics during late-life parenting.

THE LANDSCAPE OF MIDLIFE PARENTING: DEMOGRAPHY AND LIFE CHALLENGES

Midlife parenting is a remarkably prevalent status. According to Marks (chapter 2), fully 90 percent of adults between the ages of thirty-five and sixty-four are parents. Few other roles are occupied by nearly all adults. However, the midlife parenting role is not uniformly experienced. As Marks noted, "A plurality of midlife parenting organized significantly along social demographic divisions of gender, age, marital status, and race/ethnicity" (p. 73). The chapters in this volume expose the extent of this plurality.

For example, as Meyer (chapter 3) pointed out, by virtually all measures, white parents have more economic resources than members of other racial or ethnic groups, married parents have more resources than single parents, and midlife single fathers have more resources than midlife single mothers. There is a curvilinear relationship between age of midlife parents and economic well-being, with resources increasing until around the mid-fifties but falling off thereafter.

Thus, the playing field is not level, and this pattern of economic inequality sets the stage for yet an additional layer of diversity, regarding the quality of the midlife parenting experience. Umberson (chapter 13) showed that these structural differences affect the relationships between parents and children. For example, divorced midlife parents report more strain in, less social support from, and more dissatisfaction with the parent-child relationship than do married midlife parents. Parents with more years of education are more likely to value autonomy in their children than do parents with fewer years of education, who are more apt to value obedience (see Alwin, chapter 4). These effects are also felt in parental well-being. Marks found that during the midlife period, single parents more than married, women more than men, and whites more than persons of color report both physical and mental health problems.

Acknowledging the diversity inherent in parents during the midlife period and the influences of these structural factors on the experience of parenthood, parents in these different circumstances nonetheless face common challenges. All parents must deal, for example, with the biological maturity of their children and the new challenges that puberty brings to family relations. Even in this universally experienced transition, however, there is great diversity. As Graber and Brooks-Gunn (chapter 7) highlight, for girls, the normal age of menarche ranges between 9.5 and 15.5 years, and the challenges faced by parents of early- as compared with later-maturing girls are quite different.

A second common challenge of midlife parenting is the launching of adult children. Although eventually nearly all adult sons and daughters establish their own households, the home-leaving experience varies markedly. Aquilino (chapter 11) reports the startling statistic that fully 45 percent of parents between the ages of forty-five and fifty-four with children age nineteen or older have a child still living at home. This suggests that parents with two or more children have a high likelihood of having an adult child return home after he or she leaves the first time. Thus, the launching of children becomes a complex and prolonged process rather than a discrete event, although ultimately it is a task that most parents (and children) accomplish.

Another common exprience during the midlife parenting stage is holding multiple roles. In addition to being a parent (usually to more than one child), mothers and fathers are often employed outside the home. According to Marks, 81 percent of fathers and 64 percent of mothers age thirty-five to forty-four have children at home *and* are employed. It is also common for midlife parents to care for an elderly parent who has a health problem—fully 50 percent of parents in this age range have a parent with a health limitation. The role of grandparent is also prevalent, with 75 percent of men and 78 percent of women at the end of the midlife parenting stage becoming grandparents. The challenges and benefits of holding multiple roles create the context in which midlife parenting is experienced, reminding us that considerably more is going on in parents' lives than their relationship with their adolescent and young adult children.

The end of the midlife parenting experience is marked by the death of elderly parents. Marks noted that by ages fifty-five to sixty-four, 93 percent of midlife parents have lost their father, and 70 percent have lost their mother. This transition is accompanied by the emergence of age-related health problems in the midlife parent, with 20 percent having a serious health problem by the end of this stage of family life.

We have seen that the midlife parenting stage is marked by a striking degree of within-group variability. Family development/stage theories obscure the diversity of family life at a given point in time by emphasizing the differences between stages and the homogeneity of family life within each stage. However, we take an alternative view. The chapters in this volume underscore the heterogeneity linked with broad sociodemographic factors. In the following section, we consider another dimension of variability, namely, differences in the quality of the parental experience and the well-being of midlife parents. To illuminate these differences, we revisit select sociodemographic factors as well as consider social psychological processes.

Understanding Variation in the Well-Being of Midlife Parents

Midlife parents can be situated along a continuum of well-being. On the negative end of this continuum, we have seen that midlife single parents experience great economic vulnerability (see Meyer). There is also strong evidence of acute personal challenges experienced by poor African American women who are attempting to rear their adolescent children in an urban context (see Allen, Aber, Seidman, Denner, and Mitchell, chapter 8, and Spencer, Swanson, and Glymph, chapter 9). Paradoxically—and also on the negative end of the well-being continuum—Wadsworth (chapter 5) portrays the social and psychological toll of upward mobility experienced during childhood, a toll that is lifelong and continues to be manifest during the midlife period.

With regard to the middle of the well-being continuum, there is evidence that specific aspects of midlife parenting bring a mix of positive and negative outcomes. For example, it is common for midlife parents to be negatively affected by their adolescent child's pubertal development (Silverberg, chapter 6), especially during the early adolescence of the child (Graber and Brooks-Gunn). For reasons that we examine below, however, not all parents report these strains. Another common source of dissatisfaction of midlife parents is the return of adult children to the parental home. But although this transition violates parental expectations, not all parents are dissatisfied with this arrangement (Aquilino, chapter 11). Similarly, parents are affected by how they feel their adult children have "turned out" (Ryff, Schmutte, and Lee, chapter 10), although the influence of the attainment and adjustment of the adult child on parental well-being is neither straightforward nor the same for all parents.

On the positive end of the well-being continuum, we find that parents in midlife report ever-improving relationships with their children, as both parents and children age (Umberson). Even when the adult child has a disability that limits or delays passage through the landmarks of family life, the well-being of midlife parents can remain quite favorable (Seltzer et al., chapter 12). Finally, fathers—particularly affluent fathers—emerge as strong family members during the midlife period, which Nydegger and Mitteness (chapter 14) termed the "prime" of fatherhood.

A major goal of this volume was to understand the factors that contribute to these variations in midlife parental well-being. Why are some parents buoyed up by the accomplishments of their children, while others suffer from parent-child strife? What factors explain the within-stage diversity not only in social circumstances but also in personal well-being of midlife parents? The chapters in this volume point to four major classes of influences that account for the diversity of the quality of the midlife parenting experience. Two of these are macrolevel social structural factors—social class and gender—whereas the other two reflect microlevel social and psychological processes—life events and interpretive mechanisms. Together, they help to clarify variations in the well-being of midlife parents.

Social Class

If there is one factor that cuts across most chapters in this volume, social class stands out as the critical explanatory variable. The studies presented by Allen et al. and Spencer, Swanson, and Glymph show how the stresses associated with race and poverty can obscure or overwhelm the midlife parenting experience. Umberson also found that African Americans reported less social support and more parental dissatisfaction compared with other groups. In contrast, advantaged parents (fathers, in this example) have been shown to have a continuing and powerful influence in their adult child's life during this stage (Nydegger and Mitteness). The disparity between the lack of efficacy in the parents in the Allen et al. sample and the positive leverage observed by Nydegger and Mitteness underscores the importance of attending to issues of social class during the midlife parenting period.

Social class also conditions parental reactions to the growing autonomy of adolescent children. Silverberg reported that social class predicts whether mental health of parents is challenged by the growing autonomy of their adolescent children. For middle-class mothers, having a strong work orientation protects against depression in the face of pubertal development of their children. In contrast, for lower-class mothers who do not have a strong work orientation, their child's transition to adolescence takes a toll on personal well-being. Similarly, it was blue-collar fathers who reported lower life satisfaction and more intense identity concerns in the face of the emotional autonomy of their sons. In the minority context, Allen et al. found that the efficacy of African American mothers was affected by two factors: the mother's level of education and the extent to which the young adolescent experienced difficulties in the transition from elementary school to junior high. Unexpectedly, mothers with high levels of education showed highest efficacy when their adolescent experienced *greater* difficulties, although the reverse was true for mothers with low levels of education. This set of findings implies that well-educated mothers are psychologically empowered by the challenge of assisting their children with school-related difficulties, whereas such challenges appear to overwhelm poorly educated mothers.

Adding children to the class formulation, Ryff, Schmutte, and Lee found that the social class of both the midlife parents and their adult children influences the well-being of midlife parents. Specifically, when adult children overtake their parents' attainment, parental well-being is at risk. However, parental social class (as indicated by level of education) moderates this relationship. Mothers who were highly educated had higher well-being when their daughters' attainment exceeded their own, but mothers with lower levels of education had lower well-being under these circumstances. Thus, Ryff and her colleagues identified three separate but interactive processes: the social class of the parent (as indicated by level of education), the social class of the adult child (as indicated by level of attainment), and the parent's reflection on the child's attainment status vis-à-vis his or her own. These results clarify that social class has both structural and psychological components.

These findings also illuminate Aquilino's conclusion that parents with less education were more satisfied to have an adult child return home than those who were better educated. If parents with less education are negatively affected by having their child outattain them, as suggested by Ryff, Schmutte, and Lee, then having an adult child return home may indicate the opposite situation, namely, that the child has not achieved the requisite status to maintain an independent household. Thus, although having upwardly mobile children might threaten the well-being of poorly educated parents, having an adult child return home may have the opposite effect.

Although middle-class parents may be protected against various stresses associated with midlife parenting, their advantaged status brings a mix of positive and negative outcomes. For example, according to Umberson, parents of higher socioeconomic status (SES) report less social support, more strain, and more dissatisfaction in their relationship with their adult children than lower-SES parents. It is possible that high-SES parents expect more from their adult children (and are more disappointed) than their lower-class counterparts. Alternatively, it may be that less intimacy actually exists in the parent-child relationship in middle-class families. Another example of family strains evident in middle-class families was that maternal employment in fairly prestigious occupations was linked with depression in these mothers' daughters, which suggests possibly a reduction of time spent in the maternal role and lower availability to adolescent children (Graber and Brooks-Gunn).

Finally, Wadsworth's (chapter 5) data testifies to the lifelong influences following from one's social class during childhood. It is not, therefore, social class standing just during midlife but class status throughout the earlier years of the life course that impacts the well-being of the midlife parent. In addition, the extent to which midlife parents experienced upward social mobility during their formative years influenced current social and psychological well-being. Paradoxically, there are risks of social mobility—for men, less satisfaction with family, and for women, higher alcohol intake. These data suggest that the fruits of upward mobility may not be fully experienced by the generation that makes the transition to the higher social class but perhaps by *their* children, when they reach adulthood.

Gender

The chapters in this volume provide strong evidence that the gender of both parent and child influences the parental experience in midlife. Past family research has been characterized as "mother" or "wife" research because of the lack of attention to the father's perspective. The chapters by Meyer and by Nydegger and Mitteness reflect emerging interest in fathers and document how their circumstances and experiences are distinct from those of mothers. The growing phenomenon of single fatherhood is significantly changing the demography of midlife parenting, as has the recognition that both married and single fathers exert strong influences on their children during this stage of life.

Several chapters in this volume compared mothers and fathers.

They provide cumulative evidence that mothers report more closeness and involvement with their children than fathers during both the early and later years of the midlife parenting stage. Silverberg found that mothers reported more closeness than fathers in their relationships with adolescent children, particularly with their daughters. Similarly, Umberson found that mothers report more social support from their adult children than do fathers and feel more responsible for and have greater involvement with their grown sons and daughters. Ryff, Schmutte, and Lee found that mothers attached greater importance to and felt more responsible for their children's adjustment than did fathers.

However, along with greater closeness and a stronger sense of responsibility, mothers also report more conflict with their children during the midlife period than do fathers (Graber and Brooks-Gunn). Thus, greater intensity in both intimacy and conflict with children characterizes the midlife mother's as compared with the midlife father's experience.

The *effects* of conflict between parents and adolescent children are also different for mothers and for fathers. Silverberg found that mothers were more negatively affected than fathers by day-to-day struggles with adolescent children. A similar conclusion is indicated by the data reported by Pruchno, Peters, and Burant (chapter 15), who found that the well-being of fathers is predicted directly from their disagreements with their own adolescent children, whereas mothers' well-being is predicted not only by their disagreements with their adolescents but also by their husbands' disagreements. Thus, the mother suffers as a third party when her husband and adolescent children are in conflict. These findings suggest that not only do mothers report higher *levels* of conflict with their children than do fathers, they are more *emotionally vulnerable* to family conflict than fathers as well.

Especially in white-collar or middle-class families, fathers experience their child's transition to adolescence as a time of increased satisfaction and pride as a parent (Silverberg) similarly finding their adolescent's transition to adulthood to signal increased salience of their own role relative to mothers (Nydegger and Mitteness). Thus, the dimensions along which mother-child and father-child relationships are organized are different: intimacy and conflict are the cornerstones of the mother-child relationship; pride and influence are key defining features of the father-child relationship.

Wadsworth found that parenthood inclines midlife women to dissatisfaction with work, while it has the opposite effects on men. Thus, there are interactions between parental status and gender that extend beyond the realm of the family.

Finally, points of convergence were also reported between midlife mothers and fathers. Ryff and her colleagues indicated that mothers and fathers had similar hopes and dreams for their children. Both wanted their offspring to achieve happiness and educational and career success, have a happy family, find personal fulfillment, be a good person, and have good health, in descending order.

Added to the differences between mothers and fathers is a distinct set of gender-based processes pertaining to how parents are differentially affected by their sons and daughters. For example, Ryff, Schmutte, and Lee showed that the attainment and adjustment of sons, rather than daughters, explained greater variance in the well-being of both mothers and fathers, although it was social comparisons with daughters, not sons, that had greater ties to parental well-being. Silverberg's longitudinal analysis suggests that sons' mothers who have low investment in work are particularly vulnerable to midlife self-questioning and reappraisal as their sons mature. Alternatively, Allen et al. reported that authoritative African American mothers felt more competent in the face of daughters' increased difficulties in the transition from elementary to middle school than sons'.

In accounting for the salience of sons to fathers, Nydegger and Mitteness explain that fathers share a male world with their sons, which provides a commonality of experience. They view their daughters—particularly traditional (i.e., non-career-oriented) daughters—as occupying a more mysterious world. The salient feature of the father-son relationship is respect, whereas the abiding characteristic of the father–traditional daughter relationship is affection, but without much comprehension. With nontraditional daughters (i.e., those with strong career orientations), fathers fall somewhere between these two traditional profiles, but such relationships possess neither the shared experience of the father-son dyad nor the affection of the father–traditional daughter dyad.

In concert, these findings convey considerable gender diversity in the midlife parental experience. Such differences underscore the need to include fathers as well as mothers in future empirical studies of parenting as well as to attend to the complexities of same-sex and opposite-sex parent-child dyads.

Life Events and the Linkage of Life Trajectories

The midlife period is marked by a high frequency of life events, many of which are stressful. Marks reported the following common life events experienced by midlife parents: single parenthood (about 20 percent); having a child who becomes divorced, separated, or widowed (about 20 percent); coresidence with an adult child (nearly 50 percent); coresidence with an elderly parent (about 30 percent), and death of a father (93 percent) or a mother (70 percent). These events are punctuation points in the midlife parental experience, and they influence not only the well-being of parents and children but also the emotional climate of the family.

Evidence suggests that stressful life events do, indeed, affect the quality of the relations between midlife parents and their children. Pruchno, Peters, and Burant found that the greater number of negative events that are experienced by adolescents, the more disagreements they had with their fathers. Umberson reported a somewhat different pattern: midlife parents who experienced a stressful life event—the death of an elderly parent—received increased contact, supportiveness, and closeness from their adult children. In the former example, stressful events in the lives of adolescent children negatively affected relationship quality, whereas in the latter, the stressful events in the life of the midlife parent positively affected relationship quality. Thus, important issues in assessing the impact of life events are *to whom* has the event occurred and *when* in the life course of parents and children it happened.

Although considerable past research has examined the cumulative effects of stressful life events, several chapters in this volume underscore the importance of tracking factors that lead up to such events and examining their sequelae. Aquilino found, for example, that stressful events in the life of the child, such as divorce or leaving school, frequently predicted the return of an adult child to the parental home. Thus, as Pruchno, Peters, and Burant noted, a ripple effect of events is experienced in which the stresses of one family member provoke the occurrence of events in the lives of the other members of the family.

Returning adult children underscore another relevant feature of events in the lives of midlife parents, namely, the diversity of impact or consequences of such events. As Aquilino described, having an adult child return home can provoke feelings of either psychological distress or satisfaction in the parent, depending on a variety of other factors, such as the parent's level of education and the child's degree of autonomy. Thus, the same event will not be equally stressful for all midlife parents, highlighting the necessity of attending to individual differences in the meaning of the life event and the resources that parents and children bring to these experiences.

The research of Seltzer et al. challenges the usual characterization of nonnormative life events (i.e., those that are unplanned and atypical) as having negative consequences. Their data did not support predictions from family stress models, which would construe caring for a child with mental retardation as a risk factor for mothers' physical or mental health. Rather, the mothers of such adult children were found to function as well as or superior to relevant reference groups. In short, the nonnormative experience of providing decades of care for a son or daughter with mental retardation did not result in nonnormative outcomes for mothers. Furthermore, their work showed that lifelong parenting for a child with a disability did not change the way a midlife mother experiences *other* stressful events, such as residential relocation, widowhood, or declining health. Although it was predicted that a nonnormative parenting role would overwhelm other aspects of the parent's life, the data indicated that the well-being of these midlife mothers was similar to that of mothers whose child did not have a disability.

While stressful life events are one set of factors that influence the well-being of individual family members, life-course transitions also have ripple effects in the family, although they may be less abrupt than discrete events and not as stressful. Several studies found that the parental experience in midlife is tied to life-course transitions in the children. For example, Nydegger and Mitteness found that as children reach adulthood, the functions of their fathers change. Fathers relinquish the caregiving role, act less as an authority figure, and withdraw from the roles of provider and protector. At the same time, new roles emerge in their own right—friend, counselor, and companion. Thus, transitions in the lives of children influence the content of the parent role. As stated by Pruchno, Peters, and Burant, "The webs that join the lives of family members to one another are intricate and complex and have a stronghold on the lives of family members" (pp. 599–600).

A further example of how children's life-course transitions affect parental well-being concerns the years just before the launching of adult children, which have been found to be a period of great stress for parents. This pattern was reported in two chapters exploring quite different examples of midlife parenting. Silverberg observed that it is often the case that when adolescents show signs of autonomy, the well-being of parents suffers. Seltzer et al. found that when parents of adults with mental retardation make plans to launch their adult child, there is a downturn in their well-being. These two examples differ notably by the age and capacities of the child—the Silverberg sample consisted of nonhandicapped children in their teens, whereas the Seltzer et al. sample was composed of adults with mental retardation in their thirties, on average. In both groups, however, the approach of a transition in which the child would leave the proximal zone of the family signaled increased distress in the parents.

In a parallel fashion, life-course transitions in midlife parents affect the development of their adolescent and young adult children and the parent-child relationship. Marks reported that midlife parents who have had marital disruptions have adult children who are more likely to have had marital separations and to be divorced. Wadsworth found that when parents are upwardly mobile (i.e., move from lower to middle class), their children have a higher risk of personal distress than children born into the middle class.

Finally, the effects of parent or child transitions or statuses may have a positive significance for one family member and a negative outcome for another. For example, Graber and Brooks-Gunn reported that a predictor of depression in adolescent daughters was maternal employment. This finding contrasts with (but does not necessarily contradict) Silverberg's and Allen et al.'s conclusion that a strong work orientation in mothers is related to *improved* maternal well-being. Employment might buffer the stresses associated with midlife parenting for mothers, but this does not necessarily translate into a better outcome for their daughters. Thus, while the family passes through the midlife stage together, family members experience its landmarks individually.

Interpretive Mechanisms

Variation in the well-being of midlife parents is also importantly influenced by the interpretive lens they bring to their life experiences and to those of their children. Ryff, Schmutte, and Lee drew on social psychological theory to explicate certain interpretive mechanisms. One mechanism pertained to parents' perceptions of how their children compare with themselves. Extensive prior research has documented the effects of social comparison processes on self-esteem. In applying such a framework to the family, this research demonstrated that multiple aspects of parental well-being—particularly levels of self-acceptance, environmental mastery, and purpose in life—were strongly linked not only to how well children had "turned out" but also to parents' perceptions of how these children compared with themselves. Paradoxically, parents who felt their children had done better than themselves (especially in the adjustment realm) had lower levels of well-being than parents who saw their children as doing more poorly relative to themselves.

A second interpretive mechanism was derived from attributional theory, which examines what people see as the causes of particular outcomes. Applied to parenting, Ryff, Schmutte, and Lee investigated the extent to which parents saw themselves as responsible for the lives of their children. The findings suggested that parents' well-being was again predicted not only by what children had accomplished but also by perceptions that the parent had been involved in, a good role model for, and responsible for the lives of their children. Parents with the lowest levels of well-being were those who felt their children had not turned out well *and* who felt they had exercised little responsibility for children's life outcomes.

Social psychological theory also gives emphasis to the importance that people attach to their life roles. High versus low levels of importance are thus believed to moderate the consequences of various life experiences. Such hypotheses were borne out by the work of Silverberg, which demonstrated that the effects on their parents of developing adolescents were moderated by the parents' (particularly, mothers') level of investment in their work role. Thus, confronting a child who is becoming physically, psychologically, and socially mature prompts greater self-questioning and life appraisal among mothers with low investment in their occupational identity outside of the home. The implication, then, is that understanding of how children's transitions affect their parents requires knowledge of parents' self-definitions and the salience or centrality they attach to different parts of their identities.

The ways in which children's unfolding lives influence the well-being of their parents also requires knowledge of the expectations parents bring with them to the parental experience. Aquilino gave special emphasis to the importance of understanding parental expectations in evaluating the impact of the adult child's return to the parental home. Presumably, parents have implicit, if not explicit, ideas about when and how adult children will negotiate particular role transitions (e.g., begin and complete their education, enter into marriage, become parents). On a more general level, Ryff, Schmutte, and Lee's description of parents' hopes and dreams for their children illuminates the broad goals that adults bring to the parental experience. It is when such expectations or goals are violated that parental well-being may be affected, but few studies collect the data necessary to juxtapose parental expectations with the realities of children's lives. As Aquilino conveyed, future research would be enriched by including direct and detailed assessments of parents' expectations for their children.

Also implicated in parental well-being are their anticipations and plans for oncoming events in the lives of their children. Seltzer et al. showed, for example, that the mere anticipation of launching a child with mental retardation was marked by declines in parental well-being. Mothers who had added their son's or daughter's name to a waiting list had poorer well-being than those who had not taken this step. Thus, consequences for parental well-being do not follow solely from actual transitions in children's lives; just the anticipation of such changes may also affect parents. This observation points to the need for more study of anticipation processes in the midlife parental experience.

All the above examples illustrate the need to "get inside parents' heads" to illuminate the different psychological frameworks they bring to the construction of themselves and their children. Undoubtedly, investigation of inner realm provides further insight about how parenthood affects parents themselves, although getting to this level may require a more diverse array of methods than currently characterizes much parental research. Nydegger and Mitteness call for more anthropological, phenomenological approaches where the objective is to get to the meaning of the parental role to the parent him/herself. Their provocative findings regarding fatherhood strengthen the case for other qualitative endeavors, with their unique capacity to expose the phenomenology of parenthood and the interpretive mechanisms that shape it.

Issues of Social Change in the Parental Experience

The contributors to this volume addressed social change in the parental experience according to the broad sweep of historical time as well as in terms of the slower, less discernible creakings of change. Alwin's historical perspective on parental socialization values documented a shift in which younger cohorts of parents showed greater preference for imagination and independence in their children and lesser preference for social conformity and obedience than older cohorts of parents. The "economically worthless but emotionally priceless" child of the twentieth century presumably marks a profound change from viewing children primarily as helping hands to seeing them as little persons to be nurtured so as to maximize their development and well-being. Our volume brings to the fore the question, What are the implications of this change not only for children but for parents as well? While contemporary parents may reap fewer familial benefits from their children's labor, have there been gains in terms of richer, more satisfying relationships with children, particularly during adulthood?

This question may be especially relevant to Aquilino's work on the return of adult children to the parental home. If, as Alwin conveys, autonomy has become a prized quality in children, the reestablishment of dependence on parents would seem particularly problematic. However, to the extent that more recent cohorts of parents derive significant pluses from their social and emotional relationships with children, it may be that lapses in the autonomy of grown children (as signified by returning home in adulthood) can be more easily accepted.

Wadsworth also covers the broad sweep of historical time but brings to it a focus on specific moments and their long-term consequences. Study of the 1946 birth cohort offers a powerful opportunity to mark the impact of social changes in postwar Britain, specifically the dramatic gains that occurred in standard of living and educational attainment. This period of marked social change set in motion processes of upward mobility with long-term psychological as well as social consequences. In midlife, those parents whose own parents were especially enthusiastic about their educational pursuits had greater optimism about their current work and future opportunities. Wadsworth also examined the effects of such upward mobility in parents on their children when they reach adulthood, as we have described throughout this chapter.

Less dramatic but undeniably present in other chapters in the volume were themes of social change in male/female roles. Meyer, for example, drew attention to the increased numbers of single fathers among contemporary families and elaborated their specific strengths and vulnerabilities. Other chapters pointed to shifts in women's roles. Ryff, Schmutte, and Lee showed that the self-evaluations of midlife mothers are particularly influenced by perceptions of how they compare with their adult daughters, in realms of both attainment and adjustment. Because many of these mothers likely had daughters who matured in a different "opportunity climate" than their own, they are especially vulnerable to negative social comparisons with daughters. Similarly, Nydegger and Mitteness elaborated the complexities of contemporary relations between midlife fathers and their nontraditional daughters. Again, these career-oriented female offspring pose new challenges for their fathers and mothers as they mature into adult roles that are quite unlike those of their parents' or grandparents' generation.

Future lines of inquiry need to monitor social change through the later years of the parents' lives and the midlife transitions of their children. Although social change occurs both via the cumulative effects of changes within individuals and via changes affecting successive cohorts, Alwin shows that the latter process is the more powerful. Thus, an important avenue for future study is an examination of how such change processes are played out in the next generation and the ties between their grown children and their children's children.

BEYOND MIDLIFE PARENTING: LOOKING AHEAD TO THE LATER YEARS

We close the volume with a glimpse at the years that lie ahead in the parental experience. Observing that there is no "magic moment" when midlife parenting ends, Umberson described the transition out of this phase as prolonged and gradual. She noted, however, that certain experiences mark the transition, such as the onset of frailty in the parent or shifts in patterns of exchange in which adult children provide more support to the parent than is returned. The continual renegotiation and reformulation of the parenting role was further emphasized by Nydegger and Mitteness. In their view, the parenting role matures along with children. Thus, gazing ahead to the later years of parenthood raises a host of issues about possible transformations in roles and reconfigurations of the connections between parents and children. We organize our reflections about this future period around two themes: the nature of continuities and discontinuities in the parental experience, and the heightened reciprocity that characterizes aged parents' ties to their midlife children.

Our collage of the midlife parental experience reveals recurring motifs. That is, certain ideas appear and reappear, although in different contexts and different temporal locations. The topic of autonomy constitutes one such repeating motif. Alwin showed that as children age, parents value autonomy ever more strongly than obedience. Similar age-related patterns are evident from the juxtaposition of Silverberg's and Aquilino's findings. Silverberg described how children's adolescent transitions, with their accompanying physical, emotional, and social changes, pose new challenges for parents. A key task during this time is the renegotiation of the parental role to allow for the child's emerging autonomy. Aquilino, describing a later point in the life course, revisits the theme of autonomy as a lens central to understanding the significance of an adult child's return to the parental home. It is when such reentry signals a lack or loss of autonomy and independence in the adult child that familial problems are likely to occur.

We speculate that autonomy reappears as a salient motif in the later years of the parental experience, although at that time, it is the autonomy of the parent, not the child, that is center stage. To the extensive literature on caregiving to aging parents (Blieszner, Mancini, and Marek, chapter 16), we thus bring the observation that how parents relinquish their own self-sufficiency and independence may be influenced by the family history of negotiated shifts in autonomy. Parents who fostered autonomy in their own children as well as accepted occasional lapses in their children's capacities to manage for themselves may well be those who can, with equanimity, allow these children to care for them in old age. In addition, their children may be those most capable of—and concerned about—providing such care. We underscore the need in future inquiries to connect these multiple occasions of renegotiated autonomy.

Intimacy and the affectional ties that characterize parent-child relations constitute a related realm for tracking continuities and discontinuities in the parental experience. Many contributors to this volume (Wadsworth; Aquilino; Seltzer et al.; Umberson; Nydegger and Mitteness; Pruchno, Peters, and Burant) addressed the quality of the parent-child relationship, some during times of transition and stress, and others, over more gradual periods of change. Extrapolation to the later years of parenthood brings to the fore issues of whether comparable levels of interpersonal connection will be sustained, or possibly redefined, as parents age. As asked by Blieszner, Mancini, and Marek, does the quality of relationships in one era influence the quality in subsequent eras of parenting? Wadsworth took advantage of longitudinal data to conclude that the parent-child relationship during adolescence was a strong predictor of the closeness of the relationship decades later when the parents reached old age and the child was in midlife. Similarly, Nydegger and Mitteness found that the father-child relationship during the father's midlife positions him well for continued intimacy with his children as he moves into old age and as they (the children) enter midlife. And, Umberson found that social support provided by children to parents increases as the parent ages, foreshadowing positive parent-child relations during the old age of the parents.

To these findings, we note possible linkages with social change processes, particularly Alwin's description of the historical shift in parental values, with more recent cohorts paying greater attention to children's personal development than their obedience or responsiveness to authority. Perhaps the nurturing of children's personal well-being translates to greater depth in the emotional ties that parents have with their progeny as adults. Explication of these ideas requires greater understanding of continuities and discontinuities in parent-child affectional bonds.

Issues of reciprocity, while evident in the preceding examples, are brought into sharp relief via the topic of parental responsibility. Ryff, Schmutte, and Lee examined parents' views of how responsible and involved they had been in different aspects of their children's lives (e.g., educational and occupational pursuits, personal adjustment, social relationships). It was shown that parents' psychological well-being was predicted by their responsibility ratings, independent of how well children had done in life. That is, parents' views of themselves were tied to their assessments of how they exercised parental responsibility. The findings also conveyed, as did Umberson's, that mothers felt more responsibility for children than fathers. In later life, we see that *filial responsibility* emerges as a key topic in studies of caregiving to aged parents (Blieszner, Mancini, and Marek). Responsibility, like autonomy, thus persists as a theme in understanding parent-child relations across time, but again, a marked shift occurs in the later years as to *who* is responsible for *whom*. To this transition, we explore linkages with prior experiences and ask, Are expressions of filial responsibility in adult children toward their aged parents predicted by their childhood experiences of receiving responsible care and attention from these parents? Here, a key objective is to understand the long-term reach of early socialization and the extent to which responsible parents imbue within their children a comparable sense of concern for the well-being of others, including the parents themselves.

The continual negotiation of new life events for both children and parents provides yet another realm to monitor reciprocities in their ties to each other. This volume included discussions of how life stresses among adult children influenced the lives and marital relations of their parents (Pruchno, Peters, and Burant) as well as consideration of how events in the lives of midlife parents were responded to by adult children (Umberson). We point to the need to connect these realms of experience. One hypothesis is that how parents helped or hindered their children's confrontations with life stresses may influence the extent to which adult children support or ignore the older parent's encounter with difficulties of aging. Construed as such, family life provides a kind of training ground for dealing with life challenges. Midlife parents who contribute to the "smoothing" of their children's transitions and turmoils may thus convey skills and compassion that are returned to them as they deal with obstacles when growing old.

True to our theme of diversity in this volume, we postulate that all the preceding questions about continuities and reciprocities are likely characterized by wide individual differences. For example, the extent to which parents have the requisite resources to be responsibly involved in their children's lives appears to vary by race and class (Allen et al.; Spencer, Swanson, and Glymph; Umberson). This may mean that parents who were unable (economically, educationally) to invest in their children, have in old age adult children who may exercise less filial responsibility, due again to economic restrictions as well as limited prior socialization. On the other hand, higher-SES parents were found to report more strain and dissatisfaction in relationships with adult children compared with lower-SES parents (Umberson). Thus, later-life implications for interpersonal ties do not converge with patterns of individual differences observed in other realms (i.e., filial responsibility).

Gender constitutes another critical dimension of parental differences. Repeatedly, compared to fathers, mothers were found to be more involved in and influenced by their roles as parents. Thus, the preceding questions about renegotiations of autonomy, maintenance of intimacy, and expressions of filial responsibility in adult children must be examined with close consideration of possible differences between aging mothers and fathers.

Issues of reciprocity in parent-child relations in the later years make particularly dramatic the unique experiences of nonnormative parents (Seltzer et al.). Aging parents of midlife children with mental retardation cannot relinquish their independence and autonomy to such children or look to them for responsible caregiving. These families typically include other nondisabled children as well, thereby adding to the complexities of late-life parenting. To the task of managing their own challenges of aging, these parents must also negotiate the transfer of their lifelong caregiving responsibilities to another person (another family member) or setting (placement). How such changes affect emotional and affectional ties between the aged mother and the adult child with retardation is a critical issue of this transition.

In sum, our look to the future phase of parenting sketches numerous possibilities for studying renegotiated relationships. If the characterization of these later years draws heavily on themes of adult children giving back to aging parents, it is because we have throughout the volume tried to probe how parents are affected by the experience of having and raising children. It may be that the effects of children on parents are most pronounced during this final phase of parenting. However, even as parents' needs for support and assistance may rise, we argue that their influence on the lives of children remains powerful. They provide, for example, critical role models for their children's own aging. In midlife, parents may ask themselves, "How have my children turned out compared with me?" In the parents' old age, their children may ask, "How am I going to grow old compared with them?" Thus, the tale of parents' and childrens' influences on each other is a lifelong story. This volume portrays one significant but generally unexamined era in this tale: the parental experience in midlife.

CONTRIBUTORS

J. Lawrence Aber, National Center for Children and Poverty, Columbia School of Public Health.

LaRue Allen, Department of Applied Psychology, School of Education, New York University.

Duane F. Alwin, Survey Research Center of the Institute for Social Research, University of Michigan.

William S. Aquilino, Department of Child and Family Studies, University of Wisconsin-Madison.

Rosemary Blieszner, Department of Family and Child Development, Virginia Polytechnic Institute and State University.

Jeanne Brooks-Gunn, The Adolescent Study Program, Teachers College, Columbia University.

Christopher J. Burant, Myers Research Institute, Menorah Park Center for Aging.

Seung Chol Choi, Department of Sociology and Waisman Center, University of Wisconsin-Madison.

Jill Denner, Department of Psychology, New York University.

Alvin Glymph, Applied Research Center, Georgia State University.

Julia A. Graber, The Adolescent Study Program, Teachers College, Columbia University.

Jinkuk Hong, Department of Sociology and Waisman Center, University of Wisconsin-Madison.

Marty Wyngaarden Krauss, Heller School, Brandeis University.

Young Hyun Lee, Department of Sociology, University of Wisconsin-Madison.

Jay A. Mancini, Department of Family and Child Development, Virginia Polytechnic Institute and State University.

Lydia I. Marek, Department of Family and Child Development, Virginia Polytechnic Institute and State University.

Nadine F. Marks, Child and Family Studies, Institute on Aging, Center for Demography and Ecology, University of Wisconsin-Madison.

Daniel R. Meyer, School of Social Work and Institute for Research on Poverty, University of Wisconsin-Madison.

Christina Mitchell, Health Sciences Center, University of Colorado.

Linda S. Mitteness, Medical Anthropology Program, University of California, San Francisco.

Corinne N. Nydegger, Medical Anthropology Program, University of California, San Francisco.

Norah D. Peters, Department of Sociology and Anthropology, Beaver College.

Rachel A. Pruchno, Center on Aging, Bradley University.

Carol D. Ryff, Department of Psychology, Institute on Aging and Adult Life, University of Wisconsin-Madison.

Pamela S. Schmutte, Department of Psychology, University of Wisconsin-Madison.

Edward Seidman, Department of Psychology, New York University.

Marsha Mailick Seltzer, School of Social Work and Waisman Center, University of Wisconsin-Madison.

Susan B. Silverberg, Division of Family Studies, University of Arizona.

Margaret Beale Spencer, Center for Health, Achievement, Neighborhood Growth, and Ethnic Studies (CHANGES), University of Pennsylvania.

Dena Phillips Swanson, Center for Health, Achievement, Neighborhood Growth, and Ethnic Studies (CHANGES), University of Pennsylvania.

Debra Umberson, Department of Sociology and Population Research Center, University of Texas.

Michael E. J. Wadsworth, Medical Research Council National Survey of Health and Development, Department of Epidemiology and Public Health, University College/London Medical School.